DOWNHOMER
Household Almanac
& Cookbook 2

This book belongs to:

Carol Blackmore

It was received as a gift from:

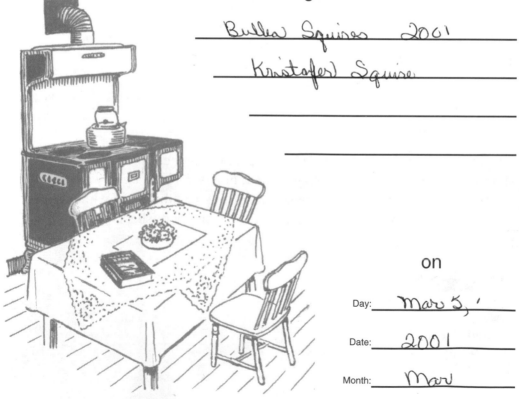

Bulla Squires 2001

Kristofer Squire

on

Day: Mar 5,

Date: 2001

Month: Mar

Year:

Editor - Ron Young

Editorial Assistants:
Dana Cooper
Paula Gale
Charlene Jenkins
Lila Mercer
Jennifer Miller
Janice Stuckless
Sandra Young

Illustrations - Mel D'Souza

Copyright 2000 by Downhome Publishing Inc.
303 Water Street
St. John's, Newfoundland, Canada
A1C 1B9
Tel: 709-726-5113
Fax: 709-726-2135
Email: mail@downhomer.com
Home Page: downhomer.com

ISBN: 1-895109-12-4

Printed in Canada
First Printing - October, 2000

QUICK REFERENCE INDEX

More Detailed Index
Pages 457 to 473

This book is dedicated to my mother, Violet Young - nee Froud.

Thank you to all the people who contributed to this book, including all of those who sent poems, stories, jokes, Life's Funny Experiences and recipes. Thank you to Loreen Haldenby-Adams, Hilda Warren, Bill and Rick Sones, Reg Wright and Bruce Stirling for their contributions. Thank you to Mel D'Souza for his imaginative illustrations that gave life to the pages of this book.

Ron Young

About this book...

A wise man once said, "When you stumble upon a good idea, run with it." (Or maybe it was "Eureka!" - something like that anyway.) Well, our first book must have been a good idea, because we've been running with it ever since it first came out in November 1996. It became a Canadian Best Seller in less than eight months and is now in its fifth printing, with no sign of slowing down.

Due to the overwhelming response to our first book, and after many requests from our readers, we decided to bring out a second book, with certain changes. We still have the recipes - all new and sprinkled with fresh tidbits and thoughts. We are introducing a kids' recipes section for whole families to enjoy. We have an all-new 'Tonic For The Soul' section. Other additions include a natural health section called 'Grassroots Healing', an astrology section, and a section for noting important birth dates called 'VIP Pages'.

We set a standard with the first book, and the least you can expect is that this one equals it.

Enjoy!

Tonic For The Soul

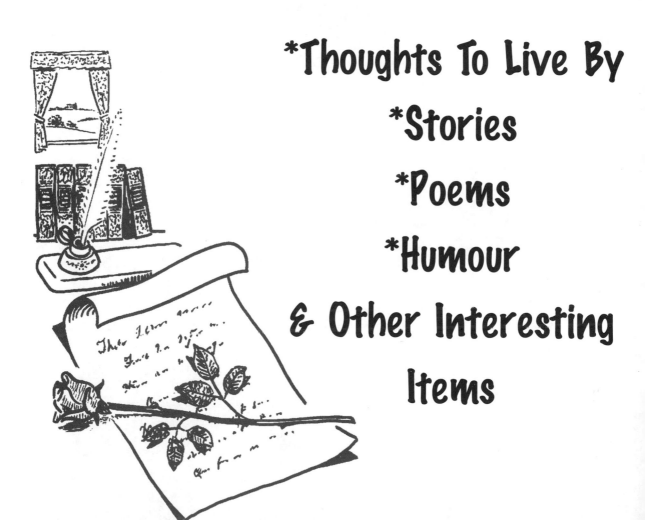

*Thoughts To Live By

*Stories

*Poems

*Humour

& Other Interesting

Items

The Window

Author Unknown

There were once two men, both seriously ill, in the same small room of a great hospital. Quite a small room, it had one window looking out on the world. One of the men, as part of his treatment, was allowed to sit up in bed for an hour in the afternoon (something to do with draining the fluid from his lungs). His bed was next to the window. But the other man had to spend all his time flat on his back.

Every afternoon when the man next to the window was propped up for his hour, he would pass the time by describing what he could see outside. The window apparently overlooked the ocean. There were sea birds, and children came to catch fish from a wharf and play games of tag. Young lovers

walked hand in hand on the beach, and there were flowers and stretches of grass nearby, and beyond a point of land, boats sailed in and out.

The man on his back would listen to the other man describe all of this, enjoying every minute. He heard how a child nearly fell into the ocean, and how beautiful the girls were in their summer dresses. His friends' descriptions eventually made him feel he could almost see what was happening outside.

Then one fine afternoon, the thought struck him: Why should the man next to the window have all the pleasure of seeing what was going on? Why shouldn't he get the chance? He felt ashamed, but the more he tried not to think like that, the worse he wanted a change. He'd do anything! One night as he stared at the ceiling, the other man suddenly woke up, coughing and choking, his hands groping for the button that would bring the nurse running. But the man watched without moving — even when the sound of breathing stopped. In the morning, the nurse found the other man dead, and quietly took his body away.

As soon as it seemed decent, the man asked if he could be switched to the bed next to the window. So they moved him, tucked him in, and made him quite comfortable. The minute they left, he propped himself up on one elbow, painfully and laboriously, and looked out the window.

It faced a blank wall.

Tonic For The Soul

Thoughts To Live By, Stories, Poems, Humour, & Other Interesting Items

Grannie's Rocker *By Bobbie Wheeler and Ivy Marsh, Lower lance Cove, Trinity Bay*

Dear old Grannie loved her chair
We're sure yours must have too
She wouldn't trade it for the world,
No matter what we'd do

'Twas not the kind that you see now,
All fancy carved and such
It was made out of a flour barrel
And had a "homey touch"

Our Grannie covered it with care
With gingham and fancy lace
You could see how much she loved it
By the smile upon her face

For underneath the cushion
Where no one else could see
Grannie kept all her remedies
As proud as she could be

It held such things as "ginger wine"
Castor oil and Donna tea

And every time someone got sick
Grannie would say, "let's see"

What I've got in the barrel for you
That will rid you of the flu
And out would come her remedies
With care we guarantee you

She'd mix balsam with some sugar
And make you drink it down
And molasses mixed with sulphur
At least a half a pound

Your eyes would water from the stuff
That Grannie used to make
It cured everything from "night blind"
To a plain old belly ache

When you awoke next morning,
Still happy to be here
With special thanks to Grannie
And her good stuff under her chair
***

Fun With Familiar Phrases

You may hurl slurs and slander me
To make my friends desert me
But *Sticks and stones may break my bones*
but names will never hurt me.
                                    -Ron Young

Rhymes & Reflections

The time when life
Is most unkind
Is when it lets the body
Outlive the mind
                        -Ron Young

***

The Lighter Side

A Little Kindergarten boy was crying, so the teacher asked him what was wrong.

"I cant find my boots," sobbed the little boy.

The teacher looked around the classroom and saw a pair of boots.

"Are these yours?"

"No, they're not mine," the boy shook his head.

The teacher and boy searched all over the classroom for his boots.

Finally the teacher gave up. "Are you **sure** these boots are not yours?"

"I'm sure," the boy sobbed, "mine had snow on them."

A Prayer From Newfoundland

By Ron Young

God our father understand
Why we worship Newfoundland
We see your works in every tree
And feel your power in the sea
More often here to you we've knelt
More often here is your presence felt
The cities of the world are grand
But they were built by mortal man

And buildings make it hard to see
The beauty that was made by thee
And please forgive our city kin
For there it's easier to sin
So God our Father with thy love
Guide them back to bay and cove
So things that you have made they'll see
And they'll know why we worship thee.

***

Life's Funny Experiences
A Long Conversation Piece

Reprinted from
Downhomer Magazine

When I was a telephone operator in Corner Brook in the '70's', I was working on the board one day when a customer from Sunnyside called in to say she had a problem. I asked her how I could help her. She said that the telephone guy had been their that day and had installed a new phone, but the cord which ran from the phone to the box on the wall was too long. She asked if I could pull back in on my end because people where tripping over it.
Submitted by Dianne Hewlett, Sparwood, British Columbia

***

Classroom Chuckles

Teacher: What is your name, son?
Jonas: My name is Jonas.
Teacher: Say "sir" when you talk to me, young man.
Jonas: Okay then, my name is Sir Jonas.

Confessions of the Rich and Famous

Ah, yes, divorce, from the Latin word meaning to rip out a man's genitals through his wallet. *- Robin Williams*

Don't Make A Bigger Word Your Choice
When The Diminutive Version Will Suffice

Many people use big words when smaller ones do the job better. Here are some well known lavish locutions that utilize voluminous words superfluously. See how many you can do without checking out the answers hidden throughout this book. The locations of the answers are indicated, in case you want to cheat, but don't do it until you have given them a good try.

1. Person's of imbecilic mentality devigate in parameters which cherubic entities approach with trepidation. *Answer hidden on next page.*

2. Scintillate, scintillate, asteroid minific. *Answer hidden on page 346.*

3. Members of an avian species of identical plumage congregate. *Answer hidden on page 14.*

4. Surveillance should precede aviation. *Answer hidden on page 37.*

5. Pulchritude possesses solely cutaneous profundity. *Answer hidden on page 17.*

6. It is fruitless to become lachrymose over precipitately departed lacteal fluid. *Answer hidden on page 25.*

7. Freedom from incrustations of grime is contiguous to rectitude. *Answer hidden on page 48.*

8. The stylus is more potent than the fencing impliment. *Answer hidden on page 55.*

9. It is fruitless to attempt to indoctrinate a superannuated canine with innovative maneuvers. *Answer hidden on page 61.*

10. Eschew the implement of correction and vitiate the scion. *Answer hidden on page 69.*

11. The temperature of the aqueous content of an unremittingly ogled saucepan does not react 212°F. *Answer hidden on page 62.*

12. All articles that coruscate with resplendence are not truly aurferous. *Answer hidden on page 15.*

13. Where there are visible vapours having their prevalence in ignited carbonaceous materials, there is conflagration. *Answer hidden on page 46.*

14. Sorting on the part of mendicants must be interdicted. *Answer hidden on page 14.*

15. A plethora of individuals with expertise in culinary techniques vitiate the potable concoction produced by steeping certain comestibles. *Answer hidden on page 60.*

16. Male cadavers are incapable of yielding any testimony. *Answer hidden on page 28.*

17. Individuals who make their abode in vitreous edifices would be advised to refrain from catapulting petrous projectiles. *Answer hidden on page 41.*

18. A revolving lithic conglomerate accumulates non congeries of small green hydrophilic plants. *Answer hidden on page 42.*

19. The person presenting the ultimate cachination possesses thereby the optimal cachination. *Answer hidden on page 77.*

20. Missiles of ligneus or petrous consistency have the potential of fracturing my osseous structure, but appellations will eternally remain innocous. *Answer hidden on page 10.*

21. Hades' scintillations. *Answer hidden on page 48.*

***

Fun With Familiar Phrases

Before you, a single thing begin always be sure to use your head and remember that *Fools rush in where angels fear to tread*

-Ron Young

Aunt Alice says:

I know what Victoria's Secret is. The secret is that nobody older than 30 can fit into their stuff.

Rhymes & Reflections

It's amazing that tourists
Stand in awe
At the beauty around us
That we never saw
-Ron Young

Fun With Familiar Phrases

You can't get just what you want for free
The successful are indifferent to losers
And people mostly give up what they
don't want
So *Beggars can't be choosers*
-Ron Young

***

Is That A Fact? *-Ron Young*

**Reprinted from
Downhomer Magazine**

Many Things are accepted as facts. Not all of them are.

Most Americans believe that Charles Lindbergh was the first person to fly nonstop across the Atlantic in his monoplane, *The Spirit of St. Louis*, in May of 1927.

The fact is that Lindbergh was the sixty-seventh man to make a non-stop flight across the Atlantic. Eight years earlier, in June of 1919, John William Hancock and Arthur Whitten Brown, in a two-engined Vickers, flew nonstop across the big pond from St. John's, Newfoundland. In July of that year, 31 people in a British dirigible, LX-126, later christened the *Los Angles*, carrying 33 people, made a one-way trip from Germany to the United States. In fact, there were others who flew the Atlantic previous to this, but flew in aircraft equipped to land on water and stopped down on the ocean in such places as the Azores, while the flights previously mentioned were all non-stop.

***

Fun With Familiar Phrases

When people have a common bond
It matters not the kind of weather
Or the type of clothes they've donned
Birds of a feather flock together
-Ron Young

Rhymes & Reflections

One thing I've learned in growing old,
No doubt you've noticed it, too:
The kids to whom you gave advice
Now give advice to you.
-F.G. Kernan

Rhymes & Reflections

Success may come
To him who waits;
But, goodness, how
It hesitates.
-Robert Dennis

Fun With Familiar Phrases

Things are not always as they seem
We are often told
Imitation jewels will often gleam
But *All that glitters is not gold*
-Ron Young

Strange but TRUE *-Bill Sones & Rick Sones Ph.D.*

Q. Have you ever had a taste for regurgitated bee spit?

A. You have if you like honey. To make a pound of it requires some 60,000 nectar loads, or four million flower visits by individual bees, totaling 100,000 miles or more, says May Berenbaum in *Bugs in the System: Insects and Their Impact on Human Affairs*.

Most nectars are around 90 percent water, honeys less than 20 percent. To concentrate honey from nectar, worker bees repeatedly eat and regurgitate it onto their tongues, hundreds of times, aerating it and drying it out, while other 'busy bees' fan their wings up to 26,000 times a minute to keep air circulating in the hive to facilitate the curing.

***

What Manner of Manners?

Manners seem like common sense, but historically, our sense wasn't so common.

An etiquette book of the 1530s says that when dining in "good society" one should remember that "It is most refined to use only three fingers of the hand, not five. This is one of the marks of distinction between the upper and lower classes." They were referring to the thumb and first two fingers; the pinkie and ring fingers were thought to be of such little use in eating that soiling them was unnecessary. Only unthinking common people would grab at food with a whole fist!

Smiles, Chuckles & Belly Laughs
Common Courtesy

Author Unknown

The other day I went to a local Bible store, where I saw a bumper sticker that read *Honk if you love Jesus*. I bought the sticker and put it on my bumper. I am really glad I did. What an uplifting experience. I was stopped at the light at a busy intersection, just lost in thought about the Lord, and didn't notice that the light had changed. The bumper sticker really worked! I found lots of people who love Jesus. Why, the guy behind me started to honk like crazy. He must **really** love the Lord because pretty soon he leaned out his window and yelled "Jesus Christ!" as loud as he could. It was like a football game With him shouting, **"Go Jesus Christ! Go,"** it was just like a football game. Everyone else started honking too so I leaned out my window and waved and smiled to all of those loving people. There must have been a guy from Hawaii back there because I could hear him yelling something about a sunny beach and saw him waving a funny way with only his middle finger stuck in the air. I asked my kids what it meant. They looked at each other and laughed and said it is a Hawaiian good luck sign. So, I leaned out the window and gave him the good luck sign back. A couple of people were so caught up in the joy of the moment that they got out of their cars and were walking towards me. I bet they wanted to pray, but just then I noticed that the light had changed to yellow and I stepped on the gas. And a good thing I did, because I was the only driver to get across the intersection. I leaned way out the window, gave them a big smile and held up the Hawaiian good luck sign as I drove away. Praise the Lord for such wonderful folks..

***

Notable Quotables -*Ron Young*

Reprinted from
Downhomer Magazine

Meanings and origins of well-known words and expressions

How did the word 'Aspirin' originate and what does it mean?

Aspirin, as sold by the Bayer company, is another name for the generic drug known as acetylsalicylic acid. The first "a" in "aspirin" is taken from the generic term. The "spir" comes from "spiraea ulmaria", a plant used in the manufacture of the drug. The "in" is merely a suffix usually applied to chemical and mineralogical goods (such as glycerin or acetin).

By the way, if you ask your druggist for acetylsalicyclic acid pills he will sell them to you in the generic form. They are the same thing (and do the same job) as aspirin at a cheaper price.

Inspirational

The Legend of the Sand Dollar *Author Unknown*

There's a pretty little legend
That I would like to tell
Of the birth and death of Jesus
Found in this lovely shell.

If you examine closely,
You'll see that you find here
Four nail holes and a fifth one
Made by a Roman's spear.

On the side of the Easter Lily,
Its center is the star
That appeared unto the shepherds
And led them from afar.

The Christmas poinsettia
Etched on the other side
Reminds us of His birthday,
Our happy, Christmastide.

Now break the centre open
And here you will release
The five white doves awaiting
To spread good will and peace.

This simple little symbol
Christ left for you and me
To help us spread His gospel
Through all eternity.

***

A Little Fellow Follows Me

Author Unknown. Submitted by Van H. Eshelman

A careful man I ought to be,
A little fellow follows me,
I do not dare to go astray
For fear he'll go the self same way.

Not once can I escape his eyes;
Whatever he sees me do he tries.
Like me he says he's going to be
That little chap who follows me.

He thinks that I am good and fine;
Believes in every word of mine.
The base in me he must not see
That little chap that follows me.

I must remember as I go,
Through summer sun and winter snow,
I'm building for the years to be
That little chap who follows me.

***

Fun With Familiar Phrases

Sometimes only the surface we see
While real beauty inside isn't shown
Which means that *Beauty is only skin deep*
While ugly goes right to the bone
                                    -Ron Young

Rhymes & Reflections

Life is more like a card game
Than a game of chess, I feel
Tho skill may bring you fortune and fame
You must count on the luck of the deal
                                    - Ron Young

Don't Quit

Author Unknown

When things go wrong
As they sometimes will,
When the road you're trudging
Seems all uphill,
When the funds are low,
And the debts are high,
And you want to smile,
But you have to sigh,
When care is pressing
You down a bit —
Rest if you must,
But don't you quit.

Success is failure
Turned inside out,
The silver tint of
The clouds of doubt;
And you never can tell
How close you are,
It may be near when
It seems afar.
So, stick to the fight
When you're hardest hit —
It's when things go wrong
That you mustn't quit.

***

Between the Boulevard and the Bay *By Ron Young*

**Reprinted from
Downhomer Magazine**

THE BOULEVARD - Police Officers and Seniors

I sized up the small bed-setting apartment which, I was sure was identical to all others on the same floor. A small chrome kitchen table with the single chair beside it was against the kitchen wall. The springs in the old vinyl chesterfield, which doubled as a bed at night, creaked and groaned as I sat down. I took out my police issue note book and looked to my left. The mate to the first kitchen chair beside me at the end of the chesterfield served as a combination end table and magazine rack. A battered old rocking chair was the only other furniture.

"Was there any money in your wallet?" I asked the old man, who appeared to be the sole occupant of the small apartment.

While I waited for his reply, a large framed photograph on the top of a less than modern television set caught my eye. It was the photograph of a lady about the same age as the man who had called to report a theft.

"No, I didn't have any money in it," he replied.

"It was black leather, and had a zipper," was how he described the wallet.

"What was in the wallet?" I asked

"Oh, just a picture of my wife and my son. My wife died a couple of years ago, officer."

I looked at the photograph on the TV, "Is that her?"

"Yes, we were married for fifty-three years."

That's when I saw what appeared to be the corner of a black leather wallet protruding from behind the picture. I fished it out and held it up to the old man, thinking that he suffered from memory lapses, the way old people do sometimes.

He probably placed it behind the photographs and forgot where he put it, I thought to myself.

When he saw the wallet his stare fell to the floor and I knew that he wasn't suffering from any memory lapse, he had being lying to me.

I could have told him that reporting a crime that hadn't been committed was a crime in itself. But I didn't. I could have asked him why he called the police, but I didn't have to. I already knew.

"Your wallet wasn't really stolen, was it?" I asked.

"No, officer," he sadly said, "I'm sorry."

Since there was no crime here to investigate, and since I was probably needed elsewhere I should have left right away, but I didn't. I couldn't. So I stayed a while and talked to the old man, because that's why he called in the first place.

"Does your son come to visit you?" I asked.

"Yes, but not very often, He's got an important job, he's a stock-broker you know. He's very busy with his work, and then there's Janet and the kids. He came by last Christmas but he couldn't stay long."

"Do you have any other relatives?"

"Except for a sister, who moved to Australia many years ago, they're all dead," he told me. "I haven't heard from her in years."

I chatted with the old man for a while and as I left his apartment I was cognizant of what it was like to be truly and utterly lonely.

At home later that night I wrote...

The Pensioner's Vigil
Nursing home
Tiny room
Staring through window
Eyeing the gloom.
Gone is the time
For taking stock,
Of waiting for
Opportunity's knock.
Just tortoise hands
On mocking clock
Incessantly shouting
Tick-tock, tick-tock
Minute hand creeping
Across the face

Years blurring by
Not leaving a trace.
Death-watch beetle
Calling its mate
Keeping cadence
With another's fate
Far away
In the wall, knock, knock
Creaking wood
Of the chair, rock, rock
Relentlessly racing
Indifferent clock
Trumpeting tapps!
Tick-tock, tick-tock!!!

THE BAY - The Third Biggest Liar in Twillingate

I used to believe that my grandfather, Pierce Young, was the biggest liar in Twillingate. My brother, Gary, believed this, too.

But Gary recently told me that he was talking to Howard Butt and Howard informed him that our grandfather was actually the third biggest liar in Twillingate. The reason that Grandfather Young took third place, according to Howard, was that his grandfather, Mose Butt, took first and second place in the liar category.

My grandfather worked on construction in New York many years ago. One of the stories he used to tell was about the time he fell off a skyscraper in the Big Apple. He claimed that he was falling to a sure death on the sidewalk below when he remembered that he had his hammer with him and nails in his pocket. According to him he pulled out a four inch nail and using his hammer drove the nail into the side of the skyscraper. Then all he had to do was hang on to the nail until help arrived.

I don't know how Mose Butt could have topped that story to the point that he could wrest first and second place liar away from my grandfather, but apparently he did.

I don't know if either of these gentlemen were really liars. Lies summon up thoughts of deceitfulness and I don't really believe that Mose Butt or Pierce Young ever told those stories to be deceitful, they just told stories. Times were tough back then and stories, true or otherwise, were nothing more than escapism from the hardship which was part of everyday life. Today, stories like the ones Grandfather and Mose told are referred to as fiction and are considered legitimate.

When Grandfather Young came back to Newfoundland after his travels abroad, he became a Salvation Army Soldier. As such he was not permitted to tell lies. He was also not permitted to partake of tobacco, but he did. He loved his chew of Jumbo. And even though he knew that chewing tobacco was sinful, he did his best to avoid telling lies about it. This was achieved to a degree by naming one of the pockets in his fisherman's coveralls; "The World". He never kept his plug of Jumbo in that pocket. So when someone asked him for a chew of that valuable commodity, he could truthfully say, "I don't have a stick in the world."

Although Grandfather was mostly a fisherman he was really a jack-of-all-trades. Come to think of it, all fishermen were jacks-of-all-trades back in those days. A fisherman not only had to know the ways of wind and water and where the fish were, he had to be a businessman, a salesman, a net maker and a net mender, a cobbler, a tailor, a boat builder and a sailor.

But Grandfather gave up fishing for a number of years and worked for the hospital. He was really a jack-of-all-trades there as well. He looked after the hospital's hens and pigs, as well as 35 or more cows. The cows all had to be milked and the milk boiled to obtain cream and skim milk. He planted ground and raised all the potatoes, turnips, carrots, cabbage, etc., required to feed the hospital's staff and patients. He also looked after the hospital's transportation and shipping needs, as well as running the ambulance service. No, he never drove an automobile or owned a driver's license.

When supplies had to be picked up in Lewisporte in the winter or a patient had to be brought in from "the Bay", grandfather harnessed up one of the hospital's three horses to a slide and off he went.

But the calling of the sea got to be too strong for Grandfather, so he gave up his job at the hospital and went back fishing. Grandfather was a poor fisherman. He never owned a motorboat like most other fishermen did. Instead, Grandfather rowed his punt to the fishing grounds early every morning and rowed back again late every night. Quite often though, a motorboat heading in the same direction would toss him a line and give him a tow.

There is a saying in Newfoundland; "A fisherman is one rogue, a merchant is many." From the stories I've heard, Grandfather was certainly a bit of a rogue. Hilda Troake told me about the day her father, Jimmy Primmer, was hauling his trawl in the fog. For some reason the long line he was hauling felt 'a little funny'. When Jimmy broke out of the fog, there was Grandfather Young hauling Jimmy's trawl from the other end.

Grandfather was a small man in stature, but was very spry and physically capable. He was not only a solo fisherman, he cured all his fish by hand with the help of his second wife Fanny (my real Grandmother Florence, nee Sheppard, of Catalina died in 1931 at a young age). Grandfather and Fanny would carry the fish all the way up Elias Young's garden on handbar or in a wheelbarrow.

In the fall, Grandfather shipped his fish by boat and train to Grand Falls where he went door-to-door peddling his product.

Grandfather never declared his barrels and boxes of fish as such to the train people. He always said they were personal clothes so he could ship them cheaper. Although Grandfather couldn't read or write, he knew the values of a dollar and a cent. I don't believe he himself ever got cheated.

His little house was just up Hospital Lane near the hospital. My father-in-law, Doug Dove, told me the story of the winter of the big snowfall. Grandfather's house was completely covered in snow after the big snowfall. The men of Twillingate got together to dig Grandfather and Fanny out. They spent all day digging, but when they got to the door it was padlocked on the outside. I don't know where Grandfather was that day, but he and Fanny weren't in the house and he didn't have to shovel any snow when they returned.

Although he was a busy man, he took the time one year to build me a wheelbarrow. That wheelbarrow was one of the nicest things I ever owned. It was made completely of wood, even the wheel. It was a real work of art.

Apart from his fishing punt, grandfather owned a small dinghy. His punt was kept moored off on-collar and the dinghy was always kept hauled up on the beach and only used for transportation back and forth to the punt. In my mind's eye I can see him now paddling his dinghy backward to the beach. He always paddled the dinghy backward, never forward.

He used to tell me that when he died the dinghy would be mine. I looked forward to one day owning that beautiful little boat, even though it was a bit cranky*.

In 1965, while still plying his trade as a fisherman, Grandfather died at the age of 72. I never did get that dinghy.

Grandfather was buried next to his first wife in the cemetery up on Platter's Head surrounded by Tuckamores**. There is a headstone above her grave but Grandfather never got one. His brother Ned, the blacksmith, is buried nearby. Ned's gravesite has a headstone, as do all the other gravesites in the burial ground. But Grandfather lies in an unmarked grave.

So he wouldn't be entirely forgotten. I wrote a poem for him.

Grandfather Young
Dwarf tuckamores stand above the sea
On a place called Platter's Head
Sentinels for years and years
Watching o're the dead

Wild Blueberries grow on Platter's Head
On a lonely piece of ground

And weeds and grasses grow there, too
On a little hummock mound

There's nothing else to indicate
That this six-foot plot of land
Holds all that's left of one, Pierce Young
Who once was a fisherman

The tides come in and the tides go out
Waves crash on the cliffs below
But the fisherman no longer cares
About the ebb of the tides and the flow

His neighbours all have headstones
To let the strangers know
A little bit about the folk
Who are resting down below

But the visiting strangers will not know
That the little unmarked mound
Holds a fisherman late of Twillingate
A few feet underground

And the sea that once was his livelihood
Still pounds on the rocky shores
Where above lies a fisherman, lost in time
Among the tuckamores

**Pierce Young,
as a young man**

*Tippy

**Dwarfted evergreen trees that are dead on the side that faces the salty, onshore winds.

Tonic For The Soul

Thoughts To Live By, Stories, Poems, Humour, & Other Interesting Items

***

SKIPPER SAYS:

A bachelor washes his own dishes, makes his own bed, puts out his own garbage, and then, a month or so later, has to do it all over again.

A Hug

Author Unknown. Submitted by Irene Watkins, Roberts Arm, Newfoundland.

It's wondrous what a hug can do!
A hug can cheer you when you're blue
A hug can say "I love you so."
Or "Gee, I hate to see you go."
A hug is "Welcome back again."
And "Great to see you! Where have you been?"
A hug can soothe a small child's pain
And bring the rainbow after rain.
The Hug; there's no doubt about it
We scarcely can survive without it!
A hug delights and warms and charms
It must be why God gave us arms!

***

Hugging

Submitted by Cora Oswald, Farmington Hills, Michigan

Hugging is healthy; it helps our bodies' immune system, it keeps you healthier, it cures depression, it reduces stress, it induces sleep, it's invigorating, it's rejuvenating, it has no unpleasant side effects, and hugging is nothing less than a miracle drug.

Hugging is all natural. It is organic, naturally sweet, no pesticides, no preservatives, no artificial ingredients, and 100% wholesome.

Hugging is practically perfect. There are no movable parts, no batteries to wear out, no periodic check-ups, low energy consumption, high energy yield, inflation proof, non-fattening, no monthly payments, no insurance requirements, theft proof, non-taxable, non-polluting, recyclable and, of course, fully returnable.

***

Classroom Chuckles

Teacher: Now remember, children, it's only fools who are certain. Wise men think before they speak.
Jonas: Are you sure, Sir?
Teacher: I'm certain, Jonas! Quite certain!

Reprinted from
Downhomer Magazine

Inspirational
When Pa Said Grace

By Carl B. Ike. Submitted by Irene Watkins, Robert's Arm, Newfoundland

When Pa said grace and bowed his head
We knew he meant each word he said
'Pears like to me we all could feel
Much more enjoyment in our meal
For he was earnest and his face
Showed thankfulness
When Pa said grace

When Pa said grace his words were few
But how they'd touch you through
and through
He'd simply ask God's blessing
rare
Upon his family gathered
there.
And , "Bless this food, Lord

to its place"
We thank thee God
When Pa said grace

When Pa said grace, it reached the spot
God's throne above and what it taught.
Has always been
so much to me
Since Pa has passed away
you see
And as I neatly close
life's race
I oft recall
When Pa said
grace

Dad's Grace

Submitted by Mary Bourgeois nee Mercer, Mount Pearl, Newfoundland

O Lord, help us to be thankful for food in a world where many walk in hunger, for faith in a world where many walk in fear, for friends in a world where many walk alone.

***

Fun With Familiar Phrases

Don't cry over spilt milk
It will only spoil your day
For there is nothing that you can do
About it any way
                    -Ron Young

Rhymes & Reflections

A good thing to remember,
A better thing to do -
Work with the construction gang,
Not with the wrecking crews.
                    -Author Unknown

The Lighter Side

The Rescue

Dear Mrs. Watkins woke up early one spring morning to find there was a flood, and the entire floor of her house was under water. Two men in a boat yelled out to her and asked if she needed help, and she replied, "No thanks, God will look after me." A short time went by and the water had risen so much that she had to go to the rooftop. A speedboat came by and offered her help, but again she replied that God would help if she needed help. Finally, the water rose so high that she was on top of her chimney and the Red Cross rescue team came by and offered her help, but she again refused. Well, she drowned and as she entered through the pearly gates, she said, "God, I thought you were going to look after me, what happened?"

God replied, "But I sent three boats."

Submitted by Roxanne Matthews, London, Ontario - Originally of Port Blandford, Newfoundland

***

Strange but TRUE *-Bill Sones & Rick Sones Ph.D.*

Q. Some animals carry around their own parachute in case of falls. Who is among this foresightful set?

A. Rats and mice, along with their smaller animal brethren. 'Terminal velocity' is the key.

A skydiver jumping out of a plane accelerates to around 160 mph, depending on body weight and positioning, then goes no faster. Small animals have more surface area for their weight, so in falling they generate more air resistance and peak at a much slower speed, with their body acting as a built-in parachute.

A mouse, for instance, can fall several thousand feet onto a hard surface and suffer little more than a daze, points out J. B. S. Haldane in his essay *On Being the Right Size*. A rat can fall out of an 11th-storey skyscraper window, then go on about its business. A much longer drop than that would probably do in the rat, but creatures smaller than mice can plunge from very great heights and go virtually unfazed.

Can This Be Me

By Bob Abbott. Submitted by Margaret Power, St. John's, Newfoundland

When alcohol has dragged you down
And its drug has numbed you brain
When friends and loved one
turn aside
'Cause you caused them
so much pain;
When you have gone and lost your
self esteem
And you got no more self-respect
You're getting there,
but have you really
Reached your bottom yet?

Your appetite for food is gone
You'd rather have a drink
Your stomach turns, your head spins
You spend more time in the sink;
You think more and more of alcohol
Whenever you're awake
It takes you longer now to shave
My, how your hands do shake!

Have you ever heard
your children ask
"Mommy, why do you cry?"
Watched your wife walk out the door

Not even wave good-bye;
Have you ever had your money gone
Bill collectors at the door
What happened to your
brand new car?
It's not in the driveway anymore!

You're sitting all alone somewhere
In a bar-room on a stool
You may think you are king, but look
around,
Others see you as a fool;
I know, cause I've been there
Lost everything I owned
And even though the place was
packed
I felt so much alone.

But I found something you can have
It's absolutely free
And it can work for anyone
Just take a look at me;
Get out to meetings, lot's of them
And you'll soon be feeling fine
Don't rush it.... Just be patient
Take it one day at a time!!!

***

Aunt Alice says:

If you love something, set it free. If it comes back, it will always be yours. If it doesn't come back, it was never yours to begin with. But, if it just sits in your living room, messes up your stuff, eats your food, uses your telephone, takes your money, and doesn't appear to realize that you had set it free...You either married it or gave birth to it.

Rhymes & Reflections

Give me a sense of humour, Lord;
Give me the grace to see a joke,
To get some happiness from life
And pass it on to other folk.

-Author Unknown

Fun With Familiar Phrases

Dead men tell no tales, they say
Can't speak once they've passed on
But with the miracle of DNA
They may have the final say
Even though they're gone

-Ron Young

Reprinted from
Downhomer Magazine

Is That A Fact? *-Ron Young*

Many things are accepted as facts. Not all of them are.

Everyone has experienced talking to someone with bad breath, and said to themselves, Why don't they use mouthwash? Some people realize they have a problem when, during a conversation the other person starts to back away. At this point they say to themselves, I wish I had some mouthwash!

The fact is that contrary to what manufacturers of mouthwash want us to believe, bad breath is not usually the result of bacteria in the mouth. Mouthwashes are only a temporary cosmetic cure and do nothing to eliminate the main causes of halitosis.

The odours from garlic and onion, do not actually originate in the mouth. The volatile oils contained in these two culprits are absorbed in the bloodstream and transported to the lungs. So the odour comes from the lungs and not the mouth. Most odours which originate in the mouth are caused by bad gums, tooth decay or infection, and should be treated by a professional.

***

Notable Quotables *By Ron Young*

Meanings and origins of well-known words and expressions

Where did the word Blazer originate?

In the 1800s the men of the British navel ship *HMS Blazer* were given smart-looking blue jackets to wear. These jackets became a fashion craze in Britain as well as in North America. The name was, of course, taken from the ship on which the jackets were first worn.

Reprinted from
Downhomer Magazine

Life's Funny Experiences
A Real 'Who-Done-It'

Reprinted from
Downhomer Magazine

When I started my second year of agricultural college, one of our courses dealt with dairy farming. The teacher started the first class by asking what experience each student had in dairy operations. I was the only student who hadn't come from a farming background, and after listening to the other students talk in great detail about the various dairy farming operations, I felt quite out of place.

Finally the teacher got around to me and asked,"Greg, what has your relationship to dairy farming been?"

Without giving it a second thought I replied, "Well people around our neighbourhood say I look like our milkman."

I think the teacher was later relieved to learn that I didn't pursue a career in farming.

Submitted by Gregory Kett, Brampton, Ontario

***

Nan's Way

Put a few drops of vanilla flavouring in a small glass in your refrigerator to banish food odors.

Blind Love
Author Unknown. Submitted by Van H. Eshelman

She knows her groceries, I guess;
She knows her onions, I confess;
She knows more than I can express
I know you couldn't realize
How much she knows, she is so wise;
On any theme she can advise.
She knows the things that I do not
(and that is saying quite a lot);
When she speaks, all I say is what?
I only wish that I could tell
The things she does one-half so well,
But I am just a plain dumbbell.
She is as wise as she can be,
But there's one thing she cannot see,
And that is - why she married me!

I Have Seen The Wind *By Ron Young*

He plays music for the waltzing trees
And finds his way through
meadow grasses
That curtsy as he passes
He's just a gentle summer breeze
It seem he's in the mood for play
And he gives the view
a sparkling motion
As he bends to kiss the ocean
I'm glad that he is meek today
I've seen his dander on the rise
When he tosses ships around
like toys

When hardy sailors fear the deep
When blood grows cold
And women weep
And I still treat him with respect
Though he gently blows
across the neck

***

Innocence and Wisdom

A mother was preparing pancakes for her sons, Kevin, five, and Ryan, three. The boys began to argue over who would get the first pancake. Their mother saw the opportunity for a moral lesson. "If Jesus were sitting here, He would say, "Let my brother have the first pancake. I can wait." Kevin turned to his younger brother and said, "Ryan, you be Jesus."

Bulletin Board

Ayres Department Store

Bargain Basement Upstairs!

Notice To All Office Staff

After coffee break, staff should empty coffee pot and stand upside down on the drain board.

What Goes Around Comes Around

by Pat Jackman

When gossip takes your life by storm
And you've nothing else to do
Try helping someone on the street
Who, but for, the grace of God, "go
you".
When other's lives is all "you" can live
And yours is full of despair
Put out your hand and help someone
And see how much they care.
If you've nothing to do but feel
sorry and sad
And talk only about "you".
Think about the deaf and dumb
With only their hands to do
If all you see is you, you, you
Then nothing else will ever be
The selfish "you" can't hide
What even the blind can see.
When you wake up in the morning
And see the morning light
And walk so freely through the day
Not a pain nor ache in sight.

You can talk and listen and get about
With all your human parts
Think of those less fortunate
With very loving hearts.
Does it make you feel just a little guilty
Or even a little sad
That you've been given so much more
Than they have ever had?
Do you feel so full of self pity that
others
Are objects of your pain?
Can't you open up your heart
And give strength where it will gain?
First give to God your old selfish ways
And turn the page to live anew
And offer, as you talk to him, the thanks
For creating "a very healthy you"
When "goes around, comes around"
Is certainly perfect meant
"Do unto others" comes back to you
With twice as much intent

***

What Manner of Manners?

Manners seem like common sense, but historically, our sense wasn't so common.

An etiquette book from the 15th century cautioned people against the following: "Do not put back on your plate what has been in your mouth."

"Do not chew anything you have to spit out again."

"It is bad manners to dip food into the salt."

Classroom Chuckles

Teacher: If Shakespeare were alive today he'd still be considered a very remarkable man.

Jonas: Of course he would. He'd be 460 years old.

Reprinted from
Downhomer Magazine

***

Tonic For The Soul

Thoughts To Live By, Stories, Poems, Humour, & Other Interesting Items

The Lighter Side

One day a duck flew into a convenience store and perched on the counter. When the man behind the counter turned around the duck said "got any duck food?"

"No," replied the man, and the duck flew away.

The next day, the duck came back and asked, "Got any duck food?"

to which the man replied, "No, I don't have any duck food," and the duck flew away.

The next day the duck returned, perched on the counter and asked, "Got any duck food?"

"No," again replied the man, "I don't have any duck food!" And the duck flew away.

The next day the duck returned, perched on the counter and again asked "got any duck food?"

Again the man replied, "NO! I told you, I do not have any duck food! If you come back again I'll nail your feet to the counter!" and the duck flew away.

The next day the duck came back, flew through the open door, and perched on the counter.

The man, quite surprised to see the duck, asked, "What do you want?" The duck looked at the man and said "Got any nails?"

The man replied "No, I don't have any nails."

"Well then, got any duck food?"

Submitted by Sonia Hallingham-Taylor, Manuels, Conception Bay South, Newfoundland

***

SKIPPER SAYS:

Old age is when you look at the menu before you look at the waitress.

Water Unto Water *-Ron Young*

Hilda Warren well remembers the year 1987. It was the year the icebergs came to the South Coast of Newfoundland. Because of the shape of Newfoundland, icebergs don't usually make their way along the South Coast, certainly not as far as the Town of Grand Bank, where Hilda lives. But in 1987 they did so in a big way. Hilda will never forget that year, and not just because of the icebergs. That was the year her husband, Harold, was told he didn't have long to live. That summer the two of them strolled together taking in the sights of the magnificent edifices. There was one large iceberg in particular that they liked. It reminded Hilda of a big cathedral, complete with a spire. *"My husband and I would drive to a little park, where we could sit and watch it, and every day it seemed a bit smaller. My husband wasn't very well; he died shortly after. I realized how much like the icebergs our lives are. Which is what prompted me to write this poem."*

To An Iceberg

O, stately, magnificent edifice
A towering beauty, still a
threat to man
Man-made cathedrals can't
compare with thee
No human hand has shaped
thy majesty
Far from some northern ice
mass hast thou come
In southern waters soon to
meet thy doom
One day we see thee, stately
high and grand
The next just water, lapping
on the land
Reminding us of the brevity
of life
So often, like the waters,
stirred by strife
All things return from
whence we came, and thus
You - water unto water,
we - dust to dust

Photo Courtesy - Falk Foto

Aunt Ethel's House

By Loreen Haldenby, Guelph, Ontario

Aunt Ethel's house was the nicest house in Milton, at least I thought so. It had two large bow windows in the front. The windows and doors were painted white and there was a large verandah which was painted white, too.

The house itself was painted buff. Now, when I think back I wonder if there was ever such a colour as buff or did we make that up. A lot of the houses in Milton were painted buff. A dark yellow colour it was. Yellow with a hint of brown thrown in.

The house was pretty nice on the inside, too, especially the parlour or the front room. Here were the pump organ, wicker chairs, a typewriter and a set of encyclopedia.

But the best thing of all in Aunt Ethel's house was the radio. Not one of these little plastic radios like we have now, but an imposing dark brown one made of wood. I'd say it was about two feet high, the top part neatly curved. When you turned on the radio, a big red light called the magic eye came on.

In 1936, neither Charlie nor I had such luxuries in our homes, but Aunt Ethel was a kindly soul, a very kindly soul and we took shameful advantage of her. But then we were wild, totally undisciplined and both of us spoiled rotten by two very indulgent mothers.

I don't know how but Charlie knew everything about radios, their programs, the various radio stations. It is no surprise to me at all that in later life he became a wizard in electronics.

"The Merry Islanders is comin' on a half-past six," he'd say, "they're on every Monday and Wednesday and Friday." So at half-past six on Mondays, Wednesdays and Fridays we stopped whatever it was we were doing and headed for Aunt Ethel's house. We didn't knock at the door for we were devoid of manners. We walked straight through the kitchen where the family was eating supper, straight through the hall to the front room and there we plopped ourselves down in the two big cushioned chairs that sat on either side of the radio.

Charlie wouldn't allow me to turn on the radio. That was his job. He fiddled with the dials until he got some station in Charlottetown, P.E.I., and there, amid the static and the wavering of the radio waves, we were first introduced to the music of Don Messer. I still sometimes listen to records of Don Messer and I get so homesick I can almost feel the spray of the salt water on my face. Or is it perhaps a tear?

There were other programs, too. Superman, and Tarzan and another program that I can't remember the name of, but it was about a boy called Jerry and his dog, Rags.

Sometimes after these programs we stayed to hear *the Barrelman* which came on at seven o'clock. *The Barrelman* was none other than Joey Smallwood himself. *The Barrelman* told Newfoundland stories and he was on station V.O.N.F. which stood for the Voice of Newfoundland. The announcer was Bob McLeod. He started off by advertising Green Label butter which we couldn't afford, having to be content with Solo butter, an almost inedible concoction. I never tasted this Green Label butter but I used to see it in the stores. It was wrapped in an off-white coloured piece of wax paper with the picture of a woman following a cow. The woman and the cow were drawn in green crayon.

I think it was the Barrelman who, on one July evening, told us an unbelievable story. He said that a man had told him that a fish came out of the water in Conception Bay and wrote on a rock with his tail, 'be ye ready on August 12'.

"Do you think that's true, Aunt Ethel." I asked, "Do you think the world is coming to an end on August 12?"

"I hope 'tis true," Aunt Ethel said, "I hope so, child. I can't wait to see my Blessed Redeemer face to face." That was no comfort to me at all. I lived in abject terror for the rest of the summer. I hardly told any lies at all and never said one single bad word as I prepared for the Judgment Day.

August 12 dawned calm and clear, but I didn't relax until the sun set peacefully in behind the blueberry barrens. After that, life got back to normal.

But the best program of all on the radio came on Saturday night at 9:30 pm. Jackie Welch on station V.O.N.F. Jackie Welch from St. John's. Can anyone remember him? Charlie and I wouldn't miss him for all the world.

Born to lose, my every hope is gone.
It's so hard to face an empty dawn.
All my life and now you say we're through
Born to lose and now I'm losing you.
sang Jackie Welch as we listened enthralled, or
I found my thrill
On Blueberry Hill

On Blueberry Hill where I first met you.

In between the songs, jigs and reels were played mostly on the accordion. *The Fisherman's Hornpipe*, *Soldier's Joy* and *The Banks of Newfoundland*. As soon as this happened, Charlie and I jumped up and pranced all around the floor in time to the music. Some of these tunes were quite ribald.

'Deed I am in love with you
Out all night in the foggy dew.
'Deed I am in love with you,
Mussels in the corner, or
Billy Peddle, Billy Peddle, did you see Billy White?
Oh, he's gone down town for to stay all night....

We sang as we jumped around the floor in time to the music.

It's a good thing that Aunt Ethel never came in to check on us. I never remember her doing that. Perhaps she was afraid of what she would find. One thing for sure, she would have knocked our heads together if she found us dancing, as dancing was a cardinal sin as far as the Methodist Church was concerned, and Aunt Ethel was an avid church-goer. "Oh, you wicked, wicked, children," she'd say if she ever caught us dancing.

Actually, I only remember one time that Aunt Ethel lost her patience with us. Charlie and I were racing up and down her staircase playing trains, our favourite game. Charlie, of course was the engineer. At the top of the stairs, hanging in the upstairs hall ceiling, was a glittering chandelier, its delicate glass prisms catching the rays of sunlight as they danced along the ceiling. In the center of this sparkle and glitz was a coal oil lamp held in place by a short chain of brass.

Charlie, the engineer, grabbed the chain to blow the whistle. "Whoo, whoo," he shouted as the chain slipped and the lamp tipped precariously.

We tried, Charlie and I. We tried hard to fix it but it was too much for our small inexperienced hands and minds. There was nothing to do but to call Aunt Ethel. She came wiping her hands on her apron. She took the lamp out of our hands and secured the chain. "Go on home, the both of yez," she said. That was the only time I can remember that she ever scolded us.

Now as I sit and reflect on the untamed wildness of my childhood, I am sometimes ridden with guilt and shame. Did we ever try to repay Aunt Ethel for her kindness and indulgence? No, we did not. Often, we stole her strawberries and rhubarb from her garden and ate them up, and worse still, we would crawl through her grass meadow flattening down the tall grass in which she took so much pride.

One thing, though, stands out in my memory. I remember myself, a child of about eight, going in the marsh (or mish as we called it) at the back of our house. In the woods around the marsh I remember picking a large bunch of ferns and buttercups which I carefully carried up to Aunt Ethel's house. I can see her now sitting on a chair in the middle of the kitchen. "These are for you, Aunt Ethel," I said, handing her the wild flowers.

To my surprise, she took the flowers and burst into tears, crying as if her heart would break. I wonder now what prompted this outburst of emotion. Is it possible that such a little act of kindness could have such an effect? I'll never know, but dear Aunt Ethel, it was little enough, considering all you did for me.

Aunt Ethel is gone now, and so I believe is her house. But the memories linger on until at last they, too, will fade away.

***

Fun With Familiar Phrases

If you always think before you act
You will ever out of trouble keep
And never fall into a trap
If you *Always look before you leap*

-Ron Young

Rhymes & Reflections

Life would be much better
And we'd easier get along
If we defended our rights
As often as our wrongs

-Ron Young

***

I Am A Fisherman *By David Boyd, Durrell, Newfoundland*

A seagull spreads its wings across the
face of dawn,
And the pulse of the restless sea throbs
across eternity.
My motor pounds me into another day,
As I come from the harbour
and into the bay
Where my nets are set -
By the headland craig and the
breaking shoal.

I'm a fisherman -
Nurtured on the salty
milk of an
island
breast
Little earthly
wealth I have, but

with riches I am blessed.
I've seen traps full of cod
Their streamlined shapes caught in a
sliver of sunlight -
Then rising full force to boil the
morning sea.

I've seen too, water-haul after water-
haul
And traps sunk with slub,
I've felt the pangs of hunger by a table
scarce of food!

But I care not much for earthly wealth,
For I've heard the call of the sea.
Her salty lips have kissed my brow,
She has whispered - free, free, free!

Remembering The Old Steam Bullet *By Ron Young*

I still see you at the station standing
Against the night - a looming giant
Admitting and discharging folks
Complacent, yet compliant
Waiting for the magic word,
Conductor shouts out, "All aboard!"
No longer are you quiet

You hiss and scream,
    releasing steam
Fuel is fired and burning
Inertia's strain you feel
    again
As motion is your yearning
You puff and pant, stamp feet and chant
Wheels slow - then faster - turning

The couplings'-clickin' tempo quickens
Clickety, clickety, clacker
Your slow-start ride enlivens stride
Whistle howls instanter

Your coal is hot - you start to trot
Then break into a canter

Clickety-clack! Clickety -lack!
Passing woodland, glen and pasture
Clickety-clickety-clickety-clack
Galloping, galloping faster
Inertia's pride is on your
    side
And rails your only
    master

And then at last you're lost to
    sight
Your presence swallowed by the night

Later still, the plaintive, sad refrain
Of your mournful whistle haunts again
Graveyards where the ghosts are
    keeping
Vigil while the world is sleeping

***

The Lighter Side

One day, shortly after the birth of their new baby, the mother had to go out to do some errands. The proud papa stayed home to watch his wonderful new son. Soon after the mother left, the baby started to cry. The father did everything he could think of, but the baby just wouldn't stop crying.

Finally, the dad got so worried he decided to take the infant to the doctor. After the doctor listened to all the father had done to get the baby to stop crying, the doctor began to examine the baby's ears, chest and then down to the diaper area. When he opened the diaper, he found it was just LOADED.

"Here's the problem," the Doctor said. "He just needs to be changed."

The father is very perplexed, "but the diaper package specifically stated it is good for up to 10 lbs!"

Submitted by Basil Packwood, Howley, Newfoundland

***

Notable Quotables By Ron Young
Meanings and origins of well-known words and expressions

What does the word 'Boycott' exactly mean, and where did it originate?

According to the *Oxford Dictionary*, Boycott means:

1. combine in refusing to have social or commercial relations with (a person, group, country, etc.) usually as punishment, or coercion.

2. refuse to handle (goods) to this end.

As to the origin; back in the 1800s, Captain Charles Boycott, worked so hard at collecting the rents, that eventually his tenants in Ireland got together and refused to work or to pay rent. They were so successful in their endeavor to bring attention to their plight that the method spread to other estates. Captain Boycott died in 1897, but his name and what it stood for back in Ireland has been with us ever since.

Innocence and Wisdom

A three-year-old went with his dad to see a litter of kittens. On returning home, he breathlessly informed his mother there were two boy kittens and two girl kittens. "How did you know?" his mother asked. "Daddy picked them up and looked underneath," he replied, "I think it's printed on the bottom."

***

Life Is A Masquerade Party

Author Unknown. Submitted by Rosemary (Dolly) Krause, (nee Stamp), New Jersey

Life is a masquerade party
We all have our own masks
to wear
While the rich pretend they
are happy
The poor pretend they
don't care.

But underneath all those
false faces
The comedy doesn't go far

For at night when we look in the
mirror
We see ourselves just as we are.

At night when the party is over
And our masks they are put on
the shelf
We may make the world think
we are happy
But we can't hide the truth
from ourself.

***

Bulletin Board

Eli's Butcher Shop

Honest scales - no two weigh's about it!

National Bank

We'll lend you all the money you need if you can prove you don't need it.

Strange but TRUE -Bill Sones & Rick Sones Ph.D.

Q. Do gorillas tell lies? Can a dolphin distinguish a reasonable request from a silly one? Will a parrot invent a new word out of the blue?

A. A female chimp named Washoe learned about 200 words of American sign language, used by many deaf people, reports Robert A. Baron in *Psychology*.

Koko, a female gorilla, mastered hundreds of signs and could string them into sentences, even creating novel concepts such as 'white tiger' to describe a zebra. On one occasion, after Koko jumped onto a sink that broke away from the wall, she accused one of the researchers of being responsible.

Akeakamai, a female dolphin, was taught 'hand gestures' symbolizing 50 objects or actions, and could comprehend sentences of up to five different gestures, such as "to place the Frisbee on her left in the basket on the right." Ake could even tell when her trainer was putting her on, ignoring such requests as "Go and fetch the swimming pool wall."

An African gray parrot named Alex could name roughly 80 objects and events and string words into sentences like "I want shower." When presented with an apple for the first time, Alex made up the word "banerry," combining banana and cherry, concepts already at his disposal.

***

Fun With Familiar Phrases

Peopled inclined to be dressed to the nines
Shouldn't throw cream pies
or custard cones
And *People who live in glass houses*
Shouldn't throw stones

-Ron Young

Rhymes & Reflections

He who learned to read
And never does, is a bigger fool
Than all the world's unfortunates
Who couldn't go to school

-Ron Young

***

What Manner of Manners?

Manners seem like common sense, but historically, our sense wasn't so common. The oldest known etiquette book is known among archaeologists as the Prisse Papyrus, and bears the title *Instructions of Ptahhotep.* It was written in about 2500 BC in the old kingdom of Egypt. Ptahhotep advises that when in the company of one's superiors

"laugh when he laughs." Do not argue when discussing philosophy with a superior, but instead agree with his views, "..so thou shalt be very agreeable to his heart." He also believes in the virtue of silence when talking to a boss: "Let thy mind be deep and thy speech be scanty," or with a wife, "Be silent, for it is a better gift than flowers."

Who Will Take Grandma?

Author Unknown. Submitted by Rachel Hollett, Cambridge, Nova Scotia.

Who will take Grandma?
Who will it be?
All of us want her
I'm sure you'll agree
Let's call a meeting
let's gather the clan,
Let's get it settled as soon as we can,
In such a big family
there's certainly one
Willing to give her
a place in the sun.

Strange how we thought that
she'd never wear out
But see how she walks
it's arthritis, no doubt
Her eyesight is faded
her memory's dim
She's apt to insist on the silliest whim
When people get older
they become such a care
She must have a home
but the question is where?

Remember the days
when she used to be spry?
Baked her own cookies
and made her own pie
Helped us with lessons
and tended our seams

Kissed away troubles
and mended our dreams?
Wonderful Grandma
we all loved her so
Isn't dreadful she's no place to go.

One little corner is all she would need
A shoulder to cry on - her bible to read
A chair by the window with sun
coming through
Some pretty flowers still
covered in dew -
Who'll warm her with
love so she won't mind
the cold?
Oh, who will take
Grandmother now that
she is old?

What Nobody wants her?
Oh, yes there is ONE
Willing to give her a place in the sun
Where she won't have to worry or
wonder or doubt -
And she won't be our problem to
bother about -
Pretty soon now
God will give her a bed -
But who'll dry our tears when dear
Grandma is dead?

***

Rhymes & Reflections

You'll never know the value
Of the harvest you yield
Until you first
Have toiled in the field

-Ron Young

Fun With Familiar Phrases

A Will-o-the-wisp will never get rich
A rolling stone gathers no moss
A travelling Gypsy has never a home
But also has never a boss

-Ron Young

Is That A Fact?   *By Ron Young*

Reprinted from
Downhomer Magazine

Many things are accepted as facts. Not all of them are.

Everyone knows that one of the greatest things which the great American president, Abraham Lincoln did was free all slaves in America with his famous Emancipation Proclamation.

The fact is that the Emancipation Proclamation only set free the slaves in the Confederacy, over which Abraham Lincoln, at that time, had no jurisdiction. In other words, it freed no slaves whatsoever. Some of the states which were part of the Union, Kentucky and Maryland, for instance, had slaves at that time, and continued to have slaves. One of the direct results of the Proclamation was that 180,000 former slaves joined the Union Army. This, along with the Proclamation itself, gave the appearance to other nations, specifically England and France, that the war being waged by the North was a war against slavery. This is probably why France and England didn't take part in the war on the side of the South, on whom they relied for most of their cotton.

***

Life's Funny Experiences

Reprinted from
Downhomer Magazine

Brown Bagging It

I went to Toronto in 1966 and after I got a job, I called a couple of my friends and told them to come up. They got work shortly after they arrived. They had trouble waking up in the morning so I went out with them while they bought an alarm clock. We found a suitable clock which we wound up to make sure that it was working. It worked fine so we bought it. On the way back we stopped in for a couple of cold beers. The three of us went to the washroom and when we came out someone yelled, "Get out now," which we did. There were police and police vehicles everywhere outside the bar. Several police officers went inside the bar and came out a short time later carrying the brown bag containing the clock that we had left ticking on the table.

Submitted by Peter Picco, Freshwater, Placentia, Newfoundland

Confessions of the Rich and Famous

I am not the boss of my house. I don't know how I lost it. I don't know when I lost it. I don't think I ever had it. But I've seen the boss's job and I don't want it.

- *Bill Cosby*

Aunt Alice says:

> Skinny people irritate me! Especially when they say things like, "You know, sometimes I just forget to eat." Now I've forgotten my address, my mother's maiden name, and my keys. But I've never forgotten to eat. You have to be a special kind of stupid to forget to eat.

***

Smiles, Chuckles & Belly Laughs

Gravitationally Challenged

This is an accident report which was printed in the newsletter of the British equivalent of the Workers' Compensation Board. This is the bricklayer's report....a true story.

Dear Sir:

I am writing in response to your request for additional information in block #3 of the accident report form. I put "Poor Planning" as the cause of my accident. You asked for a fuller explanation and I trust the following details will be sufficient. I am a bricklayer by trade. On the day of the accident, I was working alone on the roof of a new, six-story building. When I completed my work, I found I had some bricks left over which, when weighed later were found to be slightly in excess of 500 lbs. Rather than carry the bricks down by hand, I decided to lower them in a barrel by using a pulley which was attached to the side of the building at the sixth floor. Securing the rope at ground level, I went up to the roof, swung the barrel out and loaded the bricks into it. Then I went down and untied the rope, holding it tightly to ensure a slow descent of the bricks.

You will note in block #11 of the accident report form that my weight is 135 lbs. Due to my surprise at being jerked off the ground so suddenly, I lost my presence of mind and forgot to let go of the rope. Needless to say, I proceeded at a rapid rate up the side of the building. In the vicinity of the third floor, I met the barrel which was now proceeding downward at an equally impressive speed. This explains the fractured skull, minor abrasions and the broken collarbone, as listed in Section 3 of the accident report form. Slowed only slightly, I continued my rapid ascent, not stopping until the fingers of my right hand were two knuckles deep into the pulley. Fortunately by this time, I had regained my presence of mind and was able to hold tightly to the rope, in spite of the excruciating pain I was now beginning to experience. At approximately the same time, however, the barrel of bricks hit the ground and the bottom fell out of the barrel. Now devoid of the weight of the bricks, that barrel weighed approximately 50 lbs. I refer you again to my weight.

As you might imagine, I began a rapid descent down the side of the building. In the vicinity of the third floor, I met the barrel coming up. This accounts for the two fractured ankles, broken tooth and severe lacerations of my legs and lower body. Here my luck began to change slightly. The encounter with the barrel seemed to slow me enough to lessen my injuries when I fell into the pile of bricks, and fortunately only three vertebrae were cracked. I am sorry to report, however, as I lay there on the pile of bricks, in pain, unable to move, I again lost my composure and presence of mind and let go of the rope and I lay there watching the empty barrel begin its journey back onto me. This explains the two broken legs. I hope this is a satisfactory explanation.

Sincerely yours,
Name Withheld

***

Classroom Chuckles

Jonas: I eaten seven hot dogs for lunch, sir.
Teacher: Ate, Jonas! Ate!
Jonas: No sir, seven. There were eight on my plate but I only eaten seven.

**Reprinted from
Downhomer Magazine**

***

How To Bake A Cake

Anonymous

Light the oven. Get out bowl, spoons and ingredients. Grease the pan. Crack nuts. Remove 18 blocks and 7 toy autos from the kitchen table. Measure 2 cups of flour. Remove Kelly's hands from the flour. Wash flour off. Measure one more cup of flour to replace the flour on the floor. Put the flour, baking powder and salt in a sifter. Get the dustpan and brush up pieces of bowl which Kelly knocked on the floor. Get another bowl. Answer doorbell. Return to kitchen and remove Kelly's hands from bowl. Wash Kelly. Get out egg. Answer phone. Return. Take out greased pan. Remove pinch of salt from the pan. Look for Kelly. Get another pan and grease it. Answer the phone. Return to the kitchen and find Kelly. Remove the grimy hands from the bowl. Wash off Kelly who flees, knocking bowl off the table. Wash kitchen floor, wash the table, wash the walls, and wash the dishes. CALL THE BAKERY. LIE DOWN.

SKIPPER SAYS:

You can't believe everything you hear - but you can repeat it anyway.

***

The Seasons Of Your Passing *By Ron Young*

When over Summer
evening hovers
Days leftover haze
When all I ever want
to do
Is lie around and laze
And into setting sun I
find
I am inclined to gaze
I see your face reflected in
Its final dying rays

When I recall as dry leaves fall
When Autumn's almost through
Before crackling carpet on forest floor
Wilts with the rain and dew
And nature hasn't yet found out
That Winter's overdue
That I've walked through woods like
these before
So long ago with you

Comes ice and snow, when
cold winds blow
My thoughts are still the same
On cold, cold days I have my
ways
The Winter winds to tame
Sitting by my cozy fire
Reflecting on the flame
But the wind still whistles
down the flue
Calling out your name

In Spring, when gentle rain, again
Breathes life into the lawn
Reminding me that all things die
While life goes on and on
When dreams of things long past
it seems
Won't let me sleep 'til dawn
I feel you in the morning mist
'Tho many years you're gone

***

Fun With Familiar Phrases

If the clues point to a certain event
Then it probably will transpire
Dark clouds foretell impending rain
And *Where there's smoke there's fire*
-Ron Young

Rhymes & Reflections

"Better late than never"
You've often heard it said;
Still looking for a letter
Are you waiting 'til I'm dead?
-Author Unknown

Tonic For The Soul

Thoughts To Live By, Stories, Poems, Humour, & Other Interesting Items

The Lighter Side

A rabbi and a priest get into a car accident, and it's a bad one. Both cars are totally demolished but amazingly neither of the clerics is hurt. After they crawl out of their cars, the rabbi sees the priest's collar and says, "So you're a priest. I'm a rabbi. Just look at our cars. There's nothing left, but we are unhurt. This must be a sign from God. God must have meant that we should meet and be friends and live together in peace the rest of our days."

The priest replies, "I agree with you completely. This must be a sign from God."

The rabbi continues, "And look at this. Here's another miracle. My car is completely demolished but this bottle of Manishewitz wine didn't break. Surely God wants us to drink this wine and celebrate our good fortune."

Then he hands the bottle to the priest. The priest agrees, takes a few big swigs, and hands the bottle back to the rabbi. The rabbi takes the bottle, immediately puts the cap on, and hands it back to the priest. The priest asks, "Aren't you having any?"

The rabbi replies, "No...I think I'll wait for the police."

***

Life's Funny Experiences
Extended Vacation

Reprinted from
Downhomer Magazine

In May of 1995, my wife and I were visiting St. John's, Newfoundland, where I was born. One day we were out in Portugal Cove and were looking around for a restaurant as it was lunch time. Two men were in a van, parked on the wharf, waiting for the ferry to Bell Island. I parked next to them, walked over and asked if they knew of a place where we could eat.

The passenger said, "B'y, dere's a good place to eat right at the top of the hill."

Before I could leave he queried, "Yur not from around here b'y?"

"No," I said, "We live in B.C."

The driver then leaned over and said, "B'ys, me and the wife went out in '86. We had a grand time. The wife liked it so much she went back again six months later."

That's great," I said, "How did she like her vacation?"

"I don't know b'y," he replied, "I haven't seen her since."

Submitted by Bill and Rita Hogan

Rhymes & Reflections

You can be sure that yourself
You'll surely deceive
If you confuse the truth with
What you want to believe
-Ron Young

***

Fun With Familiar Phrases

There are some men who are inclined to
sin
Then hide it by giving false names
But in the end they can't hope to win
For they cannot hide from *Hell's flames*.
-Ron Young

A Birthday Message

Author Unknown. Submitted by Dorothy and John Rowe
Some folks grow older with birthdays, it's true
But others grow nicer as years widen their view.
And a heart that is young lends an aura of grace
That rivals in beauty a young pretty face.
For no one would notice a few little wrinkles,
When a kind loving heart fills the eyes full of twinkles.
So don't count your years by the birthdays you've had
But by things you have done to make other folks glad.

***

Aunt Alice says:

If men can run the world, why can't they stop wearing neckties? How intelligent is it to start the day by tying a noose around your neck?

***

Fun With Familiar Phrases

In all the ways you can be seen
You always will be at your very best
When your body and your soul is clean
For *Cleanliness is next to Godliness*
-Ron Young

Rhymes & Reflections

He who has a thousand friends
Had not a friend to spare,
And he who has one enemy
Will meet him everywhere.
-Author Unknown

Smiles, Chuckles & Belly Laughs

FARMIN'

by Bruce Stirling

My dad owned a restaurant on Water Street for many years. It was called The Sterling Restaurant. When my father named his restaurant, I imagine that he spelt Sterling with an 'E' to indicate the sterling quality of the food, as it was a time when pounds sterling and sterling silver were practically synonymous; a time when we Newfoundlanders looked eastward to the Mother Country for quality in everything.

The farmer's market was located directly behind the restaurant. Every Saturday, the area would be jammed with farm wagons loaded with produce. There would be cages with live chickens, ducks and rabbits; boxes of free kittens; and a rabble of assorted farm dogs that had followed the wagons to town. As a ten-year-old, I found the smell of horses and horse by-products, the laughter and chatter of humans mixing with the sounds of excited dogs, chickens and ducks, to be far more exciting than anything kids watch today on television.

My father got to know one of the farmers quite well. I forget the farmer's name, but I remember his farm was in the Goulds. One summer when my mother returned to England to visit her many brothers and sisters, I was sent to spend the summer with the farmer and his family, who had a son my age. I don't know what arrangements my parents made with the farmer, but I do remember that I was treated like one of the family in that I was expected to work like everybody else. I would walk behind the mower with a two-pronged hay-fork at haying time. My job was to clear away any fallen hay that might interfere with the next cut. The farmer's son, Eric and I, would stomp down the hay as it was forked up onto the long hay cart, and do the same thing again when it was forked up to the hay loft. We collected eggs, watered the horses and fed the pigs. I loved every minute of it and dreamed of having my own farm one day.

Before I could, The Second World War got in the way. The next thing I knew, I found myself married with three small sons, all of whom had large appetites. I also discovered, after winning The War, that there wasn't much of a demand in the private sector for an ex-artillery officer, no matter how qualified he might be. So I went to work for a daily newspaper, trying to become a political cartoonist in my spare time, which was very limited, as I also worked in the evenings as a waiter. I borrowed some money from my mother-in-law and bought a small restaurant of my own (actually, it was a fish and chip shop and not the gold mine that the previous owner had assured me it was). Finally, in desperation, I built and operated a motion picture theatre, at a time when television was putting small operations like mine out of business every week.

All of these ventures took place within a five-year period. It took me that long to realize that there was no place for me in the free enterprise system. Fortunately for me, the Korean War started at that time and Canada began to rebuild its armed services. The

Air Force announced its need for officers with army backgrounds, so I went back into uniform, blue instead of khaki. My dream of owning a farm had to be placed on the back burner for another 15 years.

I had almost reached retirement age before we finally bought 25 acres of farm land. Actually, it was five acres of farm land, planted in corn. The rest was scrub bush and swamp, ideal breeding ground for mosquitoes, as we discovered later.

By the time we had a local contractor build us a modest three-room bungalow in the middle of the corn field, and I had constructed a chicken house off to one side, winter had set in. So I subscribed to *The Hobby Farmer* and spent many a pleasant evening in front of the fireplace, thumbing through the magazine, planning what I would do come spring.

It was on one such evening that a caption under a photo of a pleasant looking young Black Angus caught my eye. "How To Cut Your Meat Costs In Half," the heading read. All one had to do, the article explained, was buy a young steer in the spring; let it graze until fall, then have it butchered. During all those lazy, hazy days of summer it would be putting on pound after pound of delicious steaks while it ate free grass. Sounded like a terrific investment. "Let's buy a steer," I said to my wife, Marj, "as soon as the snow's gone."

There was a butcher up the road, about a mile from our place. When I asked him where I could buy a steer, he offered to sell me one of his at cost, seeing as how I was a neighbour and all. His business was largely bulk meat for freezers, which meant a large turnover of animals. He nearly always had a dozen or more steer in his holding shed, he told me. "Just go down there when you're ready," he said, "and pick yourself an animal."

One bright and sunny afternoon, Marj drove our 13-year-old son, Steve, and me, up to the holding shed. I had 50 feet of clothes line on my lap, more than necessary to lead a steer home, of course, but I hated to cut it. The shed, a long, narrow building, contained some 30 animals of various shapes and sizes. I looked them over critically. Seeing as how I was paying a flat rate, it seemed sensible to select the largest of the lot.

With Steve watching, I made a loop at one end of the rope, as though I knew what I was doing, waited for the appropriate moment, then dropped the loop over the head of my choice. Wrapping the rope several times around my gloved hands, I yanked as hard as I could, hoping to separate my steer from the rest of the herd. All the animals promptly bolted for the opposite end of the shed, including mine. I was pulled completely off my feet, as I couldn't let go of the rope which was twisted tightly around my hand. I ploughed a trench with my upper torso through 20 feet or more of fresh manure, several inches thick. It occurred to me, as I struggled to my feet, that getting the steer home was going to be more complicated than I had thought it would be.

Thankful that I had 50 feet of rope, I gave the end to Steve, who was careful not to touch me. "Now," I said to our youngest, "when I chase all the animals up to this end of the shed, you run out the door with the rope. Make sure you close the door behind you, then tie the rope to the tree that's just outside." My plan worked beautifully. We had our steer isolated and close to the door.

Step two: "Now Steve," I instructed, "when I yell, you open the door, and I'll chase our steer out. Then you close the door." Once again my plan worked according to Hoyle, except that the steer dashed round and round the tree, shortening its leash with each revolution. We were so fascinated by the spectacle of the steer tying itself to the tree that Steve forgot to close the door. All the other animals, seeing the bright light of freedom beckoning, came charging towards us. Before we could get the door closed, three had escaped. Fortunately, the fenced area around the shed was comparatively small. We eventually got the escapees back, but not without expanding a considerable amount of energy and patience.

As Steve and I stood trying to catch our breath - and glaring at Marj, who hadn't stopped laughing since I stepped outside the shed - a car load of farm kids pulled over to see what was going on. "The only way you kin git that animal back to your place," one suggested, "is to tie it to your bumper. Here, we'll give you a hand." The five young teenagers pushed the reluctant steer to the rear of our car and tied its head to our bumper, allowing about six feet of slack. Wishing us good luck, they piled back into their car and drove away.

Just as we were about to do likewise, a passing farmer slammed on the brakes of his truck and came to a sliding halt.

"What in the name of all that's holy are you doin' with that poor animal?" he demanded.

"I'm taking it back to our place," I explained.

"God Almighty," he said. "You'll pull the poor critter's head clean off! You have to lead it back. Here, let me show you." He untied the steer, put a half hitch around its nose and handed me the rope. "Just walk it nice and easy up the road," he said. "Your son can follow behind with this stick and remind the critter from time to time what its supposed to be doin'."

Off we started up the road. Me first; then the steer, with Steve and his stick taking up the rear. Marj drove 50 feet behind the parade, still laughing.

Halfway home, we passed the long, rambling home of a wealthy neighbour. From the number of cars in the driveway, it appeared that they were entertaining. If I had kept my eyes on the steer instead of being nosey, it might not have happened. Just as we were abreast of the wide open gates, the damn steer shook its head; the rope fell off, and it made a bee-line up the driveway.

With me, still covered in ripe manure, in hot pursuit, the blasted animal galloped across the middle of two flower beds, around the corner of the house and right through the startled guests gathered at the near end of the swimming pool. (I was close behind. I wore an old felt hat that I called my farmer's hat. I pulled it down over my eyes, praying that nobody would recognize me. (Marj told me later that she wouldn't have recognized me.) Around the far side of the house we went. Across another flower bed and back out through the front gates. Once on the road, the stupid animal inexplicably stopped dead in its tracks, allowing the rope to be cinched around its nose again. It seemed to know that it had misbehaved because it followed me the rest of the way home like Mary's little lamb. Marj had tears running down her cheeks and didn't stop laughing until supper time.

After supper I walked over to the pasture fence - our corn stalks had been replaced by grass. My head of cattle was grazing peacefully - a pleasant bovine scene. In the morning, the so-and-so steer had disappeared. I was about to learn my first cattle lesson; i.e. cattle are herd animals. They don't like to be alone, especially if other animals are close by. I walked up to my neighbour's place, he was a real farmer, and collected my steer who was trying to hide in the middle of his milk cows. The next day I had to do it again. I couldn't understand how the critter got out, (I was beginning to think in farmer's language.) I checked my fence carefully. There was only two feet between the strands of barbed wire, and the wire itself was tight. That evening I saw the steer get out myself. It went through the wire sideways, like a high jump jumper. When I told my city friends that a steer can actually jump between two strands of horizontal barbed wire, horizontally, they looked at me as though I had been out in the sun too long. When I told Marj, she just started laughing again. But it's true. Believe me!

To keep the animal in my own field, I did two things. First, so it could never again hide in the bush, I spent a couple of dollars and bought the largest cow bell that the farm store had in stock. I strapped it around the critter's neck with one of my old belts. Second, I connected the horizontal strands of wire with vertical pieces midway between the fence posts.

The next afternoon when we arrived back from shopping, our field was empty again. Nor would my friends believe that a steer would stand perfectly still in the middle of dense bush, even though I was only ten feet away. The bell was useless. I took it off and hung it over a fence post where it slowly rusted in the weather. A few years later, when I decided that I really wasn't cut out to be a farmer, we held an auction, and somebody from the city bought the cow bell as an antique. Marj even thought that was funny.

Anyway, I was so annoyed that the steer kept getting out that I went a little crazy, buying coil after coil of barbed wire until our place looked like a concentration camp. And it worked! No more trudging up to the neighbour's. No more searching in the bush. There was another consolation; by the time the butcher's truck arrived to pick up our animal, it looked as though it had doubled in size. Its sides were positively bulging with extra meat.

Marj and I were dumbfounded a couple of days later when the butcher greeted us with: "Your animal was just about ready to calf. A fine little bull it would have been." I would swear on a stack of Bibles that our steer had nothing between its hind legs, which is the way that steers are supposed to be. Nor would my city friends believe that the animal didn't have an udder. "How could it feed its baby if it didn't have an udder?" they wanted to know. The thing is, it didn't have an udder. I'm positive I would have noticed if it had one when it went through the fence horizontally, that's for sure.

And to add insult to injury, there was no way that Marj would eat an animal that had given her so many good laughs, especially as it was nearly a fellow mother. So I had to trade our steer with the butcher for anonymous meat. All in all, considering the amount of barbed wire I had bought, I doubt that I broke even on the deal. Even counting the profit on the cow bell.

Is That A Fact? *By Ron Young*

**Reprinted from
Downhomer Magazine**

Many things are accepted as facts. Not all of them are.

Newfoundlanders living in Toronto who drive home every year know that the route back home is as much in a northerly direction as it is in an easterly direction. Americans think of Newfoundland as that island in the north, and of Labrador as being in the Arctic. Some Canadians believe the same thing.

The fact is that the Island of Newfoundland lies between 46° and 52° north latitude. The 49th parallel, which is for the most part the boundary between Canada and the US, cuts the island in half. In other words, the majority of Newfoundland residents live further south than all of the residents of the Prairie Provinces and British Columbia, with the exception of part of Vancouver Island. Labrador is no further north than all of Germany, Denmark and Holland, and most of England. The City of St. John's is south of Winnipeg; Calgary; Regina, Vancouver; Berlin, London, England; and even Paris, France.

***

Nan's Way

Lettuce won't "rust" in the refrigerator if it is wrapped in paper towels.

***

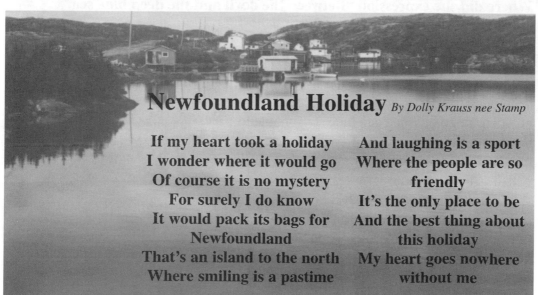

Newfoundland Holiday *By Dolly Krauss nee Stamp*

If my heart took a holiday
I wonder where it would go
Of course it is no mystery
For surely I do know
It would pack its bags for
Newfoundland
That's an island to the north
Where smiling is a pastime

And laughing is a sport
Where the people are so
friendly
It's the only place to be
And the best thing about
this holiday
My heart goes nowhere
without me

Strange but TRUE *-Bill Sones & Rick Sones Ph.D.*

Q. When a 40-year-old woman becomes pregnant, how old is the fertilized egg?

A. All or almost all female mammals are born with their full complement of eggs, so the egg in question is 40 years old - the likely reason birth abnormalities increase with the age of the mother, says Chris McGowan in *Diatoms to Dinosaurs: The Size and Scale of Living Things*.

✳✳✳

SKIPPER SAYS:

Before sixteen a boy is a boy scout, after sixteen he is a girl scout.

✳✳✳

**Reprinted from
Downhomer Magazine**

Notable Quotables By Ron Young

Meanings and origins of well-known words and expressions

Where did the expression "Between the devil and the deep blue sea" originate, and what does it mean?

The expression means the same as "Between a rock and a hard place" or "Damned if you do and damned if you don't." It conjures up images of being chased by the devil with nowhere to go but the deep blue sea, unable to swim, and without a boat of course.

In fact, the devil, in this case has to do with boats. The devil is a seam in a wooden ship's hull lying just at waterline. It was called the devil because when it sprung a leak it was difficult to reach from the inside and had to be repaired from the outside. Depending on the height of the waves and swells on the water, there wasn't much room to make repairs between the devil and the deep blue sea.

Tonic For The Soul
Thoughts To Live By, Stories, Poems, Humour, & Other Interesting Items

Inspirational
Slow Me Down, Lord
Submitted by Joe Lack

Ease the pounding of my heart
by the quieting of my mind.
Steady my hurried pace with a
vision of the eternal reach of
time.
Give me, amid the confusion of
the day, the calmness of the
everlasting hills.
Break the tensions of my nerves
and muscles with the soothing
music of the singing streams
that live in my memory.
Teach me the art of taking
minute vacations
of slowing down to look at a
flower
to chat with a friend,
to pat a dog, to smile at a child,
to read a few lines from a good
book.
Slow me down, Lord, and inspire
me to send my roots deep into the
soil of life's enduring values, that I
may grow toward my greater
destiny.
Remind me each day that the race
is not always to the swift;
that there is more to life than
increasing its speed.
Let me look upward to the
towering oak and know that it
grew
great and strong because it grew
slowly and well.

***

Aunt Alice says:

These days I wonder a lot about the hereafter -
I go to get something and then wonder,
what am I here after?

***

Fun With Familiar Phrases

Violent persuasion can never attain
What can be done with the written word
Words on paper will your point explain
For *The pen is mightier than the sword*
-Ron Young

Rhymes & Reflections

The least you lose by being rude
Is opportunity to be kind
The most you lose by being courteous
Is a moment of your time
-Ron Young

Ageless
This is a nice thing to read all the way through:

*I've learned that I like my teacher because she cries when we sing *Silent Night*. **Age 6**

*I've learned that our dog doesn't want to eat my broccoli either. **Age 7**

*I've learned that when I wave to people in the country, they stop what they are doing and wave back. **Age 9**

*I've learned that just when I get my room the way I like it, Mom makes me clean it up again. **Age 12**

*I've learned that if you want to cheer yourself up, you should try cheering someone else up. **Age 14**

*I've learned that although it's hard to admit it, I'm secretly glad my parents are strict with me. **Age 15**

*I've learned that silent company is often more healing than words of advice. **Age 24**

*I've learned that brushing my child's hair is one of life's great pleasures. **Age 26**

*I've learned that wherever I go, the world's worst drivers have followed me there. **Age 29**

*I've learned that if someone says something unkind about me, I must live so that no one will believe it. **Age 39**

*I've learned that there are people who love you dearly but just don't know how to show it. **Age 42**

*I've learned that you can make someone's day by simply sending them a little note. **Age 44**

*I've learned that the greater a person's sense of guilt, the greater his or her need to cast blame on others. **Age 46**

*I've learned that children and grandparents are natural allies. **Age 47**

*I've learned that no matter what happens, or how bad it seems today, life does go on, and it will be better tomorrow. **Age 48**

*I've learned that singing *Amazing Grace* can lift my spirits for hours. **Age 49**

*I've learned that motel mattresses are better on the side away from the phone. **Age 50**

*I've learned that you can tell a lot about a man by the way he handles these three things: a rainy day, lost luggage, and tangled Christmas tree lights. **Age 52**

*I've learned that keeping a vegetable garden is worth a medicine cabinet full of pills. **Age 52**

*I've learned that regardless of your relationship with your parents, you miss them terribly after they die. **Age 53**

*I've learned that making a living is not the same thing as making a life. **Age 58**

*I've learned that if you want to do something positive for your children, work to improve your marriage. **Age 61**

*I've learned that life sometimes gives you a second chance. **Age 62**

*I've learned that you shouldn't go through life with a catcher's mitt on both hands. You need to be able to throw something back. **Age 64**

*I've learned that if you pursue happiness, it will elude you. But if you focus on your family, the needs of others, your work, meeting new people, and doing the very best you can, happiness will find you. **Age 65**

*I've learned that whenever I decide something with kindness, I usually make the right decision. **Age 66**

*I've learned that everyone can use a prayer. **Age 72**

*I've learned that it pays to believe in miracles. And to tell the truth, I've seen several. **Age 75**

*I've learned that even when I have pains, I don't have to be one. **Age 82**

*I've learned that every day you should reach out and touch someone. People love that human touch - holding hands, a warm hug, or just a friendly pat on the back. **Age 85**

*I've learned that I still have a lot to learn. **Age 92**

Confessions of the Rich and Famous

There's very little advice in men's magazines, because men don't think there's a lot they don't know. Women do. Women want to learn. Men think, "I know what I'm doing, just show me somebody naked." - *Jerry Seinfield*

Tonic For The Soul

Thoughts To Live By, Stories, Poems, Humour, & Other Interesting Items

Look Up And Grin

Author Unknown. Submitted by Cecil Owens, Saint John, New Brunswick

The good Lawd sends me troubles
   And I got to work 'em out
   But I look around and see
     There's trouble all about

And when I see my troubles
   I jes' look up and grin
   To think of all the troubles
     That I ain't in

✳✳✳

The Heart Of The Clown

Author Unknown. Submitted by Eugene from Bulley's Cove, Newfoundland

A certain man made an appointment to see a psychologist. He arrived at the psychologist office and said to him, "Doctor, I always feel depressed. No matter what I do I still feel depressed. I just don't know what to do." The psychologist looked at him and said, "Come with me to the window." The man followed and then the psychologist pointed outside and said, "Do you see that tent over there in the distance? Well, there is a circus in town and it is really good. There are lots of acts to watch, especially the clown acts, and there is one clown in particular who is extremely funny. He will make you rock with laughter over and over again. Go and see the clown and I guarantee that you will not have reason to be depressed again!" The man turned to the psychologist with sad eyes and said, "Doctor, I am that clown!"

✳✳✳

The Lighter Side

Lots Of Signal

The whole lifestyle of Newfoundland began to change with our entry into Confederation. Television, roads and travel made the average Newfoundlander conscious of style. Women began to put their hair in curlers or visit beauty salons. Prior to this women seldom bothered.

The newfangled rollers that women began to put in their hair drew some comments. On one occasion a lady dropped into the store with her hair in curlers. The clerk, a rather observant young fellow, looked at the curlers and said, "Martha, how many stations can you get on that thing?"

SKIPPER SAYS:

I gave up eating an apple a day when I noticed that doctors don't make house calls anymore.

***

Back From The Abyss

Reprinted from
Downhomer Magazine

By Ron Young

When the pain in your chest
Feels like it will burst
And your heart palpitates
And you fear it's the worst

Your time's close at hand
That much you sure know
You've so much to do
But it's now time to go

You sped right through life
Running, sprinting and dashing
Not stopping to relish
Each moment in passing

If you could go back now
Some things you would alter
You'd make time for your friends
And your kin, without falter

The time for expression
Has now passed you by
Inner thoughts all unspoken
You're time's come to dic

So just go see your doctor
And have him confirm
Your about now to meet
The conqueror worm

II
"Your heart's fine," says the doctor
"And you're in great shape

Except for a strained muscle
On your breast plate

Just do chest expansions
And walk daily a mile
As you take these pills,
You'll be well in a while"

The twinkle of hope
Is brought back to your eye
You are still with the living
You are not going to die

You give thanks to your doctor
And you give thanks to God
That you are still on
The green side of the sod

Your life will be different
Of that much, you well know
You will savour each moment
And take life more slow

But as you dote on the life
That you thought was gone
You'll remember two things
As you carry on

Life's not a given
It is only loaned
And your death wasn't cancelled
It was only postponed

Tonic For The Soul

Thoughts To Live By, Stories, Poems, Humour, & Other Interesting Items

Life's Funny Experiences
A Time To Expire

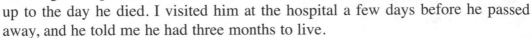

Back in November of 1996 my grandfather, who was 97, passed away after falling a couple of months earlier and breaking his hip. The man had wit, second-to-none, right up to the day he died. I visited him at the hospital a few days before he passed away, and he told me he had three months to live.

"How do you know that? "I asked.

Holding out his arm he said, "See this armband the hospital put on my arm. On one side it's got my name and my date of birth, May 16th, 1899." Then turning the band over he said, "Now see the other side, it says, EXPIRY DATE-January, 31st 1997."

Reprinted from
Downhomer Magazine

Submitted by Ed Sisk, Halifax,Nova Scotia

***

Classroom Chuckles

Teacher: Your writing is awful, Jonas. Why do you write so poorly?

Reprinted from
Downhomer Magazine

Jonas: So you won't pick up on my spelling mistakes.

***

Is That A Fact?

Many things are accepted as facts. Not all of them are.
"Can You Stand On A Dock?"

Reprinted from
Downhomer Magazine

A wharf is a structure which juts out into the water to provide a place for boats to tie up. Every Newfoundlander knows that. On the Mainland it is sometimes called a "dock".

The fact is "wharf" is correct, "dock" is not. The dock is actually the water area beside the wharf on which the boat floats. Pier levee, jetty or quay is acceptable, but dock, as a structure upon which to walk, doesn't hold any water.

***

Fun With Familiar Phrases

Too many tailors will tangle the threads
And render useless the cloth
A company won't run
with too many heads
And *Too many cooks spoil the broth*
-Ron Young

Rhymes & Reflections

Any man who says
He is happy with life
Is a man who has
A lucky wife

-Ron Young

Aunt Alice says:

> The nice part about living in a small town is that when you don't know what you're doing, someone else does.

***

Is That A Fact? *By Ron Young*

Reprinted from Downhomer Magazine

Many things are accepted as facts. Not all of them are.

Pancake Day and Mardi Gras

Some of us remember celebrating Pancake Day. We remember finding pennies, buttons, nickels and sometimes even dimes, in our pancakes. Most Newfoundlanders know Pancake Day as a Newfoundland or English tradition.

The fact is Pancake day is celebrated in most of the Christian world. Pancake day, or *Shrove Tuesday*, as it is called in some places falls between February 2 and March 9 according to the date of Easter. The word *Shrove*, which is derived from the word *Shrive*, refers to the confession of sins on preparation for Lent, a custom which dates back to the Middle Ages.

Many customs were developed from *Shrove Tuesday* celebrations. In France it's called *Mardi Gras* which means *Fat Tuesday*. The word 'Fat' is used because it was on that day that everyone stuffed themselves with all the fatty food they would be denied during Lent. Pancakes, which contain eggs and fat, were one of the popular foods on *Shrove Tuesday*.

The *Fat Tuesday* (Mardi Gras) celebrations are now a big event in New Orleans, where many French Canadians settled after being expelled from Acadia (now Nova Scotia) by the British.

Germany has its *Fetter Dienstag* and other European Countries have their version of *Fat Tuesday*.

Football and other games were much practiced in the English-speaking world, and there was much horseplay in schools and universities on *Shrove Tuesday*.

***

Fun With Familiar Phrases

You can't teach an old dog new tricks
For they've passed their learning days
And older folks are like these dogs
For they're just as set in their ways
-Ron Young

Rhymes & Reflections

A wise old owl lived in an oak;
The more he saw, the less he spoke;
The less he spoke, the more he heard;
Why can't we all be like that bird?
-Author Unknown

Smiles, Chuckles & Belly Laughs
Keeping Fit - Calorie Burning Activities *Anonymous*

Beating around the bush	75
Jogging your memory	125
Jumping to conclusions	10
Climbing the walls	150
Swallowing your pride	50
Passing the buck	25
Grasping for straws	75
Beating your own drum	100
Throwing your weight around	50 - 300
(depending on your weight)	
Dragging your heels	100
Pushing your luck	250
Making mountains out of molehills	500
Spinning your wheels	175
Flying off the handle	225
Hitting the nail on the head	75
Turning the other cheek	75
Jumping on the bandwagon	200
Balancing the books	23
Beating your head against the wall	175
Running around in circles	250
Chewing your nails	10
Eating crow	222
Fishing for compliments	50
Tooting your own horn	25
Climbing the ladder of success	775
Pulling out the stops	15
Adding fuel to the fire	150
Pouring salt on the wound	10
Wrapping it up at day's end	12

***

Fun With Familiar Phrases

It seems that time goes slower
When we anticipate
It seems *A watched pot never boils*
When we stand around and wait

-Ron Young

Rhymes & Reflections

For daily fulfillment
That never ends
Treat your friends like family
And your family like friends.

-Ron Young

Notable Quotables *By Ron Young*

Reprinted from Downhomer Magazine

Meanings and origins of well-known words and expressions

Where did the word 'Breakfast' come from?

In the middle ages (from about 400 AD to 1500 AD) most people fasted, having only two meals a day. The exceptions to this were the sick, the labourers, infants and the elderly.

Then someone decided to 'break the fast' by introducing a third meal which was eaten in the morning. This 'break fast' meal soon became an accepted practice with everybody, and the name breakfast came into common use.

***

Inspirational

Shoes

Author Unknown

As Gandhi stepped aboard a train one day, one of his shoes slipped off and landed on the track. He was unable to retrieve it as the train was moving. To the amazement of his companions, Gandhi calmly took off his other shoe and threw it back along the track to land close to the first. Asked by a fellow passenger why he did so, Gandhi smiled.

"The poor man who finds the shoe lying on the track," he replied, "will now have a pair he can use."

Confessions of the Rich and Famous

I have had my different husbands, my families. I am fond of them all and I visit them all. But deep inside me there is the feeling that I belong to show business.

- Ingrid Bergman

Strange but TRUE *-Bill Sones & Rick Sones Ph.D.*

Q. Do blind people see in their dreams?

A. They do if they once had sight, though the dream images fade over time. People born blind have no pictures but dream vividly in the other senses.

***

Nan's Way

The coldest part of any refrigerator is the top back shelf.

***

What Manner of Manners?

Manners seem like common sense, but historically, our sense wasn't so common.

When forks were first invented in eleventh-century Tuscany, they were very unsuccessful. The clergy forbid the use of them, saying that only human fingers, created by and in the image of God, were worthy to touch the food that God had provided.

Bulletin Board

To All Employees
Would the person who took the step ladder yesterday please bring it back or further steps will be taken!

Dell's Dairy Farm

FOR SALE - MANURE
Prepacked - $10 per bag
Do-it-yourself - $25 per Bag

A Special Story
(And they call some of these people "retarded?"...)
Author Unknown

A few years ago, at the Seattle Special Olympics, nine contestants, all physically or mentally disabled, assembled at the starting line for the 100-yard dash.

At the gun, they all started out, not exactly in a dash, but with a relish to run the race to the finish, and win.

All, that is, except one little boy who stumbled on the asphalt, tumbled over a couple of times, and began to cry.

The other eight heard the boy cry. They slowed down and looked back. Then they all turned around and went back. Every one of them.

One girl with Down's Syndrome bent down and kissed him and said: "This will make it better." Then all nine linked arms and walked together to the finish line.

Everyone in the stadium stood, and the cheering went on for several minutes. People who were there are still telling the story. Why? Because deep down we know this one thing: What matters in this life is more than winning for ourselves. What matters in this life is helping others win, even if it means slowing down and changing our course.

Pass it on...we need to change our hearts.

***

A Mother's Prayer
Author Unknown. Submitted by Joe Lack

Oh give me patience when wee hands
Tug at me with their small demands
And give me gentle and smiling eyes
Keep my lips from hasty replies.
And let not weariness, confusion or noise
Obscure my vision of life's fleeting joys.
So when, in years to come, my house is still
No bitter memories its rooms may fill.

Confessions of the Rich and Famous

If you can't beat them, arrange to have them beaten.
- George Carlin

The Lighter Side

An 83-year-old lady went to the doctor because she was sick. The doctor told her that in order for her to get better she would have to have sex three times a week. She said, "My husband is 87 years old, he's in the waiting room. Could you tell him."

The doctor went to speak to her husband and explain the prognosis. He said, "In order for your wife to get well she should have sex three times a week.

The husband asked, "What three days do you recommend?"

The doctor suggested, "Maybe Monday, Wednesday and Friday."

The husband looked at the doctor and offered, "Well I can drive her on Monday and Wednesday but she'll have to get the bus on Friday's."

Submitted by Debbie Smith, Mississauga, Ontario, formerly of St John's, Newfoundland

✳✳✳

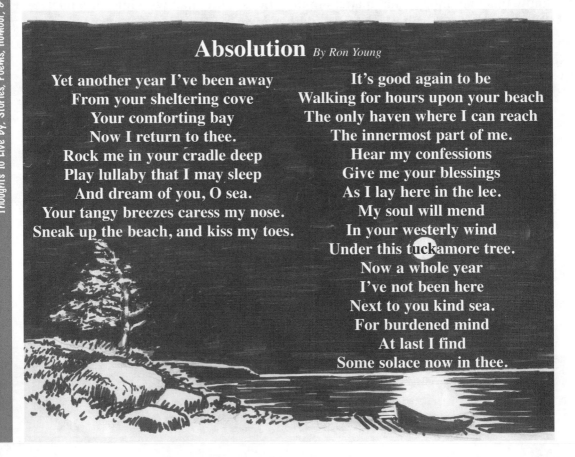

Absolution *By Ron Young*

Yet another year I've been away
From your sheltering cove
Your comforting bay
Now I return to thee.
Rock me in your cradle deep
Play lullaby that I may sleep
And dream of you, O sea.
Your tangy breezes caress my nose.
Sneak up the beach, and kiss my toes.

It's good again to be
Walking for hours upon your beach
The only haven where I can reach
The innermost part of me.
Hear my confessions
Give me your blessings
As I lay here in the lee.
My soul will mend
In your westerly wind
Under this tuckamore tree.
Now a whole year
I've not been here
Next to you kind sea.
For burdened mind
At last I find
Some solace now in thee.

Life's Funny Experiences
Benji's Better Bird

Reprinted from
Downhomer Magazine

Four years ago I married a beautiful girl from Newfoundland. She is a real sweetheart and a bright girl as well. In preparing our first Christmas meal together, she asked me to cut one leg off the turkey before we cooked it. I asked her why, as I had never heard of doing this before. Her reply was that it allowed the turkey to cook more thoroughly and besides, that was the way her 'mudder' had always cooked her turkey. I didn't protest and removed one leg from the turkey and cooked it. To tell the truth, it was delicious. The same thing happened during our second and third Christmases together, with similar results.

This Christmas we went back to Newfoundland to spend Christmas with my wife's parents and to show them their newborn grandson (their first). As Christmas dinner was being prepared I noticed my mother-in-law put the turkey into the roasting pan in one piece. I couldn't believe my eyes and just had to say something about it to her. I told her what had gone on in our house in our first three Christmases together and she said to me, "Oh yis, my son, I always did dat wit da turkey, but two year ago me 'usband bought me a bigger pan, an now I don't 'ave to no more."

Submitted by Benji in Ontario (Last name witheld for marital reasons)

***

Is That A Fact? *By Ron Young*

Reprinted from
Downhomer Magazine

Many things are accepted as facts. Not all of them are.

Actor Charles Laughton, in the movie *Mutiny On The Bounty*, portrayed Captain Bligh as a middle-aged tyrant whose career ended after the famous mutiny by Mr. Christian and the others in the crew.

The fact is that Bligh was a thirty-three year old navel lieutenant, who was referred to as captain because he captained a ship. His career did not end with the incident, as he eventually was promoted to the rank of rear admiral, which later became known as vice-admiral.

In 1805 he became governor of New South Wales, Australia. In this position, Bligh faced another mutiny. The cause of that revolt, according to Maurice Bligh, a descendant of the governor, was because corrupt officials were mistreating prisoners. According to the Encyclopedia Britannica, it was the oppressive behavior of Governor Bligh which played a major part in that revolt.

Bligh died in London in 1817.

Reprinted from
Downhomer Magazine

Classroom Chuckles

Teacher: Who was Joan of Arc, Jonas?

Jonas: Was she Noah's wife?

Teacher: Not that Ark, Jonas, The Arc I'm talking about is a place where Joan came from. She was Maid of Orleans.

Jonas: Not flesh and blood, like the rest of us?

✻✻✻

Aunt Alice says:

Now that I'm getting older I've discovered that my wild oats are kept in an All Bran box.

✻✻✻

What Manner of Manners?

Manners seem like common sense, but historically, our sense wasn't so common.

Here is some advice for children about table manners. Written by Erasmus in 1530, these were some of the things he thought were crucial for the young ones to learn anew, rather than follow the example of their parents.

"Turn away when spitting lest your saliva fall on someone. If anything purulent falls on the ground, it should be trodden upon, lest it nauseate someone."

"To lick greasy fingers or to wipe them on your coat is impolite. It is better to use the tablecloth or the serviette."

Confessions of the Rich and Famous

Always be nice to your children because they are the ones who will choose your rest home.   *- Phyllis Diller*

Innocence and Wisdom

A father was at the beach with his children when his four-year-old son ran up to him, grabbed his hand, and led him to the shore, where a seagull lay dead in the sand. "Daddy, what happened to him?" the son asked. "He died and went to heaven," the dad replied. The boy thought a moment and then said, "Did God throw him back down?"

***

Strange but TRUE
-Bill Sones & Rick Sones Ph.D.

Q. Is it common to die on the toilet?

A. It's more common to die in bed, naturally, since that's eight hours a day (By the way, the dreaming part is the riskiest). Baths, too, take their steamy, slippery toll.

By one tally of sudden deaths in Osaka, Japan, says Adam Hart-Davis in *Thunder, Flush and Thomas Crapper*, in eight percent of cases, the fatal symptoms began in the lavatory, 17 percent in the bath, 31 percent in bed.

Elvis Presley, the undisputed king, reportedly died sitting on the throne - from straining? Or was it just his time? More shocking was the guy in Ryde, on the Isle of Wight, who sat on a metal lavatory seat electrified by a faulty cable. What a way not to go!

Then there are the sad streetpeople of New York City for whom their pissoir is a subway station. Waking up, they'll "wander over to the edge of the platform, and unthinkingly pee on the live rail. Urine is a solution of salts in water; so it's a good conductor of electricity."

***

Fun With Familiar Phrases

Punishment needs to be applied
Even though your children, you adore
Spare the rod and spoil the child
And in later years they'll pay much more
-Ron Young

Rhymes & Reflections

Doing everything for your child
Isn't always for the best
At times you're doing more for them
When you're doing less
-Ron Young

Nan's Way

Rusty bolts can usually be loosened by pouring club soda on them.

Notable Quotables *By Ron Young*

Meanings and origins of well-known words and expressions

What does the term, "chewing the fat" mean and where did it originate?

'Chewing the fat' is simply having a chat. Like a lot of our well-known expressions, it originated with ships and sailors. Before refrigeration, many of the food items a ship took to sea to feed the crew were items that weren't perishable. One of these items was salt fatback pork. Because it was not the most popular of the ship's stores, it was usually eaten after everything else was gone. Having to sit around and chew on this fat usually led to much complaining and other chatter between the sailors. This caused the conversations to be called, 'chewing the fat'.

***

Life's Funny Experiences

Getting Around In Gander

While visiting Gander from Grand Falls-Windsor last summer, we made a stop at the local bank to make an instant cash withdrawal so we could go to Subway for sub sandwiches. Not being familiar with Gander, I decided to ask someone if there was a Subway in Gander. Not realizing that the next customer in line was on a visit back from the mainland, I asked him.

"No, me son, there's no subway here," he replied, "sure they don't even have a bus system in Gander!"

Submitted by Paul Johnson, Estevan, Saskatchewan

**Reprinted from
Downhomer Magazine**

***

SKIPPER SAYS:

Immigrants have always been a problem in Newfoundland - ask any Beothuk Indian!

Inspirational

Night Prayer

Now I lay me down to sleep
I pray the Lord my soul to keep
If I should die before I wake
I pray the Lord my soul to take

Morning Prayer

Now I wake and see the light
God has kept me through the night
Make me good, oh Lord I pray
Keep and guide me through the day

***

The Lighter Side

Bear Tales

Two men went bear hunting. While one stayed in the cabin, the other went out looking for a bear. He soon found a huge bear, shot at it but only wounded it. The enraged bear charged toward him, he dropped his rifle and started running for the cabin as fast as he could. He ran pretty fast but the bear was just a little faster and gained on him with every step. Just as he reached the open cabin door, he tripped and fell flat. Too close behind to stop, the bear tripped over him and went rolling into the cabin. The man jumped up, closed the cabin door and yelled to his friend inside, "You skin this one while I go and get another!"

***

Life's Funny Experiences

The Devil, You Say

Reprinted from
Downhomer Magazine

In 1967 we were heading back to Ontario and waiting in line at the ferry dock at Port aux Basques, when a young student with pen and pad in hand came up to the window and asked if we had anything such as soil, roots or potatoes aboard. I told him we had nothing. My wife told him that she had "a small tree from my mother's back yard to replant in my back yard."

When the young man saw the tree in the trunk he said, "I'm sorry ma'am but we have a soil disease here in Newfoundland and we can't let you take this tree out of the province."

My wife indignantly replied, "That's ridiculous, they let you take the devil himself out of Ontario!"

In his best St. John's brogue, the student replied, "Yes Ma'am, I knows, because we gets 'en down here sometimes!"

I laughed so hard I almost fell off the dock. That young man is probably writing for Rick Mercer or Mary Walsh these days.

Submitted by Lloyd Carter, Kitchener, Ontario

Tonic For The Soul

Thoughts To Live By, Stories, Poems, Humour, & Other Interesting Items

Ten Commandments For A Happier Life

Anonymous

1. Hold your tongue. Always say less than you think. Cultivate a low, persuasive voice. How you say a thing often counts more than what you say.

2. Make promises sparingly, and keep them faithfully, no matter what it costs you.

3. Never let an opportunity pass to say a kind and encouraging word to, or about, someone. Praise good work done, regardless of who did it. If criticism is needed, criticize helpfully, not spitefully.

4. Be interested in others: In their pursuits, their welfare, their homes and families. Make merry with those who rejoice; weep sympathetically with those who are in sorrow.

5. Try not to have a negative spirit.

6. Preserve an open mind on all debatable questions. Debate, but do not argue. It is a mark of superior minds to disagree and yet be friendly.

7. Let your virtues, if you have any, speak for themselves, and refuse to talk of another's vices. Discourage gossip. Make it a rule to say nothing of another unless it is something good.

8. Be careful of another's feelings. Wit and humour at the other fellow's expense are rarely worth the effort and may hurt where least expected.

9. Pay no attention to ill-natured remarks about you. Simply live that nobody will believe them. Disordered nerves and a bad digestion are a common cause of backbiting.

10. Do not be too anxious about your reward. Do your work, be patient, and keep your disposition sweet. Forget self and you will be compensated - sometime, somehow, somewhere.

***

In Loving Memory of Gary Holmes

By Les Adams

Fate gave me a little babe
That filled my life with heaven
Then called again and took away
The treasure he had given

Pastors and friends tried to explain
How God in His great love

Needed such a lad as mine
To be with Him above

God took him from this world of strife
That he might happy be
But why should God be kind to him
And fiercely cruel to me?

Smiles, Chuckles & Belly Laughs
Manhood and Chain Saws

**Reprinted from
Downhomer Magazine**

By Reg Wright

I remember well the day that I made the hurdle from boy to man.

I was an oily-faced, 14-year-old. My pants were quickly running out of hems to let out, and my voice had adopted a tendency to waver from Vienna Boy's Choir to candidate to primate grunt at any given millisecond.

"Son, it's time for you to learn to use something universally sacred to men," my father stammered one day, as my bear of an uncle nodded approvingly over his shoulder.

I felt a little weak, and prepared myself for a tedious, hour-long discussion where the pair would bumble through the intricacies of human reproduction.

"It's time you learned to use... The Chainsaw," said my uncle.

Now since I'd sprung from the womb, I was terrified of The Chainsaw. Every time those metal teeth would get whirling and gouts of sawdust went skyward, I would head for the hills.

The big problem was the sound of The Chainsaw. It would set my fillings a-rattle. Laaaaaaalaaaaaaaa... it would go. It sounds like someone trying to scream with their tongue twined through an eggbeater (how I know that is another story entirely).

There were other reasons to fear The Chainsaw. Chainsaw pants, for instance. The very existence of a garment to save you from The Chainsaw clearly demonstrated to my adolescent mind that the thing was dangerous. In addition, that year happened to be the same that a lumberjack in Chilliwack, BC, hit a knot when sawing some wood and Bobbittized himself. Male legs everywhere were crossed for a week.

But they paraded me out back, where The Chainsaw was propped atop a junk of wood, its toothy chained fangs glinting in the afternoon sun.

"Husqvarna," my uncle said, patting The Chainsaw affectionately, "the Rolls Royce of wood cutting equipment."

Tonic For The Soul

Thoughts To Live By, Stories, Poems, Humour, & Other Interesting Items

It was good to know I'd be torn limb from limb by the best.

"Prime it," my father directed.

So I did as I was told.

"Pull 'er over."

I tried, believe me. But Husky just coughed and sputtered and spat blue smoke.

"C'mon!" my uncle roared. "Be a man!"

So I mustered my feeble adolescent strength, put a Herculean grip on the handle, and ripped backwards... succeeding in accidentally fisting my uncle in the groin.

But Husky sputtered to life and started to wail. My uncle limped over and put a log on the saw horse.

"Now, saw!" he bellowed.

Husky's teeth started to whirl. She was surprisingly heavy and lively. I put blade to wood, and there was an explosion of spruce.

Husky was gnawing on the wood. I was going spastic. My socks rolled down. My shoes untied themselves, I was shaking like Fats Domino.

"I-I-I c-c-c-an't hold her!" I cried.

"Saw, boy, saw!" my uncle roared.

Husky was biting through the log, albeit slowly. I was quivering like a camel in the Arctic.

"N-n-ot going to make it," I wailed.

"Saw, saw!" my uncle repeated, sounding like a crow with a lisp.

And then husky bit through the log, and then through a coil of garden hose left below the wood horse. My father seized Husky and put her to sleep.

I gave a Viking bellow that shook the suburbs. Then I gave Husky a kiss. The engine was hot, but who cared about charred lips? I was a man now!

I was a man! I had conquered The Chainsaw! What was next? I could now open stuck jars, guzzle beer, watch truck and trailer pulls on television, scratch myself, ogle women and burn cow-sized steaks on the barbecue!

Looking back on those Wonder Years, you grow to realize that the test of manhood is an ongoing affair. There are new years, new challenges, new responsibilities, bigger equipment to use. My father is still seeking a way to install a V-8 motor in our weed-whacker.

You learn small lessons in life about responsibility, and then one day you understand that manhood is not handling The Chainsaw or ice fishing or chewing tobacco. It is a measure of your character, your nobility. I know a scrawny accountant in Cape Breton who swam four kilometers after a boat overturned, towing his unconscious grandfather the whole way. He's as much a man at 140 pound as Paul Bunyan ever was.

Forgive Me Love

By Ron Young (With thanks to Emily Bronte)

Forgive me love
if I sometimes forget you
Preoccupied with life
that's slipping by
You've been a part of me
since I first met you
You'll occupy that place
until I die

Lost love of youth
who once was all I lived for
My driving force in life, my will to be
To prove myself to you
was what I left for
But I never ever proved myself to me

Forgive me love for never ever writing
Not even just to tell you I was well
I was waiting 'til my life
got more exciting
But there never ever was
enough to tell

In quiet dreams of past
I find I'm walking
Beside our special place of solitude
Where we once sat for hours
without talking
In harmony, lest words should spoil
the mood

Forgive me that I never did
come back to you
Each new day brought
a brand new way to roam
My life was filled with things
that I just had to do
And way led unto way, but never
home

Through all my hopes and dreams
in life long shattered
Through all that I have met in life
I find
That I forgot at times
but still you mattered
And when alone, your memory
soothed my mind

Forgive me love
'tho others come between us
Loneliness and passion have their day
I'm mortal and I'm cursed with
human weakness
But I am true to you in my own way

Too late for us to do the things
that we once planned to
I've seen more life than I
have left to see
And 'tho I'll never share
my joy and pain with you
And 'tho I'm old
you're always young to me

And now that I have reached
my life's December
If I returned to you I fear I'd see
That you no longer are as I remember
And after all these years forgotten me

Forgive me love
if I sometimes forget you
Preoccupied with life
that's slipping by
You've been a part of me
since I first met you
You'll occupy that place until I die

Tonic For The Soul

Thoughts To Live By, Stories, Poems, Humour, & Other Interesting Items

Life's Funny Experiences
The Balls To Do It Again

Penny Wert, the wife of a friend of mine, told me about being in a bank some years ago. It was just before Christmas and all six tellers had long line-ups, all waiting to get their banking done, and on with the shopping part. There was no talking, and all faces were solemn. In one of the line-ups was a young woman, with a young, mischievous son. He was a source of embarrassment to her as he got into the garbage can, or grabbed handfuls of deposit slips from the service desk, or did some other thing he shouldn't be doing. Each time he did something, the mother would have to leave her place in line, get her son, then bring him back, and excuse herself as she took her place in the middle of the line again. In minutes he would be gone again, off on another adventure.

Then he did the unthinkable! He found a way to open the gate, and ran inside the counter, with all employees staring at him.

The mother lost her cool. She went inside the counter, and with two hands grabbed the little guy by the front of his coat, and carried him in front of her outside the counter. There were a number of chairs for waiting customers against the wall and she plucked his little butt, as hard as she could, down on the wooden chair. Pointing a finger in his face she said, "Now you stay there!"

His face distorted in pain as he looked up at her, and in a loud voice that was a half-cry he said, "You broke my balls!"

All eyes turned in the boy's direction as he stood up, and reaching into his back pocket, removed two crushed ping-pong balls.

A man left his place in the line-up, and removing his wallet, walked over to where they were standing still looking at his broken balls. He removed a ten dollar bill from his wallet and handing it to the boy said, "Here kid, you just made my day!"

Submitted by Ron Young, St. John's, Newfoundland

**Reprinted from
Downhomer Magazine**

***

Confessions of the Rich and Famous

Women complain about premenstrual syndrome, but I think of it as the only time of the month that I can be myself.
- Roseanne

Classroom Chuckles

Jonas: How do you spell 'ichael', sir,?
Teacher: 'Ichael'? I don't know that word, Jonas.
You don't mean 'Michael' do you?
Jonas: Yes sir, but I already have the 'M'.

Reprinted from
Downhomer Magazine

***

Rhymes & Reflections

No matter how much I prove and prod
    I cannot quite believe in God;
    But oh, I hope to God that He
    Unswervingly believes in me.
              -E.Y. Harburg

Fun With Familiar Phrases

You may me ridicule and make me the fool
In front of all the rest
But a lesson you'll learn when the worm
takes a turn
He who laughs last laughs best
           -Ron Young

Aunt Alice says:

God grant me the senility to forget the people I never liked anyway, the good fortune to run into the ones I do, and the eyesight to tell the difference.

***

Bulletin Board

Bethany United Church
This Is The Gate Of Heaven
Enter Ye All By This Door

(This door is kept locked because of the draft. Please use side door)

Joe's Second-Hand Shop
We exchange anything - Bicycles, Books, Bric-a-Brac, etc. Why not bring your wife along and get a wonderful bargain.

Innocence and Wisdom

A three-year-old put his shoes on by himself. His mother noticed the left was on the right foot. She said, "Son, your shoes are on the wrong feet." He looked up at her with a raised brow and said, "Don't kid me, Mom, I KNOW they're my feet."

Reprinted from
Downhomer Magazine

***

Is That A Fact?

Many things are accepted as facts. Not all of them are.
'Were Cinderella's Slippers Really Made Of Glass?'

Most children in western civilization know of Cinderella and her famous Glass slipper.

The fact is that there are many versions of the story, Cinderella, and like so many others was told verbally for many years, in many lands and languages. None ever mentioned glass slippers. Different versions had the slippers made out of different materials, and some made no mention of the type of material from which the slippers were made, but never was glass mentioned. The story was first written in French by Charles Perrault in 1697. Stories which trace back to the French version do mention glass slippers. Perrault had his slippers made of ermine mink fur. The French word for ermine is vair. The French word for glass is verre. Both words are pronounced the same. It is not likely that a storyteller would put an aspiring princess in uncomfortable glass slippers. It seems more likely that an error in translation gave Cinderella her glass slippers.

***

What Manner of Manners?

Manners seem like common sense, but historically, our sense wasn't so common.

Covering your mouth when you yawn is just good manners, right? Today we figure that it's so the people around us won't have to look at our tonsils. In fact, the custom originated long, long ago, when people were much more superstitious. It was believed that this giant exhalation might carry with it the breath of life, and the soul of the yawner, unless the mouth were covered by the hand. In ancient Rome new mothers were cautioned to cover all of their newborn's yawns because the baby, not being able to cover it's own mouth, would be in mortal danger otherwise.

UNCLE ESAU'S NET LOFT

THE HIGHWAY BETWEEN GRAND FALLS AND CORNER BROOK, A DISTANCE OF 258 KILOMETRES, WAS OPENED ON 20 SEPTEMBER 1950. NOBLE BAIRD WAS THE FIRST TO DRIVE THE HIGHWAY, A TRIP THAT TOOK 12 HOURS — AN AVERAGE SPEED OF 21.5 KMPH!

NANA, THE DOG IN JAMES BARRIE'S "PETER PAN," WAS A NEWFOUNDLAND~ NOT A SAINT BERNARD!

THE 'RODNEY' WAS NAMED FOR CAPTAIN GEORGE B. RODNEY, NAVAL HERO & GOVERNOR OF NEWFOUNDLAND IN 1749!

Reprinted from
Downhomer Magazine

FROGS, FROM PRINCE EDWARD ISLAND AND NOVA SCOTIA, ARRIVED IN NEWFOUNDLAND ABOARD HAY SCHOONERS!

JOHN COOPER OF TRINITY BAY SET THE AMERICAN FLAG ATOP FORT SANTIAGO IN THE SPANISH-AMERICAN WAR. INSPIRED BY HIS ACTION THE AMERICANS WENT ON TO WIN THE BATTLE AND THEREBY THE WAR!

OL' ROD

Confessions of the Rich and Famous

Women need a reason to have sex. Men just need a place.

- Billy Crystal

***

Pigtails *Author Unknown*

"Mommy!" The child came running through the door, her pigtails flapping wildly like distress signals, and tears running down her cheeks in grimy tracks. "Darling, what's the matter?" her mother asked, scooping up her daughter and brushing away the tears. "Why don't I have a daddy?" the little girl asked solemnly, as she rubbed her eyes and nose on her sleeve. Her mother sighed, her heart wrenching as she held her child close. "Your daddy is gone, darling," she said gently. "He abandoned us a long time ago."

The little girl sat quietly at the back of the class as her classmates bustled, laughing and yelling merrily. She watched them work happily and stared down at her own blank piece of paper. A shadow fell across her desk, bisecting the blankness, and a hand fell upon her tiny shoulder. "Why aren't you working?" the substitute teacher knelt down and asked her gently. The child looked blankly at the teacher for a brief moment before reverting her gaze back to the paper. The teacher tried again. "Come on. Don't you want to make a Father's Day card for your daddy? I'm sure that he would really like one." The child's head snapped up. "He doesn't care," she said softly, the steel in her voice belonging to one many years her age. The teacher missed it. "Oh, I'm sure that he would love it." She smiled encouragingly. The little girl jumped up, knocking her chair backwards. He doesn't care!" She ran out of the room, pigtails flapping like distress signals.

"Can I speak to Jeanette please?" a soft male voice asked politely. For an unknown reason, shivers ran down her spine. Jeanette replied cautiously, "Speaking... May I ask who's calling?" Silence drifted down the receiver. "It's...." the voice faltered. "It's... it's your father, Jeanette." Jeanette was bombarded with a mixture of emotions as she clung to the phone anxiously, unable to respond. He continued gently, "I'd like to see you, Jeanette. Please, will you meet with me next week?" Jeanette was silent as she remembered that little girl, whose pigtails flapped wildly like distress signals. "Jeanette, please?" he asked pleadingly. "I'll be there," she said softly, unsure if she was lying or not.

She stood on the doorstep of a small cottage, one hand raised to ring the doorbell. She stood there for five minutes, her hand shaking wildly as she resisted the urge to turn around and run. Suddenly the door opened and she looked hesitantly at the father she'd never had. He looked at her cautiously, silently motioning her inside, afraid that he would frighten her off. "Why?" she spat venomously. "Why did you leave us?" "Jeanette..." he looked at her sadly, holding out his hands towards her. She stayed out of touching distance. "Why?" she demanded. He lowered his hands sadly. "I'll make no excuses. Yes, I did leave you. But I always meant to keep in touch. I loved you. I love you." "Words! That's all they are to me! Where was your love when I needed it?" "I tried to see you. I tried to call. But your mother blocked me. And when she took you out of town, I lost all trace of you." She shook her head disbelievingly. "Then how did you find me?" "I hired a private investigator. He managed to track you down when you returned here." Jeanette shook her head. "Why now?" she whispered, more to herself than to him. "I had to see you again. Jeanette, I'm dying. And I needed to resolve this. I love you. I've always loved you. Please, can you find it in your heart to forgive me for leaving?" "I don't know." "I remembered every birthday. I celebrated them every year and hoped that you knew I cared." To her, he seemed to be pleading. She remembered all the special occasions in her life that he had missed. She remembered all the times she had wept because she was the odd one out because she didn't have a dad. She remembered all the times that she had blamed herself for his absence. And she knew that she couldn't stay here another moment with him. He sensed that she was about to leave. "Wait!" he cried. "I have something to give you!" She cut him off curtly and brushed him aside. "I don't want it. It's too late to start giving now." In her mind, the little girl ran with her out the door, pigtails flapping wildly like distress signals.

"May I please speak with Jeanette, please?" a woman asked politely as Jeanette picked up the phone. "Speaking," Jeanette replied. The woman spoke bluntly. "This is Martha, your father's wife. He died last night. I thought you should know." Jeanette was shocked into silence. It had been two weeks since the day she had run out on him, and since then she had refused to return his calls. "Will you attend the funeral?" Martha continued. "I don't know," Jeanette whispered. "He would like it if you came. He always loved you, you know."

Jeanette sat at the back of the room, far apart from everyone else. Thoughts floated through her mind, memories, and she barely paid attention to the service. At the end, as she was about to leave, she was approached by an elder woman. "Jeanette?" "Yes," she said, her face and voice guarded. The lady held out her hand. "I'm Martha. Thank you for coming." Jeanette shrugged non-commitedly. "I have something for you," Martha continued. "Your father wanted you to have it. I brought it today in the hope that you would come. It's in the car." They walked silently to the car, their feet crunching the gravel underfoot. Martha opened the trunk, pulling out a hugh cardboard box, with a big manila envelope taped on top. She placed it in Jeanette's arms. Jeanette looked at it curiously. It was a plain box, with no markings, and rather heavy. "What's in it?" Jeanette asked, curious despite her conflicting emotions about her father. Martha got into her car and leaned out the window. "I don't know," she replied. "He never told me." She started the engine. "Take care, Jeanette," she said and drove off, leaving Jeanette alone with her heavy burden.

Jeanette sat on the carpet, watching the box as if it would spring up and attack her. With shaking hands she pulled off the manila envelope and tipped the contents of it on to the floor. A mass of envelopes fell down into a pile. On each envelope was written a year in a bold hand. She picked one at random and tore it open.

"May 6th, 1983. Happy Birthday, my darling! My, you're turning five today! Somebody's a big girl! I wish I could be there with you on your first day of school. I'll bet that you're so excited about starting. I remember when you were a little baby, how you would have to examine any new object that you came across. I guess you take after me in that respect. I want you to remember, darling, that just because I'm not there doesn't mean that I don't think of you. I wish you the best of luck for this year, and all the years to come. Stay out of trouble. Love always, Daddy." Jeanette read it silently, feeling the tears fall down her cheeks. She brushed them away impatiently and chose another.

"December 25th, 1997. Dearest Jeanette, Merry Christmas, sweetheart! I must say that I feel extremely close to you this year. Perhaps you know that I love you and have been searching for you? The man I've hired is fairly certain that he's close to finding you. Oh, how I pray that he hurries! Not a day goes by that I don't wish I could hold you in my arms and tell you that I love you. Tonight I'll be gazing at the stars, and I know that you'll be watching them too. And when I make a wish on the brightest star in the sky, I hope that you'll see it and know that I made a wish for you. I love you always."

Jeanette put down the letter, crying uncontrollably. She pulled the lid of the box open, tears splashing on to the cardboard, to find many small packages, all wrapped in brightly coloured, patterned paper. Inside her head she could hear her father speaking. "I remembered every birthday. I celebrated them every year and hoped that you knew that I cared." Jeanette bowed her head and whispered, "I knew it, Dad. I knew it. It just got lost along the way. But I've found it again, and Dad, I love you too." Her anger had vanished, being replaced with a great love, and she knew that her father had heard her and forgiven her for her harsh words to him. And in her mind, the little girl whose pigtails waved wildly like distress signals faded away.

Grassroots Healing

by Janice Stuckless

Introducing the use of natural products for a healthier body and mind

Grassroots Healing

It is the year 2000, an age when everything is electronic, technotronic and supersonic. We aren't yet travelling in space cars or taking day trips to the moon, as was portrayed in televisions shows of the '50s and '60s, but the technical and medical advances are astounding. Computers have introduced not only a new form of communication, but an entire section of the English language as well; anyone who doesn't know what e-mail is might as well give up on ever 'fitting in with the crowd'. Telephones no bigger than a credit card (some look suspiciously like a tricorder from Star Trek) are as common as calculators. Teachers' pointers have been replaced with hand-held lasers. We have successfully cloned a sheep...

Throughout the past century and as we enter a new one, as society becomes more advanced, it seems that the diseases that plague us are becoming more advanced as well. Yes, we have found cures for some and treatments for others, but the common cold virus, for example, is still a mystery as it changes and adapts every season. Cancer and heart disease are major killers every day world wide. Billions of dollars and hundreds of research teams are invested in discovering genes and manipulating cell activity, and so on it goes.

Meanwhile, a new branch of medicine has been steadily gaining followers and popularity. Call it Eastern medicine, alternative therapies or new-age health approaches, it all comes down to one thing. More and more people are taking charge of their health and they are looking at natural ways to incorporate healing into their daily lifestyles. That is why this section has been called Grassroots Healing, and in it we will explore some of the herbs, roots, fruits, vegetables, meats and carefully chosen supplements that are being used today in society's search for better health and a longer life.

Most of these herbal products are available at alternative health food stores. Many of the alternative suggestions in this section have powerful effects and side-effects on the body which are not always obvious by the description. Some of these herbs, foods, etc. may have an adverse affect on existing conditions or conflict with medication you are already taking. It is strongly suggested to anyone who would like to try some of these remedies and alternative methods to consult a family physician or a homeopathic specialist.

Drink to Your Health

Newfoundlanders are well-known for loving a good cup of tea. But there are more kinds of tea than Tetley and Red Rose. There are many different kinds of plants that can be steeped into a beneficial brew. Teas can help alleviate everything from cold symptoms, to depression, to gout. Perhaps it's the warmth, perhaps it's the aromatherapy, perhaps it's just the act of taking time out of a busy day to enjoy a cup of tea. Whatever is at the root of it, teas have always been, in many cultures, tonics for what ails you.

Did you know that both black and green tea leaves hold the power to fight viruses, prevent cavities, and fight off cancer cells? Here are 27 more teas and their uses:

Bay leaf, cinnamon, cloves and turmeric iced tea brewed together - Add a pinch or two of each ingredient to a pot of black tea, steep for 10 minutes and drink it with ice. This brew will relieve diarrhea symptoms.

Grassroots Healing

Dandruff cures

Make an anti-flake rinse using two **rosemary** leaves and a cup of boiling water. Let the mixture brew for at least 20 minutes. Strain the liquid and use it as a rinse.

Massage this herbal mixture into clean damp hair: Simmer four heaping tbsp of **thyme** and two cups of water in a non-aluminum pot for 10 minutes. Strain the brew and let it cool before using.

Ease an Earache

Make your own eardrops that can be used three or four times a day until symptoms subside. Place 3 drops of **garlic oil** and two of **mullein oil** in the ear.

Fight Fatigue with Food

Adding dried **barley** or **wheat grass** to a salad can offset symptoms of fatigue.

Solve Stinky Feet

Soak your feet in a solution of a tablespoon each of **goldenseal** and **myrrh** in warm water. Relax in this foot bath for 10-15 minutes, once a week. Goldenseal may leave a harmless yellow stain on your feet.

Get Rid of Gas

Chew a few **fennel** seeds to avoid excess gas.

Birch bark tea - This is an oral treatment for warts. To make the tea, brew 1-2 tsp of the powdered plant in a cup of boiling water. Let it steep for 10 minutes. You can drink the tea, or let it cool and rub it directly on the wart.

Black haw tea - Drink up to three cups a day of a tea made from 2 tsp of the herb in a cup of water, boiled, strained, and cooled. This will help ease menstrual cramps and bloating.

Chamomile tea - Stir one tbsp of whole, dried chamomile flowers in a teapot and steep for 15 minutes, then strain. This is a good tonic for heartburn and indigestion and can be taken as often as needed.

Chamomile tea is also a good treatment for insomnia, stress, exhaustion, poor appetite and anxiety. It is said that the vapors from the tea have soothing powers as well.

Chasteberry tea - Steep 1 tsp of the plant in a cup of boiling water for 20 minutes, then strain. Drink up to three cups a day to lessen the effects of premenstrual syndrome.

Cinnamon tea - Steep a tbsp of dried, powdered cinnamon bark in a cup of hot water for 10-15 min. This is useful for diarrhea sufferers.

Comfrey tea - Add either the fresh leaves or the dried leaves to a pot of boiling water. Let it simmer for10 minutes and, with the cover on the pot, let it cool and strain before drinking. This is a treatment for mild chest pains and gastro-intestinal problems.

Cranberry tea - To clear a urinary tract infection, brew dried cranberries in a tea ball and steep for 20 minutes. Drink three or four cups a day until the infection is gone.

Dandelion tea - The leaves and root can be brewed as tea. Combine 1 tsp each of leaves and root, add to 1 cup of boiling water, let steep for 10 minutes, strain and drink. This tea provides benefits to the liver, kidney and joints. However, dandelion root should be avoided by those suffering from an obstruction of the bile ducts.

Echinacea tea - This is great for a fever that accompanies a cold or flu. Add 30-50 drops of echinacea extract to herbal tea and drink every 2 hours until fever breaks.

Elderflower tea - Prepare a tea of 2 tsp of elderflower in one cup of water, then allow it to steep for 15-20 minutes. Drink the solution three times a day to break a fever.

Steep the same mixture for 10 minutes, strain before drinking, and you have a brew that helps break up congestion on the lungs and in the sinuses.

Feverfew tea - Brew a tea made of 2-3 tbsp of dried feverfew in a cup of hot water and strain. Drinking this solution can help soothe a headache.

Ginger tea - Simmer a 1-inch sliver of ginger root and 2 cups of water in a covered pot for 20 minutes. Strain the tea into a cup and add the juice of half a lemon and honey for taste. This herbal tea is a cough suppressant, pain reliever and mild sedative.

Stir 1/3 cup of ginger in a cup of hot water, strain and drink the tea to alleviate a headache.

Also, 1/3 cup of ginger in a cup of hot water, and taken 20 minutes before mealtime, can prevent heartburn.

Ginseng tea - Drink a daily cup of tea made of 1 tsp of ginseng steeped in 1 cup of water, then strained, to help combat fatigue.

Horsetail tea - Make a tea using 1 tbsp of horsetail and 1 tsp of sugar in a cup of water. Bring the mixture to a boil in a pan, then let it simmer for three hours. Strain the liquid and let it cool before drinking. The silicon in this herb can help prevent osteoporosis and heal bone fractures.

Labrador Tea tea - Mix 1 tsp of the crushed leaves in a cup of boiling water. This tea is helpful in treating coughs, chest illnesses, sore throat, headaches, kidney problems, rheumatism and diarrhea. **Caution:** This tea must be made weak and not taken often; the leaves have an intoxicating quality that, if overused, could lead to paralysis or death.

Lemon balm tea - Steep 1-3 tsp of the dried plant in a cup of boiled water for 10 minutes, strain before drinking. This soothing brew will melt away insomnia and battle depression.

Licorice tea - Boost your immune system to fight off viruses such as the flu by adding 2 tbsp of licorice root to a cup of boiling water and steeping for 10 minutes. Strain before drinking.

Licorice, burdock and dandelion tea - Boil 2 tbsp of each herb in 3 cups of water. Let simmer for 15-20 minutes and strain. Drink one cup three times a day as a treatment for eczema.

Nettle, oatstraw, a red clover teas - each of these are best brewed overnight to make a stronger tea and drank over the next couple of days. These are also beneficial to osteoporosis sufferers.

Parsley tea - Steep a few sprigs of crushed, fresh parsley or 1 tsp of dried parsley in a cup of boiled water for 5-10 minutes. Drink 2-3 cups a day to clear a urinary tract infection.

Passionflower tea - Brew a tea using the dried leaf, stem or vine of this plant to relieve PMS symptoms.

Grassroots Healing

Aniseed, basil, chamomile, cinnamon, garlic, ginger, lemon, onion, oregano or rosemary. Adding any of these to a gaseous dish (such as beans) during the cooking can reduce the resulting 'emissions'.

Heartburn Help

About 20 minutes before you sit down to a spicy meal, take a **ginger** capsule.

Sting Soothers

Combine equal amount of **echinacea** and water with just enough bentonite clay to make a thick paste. Apply paste to bite, cover with bandage and change the dressing twice a day.

Mosquito Bites

Dabbing a drop of white vinegar onto a fresh insect bite should take the sting and itch right out of it. A slice of lemon rubbed onto the skin also works on taking the itch out of mosquito bites.

Gargle Away a Sore Throat

Gargle a mixture of 40 drops of **echinacea** and warm water.

Peppermint tea - 1 tbsp of dried peppermint leaves in a cup of boiling water, and steeped for 5-10 minutes, then strained, makes a tea that can be taken three or four times a day to relieve gas and indigestion. The same result can be achieved using peppermint tea bags.

Rose hips tea - Simmer, covered, 2 tbsp of rose hips in a cup of water for 20-30 minutes. Strain off the liquid, add lemon juice and honey, and drink the tea to relieve the pain of a sore throat.

Sage and eucalyptus tea - Steep 2 tsp of each in 1/2 cup of boiling water for 20-30 minutes. Let it cool, then gargle the tea to soothe a sore throat.

Walnut tea - The seratonin found in walnuts is known to fight depression and enhance sleep. To make this tea, drop a half of an English walnut into a cup of boiling water. This can be taken several times a day.

Yarrow tea - Steep for 10 minutes a tea made of 1 tbsp of yarrow in 1 cup of water as a tonic for fever. After one or two cups, if a sweat breaks out, stop treatment.

You can also combine equal amounts of dried yarrow and dried chasteberry, add 1 tsp of this mixture in a cup of boiling water and steep for 20 minutes. Drinking up to three cups of this can reduce the bloating associated with PMS.

Rejuvenating Juices

The fastest, easiest way to get a large number of essential vitamins and minerals into our bodies is to drink them. Freshly made juices enable our bodies to absorb up to 99 per cent of the needed ingredients; solid foods are not as easily digested, and the nutrient absorption only reaches about 70 per cent.

The benefits of a particular juice can be determined by its colour. **Red juices** - made from tomatoes, cherries, red cabbage or hot peppers, for example - boost blood circulation. **Orange-coloured juices** made from apricots, carrots or oranges are known to

improve mental focus, relax muscles and relieve pain. **Green juices** come from green vegetables such as barley and sprouts to calm the nerves. Pineapples, grapefruits, apples, banana and corn make great **yellow juices** that aid digestion and treat constipation. **Blue juices** are made from blueberries, plums, grapes, potatoes, celery and nuts; they are a healthy substitute for drugs when treating a headache.

To get the most out of these juices, drink them immediately after they are prepared, or keep them in a dark, air-tight container in the fridge. Exposure to air and light destroys some of the nutrients.

There are also some special plants and herbs that add healing properties to an ordinary juice drink:

Flaxseed Oil. Add a tbsp of this oil to a glass of juice each day to ease the itch of psoriasis.

Echinacea. Add 30-50 drops of echinacea extract to water or juice and drink every two hours to break the fever from a cold or flu.

Echinacea and goldenseal. Add 30 drops each of echinacea and goldenseal to juice or water and drink to ease an earache.

Common Scents

Aromatherapy has gotten more and more respect in the western world over the last few years. Surrounding yourself with specific scents can have therapeutic effects on the mind and body. Aromatherapy uses the application of essential oils, which are distilled from aromatic plants and herbs. They are extremely potent and should **always** be diluted in another oil, cream or water before they are applied to the skin. Essential oils may be used in a bath, with a massage or inhaled as a mist.

There are two ways that essential oils can reach the areas of the body that need therapy. One is through the olfactory nerve (through the nose, basically), which will carry the scent to the brain and prompt emotional and hormonal responses. The easiest way to get a quick pick-me-up from a scent is to take the cap off the vial of oil and breathe deeply, a method that's fast, effective and can be done anywhere. Another portable and convenient aromatherapy treatment is a perfume made by adding 25 drops of your favourite essential oil to water in a spray bottle. You can also add aromatic oils to potpourri, mix them with water in a spray bottle to create your own air freshening mist, or heat the oils in an aromatic diffuser (a few drops of oil are added to water in the diffuser bowl; vapours are emitted as the water is heated, usually by a candle under the bowl.)

The other channel for getting the benefits of aromatic oils is through the skin. When oils are added to a bath or used as a lotion in a body massage, they are absorbed through the skin, and the body carries the oils to the nervous and muscular systems to provide therapeutic relief. For a full bath, a dozen or so drops of the oil is enough to add to the water once the tub is filled. In a foot or hand bath, only about five drops are needed. You can even use them in a jacuzzi: it is recommended that you add three drops per person, or six drops if only one person will be in

Grassroots Healing

Wart Wisdom

Moisten a strip of **birch bark** and tape it, inner side down, over the wart. Cover the wart with crushed **basil** leaves and secure with a bandage. Reapply every 5 to 7 days.

Vapourizing Action

When suffering from sinus congestion due to a cold, inhale the vapours from several drops of eucalyptus oil in a pan of boiled water.

One Man's Uplifting Experience with Seal Meat

In June of 1999, *Downhomer* editor Ron Young met a most interesting man from Northern Arm, Newfoundland. Percy Noseworthy revealed that because of his diabetes, he had "lost his nature." Initially, he had tried taking Viagra. While it worked, it was too expensive at $42 for four pills to continue using. Then Percy discovered something so simple that he had completely overlooked it. "When I eat seal meat, I haven't got my nature gone...At

the jacuzzi. Remember also that oil and water don't mix easily, so you will have to stir the bath with your hand to get the oils evenly distributed. If you are more of a shower person, just put four or five drops of oil on a damp washcloth and rub briskly over your skin after showering.

Still with the skin absorption method, essential oils can add to the relaxing experience of a massage. Essential oils can be mixed with a regular massage oil or lotion (up to 18 drops of essential oil in one ounce of massage oil). This is a therapeutic exercise that is effective as a full body massage or as a spot massage in the most needed areas. Most useful for easing swelling and headache pain is a compress made by rinsing a cloth in a bowl of hot or cold water that has been enhanced by six drops of a healing oil.

There are many essential oils and many therapeutic uses for aromatherapy. Below are just a sampling of these products, all of which should be available at any herbal supply store.

Basil - Bathing with a few drops of basil oil in a tub of water can lift the spirits.

Camphor (spirits of) - Place 3 drops in a cup of sweetened water. Apply the solution to a cloth and dab the head and neck for headache relief.

Camphorated Oil - Massage this oil into the chest and back for relief from bronchial infections.

Cedarwood - When massaged into the skin, this oil fights skin infections.

Chamomile - Mix the oil with a lotion and rub into patches of psoriasis as often as needed.

Chickweed - Combine 15 drops of chickweed with a two-inch mound of moisturizing lotion to create a cream that is effective on eczema. Rub into the affected area immediately after a bath.

Clary sage - Using the oil from this plant with a body massage lessens the discomfort of menstruation and treats depression.

Ginger - The aroma from this root is inhaled to increase concentration and calm the emotions.

The oil of the plant can also be massaged into relevant areas of the skin to relieve pain from headaches and arthritis.

Jasmine - The sweet smell of jasmine can aid the mind and body in the areas of depression, stress and impotence.

Lavender and tea tree - Create a soothing foot rub with a combination of 3 tsp of lavender oil and 1 tsp of tea tree oil.

Or add a few drops of the essential oils to 15 drops of water and rub into the temples as a relaxation therapy. Or, in place of water, mix the oils with aloe vera or chamomile cream.

Peppermint - An 8-ounce spray bottle of water containing 15 drops of peppermint oil can be a refreshing spray to the face and the air around you, though it shouldn't be allowed to get into your eyes or mouth.

Also, peppermint oil rubbed onto an insect bite will reduce the itching and pain.

Rose - There may be a reason why giving roses is a symbol of love. Their aroma is said to be an aphrodisiac.

Rosemary - Absorb 1-3 drops of rosemary oil in a tissue, then take a whiff of the scent when you need to improve concentration and memory.

Extraordinary Benefits of Ordinary Food

It would appear that after all the decades that scientists have spent developing chemical fixer-uppers, nature knew what it was doing after all. Foods that we include in everyday meal preparation, even in our snack foods, have a plethora of positive powers to keep us healthy and strong.

Take a typical Jiggs' dinner, for example. The cabbage, even cooked, fights cancer, ulcers and viral infections. The split peas in the peas pudding are high in soluble fibre that helps lower bad cholesterol levels and regulates blood sugar levels. Carrots are high in beta-carotene which blocks cancer cell growth. Turnips, including the greens, are similar in makeup to cabbages with regards to its cancer fighting abilities. Potatoes, especially the skins, contain a high concentration of compounds that disable viruses and carcinogen (cancer-causing agents). Now, I can't say much good about the salt meat or the doughboys, but the best measure is always moderation.

I've compiled a list of just some of the foods we eat every day that have hidden healers. Some of them may even be surprising:

Apple - Yes, it's true. An apple a day, or two or three, can keep the doctor away. Like many other fruits, the pectin is the ingredient that raises levels of good cholesterol and lowers levels of bad cholesterol. Pectin has also been proven, at least in animal testing, to prevent metastisis (spread) of cancer cells. Apples also regulate blood sugar levels, kill cold viruses in the body and aid in weight loss.

first I didn't notice, but then I started to realize that every time I ate seal it used to do the same thing to me. Oh man - did I get frisky." *Downhomer* reporter Kris Mullaly followed up on Percy's story a couple of months after Ron's interview. Percy told Kris that since the original *Downhomer* article was printed, he'd had several other men tell him that the seal meat increased their sexual desire, too. Percy's family doctor, Dr. Woolfrey, believes that if the seal meat works for Percy, there's certainly no harm in it. He would also like to see a future study done on the health effects of seal meat and seal oil, specifically as it relates to impotence.

Percy said that he prefers the meat, baked or bottled, as his own personal Viagra. The seal oil doesn't have the same effect for him, but he knows that it does work for others. He suggested that men should experiment to find the right solution, as reactions to different parts of the seal varies. "I like to have the heart and liver and the fat and the penis. I really think it's coming from the fat, you know. Like

Apple Cider Vinegar - This is another very common product, used for many years in recipes and as a tonic. It has been used externally to cool sunburns and condition hair. But many people have drunk a teaspoon of apple cider vinegar a day as a health preserver. Some of the conditions claimed to be benefitted by apple cider vinegar include bowel and kidney irregularities, arthritis, colitis, headaches, dizziness, sore throat, laryngitis, hay fever, high blood pressure, teeth and gum diseases, even hiccups. The pectin, a fibre found in the apple and in most citrus fruits, in apple cider vinegar is believed to promote bowel regularity.

Incidentally, the possible cancer-fighting effects of pectin is currently being studied in American laboratories. So far, tests on animals have shown that injecting pectin into the bloodstream of animals afflicted with cancerous tumors prevents the spread of these tumors.

Most recently, though, apple cider vinegar has found new popularity among dieters. It is being claimed that apple cider vinegar is very effective in losing weight. Because the vinegar itself is very bitter, capsules are available at health food stores for those who find the taste hard to swallow.

Apricot - Apricots are a good source of beta-carotene, and therefore are great cancer-fighting fruits. Dried apricots offer a higher concentration of beta-carotene. This form of Vitamin A is most notable for protecting against lung and skin cancers.

Beans - "Beans, beans, good for your heart..." and they are. A regular menu of beans of any type can lessen heart disease by lowering bad cholesterol and blood pressure. These legumes also regulate insulin and blood sugar levels, and help to prevent and cure bowel irregularities. Hint: Soaking beans before they are cooked into a meal helps remove some of their gas-producing sugars.

Blueberry - This berry commonly grows and is commonly picked in Newfoundland. It is a great source of fibre and an effective laxative in some people. Most often, though, blueberries are useful in treating diarrhea because of their ability to kill viruses and bacteria. A compound found in the wild berries, called anthocyanoside, helps strengthen vessel walls, keeping cholesterol out, and thereby preventing hardening of the arteries by buildup of cholesterol in the blood stream.

Cayenne pepper - This can be used in several ways. Eating the pepper can help relieve symptoms of dyspepsia, diarrhea, prostration, seasickness and even scarlet fever. Gargling the seeds helps relieve the pain and swelling of ague (facial swelling due to diseased teeth or a cold).

Cherry - Cherries contain a strong antibacterial agent that blocks plaque buildup on teeth and gums and reduces the incidence of cavities.

Chili Pepper - Spicy sauces and dishes that make your eyes water and your nose run are doing your body good. Hot peppers, like the chili pepper, boost the flow of mucus and help alleviate symptoms of bronchitis and emphysema. They also serve as effective pain killers; the shock of the hot peppers causes the nervous system to release endorphins to dull the pain and sometimes create a natural high.

Coffee - The caffeine in coffee could actually cause some problems if your body is absorbing too much of it. However, two cups of coffee spread out over a day could provide some health benefits. Small doses of caffeine offer a mental and physical boost as well as a lighter mood. Caffeine also widens bronchial tubes, allowing for easier breathing, and is particulary helpful to asthmatics. Coffee, like tea, contains tannins; swishing coffee around in your mouth, or even just drinking it, coats your teeth and gums in these antibacterial agents. Decaffeinated coffee will work as well at fighting cavities. Coffee has also been proven, in laboratory tests, to block cancer cells.

Crab - You can eat crab legs to your heart's content. Literally, because the omega-3 fatty acids in crab meat lower the level of bad cholesterol in the blood, thus reducing the risk of heart disease. And, like fish, crab meat is a great mental energy booster.

Fish - Thank God we're surrounded by water. Fish, particularly fatty types like herring and salmon, are full of oils that are good for the body. Specifically, the omega-3 oils in fish can reduce the risk of heart disease, alleviate arthritic and migraine pain, boost the immune system, relieve bronchial asthma, and fight the early stages of kidney disease. It is the protein particular to fish that stimulates brain activity to promote alertness and concentration.

Garlic - It may smell, but as a natural cure it sure doesn't stink. Garlic can aid in a myriad of ailments from herpes to high cholesterol. The extract, added to a body lotion and spread between the toes, is said to cure athletes foot. Garlic in the system thins the blood and aids blood flow, thus reducing the risk of clotting and blocked arteries. It lowers blood pressure and boosts the immune system. Properties in garlic thin mucus to improve flow, great for chest cold and chronic bronchitis sufferers. It is also believed that garlic, by boosting the immune system, offers protection against the development of cancer. Gargling garlic and water kills a lot of the bacteria that leads to mouth and gum disease. Fresh garlic may not do much for your breath, but taking the capsules daily can reduce foot odor. Garlic can effectively be taken in fresh clove, powdered, or capsule form.

Grapefruit - This is another fruit that holds the advantages of pectin. Having a grapefruit with breakfast strengthens the body's defenses against cancer cell growth. It is also beneficial to the heart by lowering bad cholesterol levels.

Honey - Honey has long been recommended to soothe a sore throat, but it has other healing powers as well. Honey is a great natural disinfectant and antiseptic. Smearing an infected cut with honey speeds the healing and keeps other bacteria out. Its bacteria-fighting ability is also

the oil from the seal. But I don't get it from the seal capsules." He got 60 seal flippers for $30, much more economical than the pharmaceutical option. As for the smell of the seal cooking, Percy has found a remedy for that, too. "All you have to do is put in half an apple and a bit of french onion soup mix in with the seal flipper as you're baking it. The smell won't be anything then." Percy owns and operates 'Flipper's Last Stop' convenience and gas bar at the crossroads in Northern Arm. Percy welcomes anyone to come in and ask him anything about his experience with seal meat. "I don't mind. I want the world to know about it. Tell everybody to come and see me and I'll tell them all about it." Just prior to press time, Percy informed us that he has lost 65 pounds since adding seal meat to his diet, and his health has improved dramatically. He now takes only one cholesterol pill a day instead of twelve and one diabetes pill a day instead of the fifteen he used to take.

useful inside the body for fighting causes of diarrhea, and it has a soothing effect that promotes sleep.

Horseradish - Horseradish contains a number of vitamins and minerals that are important in maintaining good health: calcium to help prevent osteoporosis; potassium to regulate the heart beat; several vitamins including B-6, amino acids, and folates that help lower cholesterol levels and improve circulation. *Tasty Tip: Mixed with ketchup, horseradish makes a great shrimp dip.*

Lemon and Lime - Not only are these fruits an excellent source of Vitamin C, they also contain the cancer-blocking ingredient, pectin.

Milk - It is widely known that milk is good for the bones and teeth, and to soothe the symptoms of ulcers. Although whole milk with its high fat content can be bad for the arteries and cholesterol level, skim milk may actually lower cholesterol and counteract the effect of salt on blood pressure. However, young children should be fed whole milk, as consumption of low-fat milk in children can lead to diarrhea. Milk can also be used topically to moisturize the skin. Dip a cloth in milk and apply the cloth to dry skin for a few minutes to let the milk soak into the skin.

Mushroom - Magic mushrooms indeed. Some types of mushrooms, most notably shiitake, are believed to have positive effects on the blood stream, the heart and the immune system. (Shiitake mushrooms are sometimes available in most major grocery chains, and they can also be found in specialty food stores.)

Olive Oil - Choosing to cook with olive oil over butter will be good for your heart. Olive oil is the good oil that reduces bad cholesterol levels and raises levels of good cholesterol. Blood pressure is positively affected by consumption of this oil. Olive oil also contains antioxidants that slow aging and cancer development. The most beneficial is extra virgin olive oil, which is made directly from crushed olives.

Onion - The fumes from onions, the same ones that make you cry, promote mucus flow, thus breaking up congestion on the chest. Onions also thin the blood, raise good cholesterol levels, lower overall cholesterol levels, regulate blood sugar and kill bacteria. Onions provide the same benefit to your system whether they are eaten raw, roasted, stewed or fried. Also, rubbing a slice of raw onion over an insect bite can reduce the pain and swelling.

Rice - The results of several surveys and tests have shown that rice contains properties that inhibit cancer growth, regulate blood sugar levels and prevent kidney stones. Adding rice to your diet can also provide help with psoriasis.

Seal - Seal oil is rich in omega-3 fatty acids, which are known to raise good cholesterol and lower bad cholesterol levels. In addition, there are considerable levels of Vitamin E found in seal oil.

Strawberry - This delicious berry is the strongest antioxidant of all fruits. Basically, that means it has the greatest cancer-blocking ability. It is also believed to be able to fight viruses.

Tomato - The nutrient that makes tomatoes red is called lycopene, and it is known to have cancer-blocking capabilities. Including lots of tomatoes in the diet has been linked to lower incidences of stomach and lung cancer. It is also suspected that a tomato diet fortifies the skin to protect it from harmful UV (ultra-violet) rays. Most recently, tomatoes have been heralded as the newest dietary weapon against prostate cancer.

Wine - It really is beneficial to have a glass of wine each day. Wine has several health benefits: it is antiseptic and antiviral, raises the level of good cholesterol, and it is linked to lower rates of heart disease. Like many things, however, the benefits only come with moderate use.

Yogurt - The good bacteria in yogurt fights the bad bacteria sometimes found in the intestinal tract that can cause digestive problems. Eating yogurt is a good way to restore balance to the bowels in cases of diarrhea and constipation, and it coats the stomach, providing protection from ulcers. Yogurt is another cholesterol lowering food, as well.

Omega-3 Oils - In a Class by Themselves

Newfoundlanders are known to love fish dishes of all kinds. We are traditionally a fishery-based economy, and fish, shellfish and seal meat has always been a staple of our diet. Based on scientific research on fatty acids as they relate to cholesterol and other health concerns, doctors are now strongly recommending a type of fish diet that Newfoundlanders have always enjoyed.

At the centre of this research are two types of essential fatty acids that are absolutely needed by our bodies to remain healthy. The importance of these acids, which are generally described in food sources as oils, was discovered in the 1930s. One is called omega-6, and we regularly consume plenty of it without even trying. Omega-6 oils are found in such foods as chicken, eggs, beans, cereal, whole wheat bread and nuts. As well, the great health concern over heart disease began in the 1950s, and health officials were recommending a dietary switchover to polyunsaturated fats. To meet demand, commercial food industries began producing polyunsaturated food products loaded with omega-6, considered then to be the 'good fat'. And it is a beneficial oil, but only when taken in moderation, which wasn't realized until years later.

Despite public awareness and consumption of omega-6 oils, the incidence of heart disease wasn't going down; in fact, it was steadily increasing. Then, new evidence about essential oils surfaced in the early 1970s centered around the cardiovascular health of Greenland Inuit. Researchers studied the diet of these Inuit as a way to explain the extremely low incidence of heart disease among them. It was concluded that the traditional diet of fish, shellfish and seal meat provided the Inuit with an abundance of another essential oil: omega-3.

Further research on omega-3 revealed that a certain ratio of the two essential oils was necessary for optimum health. Without a solid representation of omega-3 oils in the bloodstream, the omega-6 oils go beyond their beneficial capabilities and can actually contribute to heart disease, obesity, diabetes, cancer and other health problems that essential fatty acids are meant to address. A proportionate amount of omega-3 oils in the diet will reign in the destructiveness of omega-6 overload. Scientists today believe that because so much of what we eat already contains omega-6 oils, we need to do what we can to increase omega-3 intake and restore the balance in the bloodstream. Based on the average American diet, we currently consume a 30:1 or 20:1 ratio of omega-6 to omega-3 oils. To restore damage done to our bodies and strengthen them for better living, the ratio of omega-6 to omega-3 should be at 3:1, 2:1 or, ideally, 1:1.

It is believed that today's 'industrialized' diet is much to blame for the fatty acids ratio being out of whack. In simpler times when people had to hunt for their food, families settled near water, fresh water or ocean, to be close to a protein source. Therefore, fish and shellfish were consumed regularly. In modern times, chicken and beef are the top two sources of protein for most consumers; unfortunately, they are not good sources of omega-3 oils.

But what do omega-3 oils do exactly? Essential fatty acids are necessary in the proper construction and functioning of our cells. A balance of essential omega-6 and omega-3 fatty acids, because they work best together, contributes to healthy skin, proper development and growth in babies and small children, optimum use of cholesterol in the blood stream and the production of vital substances within the body. Remember that without a strong equalizing presence of omega-3 oils, omega-6 oils can't properly do their job.

Heart disease is the number one cause of death in the world today, and has been a major health concern for much of the 20th century. A factor that leads to heart disease is called atherosclerosis, a buildup of plaque in the arteries that is often referred to as hardening. Sometimes cholesterol becomes oxidized in the bloodstream and that oxidation spurs on plaque-forming activity in the arteries. Blocked, or partially blocked, arteries then lead to the risk of blood clots which can trigger a heart attack or stroke. A healthy intake of omega-3 oils can reduce the risks associated with heart disease.

The body uses essential fatty acids to create chemicals called prostaglandins. One of these is thromboxane which promotes normal blood clotting; however, too much thromboxane in the blood can cause the arteries to constrict. Another chemical produced from the same essential fatty acids is prostacyclin which prevents constricting of the arteries. Research on essential oils has proven that omega-3 oils can reduce the amount of thromboxane while maintaining the necessary level of prostacyclin. Too much thromboxane production also leads to high blood pressure, which can also be countered by adding omega-3 oils to the diet. Omega-3 oils also thin the blood and therefore improve circulation, which is another important factor in guarding against heart disease.

Through intense research on omega-3 oils, scientists have discovered a myriad of illnesses and ailments in addition to heart disease that can be benefited by an increased intake of these essential fats. Among them are aging, Alzheimer's, arthritic pain, asthma, attention deficit hyperactivity disorder (ADHD), cancer, depression, diabetes, dry skin, eyesight, glaucoma, immune system, impotence, infertility, menopause, osteoporosis, premenstrual syndrome (PMS) and schizophrenia.

Fish has often been referred to as 'brain food'. This is probably due to its high omega-3 content. The body needs the fatty acid DHA which is abundant in omega-3 oils to compose most of the brain matter. Proper proportions of omega-3 oils aid optimum brain development in fetuses and children and boost brain functioning. Because of this evidence, a deficiency in omega-3 fatty acids has been linked to brain disorders such as ADHD, Alzheimer's, depression and schizophrenia.

The eyes need omega-3 as much as the brain does. The retina depends on the DHA fatty acid in omega-3 oils to send optical signals to the brain at top speed. As well, omega-3 fats offset blood vessel constriction that leads to glaucoma and macular degeneration.

Omega-6 oils in high concentrations can lead to inflammatory reactions in the body, contributing to skin disorders such as eczema. Inflammation also contributes to arthritic pain, asthma, lupus and inflammation of the bowel. A proportionate existence of omega-3 oils in the system keep omega-6 fatty acid activities in check, thereby reducing the symptoms of these conditions.

Diabetics should also be aware of their omega-3 intake. Again, it is the DHA fatty acid that the body needs. DHA is used by the cells to build flexible and fluid membranes that allow proper absorption of insulin from the body. Cells that become insulin-resistant lead to people at risk for diabetes.

Maintaining the proper balance of omega-6 and omega-3 fatty acids is important to a healthy immune system. A properly functioning immune system offers you the best protection against a variety of problems, from dry skin to cancer. For example, an abundance of omega-6 fatty acids in the bloodstream can actually encourage tumors to grow. Again, it is the balancing performance of omega-3 oils that stops the progression of cancerous tumors. As well, omega-3 fats have very recently shown to block the spread (metastasis) of cancer cells.

Finally, omega-3 fatty acids play a role in healthy male and female reproductive systems. In women, omega-3 oils ease the inflammation and muscle contractions associated with the monthly discomfort. For women having trouble getting pregnant due to problems with sperm survival in the body, omega-3 and omega-6 oils work together to create a more acceptable environment in the female body for sperm to survive long enough for conception. In men, omega-3 fats have been known to increase sexual desire. Men's reproductive systems use much more of the DHA than women's for normal functioning; therefore, men need a higher intake of DHA-rich omega-3 oils to keep a sufficient supply in the body. The powerful omega-3 fatty acid is also believed to have a positive effect on prostate cancer.

As mentioned early on, it is relatively easy to slip sufficient amounts of omega-6 oils into our diet. It is also easy in a ocean-reliant culture to add more omega-3 oils to a healthy lifestyle. Omega-3 oils are most concentrated in cold-water food sources because omega-3 fatty acids act as a body insulator. The greatest fish sources of omega-3 oils (and DHA) are herring, mackerel, salmon, sardines, trout, whitefish and tuna. cod, flounder, haddock, halibut, perch and smelt are just a few other fish species which contain considerable amounts of omega-3 fats. All types of shellfish (lobster, crab, mussels, etc.) contain some omega-3 oil, as do octopus and squid. Last, but not least, seals are an excellent source of omega-3 fat. The omega-3 oils can be included in your daily health regimen by eating the meat or by taking seal oil capsules, now made right here in Newfoundland.

Supplementing Good Health

Taking herbal supplements to maintain good health has become all the rage in the last number of years. Some of these capsules are derived from ancient recipes that have been in use in some cultures for centuries. For a while, many pharmaceutical companies actively dismissed the powerful properties of some of these compounds, as did most of western medicine. Through research, testing and public demand for more natural methods of healing and prevention, drug companies and doctors are giving these supplements a second look. Some established pharmaceutical companies have branched into a line of herbal products, and more doctors are considering combining alternative therapies with conventional medicine as a more focused treatment for certain conditions. *Again, it must be stressed that anyone thinking of starting a supplement regimen should first consult his or her doctor.*

Aloe Vera - The leaves of this plant soothe burns, cuts and insect bites; and ease the symptoms of bowel irregularity, arthritis, heartburn, indigestion and ulcers.

Avena Sativa - This herb is a nerve tonic and cholesterol reducer.

Bilberry - Extracted from the bilberry fruit, this supplement may improve night vision, improves and strengthens eyes overall, regulates the bowels and increases appetite.

Black Cohosh - This herb is reported to balance hormone levels and is used as a treatment for PMS and menopause.

Cat's Claw - This is a bark that provides relief from irritable bowel syndrome, Crohn's disease, and other intestinal problems. It boosts the immune system, reduces the inflammation of arthritis and fights cancerous tumors.

Coltsfoot - Taken from the leaves, this supplement breaks up mucus for asthma, bronchitis and emphysema sufferers.

Dandelion - The roots and leaves of these plants are used in homeopathic healing.

Dandelion eases constipation, menstrual cramps, bloating and chronic rheumatism. It also reduces blood pressure and may reduce the risk of iron deficiency and anemia.

Devil's Claw - These supplements are made from the root of the plant and are used to reduce swelling in arthritis and gout sufferers. **Caution:** Should not be used by pregnant women.

Dong Quai - This herbal root regulates hormones and reduces blood pressure. It is also beneficial to women with PMS or going through menopause. **Caution:** May be unsuitable for pregnant women.

Echinacea - This wildly popular root boosts the immune system, promotes healing of wounds and fights bacteria and viruses. It is an approved treatment for asthma, boils, bronchitis, cancer, chlamydia, cold sores, cold and flu, ear infection, inflammation, and tonsillitis. **Caution:** May not be suitable to people suffering from auto-immune diseases.

Evening Primrose - This plant suppresses muscle spasms; therefore, it is useful in treating PMS and multiple sclerosis. It also reduces risk of heart disease and stroke, promotes healthy skin, and treats hair loss.

Fenugreek - The seeds soothe stomach and intestinal problems and encourage the body to cough up mucus. It is suitable for sufferers of colds and flus, asthma, bronchitis, and sinus congestion.

Feverfew - The leaves of this herb have anti-inflammatory powers. This supplement can be taken to relieve arthritic swelling, back pain, migraine headaches and fevers. **Caution:** Pregnant and breastfeeding women should avoid this herb.

Ginko Biloba - The leaves of this exotic plant increase blood flow to the brain, reduce risk of blood clotting and improve mental function. These properties make ginko biloba a treatment for Alzheimer's, memory loss, ringing in the ear, dizziness, eye disorders, stress, impotence, depression, headaches, asthma, eczema and heart and kidney disorders.

Ginseng - This humble root has gained outrageous fame for its stimulating properties. It boosts the immune system, fights symptoms of fatigue, and generally improves physical and mental stamina.

Glucosamine Sulfate - This supplement is reported to promote cartilage growth and relieve the pain of osteoarthritis.

Gotu Kola - This plant is an energy booster, memory enhancer and stress reliever.

Golden Seal - It is the root that treats bed sores, canker sores, chlamydia, cold and flu symptoms, constipation, indigestion, Crohn's disease, diabetes, inflammation, psoriasis and ulcers. **Caution:** This should not be consumed by pregnant women or people with high blood pressure.

Hawthorn - The supplements are derived from the berries and are used to lower blood pressure, lessen hypertension and reduce the severity of angina attacks. The berries also have sedative and anti-spasmodic properties.

Horsetail - This is used as a herbal treatment for hair loss, brittle nails, osteoporosis, muscle cramps, back pain and inflamed or enlarged prostate.

Kava Kava - Take this supplement to relax muscles, ease overall tension and promote sleep.

Milk Thistle - Both the seeds and leaves of this plant are used in making the supplements. Milk thistle flushes the spleen, stomach, kidney and gall bladder; it is a treatment for jaundice, hepatitis and cirrhosis.

Pumpkin - Pumpkin seeds are useful for reducing an enlarged prostate and alleviating the symptoms, and they help rid the body of tapeworms.

Saw Palmetto - Extracted from the berries, this supplement treats impotence, infertility in women and urinary tract disorders.

Seal Oil - These capsules improve general cardiovascular and circulatory health. Scientists are also studying its possible benefits to infant development.

Seaweed - This ocean grass strengthens the immune system, kills bacteria, treats ulcers, lowers blood pressure and bad cholesterol, and thins the blood.

Shark Cartilage - Shark cartilage has natural anti-inflammatory properties. It is considered to be a treatment for cancer in both humans and animals. This supplement has also become popular in treating arthritis, psoriasis and many other skin disorders. It can reduce healing time in sports-related joint and muscle injuries. Generally, shark cartilage boosts the immune system for improved overall health.

Slippery Elm - The inner bark of this plant provides relief from sore throat, digestive tract disorders, upset stomach and ulcers.

St. John's Wort - This herb has gained a lot of attention as an anti-viral, anti-inflammatory and anti-depressant supplement. It is an alternative treatment for depression, stress, insomnia and migraines. **Caution:** Users of this herb must carefully monitor the amount of time spent in the sun. St. John's Wort may make the skin photosensitive.

Grassroots Healing

Downhomer

Astro Guide

A

General Horoscope

by Madam Doziac

Downhomer Astro Guide

By Madam Doziac
St. John's, Newfoundland

Astrology probably began with the shepherds of ancient Chaldea, who observed the night sky as they watched over their flocks. The points of light in the sky seemed to be arranged in patterns that looked like mythical or living things. Formations like the crab, the bull and the archer could be seen in the sky, and these became the signs of the zodiac. The wise men of Babylon, the capital of Chaldea, noticed that people born at the same period of the year showed similar personality traits. These 'astrologers' would 'cast a horoscope' or interpret the influence of heavenly bodies on human behaviour and events.

Today, many people are still very intrigued by the zodiac. Horoscopes are read daily by millions of people worldwide. It seems too coincidental that people born under the same sign exhibit similar behaviour patterns. This is by no means 100 per cent accurate for everyone. It is but one of the many tools we can use to learn more about ourselves and others.

The following is a general guide to the common characteristics and behaviours displayed by people born under the 12 signs of the zodiac.

Aries: the Ram
March 21-April 19
Ruling planet: Mars
Opposite sign: Libra

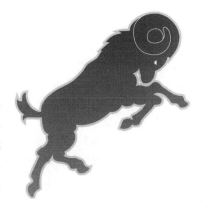

Aries is the cardinal fire sign of the Zodiac. Fire is associated with activity and enthusiasm, and this is especially true for Aries. The Arien has a quick and active mind. They are spontaneous, direct, fearless, loyal and enterprising. Rams tend to act on impulse rather than wait to work things out. They are very independent and prefer to take initiative and attack problems directly rather than avoid them. An Arien is the kind of person who will make you believe their opinion is the 'right' one.

In love: A typical Aries is very romantic and will pour this on during the dating period only. They like to be the pursuer and may avoid being chased by anyone. Aries is extremely possessive with a loved one, but does not understand when someone is possessive of them. They are very jealous and will valiantly defend their lover.

In bed: Ariens enjoy the excitement of the chase and not the conquest. They like to be the dominator but they do not want a completely submissive partner. Routine in love-making will make Aries bored and disinterested.

At work: Anyone who has a strong Aries influence is very loyal and enthusiastic about their job. They often work long hours and do not watch the clock. They get bored easily so they need to be constantly challenged. Typical occupations are: work in theatre, military, politics, sports or anything that requires being in a leadership position.

As a parent: Aries of course, do not spoil their children but they do give plenty of praise and affection. They are strict disciplinarians but will not tolerate others hurting their children. Ariens tend to push their own ideals on their children and attempt to dictate their child's future occupation.

Some positive characteristics: Is energetic, is a leader, accepts challenges, takes risks, an Aries life is an open book, independent, passionate in love.

Some negative characteristics: Is bossy, brash, jealous, poor judge of character, selfish, impulsive, stubborn, intolerant, arrogant, condescending.

Taurus: the Bull
April 20-May 20
Ruling planet: Venus
Opposite sign: Scorpio

The fixed earth sign of the zodiac is Taurus. Earth as an element is linked to practical reality. People born under the sign of Taurus require emotional and material stability. They are long-term planners and are practical and methodical in their approach to their lives and jobs. Taureans are naturally charming and friendly, and strive to make their surroundings peaceful and harmonious. They proceed through life with caution, avoiding short cuts and believe that the best is worth waiting for. Usually, Taurus folks are very sentimental and appreciative of others.

In love: Those born under the sign of Taurus are very devoted and steadfast in a relationship. Taureans will quickly settle into a long-term partnership after a short courtship. They will avoid breaking up at all costs and this stubbornness can sometimes prolong unhealthy relationships. They can be very vulnerable, but will never forgive a cheater.

In bed: When the loyal Taurean makes love it is the most physical and natural pleasure on earth. If a Taurean is being criticized they may be embarrassed about their bodies and become inhibited. But, for the most part, they enjoy sex to the fullest and enjoy being in the nude.

At work: A typical Taurus will only work at a job that they feel is respectable. They work diligently at their tasks and can't stand to be interrupted. Jobs most associated with Taureans include: banking, farming, decorating, engineering, construction, general practitioner, executive secretary, and any job that is stable in an established institution or anything involved in the acquisition of goods, investment and land.

As a parent: The Taurus parent is one who will spend hours teaching their child to tie their laces without becoming at all impatient. They don't spare hugs and kisses either. They are good at saving money for their children's college education and have high exceptions for them. They teach self love and are very encouraging and supportive, although they can be somewhat dominant and possessive with their children. As well, they have no doubts about their parenting capabilities.

Some positive characteristics: Non-critical, dependable, artistic, loving, gentle, orderly, have a good sense of time, careful, conservative, loyal, thorough.

Some negative characteristics: Stubborn, suspicious, dislikes being contradicted, materialistic, slow-moving, boring, easily embarrassed, self-indulgent, quiet, insensitive.

Gemini: the Twins
May 21-June 20
Ruling planet: Mercury
Opposite sign: Sagittarius

Gemini is the mutable air sign of the Zodiac. And like streams of air current, Gemini is constantly changing. The intelligent and quick-witted Geminian is ruled by their intellect and not their emotions. The dual personality of the Twins, one side is earthy and the other spiritual, tends to constantly change their focus. They become bored and distracted easily and find it hard to settle into one relationship. The Gemini is also sure of him/herself, is open minded and anxious to learn new things.

In love: In relationships the Gemini may frequently appear cool and distant, they appear insensitive, but deep down they hurt easily. Don't expect a Gemini to act spontaneously. A Gemini will be overwhelmed with emotion but will suppress it, this can be very frustrating to their partner. They may not say "I love you," but they do.

In bed: Talking in bed will really excite a Gemini. They enjoy variety under the sheets and little surprises. When Geminis make love they will express all their pent up emotions at once. They also want more from a partner than just sex.

At work: Geminians need variety and stimulation at work. As a boss, he or she will scrutinize and question everything employees do. They get things done and can deal with emergencies and sudden changes without batting an eyelash. Occupations associated with the Twins include: Any work in the media, artist, musician, actor, politician surgeon, scientist and anything that requires a quick mind and good dexterous abilities.

As a parent: A Gemini parent quite easily relates to their children and will jump into the sandbox and play for hours. They explain things very rationally to children but find it hard to express emotion.

Some positive characteristics: Inventive, youthful, charming, stimulating, analytical, versatile, entertaining, un-prejudiced, adaptable.

Some negative characteristics: Easily bored, restless, non-committal, nervous, has a split-personality, manipulative, impatient, irritable, gossipy, inconsiderate, sharp-tongued.

Cancer: the Crab
June 21 - July 22
Ruling planet: Moon
Opposite sign: Capricorn

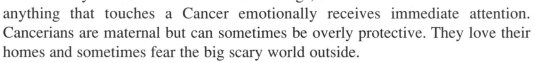

Cancer is the cardinal water sign of the Zodiac. Water is associated with sensitivity and emotion. Cancerians are like safe harbours - where boats and seafarers can find protection. Crabs have a hard shell which covers an extremely soft and sensitive interior. They are famous for their mood swings, but anything that touches a Cancer emotionally receives immediate attention. Cancerians are maternal but can sometimes be overly protective. They love their homes and sometimes fear the big scary world outside.

In love: Cancers rarely make the first move as they fear rejection. Crabs are romantics at heart and will respond to any signs of love and affection. Always the sensitive one, they hurt easily at any little criticism. Cancerians also have a tendency to put their loved-one ahead of everything else in their lives, including themselves. Separation is difficult for the Cancerian, even if it is inevitable - he or she will cling more tightly as the relationship falls apart.

In bed: Don't sleep with a Cancerian unless you want a committed relationship with them. They don't desire a complicated sex life, just a monogamous one. Cancers don't enjoy making-love out doors or in unusual places.

At work: Cancers enjoy working in comfortable and secure environments. They want responsibility, and expect to be rewarded for it. As a boss they are demanding, but generous and fair. Some typical cancer occupations include:

Anything to do with water, food, animals and children, as well as nursing, social sciences and politics.

As a parent: Cancer is the most maternal of all the signs. They worry too much about their children and can be very over-possessive. Cancers enjoy looking after and playing with children and will do anything to stimulate creative development.

Some positive characteristics: Kind, compassionate, motherly, has a good memory, helpful, protective, tenacious, domesticated, sensitive to others' needs, understanding, honest, patient.

Some negative characteristics: Fatalistic, timid, lazy, moody, sulky, crabby, manipulative, over-powering, introspective, easily-hurt.

Leo: the Lion
July 23 - August 22
Ruling planet: Sun
Opposite sign: Aquarius

Leo is the fixed fire sign of the zodiac. Like a welcoming fireplace or camp fire, Leo draws everyone into their warmth. Leos are born leaders. They are very stubborn and set in their ways, but like to transform those around them with their positive energy. Leonines are playful and crave the limelight. They are also risk-takers.

In love: Leo the lion never has trouble attracting lovers. Once in love, Leos expect to be adored. They are very romantic and don't mind showing it. The regal lion expects total commitment and will fight to the death for their lover. Leo's pride sometimes makes it difficult to end an affair. And they may act cruelly when an unwanted lover continues to cling.

In bed: Dramatic Leo is very unrestrained in bed, they make their lovers feel very special. But, they tend to get caught up in their own fantasy world and may forget about the person with them. Leonines have trouble accepting their shortcomings and will not seek out help if they have sexual problems.

At work: Leos always make a wonderful first impression during job interviews. They must be in charge of something and have the ability to get everyone working hard for them. They don't tolerate failure and sometimes take credit for others' accomplishments.

As a parent: Leonines make very conscientious parents. They are generous with their love and praise and spending money. Leo parents expect appreciation from their kids for all the sacrifices they make for them. Lions want to be proud of their offspring and sometimes may put too much pressure on their children to be successful.

Astro Guide

Some positive characteristics: Honest, loyal, always a leader, organized, generous, motivated, reliable, has dignity, proud, courageous, accepting.

Some negative characteristics: Arrogant, stubborn, smug, indifferent, cold-hearted, materialistic, sulky.

Virgo: the Virgin
August 23 - September 22
Ruling planet: Mercury
Opposite sign: Pisces

The mutable earth sign of the zodiac, Virgo, like a gardener knows how to plan and adapt their garden. Virgos are very busy people, and see things through fruition. They worry a lot and feel like they are never quite good enough. Virgoans enjoy serving others, and living a life of modesty. The Virgin is also very responsible, a good strategizer and usually has a brilliant mind.

In love: A Virgo is frightened by in-your-face romance. They will wait an eternity for Mr. or Mrs. Right. Once in love, they are warm, dedicated and steadfast. They are not likely to cause jealousy and will avoid break-ups. But, if the end of a relationship is inevitable, sensible Virgo will not hang on and will probably avoid reconciliation.

In bed: Virgos are not overly flirtatious, but will seduce using subtle charm. Virginous Virgo can tolerate periods of celibacy. They are looking for a life-long partner, not an easy one-nighter. Virgos enjoy learning all they can about sex.

At work: Virgoans work best in a supporting role, they enjoy helping others. Meticulous and disciplined, quick-thinking, the Virgin is also analytical, courteous and reliable. An ideal employee.

As a boss: Virgos may not fare that well in a large, cut-throat industry, as they expect honesty in all situations.

As a parent: Virgo parents worry immensely about their children's health and may spend too much time with them at the doctor's office. Virgos encourage their kids to ask questions and they support constructive play for them. Virgos sometimes find it difficult to show affection to their offspring.

Some positive characteristics: Organized, dedicated, gentle, humane, well-informed, charming, painstaking, observant, down-to-earth, honest, self-disciplined.

Some negative characteristics: Irritable, is a hypochondriac, nervous, worrisome, eccentric, demanding, prudish, is a perfectionist, emotionless, miserly.

Libra: the Scales
September 23 - October 22
Ruling planet: Venus
Opposite sign: Aries

Libra is the cardinal air sign of the zodiac, and can be compared to a wind instrument, playing beautiful music and promoting peace and harmony. Librans are always striving to achieve balance in their lives and are great lovers of beauty. Like the scales of justice, they try to see both side of any situation and treat others with fairness. People born under this sign are more often very refined, and quite particular about their physical appearance. They are true romantics and are great lovers of art and good food. They detest change and anything unpleasant, and never rush into things.

In love: Always the hopeless romantic, Librans will sit and wait for their prince or princess charming to come along. When in love, Libras become emotionally dependent on the other. They tend to ignore their partner's faults and will do anything to avoid hurting them. Libras expect admiration, and when they get it they allow all the world to see it. When rejected, Libras become devastated and will try to charm the other back into their life.

In bed: Libras tend to be insecure about their sexual appeal and this inhibits their love-making. Making love is not always a passionate experience for them, even though they make it appear so. They are very often interested in sex, but only if they are confident about their physical appearance.

At work: Libras take a lot of time to get things right. They tend to be overly cautious and meticulous and may require periods of rest. Their working environment should be harmonious and free from anything disturbing or upsetting. As an employer, a Libra can be unhurried but extremely stressed and restless. They believe their policy is best, but will have the answers to unusual problems.

As a parent: Librans do not make strict parents and tend to spoil their children. They don't spare the hugs and compliments but are very just and fair. Libras tend to be the dominating parent.

Some positive characteristics: Loyal, amiable, open-minded, tactful, good listener, cooperative, fair, sincere, charming, communicative, loving, romantic, artistic, refined.

Some negative characteristics: Vain, sulky, indecisive, flirtatious, insincere, materialistic, manipulative, fearful, overbearing.

Astro Guide

Astro Guide

Scorpio: the Scorpion
October 23 - November 21
Ruling planet: Mars and Pluto
Opposite sign: Taurus

Scorpio is the fixed water sign of the zodiac, like the ocean, at times ferocious and at times still, it has the power to transform even the hardest substances. Mystery shrouds the Scorpionic persona, a sexy attribute which makes them extremely attractive. They are determined and impenetrable and know what they want from life. Always strong-willed and passionate, the sting of the Scorpion is more likely to hurt themselves rather than others. Scopios hate social obligations and interruptions, but are very tender and loving. Never superficial, Scorpios may be the most loving of all signs.

In love: Scorpios want a monogamous relationship. Love is central to their life and is the cause of many of their decisions and actions. The Scorpio is very possessive, but keeps it hidden; they are not the type to kiss or hold hands in public. Probably the most attractive of all signs, they never have trouble finding a mate. But once rejected, they may become extremely vengeful and unforgiving.

In bed: As the most sensual and magnetic of all signs, Scorpions understand the importance of a good sex life. When making love, they express all of their pent up emotions and frustrations. They are very faithful and use sex as an expression of their dedication.

At work: At the office, Scorpios end up knowing everyone's secrets, without giving away their own. They are problem-solvers and tackle any task head-on. Extremely competitive, they excel in leadership positions. Calm, cool and confident in all situations, they have trouble accepting failures. Scorpios are good at getting to the root of the problem, human or mechanical.

As a parent: Scorpios are passionate and strict parents, and have high standards for their children. They enjoy their children to the fullest, taking them to movies and playgrounds; always keeping them out and about and busy. But they do find it difficult to change their own point of view, which can broaden the generation gap.

Some positive characteristics: Loving, determined, brave, hard-working, sincere, magnetic, sensual, emotional, intense, unshockable, understanding, investigative, constructive.

Some negative characteristics: Anxious, hyper-sensitive, self-destructive, moody, sadistic, intolerant, cunning, vindictive, jealous, suspicious, possessive, dangerous, secretive, ruthless, devious, unbalanced, excessive.

Sagittarius: the Archer
November 22 - December 21
Ruling planet: Jupiter
Opposite sign: Gemini

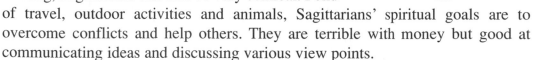

Sagittarius is the mutable fire sign of the zodiac, like the sparks from a raging fire, they are always transforming. Adaptable Sagittarius is open-minded, tolerant, honest and usually happy-go-lucky. They seek justice and hold no grudges. Sometimes overly trusting, Sagittarians can also be very comical. Fond of travel, outdoor activities and animals, Sagittarians' spiritual goals are to overcome conflicts and help others. They are terrible with money but good at communicating ideas and discussing various view points.

In love: Sagittarians hate feeling tied down, and enjoy affairs in exotic places; love to them is a romantic adventure. When in love, they are generous and happy and expect security, honesty and stimulation. Sagittarians will not stand for a jealous or possessive partner; they will move on. If a relationship becomes boring or routine, the Sagittarius will have an affair or leave the relationship.

In bed: Always the adventurer, the Archer can be a little reckless when it comes to their sexual partners. For Sagittarians, a similar intellect is an attractive sexual quality. They enjoy expressing their affection through lots of cuddling.

At work: Sagittarians need to be constantly challenged and stimulated at work. If they become bored or restless they will leave the job. It is not unlikely for Sagittarians to have more than one job. Always enthusiastic, versatile and willing, typical occupations include anything to do with travel, performance, teaching and using their intellect.

As a parent: Sagittarians have very defined moral standards for their children. They are playful and fun, enjoy their children and provide a stimulating environment. They answer questions honestly, talk openly with their children and enjoy traveling with them. But they sometimes expect too much from their children intellectually.

Some positive characteristics: Dependable, unselfish, tolerant, open-minded, jovial, optimistic, honest, fair, stimulating, sensual, spiritual.

Some negative characteristics: Restless, proud, wasteful, indulgent, argumentative, critical, impatient, uncommitted, preachy, careless.

Astro Guide

Astro Guide

Capricorn: the Goat
December 22 - January 19
Ruling Planet: Saturn
Opposite sign: Cancer

The cardinal earth sign of the zodiac, Capricorns are like the oldest and most valuable tree in the woods. Practical, serious and worrisome, they are good at saving money, business matters and planning for their future. Diligent and self-controlled, they usually achieve their goals. Often very quiet and conservative, Capricorneans avoid the spotlight so as never to appear foolish. They do display a wry and ironic sense of humour.

In love: Capricorns have great difficulty expressing their feelings, but are secret romantics at heart, who crave a perfect, secure, long-term relationship. They are not the type to make passes at strangers and are rarely flirtatious. They never lie about being in love, and when they do say those three little words, they don't feel like they need to repeat them. As a rule, Capricorns take a long time to put an end to a relationship. But, if they are betrayed, they can be quite nasty and will drop the adulterous one in a blink.

In bed: Under the sheets, Capricorneans are into it, body, mind and soul. They make the best lovers. They see no separation between love and sex and will insure the utmost satisfaction for both parties.

At work: Capricorns generally work long and hard. Diligent to the core, no obstacle is too big. They arrive at work early, leave late and dress very conservatively. So dependable and responsible at work that they may neglect their own needs. Very quiet, they are not very social but coworkers trust them. They create a private and tidy work environment, and tend to work in occupations that demand organization, smart management, but never as the front person.

As a parent: Strict, but very fair, Capricorns take parenthood seriously. Tender and sensitive, they teach good manners and provide the best in everything for their kids. Capricorns find it easier to relate to older children than younger ones.

Some positive characteristics: Organized, cautious, calm, realistic, observant, hard-working, fearless, conventional, concerned, loyal, respectful, reliable, determined.

Some negative characteristics: Over-critical, egotistical, unforgiving, fatalistic, status-seeking, perfectionist, worrisome, materialistic, greedy, bossy, narrow-minded.

Aquarius: the Water Carrier
January 20 - February 18
Ruling planet: Saturn and Uranus
Opposite sign: Leo

Aquarius is the fixed air sign of the zodiac; great thinkers, they are steadfast in their opinions. Honest and forthright, Aquarians tend to be extremely aware of their environment. They are also great humanitarians and may carry the weight of the world on their shoulders. The Water Carrier is very tolerant and avoids hurting others at all costs. Most Aquarians are very intellectual and sometimes may be viewed as eccentric or odd; quite sure of the world, but often quite unsure of their own identity. They seem to be 50 years ahead of their time.

In love: Aquarians are afraid of deep emotional involvement. Very independent, they may act aloof for the duration of a relationship and may choose to live apart. Aquarians take the dominating role in an affair and will easily drop a partner who is too demanding or jealous.

In bed: When Aquarians make love it's more of an intellectual experience than an emotional or physical one. Quite modest when it comes to sex, they are extremely adamant about cleanliness and proper contraception. Rarely jealous, Aquarians make better friends than lovers.

At work: Aquarians do very well working with a group. They dislike routine work and decision making. Aquarians are very creative and may change jobs frequently in their early years. An Aquarian's work environment must be free of emotional tension and noise. Typical jobs include writer, photographer, inventor, scientist, engineer, archaeologist, humanitarian worker; anything to do with investigation, experimentation, forward thinking or analysis.

As a parent: Aquarian parents are friends for life. They encourage independence of thought and treat their children as equals. Not very strict disciplinarians, they let their children live their own lives, but demand the best education for them.

Some positive characteristics: Honest, community-minded, respectful, thoughtful, dependable, loyal, scientific, inventive, creative, cooperative, independent.

Some negative characteristics: Voyeuristic, tactless, critical, eccentric, doubtful, unrealistic, unconventional, self-righteous.

Astro Guide

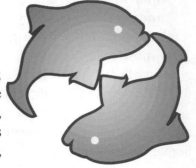

Pisces: the Fishes
February 19 - March 20
Ruling planet: Jupiter and Neptune
Opposite sign: Virgo

Pisces is the mutable water sign of the zodiac; like a constantly moving river, Pisces can change their moods a dozen times a day. Hyper-sensitive, but perceptive, charitable and compassionate, Pisces make great friends. Multi-talented, artistic and shy, they seem to exist in their own dream world. A typical Pisces is idealistic, good-natured and trustworthy, but often sad, feeling as if they've been given a bad deal in life.

In love: When a Piscean feels unloved they become very depressed. Very romantic and eager to please, Pisceans don't recognize when they are being treated badly in a relationship. They need to be constantly reassured they are loved; this can be trying in some relationships. When rejected, a Pisces will continue to hold on; the ex may have to go to extremes to be rid of them.

In bed: Pisces is less interested in the act of love-making than in the expression of love that is associated with it. Sex to them is an act of romance, not physical pleasure. Pisces may seek more than one sexual partner in order to reassure them that they are desired.

At work: Pisces enjoy work that promotes freedom of expression. When they are happy, they are loyal and get the job done. As a boss, they are a shrewd judge of character, unconventional and creative. Typical jobs are anything to do with the arts or helping people.

As a parent: Pisceans don't like disciplining their children or using harsh words. They listen with an open mind, encourage personal development and happily accommodate all of the childhood fantasies. Their children may grow up a little spoiled, as they are loved so intensely.

Some positive characteristics: Loving, trusting, dependable, giving, helpful, open-minded, romantic, creative, mystical, gentle, understanding, kind.

Some negative characteristics: Self-pitying, gullible, dependent, glum, is a sensationalist, unmotivated, permissive, easily discouraged.

Astro Guide

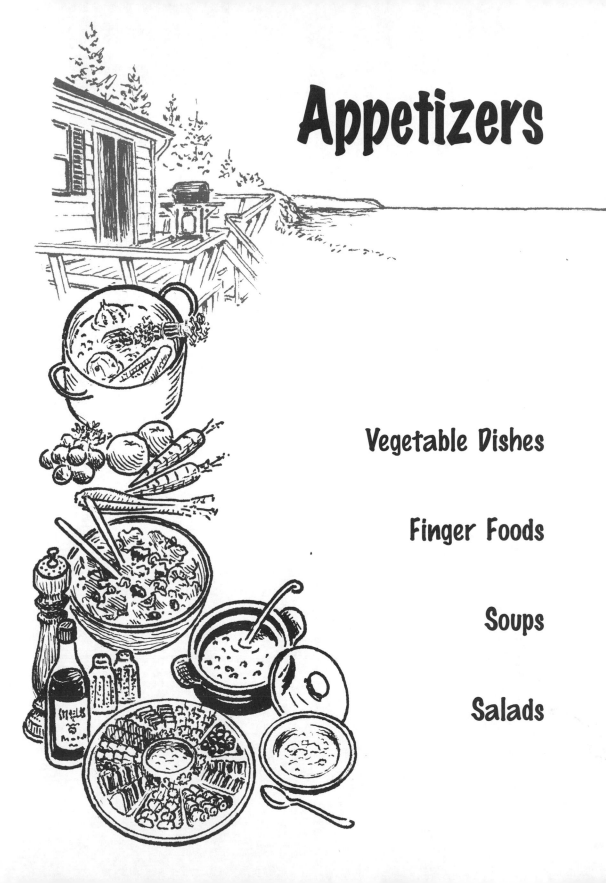

Appetizers

Vegetable Dishes

Finger Foods

Soups

Salads

Pea Soup

Ron Pumphrey, St. John's, Newfoundland

Ingredients:

2 cups dried whole or split yellow peas
8 cups cold water
2 onions, chopped
1-2 stalks celery, chopped (optional)
1 carrot, chopped (optional)
1 cooked ham bone or 3-4 slices salt pork, chopped
1-2 bay leaves (optional)
salt and pepper to taste
pinch thyme (optional)

Spice of Life

You're only young once ...after that, you have to think up some other excuse - Billy Arthur

Directions:

Wash peas, discarding any that are discoloured or shrivelled. Place in a soup pot, cover with cold water and let soak overnight. Next morning, add the chopped vegetables, ham bone and bay leaf. Bring to a boil, then lower heat and simmer gently for 3 or 4 hours. Stir mixture occasionally and add a little boiling water to keep soup at the right consistency, but the final result should be a hearty thickness. Remove ham bone and add seasonings. Serves 6-8.

Carrot Soup

Deanne Wells, St. John's, Newfoundland (formerly of Seal Cove, Fortune Bay, Newfoundland)

Ingredients:

1/4 cup butter or margarine
2 medium onions, chopped
1 garlic clove, minced
3 medium potatoes, diced
4 medium carrots, diced
5 cups chicken stock
1 bay leaf
1/4-1/2 tsp thyme
1/4 tsp pepper

Food for Thought

Religion has two children, love and hatred. - Russian proverb

Directions:

Melt butter in large saucepan. Add onion and garlic; saute until clear and soft. Add remaining ingredients using 1/4 tsp thyme. Bring to a boil; cover and simmer until vegetables are tender. Discard bay leaf. Add more thyme if desired. Makes 8 1/2 cups.

Pea Soup

Teresa Ivey, St. John's, Newfoundland

Ingredients:

1 pkg split peas
1 onion, diced
1 cup celery, diced
3 medium potatoes, diced
1/2 turnip, diced

Trivia Tidbits

The biggest gold nugget in the world weighed as much as a grown man.

Appetizers

Soups, Salads, Vegetable Dishes and Finger Foods

Appetizers

Soups, Salads, Vegetable Dishes and Finger Foods

3 carrots, diced
1 lb salt meat

Directions:
Soak meat and peas overnight. Drain off water and add more with onion and simmer for 2 hours. Add vegetables about 20 minutes before serving.

Lentil Barley Soup

Ann Bain, Tatamagouche, Nova Scotia (nee Rowe, Collins Cove, Burin, Newfoundland)

Ingredients:
1 medium onion, chopped
1/2 cup green pepper, chopped
3 cloves garlic, minced
1 tbsp butter or margarine
1 can (49 1/2 oz) chicken broth
3 medium carrots, chopped
1/2 cup dry lentils (red)
1 1/2 tsp Italian seasoning
1 tsp salt
1/4 tsp pepper
1 cup cooked chicken or turkey, cubed
1/2 cup quick-cooking barley
2 medium fresh mushrooms, chopped
1 (28oz) can crushed tomatoes, undrained

> *Food for Thought*
> To learn something new, take the same path you took yesterday.
> - John Burroughs

Directions:
In dutch oven or soup kettle, saute onion, green pepper and garlic in butter until tender. Add broth, carrots, lentils, Italian seasoning, salt and pepper; bring to a boil. Reduce heat, cover, and simmer for 25 minutes. Add chicken, barley and mushrooms, return to a boil. Reduce heat, cover and simmer for 10 - 15 minutes, or until lentils, barley and carrots are tender. Add tomatoes and heat through. Makes 8-10 servings. *Note:* Since green and brown lentils stay firm when cooked, we prefer them in a salad, rather than red lentils, which tend to go mushy.

Chicken Soup

Desiree Sheppard, Manuels, CBS, Newfoundland

Ingredients:
1 lb chicken
3 carrots
3 potatoes
1 cup rice
1/2 turnip
2 parsnip
2 small onions
salt and pepper, to taste
savoury to taste

> **Trivia Tidbits**
> North American grizzly bears can run as fast as many horses.

Directions:

Boil chicken thoroughly. Remove meat from bones, then return meat to the water. Chop vegetables finely and add to soup. Add rice, a dash of savoury, salt and pepper. Simmer 25 - 35 minutes.

Clam Chowder

Cathy Bishop, St. John's, Newfoundland

Ingredients:

1/4 cup salt pork, diced
1/2 cup onion, chopped
2 cups clam liquor or salt water
1 cup potatoes, diced
2 cups clams
2 cups milk (canned or fresh)
pepper to taste

Directions:

Fry salt pork and remove scraps. Add onions and cook slowly. Add clam juice and potatoes, simmering until tender. Add clams, milk and seasoning. Garnish with salt pork scraps and a small piece of butter.

Clam Chowder

June Gates, Woodstock, Ontario

Ingredients:

2 tbsp salt pork, diced
3 tbsp butter
2 tbsp onion, chopped
1 cup boiling water
2 cups potato cubes
1 tsp salt
dash of pepper
1 (10oz) can baby clams
2 1/2 cups scalded milk

Directions:

Saute salt pork in butter until golden brown and crisp. Add onion; cook until golden. Then add water, potatoes, salt and pepper. Cover and boil for 15 minutes, stirring occasionally. Add clams with liquid; heat. Add milk, season to taste.

Neighbourhood Bean Soup

Ann Bain, Tatamagouche, Nova Scotia (nee Rowe, Collins Cove, Burin, Newfoundland)

Ingredients:

2 cups Great Northern beans
5 cups chicken stock
3 cups water

1 large, meaty ham bone
2 - 3 tbsp chicken boullion granules
1 tsp thyme
1/2 tsp marjoram
1/2 tsp pepper
1/4 tsp sage
1/4 tsp savoury
2 medium onions
3 medium carrots
3 celery ribs

Food for Thought
The hardest job kids face today is learning good manners without seeing any. - Fred Astaire

Directions:

Wash beans and soak overnight. Add next 9 ingredients; bring to a boil. Reduce heat, cover, and simmer for 2 hours. Add onions, carrot and celery. Simmer 1 hour longer.

Best Broccoli Soup

Ann Bain, Tatamagouche, Nova Scotia (nee Rowe, Collins Cove, Burin, Newfoundland)

Ingredients:

4 cups fresh broccoli, chopped
1 cup celery, chopped
1 cup carrots, chopped
1/2 cup onion, chopped
6 tbsp butter or margarine
6 tbsp flour
3 cups chicken broth
2 cups milk
1 tbsp minced fresh parsley
1 tsp onion salt
1/2 tsp garlic powder
1/2 tsp salt

Spice of Life

Those who can, do.
Those who can't,
attend conferences.

Directions:

In dutch oven or soup kettle, bring chicken broth to a boil. Add broccoli, celery and carrots; boil 2-3 minutes. Drain, reserve liquid and set vegetables aside. In same kettle, saute onion in butter until tender. Stir in flour to form a smooth paste. Gradually add the reserved broth and milk, stirring constantly. Bring to a boil and stir for 1 minute. Add vegetables and remaining ingredients. Reduce heat, cover and simmer for 30 - 40 minutes, or until vegetables are tender. Makes 6-8 servings. Use homemade broth whenever possible.

French Onion Soup

Ben Bellefontaine, Etobicoke, Ontario
Ingredients:

6 beef cubes
6 cups hot water
5 cups onions, thinly sliced

1/4 cup butter or margarine
1/4 tsp pepper
1/4 tsp sugar
1 tbsp flour
1/2 tsp salt

Directions:

Dissolve beef cubes in 6 cups of hot water. Saute onion in butter or margarine until golden. Sprinkle with salt, pepper, sugar and flour; add beef cube mixture. Cover and simmer for 3-4 hours. Serve in bowls topped with croutons and parmesan cheese. This soup is best cooked in a slow cooker or crock pot for about 6 or 7 hours.

Hamburg Soup

Rosalind Fraser, Garson, Ontario

Ingredients:

1 lb lean hamburger meat
4 onions, diced
2 stalks celery, diced
2 large carrots, diced
2 bay leaves
1 cup small pasta shells
salt and pepper, to taste
10 cups water
3 tbsp beef bouillon
1 tin tomatoes, chopped
1 (7oz) tin tomato sauce
3 tsp chili powder
2 tsp basil

Directions:

Brown meat, onion, celery and carrot in soup pot. Once browned, add remaining ingredients. Simmer until done.

Spicy Cream of Carrot Soup

Cathy Robinson-Gill, Shelby, North Carolina, USA (formerly of Baie Verte, Newfoundland)

Ingredients:

3 to 3 1/2 cups canned reduced-sodium chicken broth, divided
4 medium carrots, sliced
1 medium yellow onion, cut into thick slices
1 medium stalk celery, sliced
4 tbsp long grain white rice
1 tsp sugar
1/8 tsp cayenne pepper, or to taste
1/2 cup milk
1/2 cup sour cream
salt to taste

Directions:

This healthy and delicious soup is rich in Vitamin A. Serve hot or cold. Preparation time: 10 mins. Cooking time: 30 mins.

In a large saucepan, combine 3 cups of broth, carrots, onion, celery, rice, sugar and cayenne pepper. Cover and bring to a boil over high heat. Reduce the heat to low and simmer until the rice and carrots are tender, about 15 to 20 minutes. Stir milk and sour cream into the carrot mixture. Using a food processor or electric blender, puree the soup, half at a time, until it is smooth. If a thinner soup is desired, blend in 1/2 cup of additional chicken broth. Return the soup to a medium size saucepan. Stir in salt and additional cayenne pepper, if desired. Reheat the soup over moderate heat until it is hot, but not boiling. Ladle the soup into bowls. Serve immediately.

Hearty Minestrone Soup

Sherry Lander, Mississauga, Ontario (formerly of Old Bonaventure, Newfoundland)

Ingredients:

3 slices bacon
1 onion, chopped
1 carrot, chopped
1 stalk celery, chopped
1 1/2 cups cabbage, chopped
4 cups water
3 (10oz) cans chicken broth
1 (19oz) can tomatoes, coarsely chopped with liquid reserved
1 cup mini pasta shells
1 (14oz) can red or white kidney beans, drained
3 cloves of garlic, minced
2 tbsp Italian parsley, chopped (fresh or dried)
parmesan cheese, grated

Spice of Life

It's not for stealing that you are punished, but for getting caught.

- Russian proverb

Directions:

Cook bacon until crisp; chop. Add onion, carrot, celery and cabbage. Cook, stirring occasionally, about 5 minutes. Stir in water, broth and tomatoes with liquid; bring to a boil. Reduce heat and simmer, covered, for 15 minutes. Stir in shells and cook, uncovered, 15 minutes longer. Stir beans, garlic and parsley into soup and cook for an additional 10 - 15 minutes. Serve topped with parmesan cheese.

Bahamian Chicken Souse (Soup)

Donna Young, Nassau, The Bahamas (originally from Newfoundland)

Ingredients:

1 large chicken, cut in pieces
1 onion, sliced
1 stalk celery, chopped
1/2 cup lime juice
2-3 cups water
3 potatoes, peeled and sliced
2 carrots, peeled and sliced

Food for Thought
A man who isn't his own worst critic is his own worst enemy. - Frank Tyger

2 bay leaves
hot sauce or peppers, to taste
salt and pepper, to taste
3-4 whole allspice
fresh lime, sliced (to garnish)
hot peppers, diced (to garnish)

> **Trivia Tidbits**
> The Mongolian rat never takes a drink of water, or anything else. It survives in the desert on the food it eats, and it derives all the liquid it needs from that food.

Directions:

Remove any excess fat from chicken. Place all ingredients in pot, cover with water. Bring to a boil and cook over medium heat for 45 minutes or until chicken is cooked. Serve a garnish of fresh lime and diced hot peppers on the side for guests to add to the souse (another name for soup).

Mushroom Potatoes

Doreen Halfrey, Framingham, Massachusetts, USA (nee Young, Black Duck Brook, Newfoundland)

Ingredients:

1 can low-fat cream of mushroom soup, undiluted
1/2 cup skim milk
1 large onion, chopped
4 medium potatoes, cooked and diced
dash of paprika

> **Spice of Life**
> If at first you don't succeed ...read the instructions.

Directions:

In a bowl, combine soup, milk and onion. Stir in potatoes. Pour into a 1 1/2 quart baking dish that has been coated with non-stick cooking spray. Sprinkle with paprika. Bake uncovered at 350°F for 30 minutes or until bubbly.

Stuffed Potatoes

Ann Bain, Tatamagouche, Nova Scotia (nee Rowe, Collins Cove, Burin, Newfoundland)

Ingredients:

1/2 cup non-fat plain yogurt
1 cup chopped turkey, ham or smoked turkey breast
1/2 cup onions, chopped
1/2 cup green peppers, chopped
1/4 tsp ground black pepper
2 large baking potatoes
shredded cheese, optional

> **Trivia Tidbits**
> It takes wine forty years to reach ideal maturity.

Directions:

Bake potatoes. Scoop out potato and mix together with first 5 ingredients. Stuff back in potato skins. Top with shredded cheese, if desired.

Cheese Scalloped Potatoes with Carrots

Ron Pumphrey, St. John's, Newfoundland

Ingredients:

2 cups water
6 potatoes, thinly sliced
4 medium onions, thinly sliced
4 medium carrots, diagonally sliced
3 tbsp margarine
2 tbsp flour
1 tsp salt
1/8 tsp pepper
dash of cayenne pepper
1 1/2 cups milk
1 1/2 cups old cheddar cheese

Food for Thought
Opportunities always look better going than coming.

Directions:

Bring water to a boil in large frying pan. Add potatoes, carrots and onions. Cover and cook for 10 minutes or until tender; drain. In another saucepan, melt butter then remove from heat. Stir in flour, salt and peppers. Add milk, blending well. Bring to a boil over medium heat, stirring until thickened and smooth. Stir in cheese and cook over low heat, stirring constantly until cheese melts. Layer half of the potatoes, onions and carrots in lightly greased 9x13 baking dish. Top with half the sauce. Repeat layers. Bake covered for 30 minutes or until potatoes are tender. Remove cover during the last 10 minutes of baking. Serves 6-8.

Crisp Cheese-Topped Potatoes

June Gates, Woodstock, Ontario

Ingredients:

4 medium potatoes
2 tbsp melted butter
dash of salt
1 1/2 cups old cheddar cheese, grated
2 cups Corn Flakes, crushed
dash of paprika

Trivia Tidbits
You can read a book while floating on your back in the Dead Sea.

Directions:

Wash potatoes and slice 1/4-inch thick; toss potato slices in melted butter. Place slices slightly overlapping on foil-lined, greased baking sheet. Sprinkle lightly with salt. Bake at 375°F for 15 minutes. Remove from oven and sprinkle with cheese. Top with crushed cereal and sprinkle lightly with paprika. Return to oven and bake for additional 25 minutes or until potatoes are tender. Serves 6.

Beef and Potato Boats

Ann Bain, Tatamagouche, Nova Scotia (nee Rowe, Collins Cove, Burin, Newfoundland)

Ingredients:

4 large baking potatoes
2 tbsp butter

1 1/4 tsp salt, divided
dash pepper
1/4 - 1/3 cup milk
1 lb ground beef
1 small onion, chopped
6 bacon strips, cooked and crumbled
1/2 cup sour cream
1/4 cup cheddar cheese, shredded

> *Food for Thought*
> He that spareth the rod
> hateth his son.
> - Proverbs 14:10

Directions:

Wash potatoes and bake at 400°F for 60-70 minutes. When done, slice a small portion off the top and scoop out the pulp leaving 1/4 inch shell. In a bowl, mash the potato that you just removed with the butter, 1/2 tsp salt, pepper and milk. Set aside. In a saucepan, over medium heat, brown beef and onion; drain and cool ten minutes. Add bacon, sour cream and remaining salt. Spoon into potato shells. Top each with a fourth of potato mixture. Sprinkle with cheese. Place potatoes on an ungreased baking sheet and bake at 400°F for 20 - 25 minutes. Makes 4 servings.

Old-Fashioned Potatoes

Ann Bain, Tatamagouche, Nova Scotia (nee Rowe, Collins Cove, Burin, Newfoundland)

Ingredients:

3 eggs, separated
2 cups potato, mashed (no butter or milk)
3/4 cup cheddar cheese, shredded
2 tsp green onion, finely chopped
2 tsp red pepper, finely chopped
salt and pepper, to taste

> **Spice of Life**
> Success covers a
> multitude of blunders.
> - George Bernard Shaw

Directions:

In a bowl, mix together potatoes, cheese, onion and pepper. In another bowl, beat egg yolks. Mix them into the potatoes. In another bowl, beat egg whites until soft peaks form. Fold into potato mixture. Add salt and pepper. Place in a greased 1 1/2 quart casserole dish. Cover and bake at 400°F for 20 minutes. Serves 4 - 6.

Baked Potatoes

Daphne Rideout, Springdale, Newfoundland

Ingredients:

Potatoes
Butter

> **Trivia Tidbits**
> If you are in a steel-
> roofed car you cannot be
> struck by lightening.

Directions:

Select medium-sized potatoes and wash with a vegetable brush to remove all particles of dirt. Soak in cold water for 1 hour. Bake at 400°F for 40 - 50 minutes or until soft. Rub skins with butter to soften them. Serve at once as they become soggy if allowed to stand.

Deep Fried Onion Rings

Bertha Smith, Clarenville, Newfoundland

Ingredients:

1 cup flour
1 cup water
2 tbsp baking powder
onions (sliced)
seasoning salt

Directions:

Mix flour, water and baking powder. Let rise for a few minutes. Dip slices of onion in batter. Deep fry. Shake with seasoning salt.

Sweet and Sour Carrots

Doreen Sooley, Perth-Andover, New Brunswick

Ingredients:

1 lb carrots
2 1/2 tbsp oil
1 1/2 tsp salt
2 cups water
2 1/2 tbsp vinegar
2 1/2 tbsp sugar
2 1/2 tbsp cornstarch

Directions:

Wash carrots but do not peel; cut into diagonal slices. Heat oil and fry carrots, stirring constantly, for 1 minute. Add salt and 1 cup of water and boil for 5 minutes. Mix together vinegar, sugar, cornstarch and remaining cup of water. Add to pan and cook until sauce is clear.

Marinated Carrots

Grace Ryan, Newman's Cove, Bonavista Bay, Newfoundland

Ingredients:

5 cups carrots, cooked and sliced
1 med onion
1 med green pepper, chopped
1 tin tomato soup
1/4 - 1/2 cup vegetable oil
1 cup white sugar
3/4 cup vinegar
1 tsp Worchestershire sauce
1/2 tsp mustard
1/2 tsp pepper
1 tsp salt

Trivia Tidbits
The substance that comes closest to the chemical construction of blood is seawater.

Food for Thought
Life is far too important a thing ever to talk seriously about.
- Oscar Wilde

Spice of Life
Many a man in love with a dimple makes the mistake of marrying the whole girl.
- Stephen Leacock

Directions:

Slice and boil carrots for 12 - 15 minutes. Boil rest of ingredients in medium saucepan for 5 minutes. Add mixture to carrots; stir well. Place in mason jars.

Glazed Carrots with Onion

Joan Brown, St. John's, Newfoundland (nee Kelly, Trinity, Trinity Bay, Newfoundland)

Ingredients:

2 cups sliced carrots
1 onion, thinly sliced
1/4 cup firmly packed brown sugar
2 tbsp butter
1/4 tsp nutmeg

Food for Thought
Nothing lasts forever ...
not even your troubles.
- Arnold H. Glasgow

Directions:

In skillet or saucepan, partially cook carrots in water (about 10 minutes) and drain. Stir in onion, sugar, butter and nutmeg. Simmer, stirring occasionally, about 15 minutes or until tender. Makes 4 servings.

Liver and Bacon Appetizers

Janice Mercer, Portugal Cove, Newfoundland

Ingredients:

1 lb chicken livers, halved
vinegar to cover
bacon strips, halved

Food for Thought
He that serves God for
money, will serve the
devil for better wages.

Directions:

Soak chicken livers in vinegar at least 2 hours. Drain well. Wrap in strips of bacon and pin with a toothpick. Bake at 300°F until bacon is crisp. Serve hot.

Macaroni Salad

Wendy Warren, North West Brook, Newfoundland

Ingredients:

2 cups macaroni, cooked
2/3 cup white sugar
1/4 cup oil
1/3 cup ketchup
1 tsp paprika
1 tsp salt
1/4 tsp pepper
1/4 cup vinegar
2 tomatoes, diced
1/2 cup green pepper, diced
1/4 cup cucumber, diced

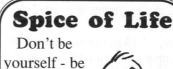

Spice of Life
Don't be yourself - be someone a little nicer.
- Mignon McLaughlin

1/2 cup onion, diced
1 tsp relish

Directions:

Mix all ingredients together except macaroni. When blended, add macaroni. Cover and let stand for 2-3 hours before serving.

Broccoli Salad

Yvonne White, Fort McMurray, Alberta

Ingredients:

1 head of broccoli
1 1/2 cups cheese, shredded
1/2 cup green onion, chopped
1/4 cup bacon bits

Dressing:

3/4 cup of Miracle Whip
4 tbsp white vinegar
1/2 cup white sugar

Directions:

In a bowl, combine broccoli, shredded cheese, green onion and bacon bits. In another bowl, combine Miracle Whip, vinegar and sugar. Blend well. Pour this dressing over the salad.

Layered Cabbage and Apple Salad

Ann Marie Traher, London, Ontario

Ingredients:

2 cups cabbage, shredded
1 (17oz) can green peas, drained
1 (8oz) can water chestnuts, drained
1/4 cup onion, chopped
3/4 cup celery, chopped
1 large red apple, unpeeled, cored and chopped
1/4 tsp salt
1/2 cup sour cream
1/2 cup mayonnaise or salad dressing
1 tsp sugar
1 cup cheddar cheese, shredded
1 cup pecans, finely chopped

Directions:

Early in the day, or night before, combine cabbage, peas, water chestnuts, onion, celery, apple and salt in a large bowl. Combine sour cream, mayonnaise and sugar; stir until blended. Spread sour cream mixture over cabbage mixture, covering to edge of bowl. Layer cheese and pecans on top. Cover salad; chill 8 hours. Toss before serving. For maximum effect, serve this pretty salad in a clear glass bowl to show off the colourful layers. Serves 8 - 10.

Spice of Life

Get married on Friday the 13th; you will always have something to blame it on.

Trivia Tidbits

Henrietta Howland Green, born in 1835, was so thrifty that she lived almost entirely off cold porridge for most of her life, rather than spend the few cents it cost to heat the porridge. She died in 1916, leaving a fortune of 95 million dollars.

Warm Spinach Salad

Connie Fowlow, Goulds, Newfoundland (nee Mason, St. John's, Newfoundland)

Ingredients:

2 oz vegetable oil
2 medium potatoes, peeled and sliced
8 oz chicken breasts, cubed
4 strips bacon, diced
1 medium onion, sliced
4 oz mushrooms, sliced
4 oz extra virgin olive oil
2 1/2 oz malt vinegar
salt and pepper, to taste
1 pkg fresh spinach

Trivia Tidbits
The town of Old Sarum in England had only six voters in 1832, but sent two MPs to Parliament nevertheless.

Directions:

Heat oil in large frying pan; saute potatoes until lightly browned. Add chicken breast and bacon; saute until chicken is cooked. Add onions, mushrooms and olive oil; stir until onions are tender. Add malt vinegar. Season with salt and pepper and pour over spinach. Serve immediately.

Jelly Pineapple Salad

Denise Hibbs (nee Jenkins), Springdale, Newfoundland

Ingredients:

1 (19oz) can crushed pineapple
1 pkg Dream Whip
1 (4oz) pkg cream cheese
1 pkg lime jelly

Spice of Life
All the world loves a lover ...except his wife.

Directions:

Drain juice from pineapple; add water to juice to make 1 1/2 cups and bring to a boil. Mix juice and water mixture after it has boiled. Let jelly set (not stiff). Mix Dream Whip as instructed on package. Add cream cheese and beat well. Add pineapple and jelly. Beat all ingredients well, then place into jelly mould. Chill.

Potato Salad

Violet Schnarr, Elmira, Ontario (nee Noseworthy, Birchy Bay, Newfoundland)

Ingredients:

8 potatoes, cooked and diced
3 hard-boiled eggs, peeled and diced
2 stalks celery, chopped
2 carrots, chopped
2 green onions
1/3 cup salad dressing
2 tbsp vinegar
1 tsp sugar
salt and pepper, to taste

Food for Thought
From what we get, we can make a living; what we give, however, makes a life. - Arthur Ashe

Directions:

In a large bowl combine potatoes, eggs, celery, carrot and green onions. Combine rest of ingredients and pour over vegetables; mix gently. Chill until ready to serve.

Broccoli and Cauliflower Salad

Violet Schnarr, Elmira, Ontario (nee Noseworthy, Birchy Bay, Newfoundland)

Ingredients:

1 head of cauliflower
1 head of broccoli
1 cup carrot, grated or sliced
6 green onions
1 green pepper
dash of Worchestershire sauce
1 cup sour cream
1 cup salad dressing
1/3 cup sugar
1 tbsp vinegar

Trivia Tidbits

Male mosquitoes are vegetarians. It's only females that bite.

Directions:

Cut vegetables into bite-size pieces and place in a large bowl. Combine remaining ingredients. Mix well and pour over vegetables. Toss well.

Pancakes

Jennifer Miller, Mount Pearl, Newfoundland

Ingredients:

1 2/3 cups flour
3 tsp baking powder
1/2 tsp salt
2 tbsp sugar
3 tbsp shortening, melted
1 egg
1 1/2 cups milk

Food for Thought

Breathes there a man, and soul so dead,
Who never to himself hath said,
This is my own, my native land.
- Walter Scott

Directions:

Preheat griddle or heavy frying pan on low heat. Sift dry ingredients. In separate bowl, beat egg until foamy; add milk and shortening. Make a well in the center of dry ingredients; add liquid ingredients all at once. Mix with an egg beater only until smooth. Grease griddle lightly for first cakes. Drop batter from tablespoon onto hot griddle and spread gently until 4 inches in diameter. Cook on one side and then turn over. Serve at once with butter and syrup.

Rice Salad

Denise Hibbs (nee Jenkins), Springdale, Newfoundland

Ingredients:

1 cup cooked rice, chilled
1/4 tsp sugar
1 can crushed pineapple
1/4 cup mayonnaise
1 pkg Dream Whip

Spice of Life

It's better to have loved a short man that never to have loved a tall.

Directions:

Combine chilled rice, pineapple and sugar. Whip Dream Whip until stiff; beat in mayonnaise. Fold into rice mixture and chill.

Five-Cup Salad

Denise Hibbs (nee Jenkins), Springdale, Newfoundland

Ingredients:

1 cup sour cream
1 cup miniature marshmallows
1 cup coconut
1 cup Mandarin oranges, drained
1 cup pineapple tidbits, drained

Directions:

Combine all ingredients and stir. Keep cool until ready to serve.

> ## Food for Thought
> Never run after a man or a streetcar; there'll be another one along in a few minutes.

Rice Mandarin Salad

Denise Maher (nee Wadden), St. John's, Newfoundland

Ingredients:

wild rice, cooked
1 tin Mandarin oranges, drained
2 tsp ground tarragon
salt and pepper, to taste
3-4 stalks green onion
1 dozen cashews (or peanuts)
chicken, boiled and cut in chunks
1 small tin water chestnuts
lemon juice (to taste)
mayonnaise (to taste)

Directions:

Mix all ingredients together except last two. Mix lemon juice and mayonnaise for the dressing. Pour over salad and serve.

> ## Trivia Tidbits
> If all the hot dogs produced in the United States in a single year were joined, end to end, they would reach the moon and back, two and a half times.

Spinach Salad

Denise Maher (nee Wadden), St. John's, Newfoundland

Ingredients:

1 pkg spinach, washed and dried
1 (8oz) can bean sprouts
1 (6oz) can water chestnuts
4 hard-boiled eggs, cut small
1/2 lb bacon, cooked and cut into small pieces

Dressing Ingredients:

1/2 cup salad oil
1/2 cup sugar

> ## Spice of Life
> Blessed are the meek, for they shall inherit the earth ...six feet of it.

Soups, Salads, Vegetable Dishes and Finger Foods

Appetizers

1/2 cup ketchup
1 tsp Worchestershire sauce
1 med onion, chopped
1/4 cup vinegar
1 tsp salt

Directions:

Combine spinach, bean sprouts, water chestnuts, eggs and bacon. For the dressing, mix oil, sugar, ketchup, Worchestershire sauce, onion, vinegar and salt.

Fluffy Fruit Salad

Valerie Hickey, Churchill Falls, Labrador (nee Adams, Burin Bay, Newfoundland)

Ingredients:

2 (20oz) cans crushed pineapple
2/3 cup sugar
2 tbsp all-purpose flour
2 eggs, slightly beaten
1/4 cup orange juice
3 tbsp lemon juice
1 tbsp vegetable oil
2 (17oz) cans fruit cocktail, drained
2 (11oz) cans mandarin oranges, drained
2 bananas, sliced
1 cup heavy cream, whipped

Directions:

Drain pineapple, reserving 1 cup juice in small saucepan. Set pineapple aside. To the juices, add sugar, flour, eggs, orange juice, lemon juice and oil. Bring to a boil, stirring constantly. Boil for 1 minute; remove from heat and let cool. In a salad bowl, combine pineapple, fruit cocktail, oranges and bananas. Fold in whipped cream and cooled sauce. Chill for several hours. Makes 12-16 servings.

Cucumber Jellied Salad

Joyce Marshall, Whitby, Ontario

Ingredients:

1 pkg lime jello
3/4 cup boiling water
3/4 cup unpeeled cucumber, grated
2 tbsp onions, grated
1 cup cottage cheese
1 cup mayonnaise
green pepper, grated (optional)

Appetizers — Soups, Salads, Vegetable Dishes and Finger Foods

Directions:

Combine jello and boiling water. Let mixture cool, but not set. Combine cucumber and onions; drain well. Add green pepper (optional). Mix in the cottage cheese and mayonnaise and set in refrigerator.

Rainbow Chicken Salad

Rosalind Fraser, Garson, Ontario

Ingredients:

2 cups Bistro rainbows (pasta)
2 cups cooked chicken, cubed
1 small red onion
3 green onions
2 cloves garlic
2 tsp Dijon mustard
1/2 tsp salt
2 tbsp red wine vinegar
1/4 cup olive oil
1/3 cup parmesan cheese

Trivia Tidbits

A 4,000-year-old skull shows that man has always suffered from tooth decay.

Directions:

Boil rainbows; drain excess water and cool. Add chicken, red and green onions. In a small bowl, combine garlic, mustard, salt, vinegar and oil. Pour over salad and toss gently. Let chill for 2 hours. Top with cheese.

Three Bean Salad

Marguerite McKinley, Hinton, Alberta

Ingredients:

1 (16oz) can green beans
1 (16oz) can whole wax beans
1 (16oz) can kidney beans
1/2 cup red onion, diced
2 cups celery, diced
1 can apple jelly
1/4 cup cider vinegar
4 tsp cornstarch
1 tsp salt

Spice of Life

Man does not live by bread alone ... he needs buttering up once in a while. - Max Rogers

Directions:

Rinse and drain all beans. Dice vegetables, mix together with beans in a large bowl. This forms the salad. Cook jelly, vinegar, cornstarch and salt until thickened. Pour over salad and mix.

Ivy's Salad

Ivy Conibear (nee Woodland), Sedona, Arizona

Ingredients:

1 (3oz) pkg lime or lemon jello
1 (20oz) can crushed pineapple

1/2 cup walnuts, chopped
1/2 cup celery, chopped
3 oz cream cheese, softened
1/2 cup mayonnaise
1/2 pint whipping cream

Spice of Life
Acquaintance: a person whom we know well enough to borrow from, but not well enough to lend to. - Ambrose Bierce

Directions:

Bring jello and pineapple to a boil and partially set. Fold in nuts and celery. Blend together cream cheese and mayonnaise; fold into jello. Fold in whipping cream and set.

Pineapple Salad

Judy Kirby, Epworth, Newfoundland

Ingredients:

3 envelopes gelatin

5 1/2 cups cold water

6 pkgs pineapple or lemon jelly

5 cups hot water5 (19oz) cans crushed pineapple, undrained

Food for Thought
Go confidently in the direction of your dreams. Live the life you have imagined.
- Henry David Thoreau

Directions:

Soak gelatin in 1/2 cup cold water. Mix jelly with hot water; add geletin mixture. Stir until dissolved. Add 5 cups cold water. Add pineapple; stir well. Pour into large rectangle dish and set. This recipe is great for a take-out cold plate or a wedding supper. If the dish is large enough it can make up to 80 servings.

Broccoli-Cauliflower Salad

Grace Ryan, Newman's Cove, Bonavista Bay, Newfoundland

Ingredients:

3 green onions, chopped
1 bunch broccoli, chopped
1 bunch cauliflower, chopped
1 tub sour cream
3/4 cup Miracle Whip
1 tsp tabasco sauce
1/3 cup sugar
1/4 cup vinegar

Trivia Tidbits
In ancient Greece, an hour was defined as one-twelfth of the day. But the day was measured from sunrise to sunset. Thus, the daytime hour was longer in summer than in winter!

Directions:

Place onions, broccoli and cauliflower in salad bowl. Mix together rest of ingredients and pour over vegetables.

Tomato Cups Provencale

Marjorie Baetzel (nee Noseworthy), St. John's, Newfoundland

Ingredients:

4 to 5 medium tomatoes
1 cup toasted croutons

2 tbsp parmesan cheese
1 clove of garlic, minced
1 tsp parsley, chopped
2 tbsp butter, melted
salt and pepper to taste

Directions:

Cut tops off tomatoes. Scoop pulp out of centre and chop. Combine this with croutons (toasted bread cut into small squares), cheese, garlic, parsley, salt and pepper. Lightly salt inside of tomatoes. Fill each tomato. Sprinkle with melted butter. Place in baking dish and bake at 350°F for 20 minutes.

Stuffed Peppers

Donna Pumphrey (nee Murphy, Bell Island, Newfoundland)

Ingredients:

8 medium green peppers
1/2 cup onion, chopped
3/4 tsp salt
2 cups shredded cheese
1 lb ground beef
1 cup cooked rice
1 (12oz) can corn
1 (8oz) can tomato sauce, seasoned
1 cup buttered bread crumbs

Directions:

Cut off tops of peppers, seed and clean; Parboil until tender, drain, sprinkle inside with salt. Brown meat and onion. Add rice, corn and tomato sauce. Simmer for 5 minutes. Add cheese and cook until melted. Stuff peppers. Stand upright in a casserole dish; top with the bread crumbs. Fill dish with about 1 inch water. Bake at 350°F degrees for 40 minutes.

Stuffed Peppers

Edna Ray Martin, LaSalle, Quebec (nee Kelsey)

Ingredients:

6 medium green peppers
1 lb lean ground beef
2 tbsp oil
1/2 cup celery, chopped
1/2 cup onion, chopped
2 cups hot, cooked rice
1 1/2 cups mozarella cheese, shredded
1 (16oz) can tomatoes, drained and chopped
1 tsp salt
1/8 tsp crushed basil
1 (16oz) tin tomato sauce
Pepper (to taste)

Directions:

Remove tops and seeds from peppers. Parboil for 5 minutes; drain. Brown ground beef in oil in frying pan; add celery and onion. Cool until tender. Blend in rice, 1 cup of cheese, tomatoes, salt, pepper and basil. Spoon into peppers. Stand them up in baking pan. Pour tomato sauce around peppers. Bake covered for 30 minutes. Remove cover. Sprinkle remaining cheese. Return to oven and bake until cheese is melted.

Tomato and Avocado Bruschetta

Joan Pike, Placentia, Newfoundland

Ingredients:

4 to 6 ripe plum tomatoes
1 avocado
2 green onions, thinly sliced
1 small garlic clove, minced
2 tbsp fresh basil, chopped
2 tbsp parmesan cheese, grated
2 tsp lime or lemon juice
1 1/2 tsp olive oil
1/2 tsp salt
pinch black pepper

> **Spice of Life**
> Everybody is entitled to his own opinion ...just so long as he keeps it to himself.
> *- L. de V. Matthewman*

Directions:

Seed and coarsley chop tomatoes. Peel and cut avocado into 1/4-inch cubes. Add to tomatoes in a small bowl. Stir in onions, garlic, basil, parmesan cheese, juice, oil, salt and pepper. Serve on sliced french bread. Makes about 2 3/4 cups.

Cunnington Quiche

June Gates, Woodstock, Ontario

Ingredients:

9-inch pie shell, unbaked
1/2 lb ground beef (ham, bacon or fish)
1/2 cup mayonnaise
1/2 cup milk
2 eggs
1 tsp cornstarch
1 1/2 cups cheddar cheese, shredded
1/3 cup green onion (or green pepper), sliced
pepper, to taste

> **Food for Thought**
> What university, school, college or any form of teaching delivers to men, depends on what men bring to carry it home in.

Directions:

Brown meat; drain. Blend milk, mayonnaise, eggs and cornstarch until smooth. Stir in meat, cheese, onion and pepper; turn into pie shell. Bake in a pre-heated oven at 350°F for 35 minutes. Garnish with crumbled bacon or shredded cheese.

Quichettes

Joy Marple, Cape Breton, Nova Scotia

Ingredients:

36 frozen tart shells
6 eggs
3 cups table cream
1/2 tsp salt
1/2 tsp white pepper

Directions:

Blend eggs, table cream, salt and pepper; pour into tart shells. Bake at 375°F on bottom rack for 18 - 20 minutes. May freeze for 1 month. When frozen, reheat at 375°F for 15 - 20 minutes.

Mini Quiche

Edna Fudge, Gimli, Manitoba

Ingredients:

8 eggs
salt and pepper, to taste
1 lb bacon, finely chopped
1 medium onion, finely chopped
2 stalks celery, finely chopped
1 (12oz) block cheddar cheese, grated
25 Ritz crackers, crushed

Directions:

Beat eggs, adding salt and pepper. Fry bacon until almost crisp, draining any excess fat. Add onion and celery. Fry for additional 3 minutes, stirring often. Drain any fat. Set aside to cool. Add eggs to cooled mixture, followed by cheese, then Ritz crackers. Grease mini muffin tins well. Fill each muffin tin well to the top. Bake at 375°F for 15 - 20 minutes. Let sit in muffin tins for 2 minutes before removing. These are excellent frozen. Reheat in microwave or oven to serve.

String Beans and Rice

Patricia Delaney, Grand Falls-Windsor, Newfoundland

Ingredients:

1 tbsp cooking oil
1 lb round steak
1 medium onion, chopped
1 tsp salt
1/4 tsp pepper
1 can green beans, drained
1 (19oz) can tomato juice
1 cup long grain rice, cooked

Spice of Life

A child learns to talk in about two years, but it takes about sixty years for him to learn to keep his mouth shut.

Food for Thought

Who of us is mature enough for offspring before the offspring themselves arrive? The value of marriage is not that adults produce children but that children produce adults.

- Peter De Vries

Trivia Tidbits

In Scotland it is considered bad luck for a bride to try on her wedding gown before her wedding day.

Appetizers

Soups, Salads, Vegetable Dishes and Finger Foods

Directions:

Cut meat into 2-inch x 1/4-inch pieces. Place cooking oil in a large saucepan, brown meat and onion, adding salt and pepper. Add tomato juice and beans. Bring to a boil and gently cook for at least one hour, until the meat is tender. Serve over rice.

Fried Rice

Frances Pelley, Edmonton, Alberta (formerly of Deer Lake, Newfoundland)

Ingredients:

2 cups Uncle Ben's converted rice
3 1/2 cups boiling water
1/4 cup oil
3/4 pkg onion soup mix
2 tsp soya sauce

Spice of Life
Youth is wasted on the young, and retirement is wasted on the old.

Directions:

Mix all ingredients in casserole dish and bake at 350°F for 45 minutes. Take out of casserole dish and place in frying pan. Add whatever you like in your fried rice (onions, peas, mushrooms, etc.)

Bahamian Peas and Rice

Donna Young, Nassau, The Bahamas formerly of Newfoundland)

Ingredients:

1/4 lb butter
1/4 lb bacon
3 medium onions, diced
1 stalk celery
1 (5oz) tin tomato paste
2 fresh tomatoes, diced
1/2 can pigeon peas (or black eyed peas)
3 cups rice
4/5 quart water
2 sprigs fresh thyme or dried, to taste
salt and pepper, to taste
hot peppers, to garnish

Trivia Tidbits
Sheridan, the famous British writer, was once so drunk that when he passed out, he was left at the tavern by his drinking companions as a pledge because the others didn't have enough money to pay the bar bill. Among Sheridan's drinking companions were King George IV and Charles James Fox (a famous politician at the time).

Directions:

Cook butter and bacon until bacon is crisp. Add onions and celery; cook until soft. Add tomato paste and fresh tomatoes. Cook for 15 minutes. Add pigeon peas, water, rice and seasonings. Cover saucepan and bring to a boil. Reduce heat and simmer for about 45 minutes or until rice is done. Hot peppers can be finely diced and served as a garnish so guests can add it to their food, according to their taste.

Enhancers

Dressings

Stuffings

Spreads

Sauces

Icings

Oils

Dips

Bakeapple Sauce

Delores LeRoux, St. George's, Newfoundland

Ingredients:

2 cups bakeapples
2 cups water
pinch of salt
sugar, to taste
cornstarch

Directions:

Boil the bakeapples in water until well done. Strain through tea strainer to remove stones. Boil liquid with a pinch of salt and enough sugar to taste. Thicken with cornstarch. Serve over pudding, cake or pancakes.

Old-Fashioned Brandy Sauce

Effie White, Loon Bay, Newfoundland

Ingredients:

2 eggs, separated
1 cup icing sugar
3 tbsp brandy

Directions:

Beat egg yolks until thickened and lemon-coloured. Add half the icing sugar, beating between additions. Beat egg whites until stiff, but not dry; fold egg whites into yolks and add brandy. Serve with your favourite Christmas pudding.

Cranberry Orange Sauce

Ann Bain, Tatamagouche, Nova Scotia (nee Rowe, Collins Cove, Burin, Newfoundland)

Ingredients:

1/4 cup sugar
2 tsp cornstarch
1/2 cup fresh or frozen cranberries
1/2 cup orange juice
1/4 cup water

Directions:

Combine sugar and cornstarch in saucepan. Add cranberries, orange juice and water. Bring to a boil over medium heat, stirring constantly for 2 - 3 minutes.

Caramel Sauce

Fanny Tucker, Portugal Cove, Newfoundland

Ingredients:

3/4 cup brown sugar
1 cup boiling water

Trivia Tidbits

Snow is not frozen rain. Snowflakes change directly from water vapour into snow, without going through an intermediary stage as rain.

Food for Thought

Sex is the poor man's opera.　　　- Italian proverb

Spice of Life

Two can keep a secret if one of them is dead.

Food for Thought

The surest cure for vanity is loneliness.
　　　　　　　　-Thomas Wolfe

Enhancers

Dressings, Stuffings, Icings, Sauces, Spreads, Oils and Dips

1 1/4 tbsp cornstarch
2 tbsp cold water
1 1 tbsp vanilla
tbsp butter

Food for Thought
To be closer to God, be closer to people.   - Kahlil Gibran

Directions:

Melt brown sugar in pot with boiling water. Mix cornstarch with cold water to form paste; add to hot mixture. Boil 5 - 10 minutes over low heat until mixture begins to thicken. Add vanilla and butter. For a sufficient amount of sauce, it is best to double the recipe.

Honey Mustard Sauce

Ann Bain, Tatamagouche, Nova Scotia (nee Rowe, Collins Cove, Burin, Newfoundland)

Ingredients:
2 tbsp cornstarch
1 cup water, divided
1/2 cup honey
1/4 cup prepared mustard

Spice of Life
Life without a friend is death without a witness. - Spanish proverb

Directions:

In saucepan, dissolve cornstarch in 1/2 cup water. Add honey, mustard and remaining water. Bring to a boil over medium heat. Boil for 1 minute, stirring constantly.

Spicy Mustard

Ann Bain, Tatamagouche, Nova Scotia (nee Rowe, Collins Cove, Burin, Newfoundland)

Ingredients:
1/2 cup tarragon or cider vinegar
1/2 cup water
1/4 cup olive or vegetable oil
2 tbsp prepared horseradish
1/2 tsp lemon juice
1 cup ground mustard
1/2 cup sugar
1/2 tsp salt

Trivia Tidbits
The years are getting shorter. Four hundred million years ago a year was over four hundred days long.

Directions:

In blender, combine all ingredients and process for 1 minute. Scrape down sides of container and process 30 seconds more. Transfer to a small saucepan and let stand 10 minutes. Cook over low heat, stirring constantly until bubbly. Cool completely. If a thinner mustard is desired, stir in 1-2 tbsp more water. Pour into small containers with tight-fitting lids. Store in fridge. *Note:* Fresh horseradish and tarragon vinegar with home grown tarragon is best.

Pippa's Mustard Sauce

Ann Bain, Tatamagouche, Nova Scotia (nee Rowe, Collins Cove, Burin, Newfoundland)

Ingredients:
2 eggs
4 tbsp dry mustard

1/2 cup sugar
1/2 cup evaporated milk
1/4 cup vinegar
1/4 tsp salt
1/8 tsp white pepper

Spice of Life

Self-praise is no recommendation
...but at least you know it's sincere.

Directions:

Beat eggs. Combine mustard and sugar, add to eggs. Add milk and blend well. Cook in double boiler, stirring until thickened. Add vinegar, blend well. Season with salt and pepper. Keeps well; store in refrigerator. Makes about 1 pint. *Note:* A wonderful mustard sauce for all kinds of sandwiches, devilled eggs or meats.

Ginger-Apricot Barbecue Sauce

Bertha Smith, Clarenville, Newfoundland

Ingredients:

3/4 cup brown sugar
2 tbsp cornstarch
1 tsp ginger
1 tsp crushed garlic
1/4 cup red wine vinegar
1/2 cup soy sauce
3 tbsp apricot preserves

Trivia Tidbits

The footprints that the astronauts left on the moon will last about ten million years.

Directions:

Stir all ingredients together, blending well. Let the sauce stand for 1 hour to blend flavours. Stir sauce before putting on spare ribs or chicken. Baste during baking.

Ketchup

Charlene Jenkins, Grand Falls-Windsor, Newfoundland (formerly of Springdale, Newfoundland)

Ingredients:

5 1/2 oz tomato paste
1/3 cup water
1/2 cup white vinegar
1/4 cup sugar
3/4 tsp onion powder
3/4 tsp salt
1/8 ground cloves
1 tbsp cornstarch
3 tbsp water
1 1/2 tsp liquid sweetener

Food for Thought

The silver lining is always easier to find in the other fellow's cloud.

Directions:

Place first 7 ingredients in saucepan. Heat and stir on medium-high heat until it boils. Mix cornstarch, water and sweetener together in small cup. Stir into liquid; return to boiling and continue stirring until thickens. Cool and store in refrigerator.

Enhancers

Pressings, Stuffings, Icings, Sauces, Spreads, Oils and Dips

Blueberry Sauce

Stan Baldwin, Stephenville, Newfoundland

Ingredients:

1/4 cup butter
1 cup water
sugar to taste
1 tsp vanilla
1/4 cup coconut (optional)

Directions:

Heat water, add butter, sugar and vanilla; let butter melt. Add coconut and serve over blueberry pudding.

Lemon Sauce

Connie Fowlow, Goulds, Newfoundland (nee Mason, St. John's, Newfoundland)

Ingredients:

2 cups water
1/2 cup sugar
1/4 cup butter
2 tsp vanilla
1 env custard powder
juice of a lemon

Directions:

Bring first 4 ingredients to a boil. Mix custard powder with 1/4 cup cold water. Add to boiled mixture. Add juice of lemon. Serve over hot chicken.

Sweet and Sour Chicken Sauce

Janice Mercer

Ingredients:

1 1/2 - 2 lbs chicken
1 cup ketchup
1/2 cup brown sugar
1/2 cup white vinegar
1 tsp mustard
1/2 tsp lemon juice
1/2 tsp Worchestershire (or soya) sauce

Directions:

Combine all ingredients. Pour over 1 1/2 - 2 lbs chicken. Bake at 350°F for 1 - 2 hours. Works well on ribs as well.

Honey Garlic Sauce

Denise Maher (nee Wadden), St. John's, Newfoundland

Ingredients:

1/4 cup soya sauce

1/4 cup water
1 cup brown sugar
3 tbsp cornstarch
3 tbsp honey
2 tsp garlic salt

Directions:

Mix together and pour over chicken.

Vegetable Dip

Beulah Cooper, Gander, Newfoundland

Ingredients:

2 eggs
3 tbsp sugar
3 tbsp vinegar
1 tsp butter
1 lg pkg cream cheese
1/4 cup onion, diced
3/4 green pepper, diced

Directions:

Whip eggs; add sugar, vinegar and butter. Heat over medium heat until custard-like. Keep stirring; beat in cream cheese. Remove from heat, add onion and green pepper. Chill.

Sweet and Sour Sauce

Beulah Cooper, Gander, Newfoundland

Ingredients:

3/4 cup water
3/4 cup brown sugar
1 tbsp soya sauce
1/8 cup vinegar
1/3 cup ketchup

Directions:

Mix all ingredients together and pour over chicken or spareribs; simmer over low heat.

Zesty Homemade Horseradish

Ann Bain, Tatamagouche, Nova Scotia (nee Rowe, Collins Cove, Burin, Newfoundland)

Ingredients:

1/2 cup half & half cream
1/4 cup vinegar
1 tbsp brown sugar
2 tsp prepared mustard
1/4 tsp salt and pepper
1 cup horseradish, peeled & chopped

Trivia Tidbits
At age 93 our heart pumps only half the blood it did when we were twenty.

Food for Thought
Even the wisest of men make fools of themselves about women, and even the most foolish women are wise about men.   - Theodor Reik

Spice of Life
It's a <u>long</u> road that has no turning, but it's a <u>strong</u> stomach that has no turning.
- Oliver Herford

Enhancers
Dressings, Stuffings, Icings, Sauces, Spreads, Oils and Dips

Directions:

Place all ingredients in blender, process until fine. Cook and stir over low heat until heated through. DO NOT BOIL. Put in small jars and store in fridge for 1 - 2 months.

Carol's Famous Taco Dip

Carol Pike, Surrey, British Columbia (husband from South Dildo, Trinity Bay)

Ingredients:

1/2 cup cream cheese
1/2 cup sour cream
garlic powder to taste
small-medium jar salsa sauce
green onions
tomatoes
bacon
shredded cheddar cheese

> ### *Food for Thought*
> It doesn't much signify whom one marries, for one is sure to find out the next morning that it was someone else.   - Samuel Rogers

Directions:

Microwave cream cheese 20-30 seconds to soften. Mix first 3 ingredients together. Spread on serving plate. Spread salsa on first layer. Chop onions, tomatoes. Cook bacon until crisp, then chop into small pieces. Sprinkle green onions on top of salsa, then chopped tomato, followed by bacon bits, and then finish with shredded cheese. Serve with round tacos.

Crab Dip

June Gates, Woodstock, Ontario

Ingredients:

2 (6 1/2oz) cans crabmeat
1 medium onion, diced
4 tbsp celery leaves, chopped
2 tbsp lemon juice
1/2 cup mayonnaise
dash Worchestershire sauce
1/4 tsp salt
2 tsp green pepper, finely chopped

Directions:

Combine all ingredients. Serve with crackers.

Melba Toast Dip

Rhonda Tulk, Aspen Cove, Newfoundland

Ingredients:

1 (250g) pkg cream cheese
1/2 cup sour cream
1/4 cup Miracle Whip
1 cup seafood (or chili or salsa) sauce

> ### Trivia Tidbits
> The most poisonous fish in the world, the puffer fish, is a delicacy in Japan, where special cooks are trained in the art of preparing them so that they are not poisonous. However, there are occasions when customers eat fish that have not been properly treated and die.
>
>

Sidebar: Enhancers — Dressings, Stuffings, Icings, Sauces, Spreads, Oils and Dips

2 cups mozzarella cheese, shredded
1 green pepper, diced
1 green onion, diced
1 tomato, diced
1 red pepper, diced

Food for Thought
'Tis better to have loved and lost than never to have loved at all.

Directions:

Beat together cream cheese, sour cream and miracle whip. Spread on a large plate to 1-inch thickness. Chill for 1 hour. Pour sauce over this. Next sprinkle on shredded mozzarella cheese, green pepper, green onion, tomato and red pepper.

Spinach and Sour Cream Dip

Karen Lushman, Eastern Passage, Nova Scotia

Ingredients:

1 bag spinach
1 cup sour cream
1 cup Hellman's mayonnaise
1 can water chestnuts
1 green onion (optional)
1 pkg Knorr vegetable soup mix
1 round loaf pumpernickel bread1 pkg

Food for Thought
Nearly all men are married. Some are married to cars, some to booze, some to money, some to power, some to fame, some to golf and some to gambling. A small minority are married to a woman.
- Richard Needham

Directions:

Using scissors, cut 1/2 bag of spinach into medium-sized pieces. Add sour cream and mayonnaise. Chop 5-7 chestnuts into 4 pieces each and add to mixture. Add green onion, soup mix and mix all ingredients by hand. Refrigerate dip until ready to use. Hollow out bread using top of bread as a lid. You can use leftover bread to dip or use crackers. When ready to serve, pour mixture into bread and cover with bread lid.

Crab Dip

Gerald Pumphrey, Middle Sackville, Nova Scotia

Ingredients:

1 (10oz) tin of mushroom soup
1 (4oz) package cream cheese
1 envelope gelatin
1/4 cup cold water
1/2 cup celery, finely chopped
1/2 cup onion, finely chopped
1 cup Miracle Whip
1 (5oz) can crab meat
1/4 tsp curry powder

Spice of Life
Women dress to please themselves, or their husbands, or their women friends. Any wardrobe that really satisfies one of these groups will enrage the other two. - Mignon McLaughlin

Directions:

Heat cheese and soup; stir until smooth. Add gelatin to cold water and let soften for 5 minutes. Add to soup mixture with crab, celery, onion, Miracle Whip and curry powder. Mix well, pour into greased mould and chill overnight; serve with potato chips or crackers.

Enhancers

Dressings, Stuffings, Icings, Sauces, Spreads, Oils and Dips

Seafood Mexican Dip

Maria Young, St. Phillip's, Newfoundland (nee Hardy, Port aux Basques, Newfoundland)

Ingredients:

1 (8oz) pkg cream cheese
1/2 cup sour cream
1/4 cup mayonnaise
1 tin crab meat or shrimp
1/2 bottle salsa
2 cups mozzarella cheese, shredded
1 cup onion, chopped
1 cup tomato, diced
1 cup green pepper, diced

> **Spice of Life**
> You cannot be in two places at once ... but with supersonic travel, you can come awfully close.

Directions:

Cream together cream cheese, sour cream and mayonnaise. Place on bottom of serving dish. Layer crab or shrimp on top of mixture. Follow with layer of salsa. Combine cheese, onion, tomato and green pepper and sprinkle on top. Can be served with crackers or Nachos.

Miracle Crab Dip

Frances Ivany, Cranbrook, British Columbia (formerly of Port Rexton, Trinity Bay, Newfoundland)

Ingredients:

1/2 cup Miracle Whip
1/2 cup sour cream
1 can flaked crab meat, drained
1 tbsp cocktail sauce
2 tbsp parmesan cheese, grated

> **Trivia Tidbits**
> The broad bean is the oldest vegetable known to man.

Directions:

Combine Miracle Whip and sour cream. Add crab meat, cheese and cocktail sauce. Microwave on high for 3 minutes. Stir once and serve immediately. *Note:* For an interesting and delicious alternative, substitute crab meat and parmesan cheese with equal amount of cream cheese and salsa.

Vegetable or Cracker Dip

Marie Quinlan, Birchy Bay, Newfoundland

Ingredients:

1 cup salad dressing
1 cup sour cream
1 cup Cheeze Whiz
1 pkg onion soup mix

> **Trivia Tidbits**
> There are approximately two and one-half times as many cattle in Argentina as there are people.

Directions:

Mix above ingredients together. Place in fridge.

Onion Chip Dip

Barbara Lucas, Barachois Brook, Newfoundland

Ingredients:

1 can Nestle's cream
3/4 cup salad dressing
3/4 pkg onion soup mix
2 tbsp vinegar

Directions:

Combine all ingredients and chill in fridge for 1/2 hour.

Spice of Life

A woman without a man is like a fish without a bicycle.
- *Women's Lib slogan, 1970s*

Nacho Dip

Joanne Wellon-Fillier, Kitchener, Ontario (formerly of Millertown, Newfoundland)

Ingredients:

1 pkg cream cheese
1 cup sour cream
1 pkg Ranch-style powdered salad dressing
1 lb cooked ground beef (optional)
1 pkg taco seasoning
1 head lettuce, shredded
2 tomatoes, chopped
1 green pepper
1 red pepper
1 bottle salsa
1/2 bunch green onions
black olives
1 block medium cheddar cheese, shredded

Trivia Tidbits

A lightening storm which once struck a sheepfold in Lapleux, France, killed every black sheep, but left all the white sheep unharmed.

Directions:

Mix cream cheese, sour cream and powdered salad dressing in blender; spread on large, flat tray. In layers, add lettuce, ground beef that's been mixed with taco seasoning, tomatoes, red and green peppers, onions salsa, and olives. Cover with cheddar cheese. Serve with tortilla chips.

Guacamole

Carolyn Pitcher, St. John's, Newfoundland

Ingredients:

1 can refried beans
2 avocados, mashed (soft ones)
1 1/2 pkgs (35g) taco seasoning
1/2 cup Miracle Whip
1 cup sour cream
2 tomatoes, finely chopped
shredded cheddar

Food for Thought

The only man who is really free is the one who can turn down an invitation to dinner without giving an excuse. - Jules Renard

Directions:

This is a 4 layered dip. The first layer is the refried beans. For 2nd layer, mash the avacados with 1/2 pkg taco seasoning. For 3rd layer, mix together Miracle Whip, sour cream, and 1 pkg taco seasoning. The 4th layer consists of the tomatoes and enough cheese to cover.

Raw Veggie Dip

Norma Clarke, Peterboro, Ontario (nee Atkinson, Herring Neck, Newfoundland)

Ingredients:

1 cup plain yogurt, low fat
1/2 cup light mayonnaise
3 tbsp onion, grated
1 tbsp honey
3 tbsp ketchup
1 tsp curry powder (or less)
1 clove garlic, minced

Spice of Life

Instead of giving a politician the keys to the city, it might be better to change the locks.
- Doug Larson

Directions:

Mix all ingredients together and refrigerate. Dip will stay fresh in a well-sealed container in refrigerator for one week. Makes 1 1/2 cups.

Chip Dip

Barbara Lucas, Barachois Brook, Newfoundland

Ingredients:

1 (8oz) pkg light cream cheese, softened
1 cup ketchup
1 cup light salad dressing
1 small onion, grated

Trivia Tidbits

The acronym LASER stands for 'Light Amplification by Stimulated Emission of Radiation'.

Directions:

Blend all ingredients together. Beat with mixer until smooth. Chill and serve.

Hot Nacho Dip

Carolyn Pitcher, St. John's, Newfoundland

Ingredients:

1 lb hamburger meat
1 pkg taco seasoning
1/2 cup mayonnaise
1/2 cup sour cream
1 pkg cream cheese
1 small bottle salsa

Food for Thought

I am a great believer in luck, and find the harder I work the more I have of it. *- Stephen Leacock*

Directions:

Brown hamburger meat; add other ingredients. Bake in oven at 350°F for 1/2 hour. Serve with tortilla or nacho chips.

Low-Fat Salad Dressing

Charlene Jenkins, Grand Falls-Windsor, Newfoundland (formerly of Springdale, Newfoundland)

Ingredients:

1/4 cup sugar
3 tbsp flour
1/2 tsp dry mustard powder
1/2 tsp salt
1 cup skim milk
1/4 cup white vinegar

```
┌─────────────────────────┐
│     Trivia Tidbits      │
│  In Lexington, Kentucky,│
│  it is illegal to carry │
│  ice cream in your      │
│  pocket.                │
└─────────────────────────┘
```

Directions:

Stir sugar, flour, dry mustard and salt together well in small saucepan. Mix in part of the milk until smooth. Whisk in remaining milk and vinegar. Heat and stir until it boils and thickens. Pour into container when cooled and store in refrigerator.

Poppy Seed Salad Dressing

Maria Young, St. Phillip's, Newfoundland (nee Hardy, Port aux Basques, Newfoundland)

Ingredients:

2 tsp dry mustard
2 tsp salt
2/3 cup cider vinegar
1/2 onion, shredded
4 1/2 tsp poppy seed
3/4 cup sugar
2 cups Mazola oil

```
┌──────────────────────────┐
│     Spice of Life        │
│  Ninety percent of the   │
│  politicians give the    │
│  other ten percent a     │
│  bad name.               │
│          - Henry Kissinger│
└──────────────────────────┘
```

Directions:

Mix together all ingredients except oil. Slowly add oil while mixing. *Note:* All ingredients should be cold when using.

Caesar Salad Dressing

Madge Witzing, London, Ontario (nee Bailey, Baie Verte, Newfoundland)

Ingredients:

3 cloves garlic, mashed or chopped
1/2 tsp salt
1/4 cup granulated sugar
1/4 cup vinegar
2 eggs
1 tsp Dijon mustard
2 cups vegetable oil
1 tbsp lemon juice (fresh or bottled)
1/2 tsp pepper
6 tbsp of parmesan cheese

```
┌──────────────────────────┐
│    Food for Thought      │
│  Men are disturbed, not  │
│  by the things that      │
│  happen, but by their    │
│  opinion of the things   │
│  that happen.            │
│              - Epictetus │
└──────────────────────────┘
```

Directions:

Put garlic in blender, food processor or mix master. Add salt, sugar, vinegar, eggs and mustard; blend. Add oil very slowly, starting with a drop at a time then trickling until oil is used. (Will not thicken if oil is put in too quickly). Add lemon juice, pepper and cheese; blend again. Keeps well in jars. Great with potato chips or cut vegetables, as well as a salad.

Oatmeal Dressing

June Osborne Buffitt, Mutton Bay, Duplessis County, Quebec

Ingredients:

3 cups Quaker oats
1 onion, finely chopped
1/2 tsp salt
1/4 tsp pepper
2/3 cup cooking oil

Directions:

Blend all above ingredients together in large mixing bowl. (Excellent stuffing for chicken.)

Creamy Herb Dressing

Rosalind Fraser, Garson, Ontario

Ingredients:

1/4 cup low-fat cottage cheese or sour cream
1/4 cup low-fat plain yogurt
1/4 tsp Dijon mustard
1/4 tsp dried oregano
1/4 tsp basil
salt and pepper, to taste

Directions:

In blender, process cottage cheese until smooth. Add remaining ingredients; blend well. Cover and refrigerate for 4 hours or up to 3 days. Use for pasta, vegetable or lettuce salads.

Dressing for Turkey or Chicken

R. Maxwell Winters, Saint John, New Brunswick

Ingredients:

1 lb sausage meat
2 cups soft bread crumbs
1 cup celery, chopped
1/4 cup onion, chopped
3 tbsp butter or margarine, melted
1/2 tsp salt
1/8 tsp pepper
dash of poultry seasoning

Directions:

Fry sausage meat until brown. Add rest of ingredients, mixing well. Stuff turkey.

Sidebar (vertical): Enhancers — Dressings, Stuffings, Icings, Sauces, Spreads, Oils and Dips

Chicken Batter

Judy Alexander, Flat Bay, Newfoundland

Ingredients:

1 egg (beaten)
8 cups flour
1/2 tsp salt
1/2 tsp MSG
3 tbsp black pepper
1 tbsp white pepper
1 tbsp garlic powder
3 tbsp oregano
1 tbsp thyme
1 tbsp paprika
1 tbsp cayenne pepper
1 1/2 tbsp cumin powder
1 1/2 tbsp cajun powder

Directions:

Combine all ingredients, except egg. Dip the chicken in the egg and then in the batter. Fry the chicken to your preference.

Turkey Stuffing

Rosalind Fraser, Garson, Ontario

Ingredients:

1 roll all-purpose pure pork sausage
4 stalks celery, finely chopped
4 green onions, chopped
1/2 cup water
2 cups fine bread crumbs
1/2 cup Minute Rice, uncooked
1 raw potato, chopped
sage and poultry seasoning

Directions:

Cook sausage in medium saucepan; add remaining ingredients. Mix well before stuffing turkey.

Shake Rattle and Roast

Jacquie Charbonneau, Bowmanville, Ontario

Ingredients:

1 cup flour
3/4 cup Bran Flakes, ground in blender
2 tsp salt
2 tsp pepper
1 tsp onion powder
1 tsp garlic powder
1 tsp oregano
1 tsp paprika

Trivia Tidbits
There are over 4000 man-made objects flying about in outer space.

Spice of Life
Politicians are the same all over. They promise to build a bridge even where there is no river.
- Nikita Khrushchev

Food for Thought
Success in marriage does not come merely through finding the right mate, but through being the right mate.
- Barnett Brickner

Enhancers

Dressings, Stuffings, Icings, Sauces, Spreads, Oils and Dips

Directions:

Mix all ingredients together. Coat chicken or pork chops. Keep refrigerated.

Herb Rub for Turkey

Joy Marple, Cape Breton, Nova Scotia

Ingredients:

3 tbsp olive oil

1 1/2 tsp paprika

2 1/2 tsp salt

1 tsp garlic, minced

1 tbsp mix of dried rosemary, sage, tarragon

1 tbsp dried thyme

1/2 tsp pepper

Directions:

Combine all ingredients in a small bowl. Rub all over turkey and drizzle some in cavity. Bake as usual.

Drawn Butter

Bethany Keeping, St. John's, Newfoundland (formerly of Port aux Basques, Newfoundland)
Bertha Smith, Clarenville, Newfoundland
Vicki Lear, Gander, Newfoundland

Ingredients:

1/4 cup butter

2 small onions, chopped

2 1/2 tbsp flour

1 1/2 cups hot water

salt and pepper, to taste

Directions:

Melt butter in a small saucepan; add onions and saute for about 2 minutes over low heat. Add flour and mix well. Add hot water; cook until thickened, stirring constantly. Add salt and pepper to taste. Remove from heat and serve over boiled or salt fish, and potatoes.

Smoked Salmon Spread

Alvina Cutler, Terrace, British Columbia

Ingredients:

1 (8oz) pkg cream cheese (room temperature)

2 tbsp onion, finely chopped

1 tbsp lemon juice

1 tbsp horseradish

1 tsp liquid smoke

1/4 tsp salt

1/2 cup pecans, chopped

2 tbsp parsley

2 cups canned pink salmon, drained

Directions:

Combine all ingredients together and mix well. Keep refrigerated.

Spice of Life

The poor ye have with you always ... despite the fact that they were never invited.

Trivia Tidbits

Seals use their hind legs to swim; sea lions use their front flippers.

Food for Thought

A great many people think they are thinking when they are merely rearranging their prejudices.

- William James

Never-Fail Meringue Pie Topping

Marjorie Baetzel, St. John's, Newfoundland (nee Noseworthy)

Ingredients:

1 tbsp cornstarch
2 tbsp cold water
1/2 cup boiling water
3 egg whites
5 to 6 tbsp sugar
1 tsp vanilla
pinch of salt

Food for Thought
The oldest words of pen or tongue:
We didn't do that when I was young.
- Suzanne Douglass

Directions:

Blend cornstarch with cold water in small saucepan. Add boiling water and cook until clear and thickened. Let stand until completely cold. Beat egg whites until stiff. Turn mixer on low and add salt, vanilla and sugar. Gradually add cold cornstarch mixture and turn up mixer to high speed until stiff peak forms. Pile meringue on cooled pie filling. Bake at 350°F for about 10 minutes, until golden brown. This is an excellent topping for lemon or custard pies.

Lemon Coconut Filling

Daphne Peddle, Barre, Massachusetts

Ingredients:

2/3 cup sugar
pinch of salt
2 tsp cornstarch
2/3 cup boiling water
2 cups coconut
juice of 1/2 lemon
grated rind of 1/2 lemon

Trivia Tidbits
Cockroaches have remained on earth unchanged for 250 million years.

Directions:

Mix sugar, salt and cornstarch well. Add boiling water and boil for 5 minutes, stirring constantly. Add lemon juice, rind and coconut; blending well. Cool. Spread between cake layers. Makes enough filling to spread between three 8-inch layers.

Double Boiler Frosting

Daphne Peddle, Barre, Massachusetts

Ingredients:

1 egg white, unbeaten
7/8 cup sugar
3 tbsp cold water
1/2 tsp light corn syrup
1/2 tsp vanilla

Spice of Life
A watched pot never boils ... especially when you forget to turn the burner on.

Directions:

Put egg white, sugar, water and corn syrup in top of double boiler; mix thoroughly. Place over rapidly boiling water and beat constantly with a hand mixer until mixture holds a peak (about 7 minutes). Remove from heat; add vanilla and beat until cool and thick enough to spread.

Mock Cream Icing

Beverly Wagner, Ladysmith, British Columbia

Ingredients:

1/2 cup soft butter
1 cup icing sugar
3 tbsp cold water
3 tbsp boiling water
1 tsp vanilla

Food for Thought

He, who is not afraid
to face the music,
may sometimes
lead the band.

Directions:

Cream butter and sugar well. Add cold water, 1 tbsp at a time, mixing well with electric beater. Add boiling water the same way. When very fluffy, add vanilla.

Grant's Simple Shrimp Dip

Grant Young, St. Phillip's, Newfoundland

Ingredients:

Horseradish
Ketchup

Food for Thought

Don't limit a child to your own learning, for he was born in another time. - Rabbinical saying

Directions:

Mix equal amounts of horseradish and ketchup in a bowl for a perfect shrimp dip. (Vary ratios to suit personal taste.)

Custard Frosting

Norma Clarke, Peterboro, Ontario (nee Atkinson, Herring Neck, Newfoundland)

Ingredients:

2 tbsp custard powder
1/2 cup water
1/2 cup butter or margarine
1 cup sugar
1/2 tsp vanilla

Trivia Tidbits

It would take you about 35 days to write the last names of a million people.

Directions:

Mix custard powder and water; boil until thick. Set aside and let cool. Cream butter, sugar and vanilla together. Gradually blend the two mixures with a spoon.

Enhancers

Pressings, Stuffings, Icings, Sauces, Spreads, Oils and Dips

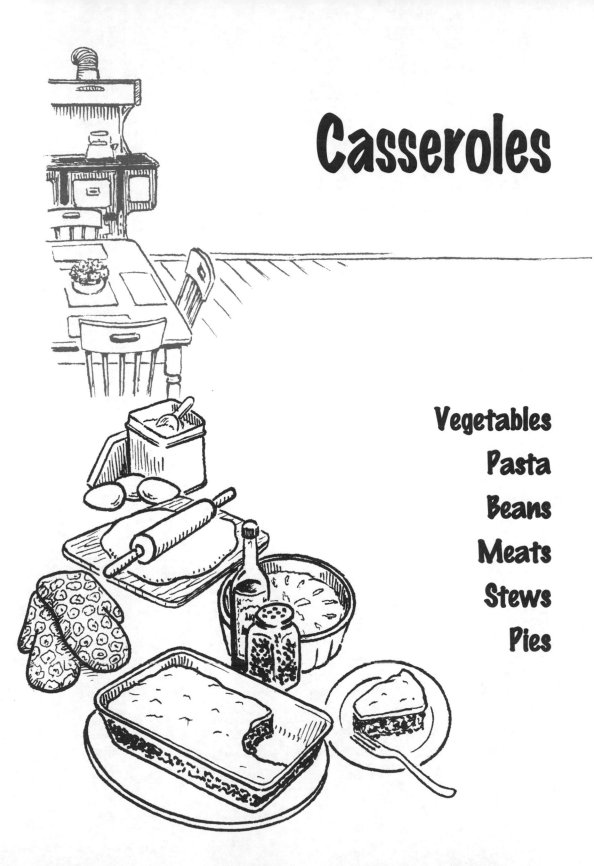

Casseroles

Vegetables
Pasta
Beans
Meats
Stews
Pies

Grandma's Fish Dinner

Mrs. Mary Caravan, Deer Lake, Newfoundland

Ingredients:

1-2 lb cod fillet
1/4 cup margarine
1 cup thinly-sliced onion
3 cups thinly-sliced potatoes
1 1/2 cups thinly sliced carrots
1 clove garlic (minced)
1 tbsp flour
1 tsp salt
3/4 cup warm milk

Food for Thought

Far away there in the sunshine are my highest aspirations. I may not reach them, but I can look up and see their beauty, believe in them and try to follow where they lead.

- Louisa May Alcott

Directions:

Melt margarine in large saucepan and saute onion until tender. Add potatoes, carrots and garlic. Fry for 5 minutes, stirring constantly. Sprinkle on the flour and salt; stir and coat well. Add milk and heat until bubbly. Spoon all into 2 qt. casserole dish, cover and bake 30 minutes in 350°F oven. Next, take it out and arrange fillet on top of the mixture. Brush with oil, cover and bake for another 25 - 30 minutes. (It's delicious!)

Macaroni Salad

Della Ivey, St. John's, Newfoundland

Ingredients:

3/4 cup mayonnaise
2 tbsp vinegar
1 tbsp prepared mustard
1 tsp sugar
1/2 tsp salt
dash pepper
2 cups macaroni, cooked
1/2 cup green onions, sliced
1/4 cup sweet pickle relish
1/2 cup celery, diced
1/2 cup red pepper, diced
1/2 cup green pepper, diced

Trivia Tidbits

After the 1745 rebellion, led by Bonnie Prince Charlie, the British government made it illegal for Scotsmen to wear tartan kilts - their national dress. The ban remained until 1832.

Directions:

In a large bowl combine mayonnaise, vinegar, mustard, sugar, salt and pepper. Mix well with remaining ingredients. Cover and chill several hours. Toss before serving. Makes 8 servings.

O'Brien Potatoes

Lori Bishop, St. John's, Newfoundland

Ingredients:

6 tbsp butter
6 tbsp flour
3 cups milk

Spice of Life

Money doesn't go as far as it used to, but at least it goes faster.

Pastas, Beans, Vegetables, Meats, Pies and Stews

Casseroles

salt and pepper, to taste
4 cups potatoes
1/4 cup pimento, chopped
1/4 cup green pepper, finely chopped
3 cups cheddar cheese, grated

> ## Spice of Life
> People who live in glass houses
> ...make interesting neighbours.

Directions:

Make white sauce with butter, flour and milk. Season to taste with salt and pepper. Stir in 2 cups potatoes in electric skillet; sprinkle with salt and pepper. Pour 1/2 the sauce over the potatoes and sprinkle with 1/2 cup cheese. Add pimento, green peppers and remaining potatoes, season and top with sauce. Sprinkle with remaining cheese. Set dial at 300°F and cook until bubbling. Turn control to 220°F and continue to cook for 30 minutes. Serves 8.

Cheesed Cauliflower

Marian Shea, Manuels, CBS, Newfoundland

Ingredients:
1 medium head of cauliflower
salt to taste
1/2 cup mayonnaise
1 tsp prepared mustard
3/4 cup cheese, shredded

> ## Food for Thought
> If a man happens to find himself,
> he has a mansion which he can
> inhabit with dignity all the days of
> his life. - James Michener

Directions:

Remove leaves and trim base from cauliflower. Wash and cook whole in boiling salted water 15 - 20 minutes, or until tender. Drain and place in ungreased shallow baking dish, sprinkle with salt. Mix mayonnaise and prepared mustard; spread over cauliflower. Top with cheese; bake at 350°F for about 10 minutes, or until cheese is melted. This recipe is also good for broccoli, or you can place 1/2 and 1/2 in the same dish.

Chicken Casserole Newfoundland-Style

Gail Corcoran (originally from St. George's, Newfoundland)

Ingredients:
7-8 fresh chicken legs (boiled)
1 can corn nibblets
1 can cream of chicken soup
1 cup of mayonnaise
1 bag of plain potato chips (the larger the bag the more casserole)

Directions:

Remove chicken from the bone, cut into small pieces and place in a large bowl. (**NOTE:** Make sure chicken was boiled in large pot on stove for at least 1 hour beforehand). After placing the chicken in the bowl, put in the corn, soup, mayonnaise and potato chips. It helps if the chips are crushed up first. Mix all ingredients together well. (It may look unappetizing, but I assure you that it is quite delicious!) Turn mixture into an ungreased baking dish and bake in a preheated 350°F oven for 20 minutes. Remove, let cool and serve.

Chicken Casserole

Mary Feehan, St. John's, Newfoundland

Ingredients:

1 1/2 cups V-8 juice
2 1/2 lbs chicken
2 tbsp vegetable oil
1/2 cup onion, chopped
1 clove garlic, minced
1/2 tsp oregano
1/4 tsp salt
1 small green pepper
1 tbsp flour

Directions:

Reserve 1/4 cup V-8 juice. Brown chicken in frying pan with vegetable oil; pour off fat. Add remaining juice, onion, garlic, oregano and salt; cover and simmer for 30 minutes. Add green pepper and cook 15 minutes, stirring occasionally. Gradually blend reserved juice into flour until smooth; slowly stir into sauce. Cook, stirring until thickened. Serves 4.

> **Trivia Tidbits**
>
> When the Wright Brothers made aviation history at Kitty Hawk, North Carolina, their initial 12-second flight spanned a distance shorter than the wingspan of a Boeing 747 jumbo jet - which measures 195.7 feet from tip to tip.

Scalloped Potatoes

Trudy Ivey, Mount Pearl, Newfoundland

Ingredients:

6 large potatoes
flour
butter
salt and pepper
milk
grated cheese

Directions:

Peel 6 large potatoes. Slice thinly and place in layers in a buttered 2-quart baking dish. Cover each layer with a sprinkle of flour, dot with butter, and season with salt and pepper. Fill dish with milk up to top layer of potatoes and sprinkle with grated cheese. Bake slowly until tender at 350°F for about 1 1/4 hours.

> **Food for Thought**
>
> Maybe they can't make you fight, said the draft officer, but they can take you to where the fighting is, and you can use your own judgement.

Mom's Seven Layer Dinner

Rosemarie Reynar, North York, Ontario (nee Stratton, Lewisporte, Newfoundland)

Ingredients:

1 lb hamburger meat
potatoes, sliced
carrots, sliced
onion, sliced
mixed vegetables (corn or peas)
cooked rice (enough to cover layer a little thick)
1 can tomato soup
salt & pepper, to taste

> **Spice of Life**
>
> Never put off until tomorrow what your secretary can do today.

Casseroles

Pastas, Beans, Vegetables, Meats, Pies and Stews

Directions:

Cook hamburger meat, season to your taste. Drain off excess fat. In a casserole dish, layer the above items, lightly seasoning each layer with salt and pepper. Bake at 350°F for 60 - 90 minutes.

Delicious Beef Crumble

Maisie Moyles, Carmanville South, Newfoundland

Ingredients:

1 tbsp Canola oil
1 1/2 lbs lean ground beef
1 onion, chopped
2 tbsp flour
1 cup bccf broth
1 tbsp tomato paste
1 tsp mixed herbs
6 fresh mushrooms, sliced
1 cup flour
1/4 cup butter
1/2 cup cheddar cheese, shredded
1/2 tsp salt
1/2 tsp pepper

Trivia Tidbits

Every person has a unique tongue print.

Directions:

Heat oil in skillet over medium heat. Add ground beef and onion, stirring occasionally for 6 minutes or until no longer pink. Stir in flour. Add broth, stirring until mixture boils. Stir in tomato paste and herbs until blended. Add mushrooms. Turn into shallow casserole dish. In bowl, rub together flour and butter to resemble fine crumbs. Stir in cheese, salt and pepper. Sprinkle over meat base. Bake in 375°F oven for 45 - 60 minutes, or until golden brown.

Ship Wreck

Bernadette Bishop, St. John's, Newfoundland

Ingredients:

1 large onion, sliced
raw potatoes, thinly sliced
1 lb minced moose meat
uncooked rice
1 can tomato soup
salt and pepper, to taste

> *Food for Thought*
> The toughest thing about success is that you've got to keep on winning.
> - Irving Berlin

Directions:

Place sliced onion in buttered baking dish. Over onion, put a layer of potato, a thick layer of meat, then a layer of uncooked rice. Season each layer with salt and pepper. Keep doing this until all meat is used up. Add a can of tomato soup with a can of boiling water. Cover and cook at 350°F for 2 hours. Add more water if necessary.

Cranberry Baked Beans

Ann Bain, Tatamagouche, Nova Scotia (nee Rowe, Collins Cove, Burin, Newfoundland)

<u>Ingredients</u>:

3 cups dry navy beans
5 cups cranberry juice
1/2 lb lean salt pork or diced bacon
1 large onion
1/2 cup ketchup
1/4 cup molasses
5 tsp dark brown sugar
1 1/2 tsp ground mustard
1 1/2 tsp salt
1/8 tsp ground ginger

> ## Trivia Tidbits
> The foundations of the great European cathedrals go down as far as forty or fifty feet. In some cathedrals the amount of stone under the ground is greater than that above ground.

<u>Directions</u>:

Wash and soak beans overnight or place beans in dutch oven; add water to cover by about 2 inches and bring to a boil for 2 minutes. Remove from heat, cover and let stand for 1 hour. Drain beans and discard liquid. Add cranberry juice to beans, bring to a boil. Reduce heat, cover and simmer for 1 hour. Drain, reserving juice. Place beans in pot, add remaining ingredients and 1 1/2 cups of juice. Cover and bake at 350°F for 3 hours. Add reserved juice as needed.

Farmer's Casserole Breakfast

Ann Bain, Tatamagouche, Nova Scotia (nee Rowe, Collins Cove, Burin, Newfoundland)

<u>Ingredients</u>:

3 cups hash browns
3/4 cup shredded cheese
1 cup cooked ham, diced
1/4 cup green onion, chopped
1/4 cup red pepper, chopped
4 eggs
1 can evaporated milk
salt and pepper, to taste

> ## Spice of Life
> It's an ill wind that blows when you leave the hairdresser.
> - Phillis Diller

<u>Directions</u>:

Place hash browns in 8x8 baking dish. Sprinkle with cheese, ham, onions and red pepper. Blend together eggs, milk, salt and pepper and pour over mixture. Cover and refrigerate overnight. Bake uncovered 350°F for 55 - 60 minutes.

Scalloped Bologna

Janice Mercer, Portugal Cove, Newfoundland

<u>Ingredients</u>:

8 medium potatoes, thinly sliced
1 large can creamed corn
1 tin evaporated milk
1 lb bologna, cubed
salt and pepper to taste

> ## Food for Thought
> It takes 15,000 casualties to train a major-general.
> - Ferdinand Foch

Directions:

Place all ingredients in large baking dish or small roaster. (The ingredients may be mixed together or layered). Add enough water to just cover. Bake at 350°F until potatoes are tender. Serves 4 - 6.

Seven Layer Dinner

Joan Brown, St. John's, Newfoundland (nee Kelly, Trinity, Trinity Bay, Newfoundland)

Ingredients:

1lb ground beef (or sausages, pork or fish fillets)
2 onions, sliced
3 medium potatoes, sliced
3 carrots, sliced
1 cup green peas (or corn)
1/4 cup raw rice
1 can tomato soup
1 can water

> **Spice of Life**
> Poverty is no sin
> ...but it's certainly an
> inconvenience.

Directions:

Fry onions until tender but not brown and spread over bottom of a 2-quart casserole dish. Add layer each of potatoes, carrots and green peas or corn (including the liquid). Sprinkle with raw rice. Arrange ground beef (sausages, pork or fish fillets) on top. Dilute tomato soup with water and pour over top. Bake, covered, at 350°F for 1 hour. Remove cover and cook for an additional 30 minutes.

Spaghetti Casserole

Lisa Gullage (nee Parsons), Kelligrews, Newfoundland

Ingredients:

1 large onion
3 celery stalks
1 medium green pepper
1 large can mushrooms, or fresh
salt and pepper to taste
2 lbs lean ground beef
1 pkg spaghetti
1 can spaghetti sauce
1 can spicy stewed tomatoes
Parmesan or grated cheddar cheese

> **Trivia Tidbits**
> On April 21, 1959, Alf Dean
> caught a 16-foot, 10-inch white
> shark which weighed 2,664
> pounds at Denial Bay, Australia -
> the largest fish ever caught by rod
> and reel.

Directions:

Cut up onions, celery, green pepper and mushrooms. Add salt and pepper, and saute in frying pan in butter or margarine. Brown ground beef and boil spaghetti. In a greased casserole dish, pour first layer of onion, celery, green pepper and mushroom mixture. Then add layer of browned, drained ground beef. Add tin of spaghetti sauce over ground beef. Place spaghetti noodles on top. Layer spaghetti with full tin of spiced tomatoes. Top off with cheese of choice. Bake at 350°F for 1/2 hour or until cheese melts.

Sweet Potato Casserole

June Gates, Woodstock, Ontario

<u>Ingredients</u>:

2 tbsp cornstarch
1 cup brown sugar
dash cinnamon
1/2 tsp salt
2 tbsp orange rind, grated
1 cup orange juice (fresh or frozen)
1 cup water
1/4 cup butter
boiled sweet potatoes, sliced

<u>Directions</u>:

Mix together all ingredients, except potatoes, and cook until slightly thickened. Slice potatoes 1/2-inch to 3/4-inch thickness. Pour mixture into casserole dish and top with potato slices. Bake at 350°F until bubbly. Sauces and potatoes may be made ahead of time and put together just before heating.

Food for Thought

You can't take it with you when you go,
There is no doubt about it;
But that's about the only place
That you can go without it.

\- Kathryn Gelander

Sausage Potato Casserole

Doreen Halfrey, Framingham, Massachusetts, (nee Young, Black Duck Brook, Newfoundland)

<u>Ingredients</u>:

1 lb bulk pork sausage
1 can cream of mushroom soup, undiluted
3/4 cup milk
1/4 cup onion, chopped
1/2 tsp salt
1/4 tsp pepper
3 cups peeled potatoes, thinly sliced
1 cup cheddar cheese, shredded

<u>Directions</u>:

In a large skillet, cook sausage until no longer pink; drain. In a bowl, combine soup, milk, onion, salt and pepper. In an ungreased 11x7x2 baking dish, layer half the potatoes, soup mixture and sausages. Repeat layers. Cover and bake at 350°F for 1 1/2 hours, or until the potatoes are tender. Uncover and sprinkle with cheese. Return to oven for 5 minutes or until cheese is melted. Yield 4-6 servings.

Spice of Life

Old jokes never die; they just sound that way.

Make Ahead Pasta Casserole

Judy Kirby, Epworth, Newfoundland

<u>Ingredients</u>:

1 lb Italian sausage, mild or hot
1 large onion, chopped
1 clove garlic, crushed
2 cups fresh mushrooms, sliced
1 cup red or green pepper, sliced

Trivia Tidbits

Her Majesty the Queen is forbidden to enter the House of Commons.

Casseroles

Pastas, Beans, Vegetables, Meats, Pies and Stews

1 (24oz) can pasta sauce
1 pkg frozen spinach or broccoli (thawed)
1 cup mozzarella cheese
5 cups rotini or penne pasta, cooked
1/2 cup parmesan cheese

Directions:

Crumble sausage into large frying pan, brown and drain off fat. Add onion, garlic, mushrooms and pepper. Cook, stirring for 5 minutes. Add pasta sauce; simmer for 5 minutes. Remove from heat and gently stir in thawed spinach, mozzarella, cooked pasta and 1/4 cup parmesan cheese. Spoon into a greased 12-cup casserole dish. Sprinkle with remaining cheese. At this point, casserole can be refrigerated for up to 24 hours. Bake covered at 350°F for 25 minutes and uncovered for 10 minutes.

Chinese Supper Dish

Beulah Cooper, Gander, Newfoundland
Ingredients:
2 cups cooked chicken
1 tin mushroom soup
2/3 tin water
1 cup onion, chopped
1 cup celery, chopped
1 tin mushrooms, drained
1 tin chow mein noodles
1 cup green pepper, chopped

Food for Thought

When dressing, don't forget to put on a smile.

Directions:
Combine all ingredients and bake in casserole dish for 1 hour at 350°F.

Salmon Ball Casserole

Cathy Gale, Codroy Valley, Newfoundland
Ingredients:
2 (7 3/4oz) cans salmon
1/2 cup long grain rice, uncooked
1/2 cup carrot, grated
1/4 cup onion, chopped
1 egg
1/2 tsp salt
1/8 tsp pepper
1 (10oz) tin cream of mushroom soup
1/2 cup water

Directions:
Put salmon and juice in a bowl. Remove skin and bones. Add rice, carrot, onion, egg, salt and pepper. Mix well, then form into 16 balls. Put in 9x9 baking dish. Mix soup and water. Pour over top. Bake covered for 1 hour at 350°F. Serves 6.

Lentil Stew

Ron Pumphrey, St. John's, Newfoundland

Ingredients:

6 cups water
2 cups green lentils
1 cup onion, chopped
1 lb mushrooms, sliced
1 tsp basil
2 tsp salt
2 stalks celery, diced
4 carrots, diced
1 (19oz) can tomatoes
1 clove garlic
2 tbsp vinegar

Directions:

(NOTE: Use ham bone for flavour.) Bring water and lentils to a boil. Simmer for 1 hour. Add rest of ingredients, except vinegar. Cook for 1 hour. Add vinegar. Serve with a green salad.

Easy Lasagna

Nicole Ryan, Newman's Cove, Bonavista Bay, Newfoundland

Ingredients:

1 1/2 lb hamburger meat
1 (14oz) tin tomato soup
1 (7oz) tin tomato paste
1 (10oz) can mushroom pieces
1 tsp onion powder
1 tsp garlic powder
1/4 tsp pepper
1/2 tsp salt
1 pkg lasagna noodles
1 lb mozzarella cheese, grated

Directions:

Brown hamburger meat. Add remaining ingredients to make a sauce. Cook noodles. Place a layer of noodles, a layer of sauce, layer of lasagna and a layer of cheese in a casserole dish. Bake at 350°F for 1/2 - 3/4 hour.

Baked Beans With Pork

Gerald Pumphrey, Middle Sackville, Nova Scotia

Ingredients:

2 cups dry beans
6 cups cold water
1/4 lb salt pork
1 medium onion, sliced
3 tbsp brown sugar
1/4 cup mild molasses

Trivia Tidbits

If you have 20/20 vision it means that at 20 feet you can read letters on a chart that any person with perfect vision is able to read. With 20/40 vision you can read at 20 feet, letters that a person with perfect vision can read at 40 feet.

Food for Thought

A boy's will is the wind's will, and the thoughts of youth are long, long thoughts.

-Henry Wadsworth Longfellow, My Lost Youth

Spice of Life

If at first you don't succeed, try again ...just to show how stubborn and stupid you can be.

Pastas, Beans, Vegetables, Meats, Pies and Stews

Casseroles

1 tsp salt
1/2 tsp mustard
pinch of black pepper
2 tbsp ketchup

Directions:

Rinse beans; soak overnight in 6 cups cold water. Simmer beans in soaking water or enough to cover for 1 1/2 to 2 hours until tender. Drain, saving liquid because it is rich in vitamins and minerals. Put pork and onion in bottom of bean pot or casserole. Add beans. Combine remaining ingredients with 1 1/2 cups hot bean liquid or water, and pour over beans. Add more water if necessary to cover them. Bake beans very slowly at 250°F for 5 - 7 hours. Remove cover during last 1/2 hour to brown beans. Add boiling water as required during baking to keep beans covered with liquid.

Chinese Casserole

Shirley MacDonald, Fredericton, New Brunswick

Ingredients:

1 lb ground beef
2 tsp soya sauce
1 can cream of mushroom soup
1 cup onions, chopped
2 cups celery
1 cup green pepper, chopped
1 (19oz) tin of bean sprouts, drained
1 large tin of Chinese noodles

Directions:

Fry together ground beef and soya sauce. Add soup, onions, celery, green pepper and bean sprouts. Place 1/2 tin of noodles on bottom of casserole dish; then add other mixture. Top with remaining noodles.

Hashbrown Casserole

Donna Pumphrey (nee Murphy, Bell Island, Newfoundland)

Ingredients:

2 lbs hashbrowns, thawed
1 tsp pepper
1 tsp salt
2 cups cheese, grated
1 cup sour cream
1 cup mushroom soup
1/4 cup melted butter (optional)
1/2 cup crushed Corn Flakes (optional)

Directions:

Mix all ingredients. Rinse out soup can with 1/4 cup of water and add it to mixture. If desired, melt butter and Corn Flakes and add over top of casserole. Bake at 300°F for 30 minutes, uncovered in a greased casserole dish.

Lasagna

Marian Shea, Manuels, Conception Bay South, Newfoundland

<u>Ingredients</u>:

1 lb ground beef
1 large tin tomatoes
8 oz tomato sauce
2 envelopes spaghetti sauce mix
2 cloves garlic, minced (optional)
8 oz lasagna noodles
6 - 8 oz mozzarella cheese, grated
1 cup cottage cheese
1/4 cup parmasen cheese
salt, to taste

Spice of Life

Watch your step - everyone else does.

<u>Directions</u>:

Brown meat slowly, spoon off excess fat, and add next 4 ingredients. Cover and simmer 40 minutes, stirring occasionally. Salt to taste. Cook noodles in boiling water. Place half the noodles in a rectangular dish. Cover with a third of sauce, add half the mozzarella, then half the cottage cheese. Repeat layers ending with sauce. Top with parmesan cheese. Bake at 350°F for 15 minutes.

Murphy's Macaroni and Cheese

Donna Pumphrey (nee Murphy, Bell Island, Newfoundland)

<u>Ingredients</u>:

1/2 pkg (8oz) elbow macaroni
1 cup milk
4 tbsp butter
1 1/2 cups ketchup
1 cup cheddar cheese
salt and pepper to taste

Spice of Life
Ye shall know the truth and the truth shall make you flee.
- Helen Wieselberg

<u>Directions</u>:

Boil macaroni in salted water until tender. Drain, and place in greased casserole dish. Add salt, pepper, butter and ketchup. Mix well. Cut cheese into small cubes. Mix into macaroni, reserving about 1/2 cup for the top of casserole. Bake at 350°F for 45 - 60 minutes.

Sweet 'n' Sour Meatballs

Donna Pumphrey (nee Murphy, Bell Island, Newfoundland)

<u>Ingredients</u>:

3/4 cup brown sugar
3/4 cup vinegar
3/4 cup water
1/4 tsp mustard
1 cup ketchup
1 - 2 lbs ground beef
dash of garlic salt

Food for Thought
I am the captain of my soul;
I rule it with stern joy;
And yet I think I had more fun
When I was cabin boy.
- Keith Parsons

2 or 3 eggs
1 cup bread crumbs
dash of salt and pepper
dash of accent salt
dash of steak spice

Directions:

In saucepan heat sugar, vinegar, water, mustard and ketchup over medium heat for 10 minutes; set aside. In large mixing bowl add meat and all other ingredients, mixing well. Once mixed, form into meatballs of desired size. Brown in a medium frying pan until meat is no longer pink. Place meatballs into casserole dish and pour sweet and sour sauce over them. Bake at 350°F for 1 hour.

Mashed Potato Casserole

Jeanette Osmond, Grand Bank, Fortune Bay, Newfoundland

Ingredients:

8 cups potatoes, cooked
1/2 cup mayonnaise
1 (8oz) pkg cream cheese, softened
1 tsp onion powder
3/4 tsp salt
1/4 tsp pepper
dash of paprika

Directions:

Mash potatoes, gradually stir in mayonnaise, cream cheese, onion powder, salt and pepper until light and fluffy. Spoon into casserole dish. Sprinkle with paprika. Bke at 350°F for 45 minutes. Serves 10 - 12.

Tuna Macaroni Casserole

Beulah Cooper, Gander, Newfoundland

Ingredients:

1 tin tuna
1 tin mushroom soup
1 cup milk
2 tbsp flour
salt and pepper
1 cup onion, chopped
1 cup green pepper, chopped
3 tbsp butter
1/2 pkg macaroni (cooked)

Trivia Tidbits

It is illegal to whistle underwater in Vermont.

Directions:

Combine tuna, soup, milk, flour, salt and pepper. In frying pan, fry onion and green pepper in butter until onion is transparent. In casserole dish, combine cooked macaroni with rest of ingredients. Bake at 350°F for 30 minutes.

Broccoli Casserole

Rhonda Tulk, Aspen Cove, Newfoundland

Ingredients:

1 pkg frozen broccoli, chopped
2/3 cup rice
1 can cream of mushroom soup
cheddar cheese, shredded

Directions:

Mix rice and equal amounts of water to soup, mix with broccoli. Sprinkle with cheese; stir. Sprinkle cheese on top; cook, covered, about 25 - 30 minutes at 350°F in greased casserole dish.

Beef Fiesta Casserole

Effie White, Loon Bay, Newfoundland

Ingredients:

1 lb ground beef
1 can tomatoes
1 can corn
1 tsp chili powder
1 1/2 cups water
1 oxo cube
1 green pepper
1 onion
1 1/3 cups rice, cooked

Directions:

Brown meat; add tomatoes, corn, water, green pepper, onion, oxo cube and chili powder. Once cooked, blend with cooked rice.

Goulash

Siobhan Coady (formerly of Grand Falls-Windsor, Newfoundland)

Ingredients:

1-2 lbs minced beef
2 tsp shortening or butter
1 medium onion
1/4 cup green pepper
salt and pepper, to taste
2 cups macaroni, cooked
1 tin tomato soup
1 cup cheddar cheese, grated

Directions:

Melt shortening (or butter) in frying pan. Fry meat with onions, salt, pepper and green pepper. Add cooked macaroni to meat mixture, along with tomato soup and cheese. Pour into 2-quart casserole dish and bake at 350°F for 20 - 25 minutes. Serves 4.

Spice of Life

Virtue is its own reward ...but has no sale at the box office. - Mae West

---

Food for Thought

Man's a kind of Missing Link, fondly thinking he can think.

- Piet Hein

Trivia Tidbits

The flooding of rice paddies has little to do with nourishing the rice, instead it is done primarily to drown the weeds.

Pastas, Beans, Vegetables, Meats, Pies and Stews

Casseroles

Sweet and Sour Meat Loaf

Rachel Hollett, Cambridge, Nova Scotia (nee Lomond, Port aux Basques, Newfoundland)

Ingredients:

1 1/2 - 2 lbs ground beef
1 large onion
2 cups tomato sauce, divided
1 cup cracker crumbs
1 egg, beaten
1/2 tsp salt
1 cup water
2 tbsp vinegar
2 tbsp mustard
2 tbsp brown sugar

> ## Food for Thought
> I have learned that only two things are necessary to keep one's wife happy. First, let her think she is having her way. And second, let her have it. *- Lyndon B. Johnson*

Directions:

Mix ground beef, onion, 1 cup tomato sauce, cracker crumbs, beaten egg and salt together. Mound in center of well-greased baking dish, leaving about 1 inch of space all around it. Combine remaining tomato sauce, water, vinegar, mustard and brown sugar; mix well and pour over meat mixture. Bake at 350°F for 1 1/2 - 2 hours.

Bahamian Style Macaroni and Cheese

Donna Young, Nassau, The Bahamas (formerly of Newfoundland)

Ingredients:

1 lb macaroni
1/2 lb margarine
1 medium sweet pepper, diced
1 medium onion, diced
3 eggs
1 can evaporated milk
thyme, to taste
paprika
1-2 hot peppers (or 4-5 dashes hot sauce)
1 1/2 lbs hard cheddar cheese, grated
salt, to taste

> ## Spice of Life
> A friend in need is a friend indeed ...but who needs friends in need?

Directions:

Preheat oven to 350°F. Cook macaroni according to package directions. Drain, but do not let it dry out completely. Let cool for 5 minutes. Add margarine and stir. Let cool for 10 minutes. Add sweet pepper, onions, eggs and evaporated milk; stir. Add thyme, paprika and hot pepper. Add half of the cheese to macaroni mixture; add extra salt and thyme, if needed. If mixture is drying out, add more evaporated milk. Grease a 5x10 baking dish with margarine. Add macaroni mixture and spread out evenly. Spread remaining cheese over top. Sprinkle with paprika. Bake, uncovered, for 25 - 30 minutes or until macaroni juices have evaporated considerably and cheese has melted.

> ## Spice of Life
> Always tell the truth, even if you have to lie to do so.

Casseroles
Pastas, Beans, Vegetables, Meats, Pies and Stews

Tourtiere

Phyllis Lemieux, Chateauguay, Quebec (nee Boyd, Herring Neck, Newfoundland)

Ingredients:

1/2 lb ground veal
1/2 lb ground pork
1/3 cup onion, chopped
1/4 cup water
1 tsp salt
1/4 tsp pepper
1 pie shell

> ### *Food for Thought*
> Justice is the insurance we have on our property and lives, and obedience is the premium we pay for it.

Directions:

Cook meats, onion, water, salt and pepper over medium heat until meat is no longer pink, but is still moist. Let cool. Prepare pastry shell as per directions, pour meat mixture into pie shell. Roll out a top crust and place over meat mixture; make slots for steam to escape. Bake at 425°F for 20 minutes or until done.

John's Hamburger Casserole

Marilyn Pumphrey, St. John's, Newfoundland

Ingredients:

1 medium onion, chopped
1 lb lean ground beef
3/4 tsp salt
1 dash pepper
2 cups (16oz) cut green beans, drained
5-6 carrots, sliced and cooked
1 can condensed tomato soup

> ### Trivia Tidbits
> No one knows for sure when Jesus Christ was born, but it was sometime between the year 8BC and 6AD.

Directions:

Cook onion until transparent. Add meat and cook at medium temperature until no longer pink. Add vegetables and soup. Mix and place in a greased 1 1/2-qt casserole dish. Bake at 350°F for 1 1/2 - 2 hours.

Chicken Hurry

Denise Hibbs (nee Jenkins), Springdale, Newfoundland

Ingredients:

2 1/2 - 3 lbs chicken parts
1/2 cup ketchup
1/4 cup water
1/4 cup brown sugar
1 envelope onion soup mix

> ### Trivia Tidbits
> There have been over 20,000 shipwrecks in Newfoundland coastal waters.

Directions:

Preheat oven to 350°F. Arrange chicken in casserole dish. Mix ingredients together and cover chicken. Cook for approximately 1 - 1 1/2 hours.

Tuna and Cheese Casserole

Leone Smith, St. Catharines, Ontario (nee Chafe, Petty Harbour, Newfoundland)

Ingredients:

2 cans tuna, drained
2 cans cream of mushroom soup
1/2 can milk
1/2 tsp thyme
1/2 tsp basil
1 tbsp parsley
1/4 cup parmesan cheese
salt and pepper, to taste
3 cups cheddar cheese, grated
4-5 cups small shell macaroni

Directions:

Combine tuna, soup, milk, thyme, basil, parsley, parmesan cheese, salt, pepper and 1 cup cheddar cheese. Cook macaroni according to package directions. Drain, stir into other ingredients and top with remaining cheddar cheese. Bake at 350°F for 30 minutes. Makes 4 servings.

> *Food for Thought*
> The world befriends the elephant and tramples on the ant.
> - Hindustani proverb

Hashbrown Casserole

Jessie Chaulk, St. John's, Newfoundland

Ingredients:

1 pkg hash browns
1/4 cup butter
1 1/2 cups cheddar cheese
1 can cream of chicken soup
1 small tub sour cream
1/2 soup can water
1/4 cup chopped onion
1 cup Corn Flakes, crushed

> **Spice of Life**
> If once a man indulges himself in murder, very soon he comes to think little of robbing; and from robbing he next comes to drinking and Sabbath-breaking, and from that to incivility and procrastination.
> - Thomas De Quincey, On Murder

Directions:

Place hash browns on bottom of a casserole dish. Melt butter and sprinkle over hash browns. Combine remaining ingredients in, except corn flakes, a separate bowl; pour over hashbrowns. Sprinkle crushed Corn Flakes on top. Bake at 350°F for 45 minutes.

> **Trivia Tidbits**
> Charlie Chaplin once won third prize in a Charlie Chaplin look alike contest.

Meats, Poultry & Game

Wild Game
Wild Fowl
Chicken
Turkey
Beef
Pork
Seal

Poultry Cooking Chart

		DIRECTIONS
Chicken 2 1/2 - 3 1/2 pounds 3 1/2 - 4 3/4 pounds 4 3/4 - up	**Time** 1 1/2 - 2 hours 2 1/4 - 2 1/2 hours 2 3/4 - 3 hours	**For Roasting** Wipe inside with damp cloth, and stuff loosely with your favourite dressing. Turn back skin on neck, fold wings across with tips touching. Tie legs together. Place bird on rack in open roaster. If desired, cover bird with parchment foil. Place in oven preheated to 325°F and cook until internal temperature of meat on the inside of the thigh reaches 195° - 200°F (using cooking thermometer), or until drumstick twists off easily.
Turkey 4 - 6 6 - 8 8 - 10 10 - 12 12 - 14 14 - 16 16 - 18 18 - 20 20 - 24	**Time** 3 - 3 3/4 hours 3 3/4 - 4 hours 4 - 4 1/2 hours 4 1/2 - 5 hours 5 - 5 1/4 hours 5 1/4 - 6 hours 6 - 6 1/2 hours 6 1/2 - 7 1/2 hours 7 1/2 - 9 hours	
Chicken **(Broilers)**	**Time** 30 - 35 minutes	Place chicken pieces, skin side down, on cold broiler rack, 5 inches from broiler, in oven preheated to 325°F. Brush top side with margarine and broil for 18 - 20 minutes. Turn over, coat remaining side with margarine and broil a further 10 - 14 minutes.
Chicken **(Fryers)**	**Time** 35 - 40 minutes	Dip pieces in seasoned flour, crumbs, etc., and brown in hot fat. Reduce heat, cover and cook until tender. Remove cover to brown and crisp quickly.
Duck	**Time** 25 - 30 minutes per pound	Roast uncovered at 325°F, with a small amount of water for 25 - 30 minutes per pound. Pour off excess fat as necessary.
Goose	**Time** 25 - 30 minutes per pound	Roast covered at 450°F, for one hour. Then pour off accumulated fat. Sprinkle with seasoned flour. Add 1 cup water and roast uncovered at 325°F for 25 minutes per pound.

Beef Cooking Chart

DIRECTIONS

Tender Cut Steaks	Thickness in Inches	Time in Minutes	
		Rare	Med
Sirloin	1/2 - 3/4	10 - 12	14 - 16
	1 - 1 1/4	15 - 20	20 - 25
Porterhouse or T-Bone	1/2 - 3/4	9 - 10	12 - 15
	1 - 1 1/4	14 - 16	18 - 20
Wing or	1/2 - 3/4	5 - 6	6 - 7
Club Steak	1 - 1 1/2	9 - 10	11 - 12
Tenderloin	1 - 1 1/4	9 - 10	11 - 12

Tender Cut Roasts	Weight	Cooking Time Minutes per pound	
		Rare	Med
Standing Rib	7 - 8 lbs	10 - 12	14 - 16
Rolled Rib	6 - 8 lbs	9 - 10	12 - 15
Rump (High quality)	5 - 7 lbs	14 - 16	18 - 20
Sirloin	5 - 6 lbs	5 - 6	6 - 7
Porterhouse & Wing	5 - 6 lbs	9 - 10	11 - 12
Round (High quality)	5 - 6 lbs	9 - 10	11 - 12

Less Tender Cuts		Cooking Time
Neck-Boneless	1 - 2 lbs	
Shank Meat	1 - 2 lbs	
Stewing Beef	1 - 2 lbs	3 hours (total time)
Brisket	1 - 2 lbs	
Flank	1 - 2 lbs	
Swiss Steak	1 - 2 lbs	
Short Rib	2 - 3 lbs	2 - 2 1/2 hours (total time)
Round Steak	2 lbs	
Brisket	2 lbs	
Blade	5 - 6 lbs	30 - 35 minutes per pound
Brisket	4 - 5 lbs	
Chuck	5 - 6 lbs	
Rolled Plate	5 - 6 lbs	10 minutes extra per pound for rolled cuts
Rump	5 - 6 lbs	
Shoulder	5 - 6 lbs	

For Broiling
Slash the fatty edge of the meat to prevent it from curling up when cooking. In an oven preheated to 325°F, place meat on a cold rack about 4 - 5 inches below the broiling element. Season and broil for half the suggested time one side; then using tongs, turn meat over and continue broiling until ready.

For Pan-Frying
Slash the fatty edge of the meat to prevent it from curling up when cooking. Preheat a heavy frying pan and add cooking oil after pan is almost hot to prevent sticking. Season and fry on one side for half the suggested time, then turn over to complete cooking. Pour off excess fat as it accumulates.

For Prime Roasting
Place tender meat, fat side up, on rack in open pan. Cook uncovered at 300°F. Do not add water or sear meat. Meat will be done Rare when internal temperature is 140°F, Medium at 160° and Well Done at 170°F. (Use a meat thermometer to determine this)

For Stewing
Cut meat in small pieces and dip in seasoned flour. Preheat pan and add oil to prevent sticking. Brown meat quickly at high temperature. Lower temperature and cover with warm water. Simmer (without boiling) until tender. Add vegetables and seasonings about 1/2 hour before meat is done. Thicken gravy if desired.

For Braising
Dip meat in well-seasoned flour. Brown on both sides in a heavy frying pan with a small amount of cooking oil. Add liquid (water, tomato juice, soup stock, pot liquor, or liquid of your choice). Cover pan and cook slowly in a 300°F oven or on stove top until tender. Add liquor as needed.

For Pot Roasting
Rub less-expensive roast with well-seasoned flour. Brown in a roasting pan, fat side up, or add a small amount of fat on top if lean. Add liquid (water, tomato juice, soup stock, pot liquor, or liquid of your choice). Cover pan and cook slowly in a 300°F oven until tender. Add liquor as needed.

Beef Cut Guide

How you prepare and cook a portion of beef depends on how tender it is, and how tasty it is. This guide is designed to help you determine the most and least tender, and the most and least tasty portions. Along the backbone of the carcass you'll find the most tender cuts, while the tastiest cuts are taken from the front and rear sections. Each side of a carcass is subdivided into the large cuts (shown along the centre), while the smaller cuts that you find at the store's meat counter are shown at the top and bottom.

Rib- This tender portion of the carcass produces bone-in or boneless steaks and roasts that are most tender the closer they are to the short loin.

Short Loin- The closer to the sirloin the more tender the meat of this portion is, yielding the very tender Top Loin, T-Bone and Porterhouse steaks. Divided lengthwise, the bottom of this section is the most tender of all beef, Tenderloin.

Sirloin- This tender section yields Flat-bone, Round-bone, Wedge-bone, and boneless Sirloin steaks.

Chuck- This portion yields tough cross rib, eye steaks and roasts, and ground beef.

Shank- This flavourful, but tough portion is best in stews or braised.

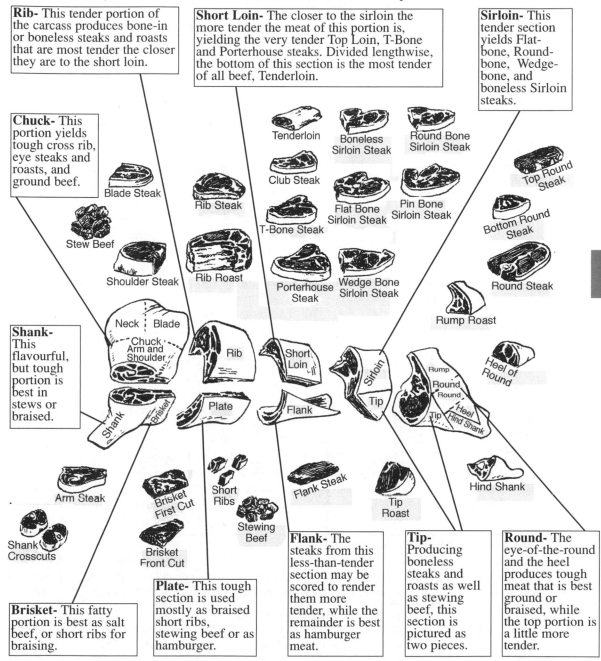

Flank- The steaks from this less-than-tender section may be scored to render them more tender, while the remainder is best as hamburger meat.

Tip- Producing boneless steaks and roasts as well as stewing beef, this section is pictured as two pieces.

Round- The eye-of-the-round and the heel produces tough meat that is best ground or braised, while the top portion is a little more tender.

Brisket- This fatty portion is best as salt beef, or short ribs for braising.

Plate- This tough section is used mostly as braised short ribs, stewing beef or as hamburger.

Pork, Lamb and Veal Cooking Chart

	DIRECTIONS

Lamb (Tender Cuts) Leg Loin Roast Crown Roast Rolled Front Front (Bone-In) Shoulder Roast	**Weight in Pounds** Weights of Lamb, Veal and Pork roasts should be about 4 - 7 pounds	**Cooking Time** 30 - 35 minutes per pound 45 minutes per pound (rolled cuts)	**For Roasting** Place meat, fat side up, on a rack in an open pan and insert meat thermometer in centre of largest muscle. Cook uncovered at 325°F. Do not sear the meat or add water. Cook lamb and veal until thermometer registers internal temperature of 180°F, and pork until 185°F is reached.
Pork Loin Roast Crown Roast Fresh Ham Fresh Pork Butt Tenderloin (stuffed) Rolled Shoulder		**Cooking Time** 40 - 45 minutes per pound	
Veal (Tender Cuts) Leg Roast (fillet) Loin Roast Rump Roast		**Cooking Time** 40 - 45 minutes per pound 45 minutes (rolled cuts)	**For Broiling** Slash the fatty edge of the meat to prevent it from curling up when cooking. In an oven preheated to 325°F, place meat on a cold rack about 4 - 5 inches below the broiling element. Season and broil for half the suggested time on one side; then, using tongs, turn meat over and continue broiling until ready.
Lamp (Less Tender Cuts) Rib Chops Loin Chops Shoulder Chops	**Thickness** 1/2 - 3/4 inches	**Cooking Time** 10 - 12 minutes (total)	
Pork Loin Chops Rib Chops Tenderloin (Frenched) Butt Chops Spareribs (Braised)	**Thickness** 1/2 - 3/4 inches	**Cooking Time** 20 - 25 minutes (total)	**For Pan Frying** Slash the fatty edge of the meat to prevent it from curling up when cooking. Preheat pan on medium heat and add oil. Place meat in pan and turn frequently to ensure even cooking. Pour off excess fat as necessary.
Veal (Less Tender Cuts) Sirloin Steak Loin Chops Veal Cutlet	**Thickness** 1/2 - 3/4 inches	**Cooking Time** 15 - 20 minutes (total)	**For Braising** Brown meat quickly in hot fat. Lower temperature and cook slowly, covered, until tender. Add water or vegetable juice to keep moist.

Stewing Less Tender Cuts of Lamb and Veal
Cut meat into small pieces, dip in seasoned flour and brown in hot fat. Cover with warm water and simmer 2 1/2 to 3 1/2 hours until tender. Do not boil. Add vegetables and seasoning about 30 minutes before meat is done. The gravy may be thickened with flour if desired.

Lamb or Veal Soup (Less tender cuts are quite satisfactory)
Cook meat (and bones) for 2 1/2 to 3 1/2 hours in gently simmering water. Celery leaves, onion slices and parsley may be added 30 minutes before meat is done. Season well before serving.

Pork Cut Guide

The front of the pig is very tough as it contains small muscles and connective tissue. Braising or poaching can render this portion more chewable. The rear section, with its larger muscles, is tender enough to roast or fry. The muscles on the pig's back are little used and very tender, while the belly may be broiled or even poached to render out the fat it contains. The diagram in the middle of the page shows the primal cuts of the pig carcass, while the smaller retail cuts are shown above and below.

Blade End-
Tender and meaty blade roasts are taken from this, the fattiest portion of the carcass, as well as blade chops.

Centre Loin-
Centre-rib roast, centre-loin roast and boneless top-loin roast comes from this, the juciest part of the pig. Bacon is also derived from this portion, which also produces butterfly chops, top-loin chops and back ribs.

Sirloin-
The tenderloin muscle which is found on the bottom of the sirloin is the most tender part of the pig. If this is removed, the top portion is usually sold as a bone-in roast or sirloin chops.

Shoulder-
Blade steaks and boneless or bone-in steaks are taken from this tough part of the carcass, which also yields cube steaks and cubed meat for stews.

Picnic Shoulder-
This tough, fatty section yields picnic shoulder roasts and arm roasts. The lower section makes hocks, while from further up, steaks are obtained. The rest becomes ground pork.

Pig's Feet-
Pig's feet are sometimes sold whole and pickled, or just used to make stock.

Belly-
After the spareribs, with their thin, tender meat removed, the remaining rind, fat and meat are used to make bacon and salt pork.

Leg (Ham)-
Large ham roasts and slices are obtained from the upper portion of the leg, while the bony, lower ham is sold as the shank end. Either may be purchased boneless or rindless.

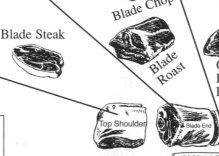

Shoulder Roast

Centre-Loin Roast

Back Ribs

Blade Chop

Top-Loin Chop

Loin Chop

Tenderloin

Blade Steak

Blade Roast

Centre Rib Roast

Rib Chop

Sirloin Roast

Cutlet

Sirloin Chop

Top Shoulder

Blade End

Centreloin

Sirloin

Spare Ribs

Belly

Ham

Picnic Shoulder

Foot

Picnic Shoulder Roast

Belly

Spareribs

Ham Butt End

Pig's Feet

Arm Roast

Hock

Ham Centre Slice

Arm Steak

Ham Shank End

Lamb Cut Guide

The meat of a young sheep is called lamb, while the meat of a mature sheep is called mutton. Although no part of a sheep's carcass is really tough, the most tender parts are on the back where the muscle is not used much. An "exploded" view of a sheep carcass is shown in the middle of the page, while above and below are some of the retail cuts. Before making a purchase, check the meat for quality. The fat on fresh, young lamb should be white, the flesh should be firm and tender, and the ends of the bones should be red, moist and porous. The meat is darker and the bones are dryer and whiter in more mature meat.

Shoulder-
Although very bony, this section is very flavourful and is sometimes cut crosswise into chops, or the bone removed and the meat rolled. It is often cut into small or bigger cubes for stew.

Rib-
This is the most pricey part of the carcass from where the 'rack of lamb'(containing 7 ribs) is taken. It also yields tender, richly marbled chops.

Loin-
The animal's tenderest meat comes from the loin. The loin roast, eye-of-loin chops, tenderloin chops and T-bone chops come from this section.

Neck-
Flavourful but tough, the neck is usually sold as bone-in slices or ground.

Foreshank-
This is a single serving of tasty and lean meat.

Breast-
The breast is very flavourful, but fatty. Sold as bone-in breast or deboned and rolled breast, this sections also yields spareribs, riblets or ground lamb.

Flank-
The toughest meat on the sheep comes from the flank which is usually ground.

Leg-
The upper part of the leg yields tender meat, which includes sirloin and center roasts as well as sirloin chops or steaks. The shank has firmer meat and produces leg roasts, leg steaks, or cubes suitable for stews.

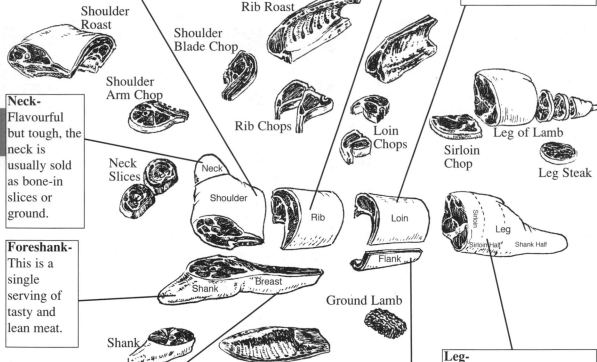

Shoulder Roast • Shoulder Blade Chop • Rib Roast • Shoulder Arm Chop • Rib Chops • Loin Chops • Leg of Lamb • Sirloin Chop • Leg Steak • Neck Slices • Neck • Shoulder • Rib • Loin • Sirloin • Leg • Sirloin Half • Shank Half • Flank • Shank • Breast • Ground Lamb • Shank • Breast • Riblets • Spareribs

Moose Cabbage Rolls

Herb Greening, Botwood, Newfoundland

Ingredients:

8 lg cabbage leaves
1 lb moose meat
1 onion, chopped
salt and pepper to taste
1 onion, grated
1/2 cup rice, cooked
2 tbsp vinegar
1/4 tsp chili powder
2 cups canned tomatoes
2 tbsp sugar

Trivia Tidbits

There is a Beaver dam in Montana that is 2,100 feet long.

Directions:

Soften cabbage leaves in boiling water. Brown meat and chopped onion in pan. Season meat with salt and pepper. Add grated onion and cooked rice, mixing well. Place a large tablespoon of mixture on a cabbage leaf, roll, and place in baking dish with rolled edge down or fasten with toothpicks. Add remaining ingredients and a little water. Simmer or bake at 325°F 1 1/2 - 2 hours.

Baked Stuffed Moose Heart

Frances Butt, Winterbrook, Newfoundland

Ingredients:

1 moose heart
1 large onion, chopped
1 tsp savoury
1 cup bread crumbs
1/4 tsp butter, melted
1/2 tsp poultry seasoning
bacon or salt pork

Food for Thought

Faith is telling a mountain to move and being shocked only if it doesn't.

Directions:

Wash heart and soak overnight in baking soda and water. Clean out vessels inside. Mix remaining ingredients and stuff heart (same as for chicken). Skewer and tie with line. Place in baking pan or roaster and place strips of bacon or salt pork on top. Add a small amount of water to pan and cover. Bake at 325°F for 4 or 5 hours. Baste occasionally. Slice and serve warm or cold with potato salad. *Note:* Salt, pepper, garlic powder, etc. may be sprinkled over the heart before baking.

Sweet and Sour Moose

Daphne Parr, St. Lunaire, Newfoundland

Ingredients:

moose
1/2 cup sugar
1/4 cup ketchup

Spice of Life

If at first you don't succeed ...find someone who knows what he's doing.

Wild Game, Wild Fowl, Chicken, Turkey, Beef, Pork, Seal

Meat Dishes

1/4 cup vinegar
3/4 cup cold water
1 tbsp cornstarch

Directions:

Slice meat into thin pieces. Fry until tender. Boil together sugar, ketchup, vinegar, cold water and cornstarch. Place meat in casserole dish and pour on sauce. Bake at 350°F for 30 minutes.

Moose Pie

Amy House, Stephenville, Newfoundland

Ingredients:

1 pkg French's meat marinade
water (as required)
2 to 3 lbs moose
flour (as required)
olive oil
2 large onions, chopped
1 pkg fresh mushrooms, sliced
1 cup red wine
1/2 tsp pepper
1/2 tsp basil
1/2 tsp oregano
1/2 tsp seasoning salt
1/2 tsp thyme spice
2 cups beef stock
3 carrots, sliced
2 cups frozen peas
non-stick cooking spray

> **Trivia Tidbits**
> During the chariot scene in 'Ben Hur', a small red car can be seen in the distance.

Directions:

Mix meat marinade according to package instructions (replace water with red wine, if desired). Cut moose into 1-inch cubes and marinate 12 to 14 hours in refrigerator. Remove moose from marinade, dredge in flour, and fry on high heat in olive oil to brown, a little at a time, transferring browned meat to roaster. Add onion, mushrooms, wine and spices. Bake at 300°F for 2 - 3 hours or until moose is tender, checking periodically to ensure it doesn't dry out. Add beef stock, carrots and peas and return to oven for 45 to 60 minutes. Remove from oven and thicken with flour and water mixture, to make a thick stew. Place stew in Pam-sprayed, 9-inch casserole dish.

Pie Crust Ingredients:

1 cup butter or margarine
2 1/4 cups flour
1/2 tsp salt
4 or 5 tbsp cold water
1 egg white
2 tbsp milk

> ***Food for Thought***
> Keep your fears to yourself, but share your courage with others.
> - Robert Louis Stevenson

Directions:

In a large bowl, cut butter or margarine into flour and salt. Using your hands, work mixture until crumbly. Add water, one tablespoon at a time, until mixture begins to stick together, using only enough water to be able to form a ball of dough in your hands. The less water you use and the less you work the dough, the flakier it will be. On a clean and floured counter, pat the ball of pastry down with your hands until it is in the shape of the casserole dish. Place a large sheet of waxed paper over the pastry and roll it out until it will cover the casserole. The pie crust may be thicker than usual but it's nice to have a thicker pastry for a meat pie. Folding the pastry in half, place it to one end of the casserole dish and unfold it to cover the stew completely, tucking edges into the side of the dish. With a butter knife, cut six or eight half-inch slits in the pastry to allow steam to escape. Bake at 425°F for 20 minutes until almost done. Beat egg white and milk mixture together, brush onto pastry and return to oven for 5 minutes or until pastry is golden brown.

Stuffed Moose Heart

Ron Strickland, St. John's, Newfoundland (formerly of St. George's, Newfoundland)

Ingredients:

1 moose heart
2 cups bread crumbs
1 tsp salt
1 tsp pepper
1 tbsp butter
salt pork

> ### Spice of Life
> Gossip that is travelling around loose is a lie, or it will be, by the time it has changed hands once more.   - John Billings

Directions:

Clean moose heart inside; do not cut. Mix bread crumbs with salt, pepper and butter and stuff heart. Place heart into roaster, add salt and pepper and pieces of salt pork. Place in oven and bake at 325°F for 3 hours.

Moose/Caribou Jerky

Jennifer Fudge, Ramea, Newfoundland

Ingredients:

moose or caribou meat
2 1/2 tsp salt
9 dashes Worchestershire sauce
1 tbsp garlic powder
4 cups warm water
1 tbsp onion powder
6 dashes tabasco sauce
soya sauce, for colouring

> ### Trivia Tidbits
> The most common first name in the world is Mohammed.

Directions:

Mix all but moose in a glass bowl; add soya sauce to make a dark colour. Cut meat into 1/4-inch strips and let soak for 6 hours in glass bowl mixture. Bake in a vented oven at 150°F with pan in underneath to catch drippings. Cook until you can bend it without breaking it.

Memory Maker Newfoundland Spaghetti

Hubert Beck, Nanisivik, Northwest Territories

Ingredients:

1 lb lean ground moose
2 cloves garlic, chopped
1 red or green pepper, chopped
8 large fresh mushrooms, sliced (or 1 can whole mushrooms)
1 (28oz) can of tomato sauce
26 oz wine (homemade or other)
chili powder, to taste
2-3 small onions, chopped
2-3 small tomatoes, chopped
olive oil
2-3 bottles home brew beer (optional)
1-2 people you love

Food for Thought
A fool does in the end what the wise man does at the beginning.

Directions:

Get all of the people to be eating together. Cook meat in a little olive oil; drain off excess fat. Everyone have a home brew (optional) while waiting. Add all other ingredients except the people and beer and only 4 oz of the wine. Simmer for 40 minutes or until tender. Serve over spaghetti noodles. Finish the rest of the wine with the meal. Enjoy the meal, and the people you are with, and tell them how much you care about them.

Venison Patties

Matthew Durnford, Calgary, Alberta

Ingredients:

moose meat
deer meat
salt and pepper, to taste

Spice of Life
The only secret a woman can keep is that of her age. - Fuller

Directions:

Grind meats fine and press together like a round steak. Cook in an iron pan at 300°F. Do not turn meat over at all until the side you are cooking is sufficiently done. When the blood turns white, turn meat over with a pancake turner. Salt and pepper the meat only after turning over, not before. Cook meat to medium or well done. Serve very hot with a little hot brandy and honey to taste. Venison paddies go well with a bottle of burgundy or Clarey.

Moose Stew

Kimberly Snow, St. John's, Newfoundland (formerly of Moreton's Harbour, Newfoundland)

Ingredients:

3 lbs moose, cut in small pieces
1/4 lb butter
salt and pepper, to taste
6 cups water
1 onion, chopped
2 carrots, sliced

Trivia Tidbits
On average, 12 newborns will be given to the wrong parents daily.

10 potatoes, cut in chunks
1 small turnip, cut in chunks
2 parsnips, sliced

Directions:

Brown moose meat in hot butter. Add water, salt and pepper. Let simmer, adding a chopped onion after about 1 hour. Cook for another hour; then add vegetables. Cook for another 30 minutes or until vegetables are tender. Make dumplings if you wish.

Wined Rabbit

Marian Shea, Manuels, Conception Bay South, Newfoundland

Ingredients:

2 - 3 lbs rabbit (jointed)
2 oz shortening
1 onion, studded with cloves
1 carrot, sliced
1 tsp sugar
1/2 lb tomato chutney
1/2 pint chicken stock
1 glass port wine
salt and pepper, to taste
milk for thickening
2 tbsp flour

Directions:

Melt shortening and fry rabbit quickly on all sides; place in casserole. Add all remaining ingredients except flour and milk and cook at 350°F for 1 hour. Remove joints. Thicken sauce with flour blended with milk and serve over rabbit.

Baked Flippers

Agnes Coady, St. John's, Newfoundland

Ingredients:

2 seal flippers
3 slices fat pork
3 carrots
1 parsnip
2 medium onions
6 potatoes
1 turnip
salt and pepper, to taste

Topping:

2 cups flour
1/2 cup shortening
1 tsp salt
2 tsp baking powder
water to make stiff dough

Spice of Life
Opportunity always knocks at the least opportune moment.

Food for Thought
If you want an accounting of your worth, count your friends. - Merry Browne

Meat Dishes

Wild Game, Wild Fowl, Chicken, Turkey, Beef, Pork, Seal

Directions:

Remove all fat from flippers carefully. Wash and cut into serving pieces. Do not parboil. Fry out salt pork and brown flippers in this. Add a little water and let simmer until partly tender. Add chopped vegetables, except potatoes. Season and add 1 cup water. Cook about 1/2 hour and then add potatoes. Cook for another 15 minutes, adding a little water if needed. Mix all topping ingredients together using enough water to make a stiff dough. Place topping flat over the pan cover and cook 15 - 20 minutes. Serve when cooked.

Baked Seal

Motey Hayley, St. John's, Newfoundland

Ingredients:

seal meat or flipper
1 tbsp baking soda
salt and pepper, to taste
strips of salt pork
1 large onion, chopped
1 cup water

> *Food for Thought*
> On the road between the homes of friends, grass does not grow.
> - Norwegian proverb

Directions:

Soak meat in cold water, to which soda has been added, for 1/2 hour. The soda makes the fat white. Remove all fat. Put meat in baking dish and season with salt and pepper. Place fat pork on top and add water. Cover and bake for 3 1/2 hours at 375°F. Add onion, and water if needed, and bake for another 1/2 hour. Remove meat from pan and make gravy, if desired. Serve with vegetables and baked pudding.

Duck

Gerry Pumphrey, Middle Sackville, Nova Scotia

Ingredients:

1 duck
1 small bottle of marmalade jam
1 cup orange juice

> *Food for Thought*
> If you were somebody else, would you want to be friends with you?

Directions:

Cooking time - 40 minutes per pound at 325°F. Place duck in roaster. Fork underneath to allow drainage of fat. Every 1/2 hour drain fat. Pour orange juice over duck 20 minutes before being done. Pour marmalade jam over top of duck. Add to regular stuffing:1/4 tsp of garlic powder; 1/4 tsp of basil (not sweet basil) and a few chopped walnuts.

Partridge in Marinade

Matthew Durnford, Calgary, Alberta

Ingredients:

partridge
olive oil (as required)
salt (to taste)
white pepper (to taste)

> **Spice of Life**
> A rose by any other name would smell as sweet ...a chrysanthemum by any other name would be easier to spell. - William J. Johnston

1 cup white wine (or as required)
thyme (to taste)
marjoram (to taste)
sweet basil (to taste)
parsley (to taste)
2 cloves garlic

Spice of Life

I can resist everything
except temptation.
- Oscar Wilde

Directions:

Divide bird into 4 pieces. Slightly brown in olive oil in an iron pan. Season with salt and pepper. Cover with equal parts of white wine and water. Add chopped garlic and herbs to taste. Bring to boil and simmer until partridge is tender.

Newfoundland Boiled Dinner with Dough Boys

Sonya Mercer, St. John's, Newfoundland

Ingredients:

2 lbs salt beef or spare ribs
1 cup split peas
6 carrots
6 potatoes
1 medium turnip
1 head cabbage

Dough Boys Ingredients:

2 1/2 cups flour
4 1/2 tsp baking powder
1 tsp salt
milk

Trivia Tidbits

The largest of all crabs is the Japanese spider crab. It has a span of more than three metres (10 feet) from claw tip to claw tip and could wrap its claws around two or three men.

Directions:

Cut salt beef in 2-inch pieces and soak in cold water overnight. Tie peas in a cloth bag and soak also. Drain off water. Bring to a boil and cook slowly for 3 hours until tender. Clean vegetables. Add turnip, potatoes and carrots 1/2 hour before serving dinner. Add cabbage during the last 15 minutes. Do not over cool. Turn peas pudding out into a bowl and mash with butter and pepper.

Dough Boy Directions:

Blend in the flour, baking powder and salt. Stir in the milk until mixture is moistened. Shape mixture into small balls and drop into liquid with the meat and vegetables of the boiled dinner (above). Cover pot tightly and cook for 15 minutes. Do not lift cover during cooking.

Sugar Cured Ham and Bacon

Clayton R Bain, Tatamagouche, Nova Scotia (formerly of Yarmouth, Nova Scotia)

Ingredients:

2 cups fine salt
2 cups brown sugar
1 cup molasses
1 tbsp salt petre

Trivia Tidbits
Warren Beatty and Shirley MacLaine are brother and sister.

Wild Game, Wild Fowl, Chicken, Turkey, Beef, Pork, Seal

Meat Dishes

1 tbsp cloves
1 tbsp cinnamon

Directions:
Dissolve all ingredients in cold water and use to cover ham. Place in beef bucket and keep turning it every 2-3 days for 2 weeks, or until it is ready to eat. Take out and drip. Hang up.

Rabbit Stew

Sherry-Lynn Loveless, Paradise, Newfoundland (formerly of Seal Cove, Fortune Bay, Newfoundland)

Ingredients:
2 rabbits, cleaned
2 cups water
1 onion, chopped
fat pork
3 tsp flour
1 cup turnip, diced
3 carrots, sliced
1 1/2 tsp salt
1/2 cup potato, diced

> **Trivia Tidbits**
>
> John Wilkes Booth's brother once saved the life of Abraham Lincoln's son.

Directions:
Cut up rabbit. Sprinkle with flour and brown in pork fat. Add vegetables and cook for 20 minutes. Thicken gravy. May be served with dumpling or a pastry baked over it.

Baked Stuffed Rabbit

Joy Pilgrim, Portugal Cove, Newfoundland (formerly of St. Anthony, Newfoundland)

Ingredients:
rabbit
4 cups fine bread crumbs
2 tbsp onions
1/4 cup soft butter
salt and pepper, to taste
2 tbsp savoury
fat pork, sliced

> **Food for Thought**
> He who chooses a job he likes, will never have to work a day in his life.

Directions:
Clean rabbit thoroughly. Prepare the bread crumbs, onions, butter, salt, pepper and savoury for dressing and fill rabbit; sew together or fasten with skewers. Place in a roasting pan and lay four or five slices of fat pork across its back. Add a little water and cover the pan. Bake at 350°F until meat is tender (about 25 - 30 minutes per pound). Remove from oven and thicken drippings for gravy. Top with your favourite pastry and return to oven. Bake at 450°F until pastry is nicely browned. Serve immediately.

Meat Dishes
Wild Game, Wild Fowl, Chicken, Turkey, Beef, Pork, Seal

Calf's Liver and Bacon

Deanne Stuckless, Kilbride, Newfoundland

Ingredients:

1 lb calf's liver
salt and pepper, to taste
flour
1/2 lb bacon (and drippings)

Directions:

Cut liver in 1/2-inch thick slices. Pour boiling water over, let it stand 5 minutes and drain. Sprinkle with salt and pepper and dredge with flour. Cook slowly in hot drippings or bacon fat. Serve with crisp bacon.

> ### Spice of Life
> As I grow older, I find that I don't have to avoid temptation any longer - now temptation avoids me.
> *- Henny Youngman*

Turr's Hearts and Livers

Alvina Stuckless, Kilbride, Newfoundland (formerly of Valley Pond, Newfoundland)

Ingredients:

1 lb turr hearts and liver
fat pork, diced
2 onions, sliced
1 cup water

Directions:

Brown hearts and livers in fat pork. Add onions and water; cover and cook for 30 minutes, adding a little more water if required.

Baked Turr or Duck

Charlene Peddle, St. John's, Newfoundland

Ingredients:

2 turrs
2 cups bread crumbs
1/2 tsp salt
1 onion, chopped fine
1/4 tsp pepper
1/4 cup butter, melted
1 tsp savoury (or more)

Food for Thought

A wise man makes his own decisions; an ignorant man follows public opinion.
- Chinese proverb

Directions:

Clean turrs, drain well. Mix dressing ingredients and stuff turrs. Place in a roaster and prick birds so fat will drain off. Sprinkle with salt and pepper. Bake at 400-425°F for 1/2 hour to render off fat. Pour fat off and lower heat to 350°F; cook for another 1 1/2 hours. Remove cover for last 1/2 hour to brown skin. After removing turrs, add more water to drippings and make gravy. Serve with turnip, cabbage, carrot, potatoes and baked pudding.

Lemon Herbed Chicken

Kathleen Ivey, St. John's, Newfoundland

Ingredients:

salt (to taste)
lemon pepper (to taste)
1 chicken, cut up
1/4 cup oil
1/4 cup butter
1/2 cup onion, chopped
2 tbsp dried parsley flakes
1/2 tsp rosemary
1/2 cup fresh lemon juice

Directions:

Salt and pepper chicken, then brown on all sides in hot oil and butter in skillet. Sprinkle with onion, parsley, and rosemary. Pour lemon juice over all. Cover and simmer until chicken is fork-tender; about 25 minutes. Serve with baked potatoes and a green vegetable.

> ## Food for Thought
> Most of us spend a lot of time dreaming of the future, never realizing that a little of it arrives each day.

Curry Chicken

Laurie Roberts, Baie Verte, Newfoundland (formerly of Little Bay Islands, Newfoundland)

Ingredients:

4-6 chicken legs
1 can cream of chicken soup
1 can tomato soup
1 can water
1 medium onion, chopped
2 tsp curry powder
2 tsp chili powder

Directions:

Place the chicken in a roaster. Mix the remaining ingredients in a bowl and pour over chicken. Bake for 1 hour in a 350°F oven. Serve with mixed vegetables and rice. This recipe is very simple to prepare and is very tasty.

> ## Spice of Life
> The best revenge is to live long enough to be a problem to your children.

Barbecued Chicken Wings

Bertha Smith, Clarenville, Newfoundland

Ingredients:

2 lbs chicken wings (cut at joints)
2 tbsp oil
salt and pepper, to taste
1 bottle chili sauce
2 dashes Worchestershire sauce
1/4 cup white sugar
1/2 cup vinegar
1 small onion, chopped

> ## Trivia Tidbits
> Playing cards were issued to British pilots in WWII. If captured, they could be soaked in water and unfolded to reveal a map for escape.

Directions:

Place chicken wings in casserole dish adding oil, salt and pepper. Bake at 325°F for 45 minutes. Remove from oven. Combine remaining ingredients; mix well and pour over chicken. Return to oven for another 45 minutes.

Chicken Fingers

Ann Bain, Tatamagouche, Nova Scotia (nee Rowe, Collins Cove, Burin, Newfoundland)

Ingredients:

6 chicken breast halves
1 egg, beaten
1 cup buttermilk
1 cup flour
1 cup bread crumbs
1 tsp salt
1 tsp baking powder

Food for Thought
People who can afford to gamble don't need money, and those who need money can't afford to gamble.

Directions:

Marinate chicken breasts in beaten egg and buttermilk mixture for at least 4 hours. Cut chicken in strips. Combine flour, bread crumbs, salt and baking powder and roll drained chicken in mixture. Fry in oil or deep fry. *Note:* Onion rings can be done in the same manner.

Oven-Baked Curry Chicken

Ann Bain, Tatamagouche, Nova Scotia (nee Rowe, Collins Cove, Burin, Newfoundland)

Ingredients:

4 tsp curry powder
1/2 tsp cinnamon
1/2 tsp cayenne
salt, to taste
1/3 cup flour
chicken
2 tbsp oil

Trivia Tidbits
Orcas (killer whales) kill sharks by torpedoing up into the shark's stomach from underneath, causing the shark to explode.

Directions:

Combine the first 5 ingredients in clear plastic zipper bag. Add chicken and shake well to coat. Place chicken on baking sheet and drizzle with oil. Bake 20 minutes at 375°F, then turn over and bake for another 20 minutes.

Chicken Fingers

Ann Bain, Tatamagouche, Nova Scotia (nee Rowe, Collins Cove, Burin, Newfoundland)

Ingredients:

1 cup Italian bread crumbs
2 tbsp parmesan cheese
1 clove garlic, minced
1/4 cup vegetable oil
6 chicken breast halves, boneless and skinless

Trivia Tidbits
Daniel Boone detested coonskin caps.

Meat Dishes

Wild Game, Wild Fowl, Chicken, Turkey, Beef, Pork, Seal

Directions:

Combine bread crumbs and parmesan cheese. In a small bowl, combine garlic and oil. Dip chicken strips in oil and dip in bread crumbs. Place on baking sheet and bake at 350°F for 20 minutes.

One-Pan Italian Chicken

Janice Mercer

Ingredients:

1 tsp oil
8 chicken thighs or breasts
1 lg tin tomato sauce
2 large onions, thinly sliced
8 slices of mozzarella cheese
salt and pepper, to taste

> ***Food for Thought***
> Blessed are those who can give without remembering, and take without forgetting.

Directions:

Heat oil on medium heat in large frying pan. Add onion and chicken; cook until browned. Add tomato sauce, salt and pepper. Simmer, covered, on low heat until chicken is cooked and tender. Place one slice of cheese on each piece of chicken, replace cover until cheese melts. Best served over rice or noodles. Serves 4 - 6.

Sweet and Sour Chicken Wings

Joan Brown, St. John's, Newfoundland (nee Kelly, Trinity, Trinity Bay, Newfoundland)

Ingredients:

chicken wings
1 cup ketchup
1 onion, diced
1 tsp thyme
1/2 cup brown sugar
1 tsp vinegar
1 cup water from boiled chicken

> **Trivia Tidbits**
> Leonardo da Vinci could write with one hand and draw with the other at the same time.

Directions:

Boil chicken wings for 10 minutes and reserve 1 cup water. Mix remaining ingredients with the reserved water and pour over chicken wings. Bake at 300°F for 2 hours. Serve over rice.

Chicken Rolls Supreme with Stuffed Mushrooms

Marjorie Baetzel, (nee Noseworthy) St. John's, Newfoundland

Ingredients:

6 boneless chicken breasts
2 1/2 cups bread crumbs
1/4 cup parmesan cheese
3/4 tsp salt
2 tsp parsley flakes
3/4 cup butter
1/2 tsp garlic (minced)

> **Spice of Life**
> Half the world is nutty - the rest are squirrels.

1 tsp mustard
1 tsp Worchestershire sauce

Stuffed Mushroom Ingredients:
15 to 20 large mushrooms
2 tbsp butter
3 tbsp onion, finely chopped
1/2 cup bread crumbs
1/4 cup sour cream
1/2 tsp parsley
dash of salt and pepper

> ## *Food for Thought*
> You have never really lived until you've done something for somebody who can never repay you.

Directions:
In a large mixing bowl combine bread crumbs, cheese, salt and parsley flakes. Blend together. In a medium sauce pan melt butter; add garlic, mustard and Worchestershire sauce. Mix together. Dip each chicken breast in butter mixture and coat well in crumb mixture. Roll and tuck ends in forming a roll. Place in a shallow baking dish. Pour any leftover butter mixture over rolls. Cover with foil and bake at 350°F for no longer than 50 minutes. Baste occasionally and keep covered until done. Serve with stuffed mushroom, baby carrots and mashed potatoes.

Stuffed Mushroom Directions:
Scrub mushrooms and cut off stems. Also scoop out moderate amount from centre cap and finely chop this as well. In a skillet melt butter. Add onion and cook, stirring for 3 minutes. Add mushroom choppings and cook further for 4 minutes. Remove from heat and add bread crumbs, sour cream, parsley, and salt and pepper. Sprinkle a few grains of salt in each cap before stuffing. Spoon above mixture into each mushroom cap. Place in ungreased shallow dish. Bake uncovered at 325°F - 350°F for 1/2 hour.

Sweet and Sour Chicken

Lisa Gullage (nee Parsons), Kelligrews, Newfoundland

Ingredients:
2 tbsp vegetable oil
3-4 skinless, boneless chicken breasts
1/2 cup carrot, grated
1/2 cup green pepper strips
1/2 cup red pepper strips
1/4 cup green onion
1 tbsp garlic
1 cup drained pineapple chunks (reserve 1/4 cup juice)
2 tbsp water
3 tbsp white vinegar
2 tbsp soya sauce
1 tbsp brown sugar
1 tbsp cornstarch
1 tbsp ground ginger
2 cups Minute Rice, cooked

Spice of Life
Never underestimate a woman - unless you're estimating her age or her weight.

Directions:

In large skillet, heat oil; add chicken. Cook over medium-high heat, stirring occasionally, until lightly browned, about 3 minutes. Add carrots, peppers, green onion and garlic; cook, stirring frequently, 2 minutes longer. In small bowl, combine reserved pineapple juice, water and remaining ingredients except rice. Pour over chicken mixture and stir in pineapple chunks. Cook until starting to boil, 2 minutes. Pour over ready-made rice. Makes 4-6 servings.

Bar-B-Qued Chicken

Marjorie Baetzel, St. John's, Newfoundland (nee Noseworthy)

Ingredients:

chicken
3/4 cup ketchup
1/8 cup vinegar
1/2 cup water
1 1/2 tbsp Worchestershire sauce
3/4 tsp mustard
1/2 tsp salt
2 tbsp brown sugar
1 cup celery, chopped
1 medium onion, finely chopped
1 cup mushrooms, sliced

Directions:

In a glass baking dish arrange your favourite chicken parts (thighs, drumsticks etc.) Combine all above ingredients and spread over chicken parts. Cover tightly with foil and bake at 350°F for 1 1/2 hours. Remove foil for last 20 minutes and brown at 400°F. Serve with baked potatoes.

Chicken Divan

Marjorie Baetzel, St. John's, Newfoundland (nee Noseworthy)

Ingredients:

4 boneless chicken breasts
2 tbsp mayonnaise
1 can cream of chicken soup
3/4 cup milk
1 tbsp onion, grated
1 tsp lemon juice
2 tbsp butter
1 cup bread crumbs
1 1/2 pkgs broccoli

Directions:

Cut chicken into small pieces. Fry pieces in a little oil for 10 minutes. In a casserole dish place broccoli that has been steamed for 10 minutes. Place cooked chicken on top of broccoli. Mix mayonnaise, chicken soup, milk, onion and lemon juice. Pour over chicken and broccoli mixture. Use fork to let mixture seep down among chicken and broccoli. Melt butter and pour over bread crumbs; tossing lightly with a fork. Sprinkle over top of casserole. Bake uncovered at 350°F for 30 - 35 minutes, until bubbly.

Chicken Breasts Diane

Gerald Pumphrey, Middle Sackville, Nova Scotia

<u>Ingredients</u>:

4 large boneless chicken breasts (halves or 8 small)
1/2 tsp salt
1/4 - 1/2 tsp black pepper
2 tbsp olive or salad oil
2 tbsp butter or margarine
3 tbsp fresh chives or green onions, chopped
juice from 1/2 lime or lemon
2 tbsp brandy or cognac, (optional)
3 tbsp parsley, chopped
2 tsp dijon-style mustard
14 cups chicken broth

<u>Directions</u>:

Place chicken breast halves between sheets of waxed paper or plastic wrap. Pound slightly with mallet. Sprinkle with salt and pepper. Heat 1 tbsp each of oil and butter in large skillet. Cook chicken over high heat for 4 minutes on each side. Do not cook longer or they will be overcooked and dry. Transfer to warm serving platter. Add chives or green onion, lime juice, brandy, parsley and mustard to pan. Cook 15 seconds, whisking constantly. Whisk in broth; stir until sauce is smooth. Whisk in remaining butter and oil. Pour sauce over chicken. Serve immediately. Makes 4 servings.

> **Spice of Life**
>
> There are several good protections against temptation, but the surest is cowardice. - Mark Twain

Chicken Chop Suey

Gerry Pumphrey, Middle Sackville, Nova Scotia

<u>Ingredients</u>:

1 - 2 lbs chicken
1 cup chicken broth
1/2 clove garlic, crushed
1/2 lb mushrooms, chopped
1/2 green pepper, cut in strips
1 onion, sliced
2 tbsps margarine
1 large can bean sprouts, drained
1 tsp salt
2 tsp cornstarch
2 tsp soya sauce
3 cups cooked rice

> **Trivia Tidbits**
>
> The leg which the Marquis of Anglesey had amputated during the Battle of Waterloo was given a full military funeral.

<u>Directions</u>:

Simmer chicken 15 minutes, drain and save stock. Discard skin and bones. Saute garlic, mushrooms, onion and green pepper in margarine. Stir in bean sprouts and salt, cover and cook for 1 minute. Uncover and stir in cornstarch; add soy sauce; add cup of chicken broth and cook 12 minutes. Serve over rice.

Crystal's Nice and Spicy Chicken

Betty Lou (formerly of Appleton, Ontario) and Syd George (formerly of Howley, Newfoundland), Gloucester, Ontario

Ingredients:

4 boneless chicken breasts
1 (14oz) tin pineapple chunks
1 bottle barbecue sauce

Directions:

Strain juice from pineapple and reserve fruit. Mix juice and barbeque sauce together. Spray non-stick skillet with cooking spray and heat on high. Brown chicken 3-5 minutes per side and add pineapple juice mixture. Lower heat to medium and cook uncovered, turning chicken once during cooking. When sauce thickens, about 20-30 minutes, check chicken for doneness. Add pineapple chunks and heat through 3-5 minutes. Serve over a bed of rice. *Note:* May substitute sliced peaches for pineapple chunks.

Peaches and Cream Chicken

Renee Davis Hillier, Kingston, Ontario (formerly of Grand Falls-Windsor, Newfoundland)

Ingredients:

2 chicken breasts
salt and pepper to taste
1 tin peaches, diced
1 cup honey dijon salad dressing
1 cup apricot jam

Food for Thought
A gossipper can give you all the details without knowing any of the facts.

Directions:

Sprinkle chicken breasts with salt and pepper on both sides and pan fry on stove. When chicken is cooked, add peaches (including juice). Mix apricot jam and salad dressing and ensure chicken is completely covered with mixture. Allow to simmer for at least 10 - 15 minutes. Serve over rice.

Baked Chicken

Ron Strickland, St. John's, Newfoundland (formerly of St. George's, Newfoundland)

Ingredients:

chicken
1 tbsp butter, fresh bacon or salt pork
salt and pepper to taste
1 small onion

Spice of Life
Procrastination is fun.
Just wait and see.

Directions:

Skin and cut up chicken. Place strips of bacon, salt pork or butter on bottom of square baking dish. Place chicken on top. Season with salt, pepper and onion. Bake at 325°F for 1 1/2 hours.

Food for Thought
Happiness is a journey, not a destination.

Meat Dishes

Wild Game, Wild Fowl, Chicken, Turkey, Beef, Pork, Seal

Chicken Casserole

Emma Martin, Catalina, Newfoundland

Ingredients:

2 cups chicken, cubed
1/2 cup green pepper, chopped
1/4 cup butter
1 onion, chopped
salt and pepper, to taste
2 cups macaroni
2 cups frozen broccoli
2 cups milk
1 tin cream of chicken soup
1 1/2 cups cheddar cheese, grated
1 tin mushrooms (optional)

Spice of Life

There's no rest for the wicked - and none for the virtuous either.

Directions:

In frying pan, cook chicken, onion, green pepper, salt and pepper in butter. In separate pan, cook macaroni; just before macaroni is cooked, add frozen broccoli and bring to a boil. Cook 4 - 5 minutes. To chicken mixture, add cream of chicken soup and milk over medium heat. Heat for 15 minutes. Add 1 cup cheese, stir until thick. Strain macaroni and brococoi mixture. Mix everything together in a 9x13 casserole dish, cover with 1/2 cup cheese. Cover and bake at 350°F for 30 minutes or until cheese is melted.

Curried-Orange Chicken

Connie Fowlow, Goulds, Newfoundland (nee Mason, St. John's, Newfoundland)

Ingredients:

2 lbs chicken breasts, skinless
2 tbsp flour
salt and pepper, to taste
2 tbsp margarine
3/4 cup orange juice
1 orange, peeled and sectioned
2 tsp curry powder
1 cup honey
2 tbsp prepared mustard

Trivia Tidbits
The number of possible ways of playing the first four moves per side in a game of chess is 318,979,564,000.

Directions:

Toss chicken breasts with seasoned flour and brown in margarine over medium-high heat. Place in a baking dish, boneside up. Combine remaining ingredients and pour over the chicken. Cover and bake at 350F for 1 hour. Makes 4 - 6 servings.

Spice of Life
Those who flee temptation usually leave a forwarding address.   *- Lane Olinghouse*

Meat Dishes

Wild Game, Wild Fowl, Chicken, Turkey, Beef, Pork, Seal

Chicken Italiano

Connie Fowlow, Goulds, Newfoundland (nee Mason, St. John's, Newfoundland)

Ingredients:

1 (48oz) can tomatoes
1/2 tsp dried basil
1/2 tsp tarragon
1/2 tsp salt
1/4 tsp pepper
2 tsp margarine or oil
1 clove garlic, finely chopped
2 lbs chicken breasts, skinless
2 tsp dried parsley (or 2 tbsp fresh)
1/2 cup mozzarella cheese, shredded

> ### *Food for Thought*
> It's nice to know that when you help someone up a hill you're a little closer to the top yourself.

Directions:

Pour tomatoes into blender or food processor. Add basil, tarragon, salt and pepper; puree until smooth. Melt margarine in large frying pan; saute garlic over medium heat for 1 minute. Add chicken breasts, fry, turning once or twice, until golden on both sides. Turn chicken fleshy side down and cover with tomato mixture. Bring to a boil; reduce heat and simmer 15 minutes until tender. Remove chicken and place fleshy side up, in a warm oven-proof dish. Stir parsley into sauce and spoon over chicken breasts. Sprinkle with cheese; place under broiler 1 minute, until cheese melts. Makes 4 servings.

Lemon Chicken

Connie Fowlow, Goulds, Newfoundland (nee Mason, St. John's, Newfoundland)

Ingredients:

8 chicken breasts, boneless
2 tbsp butter
2 tbsp milk
1/2 cup dry bread crumbs
flour
1 egg
1 cup ground almonds, toasted
1/2 tsp white pepper
3 tbsp vegetable oil

Lemon Sauce Ingredients:

2 cups water
1/2 cup sugar
1/4 cup butter
2 tsp vanilla
1 env custard powder
1/4 cup cold water
juice of a lemon

Trivia Tidbits

Ice skates did not originate in Holland, as many believe, but roller skates did.

Directions:

Pat chicken dry. Beat egg with milk. Mix almonds, bread crumbs and pepper. Lightly dust chicken with flour; dip into egg mixture, then into almond mixture and coat completely. Place on rack and cover with a tea towel. Refrigerate 1 - 6 hours. On a cookie sheet, heat oil and butter at 375°F for 5 minutes. Place chicken in pan. Bake for 20 - 25 minutes, turning over halfway through. To prepare lemon sauce, boil water, sugar, butter and vanilla. Mix custard powder with 1/4 cup cold water; add to boiling mixture. Add lemon juice and serve over hot chicken.

Honey Garlic Chicken Wings

Connie Fowlow, Goulds, Newfoundland (nee Mason, St. John's, Newfoundland)

Ingredients:

1 cup brown sugar
2 tsp dry mustard
1 tsp garlic powder
2 tbsp soya sauce
2 tbsp corn syrup
1 pkg chicken wings

Spice of Life
Opportunity knocks but once ... but temptation leans on the doorbell.

Directions:

Cut chicken wings in half, removing tips. Mix dry ingredients together. Coat chicken wings in dry mixture and place in plastic container or freezer bag. Mix soya sauce and corn syrup and pour mixture over wings. Marinate in refrigerator for 1 hour. Bake in shallow dish at 300°F for 2 hours.

Easy Chicken Cordon Bleu

Connie Fowlow, Goulds, Newfoundland (nee Mason, St. John's, Newfoundland)

Ingredients:

6 chicken breasts, boneless and skinless
6 slices cooked ham
3 slices Swiss cheese
1 egg, slightly beaten
2 tbsp milk
3/4 cup fine bread crumbs
1 (10oz) can mushroom soup
1/2 cup milk
2 tbsp white wine
paprika

Trivia Tidbits
The numbers '172' can be found on the back of the U.S. $5 dollar bill and in the bushes at the base of the Lincoln Memorial.

Directions:

Place a slice of ham on each chicken breast. Cut cheese slices into two pieces. Place 1 piece on each ham slice; roll up and secure with a toothpick. Mix egg and 2 tbsp milk; dip each roll in egg mixture. Roll in bread crumbs. Place rolls, seam side down in 13x9x2 baking dish. Heat mushroom soup and 1/2 cup milk. Add white wine. Pour sauce over chicken rolls. Cover baking dish with foil; bake at 350°F for 1 hour. Uncover; sprinkle with paprika. Bake 10 minutes longer to brown bread crumbs.

Chicken Pie

Alice Bye, Oliver, British Columbia

Ingredients:

1/2 cup butter or margarine
1/2 cup flour
1 tsp salt
1/8 tsp pepper
1 tbsp dried minced onion
3 cups chicken broth (or leftover gravy)
3 cups chicken, cooked and diced
1 cup lima beans (or peas), cooked
1 cup carrots, cooked

Directions:

Melt butter or margarine in a saucepan. Blend in flour, salt, pepper and onion. Gradually stir in broth or leftover gravy. Cook, stirring constantly until smoothly thickened. Add chicken, beans and carrots. Combine and turn into a 2 1/2-quart casserole. Cover with pastry *(See p. 59 for "Baked Pudding")*. Slash pastry to let steam escape. Bake in a preheated oven for 20 minutes or until pastry is golden brown and chicken is bubbly. (Freezes well).

> ## Spice of Life
> Talk about others, you're a gossip; talk about yourself, you're a bore.
> - Henny Youngman

Cajun Chicken Wings

Denise Hibbs (nee Jenkins), Springdale, Newfoundland

Ingredients:

1/2 cup Heinz 57 sauce
1/2 cup ketchup
1 tsp mustard
1 tbsp Worchestershire sauce
1/2-1 tsp cayenne pepper
3/4 tsp ground thyme
3/4 tsp dried oregano
3/4 tsp pepper
2 lbs chicken wings, sectioned

Directions:

Combine all ingredients, except wings. Marinate wings in sauce for 20 minutes. Bake at 350°F for 1 -1 1/2 hours, or until done.

> ## Food for Thought
> The trouble with the future is that it usually arrives before we're ready for it.

Tropical Chicken

Pearl White, Trenton, Ontario (nee Flight, Small Point, Newfoundland)

Ingredients:

3 lbs chicken pieces
1 cup orange juice
1/4 cup lemon juice
1/4 tsp garlic powder
1 tbsp parsley, chopped
salt and pepper, to taste
1/2 cup soya sauce

> ## Trivia Tidbits
> There are no clocks in Las Vegas gambling casinos.

Directions:

Put chicken in roasting pan and cover with orange and lemon juice. Add spices and bake at 350°F for 25 minutes. Baste. Add soya sauce and bake an additional 25 minutes. Serves 6.

Sweet and Sour Chicken

Denise Hibbs (nee Jenkins), Springdale, Newfoundland

Ingredients:

2 tbsp vegetable oil
4 skinless, boneless chicken breasts, cubed
1 cup carrot, grated
1/2 red pepper, cut in strips
1/2 green pepper, cut in strips
2 garlic cloves (or 1 tsp minced garlic)
1 cup pineapple chunks, drained (reserve juice)
2 tbsp water
3 tbsp white vinegar
2 tbsp soya sauce
1 tbsp brown sugar, firmly packed
1 tbsp cornstarch
1 tsp ground ginger (optional)
2 stems green onion (optional)

Trivia Tidbits
Women wrestlers are not allowed to perform in Gloversville, New York.

Spice of Life
Save a tree - eat a beaver.

Directions:

In large frying pan, heat oil; add chicken. Cook until lightly browned. Add carrots, peppers and garlic; cook, stirring frequently. In a small bowl, combine reserved pineapple juice, 2 tbsp water and remaining ingredients. Pour over chicken mixture and stir in pineapple chunks. Cook until just boiling. Serve on white rice.

Curry Chicken

Danessa Quinlan, Birchy Bay, Newfoundland

Ingredients:

2-3 lbs of chicken
1/3 cup vinegar
1/2 cup brown sugar
1 tsp salt
1 onion, chopped
1 tin tomato soup
3/4 cup diced celery
1 tbsp soya sauce
1 tbsp Worchestershire sauce
1 carrot, thinly sliced
1/2 cup water
1 apple, chopped and peeled

Food for Thought

No wind is favourable for the sailer who doesn't know in which direction he is going.

Directions:

Place chicken in roaster or casserole dish. Bake at 325°F until brown. Combine remaining ingredients. Pour over chicken; bake for 1 hour.

Margarita Chicken

Roberta Ferns, Williams Lake, British Columbia

Ingredients:

1/4 cup Tequila

3 tbsp margarita mix

2 tbsp cooking oil

1 jalapeno pepper, minced

1 tsp grated lime peel

1 tbsp honey

1 tsp salt

1 tsp dried oregano

1 large clove garlic, crushed

6 whole chicken legs, thighs attached

Directions:

Mix together all ingredients, except chicken. Pour into shallow glass baking dish. Add chicken, cover and refrigerate overnight. Place chicken on grill over hot coals. Grill 40 - 50 minutes, basting with marinade. Chicken may also be oven-broiled till tender. Serves 6.

Chicken Chili

Selina Statnyk, Leduc, Alberta

Ingredients:

2 tbsp oil

1 lb boneless chicken, cubed

2 cloves garlic, minced

1 onion, chopped

2 carrots, sliced

1 stalk celery, sliced

10 small mushrooms, sliced

1 tbsp chili powder

1 tsp oregano

1 tsp cumin

1/2 tsp paprika

1/4 tsp salt

dash of pepper

dash of Tabasco sauce

1 (19oz) can tomatoes, undrained

1 (19oz) can red kidney beans, undrained

Directions:

In large saucepan, heat oil over medium heat and brown garlic and chicken for 5 minutes or until chicken is firm. Add vegetables and cook an additional 5 minutes. Reduce heat to low and stir in seasonings. Cook, stirring often, for another 5 minutes. Stir in tomatoes and beans; bring to a boil, breaking up tomatoes. Cover and simmer for 15 minutes. Uncover and simmer for an additional 15 minutes. Serve with rice, tacos or tortillas. Garnish with sour cream, cheese and avocado. Makes 4 servings.

Food for Thought

There's no rest for the wicked, and no arrest for the wicked who are politically connected.

Trivia Tidbits

There are twenty-two more miles of canal in Birmingham, England, than in Venice, Italy.

Meat Dishes

Wild Game, Wild Fowl, Chicken, Turkey, Beef, Pork, Seal

Braised Chicken with Vegetables

Sharon L. Begin, Dundas, Ontario

Ingredients:

1/3 cup all-purpose flour
1 tsp salt
1/2 tsp paprika
1/8 tsp pepper
2 1/2 - 3 lb broiler fryer chicken, cut up
2 tbsp vegetable oil
1/4 cup water
2 medium carrots, cut in 1/4-inch slices
8 oz broccoli flowerets
1/2 small head cauliflower, separated into flowerets
1/2 tsp onion salt
1/2 tsp dried rosemary leaves
1/2 cup dairy sour cream

> *Food for Thought*
> The time to get primed for the future is when you're still in your prime.

Directions:

Mix flour, salt, paprika and pepper; coat chicken. Heat oil in skillet or Dutch oven; cook chicken over medium heat until brown, about 15 minutes. Drain fat if necessary. Add water and carrots; heat to boiling. Reduce heat, cover and simmer for 30 minutes. Add broccoli and cauliflower; sprinkle with onion salt and rosemary. Add small amount of water if necessary. Cover and simmer until thickest pieces of chicken are done and broccoli is tender-crisp, about 10 - 20 minutes. Remove chicken and vegetables to warm platter; keep warm. Stir sour cream into skillet; heat just until hot. Serve with chicken and vegetables. Yield 6 servings. *Note:* This recipe goes great with chicken-flavoured rice. Use chicken broth or Oxo instead of water while cooking rice. Also omit the salt.

Chicken Divan

Maria Young, St. Phillip's, Newfoundland (nee Hardy, Port aux Basques, Newfoundland)

Ingredients:

4 cups fresh broccoli spears, cooked
1 cup carrots, sliced (optional)
1 cup green or red pepper, sliced (optional)
1 1/2 cups chicken or turkey, cubed
1 can broccoli cheese soup
1/2 cup milk
1 tbsp butter, melted
2 tbsp dry bread crumbs

> `Trivia Tidbits`
> A newborn baby panda is smaller than a mouse.

Directions:

Place vegetables on bottom of a shallow dish. Cover with chicken. Combine milk and soup; pour over chicken. Combine butter and bread crumbs and sprinkle over top of mixture. Bake at 450°F for 10 minutes. Broil uncovered for 1 minute to brown.

Meat Dishes

Wild Game, Wild Fowl, Chicken, Turkey, Beef, Pork, Seal

Chicken Hurry

Melissa Clarke, Oshawa, Ontario

Ingredients:

2 1/2 - 3 lbs chicken parts
1/2 cup ketchup
1/4 cup water
1/2 cup brown sugar
1 envelope dry onion soup mix

Directions:

Arrange chicken parts in small roaster or casserole dish. In a small bowl, combine above ingredients; mix well. Spoon over chicken. Bake covered at 350°F for 1 hour or until tender.

> ***Food for Thought***
> The secret of happy living is not to do what you like, but to like what you do.

Oriental Chicken Drumsticks

Rosalind Fraser, Garson, Ontario

Ingredients:

12 drumsticks, skin removed
1/2 cup orange marmalade
1/4 cup Dijon mustard
2 tbsp soya sauce

Directions:

Preheat oven to 375°F. Line baking pan with foil; place drumsticks in pan. Combine remaining ingredients together and brush over chicken until coated. Bake for 20 minutes uncovered. Baste chicken; bake for 10 minutes. Baste chicken again and bake for another 10 minutes.

> **Trivia Tidbits**
> A litre of vinegar is heavier in winter than in summer.

Chicken Wings

Pat Blinn, Peterborough, Ontario

Ingredients:

2 - 2 1/2 lbs chicken wings
1 1/2 cups soya sauce
2 tbsp wine
2 tbsp lemon juice
3/4 tsp garlic salt
2 tbsp sugar
1/4 cup honey
3 drops Tabasco sauce, if desired

Directions:

Mix all ingredients together and marinate for 30 minutes. Place wings on top of rack over roasting pan. Bake at 350°F for 30 minutes. Turn over and bake for another 20 minutes or until done. Serve hot.

> **Spice of Life**
> The weaker sex is really the stronger sex because of the weakness of the stronger sex for the weaker sex.

Perfect Sweet and Sour Sauce, Chinese Style

Pat Jackman, Holland Landing, Ontario

Batter Ingredients:

1 cup white vinegar
1 cup white sugar
1/4 cup ketchup
cornstarch (for thickening)

> ## Food for Thought
> Not keeping an appointment is an act of clear dishonesty. You may as well borrow a person's money as his time.

Directions:

Bring first three ingredients to a boil; add more sugar if desired. Thicken with cornstarch. Ready to serve on chicken balls.

Easy Chicken Stew

Hilda Birkett, London, Ontario (formerly of Mutford's Cove, Newfoundland)

Ingredients:

3 boneless, skinless chicken breasts, cubed
2 cloves garlic, chopped
1 medium onion, chopped
butter, or oil
1 can cream of mushroom soup
1/2 to 1 can water

> ## Food for Thought
> If you don't have a sense of humour, you probably don't have any sense at all.

Directions:

Stir fry chicken, garlic and onion in a small amount of butter or oil until chicken is done. Add cream of mushroom soup and enough water to make a thick sauce. Season to taste. Serve over cooked rice or noodles.

Chicken Breast with Crabmeat Stuffing

Liz Bourne-Zahorodney, Blenheim, Ontario

Ingredients:

1/4 cup green pepper, chopped
1 small onion, chopped
2-3 stalks celery, chopped
2 tbsp butter
1 can crabmeat
1 cub herb seasoned stuffing mix
1 (10oz) can cream of mushroom soup
1/3 cup white wine
1 tbsp lemon juice
2 tsp Worchestershire sauce
1 tsp dry mustard
6 boneless chicken breasts

> ## Spice of Life
> Nature is a kind mother. She couldn't well afford to make us perfect, so she made us blind to our failings. - Josh Billings

Directions:

Saute green pepper, onion and celery in butter. Add crab, stuffing mix, 1/2 can soup, 2 tbsps white wine, lemon juice, mustard and Worchestershire sauce. Fill chicken breasts with stuffing

Meat Dishes

Wild Game, Wild Fowl, Chicken, Turkey, Beef, Pork, Seal

mixture and skewer chicken closed. Broil in oven or on a barbecue grill for 30 minutes, turning frequently. Combine the rest of the soup and wine and pour over chicken during last 10 minutes of grilling or broiling. Can also be dusted with flour and paprika and baked in oven at 350°F for 1 hour.

Southern Honey Chicken

Doreen Sooley, Perth-Andover, New Brunswick

Ingredients:

1 - 1 1/2 lbs chicken pieces
2 eggs yolks, slightly beaten
4 tsp soya sauce
4 tbsp lemon juice
1/2 cup honey
4 tbsp butter or margarine, melted

> ## Spice of Life
> Would it not be more economical for the governments to build asylums for the sane instead of the demented? *- Kahlil Gibran*

Directions:

Preheat oven to 325°F. Arrange drumsticks or pieces of chicken in a large square baking dish. Mix above ingredients in a large bowl; stir well. Pour over chicken, coating well. Cook for 1 hour, turning chicken often.

Foiled-Up Fowl

Carolyn Vatcher, Latabatiere, Quebec

Ingredients:

1 whole chicken, cut up
3 tbsp mustard
2 tbsp vinegar
1/4 cup water
1/2 cup brown sugar
1/2 cup ketchup
1 env onion soup mix
1 tsp salt

> ## Trivia Tidbits
> The game of chess originated in India over 1500 years ago.

Directions:

Preheat oven to 350°F. Place chicken in baking dish. Combine remaining ingredients and pour over chicken. Cover tightly with foil. Bake for 1 1/4 hours. Uncover and bake for additional 15 minutes. Serve with rice, noodles or french fries.

Sweet and Sour Chicken Wings

Joanne Wellon-Fillier, Kitchener, Ontario (formerly of Millertown, Newfoundland)

Ingredients:

2 lbs chicken wings
corn oil
1/2 cup vinegar
1/2 cup water
1/2 cup ketchup
1/2 cup sugar

1 tsp soya sauce
1 tbsp cornstarch
salt, to taste

Sauce Ingredients:
1 cup white vinegar
1 cup white sugar
1/4 cup ketchup
cornstarch

Directions:

Fry chicken wings in as little oil as possible until browned and tender. Remove from skillet and drain on paper towels. Heat vinegar, water, ketchup, sugar, salt and soya sauce in saucepan. Mix cornstarch with a small amount of water to make a paste. Stir into sauce. Cook and stir sauce until smooth, transparent and thickened. Serve hot or cold as dipping sauce for wings. Makes 12 appetizers.

Baked Herb Chicken

Lois Strickland, Owen Sound, Ontario

Ingredients:
1 three pound chicken, cut up
1 can mushroom soup
1 tsp lemon rind, grated
2 tsp lemon juice
1/2 tsp salt
1/4 tsp basil
1/4 tsp oregano

Directions:

Arrange chicken in a 9x13 baking dish. Combine remaining ingredients and pour over chicken. Bake, uncovered at 325°F for 1 1/4 hours. Serve with hot, cooked rice. Serves 6.

Chicken Wings

Barb Clarke, Oshawa, Ontario

Ingredients:
chicken wings
celery salt
paprika
salt and pepper
barbecue sauce or Diana's Gourmet Honey and Garlic sauce

Directions:

Sprinkle chicken wings with celery salt, paprika, salt and pepper; deep fry on high for 10 - 12 minutes. Dip wings in barbecue sauce. Shake off excess sauce and bake at 350°F for 15 minutes.

Meat Dishes

Wild Game, Wild Fowl, Chicken, Turkey, Beef, Pork, Seal

Chicken-A-La-'Mel'

Denise Maher (nee Wadden), St. John's, Newfoundland

Ingredients:

1/2 cup vinegar
1/2 cup brown sugar
1 apple, cut up
1 onion, diced
1 carrot, grated
1 cup celery
1 cup water
1/2 tsp salt
1 tsp soya sauce
1 tin tomato soup
chicken pieces

Food for Thought
It takes an honest person to admit if he's tired or just lazy.

Directions:

Mix together and add in chicken. Bake at 250°F for 2 hours. Serve with mashed potatoes or rice.

Chicken Rice Bake

Charlene Jenkins, Grand Falls-Windsor, Newfoundland (formerly of Springdale, Newfoundland)

Ingredients:

2 lbs skinless, boneless chicken breasts (fat removed)
1/2 tsp paprika
1/2 tsp celery salt
1/2 tsp garlic powder
2 cups boiling water
1 tbsp chicken bouillon powder (35% less salt)
1 cup long grain rice, uncooked
2 tbsp chopped pimiento
1/2 tsp parsley flakes

Trivia Tidbits
Rhubarb is a vegetable not a fruit. Tomato is a fruit not a vegetable.

Directions:

Spray frying pan with non-stick cooking spray. Mix paprika, celery salt and garlic powder; sprinkle chicken with mixture and brown both sides. Pour water into a 3-quart casserole dish; stir in bouillon powder. Stir in rice, pimiento and parsley. Lay chicken on top; cover and bake at 350°F for about 1 hour until rice is cooked, water is absorbed and chicken is tender. Fast and easy and low fat.

Chicken Cacciatore

Charlene Jenkins, Grand Falls-Windsor, Newfoundland (formerly of Springdale, Newfoundland)

Ingredients:

2 lbs skinless, boneless chicken breasts (fat removed)
1 1/4 cups onion, chopped
1 green pepper, chopped

1 cup fresh mushrooms, sliced
1 (14oz) can tomatoes, broken up
1/2 tsp salt
1/8 tsp pepper
1/4 tsp garlic powder
3 tbsp white wine

Directions:

Arrange chicken in a 2-quart casserole dish. Spray frying pan with non-stick cooking spray and add onion, green pepper and mushrooms. Saute until soft and add to chicken. Place remaining ingredients in frying pan. Stir to loosen any brown bits and pour over casserole. Cover and bake at 350°F for 1 1/2 hours or until chicken is tender. Garlic is light so you may want to add more to strengthen it.

Leg of Lamb

Austin Davis, formerly of Fortune Harbour/Grand Falls-Windsor, Newfoundland

Ingredients:

6 lbs leg of lamb
1 tsp salt
1/4 tsp black pepper
1/4 cup butter
2 cloves garlic
1 tsp rosemary
2 slices fresh ginger root
2 tbsp flour
1/2 tsp thyme

Directions:

Combine all ingredients and rub all over roast and let stand at room temperature for about an hour. Place in roaster and bake at 450°F for 30 minutes; reduce heat to 325°F and bake for another 30 minutes (rare) or additional 45 minutes (medium rare).

Leftovers Pot Pie

Janice Mercer, Portugal Cove, Newfoundland

Ingredients:

2 pie crusts (fresh or frozen)
left over turkey, beef etc.
left over vegetables
gravy
salt and pepper, to taste

Directions:

Place bottom crust in pie pan. Mix meat, vegetables and gravy together. Add salt and pepper; cover with top crust. Cut several slits in top crust. Bake as per instructions for pie crust. Serves 4 - 6. (Great for leftover turkey, roast, pork, moose, etc).

Meat Dishes

Wild Game, Wild Fowl, Chicken, Turkey, Beef, Pork, Seal

Swiss Steak

Donna Cheeseman, St. John's, Newfoundland

Ingredients:

1/2 cup flour
1 tbsp dry mustard
1 tsp brown sugar
1 1/2 lbs round steak
2 tbsp Worcestershire sauce
2 tbsp fat
1 (26oz) can tomatoes
1 cup onion, chopped
1/2 cup celery, chopped
2 - 3 carrots, diced
salt and pepper, to taste

Trivia Tidbits
A rat can last longer than a camel without water.

Directions:

Pound dry ingredients into steak with potato masher. Then brown both sides in hot fat. Place meat in bottom of dutch oven or roaster. Remainder of dry ingredients can be sprinkled on top if desired. Add rest of ingredients; cover and bake at 350°F for 1 1/2 hours or simmer on top of stove for 3 hours.

Meat Loaf

Desiree Sheppard, Manuels, CBS, Newfoundland

Ingredients:

1 (10oz) can tomato soup
2 lbs ground beef
1/2 cup fine bread crumbs
1/2 cup onion, chopped
2 tbsp parsley
1 tbsp Worcestershire sauce
1 egg, slightly beaten
1 tsp salt
dash of pepper

Food for Thought
Kindness consists of loving people more than they deserve.
- Joseph Joubert

Directions:

Combine all ingredients, mix well. Shape into loaf; place in shallow baking pan. Bake at 350°F for 1 1/2 hours. *Note:* Cream of celery, mushroom or vegetable soup may be substituted for tomato soup.

Peppered Steak

Rosemarie Reynar, North York, Ontario (nee Stratton, Lewisporte, Newfoundland)

Ingredients:

1 - 1 1/2 lbs steak
1 cup celery, chopped
1 large tin tomatoes

1 medium onion, chopped
1 tin consomme
2 green peppers, cut in strips
1 tsp salt
1/2 tsp garlic powder
2 tbsp soya sauce
2 tbsp cornstarch

Trivia Tidbits
Cats cannot taste sweet
foods.

Directions:

Cut steak into thin strips. Pan fry in oil for 5 -10 minutes, browning lightly on both sides. In baking dish, combine rest of ingredients, except cornstarch. Add steak strips. Mix cornstarch with 1/4 cup water and pour over ingredients. Cook covered for 1 1/2 hours at 325°F. When cooked, add 1 tin mushrooms if desired. Serve over cooked rice.

Steak In Sauce

Janice Mercer, Portugal Cove, Newfoundland

Ingredients:

1 large steak, cubed
1 lg onion, diced
1 tbsp oil
3 tbsp flour
1 cup water
1/2 medium green pepper, diced
1 can mushrooms with juice
1/2 cup ketchup
1 sm tin tomato sauce
1 lg tin tomatoes
3 tsp soya sauce
1 tsp garlic powder
salt and pepper, to taste

Food for Thought
Happiness is like jam - you can't spread even a little without getting some on yourself.

Directions:

In large frying pan, brown steak and onion in oil. Add flour to brown; then add water to thicken. Add remaining ingredients and simmer over low heat for 1 hour. Great over rice.

Hawaiian Spareribs

Maisie Moyles, Carmanville South, Newfoundland

Ingredients:

1 14-16oz can pineapple chunks
1/4 cup honey
1/4 cup white vinegar
1 tsp salt
1 tsp Worcestershire sauce
1/4 tsp ground ginger
5 lbs pork back ribs, cut into single rib portions

Spice of Life
If absolute power corrupts absolutely, does absolute powerlessness make you pure?
- Harry Shearer

Directions:

Drain pineapple juice into shallow roasting pan. Stir in honey, vinegar, salt, Worchestershire sauce and ginger (reserve pineapple). Add ribs, stirring to coat ribs. Cover pan tightly with foil. Bake in 325°F oven for 2 hours or until tender. During last 10 minutes, add reserved pineapple chunks. Arrange ribs and pineapple on warm platter and serve.

Chinese Green Pepper Steak

Joan Brown, St. John's, Newfoundland (nee Kelly, formerly of Trinity, Trinity Bay, Newfoundland)

Ingredients:

1 tbsp soya sauce

1 clove garlic

1/4 cup salad oil

1 lb steak, cubed or in strips

1 green pepper, chopped

1 lg onion, chopped

1/2 cup celery, chopped

1 tsp cornstarch

1/4 cup water

2 tomatoes peeled and cubed (canned tomatoes may be used)

1 can mushrooms, optional

> **Spice of Life**
> If at first you do succeed
> ...quit. Don't spoil a
> perfect record.

Directions:

Mix soya sauce, salad oil and garlic; pour over meat and marinate for 1 hour. Brown marinated meat well on all sides; add green pepper, onion and celery. Cover and cook for 5-10 minutes. Stir in cornstarch, dissolved in water. Cook until thickened. Add tomatoes and mushrooms; cover and cook for 5 minutes. Vegetables should still be firm and crunchy. Serve over hot rice. Serves 4.

Quick Hamburger Supper

Wendy Warren, North West Brook, Newfoundland

Ingredients:

1-2 lbs hamburger meat

1 onion

1 tin mushrooms

1/4 cup soya sauce

3/4 cup water

2-3 tbsp cornstarch

> **Trivia Tidbits**
> Gale warnings were first
> issued in 1861.

Directions:

Fry hamburger meat until brown; drain grease. Add onion and mushrooms and cook until onion is transparent. Mix soya sauce, water and corn starch and pour over hamburger meat to thicken. Serve over rice.

Beef Stroganoff Sandwiches

Doreen Halfrey, Framingham, Massachusetts (nee Young, Black Duck Brook, Newfoundland)

Ingredients:

2 lbs ground beef

1/2 cup onion, chopped
1 tsp salt
1/2 tsp pepper
1/2 tsp garlic powder
1 loaf French bread
butter or margarine, softened
2 cups sour cream
2 tomatoes, seeded and chopped
1 lg green pepper, diced
3 cups cheddar cheese, shredded

> ### Spice of Life
> When poverty comes in the door, love flies out the window and when pa comes in the door, ma's boyfriend flies out the window.

Directions:

In skillet, brown ground beef and onion; drain. Add salt, garlic powder and pepper. Cut bread in half lengthwise. Butter both halves and place on baking sheet. Remove meat mixture from the heat; stir in sour cream. Spoon onto the bread. Sprinkle with tomatoes, green pepper and cheese. Bake at 350°F for 20 minutes or until cheese is melted.

Pepper Steak

Grace Ryan, Newman's Cove, Bonavista Bay, Newfoundland

Ingredients:

2 lb round steak, cut in 1/2-inch strips
3 tbsp oil
1 medium onion, diced
1/4 cup soya sauce
1/4 cup sugar
1 tsp salt and pepper
2 green peppers, cut in strips
1 lg tin stewed tomatoes
1/4 cup water
1 tin mushrooms, drained
1 tbsp cornstarch

> ### Food for Thought
> Religion is what keeps the poor from murdering the rich.
> - Napoleon Bonaparte

Directions:

Brown strips of round steak in oil. Add onion, soya sauce, sugar and seasonings. Add green peppers, tomatoes, mushrooms and water. Cook for 15 minutes. Mix cornstarch with water and add to mixture; cooking for 5 minutes. May be served with rice or mashed potatoes.

Feed-Da-Bunch Chili

Dorothy Wyatt, City Councillor, St. John's, Newfoundland

Ingredients:

2 lb ground beef
2 onions (chopped)
2 (14oz) tins red kidney beans
1 tin tomato paste

> ### Spice of Life
> Poverty is no sin ...it's worse!

Wild Game, Wild Fowl, Chicken, Turkey, Beef, Pork, Seal

Meat Dishes

1 tin tomato sauce
1 tin tomato soup
1 tin tomatoes
1 green pepper
1 can mushrooms, bits and pieces
2-3 celery stalks
chili powder
salt and pepper, to taste

Directions: (Newfie Style)

Ya flings the meat in da frying pan wit oil and ya browns it. Da onions have got to be cut up right proper like and ya flings them in too, so dey gets softened up. Don't answer the phone because dis stuff will burn. Drain off the fat an' give it to the cat, soaked in chunks of bread. Don't tell the vet. Oh me nerves, dear God, I almost forgot. Ya flings in da red kidney beans. Ya simmers all dat stuff for a while an' don't answer da phone 'cause ya could spile it. Now, this is crucial: Fling in da tomato paste, tomato sauce, tomato soup and can of tomatoes. Pause for a moment. It will turn out all right. Encourage yourself! Go for da green pepper an' gut out da inside. Ya slashes dat an' cuts hit up right proper before plunging it into the proposed gourmet concoction. Ya flings in yer bits an' pieces of mushroom stuff bought on sale. Ye cleans yer celery an' cuts it up right proper like. Fling in chili powder, a bit of salt an' pepper an' simmer da works for a while. Don't answer the phone because you could blow it. Den wen yer sick an' tired of looking at it simmering, get yourself a big bowlful and stick da rest in the freezer fer da times wen company comes. Now, go answer da phone and you won't need no beano or tums me ducky, 'cause tis some perfect.

Sloppy Joes

Natalie Ryan, Newman's Cove, Newfoundland

Ingredients:

1 lb ground beef
1 onion
1 tsp chili powder
1/2 tsp salt
1 tsp Worchestershire sauce
2 tbsp brown sugar
1 (8oz) can tomato sauce
2 tbsp vinegar

Directions:

Partially brown beef; add onion. Reduce heat to low and season beef with chili powder, Worchestershire sauce and brown sugar. Add tomato paste and vinegar. Cook until most of the liquid has evaporated - about 5 minutes. Serve between hamburger buns.

Meat Loaf

Marilyn Pumphrey, St. John's, Newfoundland

Ingredients:

1/2 cup celery, finely chopped
1/2 cup onions, finely diced
margarine as needed

1 lb minced ground steak
1 tsp salt
1/4 tsp pepper
1 cup finely rolled crackers
1 tin mushroom soup
1 egg

Directions:

Soften celery and onion in margarine in frying pan. Add meat, salt and pepper. Stir and brown meat a little. Remove from stove and mix with crackers, soup and egg. Put in loaf pan and set loaf in roaster with 2 inches of water in roaster. Cook at 375°F for 50 minutes.

Pepper Steak with Rice

Ron Pumphrey, St. John's, Newfoundland

Ingredients:

3 cups hot cooked rice
1 lb lean beef round steak (1/2-inch thick)
1 tbsp paprika
2 cloves garlic, crushed
1 1/2 cups beef broth
1 cup green onions, sliced (including tops)
2 green peppers, cut in strips
2 tbsp cornstarch
1/4 cup water
1/4 cup soya sauce
2 large fresh tomatoes, cut in eights

Directions:

While rice is cooking, pound steak to 1/4-inch thickness, cut into 1/4-inch wide strips. Sprinkle meat with paprika and allow to stand while preparing other ingredients. In large skillet, brown meat in butter; add garlic and broth. Cover and simmer for 30 minutes. Stir in onion and green peppers. Cover and cook for 5 minutes more. Blend cornstarch, water and soya sauce in small bowl; stir into meat mixture. Cook, stirring until clear and thickened, about 2 minutes. Add tomatoes and stir gently. Pour over bed of fluffy rice. Makes 6 servings.

Beef Stroganoff

Siobhan Coady (formerly of Grand Falls-Windsor, Newfoundland)

Ingredients:

1 cup butter or margarine
1 1/2 cups onions, finely chopped
1 1/2 lbs fresh mushrooms, sliced (or 2-3 cans mushroom pieces, drained)
3-5 lbs beef, top round, cut 1/4 x 1/4 x 2 inch strips
6 tbsp flour
3 cups canned beef consomme
1 1/2 tsp salt
6 tbsp tomato paste
2 tsp Worchestershire sauce

1 1/2 cups sour cream
1 1/2 cups heavy cream

Directions:

Melt 1/3 cup of butter or margarine in large saucepan. Add onions and saute until golden; remove and set aside. Melt another 1/3 cup butter; add mushrooms and saute until lightly browned. Remove and set aside. Melt remaining 1/3 cup butter and add beef, which has been rolled in flour. Brown the beef thoroughly. Add onions, beef consomme, salt and tomato paste. Bring to a simmer, cover pan and allow meat to simmer for a least 2 hours. Add mushrooms and Worchestershire sauce; remove from heat. Add sour cream and heavy cream, mixing thoroughly. Nice when served over egg noodles or green salad. Serves 6-12.

Kibbee

Austin Davis (formerly of Fortune Harbour/Grand Falls-Windsor, Newfoundland)

Ingredients:

3 lbs top round steak
2 lg onions
1 1/2 cups of #10 Bulger (fine) wheat
salt and pepper, to taste
olive oil

Food for Thought
The man with a new idea is a crank until the idea succeeds. - Mark Twain

Directions:

Steak must be minced thoroughly by butcher. (At least three times through mincer). Onions must be chopped and beaten to a pulp. Wheat is soaked in cold water until soft, then squeezed dry. Mix all ingredients together, adding salt and pepper to taste. Wheat is added slowly. Pound the mixture with wooden mallet for thorough mixing. Form into light patties and fry in light olive oil. Small quantity can be consumed raw with dry biscuit or with pita bread and raw onion.

Barbequed Spareribs

Beulah Cooper, Gander, Newfoundland

Ingredients:

2 pkgs spareribs
1/2 cup brown sugar
3/4 cup vinegar
1 cup ketchup
1 tsp Worchestershire sauce
1 onion, chopped
salt and pepper, to taste

Spice of Life
It isn't whether you win or lose - it's how you place the blame.

Directions:

Place ribs in pan. Sprinkle with salt and pepper. Bake at 225°F for 2 hours. Mix together sugar, vinegar, ketchup, Worchestershire sauce and onions. Spread over ribs; bake at 375°F for 1 hour.

Sweet Mince Meat

Kelly Roach, St. John's, Newfoundland

Ingredients:

6 cups raisins
6 cups currants
2 oranges, grated
2 lemons, grated
2 cups mixed peel
2 tbsp ginger
6 cups brown sugar
2 cups dark molasses
2 cups shredded suet
4 cups apple, sliced
2 tbsp salt

Directions:

Combine raisins, currants and molasses. Boil for 15 minutes. Add a little water if necessary. Blend in grated oranges, grated lemon, mixed peel and ginger. Add brown sugar, molasses and suet. Continue to simmer. Add apple slices and salt, continue to simmer for 45 minutes, stirring occasionally to keep from sticking. Cool slightly and jar.

Spice of Life
Kissing is a bad practice; but practice makes perfect.

Sweet and Sour Spareribs

Frances Pelley, Edmonton, Alberta (formerly of Deer Lake, Newfoundland)

Ingredients:

1/2 cup vinegar
1 cup brown sugar
1 can consomme soup
2-3 tbsp cornstarch
2-3 tsp soya sauce
1 rack of ribs

Directions:

Bring vinegar, brown sugar and soup to a boil. Add cornstarch and soya sauce. Boil all together. Partially cook ribs in roaster. Drain off excess water. Add sweet and sour sauce to ribs. Cook for another 1/2 hour. *Note:* Sauce also tastes great on chicken and meat balls.

Trivia Tidbits
Valium is the most used drug on earth.

Moray Pie

Trudy Gushue, Bacon Cove, Newfoundland

Ingredients:

1 lb minced steak
2 oz butter
3 small carrots, grated
3 small onions, chopped
1/2 pt beef stock or water
salt and pepper, to taste
1 lb potatoes
parsley, to garnish

Food for Thought
Don't curse the darkness, light a candle.
- Chinese Proverb

Meat Dishes

Wild Game, Wild Fowl, Chicken, Turkey, Beef, Pork, Seal

Directions:

Fry beef in butter until brown; add carrots and onions. Fry gently for another 2 minutes. Add stock and seasonings; simmer for 30 minutes. Parboil potatoes, cut into slices about 1/4-inch thick. Put meat mixture into pie dish, top with potatoes, brush with melted butter and brown under grill. Garnish with parsley. Serves 4.

Minced Collops

Trudy Gushue, Bacon Cove, Newfoundland

Ingredients:

1 oz drippings
1 large onion, finely chopped
1 lb minced steak
1 cup beef stock
salt and pepper, to taste
1/2 cup breadcrumbs (or oatmeal)

Directions:

Melt drippings in pan and add onion; cook for a couple of minutes, then add minced steak. Brown steak, beating it well with fork to keep lump free. Add stock, and salt and pepper to taste. Simmer for 1 hour; then add bread crumbs (or for variation, use oatmeal). Cook for a few minutes more. Serve with mashed potatoes and buttered carrots. Serves 4.

Newfoundland Pork Cakes

Herb Greening, Botwood, Newfoundland

Ingredients:

1 cup minced salt pork
6 potatoes
2 cups flour
2 tsp baking powder

Directions:

Cook potatoes and mash well. Add salt pork and mix well. Add flour mixed with baking powder. Form into patties and bake at 400°F for 1/2 hour or until brown.

Spanish Noodles

Josephine Jenkins, Springdale, Newfoundland (nee Young, Twillingate, Newfoundland)

Ingredients:

4 slices bacon
1 onion, chopped
1 green pepper, diced
1 lb ground beef
salt and pepper, to taste
1 can tomatoes
1/4 cup chili sauce
1 cup egg noodles

Directions:

Fry bacon, remove from pan. Brown onion and green pepper until tender; brown meat. Season with salt and pepper. Add tomatoes and chili sauce; bring to a boil. Cook egg noodles and place on top of meat mixture. Cover and simmer for about 20 minutes. Crumble bacon and sprinkle over top.

Sloppy Joes

Josephine Jenkins, Springdale, Newfoundland (nee Young, Twillingate, Newfoundland)

Ingredients:

1 1/2-2 lbs ground beef
2 onions, diced
1 green pepper, diced
2 tsp salt
1 tsp garlic
1 tsp barbecue spice
1 large tin tomatoes
3 stalks celery, chopped
1 tin mushrooms
1 tsp pepper
1 tsp Italian seasoning
1 bay leaf

Trivia Tidbits

The albatross can fly all day without once flapping its wings

Directions:

Brown meat and onion. Add all other ingredients and simmer for 1 hour. Serve over hamburger buns.

Italian Spaghetti

Josephine Jenkins, Springdale, Newfoundland (nee Young, Twillingate, Newfoundland)

Ingredients:

1 lb ground beef
1 onion
1 green pepper
1 tin mushrooms
1 tin tomato soup
1 (5 1/2oz) tin tomato paste
1 (14oz) tin tomato sauce
1 (14oz) tin meat sauce
1 bottle chili sauce

Food for Thought
Behave toward everyone as if receiving a great gift.
– Confucius

Directions:

Brown meat and onion in frying pan. Add green pepper and mushrooms and set aside. Mix remaining ingredients in pot, then add meat mixture and simmer for 1 hour on low heat.

Meatloaf with Sauce

Marie Quinlan, Birchy Bay, Newfoundland

Ingredients:

1 lb ground beef
2 onions, chopped
2 eggs
1 cup bread crumbs
1/2 cup milk
salt and pepper, to taste

Sauce Ingredients:

1 onion, chopped
1 cup ketchup
1 tbsp vinegar
1 tsp mustard
2 tsp sugar
2 tbsp lemon juice
1 cup water
1/2 tsp Worchestershire sauce

Directions:

Mix hamburger meat, onions, eggs, crumbs, milk, salt and pepper. Place in a bread pan. Bake at 375°F for 20 minutes. For sauce, brown onion in butter. Add remaining ingredients; boil for 10 minutes. Pour sauce over meat loaf and continue baking at 375°F for 30 minutes.

Sweet and Sour Meat Balls

Josephine Jenkins, Springdale, Newfoundland (nee Young, Twillingate, Newfoundland)

Ingredients:

1 lb ground beef
3/4 cup rolled oats
1 egg
1/2 cup milk
1 onion
salt and pepper, to taste
Sauce:
3/4 cup brown sugar
1 cup ketchup
1/4 cup vinegar
1/2 cup water
1 tbsp cornstarch

Directions:

Mix meatball ingredients together, roll in balls and bake at 350°F for 30 minutes. Mix sauce ingredients and bring to a boil. Pour sauce over meatballs when ready to serve.

Spice of Life

Poverty is no sin ... but it might as well be.
- Kin Hubbard

Trivia Tidbits

In 1386, a pig was publicly hanged for killing a child.

Spice of Life

The best investment is land, because they ain't making any more of it.
- Will Rogers

Awesome Hamburgers

Selina Statnyk, Leduc, Alberta

<u>Ingredients</u>:

1 lb lean hamburger meat
1/2 cup bread crumbs
1/4 cup parmesan cheese
1 pkg onion soup mix
1 egg
1 tbsp Worchestershire sauce
1 shake Tabasco sauce
steak sauce
garlic salt
salt and pepper
parsley

<u>Directions</u>:

Mix all ingredients together and you're ready to barbecue!!

Sweet and Sour Meatballs

Pat Blinn, Peterboro, Ontario

<u>Ingredients</u>:

1 lb lean ground beef
1 egg
1 tsp onion soup mix
1 tin spaghetti sauce
1 can pineapple chunks, undrained
2 tbsp soya sauce
2 beef bouillions dissolved in 1 cup hot water
1 bay leaf
squirt of lemon juice
1/2 cup brown sugar
dash of garlic
1/2 cup white garlic

<u>Directions</u>:

Make meat balls by adding egg and soup mix to ground beef, forming into balls. Bake at 350°F for 30 minutes. Combine remaining ingredients in a medium saucepan; bring to a boil. Place meat balls in a casserole dish, covering with mixture. Continue baking at 350°F for additional 30 minutes until done.

Chinese Hamburger

Marion Scheers, Edmonton, Alberta

<u>Ingredients</u>:

1 1/2 lbs hamburger meat
1 cup celery

Spice of Life

Poverty is no sin ... as any rich man will tell you.

Trivia Tidbits

The first thermometers were so large that they took five minutes to tell a person's body temperature.

Food for Thought

The best way out of difficulty is through it.

Wild Game, Wild Fowl, Chicken, Turkey, Beef, Pork, Seal

Meat Dishes

1 cup onion, chopped
3/4 cup Minute Rice
1 1/2 cups water
1 can cream of celery soup
1 can cream of mushroom soup
1 can chop suey vegetables
noodles

Trivia Tidbits

The poison cyanide can be produced from plum stones and apple pips.

Directions:

Brown hamburger meat and drain off grease. Combine with rest of ingredients in casserole. Cook for 2 hours. Serve with noodles on top.

Veal with Tomato Sauce

Sharon L. Begin, Dundas, Ontario

Ingredients:

6 veal cutlets (about 4 oz each)
1/4 cup vegetable oil
2 cloves garlic, crushed
1 cup onion, thinly sliced
1 tin sliced mushrooms, drained
2 tbsp flour
1 tsp salt
1/4 tsp pepper
1 (8oz) can tomato sauce
2/3 cup water

Food for Thought

Men do not trip on mountains - they trip on molehills.
- Chinese proverb

Directions:

Pound veal to 1/4-inch thickness. Heat oil and garlic in a 12-inch skillet over medium-high heat. Brown veal quickly, about 5 minutes. Remove veal from skillet and reduce heat to medium. Add onion and mushrooms; cook and stir until onion is tender. Stir in flour, salt and pepper; pour in tomato sauce and water. Heat to boiling, stirring constantly. Boil and stir for 1 minute. Return veal to skillet; cover tightly and simmer until tender, about 30 minutes. Yields 6 servings.

Mexican Pork Chops

Claudine Barnes, Corner Brook, Newfoundland (nee Pye, Cape Charles, Labrador)

Ingredients:

4 pork chops
1 tsp salt
1/8 tsp pepper
1 green pepper, cut in 4 rings
4 tbsp instant rice, uncooked
1 can stewed tomatoes

Spice of Life

The best way to keep your word is not to give it. - Napoleon Bonaparte

Directions:

Brown pork chops, season with salt and pepper. Top each chop with pepper ring and fill each pepper ring with rice. Pour 1/4 cup stewed tomatoes on rice. Pour remaining tomatoes in baking dish. Cover tightly. Bake at 350°F about 1 - 1 1/2 hours.

Seafoods

Swimmers

Crawlers

&

Creepers

Fish Chowder

Donna Ivey, Manuels, CBS, Newfoundland

Ingredients:

2 tbsp butter
1 medium onion, chopped
2 cups boiling water
3 medium potatoes, sliced
2 medium carrots, sliced
2 lbs cod
2 cups milk
salt and pepper, to taste

> ## *Food for Thought*
> A man's worst enemies can't wish on him what he can think up himself.
> - Yiddish proverb

Directions:

Melt butter and cook onion until transparent. Add boiling water, potatoes and carrots. Let cook 15 minutes or until tender. Add fish cut into pieces and cook for 15 minutes more. Add milk and simmer. DO NOT BOIL. Salt and pepper, to taste

Shrimp and Scallop Linguini

Carole Ann Pye-Cooper, Denmark, Maine (father from Corner Brook area)

Ingredients:

1 lb linguini
4 tbsp olive oil
garlic (whole)
1 lb small scallops
1 lb large shrimp
1 can of small clams
cloves (to taste)
parmesan cheese (to taste)

> ## Spice of Life
> Never put off until tomorrow what you can manage to wriggle out of today. - Doug Larson

Directions:

Cook linguini aprox 6 mins and put aside. In large fry pan or wok add olive oil and gently brown garlic and remove. Put in scallops and shrimp and gently cook until shrimp turns pink (aprox. 6 mins). Add clams and return garlic along with cloves; add linguini and toss with parmesan cheese; serve immediately. Serve with garlic bread or italian bread dipped in olive oil. This healthy meal contains only good fat from seafood and olive oil. Serves up to six.

Dressed Cod Fillets

Winnie Marshall, Stephenville, Newfoundland

Ingredients:

1 lb cod fillets
1 1/2 cups bread crumbs
1 tsp savoury
2 tsp onion, minced
2 tbsp butter
1 egg, beaten
salt and pepper, to taste
flour (as required)

> ## Trivia Tidbits
> In New Orleans, every corpse is buried in a mausoleum because the ground is too damp for normal burial.

Sauce:

2 tbsp shortening

2 tbsp flour

1/2 tsp salt

1/2 tsp savoury

2 1/2 cups milk

3/4 cup tomatoes

1/2 cup bread crumbs

2 tbsp cheese, grated

Food for Thought

After God created the world, He made man and woman. Then to keep the whole thing from collapsing, He invented humour.
- Guillermo Mordillo

Directions:

Mix together bread crumbs, savoury, onion, salt and pepper. Rub in butter and add beaten egg. Place a thin layer of dressing on each fillet. Roll up like jelly roll and secure with a toothpick. Coat fillets with flour and brown in hot fat. Arrange browned fish rolls in a 1 1/2 qt casserole. To make sauce, melt shortening; blend in flour, salt and savoury. Add milk and cook until thickened. Pour sauce over fish rolls. Add tomatoes. Bake at 350°F for 30 minutes. Sprinkle with 1/2 cup bread crumbs and grated cheese. Return to oven and bake another 10 minutes.

Salmon Casserole

Todd Broomfield, Makkovik, Labrador

Ingredients:

3-4 lbs salmon fillets

6 potatoes

1 can cream of chicken or mushoom soup

1 medium onion, chopped

cheddar cheese

salt and pepper, to taste

Spice of Life

The one thing your friends will never forgive you for is your happiness. - Albert Camus

Directions:

Remove skin from salmon fillets and boil with potatoes for 10-15 minutes. Drain water and mash potatoes and salmon. Add soup, onion, salt and pepper. Mix together and put in casserole dish. Top with grated cheese and bake at 300°F for 30 minutes. (This recipe also works well with char and cod fillets).

Salmon Fondue

Trudy Ivey, Mount Pearl, Newfoundland

Ingredients:

5 slices bread

1 cup milk

2 tbsp butter

1 cup canned salmon

3 eggs, separated

salt

1/4 cup cheese, grated

Trivia Tidbits

The Vinegar River in Columbia contains so much acid that no fish can live there.

Directions:

Trim crusts from bread and cut in 1/2-inch cubes. Heat milk in upper part of double boiler. Add bread cubes, butter, liquid from salmon, and well-beaten egg yolks. Season with salt and cook until thickened, stirring constantly. Remove from heat and stir in cheese. Cool for 10 - 15 minutes. Add flaked salmon. Beat egg whites until stiff and fold into the fondue mixture. Pour into a well-greased baking dish, set dish in a shallow pan of hot water and bake at 375°F for 1 hour or until knife comes out clean when inserted.

Fresh Codfish Dressed
Herb Greening, Botwood, Newfoundland

Ingredients:

1 medium codfish

1 tsp salt

1 tsp pepper

3 cups bread crumbs

2 oz fat back pork, chopped fine

1 medium onion, chopped

Trivia Tidbits
St. John's, Newfoundland is closer to London, England than it is to Vancouver, British Columbia.

Directions:

Clean and skin codfish. Keep in shape. Sprinkle with salt and pepper. Mix together all dry ingredients and onion, fill fish and pin together with skewers. Cover fish with pieces of pork. Place in oven and bake for 1 - 1 1/2 hrs at 325°F.

Pan Fried Scallops
Marjorie Hoskins, Boswarlos, Newfoundland

Ingredients:

1/2 cup salt pork, cubed

1 lb scallops

1/3 cup flour

1/2 tsp salt

4 tbsp olive oil

4 tbsp olive oil

Spice of Life
There isn't much to talk about at some parties until after one or two couples leave.

Directions:

Render out salt pork; roll scallops in flour and salt and fry until golden brown.

Lobster Salad
Marjorie Hoskins, Boswarlos, Newfoundland

Ingredients:

2 cups lobster meat

1/2 cup onion, chopped

1/3 cup salad dressing

1 stalk celery, chopped

Food for Thought
A house is a home when it shelters the body and comforts the soul.
- Phillip Moffitt

Directions:

Mix all ingredients together; serve on lettuce with potato salad.

Crab au Gratin
Daphne Parr, St. Lunaire, Newfoundland

Ingredients:

4 tbsp butter or margarine

2 tbsp flour

1 tsp salt

1/2 tbsp pepper

2 cups milk

2 1/2 cups cooked crab

1 cup cheese, grated

Food for Thought
Learning to have and wisdom to lack
Is a load of books on an ass's back.
- Japanese proverb

Directions:

Melt butter; add flour, salt and pepper. Stir to make a paste. Add milk and cook until thick, stirring constantly. Grease casserole dish. Pour sauce over bottom, then layer crab, sauce and cheese; repeat. Sprinkle cheese on top and bake at 350°F until brown.

"Premier" Baked Fish Stew
Premier Brian Tobin, St. John's, Newfoundland

Ingredients:

1 lb haddock, cod or sole fillets, (fresh or frozen)

4 medium potatoes, peeled and quartered

4 medium carrots, scraped and cut in 2-inch pieces

1 tbsp lemon juice

1 tbsp margarine

1 1/2 tsp salt

1/4 tsp pepper

1/2 cup partially skimmed mozzarella cheese, shredded

1 - 2 tbsp chopped parsley

Spice of Life
People who live in glass houses ... should take hot baths and steam up the windows.

Directions:

Preheat oven to 375°F. Slightly grease a 13x9 baking dish. Cut fish in 2-inch square pieces and place in dish; sprinkle with lemon juice. Place carrots and potatoes between pieces, and place dabs of margarine and pieces of potato over fish. Season with salt and pepper. Sprinkle cheese over top; cover and bake for 1 hour. Serve garnished with chopped parsley. Serves 4.

Fish-in-a-Dish
Grace Ryan, Newman's Cove, Bonavista Bay, Newfoundland

Ingredients:

1 lb fresh or frozen fish fillet

1 onion, sliced

1 cup cheese, grated

Trivia Tidbits
In Greece, milk is often sold frozen on a stick to make it easier to carry.

2 cups carrots, thinly sliced
4 potatoes, thinly sliced
2 tsp margarine
4 tsp lemon juice
1/4 tsp dried parsley
1/4 tsp salt and pepper

Directions:

Cut fish in four equal servings. Lightly grease a 2.8 litre casserole dish; place fish in the centre of casserole dish. Spread onion evenly over the fish and cover with cheese; then add layer of vegetables. Dot margarine over vegetables. Sprinkle with lemon juice, parsley, salt and pepper. Cover casserole; bake at 400°F for 40 - 45 minutes or until fish is cooked and potatoes are tender.

Mussel Pie

Mary Grandy, Grand Bank, Newfoundland

Ingredients:
1 cup flour
1/2 tsp salt
1/3 cup margarine
3 - 4 tbsp cold water

Filling Ingredients:
1/2 cup margarine
5 tbsp flour
salt and pepper, to taste
2 tsp nutmeg
1 can mushroom soup
1 can mussels
1 cup milk

> ## Trivia Tidbits
> Micro-organisms have been dug out of Antarctic ice, and are still alive after half a million years.

Directions:

Combine flour and salt, cut in margarine until mixture resembles coarse meal; stir in water; pat in pie dish. For the filling, mix together margarine, flour, salt, pepper and nutmeg. Once mixed, add rest of ingredients in a medium saucepan. Cook and stir until mixture comes to a boil. Pour into a pie shell. Bake at 375°F for 20 - 25 minutes.

Crispy Baked Fillets

Jeanette Osmond, Grand Bank, Fortune Bay, Newfoundland

Ingredients:
1 lb cod fillets
1/2 cup milk
1/2 tsp salt
2 tsp lemon juice
1/2 cup Corn Flake crumbs
1 tbsp butter

> ## Food for Thought
> It is what we think we know already that often prevents us from learning. - Claude Bernard

Directions:

Combine milk, salt and lemon juice. Dip fillets in mixture, then coat with crumbs. Place in greased baking dish and dot with butter. Bake at 450°F until cooked.

Fillet Bubbly Bake

Beulah Cooper, Gander, Newfoundland

Ingredients:

1 lb cod fillet, frozen
1 can mushroom soup
2 tbsp onion, chopped
1 tbsp lemon juice
1/2 cup cheese, grated

> ## Food for Thought
> Nearly all men can stand adversity, but if you want to test a man's character, give him power. - Abraham Lincoln

Directions:

Partially thaw fillet, cut into 3-4 equal portions. Place in greased shallow pan. Combine soup, onion and lemon juice. Spoon over fillets. Top with grated cheese. Bake at 450°F for about 30 minutes.

Portuguese Salt Fish Casserole

Dave Gilbert, St. John's, Newfoundland

Ingredients:

2 lbs salt cold fish
6 to 8 potatoes
1 cup olive oil
4 onions
3/4 cup mushrooms
garlic to taste
1/2 cup black olives
4 eggs, hard-boiled and sliced

> ## Trivia Tidbits
> Man only uses about four per cent of the plants that grow on Earth.

Directions:

Boil salt fish, debone and flake. Peel and boil potatoes, making certain not to overboil, keeping them firm. Peel and slice onions. Heat olive oil in large frying pan and saute onions, mushrooms and garlic. Grease a large casserole dish. Layer sliced boiled potatoes, add layer of flaked fish and layer of onions and mushrooms. Continue until all potatoes, fish and onions have been used. Top with black olives and sliced eggs. Bake at 375°F for 25 - 30 minutes.

Ravigote Lobster

Denis Murphy, Gull Island, Newfoundland

Ingredients:

2 lbs lobster
1 potato
1 artichoke heart
1 small shallot, diced
4 cups olive oil
1/2 cup gherkin pickles

> ## Spice of Life
> Good girls go to heaven; bad girls go everywhere.
> - Helen Gurley Brown

2 tsp mustard
1/4 cup balsamic vinegar
1/4 cup wine vinegar
1/2 cup capers
1 bunch parsley (for garnish)

Directions:

Boil and de-shell lobster before it cools. Cook potato in its skin. Cook artichoke heart. Dice shallot. To make ravigote sauce, combine oil, pickles, mustard, vinegar, shallot and capers in a large size mixing bowl. Slice potato and place on warm plate with artichoke heart and lukewarm lobster. Cover with sauce and garnish with parsley.

Salmon Steaks-Baked with Mushrooms

Gerald Pumphrey, Middle Sackville, Nova Scotia

Ingredients:

2 lbs salmon steaks
1 tsp salt
pepper to taste
1 can sliced mushrooms, drained
1/4 cup oil or butter
2 tbsp lemon juice
2 tsp onion, grated

Food for Thought
It isn't the mountain that wears you out - it's the grain of sand in your shoe. - Robert Service

Directions:

Sprinkle salmon on both sides with salt and pepper. Place in well-greased baking dish. Combine mushrooms, oil, lemon juice and onion. Pour over salmon. Bake at 350°F for 30 - 35 minutes.

Crabmeat Timbales

Gerald Pumphrey, Middle Sackville, Nova Scotia

Ingredients:

2 cups crabmeat
3 eggs, separated
1 1/2 cup bread crumbs
1 1/2 tsp lemon juice
1/4 cup melted butter
1 tsp minced parsley
1/2 tsp salt
dash of pepper

Spice of Life
It is a sin to believe evil of others, but it is seldom a mistake.
- H. L. Mencken

Directions:

Beat the egg yolks, add to crabmeat, crumbs, lemon juice, butter and seasonings. Fold in egg whites, whipped stiff. Place in buttered custard cups or timbale molds and place in a pan of boiling water. Bake at 375°F for 30 minutes. When firm in the centre, remove from mold and serve with cream or sauce. Sprinkle with nuts.

Cod Au Gratin

Evelyn Davis Johnson, West Vancouver, British Columbia (formerly of Grand Falls-Windsor, Newfoundland)

Ingredients:

4 tbsp margarine
2 tbsp flour
1 tsp salt
1/2 tsp pepper
2 cups milk
2 1/2 cups fresh cod (cooked, flaked and cooled)
1 1/2 cups medium cheddar cheese, grated

Directions:

Melt margarine; add flour, salt and pepper. Stir to make a paste. Add milk and cook until thickened, stirring constantly. Grease a 2-quart casserole dish; pour a little sauce over bottom of dish. Add layer of fish, sprinkle with cheese. Repeat until all ingredients are used, ending with a layer of cheese. Bake at 350°F for 30 minutes, or until nicely browned.

Baked Codfish

Vicki Lear, Gander, Newfoundland

Ingredients:

1 whole cod fish
salt pork
3 cups soft bread crumbs
1 tbsp onion, grated
1 tbsp savoury
1 tsp salt
1/8 tsp pepper
3 tbsp butter or margarine
1 egg, beaten
1 onion, sliced

Directions:

Choose a firm fish for baking. Remove head, tail, fins and sound bone. Wash thoroughly and wipe dry. Fry out salt pork in roasting pan. Meanwhile, combine crumbs, grated onion, savoury, salt, pepper, egg and butter to make dressing. Stuff the fish; tie or skewer securely. Put fish in fried-out pork. Bake at 450°F for 10 minutes and then 400°F for 1 hour for a medium-sized fish. Baste occasionally and add onion during the last 20 minutes. Serve with vegetables and drawn butter.

Baked Haddock

Rachel Hollett, Cambridge, Nova Scotia (nee Lomond, Port aux Basques, Newfoundland)

Ingredients:

2 lbs haddock fillets
1/2 - 3/4 cup mayonnaise
1 med onion, finely chopped

Seafoods
Swimmers, Crawlers & Creepers

1 medium green pepper, finely chopped
1/2 tsp sea salt
1/4 tsp pepper
1/4 cup fresh milk

Directions:

Wash and dry fillets. Place in a baking dish. Heat together above ingredients until a sauce forms. Pour over fish and bake at 400°F for 20 - 25 minutes.

Tuna Rolls

Ron Pumphrey, St. John's, Newfoundland

Ingredients:

1 can flaked tuna
1 cup cheddar cheese, grated
3 hard boiled eggs, chopped
2 tbsp sweet relish
2 tbsp onion, minced
1/2 cup Miracle Whip
hot dog or hamburger buns

Food for Thought
The virtue of some of the rich is that they teach us to despise wealth.
- Kahlil Gibran

Directions:

Mix all ingredients. Place in hot dog rolls (or on hamburger buns). Wrap in tin foil and place in oven at 375°F for 30 minutes.

Breaded Salmon Fingers

Gordon F. Thorne, Paradise, Newfoundland

Ingredients:

1 (2-3 lb) whole salmon
1 lb flour
4 eggs
2 cups 2% milk
2 tsp salt
1 tbsp salt seasoning
1/2 tsp pepper
1/2 tsp onion powder
1 tbsp savoury
1 1/2 lbs fine bread crumbs
1/4 cup lemon (or lime) juice

Trivia Tidbits
The very first bomb dropped by the Allies on Berlin during WWII killed the only elephant in the Berlin Zoo.

Directions:

Remove both fillets from salmon. Slice cleaned salmon into 1-inch strips, leaving skin behind. In one bowl place flour. In second bowl combine eggs, milk, salt, salt seasoning, pepper, onion powder and savoury; mix well. In third pan place bread crumbs. Roll salmon fingers in flour, place in egg mixture, then in bread crumbs; and place on pan. Repeat until all fingers are used. Deep fry fingers at 350°F for 5 minutes or until golden brown. Place in oven at 300°F for 10 minutes. Place fingers on a garnished serving tray and sprinkle with lemon or lime juice.

Swimmers, Crawlers & Creepers

Seafoods

Cabbie Claw

Trudy Gushue, Bacon Cove, Newfoundland

Ingredients:

1 lb cod fillets
1 lb potatoes
2 oz butter
1/2 pt milk
salt and pepper, to taste
1 tsp corn flour
1/2 tsp dry mustard
1 hard-boiled egg
3 oz cheese, grated

Spice of Life

Advice is cheap - unless you're getting it from a lawyer.

Directions:

Cook potatocs, drain and slice them. Place cod fillets in a frying pan with butter, milk and seasoning. Simmer gently until fish is cooked. Once cooked, blend corn flour and mustard with a little of the milk. Add to fish, shaking the pan gently over heat until sauce thickens. Turn into a casserole. Chop egg and sprinkle over fish. Add potatoes. Top with grated cheese. Cook at 425°F for 15 minutes.

Fish with Vegetables

Sharon L. Begin, Dundas, Ontario

Ingredients:

1 lb fish fillets
1/2 tsp salt
1/8 tsp pepper
2 tsp margarine or butter, melted
1 tbsp lemon juice
1 medium zucchini, cut in 1/4-inch slices
1 small green pepper, cut in 1/4-inch strips
1 small red onion, sliced

Trivia Tidbits
A newly hatched crocodile is three times larger than the egg from which it comes.

Directions:

If fish fillets are large, cut into serving pieces. Place fish in ungreased baking dish; sprinkle with salt and pepper. Mix margarine and lemon juice; pour over fish. Cook uncovered at 350°F for 20 - 25 minutes or until fish flakes easily with fork. Cook zucchini, green pepper and onion in 2 tbsp margarine over medium heat, stirring occasionally for 5 - 7 minutes or until crisp-tender. Serve vegetables over fish. Yields 4 servings.

Baked Salmon in a Blanket

Dora Strowbridge, Clarenville, Newfoundland

Ingredients:

1 (1 1/2 lb) piece of salmon
1/4 cup margarine
3/4 cup flour

Food for Thought
You may give gifts without caring - but you can't care without giving. - Frank A. Clark

Seafoods
Swimmers, Crawlers & Creepers

1/4 tsp dry mustard
1/4 tsp salt
pepper, to taste

Directions:

Scale and cut salmon. Place cut side down in greased baking dish. Cream margarine and blend in sifted dry ingredients. Spread over salmon. Bake at 375°F for 50 minutes.

Hielan's Steak

Trudy Gushue, Bacon Cove, Newfoundland

Ingredients:

4 fillet steaks
2 oz butter
2 tbsp cream
2 tbsp whiskey
3 oz cheddar cheese
parsley or watercress

Spice of Life

A fashion ten years before its time is indecent. Ten years after its time, it is hideous. After a century, it becomes romantic.   - James Laver

Directions:

Fry steak on both sides in melted butter until cooked. Remove from pan. Pour cream and whiskey into pan and heat gently. Pour over steaks. Garnish with grated cheese and parsley or watercress.

Saltfish Balls and Fritters

Dora Strowbridge, Clarenville, Newfoundland

Ingredients:

1/3 cup flour, sifted
3 tsp baking powder
1 cup salt codfish, finely shredded
1/2 cup water

Trivia Tidbits
A French actor called Pierre Messie could make his hair stand on end at will.

Directions:

Mix together flour, baking powder and codfish. Add water to form a batter. Drop by spoonfuls into hot deep fat and fry until golden brown.

Newfoundland Lobster Salad

Dora Strowbridge, Clarenville, Newfoundland

Ingredients:

3 lobsters, freshly boiled and shelled
3 eggs, hard-boiled and chopped
1/2 cup mayonnaise
1/2 cup sweet pickles, chopped
1 small onion, finely chopped
salt and pepper, to taste

Food for Thought
A free society is one where it is safe to be unpopular.
- Adlai Stevenson

Directions:

Cut lobster into bite-size pieces. Combine with remaining ingredients. Serve on lettuce leaves.

Stuffed, Rolled Fish Fillets

Sharon L. Begin, Dundas, Ontario

Ingredients:

2 lbs fish fillets

2 medium onions, chopped

1/4 cup margarine or butter

2 cups soft bread crumbs

1/2 cup snipped parsley

2 tsp salt

1/2 tsp ground nutmeg

2 eggs, slightly beaten

2 tbsp margarine or butter, melted

1 tbsp lemon juice

1/8 tsp paprika

parsley, to garnish (if desired)

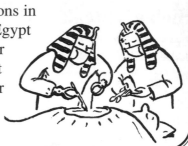

Trivia Tidbits

Surgeons in ancient Egypt had their hands cut off if their patients died.

Directions:

If fish fillets are large, cut into serving pieces. Cook and stir onions in 1/4 cup margarine until tender. Stir in bread crumbs, parsley, salt, nutmeg and eggs. Spread mixture evenly over fish fillets. Roll up fillets; secure with wooden tooth pick. Place seam side down in ungreased baking dish. Mix melted butter and lemon juice; drizzle over fish. Sprinkle with paprika. Cook uncovered at 350°F for 25 minutes until fish flakes easily with fork. Garnish with parsley and lemon slice if desired. Yields 6 servings.

Shrimp Risotto

Sharon L. Begin, Dundas, Ontario

Ingredients:

1 small onion, finely chopped

2 tbsp margarine or butter

1 can condensed chicken broth

1 soup can water

1 cup uncooked, parboiled converted rice

1/3 cup dry white wine

dash of ground thyme

1 (4 1/2oz) can tiny shrimp, rinsed and drained

1 - 2 tbsp margarine or butter

1/2 cup parmesan cheese, grated

1 tbsp snipped parsley

Food for Thought

Faith is a knowledge within the heart, beyond the reach of proof.

- Kahlil Gibran

Directions:

Cook onion in 2 tbsp margarine in 10-inch skillet over medium heat about 2 minutes. Heat broth and water just to boiling; remove from heat. Stir rice into onion mixture; cook and stir for 1 minute. Stir in wine; cook until wine is almost absorbed, about 1 minute. Stir in 1 1/4 cups broth; stir thyme into remaining broth. Cook rice mixture, uncovered, until broth is almost absorbed, about 10 minutes. Stir in remaining broth. Cook until broth is absorbed and rice is

Seafoods

Swimmers, Crawlers & Creepers

tender, about 15 minutes. Stir in shrimp and 1 - 2 tablespoons margarine; heat through. Remove from heat; stir in cheese and parsley. Yields 4 servings.

Fish Chowder

Rosalind Fraser, Garson, Ontario

Ingredients:

2 tbsp olive oil
6 potatoes, cubed
2 onions, chopped
4 stalks celery, chopped
3 large carrots, chopped
1 1/2 cups water
2 lbs fish (any kind)
1 1/2 cups milk
1 cup fresh parsley
salt and pepper, to taste
cornstarch for thickening
cold water

Trivia Tidbits
Your stomach has to produce a new layer of mucus every two weeks, otherwise it will digest itself.

Directions:

Cook potatoes, onion, celery, carrot and oil in a saucepan for 10 minutes. Add water and let simmer for 20 minutes. Add fish, let simmer for additional 10 minutes. Add parsley and milk. Thicken with cornstarch mixed with cold water.

Peppered Herb Mussels

Sue Bonderski, Ottawa, Ontario

Ingredients:

1 kg mussels
125 g butter, softened
1 tbsp crushed peppercorns
2 tbsp fresh parsley, chopped
1 tbsp fresh chives, chopped
2 tsp lemon rind, grated

Food for Thought
An enemy can never sell you out because he has nothing to offer. Only a friend has this option.
- Donald G. Smith

Directions:

Cover mussels in cold water and bring slowly to a boil; drain. Remove and discard beard and top shell from each mussel. Mix together butter, peppercorns, parsley, chives and lemon rind. Spread this mixture evenly over mussel meat in each shell. Place mussels on tray. Refrigerate for 1 hour. Cook mussels, buttered side down, on hot barbecue pan until heated through. Serves 6.

Seafood Melt

Beverly Wagner, Ladysmith, British Columbia

Ingredients:

1/4 cup butter
1/2 tsp dry mustard

Spice of Life
Actresses do things onstage today that they used to do offstage to get onstage.

Seafoods
Swimmers, Crawlers & Creepers

1/3 cup flour
1 1/3 cups milk
1 (16 1/2oz) can crab meat
1 1/2 cups cooked cod fish, diced
1/2 cup cooked shrimp
1 cup cooked scallops
4 slices French bread, toasted
salt & pepper, to taste
cheddar cheese, grated
buttered bread crumbs

Spice of Life
About the only good thing you can say about old age, it's better than being dead. - Stephen Leacock

Directions:

Preheat oven to 375°F. Melt butter in medium saucepan. Add mustard, flour and milk. Stir until thick. Once thickened, add seafood and blend well. Pour over bread in a casserole dish. Add salt and pepper to taste. Bake for 20 minutes. Sprinkle with cheddar cheese and buttered bread crumbs. Bake for additional 10 minutes. Serves 4.

Baked Codfish

Kathy Lynch, St. John's, Newfoundland

Ingredients:

1 firm whole codfish
salt pork
3 cups soft bread crumbs
1 tsp salt
1 egg, beaten
1 tbsp onion, grated
1/8 tsp pepper
1 tsp salt
1 tbsp savoury
3 tbsp butter
1 onion, sliced

Trivia Tidbits
A female ferret will die if it goes into heat and cannot find a mate.

Directions:

Remove head, tail, fins and sound bone. Wash thoroughly and wipe dry. Fry out salt pork in roasting pan. Combine remaining ingredients for bread dressing and stuff fish; tie securely and put in fried-out pork. Bake at 450°F for 10 minutes and then 400°F for 1 hour for a medium-sized fish. Baste occasionally and add sliced onion during the last 20 minutes.

Fishermen's Fresh Fish Stew

Lisa-Lynn Stockley, St. John's, Newfoundland

Ingredients:

4 slices fat pork
1 med onion or chives
5 lbs fresh codfish
potatoes
pepper
3/4 cup (or more) boiling water

Food for Thought
Most people suspend their judgement until somebody else has expressed his own, and then they repeat it. - Ernest Dimnet

Directions:

Place fat pork in a pot; fry out well. Clean fish thoroughly and remove skin; cut in 2-inch squares. Add fish to fat and then add sliced onion or chives. Slice potatoes 1/4-inch thick and cover fish with potato slices. Season with pepper and add 3/4 cup boiling water (more if needed). Cook slowly until pototoes and fish are tender, about 1/2 hour. Serves 6.

Codfish Cakes

Daisy Denny, St. John's, Newfoundland (formerly of Valley Pond, Newfoundland)

Ingredients:

6-8 cooked potatoes
1 med onion, chopped fine
2 cups salt codfish, cooked, boned and shredded
1/4 tsp pepper
1 tsp savoury
flour
pork fat

Spice of Life
The hallmark of good manners is mastering the ability to yawn without opening your mouth.

Directions:

Mash potatoes and add remaining ingredients. Form into cakes, roll in flour and fry in rendered pork fat. (Salmon may be used in place of salt codfish).

Fishermen's Brewis

Dorothy Clarke, Mount Pearl, Newfoundland (formerly of Valley Pond, Newfoundland)

Ingredients:

2 cups fat pork
1 pkg fillets or fresh cod fish
5 cakes hard bread

Directions:

Soak hard bread in cold water overnight or until soft. Fry fatback pork until a little brown. Boil fish until you can remove bones. Add hard bread and bring to a boil. Mash right away, strain, then pour rendered fatback over mixture and serve. Can be cooked within 20 minutes.

Fried Herring or Mackerel

Dale Wicks, Gander, Newfoundland (formerly of Horwood, Newfoundland)

Ingredients:

6 herring (or however many required)
flour
butter, melted

Trivia Tidbits
Money isn't made out of paper, it's made out of cotton.

Directions:

Wash herring and dry with cloth. Roll herring, which have been filleted, in flour. Place in pan and fry in a little melted butter, until brown.

Seafoods
Swimmers, Crawlers & Creepers

Spiced Herring or Mackerel

Gertie Hodder, Gander Bay, Newfoundland (formerly of Horwood, Newfoundland)

Ingredients:

6 fresh fish
1/2 cup vineger
1/2 cup water
1 small onion, chopped
1/2 tsp mustard
1/2 tsp ginger
4 cloves
1 bay leaf
1/4 tsp salt

Spice of Life
Why make the same mistake twice, when there are so many new ones available.

Directions:

Clean, fillet, wash and dry fish. Roll up head to tail and lay in greased oven dish. Mix vinegar and water together. Add other ingredients to fish. Cover and bake at 300°F for 40 minutes. Leave to cool in stock. Serve cold with salad.

Boiled Salmon

Jean Chippett, Glenwood, Newfoundland (formerly of Horwood, Newfoundland)

Ingredients:

1 salmon, cut as desired
1 tsp salt
1/2 cup salt pork scraps

Food for Thought
No man ever got lost on a straight road.

Directions:

Boil salmon in salted water with salt pork for 20 minutes or until cooked through. Salmon may also be boiled with potatoes. If so, leave out pork and add salt to taste.

Baked Herring

Wavey Hodder, St. John's, Newfoundland (formerly of Horwood, Newfoundland)

Ingredients:

4 herring
2 slices of bread crumbs
pinch of savoury
1 small onion, finely chopped
1 tbsp butter, melted
fat pork

Trivia Tidbits
A duck's quack doesn't echo. No one knows why.

Directions:

Clean herring and leave whole, if possible. Combine bread crumbs, savoury, onion and melted butter; stuff herring, secure top of herring with skewer. Cut fat pork in about 1 1/2-inch pieces in length, place on bottom of roasting pan. Lay herring on top of pork, then place pork pieces, same size, on top of herring. Bake in 325°F oven for 4 hours, remove cover and bake for another 30 minutes.

Baked Salmon

Geraldine Bennett, Stoneville, Newfoundland

Ingredients:

1 whole salmon
2 cups bread crumbs
1 onion, chopped
1 tsp poultry seasoning
2 tbsp butter, melted
1 tsp salt

Food for Thought
Ingratitude curdles the milk of human kindness.

Directions:

Clean and dry salmon; leave head and tail on but remove eyes. Combine rest of ingredients to make stuffing. Sprinkle cavity of fish with salt; stuff and skewer fish or sew up. Dot fish with butter or strips of fat pork. Wrap in foil and bake 1 hour at 350°F. Open foil for last 10 minutes.

Fried Salmon

Hilda Moss, Gambo, Newfoundland (formerly of Horwood, Newfoundland)

Ingredients:

salmon
flour
salt and pepper, to taste

Spice of Life
Time is money ... and overtime is big money.

Directions:

Once salmon is cleaned and washed, cut into pieces and dry in paper towels. Roll in flour and place in lightly greased frying pan; add salt and pepper and fry until nice and brown. (*Tip:* After washing salmon well, it may be covered with coarse salt. Let stand for 1 hour; wash off salt. Place on board and put outdoors in sun to dry for about 1 hour to stiffen. Cut into pieces for frying.)

Outer Cove Scallop Bake

Mary Dunne, Sherwood, Prince Edward Island (nee Hickey, Outer Cove, Newfoundland)

Ingredients:

1 pound scallops (more if you like)
1 tsp salt
1 cup sliced mushrooms (canned or fresh)
1 cup chopped green pepper
1/2 cup chopped celery
1/2 cup chopped onion
2 tbsp corn, vegetable or olive oil
1/2 cup butter or margarine
1/4 cup flour
2 cups milk

Trivia Tidbits
Althought Cardinal Wolsey was Archbishop of the City of York, he never once visited that English city.

Seafoods
Swimmers, Crawlers & Creepers

2 cups soft bread crumbs
1/4 cup grated cheddar cheese

Directions:

Separate scallops and sprinkle with 1 tsp salt. Fry mushrooms, green pepper, celery and onions in 2 tbsp oil for about 10 minutes until partly cooked, but not limp. Make a white sauce by combining and cooking 1/4 cup butter (margarine), flour and milk. When sauce thickens, add scallops and partly cooked vegetables. Combine thoroughly and place in a greased 1 1/2 quart casserole dish. Melt 1/4 cup butter (margarine) and mix with bread crumbs. Top the contents of the casserole dish with the buttered bread crumbs, sprinkle grated cheese on top and bake at 375° F for about 3/4 of an hour, or until mixture is bubbly around the edges and crumbs are lightly browned.

Sea Shell Seafood Chowder

Ron Young, St. John's, Newfoundland

Ingredients:

2 cups small sea shell pasta
1 pound cod cheeks (cut in chunks)
1/2 pound scallops (cut in chunks)
1/2 pound cod (cut in chunks)
1/2 pound salmon (cut in chunks)
2 cups small shrimp (frozen or thawed)
2 cans smoked oysters (drained)
2 pounds mussels in shells
1 can (19 ounce) clam chowder
3 cups milk
garlic powder (to taste)
onion powder (to taste)
pepper (to taste)
salt (to taste)

> **Trivia Tidbits**
>
> You can't always judge a dinner by the price.

Directions:

Cook mussels in boiling water until shells open, remove from shells and set aside. At the same time, cook sea shell pasta in boiling water until they are almost soft, then set aside. Place rest of ingredients in a suitable boiler, add sea shells and mussels and simmer for about 30 minutes, or until cooked to desired tenderness, stirring occasionally to prevent burning unto bottom. Add salt, pepper, onion powder and garlic powder to taste while mixture is simmering. Makes 16 regular sized bowls.

Doughy Delights

Doughnuts
Muffins
Puddings
Biscuits
Breads
Duffs
Buns
Etc.

Figgy Duff

Desiree Sheppard, Manuels, Newfoundland

Ingredients:

3 cups bread crumbs
1/2 cup flour
1 cup raisins
1/2 cup brown sugar
pinch salt
1 tsp allspice
1 tsp ginger
1 tsp cinnamon
1/4 cup butter, melted
3 tbsp molasses
1 tsp baking soda
1 tbsp hot water

Trivia Tidbits
If you spent a dollar every minute it would take you thirty average lifetimes to spend a billion dollars.

Directions:

Soak stale bread and crusts in water for a few minutes. Squeeze out water and rub between hands to make crumbs. Measure, without pressing, in a cup. Combine flour, crumbs, raisins, sugar, salt and spices; mix with a fork. Dissolve butter, molasses and soda in hot water; add to mixture. Put mixture into a dampened pudding bag; tie securely. Boil 1 1/2 hours (may be cooked in same pot with salt meat and cabbage dinner). Serve with heated molasses or salt meat dinner.

Figgy Duff

Herb Greening, Botwood, Newfoundland

Ingredients:

1/2 cup butter
2 tsp baking powder
1 cup raisins
2 cups flour
pinch salt
3/4 cup sugar
1/2 cup milk
1 egg

Food for Thought
If it's a problem that money can solve - then it isn't a problem.
- Cec Mercer

Directions:

Combine dry ingredients and add milk and egg. Place in cloth bag and boil for 1 hour. Ingredients can also be steamed in a pudding mold.

Newfoundland Figgy Duff

Frances Butt, Winterbrook, Newfoundland

Ingredients:

2 cups bread crumbs
1 cup raisins

Spice of Life
Blessed are the young, for they shall inherit the national debt. - Herbert Hoover

Doughy Delights

Puddings, Duffs, Breads, Muffins, Buns, Biscuits, Doughnuts, etc.

1/2 cup molasses
1/4 cup butter, melted
1 tsp baking soda
1 tbsp hot water
1 tsp allspice
1 tsp cinnamon
1/2 cup flour

Directions:

Soak dry bread in warm water; squeeze all water out. Add raisins, molasses and melted butter. Dissolve baking soda in hot water and add to bread mixture with spices; stir in flour. Boil in a bag or steam for 2 hours. Excellent served with Jigg's dinner.

Blueberry Pudding

Grace Ryan, Newman's Cove, Bonavista Bay, Newfoundland

Pudding Ingredients:

2 1/4 cups flour
3 tsp baking soda
3/4 cup molasses
1/2 cup hot water
1 tsp cinnamon
1/2 tsp allspice
1 cup blueberries

Custard Sauce Ingredients:

1/2 tbsp cinnamon
1/8 cup margarine
1 cup brown sugar
2 cups boiling water
4 tsp custard powder
4 tsp cold water

Trivia Tidbits

Most Canadians who own running shoes don't run in them.

Directions:

Mix all pudding ingredients together. Steam for 2 hours. To make sauce, combine cinnamon, margarine, sugar and water until dissolved. Add custard powder mixed with cold water. Stir until thickened. Serve over blueberry pudding.

Chocolate Sauce Pudding

Marjorie Baetzel (nee Noseworthy), St. John's, Newfoundland

Ingredients:

1 cup white sugar, divided
2 tbsp butter
1/2 cup milk
1 egg, beaten
1 cup flour
2 tsp baking powder

1/4 tsp salt
2 tbsp cocoa
1/2 cup chopped nuts (optional)
1/2 cup brown sugar
1/3 cup cocoa
2 cups boiling water

Directions:

Cream together 1/2 cup sugar and butter. Blend in milk and egg. Sift together flour, baking powder, salt and cocoa; add to creamed mixture. Add nuts, if using. Spread in buttered 9-inch square dish. In a bowl, mix together 1/2 cup white sugar, brown sugar and cocoa. Sprinkle over batter. Pour two cups boiling water over top. Bake at 350°F for 35 - 40 minutes. Pudding should be left at room temperature 20 minutes before serving. Serve topped with vanilla ice cream or whipped cream.

Quick Apple Pudding

Jeanette Osmond, Grand Bank, Fortune Bay, Newfoundland

Pudding Ingredients:

2 tbsp butter
1/4 cup white sugar
1 cup flour
1 tsp baking powder
1/3 tsp salt
1 cup apples, chopped
6 tbsp milk

Sauce Ingredients:

1 cup brown sugar
1 tbsp butter
dash of salt
1 1/2 cups boiling water
1 tsp vanilla

Directions:

Mix all pudding ingredients together and pour into 2-qt casserole. To make sauce, combine all sauce ingredients and pour over batter. Bake at 400°F for 30 - 35 minutes. Serve warm.

Baked Pudding

Charlotte Peddle, St. John's, Newfoundland

Ingredients:

2 cups flour
pinch salt
1/3 cup butter
2 tbsp baking powder

Doughy Delights

Puddings, Duffs, Breads, Muffins, Buns, Biscuits, Doughnuts, etc.

Directions:

Mix flour, salt and baking powder together. Cut butter into flour and add enough water to make a soft dough. Place in oven and bake for 1/2 hour, or until done (Great as covering for waterfowl as well. May be placed on top of birds last half hour of baking time).

Boiled Bread Pudding

Audra-Lee, St. John's, Newfoundland (formerly of Gander Bay, Newfoundland)

Ingredients

3 thick slices of 1-week-old homemade bread
2 tbsp cold rendered-out pork fat
pinch of salt
1 cup flour (more or less if necessary)

Spice of Life
A man is known by the company he thinks nobody knows he's keeping.
- Irv Kupcinet

Directions

Soak bread in just enough cold water to make it soft with no water left over. Then add salt, pork fat and gradually work in flour until pudding is of right consistency. Boil in pudding cloth with Jigg's dinner for 1 hour. Remove from cloth immediately when done.

Apple Pudding

Fanny Tucker, Portugal Cove, Newfoundland

Ingredients:
3 cups flour
2 1/2 tsp baking powder
3/4 cup sugar
1/2 cup butter
3 apples
1 1/2 cups water

Trivia Tidbits
Napoleon Bonaparte's mother claimed to have seen his ghost on the day he died.

Directions:

Mix flour, baking powder, sugar and butter together. Peel and cut apples in small pieces and add to dry ingredients. Add water into mixture. Pour mixture into pudding mold and boil in a covered pot for 1 1/2 hours (no less) with steady boiling. Make sure water is boiling before you place pudding in pot.

Fort Amherst Boiled Pudding

Nellie Whittle, Fort Amherst, Newfoundland

Ingredients:
1/4 cup margarine
3/4 cup sugar
2 cups flour
2 tsp baking powder
1 tsp cinnamon
1/4 tsp nutmeg

Food for Thought
To profit from good advice requires more wisdom than to give it.
- John C Collins

1 tsp allspice
pinch of salt
1/4 tsp baking soda
1/2 cup nuts
1/2 cup dates
1/2 cup raisins
milk, as needed

Directions:

Cream margarine well; add sugar and mix well. Mix dry ingredients together and add to margarine mixture. Stir in fruit. Use milk to mix until slightly moist. Put into pudding bag and boil for 2 hours. (Recipe can be halved).

Seven-Cup Pudding

Gertie Sweetapple, Glovertown, Newfoundland

Ingredients:

1 cup sugar
1 cup butter
1 cup milk
1 cup raisins
1 cup bread crumbs
1 cup flour
1 cup apple, chopped
1 tsp baking soda

Directions:

Mix all the above ingredients together and steam for three hours.

Blueberry Pudding with Rum Sauce

Gerri Hearn, St. John's, Newfoundland

Pudding Ingredients:

2 1/2 cups flour
1 tsp ginger
1 tsp allspice
1 tsp cinnamon
1 tsp salt
1/2 cup bacon drippings
1 cup molasses
1 egg
1 tsp soda
1/4 cup hot water
2 cups blueberries

Rum Sauce Ingredients:

1 tsp salt
2 cups water
2 tbsp Screech (or to taste)

Doughy Delights

Puddings, Puffs, Breads, Muffins, Buns, Biscuits, Doughnuts, etc.

2 cups dark brown sugar
2 tbsp butter
cornstarch
water

Directions:

Sift flour and spices together. Cream bacon drippings and molasses, beat in egg. Dissolve soda in water and add to molasses mixture all at once, mixing well. Add flour mixture. Beat well; fold in berries; turn into a 2-quart mold and steam for 3 hours. For sauce, boil all ingredients together and thicken with a mixture of cornstarch and water. Serve warm.

Bread and Butter Pudding

Valerie Sturge, Gambo, Newfoundland

Ingredients:

1/2 cup raisins
5 slices bread
1/4 cup butter, melted
2 eggs
1/3 cup sugar
2 cups milk
1/2 tsp vanilla

Food for Thought
Broken friendships may be patched up, but the patch is likely to show.

Directions:

Line bottom of greased casserole dish with raisins. Cut bread in 3 strips and dip in melted butter. Place bread on top of raisins. Beat rest of ingredients and pour over bread. Set dish in hot water and bake at 375°F until bread is brown and inserted knife comes out clean.

Steamed Blueberry Pudding

Bertha Smith, Clarenville, Newfoundland

Ingredients:

1/2 cup margarine
1/2 cup brown sugar
1/2 cup molasses
1 cup hot water
1 tsp baking soda
1 tsp cinnamon
2 cups blueberries
flour

Trivia Tidbits
A few drops of black paint added to a tin of white paint will make it even whiter.

Directions:

Blend together margarine, brown sugar and molasses. Add hot water, baking soda and cinnamon. Add enough flour to make a stiff dough. Add blueberries. Steam for 2 hours.

Yorkshire Pudding

Teresa Ivey, St. John's, Newfoundland

Ingredients:

1 1/4 cups flour

Spice of Life
One swallow doesn't make a summer ...but it may break a New Year's resolution.

1/4 tsp salt (or to taste)
1 cup milk
2 eggs
drippings from a roast

Directions:

Mix and sift flour and salt, add milk gradually to make a smooth paste. Add eggs and beat for 2 minutes. Cover bottom of pan about 1/4-inch with drippings from roast. Pour mixture 1/2-inch deep over the drippings. Bake at 400°F for 20 - 30 minutes in a 9x9 pan or frying pan.

Mom's Old-Fashioned Steamed Blueberry Pudding

Joan Brown St. John's, Newfoundland (nee Kelly, Trinity, Trinity Bay, Newfoundland)

Ingredients:

1/4 cup sugar
2 tbsp butter
1 egg
1 1/2 cups flour
3 1/2 tsp baking powder
pinch salt
1 cup blueberries
water to mix

> **Trivia Tidbits**
> A pint of gas has as much explosive power as a pound of dynamite.

Directions:

Mix sugar, butter and egg; add dry ingredients, stir in blueberries and add water. Place in greased tin foil pie pan and place on top of vegetables and potatoes, being careful not to let water from pot into pan. Cover and let steam until potatoes are cooked. Can be served with meal or as a wonderful dessert served with blueberry sauce.

Baked Rice Pudding

Janice Mercer, Portugal Cove, Newfoundland

Ingredients:

2 cups cooked rice
2 eggs, beaten
1/2 cup sugar
1/8 tsp salt
1 tsp vanilla
1 1/2 cups milk
nutmeg or cinnamon (optional)
raisins, dates, nuts or fruit, if desired

> **Food for Thought**
> Don't be unhappy if your dreams never come true, just be thankful your nightmares don't.

Directions:

Combine all ingredients. Pour into greased baking dish. Sprinkle with nutmeg or cinnamon (optional). Bake at 300°F for 30 - 45 minutes, or until pudding becomes firm and starts to brown on top. Serves 6.

Doughy Delights

Puddings, Puffs, Breads, Muffins, Buns, Biscuits, Doughnuts, etc.

Apple Noodle Pudding

Frances Pelley, Edmonton, Alberta (formerly of Deer Lake, Newfoundland)

Ingredients:

2 2/3 cups milk
1/2 tsp salt
2 1/2 cups broad egg noodles, broken
1/4 cup margarine, room temperature
1/2 cup sugar
3 large eggs, separated
1 1/2 tsp vanilla
2 1/2 cups sliced apples

Spice of Life

Now when I bore people at a party, they think it's their fault.
- Henry Kissinger

Directions:

In a large saucepan, bring milk to a boil, stirring occasionally. Reduce heat to medium and add salt and noodles. Simmer until tender, about 10 minutes; stirring occasionally. Remove from heat and let cool slightly. In a large bowl, beat margarine and sugar until light and fluffy. Add yolks and beat until light. Gently stir in warm noodle mixture and vanilla. In medium bowl, beat whites just until stiff peaks form, fold into noodle mixture. Spoon half the noodle mixture into a lightly greased casserole dish. Arrange apple slices over top. Spoon remaining mixture over apples. Bake uncovered at 350°F for 30 - 35 minutes until golden brown and cooked through.

Fruit Pudding

Marian Shea, Manuels, Conception Bay South, Newfoundland

Ingredients:

2/3 cup mixed citrus peel
1/2 cup dates, chopped
1/3 cup crushed pineapple (drained)
2 tbsp flour (for fruit)
1/4 tsp salt
1/4 cup sugar (brown or white)
1/3 cup raisins
1/2 cup nuts, chopped
1/4 cup butter
1 egg
1/2 cup flour
1/2 tsp baking powder
1 tbsp pineapple juice

Trivia Tidbits

The substance that comes closest to the chemical construction of blood is seawater.

Directions:

Mix all ingredients together; cover in a pudding pan and steam for about 2 hours.

Home-Made Bread

Cathy Banfield, Estevan, Saskatchewan (formerly of Bay L'Argent, Newfoundland)

Ingredients:

5 cups warm water
1/4 cup sugar

1/3 cup oil
1 tbsp salt
2 tbsp yeast
10 1/2 cups flour

<u>Directions</u>:

Combine first 5 ingredients. Add about half the flour and stir real well. Work in rest of flour, 1 or 2 cups at a time (may use more or less flour). Keep hands greased while kneading. Lightly oil top of dough. Cover with tea towel, let rise for 15 minutes. Punch down and repeat 3 more times. On fourth rise, shape into loaves or rolls, and put into well-greased pans. Poke each loaf several times with fork to pop air bubbles. Let rise for 1 hour. Bake at 350°F for 40 - 45 minutes. If baking rolls, bake for 20 - 25 minutes.

Banana Bread

June Dalley, New Brunswick (nee Howell, Carbonear, Newfoundland)

<u>Ingredients</u>:

1 cup salad dressing
1 cup sugar
2 mashed bananas
2 cups flour
2 tsp baking powder
1 tsp baking soda

> ## *Food for Thought*
> The mind once stretched by a great idea can never return to its original dimensions.

<u>Directions</u>:

Combine all ingredients. Spread evenly in a greased bread pan. Bake at 350°F for 1 hour.

Zucchini-Lemon Bread

Agnes Gaultois, Kindersley, Saskatchewan

<u>Ingredients</u>:

1 1/2 cups grated zucchini
1/4 cup butter
3/4 cup light brown sugar
1 egg
juice of 1 lemon
1 cup whole wheat flour
1 cup all-purpose flour
1/2 tsp baking soda
1/4 tsp salt
1 1/4 tsp cinnamon
1/2 tsp allspice
1/2 cup chopped walnuts (optional)
1/2 cup milk
1/4 cup vegetable oil

> ## **Spice of Life**
> It pays to advertise - a store that advertised for a night watchman was burglarized that night.
>
>

<u>Directions</u>:

Grate and peel zucchini. Place in cloth and squeeze out almost all the juice. Measure 1 1/2 cups zucchini pulp. Beat together butter, sugar and egg until creamy. Add lemon juice and zucchini, then dry ingredients and milk and oil. Preheat oven to 350°F. Place mixture in bread pans. Bake for 40 - 45 minutes or until done.

Whole Wheat Zucchini Loaf

Anita Duggan, Sechelt, British Columbia (nee Shea, Bell Island, Newfoundland)

Ingredients:

3 eggs
1 cup vegetable oil
2 cups white sugar
1 tsp vanilla
2 cups zucchini, finely grated, well-packed
1 1/2 cups all-purpose flour
1 tsp baking soda
1 1/2 tsp baking powder
1/2 cup wheat germ
1 cup whole wheat flour
1 tsp salt
2 tsp nutmeg

> *Food for Thought*
> Freedom ends when it begins to deprive another of his freedom.

Directions:

At medium speed, beat together oil, eggs, sugar and vanilla, until frothy. Beat in zucchini. At low speed, add remaining ingredients. Pour batter into loaf pans that have been greased with butter and lightly dusted with flour, then bake at 350°F for 50 minutes until loaves peak and crack.

Lebanese Bread

Agnes Gaultois, Kindersley, Saskatchewan

Ingredients:

1 pkg dried yeast
1 tsp sugar
8 cups flour
2 tsp salt
2 1/2 cups lukewarm water
3 tbsp oil

> **Trivia Tidbits**
> In 1820, a man took his wife to market and sold her for five shillings.

Directions:

Dissolve yeast in 1/4 cup lukewarm water and add sugar; set aside until dissolved (about 10-15 minutes). Sift flour and salt in large mixing bowl and place in a warm oven for a few minutes to warm slightly. Pour yeast into a well in the centre of the flour and mix by hand, adding water gradually. Knead well to a soft dough on a floured board until soft and shiny (15-20 mins). Knead in 2 tbsp oil, roll into ball and rub remainder of oil around ball. Leave in a bowl, cover with cloth and set aside for 1 - 2 hours. Pre-heat oven to hot (350°F) before beginning to bake the bread. Punch dough down in centre and draw edges to middle to reform a ball. Turn onto floured board and knead for approx. 2 minutes. Divide dough into eight equal pieces and roll each piece into a ball. Flatten each ball on a lightly floured board and roll out with a rolling pin until flat and round (about the size of a dinner plate and 1/4-inch thick). Place on slightly floured board and cover with a floured cloth. Set aside to rise nearly double (approx. 20 - 30 mins).

Place on baking tray in oven at 350°F for 5 minutes. Remove and lightly rub with oil. Place round of bread on baking tray and cook until it swells up in centre and browns slightly (approx. 4 - 8 mins), without letting a crust form. Remove from oven and allow the swelling to sink. Wrap in cloth. Continue this way until all rounds are cooked. The bread should be white, soft and chewy. When cut in half it should leave a pocket which can be filled with filling of choice. Makes 8 rounds.

Cranberry Bread

Winnie Marshall, Stephenville, Newfoundland

Ingredients:

1 cup cranberries, coarsely chopped
1 3/4 cups flour
1 1/2 tsp baking powder
1/2 tsp baking soda
1/2 tsp salt
1 cup sugar
1 egg
3/4 cup orange juice
1/4 cup vegetable oil

Spice of Life

Ye shall know the truth, and the truth shall make you free ... but first it shall make you miserable.

Directions:

Preheat oven to 350°F. Grease an 8 1/2 x 4 1/2 x 3 inch loaf pan. Sift together flour, baking powder, baking soda, salt and sugar. Stir in cranberries. Beat together egg, orange juice and vegetable oil. Add liquid mixture to dry ingredients and beat for about 30 seconds (batter may be lumpy). Turn into prepared pan. Bake for 60 minutes, or until toothpick inserted comes out clean.

Blueberry Nut Bread

Ingredients:

2 eggs
1 cup sugar
3 tbsp margarine, melted
1 cup milk
3 cups flour
4 tsp baking powder
1 tsp salt
1 cup blueberries
1/2 cup nuts

Trivia Tidbits

A man pronounced dead in 1562 was buried. Six hours later his brother felt that he might be alive and the body was disinterred. The man was found to be alive and lived another seventy years, dying at the age of 105.

Directions:

Beat eggs, add sugar gradually. Add the melted margarine and milk, mixing well. Sift the flour, baking powder and salt. Add to the liquid mixture. Stir just until blended. Mix in the blueberries and nuts. Bake at 350°F for 50 - 60 minutes.

Puddings, Puffs, Breads, Muffins, Buns, Biscuits, Doughnuts, etc.

Doughy Delights

Ron Zibelli's Italian Bread

Ann Bain, Tatamagouche, Nova Scotia (nee Rowe, Collins Cove, Burin, Newfoundland)

Ingredients: (Starter Dough)

1/4 tsp dry yeast
1/4 cup warm water
3/4 cup water, at room temperature
2 1/2 cups unbleached flour

Directions: (Starter Dough)

Make starter dough a day ahead. Stir the yeast into warm water and let stand until creamy, about 10 minutes. Stir in water and then flour, one cup at a time. Mix with electric mixer on low speed for 2 minutes, or by hand with a wooden spoon for 4 minutes. Remove dough to lightly oiled bowl. Cover with plastic wrap and allow to rise at cool room temperature for 12 - 24 hours.

Ingredients: (Bread Dough Mix)

1 tsp dry yeast
5 tbsp warm milk
1 cup water, at room temperature
1 tbsp olive oil
3 3/4 cups unbleached flour
1 tbsp salt

> **Trivia Tidbits**
> The Rock of Gibraltar is made of very soft limestone.

Directions: (Bread Dough Mix)

For bread dough, stir yeast into milk in a mixing bowl. Let stand until creamy, about 10 minutes. Add water, oil and starter dough; mix until blended. Mix the flour and salt together. Add to the bowl and mix for 2 - 3 minutes with electric mixer. Knead for 2 minutes at low speed, then 2 minutes at medium speed. Change to dough hook and knead for 2 minutes at low speed, then 2 minutes at medium speed. Knead briefly by hand on a well-floured surface. Remove dough to oiled bowl, cover with plastic wrap and allow to rise for 1 1/4 hours. For shaping and the second rise, separate dough into 3 equal pieces, knead and form by hand into 3 cylinders. Place on baking sheet spread liberally with corn meal. Cover with damp towel and allow to rise for 2 hours at room temperature. Preheat oven to 425°F for 30 minutes. Bake loaves for 25 minutes, spraying twice with water in the first 10 minutes. Bake on baking stones if possible. Cool on rack.

Cheese Bread

Ben Bellefontaine, Etobicoke, Ontario

Ingredients:

2 cups all-purpose flour
1 tbsp baking powder
1/2 tsp baking soda
1 tsp salt
4 oz cheddar cheese
2 oz parmesan cheese
2 eggs

> **Food for Thought**
> The extravagant girl usually makes a poor mother and a bankrupt father.

Sidebar (left margin): **Doughy Delights** — Puddings, Duffs, Breads, Muffins, Buns, Biscuits, Doughnuts, etc.

1 cup buttermilk
1/3 cup oil

Directions:

Combine flour, baking powder, baking soda and salt. Grate and mix in both cheeses. Break eggs into small bowl, stir in buttermilk and oil; whisk well. Stir into flour mixture. Spoon batter into greased 9x5 loaf pan. Bake at 375°F for 20 minutes. Rotate pan and bake another 20 - 25 minutes, or until done.

Cranberry Nut Bread

June Gates, Woodstock, Ontario

Ingredients:

2 cups all purpose flour
1 cup sugar
1 1/2 tsp baking powder
1/2 tsp baking soda
1 cup cranberries, coarsely chopped (or whole partridgeberries)
1 tsp salt
1/4 cup shortening
3/4 cup orange juice
1 tbsp orange rind, grated
1 egg, beaten
1/2 cup walnuts, chopped

> ## *Food for Thought*
> It's easier to admire the other fellow's thrift than to practice it yourself.

Directions:

Sift together flour, sugar, baking powder, baking soda and salt. Cut in shortening until mixture resembles coarse oatmeal. Combine orange juice and rind with well-beaten egg. Pour all at once into dry ingredients mixing just enough to dampen. Fold in berries and nuts; spoon into greased loaf pan. Bake at 350°F for 1 hour until golden brown.

Cinnamon Loaf

Joan Brown, St. John's, Newfoundland (nee Kelly, Trinity, Trinity Bay, Newfoundland)

Ingredients:

1/2 cup butter
1 cup white sugar
2 eggs
2 tsp vanilla
2 cups flour
1/2 tsp salt
2 tsp baking powder
1/2 cup milk
1 tbsp cinnamon
3 tbsp brown sugar

> ## **Spice of Life**
> A lie is an abomination unto the Lord and a very present help in time of trouble.
> - Adlai Stevenson

Directions:

Cream butter and white sugar; add eggs, one at a time, and beat well. Add vanilla. Combine flour, salt and baking powder. Add to creamed mixture alternately with milk. Mix cinnamon and brown sugar. Put 1/3 batter in bottom of pan and sprinkle 1/2 cinnamon mixture over batter. Continue in layers until all is used, ending with batter layer. Bake in well-greased pan at 325°F for 1 hour.

Pumpkin Bread

Anita A. Graham (nee Wareham), Brooklyn, New York

Ingredients:

4 eggs
3 cups sugar
1 cup salad oil
2/3 cup water
2 cups canned pumpkin
1 1/4 tsp salt
1 tsp cinnamon
3 tsp baking soda
3 1/2 cups flour, sifted

> **Food for Thought**
> Fear of criticism is the kiss of death in the courtship of achievement.

Directions:

Beat eggs and add sugar; beat until well blended. Add salad oil, water and pumpkin. Beat only until blended. Add sifted dry ingredients. Again, beat only until blended (overbeating toughens bread). Butter baking pans and flour lightly. Can be baked in 2 loaf pans or 1 larger tube pan. Bake at 350°F for 20 minutes until risen, then at 325°F for 50 minutes.

Cranberry Bread

Beulah Cooper, Gander, Newfoundland

Ingredients:

2 cups flour
1 cup sugar
1/2 tsp baking soda
1 1/2 tsp baking powder
1 tsp salt
1/4 cup shortening
3/4 cup orange juice
1 egg
1 tbsp orange rind
1 cup cranberries

> **Trivia Tidbits**
> In the history of the world there have been ten years of war to every year of peace.

Directions:

Combine dry ingredients with cranberries. Beat egg and juice with fork; add to dry ingredients. Bake at 350°F for 1 hour in loaf pan.

Doughy Delights

Puddings, Duffs, Breads, Muffins, Buns, Biscuits, Doughnuts, etc.

Irish Soda Bread

Anita A. Graham (nee Wareham), Brooklyn, New York

Ingredients:

9 cups flour
10 tsp baking powder
1 1/2 cups sugar
1 tbsp salt
1 1/2 oz caraway seeds
1 (16oz) box raisins
3 1/4 cups milk
1/4 lb butter, melted and cooled
2 eggs

Directions:

Mix all dry ingredients first. Add milk, eggs and butter. Bake at 325°F for about an hour. Makes 3 loaf pans.

Beer Batter Bread

Bev Schofield, Canning, Nova Scotia

Ingredients:

3 cups whole wheat flour
1 tsp baking powder
1/2 tsp baking soda
1/2 tsp salt
1 can or bottle of beer
2 tbsp honey
1 tbsp margarine

Directions:

Preheat oven to 325°F, grease 8-inch round pan. In medium bowl, stir together dry ingredients. With wooden spoon stir in beer and honey and mix just until dry ingredients are moistened. Turn and knead for 1 minute; spread into prepared pan. Using a sharp knife dipped in cold water, cut lines 1/2-inch deep into top of batter. Bake 40 - 45 minutes until bread pulls away from pan. Unmold onto wire rack. Rub top and side of loaf with margarine. Cool for 10 minutes.

Orange and Cranberry Bread (for Bread Machines)

Gordon Rendell, Chatsworth, Ontario

Ingredients:

1 cup milk
1 egg
1 tsp margarine
2 tsp orange peel, grated
1 tbsp sugar
1 tsp salt
3/4 cup dried cranberries

Spice of Life

Whatever goes up will go up some more after the first of the year.

Trivia Tidbits

An otter is quick enough to dodge a rifle bullet.

Spice of Life

If at first you don't succeed, try again ... when nobody's looking.

Doughy Delights

Puddings, Puffs, Breads, Muffins, Buns, Biscuits, Doughnuts, etc.

3 cups flour
2 tsp yeast

Directions:

Combine all ingredients as listed above.
For bread machine: Place in machine and bake on the 'white bread' setting.
For conventional oven: Place in loaf pan. Bake at 350°F for 45 minutes, 'til done.

Zucchini Bread

Marguerite McKinley, Hinton, Alberta

Ingredients:

3 eggs
1 1/2 cups sugar
3/4 cup oil
1 tsp vanilla
2 cups zucchini, grated
2 cups flour
1 tbsp cinnamon
1 tsp baking soda
3/4 tsp baking powder
1 tsp salt
1 cup nuts

Directions:

Beat eggs until light. Add sugar, oil and vanilla. Beat until lemon coloured. Stir in zucchini. Sift flour with cinnamon, baking soda, baking powder and salt and add to mixture; fold in nuts. Bake in loaf pan at 350°F for 1 hour. Makes 2 loaves.

No Need to Knead Brown Bread

Doreen Sooley, Perth-Andover, New Brunswick

Ingredients:

1/2 cup warm water
1/2 tsp white sugar
1 pkg dry yeast
2 cups oatmeal
2 tsp butter
boiling water
1 cup milk
3/4 cup brown sugar
1/2 cup molasses
1 tsp salt
8 cups flour

Directions:

In small bowl, mix warm water and sugar. Sprinkle yeast on top and set aside. In a large bowl, mix oatmeal and butter. Pour boiling water over oatmeal mixture; let cool. Once cooled, add

Food for Thought
There is many a tear in the heart that never reaches the eye.

Spice of Life
The way of transgressors is hard ...but it isn't lonely.

Food for Thought
Don't pray for an easier life; pray to be a stronger person.

yeast, milk, brown sugar, molasses and salt. Gradually add flour. Mix well and set overnight on kitchen counter. In the morning, pour into 4 large greased and floured juice cans, filling about 3/4 full. Let rise to top of can. Bake at 350°F for 40 - 45 minutes. Cool for 10 minutes. Bread should come out of can easily.

New French Bread

Maria Hiscock, Grand Bank, Newfoundland

Ingredients:

3/4 lb white rice
7 lbs all-purpose flour
salt, to taste
2 envelopes dry yeast
1/2 cup warm water
2-3 tsp sugar

Spice of Life
I never give them hell. I just tell the truth and they think it is hell.
— Harry S. Truman

Directions:

Place rice in pudding bag or cloth; tie securely, leaving extra room for rice to expand as it cooks. Boil 2-3 hours, until it becomes really soft (the consistency of thick paste). Dissolve yeast in water and sugar. While rice is still warm, mix with flour. Add salt to taste. Add yeast mixture and sugar. When a nice soft dough is formed, cover and let rise near a heated area (away from any drafts). When doubled in bulk, knead down and make into loaves. Makes about 13 1/2 pounds, which will keep moist much longer with the rice. Delicious and nutritious. Recipe can be cut in half, if preferred.

White Bread

Alvina Wells, Mount Pearl, Newfoundland (formerly of Seal Cove, Fortune Bay, Newfoundland)

Ingredients:

1 pkg yeast
2 cups warm water
2 tsp white sugar
12 cups all-purpose flour
1/2-3/4 cup butter, melted
2 tbsp salt
6 cups lukewarm water

Food for Thought
It would be nice if we could forget our troubles like we forget our blessings.

Directions:

Dissolve sugar in warm water and sprinkle in yeast. Let stand about 10 minutes in warm oven. Mix flour, salt and butter together; add yeast and water. Mix and knead until it has an elastic consistency. Cover and let rise for 1 hour; knead and let rise another hour. Shape into loaves and let rise again until nearly double. Bake at 375-400°F for 30 - 40 minutes.

Banana Bread

Frances Butt, Winterbrook, Newfoundland

Ingredients:

1/2 cup butter
1 cup sugar
2 eggs

Trivia Tidbits
The elephant is the only animal that has been taught to stand on its head.

3 bananas, mashed
1 3/4 cups flour
1 tsp baking powder
1 tsp baking soda
pinch of salt

Directions:

Cream butter and sugar. Add eggs; beat well. Add bananas and dry ingredients. Bake at 350°F for 1 hour.

Tea Buns

Maria Young, St. Phillip's, Newfoundland (nee Hardy, Port aux Basques, Newfoundland)

Ingredients:

1 cup coconut
3 cups flour
6 tsp baking powder
1/2 cup sugar
dash of salt
1 cup margarine
2 eggs, beaten
1 cup fresh milk

Directions:

Mix together flour, coconut, baking powder, sugar, salt and margarine until crumbly. Add eggs and milk to mixture. Blend well. Flour table or counter; pat down dough to 1 1/2-inch thickness. Cut out buns with small glass. Bake at 400°F for 10 - 15 minutes. Makes 2 dozen.

Part Whole Wheat Bread

Gail Hynes, St. John's, Newfoundland

Ingredients:

1 pkg yeast
4 cups lukewarm water
1 tsp sugar
4 tsp salt
1/2 cup sugar
4 cups unsifted whole wheat flour
7 3/4 cups sifted all-purpose flour
1/4 cup shortening, melted

Directions:

Dissolve yeast in 1 cup lukewarm water with 1 tsp sugar for 5 minutes. To the 3 cups of water add salt and 1/2 cup sugar. Combine yeast with lukewarm liquid and stir in 2 cups of whole wheat flour and half the all-purpose flour. Stir in cooled melted shortening; stir in remaining all-purpose flour and finally enough whole wheat flour to make dough barely stiff enough to knead. Knead until smooth and elastic. Cover and let rise in a warm place until it doubles in size. Shape into loaves at once; rise again until nearly double and bake at 375°F for 45 - 50 minutes. Makes 4 loaves.

Old-Fashioned Sweet Bread

Deanne Wells, St. John's, Newfoundland (formerly of Seal Cove, Fortune Bay, Newfoundland)

Ingredients:

2 pkgs yeast
4 cups lukewarm water
2 tsp sugar
1 cup molasses
3 tbsp butter
4 tsp salt
3 tsp caraway seed
12 cups sifted flour
3 cups raisins

Food for Thought
Don't be afraid to take a big step if it's required. You can't cross a chasm in two small jumps.

Directions:

Dissolve yeast in 1 cup lukewarm water, add sugar. Combine remaining 3 cups lukewarm water, molasses and butter. Sift dry ingredients; add raisins and caraway seed. Mix well and let rise until double in size. Knead and let rise again. Put in loaf pans; bake at 375°F for 1 hour. Brush top with butter while hot.

Corn Bread

Joy Greenland, Toronto, Ontario (formerly of St. John's, Newfoundland)

Ingredients:

1 cup corn meal
1 cup flour
2 tsp baking powder
1 tbsp butter
1 cup milk
3 eggs, beaten

Directions:

Mix dry ingredients; add butter warmed, but not melted. Add milk and eggs. Batter will be stiff. Bake in greased tin, mark into squares; break and serve hot.

Whole Wheat Apricot Bread

Lindsey Bartlett, Mount Pearl, Newfoundland

Ingredients:

3/4 cup dried apricots
1 slice lemon
1 cup boiling water
1 cup milk
1/4 cup sugar
1 1/2 tsp salt
1/4 cup shortening

Trivia Tidbits
Giant bamboos in South East Asia can grow up to one metre in twenty-four hours.

Doughy Delights

Puddings, Puffs, Breads, Muffins, Buns, Biscuits, Doughnuts, etc.

1 tsp sugar
1/2 cup lukewarm water
1 envelope yeast
1 egg, beaten
1 1/2 cups whole wheat flour
1 cup all-purpose flour

Spice of Life

A garden is a thing of beauty - and a job forever.

Directions:

Combine apricots, lemon and boiling water; simmer 10 minutes. Discard lemon and slice apricots. Scald milk; stir in sugar, salt and shortening; cool to lukewarm. Dissolve 1 tsp sugar in lukewarm water, sprinkle yeast and let rise 10 minutes. Stir well; add milk mixture and beaten egg. Add whole wheat and white flour; beat until smooth and elastic. Stir in apricots to make soft dough. Turn on floured board and knead until smooth. Put in greased bowl and let rise in warm place until double (about 1 hour). Knead; let rise until doubled (about 1/2 hour). Bake at 375°F for 35 - 40 minutes.

Rolled Oats Bread

Joy Hiscock, St. John's, Newfoundland

Ingredients:

2 cups boiling water
2 cups rolled oats
2 tsp salt
1/3 cup fancy molasses
1 tbsp shortening, melted
1 pkg yeast
1 cup lukewarm water
1 tsp sugar
4 1/2 cups flour

Spice of Life

Happy is the man with a wife to tell him what to do and a secretary to do it. - Lord Mancroft

Directions:

Soak rolled oats in boiling water. Add salt, molasses and shortening. Dissolve yeast in lukewarm water with sugar. When first mixture is lukewarm, add dissolved yeast. Stir in flour gradually; mix well. Knead until smooth. Place in a greased bowl and allow to stand in a warm place until doubled. Knead again and put in two greased pans. Cover, let rise in a warm place until doubled. Bake at 375°F for 50 - 60 minutes.

Squaw Bread

Angela Moss, St. John's, Newfoundland (formerly of Seal Cove, Fortune Bay, Newfoundland)

Ingredients:

4 cups flour
1 tsp salt
4 tbsp baking powder
2 tbsp soft shortening
4 cups warm water

Food for Thought

Adverse criticism from a wise man is more desirable than the enthusiastic approval of a fool.

Directions:

Mix dry ingredients; cut in shortening. Add warm water and enough extra flour to make a biscuit dough. Roll on floured board; cut into small squares. Handle as little as possible. Fry in deep hot fat.

Newfoundland Partridgeberry Bread

Ruby Marsh, Grand Falls-Windsor, Newfoundland (nee Rowsell, Leading Tickles, Newfoundland)

Ingredients:

2 cups flour
1 cup light brown sugar
1 tsp baking powder
1 tsp baking soda
1/2 cup margarine or butter
2 eggs, well beaten
rind and juice of one orange
1 cup light raisins
1 1/2 cups partridgeberries

Trivia Tidbits
In Scott, Virginia, there is a railway tunnel which was originally carved by a river through 1557 feet of solid rock.

Directions:

Place flour, sugar, baking powder and baking soda in deep pan; mix with spoon. Crumble butter or margarine with flour mixture by hand. Add raisins, beaten eggs, orange rind and juice. Add berries last. Bake at 350°F for 1 hour.

Beer Fruit Loaf

Beverly Newhook (nee Parsons), Upper Gullies, Newfoundland

Ingredients:

1/2 cup butter
3/4 cup brown sugar
2 cups flour
1 cup raisins
1 egg
1/2 cup beer
1/2 tsp soda

Trivia Tidbits
The Saxons of early England kept farm animals in their houses to help keep them warm in winter.

Directions:

Cream butter and sugar. Add flour and raisins; mix well. Combine egg, soda and beer; add to flour mixture. Mix well; place in loaf tin and bake in a moderate oven for 1 hour.

Lemon Tea Muffins

Rosemarie Reynar, North York, Ontario (nee Stratton, Lewisporte, Newfoundland)

Ingredients:

2 cups unsifted flour
2 tsp baking powder
1/2 tsp salt
1 cup butter, softened
1 cup sugar
4 eggs, separated

Trivia Tidbits
It is possible to see a rainbow as a complete circle from an aeroplane.

Puddings, Duffs, Breads, Muffins, Buns, Biscuits, Doughnuts, etc.

Doughy Delights

1/2 cup lemon juice from concentrate
1/4 cup finely chopped nuts
2 tbsp light brown sugar
1/4 tsp ground nutmeg

Directions:

Preheat oven to 375°F. In medium bowl, combine flour, baking powder and salt. In a large bowl, beat butter and sugar until fluffy. Add egg yolks; beat until light. Gradually stir in lemon juice alternately with dry ingredients (do not overmix). In a small bowl, beat egg whites until stiff but not dry. Fold 1/3 egg whites into batter; fold in remaining egg whites. Fill paper-lined or greased 2 1/2-inch muffin cups 3/4 full. In another small bowl, combine remaining ingredients. Sprinkle evenly over muffins. Bake 15 - 20 minutes or until set. Cool in pan on wire rack 5 minutes. Remove from pan. Serve warm.

Partridgeberry Yogurt Muffins

Bertha Smith, Clarenville, Newfoundland

Ingredients:

1 cup plain yogurt
1 cup rolled oats
1 cup flour
3/4 cup brown sugar
1/2 cup oil
1 cup partridgeberries
1 egg
1 tsp baking soda

> ## *Food for Thought*
> Real friends are those who, when you've made a fool of yourself, don't feel that you've done a permanent job.

Directions:

Mix yogurt and rolled oats; soak for 1 hour. Add flour, sugar, oil, berries, egg and baking soda. Mix in order given. Bake in greased muffin pans at 350°F for 15 - 20 minutes.

Quick and Easy Banana Muffins

Beverly Wagner, Ladysmith, British Columbia

Ingredients:

3 ripe bananas, mashed
1/2 cup mayonnaise
1/2 cup sugar
1 cup all-purpose flour
1 tsp baking soda
small scoop peanut butter, optional

> ## **Spice of Life**
> Two wrongs don't make a right ... and three rights will get you back on the freeway.

Directions:

Preheat oven to 400°F. Blend together bananas and mayonnaise; set aside. Mix together flour, sugar and baking soda. Fold in banana mixture. Spoon into greased or lined muffin tins and bake for 15 - 20 minutes. *Variation:* Spoon 1/2 batter into muffin tins, add a small scoop of peanut butter and top with remaining batter. Bake at 400°F for 15 - 20 minutes.

Sweets & Treats

Crumbles

Candies

Cookies

Cakes

Pies

Squares

Boston Cream Trifle

Joan Pike, Placentia, Newfoundland

Ingredients:

1 can Eagle Brand sweetened milk
1 1/2 cups cold water
1 pkg vanilla instant pudding
1 tbsp rum
2 cups whipping cream, whipped
1 pound cake, cut into 15 slices
2 oz semi-sweet chocolate, grated
3 oz semi-sweet chocolate
1 oz unsweetened chocolate
1/3 cup butter

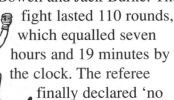

Trivia Tidbits

The longest boxing match took place in New Orleans in 1893. The combatants were Andy Bowen and Jack Burke. The fight lasted 110 rounds, which equalled seven hours and 19 minutes by the clock. The referee finally declared 'no contest' and broke up the fight.

Directions:

Combine milk and water; add pudding mix and beat well. Stir in rum. Chill until thickened (about 15 minutes). Fold in whipped cream; set aside. Place 5 cake slices in 12-cup serving bowl; spoon half of pudding mixture over cake layer. Sprinkle with half of the grated chocolate. Repeat above process, ending with a layer of cake slices. Cover all and chill overnight. Before serving, melt together semi-sweet and unsweetened chocolate with butter, stirring until smooth. Evenly spread chocolate glaze over top cake layer. Garnish as desired. Serves 10-12.

Quick Trifle

Janice Mercer, Portugal Cove, Newfoundland

Ingredients:

40 Frosted Mini Wheats
1 cup fruit juice
1/2 cup milk (more if desired)
1 small can coconut cream pie filling
1 (14oz) can fruit cocktail, well drained
1 cup whipping cream, whipped

Spice of Life

Invest in inflation. It's the only thing going up.

- Will Rogers

Directions:

Place Mini Wheats in shallow dish. Pour in juice and milk and let soak for 20 minutes. In medium size glass bowl place 1/2 mini wheats, 1/2 pie filling, 1/2 fruit. Repeat layers. Spread whipped cream on top. Garnish with fruit or coconut if desired.

Old-Fashioned Trifle

Marian Shea, Manuels, Conception Bay South, Newfoundland

Ingredients:

1 (19oz) can peach slices
1 pkg vanilla pudding mix
2 cups milk
2 cups prepared Dream Whip
1/2 cup orange juice

Food for Thought

Life is what happens to you while you're busy making other plans.

- John Lennon

Sweets & Treats

Cakes, Cookies, Squares, Pies, Candies, Crumbles

1/4 cup sherry
3 cups pound cake, 1-inch cubes
2 tbsp water
1/3 cup raspberry jam
toasted almonds and/or cherries (optional)

Spice of Life
Never put off until tomorrow
what can be avoided altogether.

Directions:

Drain peach slices, reserving 1/2 cup syrup. Combine pudding, milk and reserved syrup. Cook as directed on package. Cover and chill. Beat chilled pudding until smooth; fold in 1 cup Dream Whip. Combine orange juice and sherry; sprinkle over cake cubes in one-quart serving bowl. Stir water into jam and spoon over cake cubes. Alternately layer pudding and peach slices, ending with pudding. Top with remaining Dream Whip; chill for 2 hours. Garnish with toasted almonds and cherries, if desired.

Caramel Apple Strudel

Sharon Ashbourne, Cochrane, Alberta (nee Dyer, lly from Baie Verte, Newfoundland)

Ingredients:

12-15 Kraft caramels
2 tbsp milk
2 1/4 cups flour
1 cup sugar
1 cup pecans
1 cup butter or margarine
1 egg
1 can apple pie filling
9-inch greased pie dish

Food for Thought
There are many who dare not kill themselves for fear of what their neighbours will say.
- Cyril Connolly

Directions:

Combine caramels and milk in small bowl and microwave on high for one minute. Stir and microwave again until melted and mixes well together. Set aside. Combine flour, sugar and pecans. Cut in butter (or margarine) until crumbly, then add egg. This will make a crumbly mixture. Place 2/3 of mixture in a greased 9-inch pie dish, pressing mixture into a pie crust. Cover with apple pie filling and spread carmel mixture over top. Next cover with remaining crumble crust and bake at 350F for 45-50 minutes. This is very easy and tasty. The hardest part is peeling the wrappers off the caramels!!

Banana Dessert

Wendy Warren, North West Brook, Newfoundland

Ingredients:

1 banana cake mix
1 tin cherry pie filling

Trivia Tidbits
Bees dance to show other bees where they have found pollen.

Directions:

Mix cake mix according to directions on box. Pour 1/2 batter in cake pan. Cover with cherry pie filling. Pour remainder of batter over pie filling; spread evenly. Bake at 350°F until brown.

Barbecued Apples

Daphne Parr, St. Lunaire, Newfoundland

Ingredients:

6 apples, unpeeled
1/2 cup brown sugar, lightly packed
2 tbsp walnuts, chopped
2 tbsp butter or margarine

Directions:

Core and place each apple on individual pieces of aluminum foil. Mix together rest of ingredients. Fill centre of each apple and wrap tightly. Barbecue over medium hot coals for 30 minutes or until tender. Serves 6.

Food for Thought
One of the silliest wastes of time is figuring up how much money you'd have if you'd stayed single.
- Kin Hubbard

Raspberry Freeze

Beulah Cooper, Gander, Newfoundland

Ingredients:

1 pkg cream cheese, softened
1/3 cup sugar
1/4 cup milk
2 cups Cool Whip
1 pkg raspberries, thawed and drained

Directions:

Line a loaf pan with plastic wrap, extending slightly over sides. In a large bowl, beat cheese, sugar, milk and Cool Whip until light. Fold in raspberries with rubber spatula. Gently spread in pan. Cover and freeze for 3 hours or overnight. One hour before serving, place in fridge. Invert on serving tray and remove wrap. Cut in slices.

Spice of Life
Remember when a juvenile delinquent was a kid with an overdue library book.

Peaches 'n' Cream Brule

Betty Lou (formerly of Appleton, Ontario) and Syd George (formerly of Howley, Newfoundland), Gloucester, Ontario

Ingredients:

1/2 cup sugar
3 tbsp cornstarch
1 can 2% evaporated milk
1 egg, beaten
1 tsp vanilla extract
2 cups sliced, fresh, frozen or canned peaches
3 tbsp packed golden brown sugar

Trivia Tidbits
It's against the law to shave in Centralia, Washington, between July 26 and August 12.

Directions:

In a medium heavy saucepan, combine sugar and cornstarch. Beat milk into egg; gradually stir in sugar mixture. Cook and stir over medium heat until mixture boils and thickens. Remove from heat; stir in vanilla. Cover surface with plastic wrap; chill. Just before serving, arrange peaches in a 9-inch quiche dish or pie plate. Stir chilled custard until smooth and spoon over fruit. Sprinkle brown sugar evenly over top. Broil 4 - 5 inches from heat source, for 2 - 3 minutes, or until sugar melts and bubbles. Serve immediately.

Sweets & Treats

Cakes, Cookies, Squares, Pies, Candies, Crumbles

Lemon Angel Dessert

Connie Fowlow, Goulds, Newfoundland (nee Mason, St. John's, Newfoundland)

Ingredients:

1 angel food cake mix
1 pkg lemon pie filling
1 small tub Cool Whip
1 pt whipping cream
grated lemon rind, for garnish

Spice of Life

Let money talk, so long as it doesn't hog the conversation.

Directions:

Prepare angel food cake according to package directions. Cool. Remove from pan and break into small pieces. Prepare lemon pie filling according to package directions. Cool. Fold Cool Whip into lemon pie filling. Place cake pieces into large mixing bowl; add lemon/cream mixture. Mix all together. Thoroughly wash angel food pan. Spray with non-stick spray. Pack angel food mixture into pan; refrigerate overnight. Unmold and cover with whipping cream. Garnish with lemon rind.

Blueberry Cream Puff

Grace Ryan, Newman's Cove, Bonavista Bay, Newfoundland

Ingredients:

1 cup water
1/4 cup butter
1/2 cup flour
2 eggs
1 pkg vanilla instant pudding mix
1 1/2 cups cold milk
1 container sour cream
3 cups blueberries
1/4 cup sugar
1/4 cup cornstarch
1 pkg Dream Whip

Trivia Tidbits

Throwing confetti at weddings derived from the ancient custom of throwing grains and nuts at newlyweds and others during family celebrations. People thought that this would transfer the fertility of the seeds to the people onto which they were thrown.

Directions:

Bring 1/2 cup water and butter to a boil. Add flour; keep stirring until ball forms. Remove from heat and add eggs, one at a time. Take 1/2 the mixture and spread very thinly on lightly greased pizza pan. You can almost see the pan in places; reach as near to the edge of the pan as possible. Take other half and drop puffs all around edge. Bake 1/2 to 3/4 of an hour at 350°F. Move rack up so as not to burn. Do not open door while baking. Mix vanilla pudding powder with cold milk, as directed, until thick. Add sour cream. Bring berries and sugar slowly to a boil. Mix cornstarch with 1/2 cup water; add to berry mixture. When thickened, let cool and spread over pudding mixture. Top with Dream Whip.

Death By Chocolate

Jessie Chaulk, St. John's, Newfoundland

<u>Ingredients</u>:

1 layer of baked chocolate cake
1 large pkg of chocolate pudding
2 3/4 cups milk
1/2 cup Kahlua
2 Skor bars, crushed
1 tub Cool Whip

<u>Directions</u>:

Blend pudding mix with milk and Kahlua. Divide a layer of chocolate cake in half. Cube each half and put half in bottom of bowl. Pour half of pudding mixture; spread half Cool Whip and sprinkle with Skor bar. Repeat layers.

Food for Thought
Life is the greatest bargain; we get it for nothing. - Yiddish proverb

Layered Lemon Dessert

Frances Pelley, Edmonton, Alberta (formerly of Deer Lake, Newfoundland)

<u>Ingredients</u>:

1 pkg lemon pie filling
1 cup flour
1/2 cup soft margarine
1/3 cup ground almonds
2 tbsp sugar
1 (8oz) pkg cream cheese, softened
1/2 cup icing sugar
1/2 tsp vanilla
1 cup whipping cream, whipped
1/4 cup toasted almonds

Trivia Tidbits

Mayflies live only a few hours after they are hatched.

<u>Directions</u>:

Mix lemon pie filling according to package directions, omitting margarine. Let cool. Combine flour, margarine, almonds and sugar together and press into an 8x8 pan. Bake at 350°F for 15 - 20 minutes until golden. Beat remaining ingredients together until smooth. Fold in 1/2 of whipped cream; spread over cooled crust. Spread pie filling over cheese layer. Refrigerate until cold. Spread remaining whipped cream over lemon layer. Refrigerate. Garnish with almonds just before serving. It is best to make this dessert the day before.

Paradise Partridgeberry Treat

Judy Kirby, Epworth, Newfoundland

<u>Ingredients</u>:

2 3/4 cups cranberry juice
2/3 cup sugar
3 tbsp orange juice
2 envelopes unflavoured gelatine
1 1/4 cups partridgeberries (fresh or frozen)

Spice of Life
Life begins when the kids leave home and the dog dies.

1 pkg miniature raspberry jelly rolls*
2/3 cup Carnation evaporated milk
2 tbsp lemon juice
*Or use 1 pkg frozen pound cake, thawed and cut into 1/4 inch slices.

Directions:

In medium saucepan, combine cranberry juice, sugar, orange juice and gelatine. Chop partridgeberries and add to saucepan. Over medium heat, stir juice mixture until steaming hot, then pour into shallow bowl. Stirring occasionally, chill mixture in freezer for 1 1/2-2 hours or until it thickens to the consistency of unbeaten egg whites. Line a 9-inch spring form pan with plastic wrap. Cut jelly roll into 1/4-inch slices. Stand slices around inside edge of spring form pan. Cover bottom of pan with remaining slices. Set aside. Pour Carnation milk into a deep bowl. Chill in freezer about 15-20 minutes or until ice crystals form around edges of bowl. Beat with electric mixer until stiff (about 1 minute). Add lemon juice and continue to beat 1 to 2 minutes. Fold whipped evaporated milk into thickened jelly mixture. Pour into prepared pan and chill 1 1/2 hours, until set. Makes 8 to 10 servings.

Light Berry Breeze

Teresa Davey, Niagara Falls, Ontario (nee Anderson, Burgeo, Newfoundland)

Ingredients:

1 cup plain yogurt
1/4 cup granulated sugar
2 tsp orange rind, grated
1/4 cup orange juice
2 cups Cool Whip, thawed
1 1/2 cups blueberries
1 1/2 cups strawberries, sliced
6 slices pound cake

Food for Thought
It is unpleasant to go alone, even to be drowned. - Russian proverb

Directions:

Mix yogurt with sugar in small bowl until well blended. Fold in rind, orange juice and Cool Whip; chill. Spoon 1/4 cup sauce onto individual serving dishes. Top with 1 slice of cake and 1/4 cup more sauce. Spoon 1/2 cup berries on each serving.

Orange Buttermilk Dessert

Bertha Smith, Clarenville, Newfoundland

Ingredients:

1 (20oz) can crushed pineapple, undrained
1 (6oz) pkg orange flavoured jello
2 cups buttermilk
1 (8oz) carton whipped topping

Trivia Tidbits
A snail moves at the rate of 61 cm an hour.

Directions:

In a saucepan, bring pineapple to a boil. Remove from heat. Add jello and stir to dissolve. Add buttermilk, stirring well. Cool to room temperature. Fold in whipped topping and pour into a 11x7x2 dish. Refrigerate several hours or overnight. Cut into squares.

Fruit Juice Jello

Teresa Ivey, St. John's, Newfoundland

Ingredients:

1 (12 1/2oz) can unsweetened frozen juice concentrate, thawed
2 pkgs unflavoured gelatin
1/2 cup cold water
2 cups boiling water

Directions:

Soften gelatin in cold water. Add boiling water to gelatin mixture. Cool and add thawed juice concentrate. Pour into square pan and refrigerate until set.
*Optional: Add grapes, banana slices or other fruit before it sets.

Popcorn Ball

Ben Bellefontaine, Etobicoke, Ontario

Ingredients:

24 cups popped popcorn
3 oz raspberry flavoured gelatin (or any red gelatin)
1 cup granulated sugar
1 cup light corn syrup

> **Spice of Life**
> Wisdom doesn't necessarily come with age. Sometimes age just shows up all by itself. - Tom Wilson

Directions:

Place popped popcorn in a large bowl or pot. In saucepan, combine gelatin, sugar and syrup. Bring to a boil. Pour over popcorn, stir to coat well. Form into balls, buttering hands as needed. Makes 24 to 30 balls.

Never-Fail Pastry

Betty Lou (formerly of Appleton, Ontario) and Syd George (formerly of Howley, Newfoundland), Gloucester, Ontario

Ingredients:

4 cups flour
1/2 tsp salt
1 lb shortening
1 egg
1 tbsp vinegar cider
1 tbsp white or brown sugar
1 cup water

> *Food for Thought*
> Marriage has many pains, but celibacy has no pleasures. - Samuel Johnson
>
>

Directions:

Sift flour with salt and sugar and cut in shortening until mixture resembles bread crumbs. Beat egg; add water and vinegar. Make well in flour mixture and add enough liquid to mix the flour to a consistency that is easy to handle and roll out. Separate into four or five equal portions and roll into a ball and cover with plastic wrap and freeze for future pie shells. It can be stored for up to 2 weeks.

Apple Crisp

Marion Scheers, Edmonton, Alberta

<u>Ingredients</u>:

4 1/2 cups apples, sliced
1/2 cup sugar
2 tsp lemon juice
2 tbsp water
1/2 cup soft margarine
2/3 cup brown sugar
2/3 cup flour
1 1/2 cups rolled oats

<u>Directions</u>:

Prepare the apples; measure and arrange in an 8x8 baking dish. Sprinkle with sugar. Combine lemon juice and water. Pour over apples. Cream margarine; gradually add sugar. Blend in flour and oats. Spread over fruit. Bake in preheated oven at 350°F.

> *Food for Thought*
> We are more wicked together than separately.
> - Seneca

Blueberry Crisp

Marion Scheers, Edmonton, Alberta

<u>Ingredients</u>:

4 cups blueberries
1/3 cup white sugar
2 tsp lemon juice
1/2 cup soft margarine
2/3 cup brown sugar
2/3 cup flour
1 1/2 cups rolled oats

<u>Directions</u>:

Combine blueberries, sugar and lemon juice and put in 8x8 baking dish. Cream margarine; gradually add sugar. Blend in flour and oats. Spread over fruit. Bake in preheated oven at 350°F until pastry is golden brown.

> **Spice of Life**
> I never entertain wicked thoughts, but they sometimes entertain me.
> - Laurence Peter

Rhubarb Crisp

Marion Scheers, Edmonton, Alberta

<u>Ingredients</u>:

4 1/2 cups rhubarb, cut up
3/4 cup sugar
1/4 tsp cinnamon
1/4 tsp ginger
2 tbsp water
1/2 cup soft margarine
2/3 cup brown sugar
2/3 cup flour
1 1/2 cups rolled oats

> **Trivia Tidbits**
> A dog turns around before lying down to find which way the wind is blowing, and faces it to scent possible danger.

Directions:

Combine rhubarb, sugar, cinnamon, ginger and water; put in 8x8 baking dish. Cream margarine; gradually add sugar. Blend in flour and oats. Spread over fruit. Bake in preheated oven at 350°F. until pastry is golden brown. *Note:* May use peaches or plums in place of rhubarb.

Zucchini Apple Crisp

Marion Scheers, Edmonton, Alberta

Ingredients:

1 large zucchini
1/2 cup lemon juice
1 tsp nutmeg
1/2 cup sugar
2 tsp cinnamon

Topping:

1 1/3 cups brown sugar
1 cup flour
1 cup rolled oats
2/3 cup soft margarine

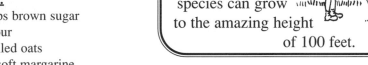

Trivia Tidbits

The bamboo is a member of the grass family. Some bamboo can grow to a foot taller in 12 hours, and another species can grow to the amazing height of 100 feet.

Directions:

Peel zucchini; remove seeds and slice as you would apples for pies (about 6 cuts). Put zucchini and lemon juice in saucepan; cover and cook over medium heat until tender, stirring occasionally (15 minutes). Add sugar, nutmeg and cinnamon. Blend well together. Remove from heat, pour into greased 13x9 pan. Mix all toppings in a bowl until crumbly. Sprinkle over zucchini. Bake at 350°F for 40 - 45 minutes until golden brown. Serve with ice cream.

Graham Wafer Cake

Marion Scheers, Edmonton, Alberta

Ingredients:

1/2 cup butter
1 egg
1 cup milk
1 tsp vanilla
1 cup sugar
2 cups graham wafer crumbs
1 tsp baking powder
pinch of salt
5 tsp flour

Food for Thought

Those who deny freedom to others deserve it not for themselves. - Abraham Lincoln

Directions :

Cream together butter, sugar, egg, milk and vanilla. Add remaining ingredients; bake at 350°F for 25 minutes. Ice.

Molasses Taffy

Christopher Sheppard, Manuels, CBS, Newfoundland

Ingredients:

2 cups molasses
1 cup sugar
2 tbsp butter
1 tbsp vinegar

Spice of Life

It's going to be fun to watch and see how long the meek can keep the earth after they inherit it. - Elbert Hubbard

Directions:

Place all ingredients in saucepan and boil until brittle - hard crack stage (when a drop put in cold water forms a ball); pour into buttered pan. Grease hands and when cool enough to handle, pull the taffy until it becomes light in colour. Cut into pieces with scissors.

Home-Made Fudge

Marian Shea, Manuels, Conception Bay South, Newfoundland

Ingredients:

4 cups sugar
1 tsp salt
1 tin milk
3 tbsp butter
1 tsp vanilla
6 large marshmallows
6 oz chocolate chips

Food for Thought

Blessed is the man who expects nothing, for he shall never be disappointed. - Alexander Pope

Directions:

Combine sugar, salt, milk and butter in a saucepan; mix well. Turn heat on high, stirring constantly until it boils; turn down to medium and boil 15 minutes. Scrape sides and stir every 2 minutes. When mixture reaches soft ball stage remove from heat. Add vanilla, marshmallows and chocolate chips. Mix well and turn into greased pan. Let stand 10 minutes, then cut into squares.

Tortoises

Claudine Barnes, Corner Brook, Newfoundland (nee Pye, Cape Charles, Labrador)

Ingredients:

1 cup chocolate chips
1 cup butterscotch chips
1 cup peanut butter
2 cups Rice Krispies
1/2 cup almond pieces

Trivia Tidbits

The Romans introduced marbles to England in the first century AD.

Directions:

Melt together chocolate chips, butterscotch chips and peanut butter over a low heat. Remove from heat and add Rice Krispies and almond pieces. Drop by tbsp on waxed paper on tray. Refrigerate about 15 minutes. Remove from wax paper onto a plate and repeat, if necessary. Makes 6 dozen cookies.

Almond Roca

Helen Dominic-Mullins, Coquitlam, British Columbia (formerly of St. John's, Newfoundland)

Ingredients:

1 lb butter
3 cups brown sugar
2 cups whole almonds (skins on)
4 cups chocolate pieces
4 cups chopped almonds (fairly small pieces)

Spice of Life
Never say never, never say always, and never say forever.
- Ann Landers

Directions:

In a pot on medium heat melt butter; add brown sugar and bring to a boil for 7 minutes, stirring constantly. (Start a timer as soon as you put the brown sugar in). Add whole almonds stirring constantly for another 7 minutes. (Should reach the hard crack stage.) Spread mixture on a greased cookie sheet. Place 2 cups chocolate pieces (I use 1/2 dark and 1/2 light chocolate) on the mixture while it is still hot. Spread chocolate evenly over whole mixture. Sprinkle with 2 cups chopped almonds. Place another cookie sheet on top of the one with the mixture. Be very careful as you should make the sheets fit exactly as you have to hold the two together and flip them so that the mixture goes into the second sheet. Repeat the steps by placing remaining 2 cups of chocolate pieces on the mixture; then the remaining almonds. Chill outside the refrigerator as it cools faster with air circulation. When chilled, break in pieces. Store in refrigerator in air-tight container. Let stand at room temperature for 1/2 hour before serving.

Fudge

Pearl White, Trenton, Ontario (nee Flight, Small Point, Newfoundland)

Ingredients:

10 oz digestive biscuits
2 oz raisins
10 squares cooking chocolate
4 oz butter
1 large tin sweetened condensed milk

Spice of Life
No matter how much money talks, nobody finds it boring.

Directions:

Crush digestive biscuits with rolling pin; add raisins. Melt chocolate, butter and milk. Mix and spread in a tin; cool. Refrigerate until set.

Brown Sugar Fudge

Norma Clarke, Peterboro, Ontario, (nee Atkinson, Herring Neck, Newfoundland)

Ingredients:

2 cups brown sugar
1 tbsp cornstarch
pinch of salt
1 tbsp butter
1/3 cup Carnation milk
1 tsp vanilla

Food for Thought
Equality may perhaps be a right, but no power on earth can ever turn it into a fact.
- Honore de Balzac

Sweets & Treats

Cakes, Cookies, Squares, Pies, Candies, Crumbles

Directions:

Combine all ingredients except for vanilla. Boil to soft ball stage. Take from heat, add vanilla and beat until creamy. Pour into buttered 8x8 pan. Mark into squares when still warm. You may want to add 1/2 cup nuts, coconut, raisins or cherries.

Maple Fudge

Norma Clarke, Peterboro, Ontario, (nee Atkinson, Herring Neck, Newfoundland)

Ingredients:

1 can sweetened condensed milk
1 cup maple syrup
1 cup brown sugar
1/4 tsp salt
1 tbsp butter
1/2 cup chopped nuts

Trivia Tidbits
There is more sugar in a kilo of lemons than in a kilo of strawberries.

Directions:

Combine all ingredients in medium saucepan. Simmer slowly, stirring until sugar disolves. Continue cooking mixture, stirring occasionally until it reaches soft ball stage or a temperature of 236°F. Cool, without stirring, to a temperature of 110°F or until mixture feels warm. Beat until thick; add nuts and pour into buttered pie pan. Allow to set until completely cooled.

Brownies

Bill Penney, St. John's, Newfoundland (formerly of St. Mary's Bay, Newfoundland)

Ingredients:

1/2 cup butter
1/4 cup cocoa
3/4 cup flour
2 eggs
3/4 cup nuts
1 tsp vanilla
1 cup sugar
2 tbsp cold water

Food for Thought
The best armour is to keep out of gunshot.

Directions:

Cream butter, vanilla and sugar. Add eggs, then dry ingredients and water. Bake in an 8x8 pan at 350°F for approximately 25 minutes.

Texas Brownies

Alice Bye, Oliver, British Columbia

Ingredients:

2 cups flour
2 cups granulated sugar
1/2 cup butter or margarine
1/2 cup shortening

Spice of Life
There is nothing new under the sun ... but a joke is brand new if you've never heard it before.

1 cup strong brewed coffee (or water)
1/4 cup dark, unsweetened cocoa
1/2 cup buttermilk
2 eggs
1 tsp baking soda
1 tsp vanilla
1 cup chopped nuts (optional)

<u>**Frosting**</u>:

1/2 cup butter or margarine
2 tbsp dark cocoa
1/4 cup milk
3 1/2 cups icing sugar, unsifted
1 tsp vanilla

Trivia Tidbits
Ants are capable of pulling weights three hundred times their own weight.

<u>**Directions**</u>:

In a large mixing bowl, combine flour and sugar. In heavy saucepan, combine butter, shortening, coffee and cocoa; stir and heat to boiling point. Pour boiling mixture over the flour and sugar. Add eggs, buttermilk, baking soda and vanilla. Mix well using a wooden spoon or electric mixer on high speed. Add nuts, if desired. Pour into a well-buttered 17 1/2x11 cookie sheet or jelly roll pan. Bake at 350°F for 20 minutes or until brownies test done in the center. For frosting, stir butter, cocoa and milk and heat to boiling. Mix in icing sugar and vanilla. Pour warm frosting over brownies as you take them out of the oven. Cut into 48 bars. (These freeze well).

Triple Chocolate Brownies

Jennifer Miller, Mount Pearl, Newfoundland

<u>**Ingredients**</u>:

1/2 cup granulated sugar
1/3 cup margarine or butter
1 egg
1 tsp vanilla
1/2 cup all-purpose flour
1/3 cup cocoa
1 tsp baking powder
1/4 cup 2% milk
1/4 cup chocolate chips

<u>**Icing:**</u>

1/4 cup icing sugar
1 1/2 tbsp cocoa
1 tbsp milk

Spice of Life
If man builds a better mousetrap, the world will beat a path to his door ... and the government will build a better mousetrap tax. - Peter's Almanac

<u>**Directions**</u>:

Preheat oven to 350°F. In bowl, beat together sugar and margarine. Beat in egg and vanilla, mixing well. In another bowl, combine flour, cocoa and baking powder; stir into butter mixture just until blended. Stir in milk and chocolate chips. Pour into 8x8 pan sprayed with vegetable spray. Bake approximately 18 minutes or until edges start to pull away from pan and centre is still wet. Let cool slightly before glazing. In small bowl, whisk together icing sugar, cocoa and milk; pour over brownies in pan.

Fudgy Oatmeal Brownies

Marion Scheers, Edmonton, Alberta

Ingredients:

1 1/4 cups sugar
1 cup oil
3 eggs
1/2 cup cocoa
2 tsp vanilla
1 cup flour
3/4 cup oats
1/4 cup wheat germ
pinch of salt
1/2 cup cold water

Food for Thought

What married couples should save for old age is each other.

Directions:

Mix sugar, oil, eggs, cocoa and vanilla. Mix rest of ingredients in order given. Pour into 9 x 13 pan. Bake at 350°F for 25 minutes.

Blonde Brownies

Wendy Warren, North West Brook, Newfoundland

Ingredients:

1/3 cup butter
1 cup brown sugar
1 egg
1 cup flour
1/8 tsp baking soda
1/4 tsp baking powder
1/2 tsp salt
1/2 cup walnuts

Trivia Tidbits

A law in Maine requires you to tip your hat when a game warden comes by.

Directions:

Melt butter in saucepan. Stir in sugar; let cool, add egg. Add rest of ingredients. Spread in 8 x 8 pan. Bake in moderate oven at 350°F for 20 - 25 minutes. When cool, cut into squares.

Awesome Brownies

Rosemarie Reynar, North York, Ontario (nee Stratton, Lewisporte, Newfoundland)

Ingredients:

3/4 cup flour
1/3 cup cocoa
1/4 tsp salt
1 cup sugar
1/2 cup butter
2 eggs
3 tbsp water
1 tsp vanilla

Food for Thought

A rolling stone gathers no moss. - Greek proverb

1/2 tsp baking powder
1 cup walnuts, optional

Directions:

Preheat oven to 325°F. Sift together flour, cocoa, salt and sugar. Stir in butter, eggs, water, vanilla and baking powder. Beat until smooth. Stir in 1 cup walnuts, if desired. Pour into greased pans. Bake for 25 - 30 minutes. When cool, top with chocolate icing.

Lemon Squares

Anita Shea, Stephenville Crossing, Newfoundland

Ingredients:

2 cups flour
1/2 cup white sugar
1 tsp baking powder
2 cups coconut
1 cup butter, melted
1 pkg lemon pie filling

> **Trivia Tidbits**
> The silk of a spider's web is stronger than a steel thread of the same diameter.

Directions:

Combine flour, coconut, sugar and baking powder. Pour melted butter over mixture; mix until crumbly. Press 3/4 of mixture into brownie pan. Mix lemon pie filling according to instructions on package. Let cool and pour over bottom mixture. Sprinkle remaining flour and coconut mixture over lemon filling. Bake at 325°F until brown for 20 - 25 minutes.

Reeses Pieces Squares

Sherry DiPaolo, Little Heart's Ease, Newfoundland

Ingredients - Base:

1 1/3 cups graham wafer crumbs
1 cup peanut butter
1 3/4 cup icing sugar
1/2 cup melted butter

Topping:

1 cup chocolate chips
3/4 cup peanut butter

Food for Thought

Saints should always be judged guilty until they are proved innocent.

Directions:

Base - Mix all ingredients well and press into an 8x8 pan and freeze.
Topping - Melt chocolate chips and peanut butter on low heat. Pour over base and freeze again. Cut into squares and refrigerate.

Old-Fashioned Buttermilk Pie

Betty Lou (formerly of Appleton, Ontario) and Syd George (formerly of Howley, Newfoundland), Gloucester, Ontario

Ingredients:

3 tsp butter, unsalted

1 1/4 cups sugar
3 eggs
1 tbsp flour
1/2 cup buttermilk
1 tsp vanilla extract
1 9-inch pie shell, unbaked

Directions:

Preheat oven to 300°F. Cream butter and sugar. Stir in eggs, flour, buttermilk and vanilla. Pour into pie shell; bake until tip of knife comes out clean, about 45 minutes. Cool slightly before serving.

Mom's Eat-Lots-More Bars

Rosemarie Reynar, North York, Ontario (nee Stratton, Lewisporte, Newfoundland)

Ingredients:

1 cup syrup
1 pkg chocolate chips
1/4 cup peanut butter
2 cups Rice Krispies
2 cups peanuts

Directions:

Melt in saucepan, syrup, chocolate chips and peanut butter. Add Rice Krispies and peanuts. Place in oblong pan. Allow to cool.

Chinese Chews

Winnie Marshall, Stephenville, Newfoundland

Ingredients:

3/4 cup flour
1/2 tsp baking powder
1/4 tsp salt
1 cup sugar
1 cup chopped dates
3/4 cup chopped walnuts
2 eggs

Trivia Tidbits

Sea otters have two coats of fur.

Directions:

Sift together flour, baking powder, salt and sugar. Stir in dates and nuts. Beat eggs until foamy and blend with dry ingredients. Turn into a greased 8x8 pan. Bake at 350°F for 25 - 30 minutes. Cool and cut into bars. Makes about 24 bars.

Fudge Squares

Wendy Warren, North West Brook, Newfoundland

Ingredients:

1 1/2 cups butter

3/4 cup brown sugar
1 egg
3/4 cup chopped walnuts
1 1/2 cups flour
1 tsp baking powder
1 tsp vanilla

Directions:

Cream butter and sugar; mix in egg and vanilla. Add flour and baking powder. Once blended thoroughly, add nuts. Spread in a greased pan. Bake for 15 minutes in moderate 350°F oven. Cool and cut into squares.

Banana Bars

June Gates, Woodstock, Ontario

Ingredients:

1/2 cup margarine
1 cup sugar
1 egg
1 tsp baking soda, dissolved in 1 tbsp water
1 tsp vanilla
1 1/2 cups sifted flour
1 tsp baking powder
1 1/3 cups mashed bananas

Icing:

2 cups icing sugar
1 tbsp butter
2 tbsp milk
1 tsp vanilla

Directions:

Cream margarine and sugar. Add egg and beat well. Stir in baking soda mixture and vanilla. Add dry ingredients, alternately with bananas, beating well. Spread into greased pan. Bake at 350°F for 25 - 30 minutes. May be iced, if desired.

Jelly Squares

Valerie Sturge, Gambo, Newfoundland

Ingredients:

2 pkgs jello
1/4 cup white sugar
3 cups boiling water
2 1/2 tbsp custard powder
1/2 cup white sugar
1 cup butter
2 cups flour
2 cups coconut
2 tsp baking powder

Food for Thought

Every woman keeps a corner in her heart where she is always twenty-one.

Spice of Life

The rain falls on the just and the unjust alike ... but if I had the management of such affairs, I would rain softly and sweetly on the just; but if I caught a sample of the unjust outdoors, I would drown him. - Mark Twain

Trivia Tidbits

Forty-two million people died as a result of the Black Death in the thirteenth century.

Directions:

Boil together jello, white sugar and water. Mix custard powder with a little water and add to the jello. Stir until thickened; let cool. Combine sugar, butter, flour, coconut and baking powder. Rub together and press into a greased pan, leaving a small amount. Pour on filling and sprinkle with remaining base. Bake in pre-heated oven at 375°F until brown.

Custard Squares

Valerie Sturge, Gambo, Newfoundland

Ingredients:

1 cup flour
1 cup coconut
1/2 cup butter
1 1/4 cups white sugar, divided
2 cups boiling water
2 pkgs custard powder
1 pkg Dream Whip
coconut

Food for Thought
True success is that which makes building stones of old mistakes.
-Arthur Guiterman

Directions:

Mix together flour, coconut, butter and 1/4 cup sugar. Spread in a greased 9-inch square pan. Bake at 350°F for 10 - 12 minutes, or until slightly brown. Let cool. In a medium-sized mixing bowl, mix 5 tablespoons custard powder in a little cold water, then add to boiling water and 1 cup sugar mixture. Stir until it thickens. Spread over base and allow to cool completely. Top with Dream Whip and sprinkle with coconut before cutting in squares.

Blueberry Squares

Beulah Cooper, Gander, Newfoundland

Ingredients:

2 cups blueberries
3 tbsp lemon juice
3 tbsp sugar
1 pkg vanilla pudding
2 cups milk
1 env Dream Whip
graham wafers

Trivia Tidbits

Bats always turn left when exiting a cave.

Directions:

Beat blueberries, lemon juice and sugar until thick. In another bowl, beat together the vanilla pudding and milk. Blend the envelope of Dream Whip together with pudding. Line 9-inch baking pan with graham wafers and pour 3/4 pudding mix on top. Add another layer of wafers and blueberry mixture. Add another layer of wafers and remaining pudding mix.

Raspberry Squares

Beulah Cooper, Gander, Newfoundland

Ingredients:

1 cup flour
1/2 cup butter
1 tbsp icing sugar
1 1/2 cups water
3/4 cup sugar
2 tbsp cornstarch
1 pkg raspberry jello
2 cups raspberries
1 pkg Nutri Whip or Dream Whip

Directions:

Mix flour, butter and icing sugar together and press into an 8-inch pan. Bake at 350°F for 10 - 15 minutes. Let cool. Bring to a boil water, sugar and cornstarch. When thickened, add jello. Place raspberries on the cooled base and cover with the jello mixture. When cool, top with Nutri Whip or Dream Whip.

Spice of Life

It isn't necessary to be rich and famous to be happy. It's only necessary to be rich.

- Alan Alda

Peanut Crunch Squares

Bernardine White, St. Lawrence, Newfoundland

Ingredients:

1/2 cup brown sugar
1 cup peanut butter
1/2 cup corn syrup
1 cup Rice Krispies
1 cup crushed Corn Flakes
1/4 cup margarine, melted
2 tbsp vanilla instant pudding powder
3 tbsp milk
2 cups icing sugar
3 tbsp margarine
3 squares semi-sweet chocolate

Food for Thought

If you travel to an underdeveloped country, you can't drink the water. If you travel to a developed country, you can't breathe the air. - Robert J. Beran

Directions:

In a sauce pan, heat brown sugar, peanut butter and corn syrup until the sugar dissolves. Remove from heat and add Rice Krispies and Corn Flakes. Press into a 9x13 pan. Chill in refrigerator. Mix together margarine, instant pudding powder and milk. Blend in 2 cups icing sugar; spread over first layer. Melt margarine and chocolate; spread over second layer. Chill and cut into small pieces.

Flannigan Shenanigan Squares

Bernardine White, St. Lawrence, Newfoundland

Ingredients:

1/2 cup peanut butter
1/3 cup cocoa
1 tsp salt
2 eggs

Spice of Life

Varicose veins are the result of an improper selection of grandparents. - William Osler

Sweets & Treats

Cakes, Cookies, Squares, Pies, Candies, Crumbles

1 cup white sugar
1 cup margarine
1 tsp vanilla
2 cups coconut
1 cup crushed walnuts
1/2 cup green cherries
4 cups graham wafer crumbs
1/2 cup red cherries, chopped

Directions:

In a sauce pan, heat peanut butter, cocoa, salt, eggs, white sugar, margarine and vanilla. Simmer over medium heat until thick. Remove from heat and add rest of ingredients. Combine well and press into pan, let cool. Top with butter icing and melted chocolate, cut into squares.

Drumsticks

Rhonda Tulk, Aspen Cove, Newfoundland

Ingredients:

1 1/2 cups graham wafer crumbs
1/2 cup peanuts, chopped
1/4 cup butter, melted
1 (250g) pkg cream cheese
1/2 cup icing sugar
1/2 cup peanut butter
2 tsp vanilla
3 eggs
1 large container Cool Whip
chocolate sundae sauce

Directions:

Mix together wafers, nuts and melted butter; press in 8x8 pan. On high speed, mix together cream cheese, icing sugar, peanut butter and vanilla. While mixing, add eggs one at a time. Fold in Cool Whip. Pour mixture over base. Drizzle chocolate sundae sauce on top and knife it through filling. Sprinkle with chopped nuts. Freeze for at least 4 - 5 hours. Keep frozen.

Pineapple Squares

Rachel Hollett, Cambridge, Nova Scotia (nee Lomond, Port aux Basques, Newfoundland)

Ingredients:

2 1/2 cups graham wafer crumbs
3/4 cup margarine
1 1/2 cups icing sugar
1 egg
1 tin crushed pineapple (well drained)
1 tin thick cream

Directions:

Rub 1/2 of the margarine and wafer crumbs together. Press little over 1/2 of it in a 9x9 pan. Bake for 8 minutes and let cool. Cream other 1/2 of the margarine, sugar and egg together; spread over wafer crumbs. Next spread with pineapple. Whip cream and spread over pineapple. Sprinkle with remaining crumbs. Store in a cool place and cut into squares.

Lively Lemon Squares
Marion Scheers, Edmonton, Alberta

Ingredients:

2/3 cup butter
2 tbsp lemon juice
3 cups graham wafer crumbs
1 (6oz) pkg lemon jelly powder
1 cup boiling water
1 (16oz) can cold milk
3/4 cup sugar
1 (14oz) can crushed pineapple and liquid
1/4 tsp salt

Directions:

Melt butter and stir in lemon juice and crumbs until combined. Reserve 1/4 cup. Press remaining crumbs into 9x13 (or larger) pan. Dissolve jelly powder in boiling water. Chill until syrupy. In large cold bowl, whip cold milk and sugar until stiff. Stir in pineapple and liquid, salt, and syrupy lemon jelly until thoroughly combined. Pour over graham crumb base. Sprinkle top with reserved crumbs. Refrigerate at least 2 hours.

Peppermint Squares

Phyllis Lemieux, Chateauguay, Quebec (nee Boyd, Herring Neck, Newfoundland)

Ingredients:

1/2 cup butter
1 egg, beaten
2 tbsp cocoa
1/2 cup white sugar
1 1/2 cups graham wafer crumbs
1/2 cup chopped walnuts
1/2 cup coconut
1/2 tsp vanilla
1/2 tsp almond extract
1/2 tsp peppermint extract

Icing:

1 tsp peppermint extract
1 1/2 cups icing sugar
2 tbsp butter
milk
2 squares unsweetened chocolate, melted

Directions:

Combine 1/2 cup butter, egg, cocoa and white sugar in double boiler. Cook for about 5 minutes and stir; remove from heat. In a mixing bowl, combine wafer crumbs, walnuts, coconut, vanilla, almond extract and 1/2 tsp peppermint extract. Combine with butter mixture and press into an 8 x 8 pan. Let cool. To make icing, mix icing sugar, 2 tbsp butter and 1 tsp peppermint extract. Add enough milk to mix. Ice squares and pour melted chocolate over top.

Plum-Filled Dessert Squares
Frances Pelley, Edmonton, Alberta (formerly of Deer Lake, Newfoundland)

<u>Ingredients</u>:

1 1/2 cups rolled oats

1 cup flour

3/4 cup margarine, room temperature

1 tsp grated lemon peel

1 tsp cinnamon

1/2 tsp nutmeg

1/4 tsp baking powder

1/3 cup brown sugar, packed

2 cups plums, chopped

> **Trivia Tidbits**
> The nail on our middle finger grows the fastest, the thumb nail the slowest.

<u>Directions</u>:

In a large bowl, combine all ingredients except plums and 2 tbsp brown sugar. Beat until well mixed. Pat half the oat mixture on bottom of greased 8x8 pan. Bake at 400°F for 12 minutes or until golden brown. Remove from oven, cover with chopped plums mixed with remaining 2 tbsp of brown sugar. Sprinkle remaining oat mixture over plums. Return to oven and bake for 20 - 25 minutes or until golden brown. Let cool.

Coconut Squares
Josephine Jenkins, Springdale, Newfoundland (nee Young, Twillingate, Newfoundland)

<u>Ingredients</u>:

2 cups graham wafer crumbs

3/4 cup sugar

3/4 cup milk

1/2 cup butter

1 cup coconut

2 tsp flour

1 tsp baking powder

1 egg, beaten

<u>Topping:</u>

1/2 cup butter

1/2 cup sugar

3 tbsp flour

3 tbsp milk

3 tbsp water

coconut

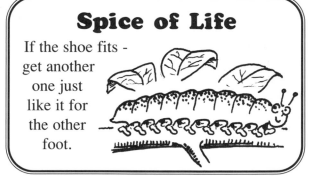

Spice of Life

If the shoe fits - get another one just like it for the other foot.

<u>Directions</u>:

Combine crumbs, sugar, coconut, flour and baking powder. Cut in butter and mix in beaten egg and milk. Press into 8x11 pan; bake at 350°F for 15 - 20 minutes. Blend all topping ingredients together. Ice squares when cool.

Nan's Coconut Squares

Josephine Jenkins, Springdale, Newfoundland (nee Young, Twillingate, Newfoundland)

Ingredients:

1/2 cup butter

1 cup sugar

2 eggs

1 tsp vanilla

2 1/2 cups flour

3 tsp baking powder

1 cup water

pinch of salt

Topping:

5 tbsp cocoa

1 cup sugar

1/2 cup hot water

1/2 cup cold water

coconut

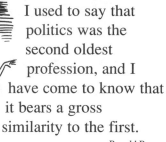

Spice of Life

I used to say that politics was the second oldest profession, and I have come to know that it bears a gross similarity to the first.

- Ronald Reagan

Directions:

Cream butter and sugar really well. Add eggs (only one, if necessary). Add remaining ingredients, mix and bake at 350°F for 1/2 hour. When cold, cut into squares. Mix cocoa, sugar and water together. Dip squares into mixture and roll in coconut.

Aero Delights

Denise Hibbs (nee Jenkins), Springdale, Newfoundland

Ingredients:

2 cups graham wafer crumbs

2 cups coconut

1/2 cup butter, melted

1 can sweetened condensed milk

4-5 Aero bars, melted

Food for Thought

Good people are good because they've come to wisdom through failure. -William Saroyan

Directions:

Mix crumbs, coconut, butter and milk; press into square, greased dish. Bake at 275°F for 10 - 12 minutes. Cool. Melt Aero bars and spread on top. Cool and cut.

Pineapple Squares

Denise Hibbs (nee Jenkins), Springdale, Newfoundland

Ingredients:

graham wafers

1/2 cup butter

3/4 cup sugar

1 egg

2 cups coconut

1 can crushed pineapple, drained

1 pkg Dream Whip

Trivia Tidbits

It was once thought unlucky to cut your nails on a Sunday.

Directions:

Layer bottom of baking dish with graham wafers. Cream butter, sugar and egg; mix well. Add coconut and drained fruit; spread over bottom. Add another layer of graham wafers over filling. Top with Dream Whip.

Triple Layer Bars

Danessa Quinlan, Birchy Bay, Newfoundland

Ingredients:

1/2 cup butter
1 1/2 cups graham wafer crumbs
2 2/3 cups flaked coconut
1 can sweet milk
1 pkg semi-sweet chocolate chips
1/2 cup peanut butter

Trivia Tidbits
There are 850,000 different kinds of insects in the world. This figure is about three times as many as all the other kinds of animals added together.

Directions:

Preheat oven to 350°F. Melt butter in 9x13 pan in oven. Sprinkle graham wafer crumbs evenly over butter and mix together; press firmly in bottom of pan. Top evenly with coconut, then with sweet milk. Bake for 25 minutes. In small saucepan over low heat, melt chocolate chips with peanut butter. Spread evenly over hot coconut layer; cool 30 minutes. Chill. Cut into bars and enjoy.

Nutty Henry Bars

Helen Duggan (nee Bransfield), Bell Island, Newfoundland

Ingredients:

1 cup brown sugar
1/2 cup milk
1/2 cup butter
1 cup crushed graham wafers
1 cup coconut
1 box whole graham wafers
1/2 cup chopped nuts

Food for Thought
It's bad form to go half-way to meet troubles which are not coming to your house. - Ethel White

Directions:

Bring brown sugar, milk and butter to a boil. Remove from heat. Add crushed graham wafers, coconut and nuts. Line bottom of a greased 9x12 pan with whole graham wafers. Pour cooked filling on top of crackers. Put another layer of graham wafers on top. Press down gently. Let cool. Cover with chocolate icing; cut into squares.

Magic Bars

Violet Schnarr, Elmira, Ontario (nee Noseworthy, Birchy Bay, Newfoundland)

Ingredients:

1/2 cup butter or margarine
1 1/2 cups graham wafer crumbs
1 can sweetened condensed milk

1 cup semi-sweet chocolate chips
1 1/3 cups flaked coconut
1 cup walnuts or pecans, chopped

Directions:

Melt butter in 9x13 pan; sprinkle with wafer crumbs. Carefully spread milk over top, as even as possible. Sprinkle chocolate chips over top, followed by coconut, then nuts. Press down firmly with your hand. Bake at 350°F for 25 - 30 minutes or until brown. Cut into squares when cooled. *Note:* May substitue 1/2 cup butterscotch chips for chocolate chips for an extra special taste.

Partridgeberry Bars

Grace Percy, Brigus, Newfoundland

Ingredients:

1 cup flour
1 cup brown sugar
1 cup rolled oats
1/2 cup butter
1 1/2 cups partridgeberry jam

Spice of Life

Misery loves company ...but it's better to have rheumatism in one leg than both.

Directions:

Preheat oven to 375°F. Grease an 8-inch cake pan. Combine flour, sugar and rolled oats. Cut in butter until crumbly; press half into prepared pan. Spread with jam. Cover with remaining crumbs and pat smooth. Bake at 375°F for 35 minutes or until lightly browned. Cool and cut into bars. Can be served hot with ice cream.

Peach Squares

Amanda Brock, Bowmanville, Ontario

Ingredients:

1/2 cup butter
3/4 cup white sugar
1 egg
1 cup coconut
1 tin peaches (or strawberries), drained & chopped
graham wafers
1 container Cool Whip

Food for Thought

Under capitalism, man exploits man; under socialism, the reverse is true. - Polish proverb

Directions:

Cream together butter, sugar and egg. Add coconut and chopped peaches. Line a square pan with graham wafers. Pour mixture over wafers. Top with another layer of wafers. Spread Cool Whip over top and sprinkle with coconut. Refrigerate.

Chocolate Confetti

Sherry Lander, Mississauga, Ontario (formerly of Old Bonaventure, Newfoundland)

Ingredients:

1/4 cup butter or margarine
1/2 cup peanut butter

1 cup semi-sweet chocolate chips
1 (8oz) bag miniature marshmallows (white or coloured)
1/2 cup walnuts (optional)
1/2 cup medium coconut (optional)

```
Trivia Tidbits
Middle names were once
illegal in England.
```

Directions:

Melt butter and peanut butter in large saucepan. Stir in chips until melted. Cool enough so that you can hold your hand on the bottom of pan. Add marshmallows and stir until all are coated. Add walnuts and coconut, if desired. Pack in a 9x9 pan that has been lined with waxed paper for easy removal. Cut and refrigerate or freeze. Makes 36 squares.

Sweet Success

Danessa Quinlan, Birchy Bay, Newfoundland

Ingredients:

2 cups chocolate wafer crumbs
1/2 cup melted butter
1 pkg cream cheese, softened
1/4 cup sugar
1 tub Cool Whip, thawed
1 cup chocolate covered toffee bars (4 bars), chopped
2 1/2 cups cold milk
2 pkgs chocolate instant pudding

Food for Thought
Only he who attempts the ridiculous can achieve the impossible. - Will Henry

Directions:

Combine crumbs and butter; press firmly in 9x13 baking pan. Chill. Beat cream cheese and sugar in medium bowl with electric mixer until smooth. Stir in half of Cool Whip. Spread evenly over crust. Sprinkle chopped candy bar over top. Pour milk into large bowl; add pudding. Beat with wire whisk or electric beater. Pour over chopped candy bar layer. Let stand 5 minutes or until thickened. Spread remaining Cool Whip over top. Refrigerate 2 hours. Garnish with additional bar. Makes 15-18 servings.

Pioneer Cookies

Emily Gallant, St. John's, Newfoundland (formerly of Mount Pearl, Newfoundland)

Ingredients:

1 cup brown sugar
1 cup raisins
1 1/2 cups water
1/2 cup butter
1 tsp cinnamon
1 tsp nutmeg
2 cups flour
1 tsp baking soda
1 tsp baking powder
1/2 tsp salt

Food for Thought
What passes for woman's intuition is often nothing more than man's transparency. - George Jean Nathan

Sweets & Treats
Cakes, Cookies, Squares, Pies, Candies, Crumbles

Directions:

Mix brown sugar, raisins, water, butter, cinnamon and nutmeg in saucepan and simmer for 5 minutes. Let cool completely. Mix flour, baking soda, baking powder and salt. Pour brown sugar mixture into flour mixture; blend together. Pour into greased 8x8 pan. Bake at 350°F for 30 minutes. Cool and cut into squares.

Date Squares

Josephine Hynes, St. John's, Newfoundland (nee Elliott, Twillingate, Newfoundland)

Ingredients:

1 1/2 cups rolled oats
1 cup soft butter
1 tsp soda
3/4 cup brown sugar, well-packed
1/8 tsp salt
1 1/2 cups flour
2 cups dates
1 cup brown sugar
1 cup hot water

Spice of Life

The hallmark of good manners is mastering the ability to yawn without opening your mouth.

Directions:

To make filling, cook dates, brown sugar and water until dates are soft; mash. Mix rest of ingredients until crumbly. Press half the mixture into a greased 9x9 pan. Spread on filling. Pat on remaining crumbs. Bake at 350°F for 20 - 25 minutes. Cut in squares. (*Note:* May use 1 1/2-2 cups partridgeberry jam or apricot jam in place of date filling.)

Soft Molasses Drops

Eleanor LaFosse Edison, Dryden, Ontario (formerly of Isle aux Morts, Newfoundland)

Ingredients:

2 cups all-purpose flour
4 cups sugar
1 tsp cinnamon
2 tsp salt
4 cups molasses
4 cups butter or margarine, softened
1 egg
2 tsp baking soda
2 cups hot coffee

Trivia Tidbits
John Bunyan wrote Pilgrim's Progress while serving a twelve-year prison term.

Directions:

Measure first 7 ingredients in order given into mixing bowl. Stir baking soda into hot coffee. Add and beat dough until thoroughly blended. Drop by tablespoons onto greased cookie sheet. Bake in 375°F oven for 10 to 12 minutes. Makes 5 dozen.

Sweets & Treats

Cakes, Cookies, Squares, Pies, Candies, Crumbles

Peanut Butter Cookies
Desiree Sheppard, Manuels, Newfoundland

Ingredients:

1/4 cup shortening
1/4 cup butter
1/2 cup peanut butter
1/4 cup sugar
1/2 cup brown sugar
1 egg
1/4 tsp salt
1 1/4 cups flour
3/4 tsp baking soda
1 pkg chocolate chips

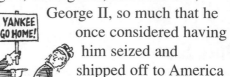

Trivia Tidbits

George I, of England, hated his son, George II, so much that he once considered having him seized and shipped off to America "where he should never be heard of any more."

Directions:

Beat shortening, butter, peanut butter, sugar, brown sugar and egg until light and fluffy. Add flour, baking soda and salt; blend well. Stir in chocolate chips. Drop from teaspoon onto ungreased baking sheet; flatten with fork. Bake at 375°F for 10 - 12 minutes. Makes 3 dozen.

Easiest & Best Shortbread Cookies
Carolyn Hanlon, Mount Pearl, Newfoundland (formerly of Grand Falls-Windsor, Newfoundland)

Ingredients:

1/2 cup cornstarch
1/2 cup icing sugar
1 cup flour
1 cup butter or margarine

Spice of Life
All men are created equal ... then some get married.

Directions:

Sift together cornstarch, icing sugar and flour. If using margarine add touch of salt. Blend in butter and work with hands until creamy. Shape into balls and flatten with a fork. Put on an ungreased cookie sheet and bake in slow oven at 300°F until edges are slightly browned.

Brown Sugar Cookies
June Dalley, Bathurst, New Brunswick (nee Howell, Carbonear, Newfoundland)

Ingredients:

2 cups brown sugar
1 cup margarine
1 egg
1/2 tsp salt
3/4 cup sour milk
2 tsp baking soda
1 tsp cream of tartar
1 tsp vanilla
4-5 cups flour

Food for Thought
Rabbi Noah of Lekivitz was asked, "Why do you not conduct yourself like your father, the late rabbi?" Replied Rabbi Noah, "I do conduct myself like him. He did not imitate anybody, and I do likewise."

Directions:

Blend all ingredients together. Roll into little balls and lay on a greased baking pan. Press down lightly with a fork. Bake at 475°F for 8 - 10 minutes.

No-Bake Cherry Cheese Deluxe Pie

Denise Hibbs (nee Jenkins), Springdale, Newfoundland

Ingredients:

1 pkg Dream Whip
1/2 cup milk
1 tsp almond extract (optional)
1 (250g) pkg cream cheese, softened
1/2 cup sugar
1 9-inch crumb crust
1 cup canned cherry pie filling
toasted sliced almonds

> ## Food for Thought
> When someone else decides when you are through, it's work. - Donald G. Smith

Directions:

Prepare Dream Whip as directed with milk and almond extract. Beat cream cheese with sugar until creamy. Blend 3/4 of topping into cream cheese mixture at low speed. Pour into crumb crust. Top with pie filling and remaining topping. Chill at least one hour.

Molasses Cookies

June Dalley, Bathurst, New Brunswick (nee Howell, Carbonear, Newfoundland)

Ingredients:

1 cup molasses
1 tsp ginger
1 cup margarine
1 tsp cinnamon
1 tsp salt
2 tsp baking soda
2 eggs
1/2 cup strong tea
4-5 cups flour

> ## Trivia Tidbits
> You could burn off 100 calories by jogging a mile, but you could also burn off 100 calories by playing cards for an hour. Incidentally, you would have to jog a mile a day for a year just to drop 10 pounds.

Directions:

Mix all ingredients together. Roll into little balls and lay on a greased baking pan. Press down lightly with a fork. Bake at 475°F for 8 - 10 minutes.

Granny's Peanut Butter Cookies

Rosemarie Reynar, North York, Ontario (nee Stratton of Lewisporte, Newfoundland)

Ingredients:

1 cup butter
3/4 cup brown sugar
3/4 cup white sugar
1 tsp vanilla
1 cup peanut butter
2 eggs, beaten
1 1/4 cups flour
1 cup bran
3/4 cup rolled oats
2 tsp baking powder

> ## Spice of Life
> The big difference between sex for money and sex for free, is that sex for money usually costs a lot less. - Brendan Behan

Sweets & Treats

Cakes, Cookies, Squares, Pies, Candies, Crumbles

Directions:

Melt butter. Beat together with sugars, vanilla, peanut butter and eggs. In separate bowl, mix flour, bran, oats and powder. Stir mixture into batter. Drop by teaspoon onto ungreased cookie sheet. Bake at 350°F for 15 - 18 minutes. Let cool.

Nellie's Jam Drops

Winnie Marshall, Stephenville, Newfoundland

Ingredients:

1 cup butter
3/4 cup sugar
1 egg yolk
2 cups flour
2 tsp baking powder

> *Food for Thought*
> The inherent vice of capitalism is the unequal sharing of blessings: the inherent vice of communism is the equal sharing of miseries.   - Winston Churchill

Directions:

Cream butter and sugar. Add egg yolk, then flour and baking powder, mixing well. Roll into marble size and dent each with your finger. Bake for 10 minutes at 350°F. Fill with jam.

Mom's Soft Molasses Cookies

Winnie Marshall, Stephenville, Newfoundland

Ingredients:

1 cup molasses
1 cup sugar
1 cup shortening, melted
1 tsp ginger
1 tsp cinnamon
1/2 tsp salt
1 tsp baking soda
2 eggs, beaten
1 1/2 cups raisins
1 cup sour milk
3 tsp baking powder
4 cups flour

> **Spice of Life**
> There's no nagging in heaven, but there is harping.

Directions:

Mix together molasses, sugar and shortening. Add ginger, cinnamon, salt and soda (dissolved in one tbsp cold water). Add eggs, raisins and sour milk. Add baking powder to flour and stir into mixture. Drop by teaspoon on greased baking sheet. Bake at 350°F for 10 - 15 minutes.

Angel Bites

Winnie Marshall, Stephenville, Newfoundland

Ingredients:

1 cup chopped dates
1/2 cup chopped walnuts
3/4 cup sugar

> **Trivia Tidbits**
> The insulation in the fuel tanks of rockets is so effective that it would take an ice cube eight years to melt.

1/2 cup butter
2 eggs, beaten
1/2 tsp salt
2 cups Corn Flakes
1 cup coconut
1 tsp vanilla or rum flavouring

Directions:

In a saucepan combine dates, nuts, sugar, butter, eggs and salt. Cook over a low heat until dates are softened (about 10 minutes). Cool for about 5 minutes and blend in Corn Flakes, coconut and vanilla or rum flavouring. Shape into 1-inch balls and roll in coconut. Makes 3 dozen cookies.

Butter Pecan Balls

Maisie Moyles, Carmanville South, Newfoundland

Ingredients:

1 cup butter
2 tsp vanilla
1 3/4 cups flour
1/3 cup icing sugar
1/4 tsp salt
3 tbsp cold water
2 cups finely chopped pecans

Directions:

In mixing bowl, cream butter until fluffy. Add vanilla and beat well. In bowl combine flour, sugar and salt. Add half to creamed mixture, beat to combine. Add water and beat well. Stir in remaining flour mixture and beat until blended. Fold in pecans. Refrigerate dough for 20 minutes or until firm. Form into 1-inch balls. Place on lightly buttered baking sheets, 1 1/2 inches apart. Bake in 300°F oven for 30 minutes, or until golden.

Soft Molasses Cookies

JM (email submission)

Ingredients:

1/2 cup shortening
1/2 cup margarine
1 cup white sugar
1 cup molasses
1 egg
3 tsp baking soda
3/4 cup boiling water
1 tbsp vanilla
4 cups flour
1 tsp cream of tartar
1 tsp salt
1/2 tsp cinnamon
1/2 tsp ginger
1/2 tsp cloves

Directions:

Cream together shortening and margarine. Add the sugar and beat until light. Blend in the molasses and egg. Dissolve the soda in boiling water and add to the mixture. Add vanilla. Sift together the dry ingredients, including spices and mix in gradually to make a soft dough. Cool. Roll out to a 1/4-inch thick. A little more flour may be added, but just enough to make the dough easy to handle. Cut out cookies. Bake at 375°F for 8-10 minutes. These are the best molasses cookies I have made.

Whipped Shortbread Cookies

Janice Mercer, Portugal Cove, Newfoundland

Ingredients:

3/4 cup icing sugar
1 cup margarine or butter
1 1/2 cups flour

> *Food for Thought*
> Life is a gamble, at terrible odds - if it was a bet, you wouldn't take it.
> - Tom Stoppard

Directions:

Whip butter and icing sugar with mixer on high speed. Add flour slowly, mixing on slower speed. Roll out on floured surface and cut in shapes or drop by teaspoon onto cookie sheet. Bake at 350°F for about 10 minutes or until edges turn golden brown. Let cool. Decorate if desired.

Newfoundland Snow Balls

M. White, Brampton, Ontario

Ingredients:

1/2 cup margarine
1 can sweetened milk
3 tbsp cocoa
1 tsp vanilla
1 1/2 cups fine coconut
2 cups graham wafer crumbs
1 pk medium-size marshmallows

> *Food for Thought*
> Fear of losing is what makes competitors so great. Show me a gracious loser and I'll show you a perennial loser. - O.J. Simpson

Directions:

In top of a double boiler, melt margarine. Blend in milk, cocoa and vanilla. Remove from heat and blend in coconut and graham wafer crumbs. Wrap each marshmallow with mixture. (A bowl of water nearby helps to keep hands moist). Roll each one in coconut. Place on a cookie sheet to freeze. Keep in tightly covered tin in freezer.

Pineapple Raisin Cookies

Joan Brown, St. John's, Newfoundland (nee Kelly, Trinity, Trinity Bay, Newfoundland)

Ingredients:

1/2 cup shortening
1 egg, beaten
3/4 cup crushed pineapple
2 cups flour
1/2 tsp baking soda
1 cup brown sugar

> **Trivia Tidbits**
> Red rain fell on the coast of Newfoundland in 1890.

1 tsp vanilla
1/2 tsp baking powder
1/2 tsp salt
1/2 cup raisins (floured)

Directions:

Blend shortening and sugar. Add egg, vanilla and pineapple. Sift in dry ingredients and add raisins. Drop on greased cookie sheet. Bake at 375°F for 12 - 15 minutes.

No-Bake Marshmallow Balls

Barbara Lucas, Barachois Brook, Newfoundland

Ingredients:

25 marshmallows
1/2 cup sweet milk
1/4 cup cherries
1/4 cup nuts
1 cup coconut

> ## Trivia Tidbits
> Guinness Book of Records holds the record for being the book most often stolen from public libraries.

Directions:

Soak marshmallows in milk; and add cherries and nuts. Form into balls. Roll in coconut and let sit in a cool place for 15 - 30 minutes.

Sugar Cookies

June Gates, Woodstock, Ontario

Ingredients:

1 cup butter or margarine, softened
1 1/2 cups icing sugar
1 egg
1 tsp vanilla
1/2 tsp almond extract
2 1/2 cups all-purpose flour
1 tsp baking soda
1 tsp cream of tartar

Spice of Life
Happy are physicians! Their success shines in the sunlight and the earth covers their failures.
- Michel de Montaigne

Directions:

Mix butter, sugar, egg, vanilla and almond extract. Blend in flour, baking soda and cream of tartar. Cover and chill for 2 - 3 hours. Preheat oven to 375°F. Roll out dough onto floured board. Cut into shapes and sprinkle with sugar. Bake 7 - 8 minutes or until edges are brown.

Kathy's Mexican Fruit Cake

Doreen Sooley, Perth-Andover, New Brunswick

Ingredients:

2 cups white sugar
2 eggs, slightly beaten
1 (19oz) can crushed pineapple, undrained
1/2 cup walnuts

> ## Spice of Life
> Half a loafer is better than no husband at all.
> - Louis Safian

Frosting:

2 cups icing sugar
1/2 cup margarine
1 (8oz) pkg cream cheese
1 tsp vanilla

Directions:

Grease a 9x13 baking dish. In large bowl combine sugar, slightly beaten eggs, pineapple and juice and walnuts. Blend well and add to pan. Bake at 350°F for 45 minutes. Set aside to cool. Combine frosting ingredients and ice cooled cake.

Spice of Life

Money isn't everything ...but it keeps you in touch with the kids.

Blueberry Cake

Beulah Cooper, Gander, Newfoundland

Ingredients:

1 cup butter
1 1/2 cups sugar
2 eggs
1 tsp vanilla
2 cups flour
1 tsp salt
2 tsp baking powder
1 cup milk
2 cups blueberries

Trivia Tidbits

Filipinos wait until an egg is just about to hatch before they cook it.

Directions:

Gradually cream butter and sugar together. Add eggs and vanilla; beat well. In separate bowl, blend dry ingredients together. Gradually add flour mixture and milk to batter. Fold in blueberries. Bake at 350°F for 50 minutes in greased 9-inch pan.

Granny's Molasses Spice Cookies

Anita A. Graham, nee Wareham, Brooklyn, New York

Ingredients:

1/4 lb unsalted butter, cut into 1/2-inch pieces
4 tbsp unsalted butter
1/4 cup dark molasses
1 tsp vanilla extract
2 cups flour
1 1/3 cups sugar, divided
2 tsp baking soda
2 tsp ginger
2 tsp cinnamon
1/4 tsp nutmeg
1/4 tsp cloves
1/4 tsp salt
1 egg, lightly beaten

Trivia Tidbits

Mary, Queen of Scots, was a very skillful billiard player.

Directions:

Preheat the oven to 375°F. In a small saucepan, melt butter over low heat. Remove and stir in molasses and vanilla. Set aside to cool. In a medium bowl, sift flour with 1 cup of the sugar and baking soda, ginger, cinnamon, nutmeg, cloves and salt. Add the beaten egg to the cooled butter mixture and mix well with a fork. Using a rubber spatula, fold the butter mixture into the flour. Cover tightly and refrigerate until firm, about 15 minutes. Put the remaining 1/3 cup of sugar in a small bowl. Roll into 1-inch balls. Toss the balls in the sugar to coat completely and place on ungreased baking sheets, about 2 inches apart. Bake for 10 minutes, or until the bottoms begin to brown. The cookies will be a little soft but will remain chewy. Let cool on baking sheet for about 5 minutes, then transfer to a rack to cool completely.

Oatmeal Cookies
Anita A. Graham, nee Wareham, Brooklyn, New York

Ingredients:

1 cup vegetable shortening (not butter)
1 cup light brown sugar
1 cup white sugar
2 eggs
1 tsp vanilla
3 cups rolled oats (not quick cooking)
1 1/2 cups flour, sifted
1 tsp baking soda
1 tsp salt
1 cup pecans, chopped
1 cup golden raisins

> ### Trivia Tidbits
> Light from Pluto takes six years to reach Earth.

Directions:

Preheat oven to 350°F. Cream shortening and sugars only enough to blend well. Add eggs and vanilla; beat until thoroughly mixed. Add oats and mix again. Sift flour together with baking soda and salt; add to oat mixture, mixing well. Add nuts and raisins. Drop by spoonful onto a greased cookie sheet. Bake for 15 minutes or until golden brown. Yields about 60 cookies. They are both chewy and crisp and keep well in tins or plastic bags.

Carrot Cookies
Shirley MacDonald, Fredericton, New Brunswick

Ingredients:

1 cup margarine
3/4 cup white sugar
2 eggs
2 cups flour
2 1/2 tsp baking powder
1 tsp salt
3/4 cup coconut
1 cup carrots, cooked and mashed

Icing: Ingredients:

3 tbsp butter

Spice of Life
Think twice before you think.
- E. E. Cummings

1 1/2 cups icing sugar
2 tbsp orange rind, grated
1 tbsp orange juice

Directions:

Cream margarine and sugar; add eggs, flour, baking powder and salt. Blend in carrots and coconut. Drop by teaspoon on oiled cookie sheet. To ice, combine icing ingredients. Frost cookies when cooled.

Peanut Butter Cookies

Beulah Cooper, Gander, Newfoundland

Ingredients:

1 cup butter

1 cup white sugar

2 eggs

1 cup peanut butter

2 cups flour

1 cup brown sugar

2 tsp baking soda

1/4 tsp salt

1 cup coconut

Trivia Tidbits
Mrs. Fanny Miles of Cincinnati had feet which measured 25 inches long.

Directions:

Cream butter until fluffy; add sugars, gradually mixing until creamy. Beat in unbeaten eggs and mix well. Add peanut butter and blend well. Add flour, soda and salt, blend well. Mix in coconut. Drop by teaspoonful onto ungreased baking sheet. Press flat with fork. Bake at 375°F for 12 - 15 minutes. Makes 6 dozen.

Shortbread

Rosalind Power, nee Wareham, Kilbride, Newfoundland

Ingredients:

1 cup margarine, or butter

1/4 tsp vanilla flavouring

1/2 cup icing sugar

1 1/4 cups flour

1/2 cup cornstarch

pinch of salt

Food for Thought
Men occasionally stumble over the truth, but most of them pick themselves up and hurry off as if nothing had happened. - Winston Churchill

Directions:

Cream margarine (or butter) well; add vanilla and icing sugar, continue to cream. Mix flour, cornstarch and salt together. Add dry ingredients to butter mixture with hands, don't work too much. Roll 1/4-inch thick and cut into shapes. Bake at 300°F for 25 minutes.

Chocolate Balls

Patricia Delaney, Grand Falls-Windsor, Newfoundland

Ingredients:

2 cans sweetened condensed milk
2 squares Baker's unsweetened chocolate
1 tsp vanilla flavouring
1 pkg graham cracker crumbs
fine, unsweetened, shredded coconut

Directions:

Place milk and squares in a microwave oven-safe bowl. Heat on high for 3 minutes. Leave in the oven for another 5 minutes. Stir the milk and chocolate until completely blended. Add vanilla and stir. Place the cracker crumbs in a large bowl. Add the liquid and mix thoroughly. Spoon out, shape into balls and roll in coconut. These can be wrapped and placed in a freezer until served, or may be kept wrapped in the refrigerator for immediate use. Makes about 4 dozen (depending on size of balls).

> *Food for Thought*
> The graveyard is too lonesome. Give me my flowers now.
> - Old postcard

Quick Cookies

Joy Marple, Cape Breton, Nova Scotia

Ingredients:

unsalted crackers
1 cup brown sugar
1 cup butter
2 cups chocolate chips
nuts (optional)

Directions:

Cover ungreased cookie sheet or jelly roll pan with crackers. Melt together sugar and butter. Spread over crackers. Cover with chocolate chips (or 1 cup white and 1 cup dark chocolate chips) and nuts. Bake at 400°F for 8 minutes or until bubbles form. Cool and break into pieces.

> **Trivia Tidbits**
> In 1970, hailstones measuring 7 1/2 inches in diameter fell in the US state of Kansas.

Peanut Butter Honey Bees

Alice Vezina, Renfrew, Ontario

Ingredients:

1/2 cup creamy peanut butter
2 tbsp butter or margarine, softened
1/2 cup confectioner's sugar
3/4 cup graham cracker crumbs
1 square semi-sweet chocolate
1/3 cup sliced almonds, toasted

> **Spice of Life**
> You're only young once ...after that, you have to think up some other excuse. Billy Arthur

Directions:

Combine peanut butter, butter and sugar; blend in crumbs thoroughly. Shape mixture into 1 1/4-inch ovals. Place on waxed paper-lined baking sheet. Melt chocolate and place in a resealable plastic bag. Cut a small hole in corner of bag. Paint three stipes on each bee. Insert two almonds in each bee for wings. Use a toothpick to poke holes for eyes. Store in refrigerator. Yields 4 dozen.

Easy Peanut Butter Cookies

Alice Vezina, Renfrew, Ontario

Ingredients:

1 cup peanut butter
1 cup sugar
1 egg, beaten
1 tsp vanilla

Directions:

In a bowl, stir all ingredients until combined. Shape level tablespoons into balls. Place 2" apart on ungreased baking sheet. Flatten with fork. Bake at 350°F for 16 - 18 minutes or until done. Let cool for 5 minutes. Makes 2 dozen.

Food for Thought

The evils of the world flow from the envy of the have-nots, and the selfishness of the haves.

Alma's Jam Jam's

Maria Young, St. Phillip's, Newfoundland (nee Hardy, Port aux Basques, Newfoundland)

Ingredients:

1 cup butter, or margarine
1 cup sugar
1 egg
1 tbsp vanilla
2 tsp baking powder
dash of salt
2 cups flour
raspberry or strawberry jam

Trivia Tidbits
The hair spring of a watch was originally a pig's hair.

Directions:

Cream together butter (or margarine) and sugar; add egg and vanilla. Add dry ingredients. Roll into 1-inch balls. Flatten lightly with fork. Bake at 350°F for 10 minutes. When cooked, put raspberry or strawberry jam on flat side, place another cookie on top.

Peanut Butter No-Bake Cookies

Doreen Sooley, Perth-Andover, New Brunswick

Ingredients:

1/2 cup peanut butter
1/4 cup butter or margarine
16 large marshmallows
1/2 cup coconut
1 cup oatmeal

Spice of Life

The successful man puts his trust in God, and works like the devil.

Directions:

Melt peanut butter, marshmallows and butter or margarine over low heat. Stir until smooth; remove and stir in oatmeal and coconut. Drop from spoon on waxed paper and chill.

Newfie Rocks

Doreen Sooley, Perth-Andover, New Brunswick

Ingredients:

1 tsp baking soda
1 tbsp boiling water
1 1/2 cups brown sugar
1 cup margarine
3 eggs, well beaten
3 cups flour, sifted
1 tsp cinnamon
1/4 tsp salt
2 cups raisins
1 cup crushed nutmeats

Directions:

Dissolve baking soda in 1 tbsp boiling water. Cream margarine and beat sugar in slowly; add eggs. Sift flour, cinnamon and salt and dust some of this over the raisins and nuts. Beat flour mixture, nuts, and raisins into creamed mixture. Add dissolved baking soda. Drop on cookie sheet, leaving space between each one. Bake at 400°F until done when touched. Makes 92 cookies.

Food for Thought

War leaves the country with three armies: an army of cripples, an army of mourners, and an army of thieves.

- German proverb

Healthful Drop Cookies

Marion Scheers, Edmonton, Alberta

Ingredients:

1 cup margarine
1 cup brown sugar
1/2 cup molasses
3 eggs
1 cup raisins
1/2 cup natural bran
1/2 cup wheat germ
1 1/2 cups white flour
1/2 cup whole wheat flour
pinch of salt
1/2 tsp baking soda
1/2 tsp nutmeg
1/2 tsp vanilla

Spice of Life

Women's lib slogan: Don't iron while the strike is hot!

ON STRIKE

Directions:

Cream margarine and sugar. Beat in eggs and molasses. Beat in rest of ingredients. Drop on cookie sheet by spoonfuls; bake at 375°F for 10 minutes.

Ginger Snaps

Marion Scheers, Edmonton, Alberta

Ingredients:

1 cup margarine
2/3 cup molasses

Food for Thought

Chastity is no more a virtue than malnutrition. - Alex Comfort

Sweets & Treats

Cakes, Cookies, Squares, Pies, Candies, Crumbles

1/3 cup brown sugar
2 tsp baking soda
1 tsp ginger
1/4 tsp nutmeg
3 cups flour

Directions:

Blend all dry ingredients. Cut in margarine. Add molasses; knead together thoroughly. Roll and cut with cookie cutter or make round balls in your hand, flatten in palm and place on greased cookie sheet. Bake at 350°F for 8 minutes.

Ginger Snaps

Jamie Senior, St. John's, Newfoundland (formerly of Burin, Newfoundland)

Ingredients:

3/4 cup butter
1/4 cup molasses
1 cup white sugar
1 egg
2 tsp baking soda
2 tsp ginger
1/2 tsp salt
1/2 tsp cloves
2 tsp cinnamon
2 cups flour

Directions:

Melt butter in saucepan and add molasses. Remove from heat and allow to cool. Add sugar and egg; beat well. Add dry ingredients and mix well. Chill thoroughly. Form into balls and roll in sugar. Bake at 375°F for 8 - 10 minutes.

Raisin Cookies

Vince Marsh, St. John's, Newfoundland

Ingredients:

1 cup boiling water
2 cups raisins
1 cup shortening
2 cups sugar
3 eggs
1 tsp vanilla
4 cups flour
1 tsp baking powder
1 tsp soda
2 tsp salt
1/4 tsp allspice
1/2 tsp nutmeg
1 1/2 tsp cinnamon
1 cup chopped nuts

Spice of Life

Rats desert a sinking ship - and so do people if they have any sense.

Directions:

Boil water and raisins for 5 minutes and cool. Cream shortening and sugar; add eggs and beat well. Blend in cooled raisin mixture and vanilla. Combine dry ingredients, including nuts and add to shortening mixture; blend well. Chill. Drop from a teaspoon onto greased baking sheets. Bake at 400°F for 12 - 15 minutes. Makes 6-7 dozen.

Macaroons

Paulette Curtis, St. John's, Newfoundland (formerly of Howley, Newfoundland)

Ingredients:

2 egg whites, beaten stiff
1/2 tsp vanilla
3/4 cup white sugar
1/4 tsp salt
2 1/2 cups coconut
maraschino cherries

Directions:

Beat egg whites stiff; add sugar, vanilla and salt slowly. Beat again and fold in coconut. Mold into small balls. Cook in moderate oven (350°F) until brown. Add cherry to top.

Molasses Cookies

Sandra Young, Kilbride, Newfoundland (nee Dove, Twillingate, Newfoundland)

Ingredients:

3/4 cup shortening
1 cup sugar
2 eggs, well beaten
1 cup light molasses
4 cups flour
1 tsp soda
1 tsp ginger
1 tsp salt
2 tsp cinnamon
3/4 cup cold, strong coffee

Directions:

Cream shortening and sugar well. Add eggs and molasses, beat well. Add dry ingredients alternately with coffee. Drop from teaspoon onto greased sheet. Bake at 350°F for 15 minutes. Makes 7 dozen.

Dad's Cookies

Paula Gale, St. John's, Newfoundland (formerly of Stephenville, Newfoundland)

Ingredients:

1 cup butter
1 cup white sugar
1 cup brown sugar
1 egg

1 1/2 cups flour
1 tsp baking powder
1 tsp baking soda
1 tsp salt
3/4 cup coconut
1 1/2 cups rolled oats

Directions:

Cream butter and sugars until light and fluffy. Add egg; beat well. Add flour sifted with baking powder, soda and salt; blend. Add coconut and rolled oats. Roll in small balls and flatten with fork. Bake at 350°F until brown.

Shortbread

Ron Young, St. John's, Newfoundland (formerly of Twillingate, Newfoundland)

Ingredients:

1/4 cup sugar
1/2 cup butter
1 cup sifted flour

Directions:

Cream butter and sugar well. Sift flour 3 times. Add to creamed mixture and combine. Roll out on board, cut in desired shapes. Bake at 350°F for 20 minutes.

Oatmeal Cookies

Ron Fowlow, Goulds, Newfoundland (formerly of Cavendish, Trinity Bay, Newfoundland)

Ingredients:

1 cup sifted flour
1 tsp salt
1/2 tsp baking soda
3/4 cup shortening
1/2 cup white sugar
1 cup brown sugar
1 egg
1 tsp vanilla
1/4 cup water
3 cups rolled oats

Directions

Sift flour, salt and baking soda on waxed paper. Beat shortening, sugars, egg, vanilla and water in large bowl with electric mixer until smooth. Stir in flour mixture and blend well. Stir in oats. Drop by teaspoon on greased cookie sheet 1-inch apart. Bake at 350° until brown. Cool on rack.

Chocolate Caramel Delights

Valerie Hickey, Churchill Falls, Labrador (nee Adams, Burin Bay, Newfoundland)
Ingredients:

2/3 cup sugar

1/2 cup butter
1 egg, separated
2 tbsp milk
1 tsp vanilla
1 cup flour
1/3 cup cocoa
1/4 tsp salt
1 cup pecans, finely chopped
1/2 cup semi-sweet chocolate chips
1 tsp shortening

Food for Thought
If you drink, you die.
If you don't
drink you die.
So it is
better to drink.
- Russian proverb

Caramel Filling:

16 caramels, unwrapped
3 tbsp whipping cream

Directions:

In small bowl beat sugar, butter, egg yolk, milk and vanilla until blended. Stir together flour, cocoa and salt. Blend in butter mixture. Chill dough at least 1 hour. Preheat oven to 350°F. Lightly grease cookie sheet. Beat egg white slightly. Shape dough into 1-inch balls; dip each ball into egg white and roll in pecans to coat. Place 1-inch apart on cookie sheet; press thumb gently in center of each ball. Bake 10 - 12 minutes or until set. While baking, prepare caramel filling. In small saucepan combine caramels and whipping cream. Cook over low heat stirring frequently until caramels are melted and mixture is smooth. Press center of each cookie again. Immediately spoon about 1/2 tsp caramel filling in each cookie. Carefully remove to cooling rack. Melt chocolate chips and shortening together in microwave, about 1 minute. Drizzle chocolate over top of cookie.

Bacardi Rum Balls
Teresa Davey, Niagara Falls, Ontario (nee Anderson, Burgeo, Newfoundland)

Ingredients:

1 1/2 cups vanilla wafer crumbs
1/4 cup Barcardi Rum (Gold or Spice)
1/4 cup honey
2 cups ground walnuts
confectioner's sugar

Spice of Life
Time is a great teacher, but unfortunately it kills all its students. - Hector Berlioz

Directions:

In medium bowl, combine all ingredients except sugar. Shape into 1-inch balls. Roll in sugar. Store in tightly covered container. Makes 30.

Chocolate Chip Applesauce Cake
Josephine Jenkins, Springdale, Newfoundland (nee Young, Twillingate, Newfoundland)

Ingredients:

1 cup butter
2 cups sugar
3 eggs
1/2 cup water

Trivia Tidbits
A fully grown walrus yields seventy gallons of pure oil.

1 tbsp vanilla
2 1/2 cups flour
2 tbsp cocoa
1 tsp baking soda
1 tsp cinnamon
1 tsp cloves
1 tsp allspice
1 tsp nutmeg
1 (10g) tin apple sauce
1 (6oz) pkg chocolate chips

Food for Thought
Don't aim for success if you want it; just do what you love and believe in, and it will come naturally. - David Frost

Directions:

Cream butter and sugar. Beat in eggs, one at a time. Add water and vanilla. Add dry ingredients to butter mixture; stir in apple sauce then chocolate chips. Bake in tube pan at 325°F for 1 1/2 - 2 hours.

Apricot Cake

Karen Chipman, nee Keats, Twillingate, Newfoundland

Ingredients:

1 cup golden raisins
1/4 cup white sugar
1 cup dried apricot, diced
2 cups water
1 cup butter
1 (8 oz) pkg cream cheese
1 1/2 cups sugar
1 tsp vanilla
4 eggs
2 1/2 cups flour
2 tsp baking powder

Spice of Life
All the world's a stage ... and it's putting on a mighty poor show.
- Edward H. Dreschnach

Directions:

Bring to boil raisins, 1/4 cup white sugar, dried apricots and water; simmer for 15 minutes. Cream together butter, cream cheese, 1 1/2 cups sugar and vanilla. Beat in eggs, one at a time. Gradually add flour and baking powder. Add fruit mixture. Grease tube pan and coat with flour. Bake at 325°F for 65 - 70 minutes.

Cherry Cake

Marian Shea, Manuels, Conception Bay South, Newfoundland

Ingredients:

1 cup butter
1 3/4 cups sugar
3 eggs
1 tsp vanilla
3 cups flour
2 tsp baking powder

Food for Thought
Whatsoever a man soweth, that shall he also reap. - Galatians 6:7

1 tsp salt
2/3 cup warm milk
2 cups cherries (floured)

Directions:

Cream butter and sugar, add eggs one at a time with vanilla. Add flour, baking powder and salt and mix together. Add milk and stir well. Fold in cherries. Bake at 325°F for 1 1/2 - 2 hours or until done.

Molasses Cake

Lew Mercer, Portugal Cove, Newfoundland (formerly of Bay Roberts, Newfoundland)

Ingredients:

1/2 lb butter
1 cup sugar
2 or 3 eggs
1 cup molasses
1 cup coffee
3 cups flour
1 tsp soda in a little hot water
1 lb raisins
4 tsp cocoa
1 tsp ginger
1 tsp cinnamon
1 tsp allspice

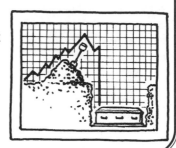

Spice of Life

Whatever goes up must come down ...except the cost of living.

Directions:

Cream butter and sugar; add eggs and molasses. Sift dry ingredients and mix with creamed mixture alternately with coffee. Bake in tube pan at 375°F for approximatly 2 hours.

Rhubarb Cake

Karen Chipman, nee Keats, Twillingate, Newfoundland

Ingredients:

2 cups flour
1/4 tsp salt
1 tsp baking soda
1 1/2 cups brown sugar
1 egg
1 tsp vanilla
1/2 cup butter
1 cup milk
2 1/2 cups rhubarb, chopped

Cake Topping Ingredients:

1/4 cup white sugar
1/2 tsp cinnamon
1/4 cup brown sugar
nutmeg (optional)

Spice of Life

Money makes the mare go ...and the woman makes the money go.

Trivia Tidbits

Burning at the stake was a legal execution as late as 1800 in the USA.

Sweets & Treats

Cakes, Cookies Squares, Pies, Candies, Crumbles

Directions:

Mix flour, salt and baking soda and set aside. Cream brown sugar, egg, vanilla, butter, milk and rhubarb. Mix flour and milk alternately to creamed mixture, making sure rhubarb is added last. Pour into greased 9x13 pan. Mix sugar, cinnamon, brown sugar and nutmeg and sprinkle over cake. Bake at 350°F for 40 minutes. Serve warm with ice cream.

Light Gumdrop Cake

June Dalley, Bathurst, New Brunswick (nee Howell, Carbonear, Newfoundland)

Ingredients:

1 cup margarine
4 eggs
4 cups flour
2 tsp vanilla
1 lb gumdrops
1 pkg red cherries
2 cups brown sugar
2 cups warm milk
2 tsp baking powder
2 tsp almond flavouring
1 lb raisins
1 cup walnuts

Trivia Tidbits

The ancestor of the modern horse, eohippus, lived about 60 million years ago. It was about the size of a spaniel or terrier and it had four toes instead of a single hoof.

Directions:

Combine all ingredients together blending thoroughly. Spread evenly into a greased tube pan. Bake in a slow oven at 300°F for 1 1/2 - 2 hours.

Cinnamon Streusel Coffee Cake

Claudine Barnes, Corner Brook, Newfoundland (nee Pye, Cape Charles, Labrador)

Ingredients:

1/3 cup brown sugar
2 tsp cinnamon
3/4 cup margarine, melted
1 cup sugar
2 eggs
1 cup sour cream
1 tsp vanilla
2 cups all-purpose flour
1 tsp baking soda
1 tsp baking powder
1/2 tsp salt

Food for Thought

Some men see things as they are and say "Why?" I dream things that never were and say "Why not?" - George Bernard Shaw

Directions:

To make the streusel, combine brown sugar and cinnamon in small bowl and set aside. In a large bowl, cream together margarine and sugar; beat in eggs, sour cream and vanilla. Add dry ingredients, stirring until smooth. Pour 1/2 the batter into greased 9-inch square pan. Sprinkle 1/2 streusel mixture over batter, spoon remaining batter on top. Sprinkle remaining streusel on top. Bake at 350°F for 40-45 minutes. Place on wire rack to cool. Serve warm or cold.

Molasses Pound Cake

Claudine Barnes, Corner Brook, Newfoundland (nee Pye, Cape Charles, Labrador)

Ingredients:

2/3 cup butter
3/4 cup sugar
2 eggs
2/3 cup molasses
2/3 cup sour milk
2 cups flour
3/4 tsp baking soda
1 tsp allspice
1 tsp cloves
1 tsp cinnamon
1 tsp nutmeg
1 cup raisins, optional

> **Trivia Tidbits**
> A raisin dropped in a glass of fresh champagne will bounce up and down continually from the bottom of the glass to the top.

Directions:

Cream butter and sugar together until light and fluffy; beat in eggs one at a time. Blend in molasses; add milk alternately with dry ingredients. Add raisins. Pour into greased 9x13 pan and bake at 350°F for 1 hour.

Partridgeberry Spice Cake

Daphne Parr, St. Lunaire, Newfoundland

Ingredients:

1/2 cup shortening
1 cup sugar
1 egg, beaten
1 1/4 cups flour, sifted
1/2 tsp cloves
1 tsp baking soda
1 tsp baking powder
1 tsp cinnamon
1/2 cup nuts, chopped
1 cup raisins
1/2 tsp salt
1 cup partridgeberries
1/4 cup water

Spice of Life

Travel broadens the mind ...and reduces the bank balance.

Directions:

Cream shortening and sugar. Add beaten egg. Sift together flour, cloves, baking soda, baking powder and cinnamon. Add nuts, raisins, salt and partridgeberries. Mix into creamed mixture alternately with water. Bake in a moderate (350°F) oven until done.

Sweets & Treats
Cakes, Cookies, Squares, Pies, Candies, Crumbles

Apricot Cake

Josephine Tobin, Lasalle, Quebec

Ingredients:

2 cups water
1/2 cup sugar
1/2 cup light raisins
1 1/4 cups apricots, chopped
1 1/2 cups sugar
1 cup butter
4 eggs
1 (8 oz) pkg cream cheese
1 1/2 tsp vanilla
2 1/4 cups flour
1 1/2 tsp baking powder

Directions:

Boil together water, sugar, raisins and apricots; simmer for 15 minutes and let cool. Cream together sugar, butter, eggs (added one at a time), cream cheese and vanilla. Add apricot mixture and stir. Add flour and baking powder. Bake in a greased bundt pan at 350°F for 1 1/2 hours, or until golden brown.

Boiled Raisin Cake

Josephine Tobin, Lasalle, Quebec

Ingredients:

1 cup butter
1 cup white sugar
1 cup brown sugar
1 cup raisins
2 tsp cinnamon
1 1/2 tsp cloves
1/2 tsp salt
2 cups boiling water
3 1/2 cups flour
2 tsp baking soda

Directions:

Boil butter, sugars, raisins, cinnamon, cloves, salt and water until butter is melted. Let cool. Add flour and baking soda. Bake in bundt pan at 325°F for 1 hour.

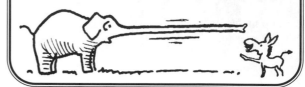

Spice of Life

If the Republicans will stop telling lies about us, we will stop telling the truth about them. - Adlai Stevenson

Food for Thought

Only madmen and fools are pleased with themselves; no wise man is good enough for his own satisfaction.

- Benjamin Whichcote

Bottles & Jars

Jams
Jellies
&
Preserves

Pear and Pineapple Jam

Charlotte Goodwin, Lynn Lake, Manitoba (nee Gallant, Stephenville Crossing, Newfoundland)

Ingredients:

3 cups pears, peeled and chopped fine
1 cup crushed pineaple, drained
1 tbsp finely grated lemon rind
1/2 cup lemon juice
6 1/2 cups white sugar
1 pkg liquid Certo

> *Food for Thought*
> Real troubles can be overcome; only the imaginary ones are unconquerable.
> - Theodor Vail

Directions:

Prepare as per directions on Certo pkg. Makes 4 - 500ml bottles.

Heavenly Jam

Patti Stanley, Sharon, Ontario (nee O'Neal, St. John's, Newfoundland)

Ingredients:

1 (6 qt) basket blue grapes
juice of 3 oranges
3/4 lb seedless raisins
sugar

> **Trivia Tidbits**
> Sixty-two per cent of vacationers prefer daytime activities, 14percent prefer nighttime activities and the remaining 24percent have no preference.

Directions:

Slip skins off grapes, set aside. Place pulp in a kettle with just enough water to keep it from burning. After a few minutes simmering, the seeds will come away quite easily, after which the pulp may be put through a colander or sieve. Add finely chopped skins to pulp; add juice from oranges. Add raisins; mix all together and bring to boiling point. Simmer gently for about 25 minutes. Measure pulp, alloting 3/4 cup of sugar to each cup of pulp. Boil until mixture shows jelly test (with wooden spoon dip in mixture and let drip. When it only drips 2 or 3 times and then sets it is done). Bottle in sterile jars, store in a cool dark place.

Blueberry and Rhubarb Jam

Charlotte Goodwin, Lynn Lake, Manitoba (nee Gallant, formerly of Stephenville Crossing, Newfoundland)

Ingredients:

8 cups blueberries
4 cups rhubarb (fresh or frozen)
1 cup water
4 cups sugar

> **Spice of Life**
> Money talks ... or does it just snicker?

Directions:

Thaw fruit, if frozen. Do not drain. Combine fruits in large saucepan or pot. Add water, bring to a full boil and simmer for 10 - 12 minutes. Add sugar, stirring to dissolve. Bring to simmer, stirring frequently. Boil to jam stage (about 20 - 25 minutes). Remove from heat; stir and skim foam. Let sit 10 minutes. Pour into hot jars; seal. Makes 12 cups.

Rhubarb and Apple Jam

Anita A. Graham (nee Wareham) Brooklyn, New York

Ingredients:

1 lb apples (Granny, if possible)
1 lb rhubarb
1/3 cup water
3 cups sugar

Directions:

Peel, core and chop apples. Wash, dry, trim and chop rhubarb. Put fruit in large saucepan with water. Heat gently; simmer until tender, about 20 minutes, stirring all the time. Check often to see no sticking occurs. When tender, add the sugar; stirring until dissolved. Boil rapidly at first, stirring, then boil more carefully until set (about 20 minutes), stirring frequently. Cover pot as it cooks down. Ladle into hot sterilized jars leaving 1/4-inch headspace. Wipe rims clean, put lids in place and tighten down. Invert for a few minutes, then return to upright position and let cool completely. Check the seals; label and store in a cool dry place. Excellent with pork chops.

> **Spice of Life**
> The wages of sin are unreported.

Heavenly Jam

Donna Cheeseman, St. John's, Newfoundland

Ingredients:

2 pkgs strawberry jello
20 oz crushed pineapple
5 cups rhubarb, diced
5 cups sugar

Directions:

Place rhubarb, pineapple and sugar in a large kettle; stir to blend well. Place over high heat until it boils. Reduce heat and boil hard for 20 minutes. Stir in jello until dissolved. Remove from heat and skim carefully. Pour into sterilized jars and seal with paraffin. Adjust covers when paraffin has set, wipe outside of jars and store in cool, dry place. This can be used with frozen, unsweetened rhubarb.

> **Trivia Tidbits**
>
> Thrushes can sing fifty-five songs without repeating themselves.

Rhubarb Jam

Renee Davis Hillier, Kingston, Ontario (formerly of Grand Falls-Windsor, Newfoundland)

Ingredients:

6 cups chopped rhubarb
1 1/2 cups + 3 tbsp sugar

> **Food for Thought**
> The ideal diet is expressed in four words: No more, thank you.

Directions:

Put rhubarb in large pot; cover with sugar. Place on minimum heat on burner. When liquid reaches about 1 inch in the pot, increase temperature to medium heat (4 or 5). Once boiled, turn on low, stirring occassionally for 1/2 hour. Pour into sterilized jars.

Partridgeberry Jam

Della Ivey, St. John's, Newfoundland

Ingredients:

6 cups partridgeberries
3 cups sugar

Directions:

Cook berries in about 2 cups of water or enough to keep pot from burning. After adding sugar, cook quickly for 15 minutes. Seal in hot sterile jars.

Heavenly Jam

Jeanette Osmond, Grand Bank, Fortune Bay, Newfoundland

Ingredients:

5 cups rhubarb
1 tin crushed pineapple
3 1/2 cups sugar
2 pkgs strawberry jelly

Directions:

Cut rhubarb into 1/2-inch pieces; place in large saucepan. Add pineapple and sugar. Stir well and place over high heat until it boils. Reduce heat and boil 20 minutes. Stir in jelly powder. Remove from heat. Skim and bottle. Red rhubarb is best used in this recipe.

> **Spice of Life**
> Old fishermen never die; they just smell that way.

Rhubarb Jelly

Joyce Marshall, Whitby, Ontario

Ingredients:

3 lbs rhubarb
1 cup water
7 cups white sugar
1 (6oz) bottle liquid pectin

> **Food for Thought**
> Always do unto others as though you were the others.

Directions:

Wash rhubarb and cut into 1/4-inch pieces. Measure 6 cups into saucepan; add water and simmer for 10 minutes, stirring as needed. Pour rhubarb in cheesecloth, twisting the corners and pressing with spoon or potato masher to extract liquid (need 4 cups juice). Pour juice into large saucepan; add sugar. Bring to a full boil. Add pectin; continue boiling, stirring constantly for 1 minute. Remove from heat. Skim foam from surface using metal spoon. Pour into sterilized jars. Cover with thin layer of paraffin. Jelly should be firm in 3 - 4 hours.

Cranberry Conserve

Anita A. Graham (nee Wareham), Brooklyn, New York

Ingredients:

1 lb cranberries
2 cups sugar
few strips orange rind
1/2 cup Grand Marnier

> **Trivia Tidbits**
> The word 'idiot' is derived from a Greek word that originally meant merely a private citizen. Thus, all men not in public office were 'idiots'.

Directions:

Place ingredients in a low glass casserole dish. Let stand at room temperature for 30 minutes. Cover with foil and bake in a pre-heated oven at 325°F for 40 minutes, stirring once during cooking time. Will keep for several months in the refrigerator.

Orange Marmalade

Ruby Pitcher, St. John's, Newfoundland

Ingredients:

6 oranges
3 grapefruit
3 lemons
sugar

Food for Thought
The inequalities between people often occur because of their goals and their use of time. - Clifton Burke

Directions:

Put oranges, grapefruit and lemons through food processor at chop setting and soak in 12 cups of water overnight. Boil for 1/2 hour and measure. For every cup of fruit and juice, add 3/4 cup sugar. Boil for 1 hour or until thick and amber-coloured.

Carrot Marmalade

Marion Scheers, Edmonton, Alberta

Ingredients:

4 cups raw carrots, grated
5 1/2 cups sugar
2 lemons, seeded and chopped
1 large navel orange, seeded and chopped
1/3 cup rind of lemon
1/3 cup rind of orange

Food for Thought
Nobody can make you feel inferior without your consent.
- Eleanor Roosevelt

Directions:

Place carrots in medium saucepan; bring to a boil. When partially cooked, drain off any excess water. Combine carrots and sugar; stir over medium heat until sugar is dissolved. Add remaining ingredients and cook over low heat for about 40 minutes. Pour into jars leaving head space at top.

Rhubarb Marmalade

Ruby Pitcher, St. John's, Newfoundland

Ingredients:

6 cups rhubarb, chopped
6 cups sugar
3 oranges - 2 peeled, 1 unpeeled
1 package of orange Jello

Spice of Life
If you keep your mouth shut you will never put your foot in it.
- Austin O'Malley

Directions:

Chop oranges and add to rhubarb and sugar. Boil for 20 minutes. Remove from heat and add Jello. Stir until Jello is melted and pour into sterilized bottles.

Bottles & Jars
Jams, Jellies and Preserves

Rhubarb Relish

Doris Alexander, Saint John, New Brunswick (formerly of Stephenville Crossing, Newfoundland)

Ingredients:

2 qts rhubarb
6 onions
1 qt cider vinegar
2 tsp salt
3 lbs brown sugar
2 tsp cinnamon
2 tsp allspice
2 tsp pepper

Food for Thought

Sometimes a man's tongue can make him deaf.

Directions:

Cook rhubarb, onions, vinegar and salt for 20 minutes. Add sugar and spices. Cook slowly for one hour. Bottle.

Corn Relish

Marguerite McKinley, Hinton, Alberta

Ingredients:

4 cups corn
1/2 cup onion, chopped
1/2 cup green pepper, chopped
1/2 cup red pepper, chopped
1 cup celery, chopped
1 1/2 cups vinegar
1/2 cup water
2 cups sugar
1 1/2 tsp salt
1 tsp mustard seed
1 tsp celery seed
1 1/2 tsp dry mustard
1/2 tsp tumeric
1/4 cup flour
1/2 cup water

Trivia Tidbits

Drinking 100 cups of coffee over a four-hour period, will furnish enough caffeine to kill the average person. However, small doses of caffeine, which can be found in, not only coffee but tea, cola drinks and other foods, are not harmful to the human body.

Directions:

Place corn in a large pot. Add onion, green pepper, red pepper, celery, vinegar, water, sugar, salt and seeds and bring to a boil. Let simmer for 10 minutes. Mix mustard, tumeric, flour and water. Gradually stir paste into boiling relish. Cook for 10 minutes. Once cooled, pour into sterilized jars.

Cabbage Relish

Matthew Durnford, Calgary, Alberta

Ingredients:

5 lbs green cabbage, shredded
3 lbs onions, chopped

Spice of Life

Better to remain silent and be thought a fool, than to speak and remove all doubt.

- Abraham Lincoln

4 cups sugar
1 tsp dry mustard
2 tsp tumeric
4 cups white vinegar
1 tbsp cornstarch
5 tbsp cold water

Directions:

Soak onions and cabbage in salted water over night; drain off water in the morning. Add remaining ingredients and boil until tender. Just before removing from heat, stir in 1 tbsp cornstarch mixed with 5 tbsp cold water. Let cool. and bottle.

Partridgeberry Pickles

Bertha Smith, Clarenville, Newfoundland

Ingredients:

1 qt partridgeberries
1 qt chopped onion
1 cup white vinegar
1 1/2 tsp allspice
1/2 tsp cinnamon
1/2 tsp cloves
2 1/2 cups sugar
1/4 tsp salt
dash pepper

Directions:

Combine all ingredients, stirring well. Boil for 1 hour. Pour into hot sterilized jars and seal.

English Relish

Elizabeth Robertson-Ledbury, Toronto, Ontario (formerly of Windsor, Nova Scotia)

Ingredients:

2 qts small, white whole onions
12 cucumbers
1 large cauliflower
1 head celery
salt
6 cups white sugar
3/4 cup flour
1/2 cup dry mustard
2 tbsp white mustard seed
1 tbsp celery seed
1 qt white vinegar

Directions:

Put cucumbers, cauliflower and celery through food grinder; add to onions. Cover with boiling

Bottles & Jars
Jams, Jellies and Preserves

water and one handful of salt. Let stand overnight; then drain off water. Mix sugar, flour, mustard, mustard seed, celery seed and vinegar in medium sized boiler. Mix and boil until mixture thickens. Add vegetables and boil for 15 minutes. Bottle and seal.

Bottled Cod

Delores LeRoux, St. George's, Newfoundland

Ingredients:

cod (amount you require)
salt pork (small amount to flavour)
1/4 tsp salt

Directions:

Remove bones from fresh cod. Put the cod into pint bottles with a slice of salt pork and salt. Boil in the open bottles for 2 1/2 hours. Seal.

Apple and Onion Pickles

Grace Ryan, Newman's Cove, Bonavista Bay, Newfoundland

Ingredients:

6 apples
6 onions
2 large tins tomatoes
2 cups vinegar
2 cups sugar
2 tsp pickling spice
2 tsp salt
1/4 head cabbage

Directions:

Boil all ingredients together for 1/2 hour. Simmer until soft, then cover slightly. Pour into hot sterilized jars. Seal immediately.

Mustard Pickles

Ruby Pitcher, St. John's, Newfoundland

Ingredients:

2 qts cucumber
2 lbs cauliflower
3 lbs onions
3 lbs green tomatoes
1/4 cup salt
1 cup flour
1 tbsp tumeric
3 cups white sugar
6 tbsp dry mustard
1 1/2 pts white vinegar

Food for Thought

Everyone has a future - some people plan theirs.

- Clifton Burke

Spice of Life

Social tact is making your company feel at home, even though you wish they were.

Trivia Tidbits

Awakened from his sleep by his crossword-puzzle-buff wife four times in one night to ask for assistance, a West German man became so upset that he strangled her to death. He was later acquited by a court on the grounds of temporary insanity.

Bottles & Jars
Jams, Jellies and Preserves

Directions:

Make a brine using salt along with some water. Add vegetables and ensure there is enough water to cover vegetables. Let mixture stand overnight. In the morning, heat mixture to boiling point, then strain. Mix mustard and vinegar together. Add other ingredients and boil until thickened. Add to vegetable mixture and heat through, but do not boil.

Pickled Cole Slaw

Rachel Hollett, Cambridge, Nova Scotia (nee Lomond, Port aux Basques, Newfoundland)

Ingredients:

1 large cabbage, grated
3 onions, grated
1 cup sugar
1 tsp salt
1 cup vinegar
2 tsp prepared mustard
3 tsp celery salt
3/4 cup salad oil

> ## Food for Thought
> Those men who try to do something and fail are infinitely better than those who try nothing and succeed beautifully.
> — Jenkin Lloyd Jones

Directions:

Combine cabbage, onions, 3/4 cup sugar and salt. Put aside. Bring remaining ingredients to a boil for 3 minutes. When dressing cools, pour over cabbage mixture.

Green Tomato Chow Chow

Doris Alexander, Saint John, New Brunswick (formerly of Stephenville Crossing, Newfoundland)

Ingredients:

9 lbs tomato
6 lbs onions
1/2 cup pickling salt
4 cups vinegar
2 cups water
5 lbs sugar
1 red pepper
1/2 cup cornstarch
2 tsp dry mustard
1 tsp tumeric

> ## Spice of Life
> Experience is what you've got when you're too old to get a job.

Directions:

Combine tomatoes, onions and pickling salt; let stand overnight. Drain in the morning, and add vinegar, water, sugar and red pepper. Boil until tender. Once boiled, add cornstarch, dry mustard and tumeric. Place into jars.

Bottles & Jars
Jams, Jellies and Preserves

Beverages

Alcoholic and
Non-Alcoholic
Punches and Slushes
for Sunny Days or
Festive
Occasions

Holiday Punch (Non-Alcoholic)

Bernadette Bishop, St. John's, Newfoundland

Ingredients:

2 cups cranberry juice
4 cups lemonade
1 cup orange juice
maraschino cherries
lemon slices
18 oz ginger ale

Directions:

Mix all ingredients, except ginger ale. Chill. Add ginger ale just before serving. Makes 18 cups.

Fruit Punch for 24 (Non-Alcoholic)

Kathleen Ivey, Mount Pearl, Newfoundland

Ingredients:

1 1/2 cups sugar
1/2 cup water
1 qt grape juice
juice of 6 lemons
juice of 6 oranges
crushed mint leaves
1 qt ginger ale
1 qt soda water
1 pt ice water

Directions:

Boil sugar in 1/2 cup water until dissolved. Cool and mix fruit juices with mixture and mint. Let stand for one hour. Strain into large punch bowl and add ginger ale and soda water just before serving. Dilute with ice water if necessary and serve with crushed ice.

Marian's Surprise Punch (Alcoholic)

Marian Shea, Manuels, Conception Bay South, Newfoundland

Ingredients:

12 oz apple juice
12 oz orange juice
1 qt ginger ale
1/4 cup sugar, or to taste
12 oz lemonade
6 oz cranberry juice
1 qt soda water
1/2 bottle champagne
cherries (to decorate/garnish)
lemon slices (to decorate/garnish)
lime slices (to decorate/garnish)
orange slices (to decorate/garnish)

Food for Thought
If you can't have the best of everything, make the best of everything you have.

Spice of Life
If at first you do succeed ...try to hide your astonishment.

Trivia Tidbits
The first vehicle to have seat belts was the 1959 Nash Rambler.

Beverages

Alcoholic and Non-Alcoholic Punches and Slushes for Sunny Days or Festive Occasions

Directions:

Mix all ingredients together. May adjust ingredients to taste. Place a large piece of ice in the middle and it does not dilute the mixture. Place cherries, slices of lemon, lime and oranges in or around the bowl (your preference).

Fruit Punch (Alcoholic)

June Gates, Woodstock, Ontario

Ingredients:

1 (48oz) can unsweetened pineapple juice
1 (12oz) can frozen limeade, undiluted
1 large bottle ginger ale
1 pt lime or raspberry sherbet

Directions:

Blend all ingredients together.

Banana Slush (Non-Alcoholic)

Beverly Martin Jenkins, Dawson Creek, British Columbia (originally from Springdale, Newfoundland)

Ingredients:

2 cups sugar
8 cups water
1 large tin unsweetened pineapple juice
4 cups lemon juice
1 can frozen unsweetened orange juice
2 well-mashed bananas
7-UP or Sprite
marachino cherries

Directions:

Boil water and sugar together for 15 minutes. Let cool completely. Add remaining ingredients and mix well. Pour into containers and freeze. To serve, put 2 scoops of slush into a glass and add 7-UP or Sprite, a marachino cherry and a straw. Very refreshing drink on a hot summer day or a taste bud pleaser at Christmastime.

Slush (Alcoholic)

Bertha Smith, Clarenville, Newfoundland

Ingredients:

1 tin frozen orange juice
1 tin frozen lemonade
1 flask vodka or gin
1 cup hot water
1 cup sugar
7-UP or ginger ale

Directions:

Mix all ingredients in a bowl. Transfer to clean beef bucket and freeze. Serve with 7-Up or ginger ale.

Trivia Tidbits
If a drop of whiskey is squirted on a scorpion's back, it will sting itself to death.

Spice of Life
To cease smoking is the easiest thing I ever did. I ought to know because I've done it a thousand times. — Mark Twain

Trivia Tidbits
In the 18th-century people would carve ugly human faces on the outside of drinking mugs, which is why the face is sometimes called the mug today.

Pina Colada Slush (Alcoholic)

Cathy Gale, Codroy Valley, Newfoundland

Ingredients:

1 large can unsweetened pineapple juice
1 tin coconut syrup
1 (26oz) bottle vodka
ginger ale or 7-UP

Directions:

Combine all ingredients and freeze. Serve with ginger ale or 7-Up.

> ## *Food for Thought*
> Always speak well of your enemies - remember, you made them.

Eggnog (Alcoholic)

Crista Doyle, Kelligrews, Newfoundland

Ingredients:

4 eggs
4 tbsp sugar
1/4 tsp salt
1 tsp vanilla
4 cups milk
nutmeg

> ## **Spice of Life**
> The wages of sin is an income for life.
> - William Irish

Directions:

With an egg beater, mix eggs, sugar and salt and beat until thick and lemon coloured. Add vanilla and milk and beat until well mixed. Pour into a punch bowl and sprinkle with nutmeg.

Newfoundland Eggnog (Alcoholic)

Herb Greening, Botwood, Newfoundland

Ingredients:

1 bottle Newfoundland Screech
1 qt fresh milk
1 tin evaporated milk
6 eggs
1/2 cup white sugar
nutmeg

> ## *Food for Thought*
> There are only two ways to be contented; one is doing what you like, and the other is liking what you do. But you'll be contented longer with the latter.

Directions:

Separate eggs and beat yolks with 1/4 cup sugar, and whites with 1/4 cup sugar. In large container, combine entire bottle of Screech, fresh milk and evaporated milk. Add egg yolk mixture. Beat for 2 minutes then top with egg whites. Sprinkle with nutmeg. It'll blow your socks off!!

Yogurt Smoothie (Non-Alcoholic)

Effie White, Loon Bay, Newfoundland

Ingredients:

1 pouch strawberry-kiwi Crystal Light
1 1/2 cups plain yogurt

1 banana
2 cups water
1 cup ice cubes

<u>Directions</u>:
Blend all ingredients together until smooth.

> **Food for Thought**
> The bank of friendship cannot exist for long without deposits.

Pink Lady (Alcoholic)

Viola Mauger, Port aux Basques, Newfoundland

<u>Ingredients</u>:
1 1/4 oz gin
1/2 oz of cream
1/2 oz of sugar syrup
1/2 oz strawberry syrup
ice cubes

<u>Directions</u>:
Combine all ingredients in blender. Blend well. Makes 1 drink.

Creme De Menthe (Alcoholic)

Ron Pumphrey, St. John's, Newfoundland

<u>Ingredients</u>:
3 cups white sugar
3 cups water
5 - 6 tsp essence of peppermint (purchase at drug store)
green food colouring
1 (25oz) bottle of Borealis Vodka

> **Spice of Life**
> Keep smiling. It makes people wonder what you've been up to.

<u>Directions</u>:
Boil water and sugar slowly for 1 hour, stirring occasionally. Cool slightly and add essence of peppermint and green food colouring. Add one bottle of Borealis Vodka. Stir well and bottle. Let stand for 5 days.

Peach or Apricot Brandy (Alcoholic)

Pearl White, Trenton, Ontario (nee Flight, Small Point, Newfoundland)

<u>Ingredients</u>:
1 large tin peaches (or apricots)
1 pkg raisins
1 pkg yeast
5 cups white sugar
10 cups boiling water

> **Trivia Tidbits**
> In Madagascar the silk from spiders' webs is woven into cloth.

<u>Directions</u>:
Place fruit, yeast and sugar into large container; add boiling water. Let stand for two weeks; strain well. Bottle and keep for three months. Leave corks loose.

Christmas Cocktail (Alcoholic)

Joy Marple, Cape Breton, Nova Scotia

Ingredients:

25 ounce wild raspberry liquor
25 ounce sparkling white wine (or liquor of choice)

Directions:

Mix the above ingredients; serve in chilled glasses.

Snappy Lemonade (Non-Alcoholic)

Irene Ivany, Kippens, Newfoundland

Ingredients:

3 lemons
2 cups white sugar

Directions:

Cut lemons into 6 to 8 pieces and put in blender. Add sugar and fill blender with cold water and about 6 ice cubes and blend.

Pink Pony (Alcoholic)

Ron Young, St. John's, Newfoundland

Ingredients:

600 ml Orange Julip
150 ml soda water or ginger ale (half a 300 ml can)
6 ounces rye whiskey
2 tbsp Grenadine

Directions:

Blend all ingredients in a blender for 30 seconds and serve over ice cubes or crushed ice, in a large wine glass.

Madonna's Eggnog in a Punchbowl (Alcoholic)

Madonna Cole, St. John's, Newfoundland

Ingredients:

12 eggs
1 cup white sugar
2 cups 2% milk
12 ounces brandy
25 ounces rum
3 cups whipping cream

Directions:

Separate the yolks of the eggs from the whites and place the yolks in a large punch bowl. Add the sugar and beat until the mixture is lemon-coloured and thick. Then slowly add the milk, brandy and rum. Beat well and chill for several hours. Beat the egg whites in a separate bowl until they are stiff. Beat the whipping cream in a large bowl, then fold the egg whites into the whipping cream. Add this to the egg yolk mixture in the punch bowl.

Iceberg Alley (Alcoholic)

Ron Young, St. John's, Newfoundland

Ingredients:

1/4 lime
1/8 lemon
1 ounce vodka
Diet 7-Up or diet Sprite

Directions:

Fill a tall glass with ice cubes, then squeeze in and throw in the lemon and lime. Fill glass with 7-Up or Sprite. Makes a very refreshing, hot-day drink.

Maidenhair Teaberry Delight (Alcoholic)

Lila Mercer, St. John's, Newfoundland

Ingredients:

2 quarts ice cream
6 ozs creme de menthe liqueur
6 ozs brandy

Directions:

Let ice cream melt, then blend all ingredients in blender and serve.

Summer Fog (Alcoholic)

Ron Young, St. John's, Newfoundland

Ingredients:

Screech rum
2 cups brown sugar
4 cups icing sugar
1 quart vanilla ice cream (melted)
1 1/2 tsp cinnamon
1/2 tsp allspice

Trivia Tidbits
Don't brag. It isn't the whistle that pulls the train.

Directions:

Blend all ingredients (except Screech) in blender and store in freezer until ready to use. To use, pour 1 1/2 ounces of Screech into a coffee mug, then add 1 1/2 ounces of frozen mixture and boiling water. Stir and enjoy.

Fuzzy Navel (Alcoholic)

Gordon and Dolly (Stamp) Krauss, New Jersey, USA

Ingredients:

3 ounces vodka
9 ounces Peach Snapps
2 cups orange juice
2 cups ice cubes or 1 1/2 cups crushed ice

Directions:

Blend all ingredients in blender and serve. (Serves 5 to 6 people)

Crybaby (Alcoholic)

Stan Baldwin, Stephenville, Newfoundland

Ingredients:

1/2 oz extra dry vermouth
1 oz extra dry gin
2 pearl onions
ice cubes

Directions:

Place ice cubes in a highball glass and add vermouth. Pour vermouth out leaving only vermouth that sticks to glass and ice. Add gin and stir for 30 seconds to ensure drink is well chilled. Strain into a martini glass (either on the rocks or straight up). Skewer two pearl onions on a toothpick, add to drink and serve.

Brandy Alexander (Alcoholic)

Stan Baldwin, Stephenville, Newfoundland

Ingredients:

3/4 oz brandy
3/4 oz creme de cacao
3/4 oz table cream
1 whole nutmeg (grated to decorate)

Directions:

Half fill a cocktail shaker with ice cubes and pour in the brandy and creme de cacao. Add the table cream and shake for 15 seconds. Strain the mixture into a small wine glass and grate nutmeg over the top.

Margarita (Alcoholic)

Stan Baldwin, Stephenville, Newfoundland

Ingredients:

1 wedge fresh lime
fine salt crystals
ice cubes
1 oz tequila
3/4 oz cointreau
1 tbsp lime juice
1 long strip cucumber peel

Directions:

Rub the lime wedge over the rim of a small wine glass. Rub the glass rim in the salt crystals to coat entire rim. Put ice cubes, tequila, cointreau and lime juice in a cocktail shaker and shake for

---

Food for Thought
Everybody is ignorant, only on different subjects. - Will Rogers

Trivia Tidbits
The button was originally developed as a means of decoration.

Spice of Life
Women's styles may change, but their designs remain the same.
- Oscar Wilde

Beverages

Alcoholic and Non-Alcoholic Punches and Slushes for Sunny Days or Festive Occasions

15 seconds. Carefully strain the mixture into a wine glass. Cut a long, narrow, thin sliver of peel from a full cucumber and skivver it around the toothpick in a serpentine fashion and add to drink for decoration.

B52 (Alcoholic)

Stan Baldwin, Stephenville, Newfoundland

Ingredients:

1/2 oz Kahlua
1/2 oz Grand Marnier
1/2 oz Bailey's Irish Cream

> *Food for Thought*
> The fellow who says he is too old to learn new tricks probably always was. - A J Marshall

Directions:

Pour the Kahlua into a small shooter glass. Hold a cold teaspoon upside down, just touching the side of the glass and the top portion of the Kahlua, then carefully pour the Grand Marnier over the bottom of the upside-down teaspoon, then create a second layer. In the same manner, add the Bailey's to create another, which will fit itself in between the Kahlua and Grand Marnier to become the second layer.

George Street Stoplight (Alcoholic)

Ron Young, St. John's, Newfoundland

Ingredients:

ice cubes
1 oz creme de menthe
1 oz creme de cacao
1 oz table cream
3 partridgeberries
3 bakeapples

> **Spice of Life**
> Said one woman to her friend, "They say if you give a man enough rope he'll hang himself." Replied the friend, "I gave mine enough rope and he skipped!"

Directions:

Place ice cubes, creme de menthe, creme de cacao and table cream into a blender and blend for 10 or more seconds. Pour into appropriate glass. Skiver partridgeberries and bakeapples unto a toothpick and add to drink to decorate and flavour.

Iceberg Blue (Alcoholic)

Stan Baldwin, Stephenville, Newfoundland

Ingredients:

3/4 oz blue curacao liqueur
3/4 oz coconut cream liqueur
1 1/2 ozs Iceberg Vodka
1 1/2 ozs pineapple juice
1 wedge of lime
1 marachino cherry
crushed ice

> **Trivia Tidbits**
> Shark skin used to be used as sand paper.

Directions:

Place all ingredients (except crushed ice, lime and cherry) into blender and blend until the colour is an even blue. Fill a large glass with crushed ice and add mixture. Garnish with lime wedge and cherry.

Mai Tai (Alcoholic)

Stan Baldwin, Stephenville, Newfoundland

Ingredients:

3/4 oz Screech
3/4 oz Aurora Borealis Vodka
3/4 oz Apricot Brandy
2 1/4 ozs chilled orange juice
2 1/4 ozs chilled pineapple juice
2 tbsp grenadine
crushed and cubed ice

Food for Thought

You can judge a man by his enemies as well as by his friends.

Directions:

Put crushed ice in cocktail shaker and add liqueurs and juices. Shake until the outside of shaker feels cold (about 20 seconds). Put ice cubes in tall glass and strain in mixture. Slowly pour in the grenadine, letting it go to the bottom, and serve.

Raspberry Punch (Non-Alcoholic)

Mary (Peggy) Bourgeois (nee Mercer), St. John's, Newfoundland

Ingredients:

30 ozs frozen raspberries
2/3 cup white sugar
ice cubes
2 cups chilled orange juice
1 (6oz) can frozen lemonade (thawed)
1 litre bottle chilled ginger ale

Spice of Life

I put up a motto that reads, 'There's no place like home', but my mother-in-law takes it down every time she visits.

Directions:

Thaw raspberries and press them through a sieve to remove seeds. Discard seeds and combine raspberry puree with sugar and stir until sugar is dissolved. Put 2 to 3 trays of ice cubes in a punch bowl and add raspberry puree, orange juice and thawed lemonade. Pour in ginger ale slowly. Makes about twenty 4-ounce servings.

Screech Punch (Alcoholic)

Josephine Jenkins, Springdale, Newfoundland

Ingredients:

1 (40oz) bottle Screech
2 litre bottle ginger ale
juice of 12 oranges
6 ozs pineapple juice
3/4 cup white sugar
ice cubes

Trivia Tidbits

In 1935, the Illinois State Legislature passed a bill designating 'the American language' as the official tongue of that state. 'English' was outlawed.

Beverages

Alcoholic and Non-Alcoholic Punches and Slushes for Sunny Days or Festive Occasions

Directions:

Put two to three trays of ice cubes in large punch bowl and add other ingredients, stirring slowly.

Screech Daiquiri (Alcoholic)

Stan Baldwin, Stephenville, Newfoundland

Ingredients:

2 ozs Screech
juice of 1/2 lime
1/2 teaspoon white sugar
crushed ice

Directions:

Shake all ingredients well in cocktail shaker and strain into a champagne glass.

Tom Collins (Alcoholic)

Josephine Jenkins, Springdale, Newfoundland

Ingredients:

1 1/2 oz gin
1 tsp white sugar
juice of 1/2 lemon
Club Soda
crushed ice and ice cubes
maraschino cherry or slice of orange

Directions:

Shake gin, sugar, lemon juice and crushed ice in cocktail shaker and strain ice cubes, club soda and stir well. Decorate with cherry or orange slice.

Whiskey Sour (Alcoholic)

Gary Young, Twillingate, Newfoundland

Ingredients:

1 1/2 ozs rye whiskey
1/2 tbsp white sugar
1/2 oz lemon juice
ice cubes
maraschino cherry or slice of orange

Directions:

In cocktail shaker, shake whiskey, sugar and lemon juice together well. Pour over ice cubes in highball glass and add cherry or orange slice to decorate.

Vegfruitberry Delight (Non-Alcoholic)

Charmaine Young, Twillingate, Newfoundland

Ingredients:

1 apple (cored, peeled and diced)

Trivia Tidbits
The Geodesic Dome is the only man-made object that becomes structurally stronger as it increases in size.

Food for Thought
I sought my soul but my soul I could not see.
I sought my God but my God eluded me.
I sought my brother - and I found all three.
- Prayer printed in London Church News, May 1986

Spice of Life
Save energy - shower with a friend.

1 cantelope (peeled and diced)
3 carrots (peeled and diced)
5 ozs freshly squeezed orange juice
18 - 20 raspberries (de-husked)
ice cubes
1 orange slice (to decorate)

> ## Food for Thought
> Immature love says, "I love you because I need you." Mature love says, "I need you because I love you." - Erich Fromm

Directions:

Place the apple, cantelope and carrots in a blender and process to a pulp. Add orange juice and raspberries and process again. Strain through a sieve, pressing out all the juice with the back of a wooden spoon and discard pulp. Pour into ice-filled tumbler and serve with sliced orange.

Wedding Punch (Alcoholic)

Mary (Peggy) Bourgeois (nee Mercer), St. John's, Newfoundland

Ingredients:

3/4 cup white sugar
1/2 cup lemon juice
48 oz can pineapple juice
2 - 3 trays ice cubes
2 litre bottles Canadian white wine
2 litre bottles Canadian champagne
fresh mint sprigs

> ## Trivia Tidbits
> King Richard I, better known as the 'Lion Heart', only spent six months of his ten-year reign in England. He spent most of his time at the Crusades.

Directions:

Combine sugar, lemon juice and pineapple juice and stir until sugar has dissolved. Put 2 - 3 trays ice cubes in large punch bowl and add pineapple mixture. Add white wine then champagne. Garnish with mint twigs and serve. Makes about forty 4-ounce servings.

Peachy Keen (Alcoholic)

Charmaine Young, Twillingate, Newfoundland

Ingredients:

3 peaches
2 tsp lemon juice
2 tsp sugar syrup
1 1/2 ozs Peach Schnapps
1 litre bottle Canadian champagne (chilled)

> ## Spice of Life
> When I was a young man I vowed never to marry until I found the ideal woman. Well, I found her but, alas, she was waiting for the ideal man. - Robert Schuman

Directions:

Put peaches in boiling water for 2 minutes to loosen skins. Peel off skins, remove stones and discard both. Process the peaches and lemon juice in a blender until you have a smooth puree. Sweeten to taste with sugar syrup. Add the Peach Schnapps to the peach mixture and mix together with the champagne and serve.

Mixed Fruit Punch (Non-Alcoholic)

John Jenkins, Springdale, Newfoundland

Ingredients:

8 cups water
1 cup sugar
3 (6oz) cans frozen lemonade (thawed)
1 (48oz) can apple juice (chilled)
1 (48oz) bottle cranberry juice (chilled)
2 cups orange juice (chilled)
2 cups strong tea (chilled)
ice

Directions:

Combine water and sugar in medium saucepan and bring to a boil for 5 minutes, then cool. Pour this mixture over a block of ice in a large punch bowl along with the other ingredients. Stir and serve.

> *Food for Thought*
> If it weren't for the last minute, nothing would get done.

Red Tartan (Alcoholic)

Ron Young, St. John's, Newfoundland

Ingredients:

1 oz scotch whiskey
1 oz vermouth
1 dash bitters
1 tsp Purity raspberry syrup
ice

Directions:

Combine all ingredients in highball glass and stir.

> **Trivia Tidbits**
> The name nickel comes from the German Kupfernickel, which means 'Nickel's copper'. Nickel was supposed to be a goblin who lived in German copper mines. He was responsible for mischievously creating the metal (nickel) that looked like copper, but was not really copper.

Henhouse (Alcoholic)

Ron Young, St. John's, Newfoundland

Ingredients:

1 whole egg
1 tsp icing sugar
2 ozs rye whiskey
crushed ice

Directions:

Put all ingredients in shaker and shake until outside of shaker becomes cold. Strain into a glass and serve.

> **Spice of Life**
> If at first you don't succeed ... destroy all evidence that you tried.

Kids' Recipes

DANGER!

NOTE TO CHILDREN

Parents should be involved before trying to do any of these recipes.

Halloween Witches' Brew

Melissa Thomas, St. John's, Newfoundland

<u>**Ingredients**</u>:

orange sherbet
ginger ale

<u>**Directions**</u>:

Place a scoop of orange sherbet in a tall glass. Pour ginger ale slowly over sherbet.

Clowning Around

Wilhelmena Hardy, Port aux Basques, Newfoundland

<u>**Ingredients**</u>:

1 pint vanilla ice cream
4 sugar cones
4 maraschino cherries
12 raisins
8 chocolate bits
whipped cream

<u>**Directions**</u>:

Place scoops (balls) of ice cream on dessert plates. Top each ice cream ball with a sugar cone for the clown's hat; place two chocolate bits for eyes, three raisins for the mouth and a cherry for the nose. Put whipped cream around the clown for his neck ruffle. Makes 4.

Food for Thought
Every bigot was once a child free of prejudice.
- Mary de Lourdes

Pink Smoothie

Philip Hardy, Port aux Basques, Newfoundland

<u>**Ingredients**</u>:

1 can frozen lemonade
maraschino cherries
2 cups cranberry juice

Spice of Life
If you want to keep a secret, keep it to yourself.
- Geoffrey Chaucer

<u>**Directions**</u>

In a large pitcher, mix lemonade as directed. Add cranberry juice and stir. Pour over ice cubes and serve a straw in each glass with a cherry on top.

Healthy Party Snack

Clark LeRiche, Port aux Basques, Newfoundland

<u>**Ingredients**</u>

1 bag popcorn (popped)
1 can peanuts (salted)
1 medium box raisins

<u>**Directions:**</u>

Mix everything together in a large serving bowl. Eat.

Trivia Tidbits
For its size, the lion has the smallest heart of all beasts of prey.

Gone Bananas

Jeremy Hardy, Port aux Basques, Newfoundland

Ingredients:

1 ripe banana
1 cup milk (cold)
1/2 teaspoon vanilla
1 scoop vanilla ice cream

Directions

Peel the banana and mash with fork in a bowl. Add the milk and vanilla and beat until well mixed. Pour into a tall glass and float a scoop of ice cream on top.

Spice of Life

Doctors will tell you that if you eat slowly, you will eat less. That is especially true if you are a child in a big family.

Coconut Bread Squares

Alma Hardy, Port aux Basques, Newfoundland

Ingredients:

1 can sweetened condensed milk
5 or 6 slices white bread
3/4 cup shredded coconut

Directions:

Trim crusts off bread and cut into 1-inch squares. Pour condensed milk in one bowl and coconut in another. Dip the bread squares first in milk and then in coconut. Place on cookie sheet and broil 4 inches from the heat, watching carefully so they don't burn. Remove to platter to cool when golden brown.

Fun With Familiar Phrases

Twinkle, twinkle, little star
But stay, my darling, where you are;
Into my life if you should fall,
I'd never see you shine at all.
                    -Samual Hoffenstein

Frosted Drink

Mackenzie Wicks, St. John's, Newfoundland

Ingredients:

1/2 pt strawberries
1/4 cup sugar
3 cups milk (cold)
1/2 pt strawberry ice cream

Directions:

Wash, drain and remove stems from berries. Mash with a fork in small bowl. Stir in sugar and milk gradually, beating with an egg beater. Add ice cream and stir until it starts to melt. Serve in tall glasses.

Food for Thought

Mothers are those wonderful people who get up before they smell the bacon cooking.

Apple Saucy Ice Cream

Sara Wicks, St. John's, Newfoundland

Ingredients:

1 medium can (or jar) apple sauce
1/2 tsp cinnamon
vanilla ice cream

Trivia Tidbits

There are about 5.5 million cats in Canada.

Directions:

In saucepan, warm apple sauce and stir in cinnamon. Spoon into dessert dishes and top with a scoop of ice cream. Serve immediately.

Fruity Eggnog

Colby Young, St. Philips, Newfoundland

Ingredients

1 cup cold milk
1 raw egg
1/4 tsp vanilla
1/4 cup orange juice
1 tbsp powdered sugar

> # Spice of Life
> Most kids only eat spinach so they'll grow up to be big and strong enough to tell Mom what she can do with her spinach.

Directions:

Mix all ingredients together in bowl and beat for two minutes with an egg beater. Pour into glasses and serve.

Baked Fruit Delight

Barbara Wicks, St. John's, Newfoundland

Ingredients:

4 large red cooking apples
3/4 cup granulated sugar
2 tbsp brown sugar
1 cup water

> # *Food for Thought*
> Kindness is something you can't give away, since it always comes back.

Directions:

Wash and core apples. Peel 1/3 of the way down from the top. Place stem end down in baking dish. Boil granulated sugar and water for 10 minutes. Pour over apples. Bake at 350°F for 45 minutes until apples are tender when pierced with a fork. Remove from the oven and sprinkle with brown sugar. Return to oven until sugar is melted.

Root Beer Float

Brianna Young, St. Philips, Newfoundland

Ingredients:

vanilla ice cream
root beer, ice cold

> # Trivia Tidbits
> Dogs have sometimes had litters as large as 23 puppies.

Directions:

Put two scoops of vanilla ice cream in two tall glasses. Slowly fill glass with root beer.

Li'l Splits

Cindy Smart, Ontario

Ingredients:

4 bananas

1 pt ice cream
maraschino cherries
1 jar pineapple topping
canned whipped topping

Directions:

Peel bananas and slice them lengthwise and then crosswise. In flat dessert dish arrange bananas in a 4-pointed cross, rounded ends out. Put a scoop of ice cream on top of bananas. Spoon on pineapple topping, some whipped cream topping, and dot with a cherry.

Breakfast Salad

Mariah Smart, Ontario
Ingredients:

2 oranges
2 bananas
small bunch grapes
1/4 cup shredded coconut

Directions:

Peel oranges and bananas and cut into bite-size pieces. Slice grapes in half, removing any seeds. Toss fruit and refrigerate until very cold. At the last minute, add coconut and toss lightly.

Chicken Little Casserole

Karen George, New Harbour, Newfoundland
Ingredients:

1 cup water
1 can mushroom soup
1 pkg onion soup mix
1 cup long grain rice
1 can cream of chicken soup
8 piece of chicken (boneless, skinless)

Directions:

Mix all ingredients in a casserole dish, placing chicken pieces on top. Bake at 375°F for 1 hour.

Ham Steak with an Edge

Julie Ann George, New Harbour, Newfoundland
Ingredients:

4 ham steaks (single size servings)
1/3 cup brown sugar
1/3 cup water
2 tbsp prepared mustard
1/4 cup vinegar
1/2 tsp salt

Food for Thought
If you really want to annoy your enemy, keep silent and leave him alone. - Arabic proverb

---

Spice of Life
Ever notice that the Jolly Green Giant stands around laughing his head off while the little people do all the work canning vegetables?

Trivia Tidbits
Every day a child is killed accidentally by a gun that is left loaded in the house. Who says that guns don't kill people?

Directions:

Place ham in baking dish. Mix remaining ingredients together; spoon over ham. Cover; bake at 425°F for 20 - 30 minutes until sauce is bubbly and ham is cooked. Serves 4.

Fuzzy Sundae

Nolan Smart, Ontario

Ingredients:

4 peach halves (canned or fresh)
1 pt vanilla ice cream
1 pkg frozen raspberries, thawed

> *Food for Thought*
> You can't have everything.
> Where would you put it?

Directions:

Arrange peach halves in dessert dishes. Spoon ice cream into peaches. Top with raspberries and serve.

Fisherman's Casserole

Sarah George, New Harbour, Newfoundland

Ingredients:

onions
potatoes
fish
Kraft cheese slices
1 can cream of mushroom soup
1 can water

> **Spice of Life**
> Every young man should serve a term in the armed forces. He'll learn how to take orders, he'll learn to make beds, he'll learn never to volunteer, and many other things he'll need to know when he gets married.

Directions:

In a casserole dish, place a layer of onions, potatoes, fish and Kraft cheese slices. Repeat layers. Add cream of mushroom soup and can of water. Bake for 1 hour at 350°F.

Porky Pig Casserole

Rachel Snow, St. John's, Newfoundland

Ingredients:

1 cup raw rice (Dainty)
1 can cream of mushroom soup
1 pkg onion soup mix
1 can water
pork chops
paprika

> **Trivia Tidbits**
> Moths cannot eat: they have neither mouths nor stomachs.

Directions:

Mix rice, mushroom soup, onion soup mix and water in a bowl. Pour into a pan. Place pork chops on top and push to sink them into mixture. Sprinkle with paprika. Cover with foil wrap and bake at 350°F for 1 1/2 hours or until meat is tender. Serve with carrots, peas or tossed salad.

Cheesy Mashed Potatoes

Michelle Miller, Mount Pearl, Newfoundland

Ingredients:

potatoes
butter
3/4 cup milk
1 tbsp vinegar
cheese

Directions:

Boil potatoes and mash them. Add butter, milk and vinegar. Grate cheese and mix some of the cheese in with the potatoes and put the remaining cheese on top. Placc in greased dish and bake at 400°F for 30 minutes. Do not cover.

Spice of Life
Out of the mouths of babes, too often, comes cereal.

Jack-In-The-Bean-Stalk Salad

Jordan Seward, Mount Pearl, Newfoundland

Ingredients:

1 (15oz) can green beans
1 (15oz) can yellow wax beans
1 (15oz) can lima beans
1 (15oz) can kidney beans
1 green pepper, chopped
2 onions, ringed
3/4 cup white sugar
1/2 cup salad oil
1/2 cup vinegar
1 tsp salt
1/2 tsp black pepper

Directions:

Toss all ingredients together lightly. Let stand for 2 hours. This salad will keep up to 3 weeks in the refrigerator.

Food for Thought
A child is a person who can't understand why someone would give away a perfectly good cat.

Pizza in a Pocket

Ryan Scott, Mount Pearl, Newfoundland

Ingredients:

pita bread
pizza sauce
mozzarella cheese, grated
pepperoni, sliced
mushrooms, sliced
green pepper, chopped

Directions:

Cut pita bread in half to form two

Trivia Tidbits
Goldfish will turn white if they are left in a dark room for a long while.

pockets. Spread inside surfaces of each pita with pizza sauce. Stuff pita with cheese, pepperoni, mushrooms and green pepper. Place on a baking sheet; broil 3 to 5 minutes or until cheese is melted and filling is hot.

Veggie Dip

Stacey Seward, Mount Pearl, Newfoundland

Ingredients:

1 container of sour cream
1/2 pkg onion soup mix

Directions:

Mix all ingredients together and serve with raw vegetables.

Applesicles

Erin Scott, Mount Pearl, Newfoundland

Ingredients:

1 (14oz) jar apple sauce
1 3/4 cups apple juice

Directions:

Whisk together sauce and juice. Pour into popsicle molds and freeze until firm.
Variations: Try both sweetened and unsweetened apple sauce. Can use other fruit juices in the same proportion as sauce to find the flavours and sweetness level that you like best.

Food for Thought

You've found a friendship that has no end
If ever you should, a child befriend.

- Ron Young

The Three Little Bears' Favourite Wings

Emily Mercer, St. John's, Newfoundland

Ingredients:

1 lb chicken wings
2 tbsp brown sugar
2 tbsp lemon juice
2 tbsp honey
salt and pepper, to taste
3 tbsp vinegar
2 tbsp soya sauce
2 tbsp Mazola oil
shake of garlic

Trivia Tidbits

Forty per cent of McDonald's profits come from the sales of Happy Meals.

Directions:

Mix well all ingredients, except chicken. Pour over chicken and marinate for 1 hour. Bake at 350°F for 1-1 1/2 hours.

Chick'n Honey

Melanie Lynch, St. John's, Newfoundland

Ingredients:

1/2 cup liquid honey
4 tsp curry powder (or less)

Spice of Life

As every intelligent husband knows, the best time to wash dishes is right after his wife tells him.

1/4 cup margarine
1/4 cup mustard
chicken pieces

Directions:

Mix sauce ingredients together and cook over low heat. Pour sauce over chicken parts. Bake at 350°F for 1 1/2 hours.

Party Spuds

Ashley Scott, Mount Pearl, Newfoundland

Ingredients:

2 lb frozen hashbrowns
1 cup onions, diced
1 tub sour cream
salt and pepper, to taste
1 cup cheese, grated
1 can cream of chicken soup
1/4 cup margarine, melted

Directions:

Mix all ingredients together. Bake at 350°F for 1 1/2 hours.

Summer Casserole

Tyler Belben, Mount Pearl, Newfoundland

Ingredients:

1 lb ground beef
1 medium onion
1 tsp salt
2 tsp cornstarch
1 cup ketchup
1 (14oz) can pineapple chunks
1/2 cup brown sugar
2 tsp dry mustard
1 can kidney beans

Directions:

Cook ground beef until lightly browned. Add onions and cook for a few more minutes. Combine remaining ingredients and add to meat. Bake at 350°F for 45 minutes.

Mud Pie

Kaitlyn Hibbs, Springdale, Newfoundland

Ingredients:

chocolate wafer crumbs
butter, melted
1 pkg chocolate instant pudding

Food for Thought
It's a feather in
A grandfather's cap
When the little ones fight
For a place on his lap
- Ron Young

Trivia Tidbits
Abracadabara was originally a charm to cure hay fever.

Spice of Life
Give a boy enough rope and he'll bring home a stray dog at the end of it.

1 cup cold milk
1 container of Cool Whip
1 1/2 cups miniature marshmallows
Gummi worms

Directions:

Make bottom using chocolate wafer crumbs and melted butter. Pat in square pan. Combine chocolate instant pudding with milk; add Cool Whip and marshmallows. Spread over the bottom. Sprinkle with chocolate crumbs. Add gummi worms on top.

Mellow Fellows

Amelia Wicks, Gander, Newfoundland

Ingredients:

1 (6oz) pkg chocolate chips
3 tbsp peanut butter
1 pkg miniature marshmallows
coconut

Directions:

Melt chocolate chips over low heat; add peanut butter and stir. Let cool and add miniature marshmallows. Shape into two rolls and roll in coconut. Slice as needed.

Food for Thought

Childhood is that wonderful time when all you have to do to lose weight is take a bath.

Chocolate Kisses

Chelsea Hibbs, Springdale, Newfoundland

Ingredients:

1 cup smooth peanut butter
1/4 cup cocoa powder
1 tsp vanilla extract
1 cup granulated sugar
2 eggs
36 Hershey Kisses

Directions:

Place all ingredients, except Kisses, in a medium bowl. Blend well with a spatula or wooden spoon. With hands, roll mixture into 1-inch balls and place on ungreased cookie sheet 2-inches apart. Gently press an unwrapped Hershey Kiss into centre of ball. Bake in a 350°F oven for 8 - 10 minutes. Remove from oven and let cool on sheet for 2 minutes before removing to racks.

Spice of Life

Hair today - gone tomorrow

Delightful Gingerbread

Renee Bennett, Stoneville, Newfoundland

Ingredients:

1 cup sugar
1 cup oil
2 cups flour
1 tsp cinnamon
1 tsp ginger

Trivia Tidbits

The largest living animal without a back bone is the giant squid.

1 tsp allspice
1 tsp cloves
1 tsp salt
2 tsp baking soda
2 tbsp hot water
2 eggs
1 cup molasses
1 cup boiling water

Directions:

Mix baking soda with 2 tbsp hot water. Mix rest of the above ingredients in a mixing bowl and then pour into a greased 13x9 baking pan. Bake at 350°F for 35 minutes.

Cottage Cheese Salad

James Hudson, Goose Bay, Labrador

Ingredients:

1 can mandarin oranges
1 (14oz) can fruit cocktail
1 (14oz) can crushed pineapple
1 container Cool Whip
1 pkg cottage cheese

Directions:

Drain fruit; mix all together with cottage cheese and Cool Whip. Let stand in refrigerator overnight. Serve as a salad or as a dessert.

Easy Treats

Aimee Bennett, Stoneville, Newfoundland

Ingredients:

24 graham crackers
1 cup flaked coconut
1 cup chocolate chips
3/4 cup walnuts, coarsely chopped
1 can condensed milk

Directions:

Preheat oven to 350°F. Grease a 13x9 pan. Place graham crackers in a blender and process until crackers form fine crumbs. Measure 2 cups of crumbs and combine with chocolate chips, coconut and walnuts in medium bowl; stir to blend. Add milk; stir with mixing spoon until blended. Spread batter evenly into prepared pan and bake 15 - 18 minutes or until edges are golden brown. Let pan stand on wire rack until completely cooled. Cut into bars. Store tightly covered at room temperature or freeze up to 3 months.

Food for Thought
A man never knows how to be a son until he becomes a father.

Spice of Life
A baby first laughs at the age of four weeks, at the same time that his or her eyes focus well enough to see you clearly.

Trivia Tidbits
7-Up got its name because it was originally sold in a seven ounce container.

Kids' Recipes
Fun Foods for Little People

Yummy Squares

Amber Wicks, Gander, Newfoundland

<u>Ingredients</u>:

1 pkg Jello (any flavour)
6 slices of bread
1 pkg Dream Whip

<u>Directions</u>:

Cut crust off bread. Prepare Jello according to package directions. Pour over bread. Chill until set and then prepare Dream Whip. Spread this on top of the cooled jello mixture. Cut into squares.

<u>Spice of Life</u>
The trouble with a kitten is that eventually it becomes a cat
- Odgen Nash

Red Bread

Devin Wells, Mount Pearl, Newfoundland

<u>Ingredients</u>:

2/3 cup white sugar
2 eggs
1/3 cup oil
1 tsp vanilla
1 cup flour
1/2 tsp salt
1/2 tsp baking soda
1 tsp cinnamon
2/3 cup crushed strawberries

Food for Thought
Be like a duck - above the surface composed and unruffled - below the surface, paddle like crazy.

<u>Directions</u>:

Beat together eggs, sugar, oil and vanilla until light and fluffy. Add dry ingredients sifted together; beat well. Add strawberries and pour into small loaf pan. Bake at 350° F for 50 - 55 minutes.

Nanna Wanna Bread

Timothy Bennett, Stoneville, Newfoundland

<u>Ingredients</u>:

1/3 cup margarine
2/3 cup sugar
2 eggs, well beaten
1 large banana, mashed
1 3/4 cups flour
2 tsp baking powder
1/4 tsp baking soda

Trivia Tidbits
Only monkeys from the American Continent can hang by their tails. Asian and African monkeys cannot.

<u>Directions</u>:

Cream margarine and sugar. Add eggs and mix. Mix in banana; add dry ingredients. Bake at 325°F for 45 - 50 minutes.

Kids' Recipes
Fun Foods for Little People

Abra Cadabra Bars

Jonathan Hudson, Goose Bay, Labrador

Ingredients:

1/2 cup butter or margarine
1 1/2 cups graham wafer crumbs
1 cup coconut
1 can condensed milk
1/2 cup nuts, chopped
1 pkg unsweetened chocolate chips
1/2 cup cherries, chopped

Food for Thought
If you think you can or can't, you're right.
- Henry Ford

Directions:

In an 8x8 baking pan, melt margarine. Mix in crumbs. Spread in pan. Spread 2/3 cup coconut, condensed milk, chopped nuts, chocolate chips, cherries and the other 1/3 cup coconut over crumb mixture. Bake at 350°F for 30 minutes or until brown.

Martian Mallow Squares

Pamela Dean, St. John's, Newfoundland

Ingredients:

1 pkg miniature marshmallows
1 can condensed milk
2 cups graham wafer crumbs
dash salt
1 tsp vanilla
1/2 cup cherries, cut up
2 1/2 cups coconut

Spice of Life
People who wouldn't think of talking with their mouths full often speak with their heads empty.

Directions:

Blend marshmallows, milk, crumbs, salt, vanilla and cherries. Line 8x8 pan with half coconut. Add mixture; press well. Place rest of coconut on top. Place in fridge for 24 hours.

Holly Dollies

Michelle Dean, St. John's, Newfoundland

Ingredients:

1 cup graham wafer crumbs
1/2 cup butter, melted
1 cup coconut
1 cup chocolate chips
1 cup walnuts
1 can sweetened condensed milk

Trivia Tidbits
The dog who lived the longest on earth is believed to be a Labrador Retriever named 'Adjutant' who died on November 30, 1963, at the age of 27 years.

Directions:

Mix melted butter and graham wafer crumbs and press in 8x8 pan. Put the next 3 ingredients in layers. Pour sweetened milk over all. Bake at 350°F for 30 minutes or until golden brown.

Coconut Squares

Cameron Hodder, St. John's, Newfoundland

Ingredients:

2 1/2 cups Corn Flakes cereal (or other flake cereal)
1 pkg medium coconut
1/2 cup raisins or maraschino cherries, drained and chopped
1/2 cup nuts, chopped
1 can sweetened condensed milk

Directions:

With a large spoon, crush cereal to reduce volume by about half. Add coconut, raisins or cherries, nuts and condensed milk; stirring until thoroughly combined. Turn into a greased 8 x 8 glass baking dish, lightly pressing mixture into dish. Microwave at HIGH for 3 minutes. Rotate dish 1/4 turn; microwave at MEDIUM-HIGH for 6 minutes, rotating dish 1/4 turn and removing shields after 3 minutes. Let stand directly on countertop for 10 minutes. Using a sharp, wet knife, cut into squares; remove from pan, cool thoroughly. (Squares will be slightly crumbly until thoroughly cooled). Makes 25 squares.

Jelly-In-Your-Belly Dessert

Andrea Loveless, Seal Cove, Fortune Bay, Newfoundland

Ingredients:

2 pkgs red jelly
2 cups hot water
1 pkg strawberries
1 can crushed pineapple
3 bananas, sliced

Directions:

Mix all ingredients together. Chill and serve with ice cream.

Food for Thought
The people to get even with are the ones who helped you.

French Poodles

Sandra LeRiche. Port aux Basques, Newfoundland

Ingredients:

3 cups coconut
1 tin sweetened condensed milk
1 pkg chocolate chips

Spice of Life
Share and share alike ... pleads the latecomer. "First come, first served," says he who got there first.

Directions:

Mix all ingredients together well. Roll into balls; roll in extra coconut. Bake at 350°F for 10 - 15 minutes or until golden brown.

Monster Grouch Cookies

Jessica Miller, Mount Pearl, Newfoundland

Ingredients:

1 cup white sugar

1/2 cup butter
1 cup brown sugar
3 eggs
1 1/2 cups peanut butter
3/4 tsp vanilla
3/4 tsp pancake syrup
2 tsp baking soda
4 1/2 cups rolled oats
1 cup M&M's
1 cup chocolate chips

Directions:

Cream butter, sugars and eggs. Add peanut butter, vanilla and pancake syrup. Stir in baking soda; add rolled oats, M&Ms and chocolate chips. Drop onto cookie sheet. Bake at 350°F for 9 - 11 minutes. Be careful, do not overbake. Cookies are chewy.

Kid-Style Chicken

Sarah Kerner, Glenwood, Newfoundland

Ingredients:

1 can cream of mushroom soup
3/4 cup milk
1 tbsp onion, finely chopped
1 tbsp parsley, chopped
2 lbs chicken parts
1 cup bread crumbs
2 tbsp butter, melted

Directions:

Mix 1/3 cup of soup, 1/4 cup of milk, onion and parsley. Dip chicken in soup mixture, then roll in bread crumbs. Place in shallow baking dish. Drizzle with butter. Bake at 400°F for 1 hour. Meanwhile, combine remaining soup and milk; heat, stirring occasionally. Serve over chicken.

Kid's Quesadillas

Stephanie Kerner, Glenwood, Newfoundland

Ingredients:

7-inch soft tortilla
1/2 tsp dijon mustard
1/3 cup old cheddar cheese, grated
1 tbsp green onion, sliced
1 tsp parsley

Directions:

Spread dijon on tortilla. Sprinkle with cheese, onion and parsley. Roll snugly. Cover with plastic wrap. Microwave for 20 - 25 seconds or wrap in foil and bake at 350°F for 12 minutes. Slice into 1-inch pieces and serve warm with salsa or sour cream. Each tortilla makes 6 pieces.

Kids' Recipes
Fun Foods for Little People

Banana Punch

Andrew Miller, Mount Pearl, Newfoundland

Ingredients:

6 cups water
2 cups sugar
1 can frozen orange juice
1 can frozen lemonade
1 (48oz) can pineapple juice
5 mashed bananas

Directions:

Combine all ingredients. Let freeze like slush. Serve mixed with ginger ale.

Tuna Tarts

Rikki Pilgrim, Portugal Cove, Newfoundland

Ingredients:

1 can tuna
1 cup cheddar cheese, grated
2 tbsp relish
2 tbsp onion, chopped
2 tbsp prepared mustard
12 slices buttered bread, crusts removed

Directions:

Drain and flake tuna. Combine with cheese, relish, onion and mustard. Place bread, buttered side down, in large muffin cups; fit in place. Spoon in mixture. Heat at 450°F for 10 minutes.

Five-Cup Salad

Colin Miller, Mount Pearl, Newfoundland

Ingredients:

1 cup sour cream
1 cup miniature marshmallows
1 cup orange sections
1 cup pineapple tidbits
1 cup coconut

Directions:

Drain juice from fruit. Mix all ingredients together and chill overnight.

Fuzzy Wuzzy Freeze

Robyn Miller, Mount Pearl, Newfoundland

Ingredients:

3/4 cup cold milk
3/4 cup chilled peaches
1/4 tsp salt

Trivia Tidbits
Most lipstick contains fish scales.

Food for Thought
Usually it is easier to forgive an enemy than a friend.

Spice of Life
As you go through life, you are going to have many opportunities to keep your mouth shut. Take advantage of all of them.

Trivia Tidbits
Donald Duck comics were banned from Finland because he doesn't wear pants.

Kids' Recipes
Fun Foods for Little People

3 drops almond extract
1/2 cup vanilla ice cream

Directions:

Blend milk, peaches, salt and almond extract until smooth. Add ice cream; blend until smooth. Makes 2 servings.

Barney's Blueberry Muffins

Melinda Thomas, St. John's, Newfoundland

Ingredients:
1/2 cup butter
1 cup sugar
2 eggs
3/4 cup milk
2 cups flour
1 cup blueberries
1/4 tsp vanilla
2 tsp baking powder

Trivia Tidbits

There are many underground streams in the Sahara Desert, and if a person dug down through the sand he could actually catch fresh-water fish.

Directions:

Mix all ingredients together and bake in muffin pan at 350°F until done.

Pineapple Delight

Kayla Kennedy, Mount Pearl, Newfoundland

Ingredients:
graham wafers
1/2 cup butter
1 egg
1 cup icing sugar
crushed pineapple
Dream Whip (or whipped cream)

Food for Thought

A person becomes wise by watching what happens when he isn't.

Directions:

Line an 8x8 pan with graham wafers. Cream together butter, icing sugar and egg. Pour mixture over graham wafers; spread crushed pineapple over this. Top with Dream Whip or whipped cream. Sprinkle a few crumbs on top. Refrigerate.

Chocolate Ants

Amanda Kennedy, Mount Pearl, Newfoundland

Ingredients:
6 squares semi-sweet chocolate
1 cup Bakers butterscotch chips
2 cups chow mein noodles
1 cup salted peanuts
1 cup miniature marshmallows

Spice of Life

There's always room at the top ...as the man said, who looked for the gas leak with a candle.
- B. Flynn

Kids' Recipes Fun Foods for Little People

Directions:

Melt chocolate and butterscotch chips over hot water or in microwave, on medium power 3-4 minutes, stirring until smooth. Add noodles, peanuts and marshmallows, stirring until coated with chocolate mixture. Drop from teaspoon onto waxed paper. Chill until firm; store in airtight container in refrigerator. Makes about 3 dozen.

Snowballs

Eric Moss, Edmonton, Alberta

Ingredients:

2 tbsp butter
3 tbsp cocoa
1 can sweetened condensed milk
2 cups graham wafer crumbs
1 cup coconut

> *Food for Thought*
> Chance makes our parents,
> but choice makes our friends.

Directions:

Melt butter; add cocoa. Stir in milk and mix well. Add graham wafer crumbs and coconut. Roll into balls and roll in coconut. Place in fridge for 1 1/2 to 2 hours.

Chicken A La Tsar

Philip Snow, St. John's, Newfoundland

Ingredients:

1 bottle Russian dressing
1 envelope chicken soup mix
3-4 tbsp apricot jam
chicken pieces

> **Spice of Life**
> When you hit the ketchup bottle,
> First none'll come out and then a lot'll.
> - Ogden Nash

Directions:

Mix together dressing, soup and jam. Pour over chicken and bake at 350°F for 1 1/2 hours.

Snowball Cake

Rachel Snow, St. John's, Newfoundland

Ingredients:

2 small pkgs pineapple Jello (or 1 large)
2 pkgs Dream Whip
angel food cake
coconut

> **Trivia Tidbits**
> Ketchup was sold in the
> 1830s as medicine.

Directions:

Set Jello according to package directions. When almost set, fold in whipped Dream Whip. In round bowl, place layer of angel food cake then layer of jello alternately until all are used up. When set, unmould on plate. Frost with Dream Whip. Cover with coconut.

Nuts & Bolts TV Snack

Colby Young, St. Phillip's, Newfoundland

<u>Ingredients</u>:

1 lb margarine or butter

2 tbsps Worcestershire sauce

1 tbsp garlic powder

1 1/2 tsps onion salt

4 cups Cheerios cereal

4 cups 'Life' cereal

4 cups Shreddies or Wheat Chex cereal

2 boxes pretzels

2 cups peanuts

1 box Bugles

1 box Cheeze Nips or Cheeze Bites

Trivia Tidbits

In the Arctic a conversation can be heard two miles away.

<u>Directions</u>:

Heat oven to 250° F. Place margarine or butter in very large roaster and put in oven to melt while oven is preheating. Add all the ingredients and stir well to coat evenly with butter. Be sure to ask for Mom or Dad's help while doing this, and be very careful because the oven and the pan will be hot. Bake for 1 and 1/2 hours, but you must make sure that the mixture is stirred every half hour. Get help and be careful while doing this. When it is cooled you will have a great TV snack for you and your friends.

Unicorns Are Forever

By Ron Young

When the moon is full
the unicorn
Comes prancing
down the beams
He slips into my
slumberings
And gallops through
my dreams

He's been around
a while, it seems
Since I remember,
yet

I've changed since I first
met him, but
He hasn't changed a
bit

He likes to run, he's
loads of fun
He's handsome and
he's clever
It's nice to know
he'll never go
He'll live and live
forever

V.I.P. Pages

The birthdates and anniversaries of the Very Important People in your life

Also a thought to live by for each day and historical events,
down through the years, for each day

On This Date in...

- **44 BC** Julius Caesar, founder of the Roman Empire, introduced the Julian Calendar.
- **1538** German and Swiss states introduced the Gregorian calendar.
- **1735** Paul Revere, American Silversmith and patriot who made the famous midnight ride, was born.
- **1959** After 25 months of fighting, popular hero Fidel Castro over-threw the hated Cuban Batista regime.
- **1984** The Sultan of Brunei, said to be the world's richest man, declared himself Prime Minister as the tiny oil-filled island nation gained its independence.

Very Important Birthdates   **1**   **JANUARY**

Name(print) _____

Comments _____

Autograph _____ Year of Birth _____

Never judge a man by his relatives; he did not choose them.

Name(print) _____

Comments _____

Autograph _____ Year of Birth _____

On This Date in...

- **1900** Queen Victoria wrote her famous line using the imperial pronoun, "We are not amused."
- **1903** President Roosevelt closed a Missouri post office for refusing to employ a black post mistress.
- **1920** Isaac Asimov, scientist and author, was born.
- **1979** Trial began for Sid Vicious, 21-year-old singer of the crusty punk group The Sex Pistols, for the murder of his girlfriend, Nancy Spungen.
- **1988** A New York accountant claimed a $3M lottery which he had actually won 45 days earlier. By waiting until the new year he saved $15,000 in taxes.

Very Important Birthdates   **2**   **JANUARY**

Name(print) _____

Comments _____

Autograph _____ Year of Birth _____

It takes an honest person to admit if he's tired or just lazy.

Name(print) _____

Comments _____

Autograph _____ Year of Birth _____

On This Date in...

- **1521** Martin Luther, founder of protestantism, was excommunicated from the Catholic Church.
- **1777** George Washington defeated the British at the Battle of Princeton.
- **1868** 16-year-old Japanese Emperor Meiji seized power, ending 700 years of military rule.
- **1924** Howard Carter discovered the sarcophagus of the boy king Tutankhamen in the Valley of Kings. A curse written on the tomb was completely ignored.
- **1988** The first advertisements in a Soviet newspaper appeared in *Izvestia*.

Very Important Birthdates   **3**   **JANUARY**

Name(print) _____

Comments _____

Autograph _____ Year of Birth _____

Humor is the hole that lets the sawdust out of a stuffed shirt.

Name(print) _____

Comments _____

Autograph _____ Year of Birth _____

On This Date in...

- **1885** The first successful appendix operation was performed by Dr. Williams West Grant, in Iowa.
- **1932** Gandhi's National Congress of India was declared illegal by the British administration, and he was arrested.
- **1948** Burma became a fully independent country outside the British Commonwealth.
- **1951** Seoul, the South Korean capital, was captured by the North Korean army during the Korean War.
- **1961** A strike in Copenhagen by apprentice barbers that began in 1938, finally ended.

Very Important Birthdates   **JANUARY**

Name(print) _____

Comments _____

Autograph _____ Year of Birth _____

Nothing dies more quickly than a new idea in a closed mind.

Name(print) _____

Comments _____

Autograph _____ Year of Birth _____

VIP Birthdates - 1 Year Calender

5 JANUARY — Very Important Birthdates

Name(print) _____

Comments _____

_____

Autograph _____ Year of Birth _____

He who says what he likes, hears what he does not like.
- Leonard L. Levinson

Name(print) _____

Comments _____

_____

Autograph _____ Year of Birth _____

On This Date in...

• **1896** The first demonstration of X-rays was given by German physicist, Rontegen.
• **1940** FM (Frequency Modulation) Radio was demonstrated for the first time in the US. The first actual broadcast took place a year later.
• **1960** The world's oldest railway, the Mumbles Railway, which ran from Swansea to Mumbles Head, Wales, made its final run before being shut down.
• **1981** The Yorkshire Ripper, Peter Sutcliffe, was charged with the murder of 13 women over a four-year period.

6 JANUARY — Very Important Birthdates

Name(print) _____

Comments _____

_____

Autograph _____ Year of Birth _____

Everybody has to be somebody to somebody. *-Malcolm S. Forbes*

Name(print) _____

Comments _____

_____

Autograph _____ Year of Birth _____

On This Date in...

• **871** King Alfred the Great of Wessex defeated the Danes at the Battle of Ashdown.
• **1540** King Henry VIII married Anne of Cleves, his fourth wife.
• **1838** US inventor Samuel Morse gave the first demonstration of his electric telegraphic system.
• **1938** The famous Austrian psychoanalyst, Sigmund Freud, arrived in London with several of his students to escape Nazi persecution of the Jews in Vienna.
• **1977** The notorious punk group The Sex Pistols were fired by their record label, EMI.

7 JANUARY — Very Important Birthdates

Name(print) _____

Comments _____

_____

Autograph _____ Year of Birth _____

A rumour is like a cheque - never endorse it until you are sure it is genuine. *-Will Henry*

Name(print) _____

Comments _____

_____

Autograph _____ Year of Birth _____

On This Date in...

• **1450** Glasgow University, Scotland, was founded.
• **1558** The French seized the port of Calais, the last foothold of the English invaders.
• **1610** Galileo discoverd four moons circling Jupiter.
• **1927** The transatlantic telephone service between New York and London opened.
• **1975** OPEC agreed to raise crude oil prices 10%. This caused world economic inflation and near bankruptcy for developing nations.
• **1990** The famous leaning tower of Pisa was closed for the first time since 1275 for safety reasons.

8 JANUARY — Very Important Birthdates

Name(print) _____

Comments _____

_____

Autograph _____ Year of Birth _____

Faith heightens guilt, it does not prevent sin. *- Cardinal Newman*

Name(print) _____

Comments _____

_____

Autograph _____ Year of Birth _____

On This Date in...

• **1806** Britain occupied the Cape of Good Hope (South Africa), formerly held by the Dutch.
• **1815** The British were defeated at New Orleans by the Americans in the last battle of the War of 1812.
• **1926** Ibn Saud became King of Hejaz and renamed it Saudi Arabia.
• **1935** Super singing star Elvis Presley was born.
• **1959** General Charles de Gaulle became president of the French Fifth Republic.
• **1961** Canadian Gordon Lonsdale and four others were arrested for spying on the British.

On This Date in...

• **1799** Income tax was introduced in Britain to help finance the Napoleonic Wars. The rate was two shillings on the pound.
• **1806** Viscount Horatio Nelson, British naval hero, was buried at St. Paul's Cathedral, London.
• **1811** The first women's golf tournament took place in Scotland between locals in Musselburgh.
• **1902** The state of New York introduced a bill to outlaw flirting in public.
• **1920** The Bolsheviks defeated the last of the White Russian troops under Admiral Koltchak.

Very Important Birthdates **9** **JANUARY**

Name(print) _____
Comments _____
_____
Autograph _____ Year of Birth _____
Beaten Paths are for beaten men. *-Eric Johnson*
Name(print) _____
Comments _____
_____
Autograph _____ Year of Birth _____

On This Date in...

• **1645** William Laud, Archbishop of Canterbury and supporter of King Charles I, was beheaded.
• **1839** Inexpensive Indian tea was auctioned for the first time in Britain, making it affordable enough to become the national drink.
• **1863** The London Underground Railway was opened.
• **1920** The League of Nations was inaugurated.
• **1946** The United Nations Assembly held its first meeting in London, England, replacing the Leage of Nations.

Very Important Birthdates **10** **JANUARY**

Name(print) _____
Comments _____
_____
Autograph _____ Year of Birth _____
Saying you can do a thing makes the doing of it more sure.
-Clifton Burke
Name(print) _____
Comments _____
_____
Autograph _____ Year of Birth _____

On This Date in...

• **1569** The first state lottery was held in England.
• **1813** Joachim Murat, King of Naples, deserted Napoleon and joined the Allies.
• **1815** Canada's first prime minister, Sir John Alexander MacDonald, was born.
• **1922** At Toronto General Hospital, 14-year-old Leonard Thompson became the first diabetic to be treated with insulin.
• **1928** Author Thomas Hardy died at age 87. His body was buried in Westminster near his second wife, his heart in the grave of his first wife in his native Wessex.

Very Important Birthdates **11** **JANUARY**

Name(print) _____
Comments _____
_____
Autograph _____ Year of Birth _____
The winners decide what were war crimes. - Gary Wills
Name(print) _____
Comments _____
_____
Autograph _____ Year of Birth _____

On This Date in...

• **1876** American adventurist and author Jack London was born. His books include *Call of the Wild*.
• **1905** Cowboy singing star Tex Ritter was born.
• **1964** The Sultan of Zanzibar was banished and the country declared itself a republic.
• **1970** A Boeing 747 jet landed at Heathrow Airport in London, at the end of its first trans-Atlantic flight from New York.
• **1976** Detective novelist Agatha Christie died.
• **1989** Former Ugandan leader Idi Amin was expelled from Zaire and took refuge in Senegal.

Very Important Birthdates **12** **JANUARY**

Name(print) _____
Comments _____
_____
Autograph _____ Year of Birth _____
The dictionary is the only place where success comes before work.
-Mark Twain
Name(print) _____
Comments _____
_____
Autograph _____ Year of Birth _____

VIP Birthdates - 1 Year Calendar

13 JANUARY — Very Important Birthdates

Name(print) _____

Comments _____

_____

Autograph _____ Year of Birth _____

In order to have friends, you must first be one. -Elbert Hubbard

Name(print) _____

Comments _____

_____

Autograph _____ Year of Birth _____

On This Date in...

• **1893** The Independent British Labour Party was formed by Keir Hardie.
• **1964** Capitol Records reluctantly released the first Beatles record in the US. *I Wanna Hold Your Hand* became the fastest-selling single ever.
• **1974** The world's largest airport was opened in Dallas, Texas.
• **1978** NASA selected its first female astronauts.
• **1982** A Boeing 737 crashed into a bridge and five ships on the Potomac River in Washington, DC, killing 78 people.

14 JANUARY — Very Important Birthdates

Name(print) _____

Comments _____

_____

Autograph _____ Year of Birth _____

The curve of a smile can set a lot of things straight.

Name(print) _____

Comments _____

_____

Autograph _____ Year of Birth _____

On This Date in...

• **1814** The King of Denmark ceded Norway to Sweden, which sparked a rebellion in Norway.
• **1907** An earthquake in Kingston, Jamaica, killed over 1000 people and virtually destroyed the city.
• **1918** Former French Prime Minister Joseph Caillaux was arrested for treason after advocating a peace settlement with Germany.
• **1938** Walt Disney Studios' first full-length Technicolor cartoon, *Snow White And the Seven Dwarfs*, was first shown in the US.
• **1957** US film actor Humphrey Bogart died.

15 JANUARY — Very Important Birthdates

Name(print) _____

Comments _____

_____

Autograph _____ Year of Birth _____

There is no future in any job. The future lies in the man who holds the job. -Dr G W Grave

Name(print) _____

Comments _____

_____

Autograph _____ Year of Birth _____

On This Date in...

• **1559** Elizabeth I, daughter of King Henry VIII and Anne Boleyn, was crowned Queen of England.
• **1790** Fletcher Christian and eight others of the *Bounty's* mutineers landed on Pitcairn Island.
• **1878** The telephone was first used to report an emergency when 21 doctors were summoned to a railway disaster at Tarifville, Connecticut.
• **1878** Women received degrees for the first time at the London University.
• **1973** Golda Meir became the first Israeli head of state to be received by the Pope.

16 JANUARY — Very Important Birthdates

Name(print) _____

Comments _____

_____

Autograph _____ Year of Birth _____

If you can't see where you're going you may not like where you end up.

Name(print) _____

Comments _____

_____

Autograph _____ Year of Birth _____

On This Date in...

• **1920** The US introduced prohibition, making the consumption of alcoholic beverages illegal.
• **1944** General Eisenhower was appointed Supreme Commander of Allied Forces in Europe.
• **1963** Yvonne Pope of England became the first woman to fly an international airline route when she took off from Gatwick, England for Dusseldorf.
• **1966** American folk singer Joan Baez was arrested today at an anti-Vietnam War protest in Oakland, CA.
• **1970** Colonel Gaddafi became Chairman of the Revolutionary Command Council in Libya.

On This Date in...

- **1706** Ben Franklin, the American statesman and scientist who helped draft the American Declaration of independence, was born.
- **1820** English author Anne Brontë was born.
- **1827** The Duke of Wellington was appointed Commander-in-Chief of the British army.
- **1966** A B-52 carrying four hydrogen bombs and the refueling tanker it collided with, both crashed.
- **1977** Gary Gilmore, who was convicted of double murder, became the first person to be executed since the US reintroduced the death penalty in 1976.

Very Important Birthdates **17** **JANUARY**

Name(print) _____
Comments _____
_____
Autograph _____ Year of Birth _____

Joys shared are doubled - sorrows shared are halved.

Name(print) _____
Comments _____
_____
Autograph _____ Year of Birth _____

On This Date in...

- **1778** Captain Cook discovered the Sandwich Islands, now known as Hawaii.
- **1911** Eugene Ely became the first pilot to land his aircraft on a ship, when he landed his bi-plane on the US cruiser, *Pennsylvania*.
- **1919** The Versailles Peace Conference opened.
- **1934** The first arrest was made in Britain as a result of issuing 'pocket' radios to policemen.
- **1943** During World War II, after a 16-month siege by the Germans, the Soviet army finally broke through to a relieved Leningrad.

Very Important Birthdates **18** **JANUARY**

Name(print) _____
Comments _____
_____
Autograph _____ Year of Birth _____

Seeing is not believing - believing is seeing. *-Dr Jim Parker*

Name(print) _____
Comments _____
_____
Autograph _____ Year of Birth _____

On This Date in...

- **1793** Louis XVI, king of France, was found guilty of treason and guillotined.
- **1809** US writer and poet Edgar Allan Poe was born.
- **1870** Americans Victoria Caffin Woodhall and Tenessee Caffin, two New York sisters, became the world's first female stockbrokers.
- **1915** German Zeppelins bombed England for the first time, causing casualties.
- **1942** The Japanese invaded Burma.
- **1966** Indira Gandhi became the first woman to be prime minister of India.

Very Important Birthdates **19** **JANUARY**

Name(print) _____
Comments _____
_____
Autograph _____ Year of Birth _____

You can do anything you want to do. You can be anything you want to be.

Name(print) _____
Comments _____
_____
Autograph _____ Year of Birth _____

On This Date in...

- **1841** Hong Kong was occupied by the British.
- **1892** In Springfield, Massachusetts, the first game of basketball, devised by Canadian Dr. James Naismith, was played at the YMCA.
- **1958** Sir Edmund Hillary, of Mt. Everest fame, became the second explorer to reach the South Pole.
- **1981** After being held in Tehran for 444 days, the 52 American hostages were released.
- **1987** Special envoy to the Archbishop of Canterbury, Terry Waite, was last seen just before 7 p.m. in Beirut prior to being kidnapped.

Very Important Birthdates **20** **JANUARY**

Name(print) _____
Comments _____
_____
Autograph _____ Year of Birth _____

There are few empty seats on the gravy train.

Name(print) _____
Comments _____
_____
Autograph _____ Year of Birth _____

VIP Birthdates - 1 Year Calendar

VIP Birthdates – 1 Year Calendar

21 JANUARY — Very Important Birthdates

Name(print) _____

Comments _____

_____

Autograph _____ Year of Birth _____

The behaviour of some children suggests that their parents embarked on the sea of matrimony without a paddle.

Name(print) _____

Comments _____

_____

Autograph _____ Year of Birth _____

On This Date in...

- **1846** The first edition of *The Daily News*, edited by Charles Dickens, was published in London.
- **1907** Taxi cabs were officially recognized by the British government.
- **1911** The first Monte Carlo rally began.
- **1941** The *Daily Worker*, the British communist newspaper, was suppressed in wartime London.
- **1954** The US launched the first nuclear submarine, the *Nautilus*.
- **1976** A British Airways (then BOAC) Concorde made its inaugural flight to Bahrain.

22 JANUARY — Very Important Birthdates

Name(print) _____

Comments _____

_____

Autograph _____ Year of Birth _____

The reason some parents no longer lead their children in the right direction is that they aren't going that way themselves.

Name(print) _____

Comments _____

_____

Autograph _____ Year of Birth _____

On This Date in...

- **1905** The infamous 'Red Sunday' in St. Petersburg occurred when Russian troops fired on workers protesting against repressive conditions.
- **1924** Stanley Baldwin resigned as British prime minister at the end of an unsuccessful election.
- **1944** The Allied landings in Anzio, Italy, began.
- **1949** Mao Tse-Tung's army marched into Peking.
- **1964** Kenneth Kaunda became the first Prime Minister of Northern Rhodesia (later named Zambia).
- **1972** The United Kingdom, the Irish Republic and Denmark joined the Common Market.

23 JANUARY — Very Important Birthdates

Name(print) _____

Comments _____

_____

Autograph _____ Year of Birth _____

A pessimist is someone who feels bad when he feels good for fear he'll feel worse when he feels better. -Thomas Jefferson

Name(print) _____

Comments _____

_____

Autograph _____ Year of Birth _____

On This Date in...

- **1556** An earthquake in Shanxi Province, China, was thought to have killed some 830,000 people.
- **1931** Russian prima ballerian Anna Pavlova died.
- **1938** 16 oil companies were convicted in the US under the Anti-Trust laws for price fixing.
- **1943** The British captured Tripoli from the Germans.
- **1968** North Korean patrol boats boarded the US 'spyship' *Pueblo*, which they claimed was within their territorial waters. Several of the *Pueblos'* crew were killed or wounded.
- **1989** Spanish surrealist artist Salvadore Dali died.

24 JANUARY — Very Important Birthdates

Name(print) _____

Comments _____

_____

Autograph _____ Year of Birth _____

A pessimist always looks both ways when he crosses a one-way street.

Name(print) _____

Comments _____

_____

Autograph _____ Year of Birth _____

On This Date in...

- **1848** Just a week before the peace treaty with Mexico, James Marshall discovered gold in California. The gold rush would follow.
- **1916** Conscription was introduced in Britain to bolster failing volunteer numbers, and to provide more fodder for the trenches on the Western Front.
- **1976** The *Olympic Bravery*, a 270,000 ton oil tanker, ran aground off France. It was the largest shipwreck ever recorded.
- **1978** An orbiting Russian satellite crashed near Yellowknife in Canada's Northwest Territories.

On This Date in...

• **1878** A Turkish steamer was sunk by the first torpedo fired in war from a Russian torpedo boat.
• **1899** Manufacture of the first radio sets began at the Wireless Telegraph & Signal Company.
• **1917** It cost the US $25 million to buy the Virgin Islands (formerly the Danish West Indies).
• **1924** The first Winter Olympics began at Chamonix, France. Scandinavians won quite a few of the awards.
• **1971** Charles Manson, along with three members of his family, was found guilty of the brutal murder of Sharon Tate, wife of movie director Roman Polanski.

Very Important Birthdates **25** JANUARY

Name(print) _____
Comments _____
_____
Autograph _____ Year of Birth _____

Hard work doesn't hurt those who don't do any.

Name(print) _____
Comments _____
_____
Autograph _____ Year of Birth _____

On This Date in...

• **1788** The first convicts arrived in Sydney, Australia.
• **1875** The first battery-powered dentist drill was patented by George F. Green.
• **1880** Douglas MacArthur, US general and Supreme Commander of the Allied Forces in the Pacific in the Second World War, was born.
• **1908** The first Boy Scout group (the 1st Glasgow) was registered.
• **1931** Mahatma Gandhi was released from prison to have discussions with the British government in India.
• **1965** Hindi became the official language of India.

Very Important Birthdates **26** JANUARY

Name(print) _____
Comments _____
_____
Autograph _____ Year of Birth _____

A bridle for the tongue is an excellent piece of harness.

Name(print) _____
Comments _____
_____
Autograph _____ Year of Birth _____

On This Date in...

• **1756** Austrian composer and child prodigy Wolfgang Amadeus Mozart was born.
• **1822** Following war against Turkey, Greece won her independence.
• **1926** John Logie Baird gave a special public demonstration of television to members of the Royal Institution in London.
• **1952** Cairo's famous Shepheard Hotel burned down.
• **1967** Three US astronauts in the *Apollo 1* died just 218 feet above the ground at Cape Kennedy.
• **1973** US action in Vietnam ended.

Very Important Birthdates **27** JANUARY

Name(print) _____
Comments _____
_____
Autograph _____ Year of Birth _____

Time may be a great healer, but it's no beauty specialist.

Name(print) _____
Comments _____
_____
Autograph _____ Year of Birth _____

On This Date in...

• **1807** London's Pall Mall was the first street in any city to be illuminated by gaslight.
• **1896** The first speeding fine was handed out to a british motorist, for exceeding 2 mph in a built up area. He was doing 8 mph.
• **1896** The first radiation treatment for breast cancer was given.
• **1935** Iceland became the first country to introduce legalized abortion.
• **1986** The US space shuttle *Challenger* blew up, killing five men and two women.

Very Important Birthdates **28** JANUARY

Name(print) _____
Comments _____
_____
Autograph _____ Year of Birth _____

One moment of folly can mean a lifetime of regret.

Name(print) _____
Comments _____
_____
Autograph _____ Year of Birth _____

VIP Birthdates – 1 Year Calendar

VIP Birthdates – 1 Year Calendar

29 JANUARY — Very Important Birthdates

Name(print) _____

Comments _____

_____

Autograph _____ Year of Birth _____

Most people would learn from their mistakes if they weren't so busy trying to place the blame on someone else.

Name(print) _____

Comments _____

_____

Autograph _____ Year of Birth _____

On This Date in...

• **1853** Napoleon III married Eugénie de Montijo at the Tuilleries, Paris.
• **1856** Queen Victoria instituted Britain's highest military decoration, the Victoria Cross.
• **1879** US comedian W. C. Fields was born.
• **1916** British military tanks had their first trials in Hertfordshire, while German Zeppelins bombed Paris for the first time.
• **1947** Buckingham Palace was lit by candles due to a nation-wide blackout caused by the temperature dropping to an all time low of -16°F.

30 JANUARY — Very Important Birthdates

Name(print) _____

Comments _____

_____

Autograph _____ Year of Birth _____

Opportunity is missed by most people because it is dressed in overalls and looks like work. -Thomas Edison

Name(print) _____

Comments _____

_____

Autograph _____ Year of Birth _____

On This Date in...

• **1933** Adolf Hitler was appointed chancellor by the president of Germany, von Hindenburg.
• **1961** The contraceptive pill went on sale in Britain. It was not available through the National Health Service until December.
• **1965** The state funeral of Sir Winston Churchill, former prime minister of England, took place.
• **1972** On what became known in Northern Ireland as Bloody Sunday, British paratroopers, believing they were under fire, opened fire themselves on rioting Catholic protestors, killing 13 civilians.

31 JANUARY — Very Important Birthdates

Name(print) _____

Comments _____

_____

Autograph _____ Year of Birth _____

Doing housework for thirty dollars a day is domestic service; doing it for nothing is matrimony.

Name(print) _____

Comments _____

_____

Autograph _____ Year of Birth _____

On This Date in...

• **1606** Guy Fawkes, the chief conspirator in the Gunpowder Plot, was hanged, drawn and quartered.
• **1747** The first VD (Venereal Disease) clinic opened at London Lock Hospital.
• **1876** All US Indians were forced to move onto reservations, or be deemed hostile.
• **1928** 3M began marketing clear Scotch tape.
• **1943** Field Marshall Paulus surrendered to the Russians at Stalingrad, in defiance of Hitler.
• **1958** *Explorer I*, the first US Earth satellite, was launched at Cape Canavarel.

1 FEBRUARY — Very Important Birthdates

Name(print) _____

Comments _____

_____

Autograph _____ Year of Birth _____

Even when a marriage is made in heaven, the maintenance work has to be done here on earth.

Name(print) _____

Comments _____

_____

Autograph _____ Year of Birth _____

On This Date in...

• **1790** The first meeting of the US Supreme Court took place.
• **1840** The first dental college opened in Baltimore, Maryland, US.
• **1884** The first edition of the *Oxford English Dictionary* was published.
• **1920** The North West Mounted Police ('The Mounties', who always got their man) became the Royal Canadian Mounted Police.
• **1979** Ayatollah Khomeini returned from many years of exile in France to become the Iranian leader.

On This Date in...

- **1801** The first parliament of Great Britain in which Ireland was represented was assembled.
- **1848** The war between the US and Mexico ended after the signing of the Treaty of Guadalope Hidalgo.
- **1914** Cub Scouts were invented in England, the first pack being formed in Sussex.
- **1972** The British Embassy in Dublin burned down during riots over the deaths of 13 Catholics in Londonderry the previous Sunday.
- **1986** Women were allowed to vote for the first time in Liechtenstein.

Very Important Birthdates **2** FEBRUARY

Name(print) _____
Comments _____
_____
Autograph _____ Year of Birth _____

Some careers are carved; others, chiseled.

Name(print) _____
Comments _____
_____
Autograph _____ Year of Birth _____

On This Date in...

- **1730** The first stock exchange quotations were published in the *Daily Advertiser*, London.
- **1916** Canada's parliament building in Ottawa was destroyed by fire.
- **1919** The first meeting of the League of Nations was held in Paris, France, with American President Woodrow Wilson as chairman.
- **1945** The Allies used over 1000 planes on daylight bombing raids on Berlin.
- **1966** The first controlled landing on the moon was made by the USSR unmanned spacecraft, *Luna IX*.

Very Important Birthdates **3** FEBRUARY

Name(print) _____
Comments _____
_____
Autograph _____ Year of Birth _____

It is better to be faithful than famous.

Name(print) _____
Comments _____
_____
Autograph _____ Year of Birth _____

On This Date in...

- **1861** The Confederate States of America, an alliance of secessionist states which met at Montgomery, Alabama, was formed.
- **1904** The Russo-Japanese War began over the former's occupation of Manchuria.
- **1938** Adolf Hitler assumed command of the German Army. Von Ribbentrop became Foreign Minister.
- **1948** Ceylon became independent. It later changed its name to Sri Lanka.
- **1976** An earthquake in the South American country of Guatemala killed 23,000 people.

Very Important Birthdates **4** FEBRUARY

Name(print) _____
Comments _____
_____
Autograph _____ Year of Birth _____

Among the best home furnishings are children.

Name(print) _____
Comments _____
_____
Autograph _____ Year of Birth _____

On This Date in...

- **1945** US troops under the command of General MacArthur entered Manila.
- **1957** Bill Haley and the Comets arrived in London at the start of their British tour.
- **1974** 19-year-old heiress, Patty Hearst, was kidnapped by the Symbionese Liberation Army.
- **1983** Nazi war criminal Klaus Barbie was flown to France to face prosecution for war crimes.
- **1983** Amongst old papers in Odense, Denmark, an unknown symphony by a nine-year-old Mozart was discovered.

Very Important Birthdates **5** FEBRUARY

Name(print) _____
Comments _____
_____
Autograph _____ Year of Birth _____

We under-rate that which we do not possess.

Name(print) _____
Comments _____
_____
Autograph _____ Year of Birth _____

VIP Birthdates – 1 Year Calendar

6 FEBRUARY — Very Important Birthdates

Name(print) _____

Comments _____
_____

Autograph _____ Year of Birth _____

Troubles in marriage often start when a man is so busy earning his salt that he forgets his sugar.

Name(print) _____

Comments _____
_____

Autograph _____ Year of Birth _____

On This Date in...

• **1788** Massachusetts became the sixth state in the Union of American States.
• **1865** General Robert E. Lee became commander in chief of the Confederate armies.
• **1911** Ramsay MacDonald was elected Chairman of the British Labour Party.
• **1919** The German airline Lufthansa was established, flying between Berlin and Weimar.
• **1952** Queen Elizabeth succeeded to the British throne, upon the death of her father, King George VI.

7 FEBRUARY — Very Important Birthdates

Name(print) _____

Comments _____
_____

Autograph _____ Year of Birth _____

Let us endeavour to so live that when we come to die even the undertaker will be sorry. -Mark Twain

Name(print) _____

Comments _____
_____

Autograph _____ Year of Birth _____

On This Date in...

• **1301** Edward of Caernarvon (later King Edward II) became the first Prince of Wales.
• **1863** The *HMS Orpheus* was wrecked on the New Zealand coast with the loss of 185 lives.
• **1974** Grenada became independent. Eric Gairy became their first prime minister.
• **1976** Joan Bazely became the first woman football referee of an all-male match at Croydon, England.
• **1990** The Soviet Union agreed to change its 'full authority' constitution; their first step towards democracy after 70 years of communist government.

8 FEBRUARY — Very Important Birthdates

Name(print) _____

Comments _____
_____

Autograph _____ Year of Birth _____

Man - that inconsistent creation who is always insisting on hotel service around home and home environment at hotels.

Name(print) _____

Comments _____
_____

Autograph _____ Year of Birth _____

On This Date in...

• **1740** The Great Frost of London, which started on Christmas Eve 1739, came to an end.
• **1910** The Boy Scouts of America movement was formally incorporated.
• **1931** US actor James Dean was born.
• **1964** The Beatles arrived at John F. Kennedy Airport in New York to start their first US tour.
• **1969** The world's biggest passenger plane, the Boeing 747, made its maiden flight.
• **1983** The Derby-winning horse Shergar was kidnapped in Ireland. He was never seen again.

9 FEBRUARY — Very Important Birthdates

Name(print) _____

Comments _____
_____

Autograph _____ Year of Birth _____

With the fearful strain that is on me night and day, if I did not laugh I should die. -Abraham Lincoln

Name(print) _____

Comments _____
_____

Autograph _____ Year of Birth _____

On This Date in...

• **1649** The funeral of King Charles I took place. He was buried at Windsor.
• **1865** General Robert E. Lee took command of the Confederate Armies in the American Civil War.
• **1923** The Russian state airline, known as Aeroflot, was formed.
• **1972** Britain and East Germany established diplomatic relations.
• **1986** Halley's Comet made its expected return but poor weather conditions reduced opportunities to see it with the naked eye.

On This Date in...

- **1763** Following the Seven Years War, the Treaty of Paris was signed. France ceded Canada to Britain.
- **1774** Andrew Becker demonstrated his practical diving suit in the Thames River, London.
- **1840** Queen Victoria of England married her first cousin, Prince Albert.
- **1889** The Church of England authorized the use of the revised version of the Bible in church services.
- **1931** New Delhi became the capital of India.
- **1942** Glenn Miller, US bandleader and composer, was presented with the first-ever golden disc.

Very Important Birthdates **10** **FEBRUARY**

Name(print) _____
Comments _____
_____
Autograph _____ Year of Birth _____

It's easier to get facts than it is to face them.

Name(print) _____
Comments _____
_____
Autograph _____ Year of Birth _____

On This Date in...

- **1810** Napoleon, having divorced his first wife Joséphine, married Marie-Louise of Austria.
- **1858** Bernardette Soubirous, a young French girl, saw a vision of the Virgin Mary at Lourdes.
- **1878** The first weekly weather report was published by the meteorological office.
- **1975** Margaret Thatcher became the first woman leader of a British political party.
- **1990** The world's most famous political prisoner, Nelson Mandela, walked to freedom after serving more than 27 years in prison.

Very Important Birthdates **11** **FEBRUARY**

Name(print) _____
Comments _____
_____
Autograph _____ Year of Birth _____

Stopping at third base adds no more to the score than striking out.

Name(print) _____
Comments _____
_____
Autograph _____ Year of Birth _____

On This Date in...

- **1818** Chile's independence was proclaimed in Santiago.
- **1831** Rubber galoshes were first marketed by J.W. Goodrich, Boston, United States.
- **1851** A discovery in New South Wales, Australia, set off a gold rush.
- **1912** China became a republic with the overthrow of the Manchu dynasty.
- **1954** The British Standing Advisory Committee on cancer claimed that the illness had a definite link with cigarette smoking.

Very Important Birthdates **12** **FEBRUARY**

Name(print) _____
Comments _____
_____
Autograph _____ Year of Birth _____

Conscience is that small, still voice that makes you feel smaller.

Name(print) _____
Comments _____
_____
Autograph _____ Year of Birth _____

On This Date in...

- **1692** The MacDonald's massacre at Glencoe in Scotland was carried out by English forces lead by John Campbell, Earl of Breadalbane.
- **1793** Britain, Prussia, Austria, Holland, Spain and Sardinia formed an alliance against France.
- **1832** The first cases of Asiatic influenza were reported in London.
- **1866** The James-Younger gang carried out their first bank robbery in Liberty, Missouri. Jesse James was just 19 years old.
- **1941** Penicillin was first used on a human.

Very Important Birthdates **13** **FEBRUARY**

Name(print) _____
Comments _____
_____
Autograph _____ Year of Birth _____

Facts do not cease to exist just because they are ignored.

Name(print) _____
Comments _____
_____
Autograph _____ Year of Birth _____

VIP Birthdates – 1 Year Calendar

VIP Birthdates – 1 Year Calendar

14 FEBRUARY — Very Important Birthdates

Name(print) _____

Comments _____

_____

Autograph _____ Year of Birth _____

Nothing gives a person more pleasure than doing a good deed in secret and having it found out by accident.

Name(print) _____

Comments _____

_____

Autograph _____ Year of Birth _____

On This Date in...

- **1477** Probably the world's first known Valentine was sent to John Paston in Norfolk.
- **1893** Hawaii was annexed by the US.
- **1922** Marconi began broadcasting regular transmissions from Essex, England.
- **1929** 'The St. Valentine's Day Massacre' took place.
- **1939** The 35,000-ton German battleship, the *Bismarck*, was launched.
- **1956** Nikita Kruschev denounced the policies of Joseph Stalin at the 20th Soviet Communist Party Conference.

15 FEBRUARY — Very Important Birthdates

Name(print) _____

Comments _____

_____

Autograph _____ Year of Birth _____

Experience is not only an expensive teacher, but by the time you get through her school, her life is over.

Name(print) _____

Comments _____

_____

Autograph _____ Year of Birth _____

On This Date in...

- **1564** Italian astronomer, physicist and mathematician Galileo Galilei was born.
- **1898** The US sent their battleship *Maine* to Havana on a goodwill mission. She struck a mine and sank, which sparked the Spanish-American War.
- **1933** An attempt to assassinate US President Franklin D. Roosevelt failed.
- **1942** WWII - The Japanese captured Singapore.
- **1945** WWII - British troops reached the Rhine.
- **1982** A violent storm off Newfoundland capsized the *Ocean Ranger* oil platform, killing 84 people.

16 FEBRUARY — Very Important Birthdates

Name(print) _____

Comments _____

_____

Autograph _____ Year of Birth _____

Discipline, once considered 'standard household equipment', has fallen on hard times, and in its place permissiveness reigns.

Name(print) _____

Comments _____

_____

Autograph _____ Year of Birth _____

On This Date in...

- **1659** The first British cheque was written.
- **1923** French fashion-setter Coco Chanel set a new style for the new age: finally, an end to the corset!
- **1935** Sonny (Salvatore) Bono, one-time singing partner and former husband of Cher, was born.
- **1937** Dr. Corothers and his American research team patented nylon.
- **1945** US forces captured Bataan in the Philippines.
- **1959** Fidel Castro became president of Cuba.
- **1960** The US *Triton*, the first nuclear submarine to travel around the world underwater, began its journey.

17 FEBRUARY — Very Important Birthdates

Name(print) _____

Comments _____

_____

Autograph _____ Year of Birth _____

The problem with second opinions is that that's exactly how long most people think before they offer them.

Name(print) _____

Comments _____

_____

Autograph _____ Year of Birth _____

On This Date in...

- **1880** A bomb exploded in an attempt to assassinate the Tsar of Russia, Alexander II.
- **1883** Mr. A. Ashwell of Herne Hill, south London, patented Vacant/Engaged signs for toilet doors.
- **1929** Yasser Arafat, President of the Palestine Liberation Organization (PLO) was born.
- **1968** Austrian Jean-Claude Killy won three Gold medals at the Winter Olympics, Grenoble.
- **1972** The British parliament voted to join the European Common Market.
- **1982** Jazz (bop) pianist Thelonius Monk died.

On This Date in...

• **1517** Mary I, Queen of England, 'Bloody Mary' or 'Mary Tudor', was born.
• **1678** *Pilgrim's Progress* was published. Bunyan began it during his second term in prison for preaching on behalf of the Baptists.
• **1876** A direct telegraph line was established between Britain and New Zealand.
• **1911** The first official airmail from Allahabad to Naini Junction in India, by Henri Pecquet, took place.
• **1930** At Lowell Observatory in the US, Clyde Tombaugh discovered the planet Pluto.

Very Important Birthdates **18** FEBRUARY

Name(print) _____
Comments _____
_____
Autograph _____ Year of Birth _____
A wise man is one who has an open mind and a closed mouth.

Name(print) _____
Comments _____
_____
Autograph _____ Year of Birth _____

On This Date in...

• **1800** Napoleon established himself as first Consul after overthrowing the French government. His new government was a dictatorship.
• **1906** William S. Kellogg formed a cornflake company to make a breakfast cereal he had invented for patients suffering from mental disorders.
• **1909** President Theodore Roosevelt called for a world conference on nature conservation.
• **1976** Diplomatic relations between Britain and Iceland ended when the two countries failed to agree on limits in the 'cod war' fishing dispute.

Very Important Birthdates **19** FEBRUARY

Name(print) _____
Comments _____
_____
Autograph _____ Year of Birth _____
Kind words will never die, neither will they buy groceries.

Name(print) _____
Comments _____
_____
Autograph _____ Year of Birth _____

On This Date in...

• **1653** Admiral Blake defeated the Dutch fleet under Van Tromp, off Portsmouth.
• **1811** Austria informed the world she was bankrupt.
• **1861** Crystal Palace was damaged and the steeple was blown off Chichester cathedral when violent storms hit England.
• **1971** Major General Idi Amin promoted himself to general and president of Uganda.
• **1985** The Irish Republic made the sale of contraceptives legal for the first time.

Very Important Birthdates FEBRUARY

Name(print) _____
Comments _____
_____
Autograph _____ Year of Birth _____
Faults are thick where love is thin.

Name(print) _____
Comments _____
_____
Autograph _____ Year of Birth _____

On This Date in...

• **1858** The first electric burglar alarm was installed in Boston, Massachusetts.
• **1885** The 555ft-high George Washington Memorial obelisk was inaugurated in Washington, DC.
• **1916** World War I: The Battle of Verdun began. It lasted until December 16th.
• **1943** American General Dwight D. Eisenhower became Supreme Commander of the Allied forces in North Africa.
• **1947** The first television soap opera, *A Woman to Remember*, began in the US.

Very Important Birthdates **21** FEBRUARY

Name(print) _____
Comments _____
_____
Autograph _____ Year of Birth _____
An expert knows all the answers - if you ask the right questions.

Name(print) _____
Comments _____
_____
Autograph _____ Year of Birth _____

VIP Birthdates - 1 Year Calendar

22 FEBRUARY — Very Important Birthdates

Name(print) _____

Comments _____

_____

Autograph _____ Year of Birth _____

The secret of happiness is to count your blessings while the others are adding up their troubles.

Name(print) _____

Comments _____

_____

Autograph _____ Year of Birth _____

On This Date in...

• **1732** George Washington was born in Virginia. He became president in 1789.
• **1797** The French landed in Britain at Fishguard, but were soon captured and no other foreign force has managed to invade Britain since.
• **1862** Jefferson Davis was inaugurated as President of the Confederate States of America.
• **1879** Frank Winfield Woolworth opened his first 'five and ten cent' store in Utica, New York.
• **1886** *The Times* ran the first-ever classified personal column.

23 FEBRUARY — Very Important Birthdates

Name(print) _____

Comments _____

_____

Autograph _____ Year of Birth _____

One thing about the school of experience is that it will repeat the lesson if you flunk the first time.

Name(print) _____

Comments _____

_____

Autograph _____ Year of Birth _____

On This Date in...

• **1836** General Santa Anna's Mexican army began the siege of the Alamo in San Antonio, Texas.
• **1905** The Rotary Club was founded in Chicago.
• **1917** The February Revolution began in Russia.
• **1945** The 'Stars and Stripes' flag was raised by US forces on the island of Iwo Jima, only 750 flying miles from Tokyo.
• **1981** It was announced that the heir to the British throne, Charles, Prince of Wales, would marry 19-year-old Lady Diana Spencer.
• **1987** US pop art icon Andy Warhol died.

24 FEBRUARY — Very Important Birthdates

Name(print) _____

Comments _____

_____

Autograph _____ Year of Birth _____

Education is what you get from reading the small print in a contract. Experience is what you get from not reading it.

Name(print) _____

Comments _____

_____

Autograph _____ Year of Birth _____

On This Date in...

• **303** The persecution of the Christians officially began in Rome with the issuing of an edict by Galerius Valerius Maximianus.
• **1887** The first two cities to be linked by telephone were Paris and Brussels.
• **1938** A nylon toothbrush went on sale in New Jersey. The first nylon product ever.
• **1946** Juan Perón was elected President of Argentina.
• **1969** The unmanned *Mariner 6* was launched by the US to fly close to Mars.
• **1987** US blues singer Memphis Slim died in Paris.

25 FEBRUARY — Very Important Birthdates

Name(print) _____

Comments _____

_____

Autograph _____ Year of Birth _____

Fortitude: the courage with which some people go through life bearing the misfortunes of others.

Name(print) _____

Comments _____

_____

Autograph _____ Year of Birth _____

On This Date in...

• **1308** Edward II of England was crowned.
• **1570** Queen Elizabeth I was excommunicated by Pope Pius V who declared her an usurper.
• **1862** 'Greenbacks' (green paper dollars) were introduced by Abraham Lincoln during the American Civil War.
• **1913** Federal Income Tax was introduced in the US.
• **1943** George Harrison, former Beatle who became a film producer with Handmade Films, was born.
• **1946** The first bananas arrived in Britain following the war, but a Bridlington girl died after eating four.

On This Date in...

• **1531** Severe earthquakes caused the death of 20,000 people in Lisbon, Portugal.
• **1928** 'Fats' Domino, US singer and pianist who composed and performed 'Blueberry Hill', was born.
• **1932** US country singer, guitarist and film actor, Johnny Cash, was born.
• **1936** Hitler launched the 'people's car', the Volkswagen, designed by Ferdinand Porsche.
• **1951** With the passage of the 22nd Amendment, it was decided that US presidents could serve no more than two terms of four years.

Very Important Birthdates **26** FEBRUARY

Name(print) _____
Comments _____
_____
Autograph _____ Year of Birth _____
Practicing the Golden Rule is not a sacrifice, it is an investment.
Name(print) _____
Comments _____
_____
Autograph _____ Year of Birth _____

On This Date in...

• **1807** Henry Wadsworth Longfellow, American poet who wrote the epic *Hiawatha,* was born.
• **1900** The British Labour Party was founded. Ramsay MacDonald became secretary.
• **1939** Britain's most haunted house, Borley Rectory, was mysteriously destroyed by fire.
• **1952** The United Nations held its first session in its new building in New York.
• **1980** Michael Jackson was awarded his first Grammy.
• **1991** The Gulf War ended.

Very Important Birthdates **27** FEBRUARY

Name(print) _____
Comments _____
_____
Autograph _____ Year of Birth _____
You can't put things across by getting cross.
Name(print) _____
Comments _____
_____
Autograph _____ Year of Birth _____

On This Date in...

• **1784** John Wesley signed the 'deed of declaration' of the Wesleyan faith.
• **1912** Albert Berry made the first parachute jump from a plane over Missouri.
• **1966** The Cavern Club, Liverpool, where the Beatles and other pop groups began, was forced into liquidation.
• **1972** The French police seized 937 lbs of pure heroin at Marseilles. The operation was later immortalized in the film *The French Connection*.
• **1976** Spain withdrew from the Spanish Sahara.

Very Important Birthdates **28** FEBRUARY

Name(print) _____
Comments _____
_____
Autograph _____ Year of Birth _____
You must speak up to be heard, but you have to shut up to be appreciated.
Name(print) _____
Comments _____
_____
Autograph _____ Year of Birth _____

On This Date in...

• **1880** The St. Gotthard tunnel linking Switzerland and Italy was completed. The rail link ran just over nine miles.
• **1908** Dutch scientists produced solid helium.
• **1916** The German Navy was ordered to sink any armed merchantmen on sight.
• **1956** Pakistan became an Islamic republic.
• **1960** Hugh Heffner opened his first Playboy club in Chicago, introducing the Bunny girls.
• **1984** Canadian prime minister Pierre Trudeau resigned as leader of the Liberal Party.

Very Important Birthdates **29** FEBRUARY

Name(print) _____
Comments _____
_____
Autograph _____ Year of Birth _____
Ambition never gets anywhere until it forms a partnership with work.
Name(print) _____
Comments _____
_____
Autograph _____ Year of Birth _____

VIP Birthdates - 1 Year Calendar

1 MARCH — Very Important Birthdates

Name(print) _____

Comments _____

_____

Autograph _____ Year of Birth _____

Diplomacy is the ability to take something and make the other fellow believe he is giving it away.

Name(print) _____

Comments _____

_____

Autograph _____ Year of Birth _____

On This Date in...

- **1932** US aviator Colonel Charles Lindberg's 20-month-old son was kidnapped from his nursery.
- **1940** Vivien Leigh won the Oscar for Best Actress for her role as Scarlett O'Hara in *Gone with the Wind*.
- **1950** Klaus Fuchs was found guilty of passing British atomic secrets to Soviet agents. He eventually served seven years in prison.
- **1961** President Kennedy formed the Peace Corps of Young Americans to work overseas as part of US aid to developing nations.

2 MARCH — Very Important Birthdates

Name(print) _____

Comments _____

_____

Autograph _____ Year of Birth _____

A good leader inspires men to have confidence in him; a great leader inspires them to have confidence in themselves.

Name(print) _____

Comments _____

_____

Autograph _____ Year of Birth _____

On This Date in...

- **1717** The first ballet was performed in England by dancing master, John Weaver.
- **1855** Nicholas I, Tsar of Russia, died.
- **1882** Robert Maclean tried unsuccessfully to assassinate Queen Victoria at Windsor.
- **1946** Communist leader Ho Chi Minh was elected President of North Vietnam.
- **1955** Severe floods in North and Western Australia killed 200 people, leaving 44,000 homeless.
- **1974** The US Grand Jury said Nixon was involved in the Watergate cover-up.

3 MARCH — Very Important Birthdates

Name(print) _____

Comments _____

_____

Autograph _____ Year of Birth _____

A pat on the back will develop character if given young enough, often enough, low enough, and hard enough.

Name(print) _____

Comments _____

_____

Autograph _____ Year of Birth _____

On This Date in...

- **1802** Beethoven's *Moonlight Sonata*, the most famous piano composition in the world, was published.
- **1895** In Munich, bicyclists had to pass a test and display licence plates.
- **1931** The US Congress adopted *The Star-spangled Banner* as the US national anthem.
- **1933** The world premiere of the famous monster gorilla movie *King Kong* was held in New York.
- **1959** Lou Costello (Louis Francis Cristello), US comedian, the other half of Bud Abbott, died.

4 MARCH — Very Important Birthdates

Name(print) _____

Comments _____

_____

Autograph _____ Year of Birth _____

Judging by the number of divorces, too many couples were mis-pronounced husband and wife.

Name(print) _____

Comments _____

_____

Autograph _____ Year of Birth _____

On This Date in...

- **1791** Vermont became the 14th state of the Union.
- **1877** The first performance of *Swan Lake* was staged by the Russian Imperial Ballet in Moscow.
- **1890** The 1710ft Forth railway bridge in Scotland, the longest bridge in Britain, was opened by the Prince of Wales.
- **1958** The US nuclear submarine *Nautilus* became the first to travel under the North Pole ice cap.
- **1964** Malta became fully independent.
- **1971** Canada's Prime Minister, Pierre Trudeau, married 22-year-old Margaret Sinclair in secret.

On This Date in

- **1461** Henry VI of England was deposed, and succeeded by Edward IV.
- **1770** British troops opened fire on a crowd in Boston, Massachusetts, killing five in what was called 'The Boston Massacre'.
- **1946** British Prime Minister Winston Churchill, made his famous speech about Russia, saying that "An iron curtain has descended across Europe."
- **1960** Elvis Presley was discharged from the US army, having completed his service in Germany.
- **1982** US star John Belushi died of a drug overdose.

Very Important Birthdates **5** **MARCH**

Name(print) _____

Comments _____

_____

Autograph _____ Year of Birth _____

A fellow doesn't have to make a lot of noise to be a big shot.

Name(print) _____

Comments _____

_____

Autograph _____ Year of Birth _____

On This Date in...

- **1806** Romantic English poet Elizabeth Barrett Browning, who defied an oppressive father to marry likewise poet Robert Browning, was born.
- **1834** In Upper Canada, York was incorporated as a city under the name Toronto; its first mayor was W.L. Mackenzie.
- **1899** A new wonder drug was introduced in the US, called 'aspirin', relieving all sorts of pain.
- **1911** Former US president Ronald Regan was born.
- **1926** Fire completely destroyed The Shakespeare Memorial Theatre in Stratford-upon-Avon, England.

Very Important Birthdates **6** **MARCH**

Name(print) _____

Comments _____

_____

Autograph _____ Year of Birth _____

A worry a day drains vitality away.

Name(print) _____

Comments _____

_____

Autograph _____ Year of Birth _____

On This Date in...

- **1876** Alexander Graham Bell patented the first telephone capable of sustained articulate speech.
- **1912** Frenchman Henri Seimet became the first aviator to fly non-stop from Paris to London. The flight took three hours.
- **1917** The world's first jazz record, *The Dixie Jazz Band One-Step* was issued by US Victor Company.
- **1989** A convicted murderer in South Carolina who successfully appealed electrocution was accidentally electrocuted while fixing a set of earphones on the toilet.

Very Important Birthdates **7** **MARCH**

Name(print) _____

Comments _____

_____

Autograph _____ Year of Birth _____

Love is the only game in which two can play and both lose.

Name(print) _____

Comments _____

_____

Autograph _____ Year of Birth _____

On This Date in...

- **1910** The first female pilot's licences were granted to a Britishman and a French woman.
- **1943** English actress Lynn Redgrave was born.
- **1952** An artificial heart was used for the first time on a 41-year-old man. It kept him alive for 80 minutes; his death was unrelated to the heart machine.
- **1973** Paul McCartney was charged with growing pot on his farm in Scotland.
- **1988** Soap opera writers in the US went on strike for improved terms, threatening major shows such as *Dynasty* and *Dallas*.

Very Important Birthdates **8** **MARCH**

Name(print) _____

Comments _____

_____

Autograph _____ Year of Birth _____

Live your life that your autograph will be wanted, not your fingerprints.

Name(print) _____

Comments _____

_____

Autograph _____ Year of Birth _____

VIP Birthdates - 1 Year Calendar

9 MARCH — Very Important Birthdates

Name(print) _____

Comments _____

_____

Autograph _____ Year of Birth _____

Your mind is a sacred enclosure into which nothing harmful can enter except by your permission.

Name(print) _____

Comments _____

_____

Autograph _____ Year of Birth _____

On This Date in...

• **1562** Kissing in public was banned in Naples, contravention being punishable by death.
• **1796** Napoleon married Josephine de Beauharnais, the widow of a former French officer guillotined during the Revolution.
• **1864** General Ulysses Grant was appointed General-in-Chief of the Union Forces in the US Civil War.
• **1891** Four days of storms began off England's south coast, sinking 14 ships.
• **1932** Pu-Yi, the last Chinese emperor, was installed as head of the Japanese puppet state of Manchukuo.

10 MARCH — Very Important Birthdates

Name(print) _____

Comments _____

_____

Autograph _____ Year of Birth _____

You do not make money in the stock market. You merely take it from somebody else who guessed wrong.

Name(print) _____

Comments _____

_____

Autograph _____ Year of Birth _____

On This Date in...

• **1906** London Underground opened the Baker Street to Waterloo section and named it the Bakerloo line.
• **1910** Director D.W. Griffith found a small village with perfect natural light. Its name: Hollywood.
• **1964** Prince Edward, youngest son of Queen Elizabeth II of England, was born.
• **1969** James Earl Ray pleaded guilty to the murder of Martin Luther King. His sentence: 99 years in jail.
• **1974** A Japanese soldier was discovered on Lubang Island in the Philippines. He still believed the Second World War was being fought.

11 MARCH — Very Important Birthdates

Name(print) _____

Comments _____

_____

Autograph _____ Year of Birth _____

When a man sits down to wait for his ship to come in, it usually turns out to be a receivership.

Name(print) _____

Comments _____

_____

Autograph _____ Year of Birth _____

On This Date in...

• **1702** The first successful English newspaper, a single broadsheet called *The Daily Courant*, was published in London.
• **1845** Henry Jones invented self-raising flour.
• **1864** A water reservoir near Sheffield, England, burst its banks, killing 250 people.
• **1941** The US Congress passed the Lend-Lease Bill enabling Britain to borrow millions of dollars to purchase food and arms for the Second World War.
• **1985** The Al-Fayed brothers won control of the House of Fraser group to become owners of Harrods.

12 MARCH — Very Important Birthdates

Name(print) _____

Comments _____

_____

Autograph _____ Year of Birth _____

The reason ideas die so quickly in some heads is because they can't

Name(print) _____

Comments _____

_____

Autograph _____ Year of Birth _____

On This Date in...

• **1609** Bermuda became a British colony.
• **1912** The Girl Guides (later called Scouts) were founded in the US by Juliette Gordon Low.
• **1913** Canberra became the federal capital of Australia. Five years later, in 1918, Moscow was designated the capital of Russia.
• **1969** George Harrison and his wife Patti were arrested and charged with possession of 120 marijuana joints at their home.
• **1969** Paul McCartney married US photographer, Linda Eastman.

On This Date in...

- **1781** German astronomer Herschel discovered a seventh planet besides Earth. He called it Uranus.
- **1894** The first professional strip-tease performance took place at the Divan Fayonau Music Hall, Paris.
- **1928** Flooding from a burst dam near Los Angeles drowned 450 people and caused extensive damage.
- **1939** US singer and pianist Neil Sedaka was born.
- **1961** Pablo Picasso, 79, married his model, Jacqueline Rocque, 37, in Nice, France.
- **1974** The Charles de Gaulle Airport was opened in Paris, named after the beloved French leader.

Very Important Birthdates **13** **MARCH**

Name(print) _____

Comments _____

_____

Autograph _____ Year of Birth _____

The only sure thing about luck is that it will change.

Name(print) _____

Comments _____

_____

Autograph _____ Year of Birth _____

On This Date in...

- **1879** German-born Swiss physicist Albert Einstein, author of the theory of relativity ($e=mc^2$), was born.
- **1883** Founding Communist theorist Karl Marx died.
- **1885** Gilbert and Sullivan's *The Mikado* was first performed at the Savoy Theatre in London.
- **1891** Telephone cable was laid along the English Channel bed by the submarine *Monarch*.
- **1953** Nikita Krushchev replaced Malenkov as First Secretary of the Communist Party.
- **1964** Jack Ruby was found guilty in Dallas, Texas, of killing J. F. Kennedy assassin Lee Harvey Oswald.

Very Important Birthdates **14** **MARCH**

Name(print) _____

Comments _____

_____

Autograph _____ Year of Birth _____

The man who has a right to boast doesn't have to.

Name(print) _____

Comments _____

_____

Autograph _____ Year of Birth _____

On This Date in...

- **44BC** Roman Emperor Gaius Julius Caesar was assassinated by conspiring members of the Senate.
- **1767** 7th US President Andrew Jackson was born.
- **1820** Maine became the 23rd state of the Union.
- **1907** Women in Finland (the only female voters in Europe) won their first seats in the parliament.
- **1937** Bernard Faustus set up America's first central blood receiving center. He called it a 'blood bank'.
- **1941** Mike Love of the Beach Boys was born.
- **1956** *My Fair Lady* with Julie Andrews and Rex Harrison opened on Broadway.

Very Important Birthdates **15** **MARCH**

Name(print) _____

Comments _____

_____

Autograph _____ Year of Birth _____

A grouch is a guy who has sized himself up and got sore about it.

Name(print) _____

Comments _____

_____

Autograph _____ Year of Birth _____

On This Date in...

- **1802** The famous US Military Academy at West Point was established.
- **1815** William of Orange was proclaimed King of the Netherlands and became King William I.
- **1918** The famous 'stuttering' song, *'K-K-K-Katy'* was published, words and music by Canadian Geoffrey O'Hara.
- **1935** Hitler renounced the Versailles Treaty and introduced conscription.
- **1973** Queen Elizabeth II opened the new London Bridge over the river Thames.

Very Important Birthdates **16** **MARCH**

Name(print) _____

Comments _____

_____

Autograph _____ Year of Birth _____

Loose conduct can do a fine job of getting you in a tight place.

Name(print) _____

Comments _____

_____

Autograph _____ Year of Birth _____

VIP Birthdates – 1 Year Calendar

17 MARCH — Very Important Birthdates

Name(print) _____

Comments _____

Autograph _____ Year of Birth _____

A small boy is a pain in the neck when he is around, and a pain in the heart when he is not.

Name(print) _____

Comments _____

Autograph _____ Year of Birth _____

On This Date in...

• **1845** Elastic bands were patented by Stephen Perry at a rubber company in London, England.
• **1899** The first radio distress call was sent from a ship off the coast of England to the nearest lighthouse.
• **1917** US singer and pianist Nat King Cole was born.
• **1921** The first birth control clinic, run by Dr. Marie Stopes, opened in London, England.
• **1969** 70-year-old grandmother Golda Meir became Prime Minister of Israel.
• **1978** The tanker *Amoco Cadiz* ran aground on the Brittany coast, spilling massive amounts of oil.

18 MARCH — Very Important Birthdates

Name(print) _____

Comments _____

Autograph _____ Year of Birth _____

There are two kinds of bachelors: those too fast to be caught, and those too slow to be worth catching.

Name(print) _____

Comments _____

Autograph _____ Year of Birth _____

On This Date in...

• **1662** Paris ran the first public buses; they were for the poor of the city who could not afford carriages.
• **1850** The American Express Company was set up in Buffalo, New York.
• **1931** Electric razors were first manufactured by Schick Incorporated, Stanford, Connecticut.
• **1932** The world's longest single-arch bridge, the Sydney Harbour bridge, was opened.
• **1947** Prince Philip became a naturalized Briton.
• **1949** Britain and seven other European countries set up NATO (The North Atlantic Treaty Organization).

19 MARCH — Very Important Birthdates

Name(print) _____

Comments _____

Autograph _____ Year of Birth _____

Between saying and doing, many a pair of shoes is worn out. -Italian proverb

Name(print) _____

Comments _____

Autograph _____ Year of Birth _____

On This Date in...

• **721BC** The Babylonians experienced the first recorded solar eclipse in human history.
• **1848** US lawman Wyatt Earp was born.
• **1920** Fearing they would have to go to war again if another member state was invaded, the US Senate voted against joining the League of Nations.
• **1931** Alka-Seltzer was first marketed in the US.
• **1958** The first planetarium opened at Madame Tussaud's, London, England.
• **1976** After 15 years of marriage, Princess Margaret and her husband Lord Snowdon, separated.

20 MARCH — Very Important Birthdates

Name(print) _____

Comments _____

Autograph _____ Year of Birth _____

Do something. Either lead, follow or get out of the way.
-Ted Turner

Name(print) _____

Comments _____

Autograph _____ Year of Birth _____

On This Date in...

• **1602** The Dutch East India Company was formed by the Netherlands government. During its 96-year history, it became very powerful.
• **1806** The foundation stone of Dartmoor prison in Devon, England was laid.
• **1819** Burlington Arcade (which is still very elegant and exclusive) opened in London, England.
• **1852** Harriet Beecher Stowe's anti-slavery novel, *Uncle Tom's Cabin*, was published.
• **1934** The first demonstration of Radar was in Kiel Harbour. It was developed by Dr. Rudolf Kuhnold.

On This Date in...

• **1908** The French aviator, Henri Farman, took up the first passenger and flew over Paris.
• **1960** A peaceful demonstration in Sharpeville, South Africa, against the government's oppressive pass laws, turned into a massacre.
• **1963** San Francisco's notorious Alcatraz Prison, which had housed such infamous prisoners as Al Capone and the Birdman of Alcatraz, was closed.
• **1990** Over 417 people were injured, 341 arrested, when a massive poll tax demonstration in Trafalgar Square turned into a riot.

Very Important Birthdates **21** **MARCH**

Name(print) _____
Comments _____
_____
Autograph _____ Year of Birth _____

If you are not big enough to stand criticism, you are too small to be praised.

Name(print) _____
Comments _____
_____
Autograph _____ Year of Birth _____

On This Date in...

• **1774** *Tommy Thumb's Song Book*, one of the first-ever collections of nursery rhymes, was published.
• **1903** The American side of the Niagara Falls ran short of water due to a drought.
• **1907** The first taxis with meters began operating on the streets of London, England.
• **1942** The British Broadcasting Company sent its first morse code messages to the French Resistance.
• **1988** In Melbourne, Australia the first official mercy killing took place when doctor and family agreed to end life support systems for a terminally-ill patient.

Very Important Birthdates **22** **MARCH**

Name(print) _____
Comments _____
_____
Autograph _____ Year of Birth _____

Take life as you find it, but don't leave it so.

Name(print) _____
Comments _____
_____
Autograph _____ Year of Birth _____

On This Date in...

• **1752** The first Canadian newspaper, The *Halifax Gazette*, was published.
• **1861** The first tram cars began operating from Bayswater, London, England.
• **1908** US film actress Joan Crawford was born.
• **1919** Benito Mussolini, Italian Socialist journalist, formed the Fascist Party to fight liberalism and communism in Italy.
• **1925** The teaching of Darwin's theory of evolution was banned by the state of Tennessee.
• **1933** Hitler became dictator of Germany.

Very Important Birthdates **23** **MARCH**

Name(print) _____
Comments _____
_____
Autograph _____ Year of Birth _____

Chewing gum proves you can have motion without progress.

Name(print) _____
Comments _____
_____
Autograph _____ Year of Birth _____

On This Date in...

• **1603** Following the death of Elizabeth I, James I, son of Mary, Queen of Scots, united the English and Scottish crowns when he acceded to the throne.
• **1905** Science fiction author Jules Verne, author of *20, 000 Leagues Under the Sea*, died at age 77.
• **1926** The first Safeways supermarket in Maryland was started by Marian B. Skaggs.
• **1976** Isabel Perón was deposed as president of Argentina in a bloodless coup.
• **1978** 50,000 tons of crude oil polluted the French coastline after the tanker *Amoco Cadiz* split in two.

Very Important Birthdates **24** **MARCH**

Name(print) _____
Comments _____
_____
Autograph _____ Year of Birth _____

There are people so addicted to exaggeration they can't tell the truth without lying.

Name(print) _____
Comments _____
_____
Autograph _____ Year of Birth _____

VIP Birthdates – 1 Year Calendar

25 MARCH — Very Important Birthdates

Name(print) _____

Comments _____

_____

Autograph _____ Year of Birth _____

Advice after injury is like medicine after death. -Danish proverb

Name(print) _____

Comments _____

_____

Autograph _____ Year of Birth _____

On This Date in...

• **1306** Robert the Bruce, the eighth Earl of Carrick, was crowned King of the Scots, becoming Robert I.
• **1807** As a result of the campaigning of Wilberforce and the Quakers, the British parliament abolished the English slave trade.
• **1876** The Scots won 4-0 in the first ever Scotland vs. Wales football match at Glasgow.
• **1942** Aretha Franklin, the Queen of Soul, was born.
• **1949** *Hamlet* became the first British film to win an Academy Award (known as an 'Oscar').
• **1990** In New York, 87 people died in a disco fire.

26 MARCH — Very Important Birthdates

Name(print) _____

Comments _____

_____

Autograph _____ Year of Birth _____

The cure for boredom is curiosity. There is no cure for curiosity.
-Ellen Parr

Name(print) _____

Comments _____

_____

Autograph _____ Year of Birth _____

On This Date in...

• **1780** The *British Gazette and Sunday Monitor* was the first Sunday newspaper published in Britain.
• **1827** The 57-year-old German composer Ludwig van Beethoven died. Two days later, his funeral in Vienna was attended by more than 10,000 people.
• **1964** Barbra Streisand established herself as a star during her first performance of *Funny Girl* on Broadway.
• **1979** President Sadat for Egypt and Prime Minister Begin for Israel signed a peace treaty at the White House, witnessed by President Jimmy Carter.

27 MARCH — Very Important Birthdates

Name(print) _____

Comments _____

_____

Autograph _____ Year of Birth _____

Cooperation is spelled with two letters: WE. *- G.M. Verity*

Name(print) _____

Comments _____

_____

Autograph _____ Year of Birth _____

On This Date in...

• **1794** The US Navy was officially created.
• **1914** In a Brussels hospital the first successful blood transfusion took place.
• **1924** Jazz singer Sarah Vaughan was born.
• **1958** Nikita Krushchev toppled Marshal Bulganin to become the Soviet leader.
• **1961** The first female traffic wardens began ticketing in Leicester, England.
• **1977** Two jumbo jets collided on the ground at Tenerife airport killing 574 people. It was the world's worst air disaster.

28 MARCH — Very Important Birthdates

Name(print) _____

Comments _____

_____

Autograph _____ Year of Birth _____

Most people are about as happy as they make up their minds to be.
-Abraham Lincoln

Name(print) _____

Comments _____

_____

Autograph _____ Year of Birth _____

On This Date in...

• **1910** The first seaplane, designed by Henri Fabre, took off near Marseilles.
• **1917** Britain's first women's service unit, The Women's Army Auxiliary Corps, was formed.
• **1920** The King and Queen of Hollywood, Douglas Fairbanks and Mary Pickford, were married.
• **1939** The Spanish Civil War ended as Franco and his Nationalist troops took Madrid.
• **1941** Seven Italian warships were destroyed by the British naval forces without any loss of lives.
• **1945** The last German V2 rocket fell on Britain.

On This Date in...

• **1871** Queen Victoria opened The Royal Albert Hall.
• **1891** British explorer Robert Falcon Scott died in Antarctica after reaching the South Pole.
• **1920** Sir William Robertson became the first man to rise from private to field marshal in the British Army.
• **1929** Britain's suffragettes win their battle when parliament passed a bill that gave the right to vote to all women over the age of 21.
• **1951** Yul Brynner and Gertrude Lawrence starred in the Broadway performance of *The King and I*.
• **1973** US troops pulled out of South Vietnam.

Very Important Birthdates **29** MARCH

Name(print) _____
Comments _____
_____
Autograph _____ Year of Birth _____

A lot of good behaviour is due to poor health.

Name(print) _____
Comments _____
_____
Autograph _____ Year of Birth _____

On This Date in...

• **1842** Ether was first used as a surgery anaesthetic.
• **1858** A pencil with an eraser attached to one end was patented by Hyman Lipman of Philadelphia.
• **1867** Russia sold Alaska to the US for $7.2 million.
• **1943** The first Broadway performance of Rodgers and Hammerstein's musical, *Oklahoma!*, was given.
• **1945** British guitar legend Eric Clapton was born.
• **1981** John Hinkley III's assasination attempt wounded President Reagan and three other men.
• **1989** US actor Kurt Russell proposed marriage to actress Goldie Hawn, on stage at the Oscars.

Very Important Birthdates **30** MARCH

Name(print) _____
Comments _____
_____
Autograph _____ Year of Birth _____

Laziness travels so slowly that poverty soon overtakes it.

Name(print) _____
Comments _____
_____
Autograph _____ Year of Birth _____

On This Date in...

• **1901** The first car was turned out by the Daimler factory, named Mercedes after the inventor's daughter.
• **1913** New York's Ellis Island received a record 6745 immigrants in one day.
• **1924** The first British national airline, Imperial, was founded at Croydon Airport.
• **1934** John Dillinger, the most wanted man in the US, blasted his way out of a police trap after escaping from prison.
• **1959** Following Chinese repression, the Dalai Lama fled Tibet and sought asylum in India.

Very Important Birthdates **31** MARCH

Name(print) _____
Comments _____
_____
Autograph _____ Year of Birth _____

The bigot agrees there are two sides to every question: his side and the wrong side.

Name(print) _____
Comments _____
_____
Autograph _____ Year of Birth _____

On This Date in...

• **1204** Eleanor of Aquitaine, wife of Henry II of England, died.
• **1867** The Paris World Fair showcased the thorough remodelling of the French capital by Baron Georges Haussmann.
• **1891** The telephone link between London and Paris began operating.
• **1945** US forces invaded Okinawa, Japan.
• **1960** The US launched its first weather satellite.
• **1984** During a violent row on the eve of his 45th birthday, Marvin Gaye Jr. was shot dead by his father.

Very Important Birthdates **1** APRIL

Name(print) _____
Comments _____
_____
Autograph _____ Year of Birth _____

Character is not made in a crisis, it is only exhibited.

Name(print) _____
Comments _____
_____
Autograph _____ Year of Birth _____

VIP Birthdates – 1 Year Calendar

2 APRIL   Very Important Birthdates

Name(print) _____

Comments _____

Autograph _____ Year of Birth _____

Happiness is having a scratch for every itch. -Ogden Nash

Name(print) _____

Comments _____

Autograph _____ Year of Birth _____

On This Date in...

• **1792** The US mint was established in the nation's then-capital of Philadelphia.
• **1860** The first Italian parliament met at Turin.
• **1884** Britain's notorious Fleet Prison, now in an appalling state, was finally closed.
• **1905** The Simplon Tunnel under the Alps, linking Switzerland and Italy, was officially opened.
• **1979** The first Israeli leader to visit Egypt, Israeli Prime Minister Begin, met President Sadat in Cairo.
• **1982** Argentina invaded the Falkland Islands.
• **1991** Coal miners go on strike across the USSR.

3 APRIL   Very Important Birthdates

Name(print) _____

Comments _____

Autograph _____ Year of Birth _____

Common sense isn't as common as it used to be. -Will Rogers

Name(print) _____

Comments _____

Autograph _____ Year of Birth _____

On This Date in...

• **1860** The Pony Express started its regular run from St. Joseph, Missouri to San Francisco.
• **1922** In Russia, Joseph Stalin was appointed General Secretary of the Communist Party.
• **1947** The private medical care service, BUPA, was founded in Britain.
• **1981** Riots broke out in the south London district of Brixton. Mobs of youths went on a rampage. Police excesses and racial harrasment were cited as causes.
• **1987** The auction of the late Duchess of Windsor's jewels fetched £31million for medical research.

4 APRIL   Very Important Birthdates

Name(print) _____

Comments _____

Autograph _____ Year of Birth _____

Good ideas need landing gear as well as wings. -C.D. Jackson

Name(print) _____

Comments _____

Autograph _____ Year of Birth _____

On This Date in...

• **1581** Sir Francis Drake returns after having made the second successful circumnavigation of the globe.
• **1896** Gold was discovered in the Yukon.
• **1900** A teenaged French anarchist attempted to assassinate Prince Edward, heir to the English throne.
• **1915** American blues man Muddy Waters was born.
• **1929** German automobile engineer Karl Benz died.
• **1963** The Beatles held all of the top-five places on the American singles charts.
• **1968** Civil rights leader Martin Luther King was assasinated at a motel in Memphis, Tennessee.

5 APRIL   Very Important Birthdates

Name(print) _____

Comments _____

Autograph _____ Year of Birth _____

Joy is the feeling of grinning inside. -Dr. Melba Colgrove

Name(print) _____

Comments _____

Autograph _____ Year of Birth _____

On This Date in...

• **1724** The world-famous Italian lover, adventurer and intellectual Giovanni Casanova was born.
• **1794** Georges Jacques Danton, popular leader of the French Revolution, was guillotined for corruption.
• **1895** English playwright Oscar Wilde was accused of sodomy and arrested. His career was ruined.
• **1908** US actress Bette Davis was born.
• **1910** Kissing was banned on French railways because it could cause delays.
• **1955** Winston Churchill resigned as Prime Minister.
• **1960** *Ben Hur* won a record ten Oscars.

On This Date in...

- **1830** The Church of Jesus Christ of Latter Day Saints was founded in New York by Joseph Smith.
- **1896** The first modern Olympic Games, revived by Baron de Coubetin, was held in Athens, Greece.
- **1909** US Commander Robert Peary reached the North Pole accompanied by Matthew Henson.
- **1917** The US entered the First World War.
- **1965** The first commercial communications satellite, *Early Bird*, was launched by the US.
- **1968** Pierre Trudeau succeeded the retiring Lester Pearson as Canada's Prime Minister.

Very Important Birthdates **6** **APRIL**

Name(print) _____

Comments _____

Autograph _____ Year of Birth _____

If you can't be grateful for what you receive; be grateful for what you escape.

Name(print) _____

Comments _____

Autograph _____ Year of Birth _____

On This Date in...

- **1739** Notorious British highwayman Dick Turpin was hanged at York. His body was taken by a mob.
- **1832** In England, Joseph Thompson, a farmer, sold his wife for 20 shillings and a Newfoundland dog.
- **1862** General Ulysses Grant forced the Confederate troops to retreat at the Battle of Shiloh.
- **1906** In Italy, more than 100 people were killed when the unpredictable Mount Vesuvius erupted.
- **1943** LSD (hallucinogenic drug known as acid) was first synthsized by Swiss scientist Albert Hoffman.
- **1947** Henry Ford, US motor car manufacturer, died.

Very Important Birthdates **7** **APRIL**

Name(print) _____

Comments _____

Autograph _____ Year of Birth _____

Any golfer can be devout on a rainy Sunday.

Name(print) _____

Comments _____

Autograph _____ Year of Birth _____

On This Date in...

- **1513** Juan Ponce de Leon claimed a new American province for Spain. He named it 'Florida,' as it was sighted on Pascua Florida, or Easter Day.
- **1973** Spanish abstract painter and sculpter Pablo Picasso, inventor of Cubism, died at the age of 91.
- **1986** Clint Eastwood, 55, of *Dirty Harry* fame was elected Mayor of Carmel, California. He promised to "clean up the town."
- **1988** The first self-extinguishing armchair was unveiled in Britain. It had its own heat detector and heat-activated sprinkler system.

Very Important Birthdates **8** **APRIL**

Name(print) _____

Comments _____

Autograph _____ Year of Birth _____

Every time you lend money to a friend you damage his memory.

Name(print) _____

Comments _____

Autograph _____ Year of Birth _____

On This Date in...

- **1865** General Robert E. Lee of the Confederate army surrendered to Union General Ulysses S. Grant, marking the end of the American Civil War.
- **1869** The Hudson Bay Company agreed to cede its considerable northern territorial rights to Canada.
- **1926** *Playboy* publisher Hugh Heffner was born.
- **1959** "The physician can bury his mistakes, but the architect can only advise his client to plant vines." - US architect Frank Lloyd Wright, who died today.
- **1966** Carlo Ponti, who was still technically married to his wife in Italy, married Sophia Loren in Paris.

Very Important Birthdates **9** **APRIL**

Name(print) _____

Comments _____

Autograph _____ Year of Birth _____

You can always tell a failure by the way he criticizes success.

Name(print) _____

Comments _____

Autograph _____ Year of Birth _____

VIP Birthdates – 1 Year Calendar

10 APRIL   Very Important Birthdates

Name(print) _____

Comments _____

Autograph _____ Year of Birth _____

God help the sheep when the wolf is judge. -Danish proverb

Name(print) _____

Comments _____

Autograph _____ Year of Birth _____

On This Date in...

- **1633** The exotic fruit called bananas were displayed in a shop window for the first time ever in Britain.
- **1820** The first British settlers arrived at Algoa Bay in the eastern Cape Province of South Africa.
- **1849** The safety pin was first patented in America by Walter Hunt of New York.
- **1919** Mexican rebel leader and people's champion Emiliano Zapata was killed by government troops.
- **1921** Sun Yat-sen was elected President of China.
- **1924** The first crossword puzzle book was published in New York.

11 APRIL   Very Important Birthdates

Name(print) _____

Comments _____

Autograph _____ Year of Birth _____

Don't expect to enjoy the cream of life if you keep your milk of human kindness all bottled up.

Name(print) _____

Comments _____

Autograph _____ Year of Birth _____

On This Date in...

- **1713** In the Treaty of Utrecht, Gibraltar and Newfoundland were ceded to Britain by France.
- **1929** The cartoon character Popeye appeared for the first time in a William Hearst newspaper.
- **1934** Tornados and dust storms destroyed fragile crops and left thousands homeless in the US praires.
- **1961** An unknown folk singer named Bob Dylan made his live debut, opening for John Lee Hooker.
- **1961** Nazi war criminal Adolf Eichmann's trial began in Jerusalem. He was found guilty and hanged.

12 APRIL   Very Important Birthdates

Name(print) _____

Comments _____

Autograph _____ Year of Birth _____

Be kind. Remember, everyone you meet is fighting a hard battle.
-Harry Thompson

Name(print) _____

Comments _____

Autograph _____ Year of Birth _____

On This Date in...

- **1606** The Union Jack became England's official flag.
- **1709** *Tattler* magazine was first published in Britain.
- **1838** English settlers in South Africa vanquish the Zulus in the Battle of Tugela.
- **1945** Franklin Delano Roosevelt, the 32nd US president, died of a stroke at the age of 63.
- **1961** The USSR put the first man in space, Yuri Gagarin, for a single orbit of the earth.
- **1989** Britain's longest running musical, Andrew Lloyd Webber's *Cats*, was performed for the 3,358th time at the New London Theatre, Drury Lane.

13 APRIL   Very Important Birthdates

Name(print) _____

Comments _____

Autograph _____ Year of Birth _____

Death - the poor man's doctor. -German proverb

Name(print) _____

Comments _____

Autograph _____ Year of Birth _____

On This Date in...

- **1668** British poet and critic John Dryden was made the first Poet Laureate and Royal Historiographer.
- **1742** In Dublin, the first performance of Handel's *Messiah* meets with great success.
- **1743** Thomas Jefferson, American president responsible for founding the Democratic party and drafting the Declaration of Independence, was born.
- **1935** Imperial Airways and QUANTAS inaugurated their London to Australia air service.
- **1964** Sydney Poitier became the first black actor to win an Oscar, for his role in *Lillies of the Field*.

On This Date in...

- **1865** President Abraham Lincoln was shot in the head in a Washington theatre by John Wilkes Booth.
- **1900** M. Loubet, The French President, opened the Paris International Exhibition.
- **1903** Dr. Harry Plotz discovered the typhus vaccine.
- **1931** King Alfonso of Spain abdicated. The country subsequently became a republic.
- **1932** Violent riots erupted in New Zealand when civil servants were told of major pay cuts.
- **1983** The first cordless telephone was introduced in Britain.

Very Important Birthdates **14** **APRIL**

Name(print) _____

Comments _____

Autograph _____ Year of Birth _____

A bargain is usually a transaction in which each party thinks he is cheating the other.

Name(print) _____

Comments _____

Autograph _____ Year of Birth _____

On This Date in...

- **1852** The first screw-top bottles were patented by Francois Joseph Belzung of Paris.
- **1901** A motor hearse was used for the first time at a British funeral.
- **1912** On her maiden voyage, the *Titanic* struck an iceberg and sank with a loss of 2,206 passengers.
- **1945** Art treasures looted by the Nazis were discovered down an Austrian mine.
- **1964** Ian Smith became Prime Minister of Rhodesia.
- **1970** Canon Business Machines of Japan announced the first hand-held electronic pocket calculator.

Very Important Birthdates **15** **APRIL**

Name(print) _____

Comments _____

Autograph _____ Year of Birth _____

Small minds discuss people; normal minds discuss events; great minds discuss ideas.

Name(print) _____

Comments _____

Autograph _____ Year of Birth _____

On This Date in...

- **1867** Orville and Wilbur Wright developed the first real powered aircraft while working in a cycle shop.
- **1912** Harriet Quinby, the first woman to fly the English Channel, made her historic flight.
- **1924** US composer of *Moon River* and *The Pink Panther*, Henry Mancini, was born.
- **1953** The royal yacht *Britannia* was launched.
- **1964** Geraldine Monk of West Germany became the first woman to fly solo around the world.
- **1975** Cambodia fell to the Communist Khmer Rouge when the capital, Phnom Penh, surrendered.

Very Important Birthdates **16** **APRIL**

Name(print) _____

Comments _____

Autograph _____ Year of Birth _____

Modesty is the art of encouraging people to find out for themselves how important you are.

Name(print) _____

Comments _____

Autograph _____ Year of Birth _____

On This Date in...

- **1421** An estimated 100,000 people were drowned in Dort, Holland, when the sea broke through the dykes.
- **1521** Nonconformist German priest Martin Luther was excommunicated from the Catholic Church.
- **1790** Benjamin Franklin, American author, scientist and diplomat, died.
- **1894** Nikita Khrushchev, USSR leader, was born.
- **1929** Dutch bank leader James Last was born.
- **1953** Beloved silent film actor Charlie Chaplin announced that because of McCarthyist persecution he would never return to the United States.

Very Important Birthdates **17** **APRIL**

Name(print) _____

Comments _____

Autograph _____ Year of Birth _____

It's not the liberty we have, but the liberty we take, which causes most of the trouble.

Name(print) _____

Comments _____

Autograph _____ Year of Birth _____

VIP Birthdates - 1 Year Calendar

18 APRIL — Very Important Birthdates

Name(print) _____

Comments _____

_____

Autograph _____ Year of Birth _____

Laugh at yourself first, before anyone else can. -Elsa Maxwell

Name(print) _____

Comments _____

_____

Autograph _____ Year of Birth _____

On This Date in...

- **1775** Paul Revere made his famous ride from Charlestown to Lexington to warn the minutemen (civil militia) of the advance of the British forces.
- **1881** London's Natural History Museum opened.
- **1906** At 5:13 am the most violent earthquake ever recorded destroyed the city of San Francisco.
- **1934** The first launderette or 'washeteria' was opened in Fort Worth, Texas.
- **1954** While President Neguib was away from the capital, Colonel Nasser seized power and became Prime Minister of Egypt.

19 APRIL — Very Important Birthdates

Name(print) _____

Comments _____

_____

Autograph _____ Year of Birth _____

There are two periods in a man's life when he doesn't understand women - before and after marriage.

Name(print) _____

Comments _____

_____

Autograph _____ Year of Birth _____

On This Date in...

- **1882** Charles Darwin, the most controversial scientist of the last two centuries, died at age 73.
- **1903** Eliot Ness, famous US government agent who succeeded in fighting Mafia gangsters, was born.
- **1927** Mae West was found guilty of 'indecent behaviour' for her hit Broadway play, *Sex*.
- **1956** In a whirlwind storybook romance, Prince Rainier of Monaco married film star Grace Kelly.
- **1971** The USSR launched the *Salyut* space station.
- **1988** China radio began broadcasting western pop music for the first time.

20 APRIL — Very Important Birthdates

Name(print) _____

Comments _____

_____

Autograph _____ Year of Birth _____

Who will not mercy on others show, how can he mercy ever hope to have? -Edmund Spenser

Name(print) _____

Comments _____

_____

Autograph _____ Year of Birth _____

On This Date in...

- **1657** The British Admiral Blake destroyed the Spanish fleet in the harbour of Santa Cruz.
- **1768** Pontiac, Chief of the Ottawa Indians, died.
- **1770** During his search for the southern continent, Captain James Cook of the ship *Endeavour* discovers the islands of New Zealand off the Australian coast.
- **1883** French painter Edouard Manet died.
- **1889** Adolf Hitler, the Austrian-born housepainter who became a German dictator, was born.
- **1988** The world's largest termite mound, around 21 feet high, was found in the Australian outback.

21 APRIL — Very Important Birthdates

Name(print) _____

Comments _____

_____

Autograph _____ Year of Birth _____

Being kidnapped and held for ransom never worries the poor man! -Proverbs 13:8

Name(print) _____

Comments _____

_____

Autograph _____ Year of Birth _____

On This Date in...

- **1509** Henry VIII accended to the throne of England.
- **1816** Charlotte Brontë, eldest of the three Brontë sisters and author of *Jane Eyre*, was born.
- **1836** The Mexicans were defeated by the Texans at the Battle of San Jacinto.
- **1894** George Bernard Shaw's *Arms and the Man* was performed for the first time in London.
- **1917** Vimy Ridge was taken by the Canadian Forces after the WWI battle which started on April 9, 1917..
- **1989** A crowd of more than 10,000 people gathered in Tianamen Square, Beijing, China.

On This Date in...

- **1500** Pedro Alvarez Cabral accidentally discovered Brazil on his way to India, and claimed it for Portugal.
- **1760** The first known pair of roller-skates was worn.
- **1838** The British packet steamer, *Sirius*, became the first steamship to cross the Atlantic to New York from England.
- **1889** The American government allowed a land run on the Oklahoma territory. More than 200,000 people were present to stake their claims to the prairie.
- **1959** Australian angler Alf Dean caught a huge great white shark. It weighed 2664 lb and was 16'10" long.

On This Date in...

- **1616** William Shakespeare died at age 52.
- **1661** Charles II was crowned King of England.
- **1897** Lester Pearson, Canadian prime minister, who won a Nobel Peace Prize in 1957 for his role in settling the Suez crisis, was born.
- **1928** Shirley Temple Black, American child film star who became the US ambassador to Ghana, was born.
- **1968** The first decimal coins appeared in Britain.
- **1969** Robert F. Kennedy's assassin, Sirhan Bishara Sirhan, was found guilty and sentenced to execution in the gas chamber.

On This Date in...

- **1792** The French national anthem, the Marseillaise, was composed by Claude-Joseph Rouget de Lisle.
- **1930** Amy Johnson, the first woman to fly solo from Britain to Australia, landed her Gypsy Moth in Darwin. She was an instant public heroine.
- **1936** English actress Jill Ireland was born.
- **1942** Actress and singer Barbra Streisand was born.
- **1967** Russian cosmonaut Vladimir Komarov was killed when the spacecraft *Soyuz I* crashed to earth.
- **1990** The Hubble Space Telescope was launched from the space shuttle *Discovery*.

On This Date in...

- **1719** Daniel Defoe's *Robinson Crusoe* was first published in London, England.
- **1848** After suffering serious damage when it was first floated, the first Royal yacht, *Victoria and Albert*, was launched at Pembroke Docks.
- **1859** Ferdinand de Lesseps saw his great plan initiated when work began on the Suez Canal.
- **1964** The head of the famous Little Mermaid statue in Copenhagen harbour was sawn off and stolen.
- **1980** The US made a disastrous attempt to rescue hostages from the US Embassy in Tehran.

Very Important Birthdates **22** APRIL

Name(print) _____
Comments _____

Autograph _____ Year of Birth _____
An upright man can never be a downright failure.

Name(print) _____
Comments _____

Autograph _____ Year of Birth _____

Very Important Birthdates **23** APRIL

Name(print) _____
Comments _____

Autograph _____ Year of Birth _____
Luck is a wonderful thing. The harder a person works, the more of it he seems to have.

Name(print) _____
Comments _____

Autograph _____ Year of Birth _____

Very Important Birthdates **24** APRIL

Name(print) _____
Comments _____

Autograph _____ Year of Birth _____
Many a meal has been ruined by ample servings of cold shoulder and hot tongue.

Name(print) _____
Comments _____

Autograph _____ Year of Birth _____

Very Important Birthdates **25** APRIL

Name(print) _____
Comments _____

Autograph _____ Year of Birth _____
Luck is always against the man who depends on it.

Name(print) _____
Comments _____

Autograph _____ Year of Birth _____

VIP Birthdates – 1 Year Calendar

26 APRIL — Very Important Birthdates

Name(print) _____

Comments _____

_____

Autograph _____ Year of Birth _____

Money doesn't make you completely happy - but it sure quiets the nerves.

Name(print) _____

Comments _____

_____

Autograph _____ Year of Birth _____

On This Date in...

- **1452** Italian painter Leonardo da Vinci was born.
- **1785** US naturalist John James Audubon was born.
- **1895** The trial of Oscar Wilde for homosexuality (illegal at the time) began. Wilde was released on bail.
- **1900** A 12-hour fire destroyed vast areas of Ottawa and Hull, Ontario, leaving 12,000 homeless.
- **1936** American comedian Carol Burnett was born.
- **1970** The famous actor, writer, Burlesque dancer and TV host, Gypsy Rose Lee, died at the age of 56.
- **1986** The world's worst nuclear accident occurred at the Chernobyl power station near Kiev, Russia.

27 APRIL — Very Important Birthdates

Name(print) _____

Comments _____

_____

Autograph _____ Year of Birth _____

If you had your life to live over again, you'd need more money.

Name(print) _____

Comments _____

_____

Autograph _____ Year of Birth _____

On This Date in...

- **1822** American General Ulysses S. Grant was born.
- **1828** The London Zoological Gardens in Regents Park, London, were opened.
- **1882** American poet, essayist and philosopher, Ralph Waldo Emerson, died at the age of 78.
- **1937** San Francisco's Golden Gate Bridge, under construction for the past four years, was opened.
- **1968** Britain legalized abortion as a result of the Abortion Act presented by Liberal MP, David Steele.
- **1970** US actor Tony Curtis was fined £50 in London for being in possession of marijuana.

28 APRIL — Very Important Birthdates

Name(print) _____

Comments _____

_____

Autograph _____ Year of Birth _____

Money isn't everything, but is sure keeps you in touch with the children.

Name(print) _____

Comments _____

_____

Autograph _____ Year of Birth _____

On This Date in...

- **1770** The famous explorer Captain James Cook landed the *Endeavour* at Sting Ray Bay, Australia. It was later renamed Botany Bay for its great flora.
- **1789** The mutiny of the crew of the *Bounty* took place. Captain William Bligh and 18 faithful men were set adrift from the captured vessel.
- **1953** The Japanese were reallowed self-government, which they had been stripped of after WWII defeat.
- **1969** French president Charles De Gaulle resigned when the response to his referendum for major government reforms was 'non'.

29 APRIL — Very Important Birthdates

Name(print) _____

Comments _____

_____

Autograph _____ Year of Birth _____

An ounce of mother is worth a pound of clergy. -Spanish proverb

Name(print) _____

Comments _____

_____

Autograph _____ Year of Birth _____

On This Date in...

- **1376** Sir Peter de la Mare, the first Speaker of the British House of Commons, took office.
- **1885** Women were granted permission to be admitted to Oxford University examinations.
- **1930** The United Kingdom to Australia telephone service was inaugurated.
- **1945** The Nazi concentration camp of Dachau was discovered and liberated by Allied troops.
- **1967** Because he refused to fight in the Vietnam War, boxer Muhammed Ali was stripped of his world heavyweight champion title.

On This Date in...

- **1789** General George Washington was inaugurated as the first President of the United States.
- **1803** New Orleans and Louisiana were purchased from the French by the US.
- **1900** The Republic of Hawaii ceded itself to the US.
- **1905** Alfred Binet, the French psychologist, explained his new 'intelligence tests'.
- **1945** Adolf Hitler commited suicide.
- **1975** Following America's withdrawl from the war, Saigon, the capital of South Vietnam, fell to the invading communist forces.

Very Important Birthdates **30** APRIL

Name(print) _____

Comments _____

Autograph _____ Year of Birth _____

Let us not pray for lighter burdens but for stronger backs.

Name(print) _____

Comments _____

Autograph _____ Year of Birth _____

On This Date in...

- **1840** The first Penny Black stamps, featuring the head of Queen Victoria, went on sale five days early.
- **1927** The first hot meals on a flight from London to Paris were served by Imperial Airways.
- **1931** The Empire State Building, the world's tallest building, was opened by President Hoover.
- **1945** The German Army in Italy surrendered to the Allies, heralding the end of WWII.
- **1960** The USSR shot down the US U-2 spy aircraft piloted by Gary Powers.
- **1967** Elvis Presley married Priscilla Beaulieu.

Very Important Birthdates **1** MAY

Name(print) _____

Comments _____

Autograph _____ Year of Birth _____

Many a person's mind has been closed for years - but not for repairs or alterations.

Name(print) _____

Comments _____

Autograph _____ Year of Birth _____

On This Date in...

- **1729** Catherine II, Empress of Russia, was born.
- **1904** US crooner and actor Bing Crosby was born.
- **1923** Lieutenants Kelly and Macready in a Fokker T-2, made the first non-stop flight across the US from Long Island to San Diego.
- **1965** Over 300 million viewers in nine countries watched the first satellite television programme.
- **1973** The Lebanese Civil War began when 29 died as the army clashed with Palestinian refugees.
- **1980** Pink Floyd's hit *Another Brick In The Wall* was banned by the South African Government.

Very Important Birthdates **2** MAY

Name(print) _____

Comments _____

Autograph _____ Year of Birth _____

The surest rule for a long life is to get somebody else to do the worrying for you.

Name(print) _____

Comments _____

Autograph _____ Year of Birth _____

On This Date in...

- **1469** Niccolo Machiavelli, Italian political theorist who wrote *The Prince*, was born.
- **1494** On his second expedition in search of a route to the Orient, Columbus discovered Jamaica.
- **1788** London's first daily evening newspaper, The *Star and Evening Advertiser*, began publishing.
- **1808** The first duel fought from two hot air balloons took place above Paris.
- **1898** Israeli Prime Minister Golda Meir was born.
- **1968** Britain carried out the first heart transplant operation on a 45 year old man.

Very Important Birthdates **3** MAY

Name(print) _____

Comments _____

Autograph _____ Year of Birth _____

No man has a right to do as he pleases, except when he pleases to do it right.

Name(print) _____

Comments _____

Autograph _____ Year of Birth _____

VIP Birthdates - 1 Year Calendar

4 MAY — Very Important Birthdates

Name(print) _____

Comments _____

_____

Autograph _____ Year of Birth _____

A man is seldom as smart as his mother thinks, or as dumb as his mother-in-law says he is.

Name(print) _____

Comments _____

_____

Autograph _____ Year of Birth _____

On This Date in...

- **1942** US country singer Tammy Wynette was born.
- **1970** US National Guards shot four students and injured eleven at Kent State University during an anti-war demonstration over Nixon's Cambodian action.
- **1989** Colonel Oliver North was convicted of three charges and had nine others dismissed, regarding his action in supplying arms to the Nicaraguan Contras from money made by selling arms to Iran.
- **1989** Christine (George) Jorgensen, former US army private who shocked the world by having the first ever sex change operation, died of cancer.

5 MAY — Very Important Birthdates

Name(print) _____

Comments _____

_____

Autograph _____ Year of Birth _____

Whoever is capable of giving is himself rich. - *Erich Fromm*

Name(print) _____

Comments _____

_____

Autograph _____ Year of Birth _____

On This Date in...

- **1760** The first hanging took place at Tyburn near London's Hyde Park. Earl Ferrers was executed.
- **1818** German philosopher Karl Marx was born.
- **1821** Napoleon Bonaparte died in exile on the isolated British island of St. Helena. He was 51.
- **1968** Paris came to a standstill when 30,000 rioting students, led by Daniel Cohn-Bendit, barricaded the streets. French workers added their support as they clashed with police in violent confrontations.
- **1988** Japanese television transmitted the first live broadcast from the summit of Mount Everest.

6 MAY — Very Important Birthdates

Name(print) _____

Comments _____

_____

Autograph _____ Year of Birth _____

Let France have good mothers, and she will have good sons. -*Napoleon Bonaparte*

Name(print) _____

Comments _____

_____

Autograph _____ Year of Birth _____

On This Date in...

- **1642** Montreal was officially established under its original name 'Ville Marie'.
- **1851** US inventor Linus Yale patented his Yale lock.
- **1915** US actor and writer, Orson Welles, was born.
- **1937** The German dirigible *Hindenburg* exploded as it landed in New Jersey. Thirty-five of her 97 passengers died. This was the fifth airship crash and marked the end of their use as transportation.
- **1959** At the height of the fishing rights conflict (dubbed the 'Cod Wars') between the two nations, Icelandic gunboats fired on British fishing trawlers.

7 MAY — Very Important Birthdates

Name(print) _____

Comments _____

_____

Autograph _____ Year of Birth _____

All that I am, or hope to be, I owe to my angel mother. -*Abraham Lincoln*

Name(print) _____

Comments _____

_____

Autograph _____ Year of Birth _____

On This Date in...

- **1763** The chief of the Ottawa Indians, Pontiac, rose up against the English garrison at Detroit and laid siege to it for five months.
- **1888** George Eastman patented the Kodak box camera. Slogan: You push the button, we do the rest.
- **1926** Women's suffrage in Britain was lowered from the age of 30 to 21 years and over.
- **1960** Leonid Brezhnev became the new head of the USSR.
- **1988** People claiming to have been abducted by aliens meet as a group for the first time in Boston.

On This Date in...

- **1429** Joan of Arc, a peasant girl, led an army to victory against the English in the siege of Orléans. She was said to have heard holy voices telling her to rid France of the English since she was 13 years old.
- **1876** Tuganini, the last Tasmanian aborigine, died.
- **1921** Sweden abolished capital punishment.
- **1945** VE Day (Victory in Europe) was celebrated.
- **1962** London's trolley buses ran for the last time.
- **1984** The Thames Barrier, designed to prevent the river from flooding central London, was opened.
- **1988** Science fiction writer Robert Heinlein died.

Very Important Birthdates **8** MAY

Name(print) _____

Comments _____

Autograph _____ Year of Birth _____

Good conduct is commendable, but is extremely difficult to become famous by.

Name(print) _____

Comments _____

Autograph _____ Year of Birth _____

On This Date in...

- **1492** Lorenzo the Magnificent, Medici ruler of the Italian city of Florence, died after a tyrranous but cultured 23-year reign. The city mourned him.
- **1671** The Irish Colonel Thomas Blood, disguised as a priest, snuck into the Tower of London and made off with the crown jewels. He was later apprehended.
- **1887** *Buffalo Bill's Wild West Show* opened as part of the America Exhibition at West Brompton.
- **1946** Italian monarch since 1900, Victor Emmanuel III, abdicated as Italy became a republic.
- **1949** Britain's first launderette opened in London.

Very Important Birthdates **9** MAY

Name(print) _____

Comments _____

Autograph _____ Year of Birth _____

It is well for a girl with a future to avoid the man with a past.

Name(print) _____

Comments _____

Autograph _____ Year of Birth _____

On This Date in...

- **1869** The railways linking the east and west coasts of the United States were completed in Utah.
- **1907** Mother's Day was first celebrated by Anna Jarvis of Philadelphia as part of her women's suffrage and temperance movement.
- **1940** Following furious Parliament arguments, Winston Churchill was chosen as prime minister of England. He promised "blood, toil, tears and sweat."
- **1942** After 11,000 missions, German and Italian warplanes stopped their blanket bombing of Malta.
- **1957** Sex Pistols member Sid Vicious was born.

Very Important Birthdates **10** MAY

Name(print) _____

Comments _____

Autograph _____ Year of Birth _____

We should be as careful of the books we read as of the company we keep.

Name(print) _____

Comments _____

Autograph _____ Year of Birth _____

On This Date in...

- **868** *Diamond Sutra*, the first printed book, was published in China. It was found in 1900.
- **1857** Indian troops mutinied against British forces, taking Meerut and marching on Delhi.
- **1858** Minnesota became the 32nd US state.
- **1949** Siam changed its name to Thailand.
- **1960** The *SS France*, the world's longest liner, was launched at St. Nazaire by General de Gaulle.
- **1981** Andrew Lloyd Webber's musical *Cats* premiered on this day in London, England.
- **1981** Jamaican musician Bob Marley died of cancer.

Very Important Birthdates **11** MAY

Name(print) _____

Comments _____

Autograph _____ Year of Birth _____

Man is the only animal that blushes, and the only one that needs to.

Name(print) _____

Comments _____

Autograph _____ Year of Birth _____

VIP Birthdates – 1 Year Calendar

12 MAY — Very Important Birthdates

Name(print) _____

Comments _____

_____

Autograph _____ Year of Birth _____

The joys of motherhood are never fully experienced until all the children are in bed.

Name(print) _____

Comments _____

_____

Autograph _____ Year of Birth _____

On This Date in...

• **1820** Florence Nightingale, the English nurse and hospital reformer, was born.
• **1870** Manitoba, which was called the Red River Colony, was purchased from the Hudson Bay Company by Canada and became a province.
• **1926** Britain's General Strike of Trade Unions in sympathy with the miner's strike came to an end.
• **1935** Alcoholics Anonymous was founded by 'Bill W' (William Wilson) in Akron, Ohio.
• **1937** The BBC transmitted its first outside television broadcast of King George VI's coronation procession.

13 MAY — Very Important Birthdates

Name(print) _____

Comments _____

_____

Autograph _____ Year of Birth _____

The greatest teacher I ever had was my mother. -George Washington

Name(print) _____

Comments _____

_____

Autograph _____ Year of Birth _____

On This Date in...

• **1717** Maria Theresa, Queen of Hungary and Bohemia, who reigned for 40 years, was born.
• **1846** The United States declared war on Mexico.
• **1914** US World heavyweight boxing champion Joe Louis (Joseph Louis Barrow) was born.
• **1950** Blind musician Stevie Wonder was born.
• **1959** Premier Joey Smallwood announced plans to build a new campus in St. John's for the Memorial University of Newfoundland.
• **1981** Pope John Paul II was shot by a Turkish gunman. He made a full recovery.

14 MAY — Very Important Birthdates

Name(print) _____

Comments _____

_____

Autograph _____ Year of Birth _____

Mothers understand what children do not say. -Jewish proverb

Name(print) _____

Comments _____

_____

Autograph _____ Year of Birth _____

On This Date in...

• **1643** Louis XIV, who reigned for 72 years, became King of France at the death of his father, Louis XIII. He was only four years old.
• **1767** The American War of Independence started at the Boston Tea Party as a protest against the British tax on importing tea into America.
• **1796** The first successful vaccination against smallpox was carried out by Edward Jenner.
• **1955** The Eastern bloc signed the Warsaw Pact.
• **1973** The first US space station, *Skylab I*, was launched. Its inhabitants followed soon after.

15 MAY — Very Important Birthdates

Name(print) _____

Comments _____

_____

Autograph _____ Year of Birth _____

Motivation is what gets you started. Habit is what keeps you going.
-Jim Ryun

Name(print) _____

Comments _____

_____

Autograph _____ Year of Birth _____

On This Date in...

• **1862** The first baseball stadium was opened at Union Grounds, Brooklyn.
• **1886** Emily Elizabeth Dickinson, whose poems remained unpublished until after her death, died.
• **1918** The world's first regular airmail service began between New York and Washington, operated for the US Post Office by the US Army.
• **1940** Nylon stockings went on sale for the first time. All competing brands went on sale simultaneously.
• **1957** Britain's first H-bomb was dropped as a test on the Christmas Island in the Indian Ocean.

On This Date in...

- **1905** American actor Henry Fonda was born.
- **1929** The first Academy Awards ceremony was held.
- **1952** The British parliament voted in favour of equal pay for women.
- **1980** Dr. George Nickopoulos was indicted on 14 counts of over-prescribing drugs to Elvis Presley.
- **1990** The most expensive painting in the world, Van Gogh's portrait of Dr. Gachet, was sold for $82.5 million dollars.
- **1991** Edith Cresson became France's first female prime minister.

On This Date in...

- **1620** The earliest record of the first merry-go-round to be set up was at a fair in Philippolis, Turkey.
- **1890** In London, England, Alfred Harmsworth published the first weekly comic paper, *Comic Cuts*.
- **1916** The summer time Daylight Saving Act was passed in Britain.
- **1969** The first transatlantic solo crossing in a rowing boat took place when Tom McClean from Dublin rowed from Newfoundland to Blacksod Bay.
- **1978** After being stolen, Charlie Chaplin's coffin turned up ten miles from its original Swiss cemetery.

On This Date in...

- **1868** Nicholas II, the last Russian Tsar, was forced to abdicate at the start of the Russian Revolution.
- **1910** Despite predictions of tidal waves, plagues and other disasters, Halley's Comet passed the sun and nothing happened.
- **1936** The BBC's first women announcers, Elizabeth Cowell and Jasmine Bligh, started on this day.
- **1975** Japanese climber Junko Tabei became the first woman to reach the summit of Mount Everest.
- **1979** Karen Silkwood, a nuclear plant worker suffering nuclear contamination, won $10.5M dollars.

On This Date in...

- **1802** For civil and military distinction of the highest order, Napoleon instituted the Légion d'Honneur.
- **1900** In the South Pacific, Tonga, 'The Friendly Islands', were annexed by Britain.
- **1909** The Simplon rail tunnel between Switzerland and Italy was officially opened.
- **1945** Pete Townshend, English guitarist and member of The Who, was born.
- **1980** Mount St. Helens erupted, killing eight people in northwestern America and sending ashes into the air which drifted hundreds of miles.

Very Important Birthdates **16** **MAY**

Name(print) _____
Comments _____
_____
Autograph _____ Year of Birth _____

An old error is always more popular than a new truth.

Name(print) _____
Comments _____
_____
Autograph _____ Year of Birth _____

Very Important Birthdates **17** **MAY**

Name(print) _____
Comments _____
_____
Autograph _____ Year of Birth _____

Some men believe in dreams until they marry one.

Name(print) _____
Comments _____
_____
Autograph _____ Year of Birth _____

Very Important Birthdates **18** **MAY**

Name(print) _____
Comments _____
_____
Autograph _____ Year of Birth _____

The only way to entertain some folks is to listen to them.

Name(print) _____
Comments _____
_____
Autograph _____ Year of Birth _____

Very Important Birthdates **19** **MAY**

Name(print) _____
Comments _____
_____
Autograph _____ Year of Birth _____

He who has no fire in himself cannot warm others.

Name(print) _____
Comments _____
_____
Autograph _____ Year of Birth _____

VIP Birthdates – 1 Year Calendar

20 MAY — Very Important Birthdates

Name(print) _____

Comments _____

_____

Autograph _____ Year of Birth _____

Train up a child in the way he should go - and walk there yourself once in a while. *-Josh Billings*

Name(print) _____

Comments _____

_____

Autograph _____ Year of Birth _____

On This Date in...

• **1867** The foundation for the Albert Hall was laid by Queen Victoria.
• **1932** Amelia Earhart took off from Harbour Grace, Newfoundland, on her historic 15-hour flight across the Atlantic.
• **1939** Pan-American Airways commenced regular commercial flights between the US and Europe.
• **1956** The first H-bomb was dropped over the Bikini Atoll during a test by the US.
• **1980** Quebecers voted against a move to separate their French-speaking province from Canada.

21 MAY — Very Important Birthdates

Name(print) _____

Comments _____

_____

Autograph _____ Year of Birth _____

We never know the love of the parent till we become parents ourselves. *-Henry Ward Beecher*

Name(print) _____

Comments _____

_____

Autograph _____ Year of Birth _____

On This Date in...

• **1471** German painter Albrecht Durer was born.
• **1780** Elizabeth Gurney, the English prison reformer who worked to help the poor and homeless, was born.
• **1804** The famous Pére Lachaise cemetary, burial place of glamourous people, opened in Paris.
• **1840** New Zealand was proclaimed a British colony.
• **1856** The first eight-hour working day was achieved by Australian stonemasons in Victoria.
• **1927** Charles Lindbergh landed in Paris after his historic first solo flight across the Atlantic.
• **1979** Elton John performed in the USSR.

22 MAY — Very Important Birthdates

Name(print) _____

Comments _____

_____

Autograph _____ Year of Birth _____

Really, the younger generation isn't so bad. It's just that they have more critics than models.

Name(print) _____

Comments _____

_____

Autograph _____ Year of Birth _____

On This Date in...

• **337** Constantine the Great is baptized on his deathbed. He was the first Christian Roman Emperor.
• **1915** Britain's worst rail disaster took place when a troop train collided with a passenger train at Gretna Green in Scotland, killing 227 people.
• **1972** Richard Nixon, the first US President to visit Russia, signed a pact with Leonid Brezhnev to reduce the risk of military confrontation.
• **1981** Peter Sutcliff, 'The Yorkshire Ripper,' was found guilty of the murder of 13 women and the attempted murder of seven others.

23 MAY — Very Important Birthdates

Name(print) _____

Comments _____

_____

Autograph _____ Year of Birth _____

A mind is a terrible thing to waste ...the waist is a terrible thing to mind.

Name(print) _____

Comments _____

_____

Autograph _____ Year of Birth _____

On This Date in...

• **1533** Henry VIII divorced Catherine of Aragon to marry Anne Boleyn, wife number two.
• **1701** The execution took place of Captain William Kidd, Scottish privateer-turned-pirate.
• **1873** The Northwest Mounted Police were formed in Canada.
• **1887** The French crown jewels went on sale and raised six million francs.
• **1928** US singer Rosemary Clooney was born.
• **1934** The young US outlaws, Bonnie and Clyde, died in a hail of bullets in Louisiana.

On This Date in...

- **1862** London's Westminster Bridge opened, as did Brooklyn Bridge over the East River this day in 1883.
- **1929** The Marx Brothers comedy team premiered their first movie, *The Coconuts*, in New York.
- **1941** The HMS *Hood* sank in a battle with the German ship *Bismarck*. Nearly 1400 drowned.
- **1941** American folk musician Bob Dylan was born.
- **1959** The former Empire Day, first celebrated in 1902, was renamed Commonwealth Day.
- **1988** Snow fell on the Syrian desert and the city of Damascus for the first time in 50 years.

Very Important Birthdates **24** MAY

Name(print) _____
Comments _____
_____
Autograph _____ Year of Birth _____
Fear tends always to produce the thing that it is afraid of.

Name(print) _____
Comments _____
_____
Autograph _____ Year of Birth _____

On This Date in...

- **1833** The Royal Horticultural Society in Chiswick, west London, had the first flower show in Britain.
- **1850** The first hippopotamus arrived in London, destined for the Regent's Park Zoo.
- **1925** The trial of Tennessee school teacher John T. Scopes began. The charge was teaching Darwin's theory of evolution despite a state law which prohibited it.
- **1965** Sonny Liston was knocked out by Cassius Clay in the first round of their fight at Lewiston, Maine. Clay retained his heavyweight boxing title.

Very Important Birthdates **25** MAY

Name(print) _____
Comments _____
_____
Autograph _____ Year of Birth _____
Never give an excuse that you would not be willing to accept.

Name(print) _____
Comments _____
_____
Autograph _____ Year of Birth _____

On This Date in...

- **1868** The last execution in England took place, of an Irish nationalist who was responsible for the deaths of 13 people at the Clerkenwell Outrage.
- **1907** American movie star John Wayne, who appeared in more than 250 films, was born.
- **1908** A major oil strike was made in Persia (Iran), the first in the Middle East.
- **1966** Olympic runner Zola Budd was born.
- **1975** While attempting to leap 13 buses, Evel Knievel, the US stuntman, suffered serious spinal injuries in Britain when his car crashed.

Very Important Birthdates **26** MAY

Name(print) _____
Comments _____
_____
Autograph _____ Year of Birth _____
Better try something and fail, than try nothing and succeed.

Name(print) _____
Comments _____
_____
Autograph _____ Year of Birth _____

On This Date in...

- **1703** Tsar Peter the Great proclaimed St. Petersburg the new Russian capital.
- **1923** US statesman Dr. Henry Kissinger was born.
- **1941** The *Bismark*, a German battleship, was sunk by aircraft from the *Ark Royal, HMS Rodney, Prince of Wales* and *King George V*.
- **1958** American rock and roller Jerry Lee Lewis cut short his UK tour after a scandal broke out over his 13-year-old wife (who was also his first cousin.)
- **1963** Jomo Kenyatta was elected Kenya's first prime minister.

Very Important Birthdates **27** MAY

Name(print) _____
Comments _____
_____
Autograph _____ Year of Birth _____
If you want an enemy, just convince a fool that he is wrong.

Name(print) _____
Comments _____
_____
Autograph _____ Year of Birth _____

VIP Birthdates - 1 Year Calendar

28 MAY — Very Important Birthdates

Name(print) _____

Comments _____

_____

Autograph _____ Year of Birth _____

Do not handicap your children by making their lives easy. *-Robert Heinlein*

Name(print) _____

Comments _____

_____

Autograph _____ Year of Birth _____

On This Date in...

- **1742** The first indoor swimming pool in England opened in London.
- **1891** The first world weightlifting championships were held in Piccadilly, London, England.
- **1932** The world's largest sea dam was completed in Holland. It stretched for 2000 metres.
- **1968** Australian pop star Kylie Minogue was born.
- **1987** A West German teenager flew his small aircraft through Soviet air space, landing right in Red Square.
- **1990** The yacht *Maiden* became the first to complete The Round the World Race with an all-woman crew.

29 MAY — Very Important Birthdates

Name(print) _____

Comments _____

_____

Autograph _____ Year of Birth _____

One of the greatest things about life is not so much where we stand as what direction we are going.

Name(print) _____

Comments _____

_____

Autograph _____ Year of Birth _____

On This Date in...

- **1453** After a year-long siege, Constantinople (now known as Istanbul) fell to the Turkish army.
- **1848** Wisconsin became the 38th state of the Union.
- **1914** Over 1000 people perished when *The Empress of Ireland*, a Canadian Pacific liner, was wrecked in the St. Lawrence River.
- **1917** US president John F. Kennedy was born.
- **1953** Edmund Hillary and his Sherpa guide became the first people to climb the summit of Mount Everest.
- **1982** Pope John Paul II became the first Pope to step on to British soil in 450 years.

30 MAY — Very Important Birthdates

Name(print) _____

Comments _____

_____

Autograph _____ Year of Birth _____

When you're dying of thirst, it's too late to think about digging a well. *-Japanese proverb*

Name(print) _____

Comments _____

_____

Autograph _____ Year of Birth _____

On This Date in...

- **1536** Jane Seymour became Henry VIII's third wife, 11 days after he had Anne Boleyn (wife #2) beheaded.
- **1431** Joan of Arc was burned at the stake for heresy. King Charles VII did nothing to help her.
- **1498** Christopher Columbus set sail on his third voyage, sponsored by the Spanish King and Queen.
- **1842** An assassination attempt was made by Jon Francis on Queen Victoria as she rode in her carriage.
- **1909** Benny (Benjamin David) Goodman, bandleader, clarinettist, child prodigy, was born.
- **1911** The first Indianapolis 500 race took place.

31 MAY — Very Important Birthdates

Name(print) _____

Comments _____

_____

Autograph _____ Year of Birth _____

More things are wrought by prayer than this world dreams of.
-Alfred, Lord Tennyson

Name(print) _____

Comments _____

_____

Autograph _____ Year of Birth _____

On This Date in...

- **1859** Big Ben began telling the time from this day.
- **1902** With the signing of the Treaty of Vereeniging, the Boer War came to an end.
- **1910** Lord Baden-Powell's sister, Agnes, announced the formation of the Girl Guides.
- **1930** Clint Eastwood, US actor, director and former mayor of Carmel, California, was born.
- **1938** The first television panel game, *Spelling Bee,* was broadcast on BBC.
- **1965** Brooke Shields, US actress and child model who starred in *Pretty Baby*, was born.

On This Date in...

- **1792** Kentucky became the 15th state of the union.
- **1926** Marilyn Monroe, US actress, was born.
- **1935** Britain introduced the first motorist's test.
- **1966** Bob Dylan had purist fans booing at Albert Hall when he used an electric guitar for the first time on his British tour.
- **1967** The Beatles' distinctive album *Sergeant Pepper's Lonely Hearts Club Band* was released.
- **1979** Rhodesia changed its name to Zimbabwe.
- **1989** Dustin Hoffman played his first Shakespearian role as Shylock, in *The Merchant of Venice*.

Very Important Birthdates **1** JUNE

Name(print) _____

Comments _____

Autograph _____ Year of Birth _____

No law has ever been made that will keep a man from acting a fool.

Name(print) _____

Comments _____

Autograph _____ Year of Birth _____

On This Date in...

- **1896** Italian physicist Marconi patented the first wireless telegraphy apparatus. Its range: 12 miles.
- **1953** The coronation of Queen Elizabeth II. The first to be televised; it was seen by more than 2 million.
- **1962** The first legal casino opened at the Metropole, Brighton, in Britain.
- **1964** The PLO (Palestine Liberation Organization) was formed in Jerusalem.
- **1979** When he returned to his homeland, Poland, for a visit, Pope John Paul II became the first Pope to visit a communist country.

Very Important Birthdates **2** JUNE

Name(print) _____

Comments _____

Autograph _____ Year of Birth _____

Enthusiasm is a good engine, but it needs intelligence for a driver.

Name(print) _____

Comments _____

Autograph _____ Year of Birth _____

On This Date in...

- **1665** The Dutch Fleet was defeated by the Duke of York off the coast of Suffolk.
- **1937** Former King Edward VIII of England, the Duke of Windsor, married commoner Wallis Simpson privately in a chateau near Tours, France.
- **1946** The first 'bikini' bathing suit, invented by Louis Reard, was unveiled in Paris.
- **1971** The world's longest running comedy, *No Sex Please, We're British*, opened in London, England.
- **1972** Sally Priesand, the first woman rabbi, was ordained in Cincinatti, Ohio.

Very Important Birthdates **3** JUNE

Name(print) _____

Comments _____

Autograph _____ Year of Birth _____

A cynic is a man who, when he smells flowers, looks around for a coffin.

Name(print) _____

Comments _____

Autograph _____ Year of Birth _____

On This Date in...

- **1798** Giacomo Casanova, Venitian writer, diplomat, spy, adventurer and lover, died in Bohemia at 73.
- **1844** Scientists discover the great auk in Iceland.
- **1937** The first shopping cart rolled down the aisles of an Oklahoma supermarket.
- **1944** WWII - Rome was liberated by the Allies.
- **1946** Juan Peron became President of Argentina.
- **1989** In China, thousands of unarmed students and workers who had been peacefully protesting for democratic reforms were killed when tanks rolled into Beijing's Tiananmen Square to quell the unrest.

Very Important Birthdates **4** JUNE

Name(print) _____

Comments _____

Autograph _____ Year of Birth _____

Ignorance needs no introduction; it always makes itself known.

Name(print) _____

Comments _____

Autograph _____ Year of Birth _____

VIP Birthdates - 1 Year Calendar

VIP Birthdates – 1 Year Calendar

5 JUNE — Very Important Birthdates

Name(print) _____

Comments _____

_____

Autograph _____ Year of Birth _____

Pray to God, but row towards the shore. -Russian proverb

Name(print) _____

Comments _____

_____

Autograph _____ Year of Birth _____

On This Date in...

• **1947** The 'Marshall Plan' was announced to help Europe recover from near bankruptcy after WWII.
• **1967** The Six-day War began between Jewish Israel and her Arab neighbours Egypt, Jordan, and Syria.
• **1968** Senator Robert Kennedy was fatally shot by Palestinian Sirhan Sirhan in Los Angeles, California.
• **1975** The President of Egypt, Anwar Sadat, reopened the Suez Canal after an eight-year closure.
• **1989** In Poland, the Solidarity political party defeated the Communists in the first free elections since the end of the Second World War.

6 JUNE — Very Important Birthdates

Name(print) _____

Comments _____

_____

Autograph _____ Year of Birth _____

Luck is what happens when preparation meets opportunity. -Elmer Letterman

Name(print) _____

Comments _____

_____

Autograph _____ Year of Birth _____

On This Date in...

• **1844** The first baseball match took place between the New York Nine and the Knickerbocker Club, N.J.
• **1844** The YMCA was founded by George Williams in London, England.
• **1891** Sir John A. MacDonald, Canada's first prime minister, died.
• **1933** The first drive-in movie opened in Camden, New Jersey. There was room for 400 cars to watch.
• **1944** WWII D-DAY: Under the command of General Dwight Eisenhower, Allied troops landed on the beaches of Normandy, France.

7 JUNE — Very Important Birthdates

Name(print) _____

Comments _____

_____

Autograph _____ Year of Birth _____

Pride breakfasted with plenty, dined with poverty, and supped with infamy. -Benjamin Franklin

Name(print) _____

Comments _____

_____

Autograph _____ Year of Birth _____

On This Date in...

• **1905** Norway refused to recognize the Swedish king and declared its independence.
• **1929** The Papal State, which had not existed since 1870, was revived and the Vatican City was established in Rome.
• **1933** The first performance of *The Seven Deadly Sins* took place in Paris.
• **1973** The Chancellor of West Germany, Willy Brandt, began a historic and emotional visit to Israel.
• **1977** Queen Elizabeth II's Jubilee celebrations began to mark her 25 years on the throne.

8 JUNE — Very Important Birthdates

Name(print) _____

Comments _____

_____

Autograph _____ Year of Birth _____

The only way to get the best of an argument is to avoid it. -Dale Carnegie

Name(print) _____

Comments _____

_____

Autograph _____ Year of Birth _____

On This Date in...

• **632** Mohammed, the prophet and founder of Islam, was said to have died on this day in Mecca.
• **1847** Britain made a new law limiting women and children under 14 to a ten-hour working day.
• **1942** WWII - Sydney and New Castle, Australia became targets for Japanese bombers.
• **1968** James Earl Ray, who was travelling under an assumed name with a Canadian passport, was arrested in London for the murder of Martin Luther King.
• **1978** New Zealander Naomi James became the first woman to sail solo around the world.

On This Date in...

- **AD68** Emperor Nero of Rome took his own life, amid hostility and unrest in his empire.
- **1870** Beloved British writer Charles Dickens, whose works highlighted the stuggles of the people of the Industrial Revolution era, died at home of a stroke.
- **1898** Britain took a 99-year lease from China on the island city of Hong Kong.
- **1934** Disney's second cartoon character, Donald Duck, made his debut in *The Wise Little Hen.*
- **1970** Folk singer Bob Dylan was given an honorary degree from Princeton University.

Very Important Birthdates **9** JUNE

Name(print) _____
Comments _____
_____
Autograph _____ Year of Birth _____

If the truth stands in your way, it's time to change directions.

Name(print) _____
Comments _____
_____
Autograph _____ Year of Birth _____

On This Date in...

- **1692** Hangings from the Salem witch trials began.
- **1909** The SS *Slavonia* sent out the first ever SOS signal when she was wrecked off the Azores.
- **1922** American sweetheart actress Judy Garland, star of *The Wizard of Oz*, was born.
- **1948** The first heart operations to unblock valves were carried out on 'blue babies', so named because of the lack of oxygen in their blood.
- **1991** The eruption of Mount Pinatubo in the Philipines forced the evacuation of 14,500 American personnel from the Clark Air Base.

Very Important Birthdates **10** JUNE

Name(print) _____
Comments _____
_____
Autograph _____ Year of Birth _____

Jealousy is nothing but poison envy.

Name(print) _____
Comments _____
_____
Autograph _____ Year of Birth _____

On This Date in...

- **1509** King Henry VIII of England married wife #1, his former sister-in-law, Catherine of Aragon.
- **1727** Following the death his father, George I, George II acceded to the English throne.
- **1935** US actor Gene Wilder was born.
- **1955** PC John G. Diefenbaker became Canada's new prime minister.
- **1977** Dutch marines stormed a train at Assen where South Moluccan terrorists held 55 hostages for 20 days. Six terrorists and two hostages where killed.
- **1979** Tough-guy actor John Wayne died at age 72.

Very Important Birthdates **11** JUNE

Name(print) _____
Comments _____
_____
Autograph _____ Year of Birth _____

People are generally about as happy as they make up their minds to be.

Name(print) _____
Comments _____
_____
Autograph _____ Year of Birth _____

On This Date in...

- **1839** Abner Doubleday invented baseball at Cooperstown, New York.
- **1929** Anne Frank, the Dutch Jewish girl whose now-famous diary was written while in hiding from Nazi persecution, was born.
- **1931** Infamous gangster Al 'Scarface' Capone was captured by the Chicago 'Untouchables'(Police elite) and charged with 5000 separate prohibition offences.
- **1978** The New York serial killer David Berkowitz, 'Son of Sam', was given life imprisonment for each of the six people he killed.

Very Important Birthdates **12** JUNE

Name(print) _____
Comments _____
_____
Autograph _____ Year of Birth _____

Quite a bit of indigestion is caused by people having to eat their own words.

Name(print) _____
Comments _____
_____
Autograph _____ Year of Birth _____

VIP Birthdates - 1 Year Calendar

13 JUNE — Very Important Birthdates

Name(print) _____

Comments _____

_____

Autograph _____ Year of Birth _____

A quarrelsome man has no good neighbours. -Benjamin Franklin

Name(print) _____

Comments _____

_____

Autograph _____ Year of Birth _____

On This Date in...

• **1381** The first popular rebellion in English history occured, against poll taxes and the maximum wage. Called the Peasants' Revolt, it was led by Wat Tyler.

• **1774** Rhode Island became the first American abolitionist colony, banning the importation of slaves and assuring them their freedom upon arrival.

• **1893** The first Women's Golf Championship, held at Royal Lytham, was won by Lady Margaret Scott.

• **1914** Rasputin, the 'Richelieu of Russia,' was killed.

• **1988** Maria Kalinina won the title of Miss Moscow in the controversial first-ever Soviet beauty pageant.

14 JUNE — Very Important Birthdates

Name(print) _____

Comments _____

_____

Autograph _____ Year of Birth _____

It's great to be great, but it's greater to be human. -Will Rogers

Name(print) _____

Comments _____

_____

Autograph _____ Year of Birth _____

On This Date in...

• **1777** The US Congress adopted the 'Stars and Stripes' as the official flag.

• **1789** Captain Bligh and his castaway crew finally drifted ashore on the island of Timor, after the infamous mutiny on the *Bounty.*

• **1907** The Norwegian Parliament, The Storting, allowed all tax-paying women the right to vote.

• **1909** US folk singer and actor Burl Ives was born.

• **1928** Revolutionary leader Che Guevera was born.

• **1964** Black South African leader Nelson Mandela, was sentenced to life imprisonment.

15 JUNE — Very Important Birthdates

Name(print) _____

Comments _____

_____

Autograph _____ Year of Birth _____

I couldn't wait for success, so I went ahead without it. -Jonathan Winters

Name(print) _____

Comments _____

_____

Autograph _____ Year of Birth _____

On This Date in...

• **1215** The Magna Carta, which limited the king's power, was sealed by King John and his Barons.

• **1752** To prove lightening is attracted to metal, Benjamin Franklin flew a kite with a metal frame during a storm. Scientific dedication or stupidity?

• **1836** Arkansas became the 25th state of the Union.

• **1846** The 49th parallel was established as the border between Canada and the USA.

• **1860** Florence Nightingale started her School for Nurses, the first such school in the world.

• **1888** Emperor Frederick III of Germany died.

16 JUNE — Very Important Birthdates

Name(print) _____

Comments _____

_____

Autograph _____ Year of Birth _____

Gratitude is the heart's memory. -French proverb

Name(print) _____

Comments _____

_____

Autograph _____ Year of Birth _____

On This Date in...

• **1903** The one-year-old Pepsi Cola Company registered its trade name.

• **1935** Roosevelt's 'New Deal,' a recovery program to beat the Depression, was passed by the US Congress.

• **1958** Yellow no-parking lines appeared on the streets of Britain for the first time ever.

• **1963** As the Soviet *Vostok 6* blasts off, its occupant, Valentina Tereshkova of the Soviet Union, became the first woman in space.

• **1978** The 'Space Invaders' electronic video game was demonstrated by Taito Corporation of Tokyo.

On This Date in...

• **1579** Sir Francis Drake anchored the *Golden Hind,* just north of what would become San Francisco Bay.
• **1775** The Battle of Bunker Hill took place during the Siege of Boston. It was one of the earliest battles of the American War of Independence.
• **1944** Iceland became an independent republic.
• **1950** In Chicago, the first kidney transplant was carried out.
• **1972** While attempting to bug the Democratic National Committee offices, five men were arrested at the Watergate complex in Washington.

Very Important Birthdates **17**   **JUNE**

Name(print) _____
Comments _____
_____
Autograph _____ Year of Birth _____
One blessing about being poor, honest and hard-working, is that nobody envies you.
Name(print) _____
Comments _____
_____
Autograph _____ Year of Birth _____

On This Date in...

• **1583** The first life insurance policy was sold.
• **1815** The combined forces led by English General Wellington and Prussian Field Marshall Blucher finally defeated Napoleon at the Battle of Waterloo.
• **1928** Amelia Earhart became the first woman to fly the Atlantic when she landed safely in Wales.
• **1975** The first crude oil taken from a well in the North Sea came ashore aboard a Liberian tanker.
• **1979** At the signing of the Strategic Arms Limitation Treaty, elated President.Carter kissed Russian President Brezhnev.

Very Important Birthdates **18**   **JUNE**

Name(print) _____
Comments _____
_____
Autograph _____ Year of Birth _____
A great many people don't care what happens so long as it doesn't happen to them.
Name(print) _____
Comments _____
_____
Autograph _____ Year of Birth _____

On This Date in...

• **1846** The first official game of baseball was played at the Elysian Fields in Hoboken, New Jersey.
• **1947** British novelist Salman Rushdie was born.
• **1953** Ethel and Julius Rosenberg became the first married couple to be executed for espionage in the US. They went to the electric chair after they were found guilty of spying on the A-bomb for the USSR.
• **1963** In Britain, the contraceptive pill was made available free to women for the first time.
• **1970** The Russian spacecraft *Soyuz 9* landed safely after a record 17 days in space.

Very Important Birthdates **19**   **JUNE**

Name(print) _____
Comments _____
_____
Autograph _____ Year of Birth _____
Initiative is doing the right thing without being told.
Name(print) _____
Comments _____
_____
Autograph _____ Year of Birth _____

On This Date in...

• **1819** The paddlewheel steamship *Savannah,* the first steamship to cross the Atlantic, arrived at Liverpool.
• **1837** Following the death of her uncle, William IV, Queen Victoria ascended to the English throne at 18.
• **1935** Charles Lindbergh and Nobel-prize-winner Alex Carrel announced the invention of a chamber for keeping vital organs alive outside the body.
• **1990** London's red doubledecker buses were phased out. Thought to be the best designed bus of all time, they nonetheless hadn't been replaced in more than 30 years, and were falling apart.

Very Important Birthdates **20**   **JUNE**

Name(print) _____
Comments _____
_____
Autograph _____ Year of Birth _____
Horse power was much safer when only the horses had it.
Name(print) _____
Comments _____
_____
Autograph _____ Year of Birth _____

VIP Birthdates – 1 Year Calendar

VIP Birthdates – 1 Year Calendar

21 JUNE — Very Important Birthdates

Name(print) _____
Comments _____
_____
Autograph _____ Year of Birth _____

Don't let yesterday use up too much of today. - *Will Rogers*

Name(print) _____
Comments _____
_____
Autograph _____ Year of Birth _____

On This Date in...

• **1675** Sir Christopher Wren began to rebuild St. Paul's Cathedral in London, England, replacing sections which had been destroyed by the Great Fire.
• **1868** The first performance of Wagner's opera *Die Meistersinger Von Nurnburg* took place in Munich.
• **1970** Brazil's soccer team won their third World Cup in a row. The last goal, scored three minutes before the end of the game, received a standing ovation.
• **1982** Diana, the Princess of Wales, gave birth to a son named Prince William. His father, Prince Charles, described him as having "sort of blondish hair."

22 JUNE — Very Important Birthdates

Name(print) _____
Comments _____
_____
Autograph _____ Year of Birth _____

He who forgets the language of gratitude can never be on speaking terms with happiness.

Name(print) _____
Comments _____
_____
Autograph _____ Year of Birth _____

On This Date in...

• **1910** German bacteriologist Paul Ehrlich announced his discovery of the definitive cure for syphilis.
• **1921** King George V opened the Northern Ireland Parliament; pleading for peace and reconciliation.
• **1936** American singer, songwriter and actor, Kris Kristofferson was born.
• **1949** American actress Meryl Streep was born.
• **1969** Actress Judy Garland was found dead in her London home. She was 47.
• **1984** The first Virgin Atlantic flight left Gatwick for New York, with tickets priced £99.

23 JUNE — Very Important Birthdates

Name(print) _____
Comments _____
_____
Autograph _____ Year of Birth _____

Since time flies, it's up to you to be the navigator.

Name(print) _____
Comments _____
_____
Autograph _____ Year of Birth _____

On This Date in...

• **1757** British troops under Robert Clive overthrew the Nawab of Bengal at the Battle of Plassey, Bengal.
• **1848** Adolphe Sax was awarded a patent for the saxophone.
• **1956** General Nasser became the first president of Egypt in an unopposed election.
• **1985** Sikh terrorists planted a bomb in an Air India Boeing 747 from Canada which exploded over the sea 120 miles off Ireland, killing 325 people.
• **1987** The US Supreme Court backed the use of hypnosis to obtain testimony in a murder trial.

24 JUNE — Very Important Birthdates

Name(print) _____
Comments _____
_____
Autograph _____ Year of Birth _____

Only a mediocre person is always at his best.

Name(print) _____
Comments _____
_____
Autograph _____ Year of Birth _____

On This Date in...

• **1876** Though greatly outnumbered, American General Custer took his 'last stand' against Chief Crazy Horse and the Sioux Indians.
• **1901** Artist Picasso's first exhibition at the Ambrose Volard Gallery in Paris met with great success.
• **1953** The engagement of Jacqueline Bouvier to US Senator John F. Kennedy was announced.
• **1983** Sally Ride, the first US spacewoman, made up one of the five crewmembers on the *Challenger*.
• **1990** For the first time ever, two women deacons in the Anglican church were ordained as ministers.

On This Date in...

- **1788** Virginia became the tenth US state.
- **1867** Barbed wire was patented in Kent, Ohio.
- **1903** British novelist and political pundit George Orwell, author of *1984* and *Animal Farm*, was born.
- **1903** Marie Curie presented her thesis at the University of Paris on the discovery of radium.
- **1925** The first car telephone is shown in Germany.
- **1945** Singer and songwriter Carly Simon was born.
- **1950** North Korea invaded South Korea. The United States promised aid against the Communist North.

Very Important Birthdates **25** JUNE

Name(print) _____
Comments _____
_____
Autograph _____ Year of Birth _____

Hating people is like burning your house down to get rid of a rat.

Name(print) _____
Comments _____
_____
Autograph _____ Year of Birth _____

On This Date in...

- **1857** The first investiture ceremony of Victoria Crosses took place at Hyde Park. Queen Victoria awarded 62 servicemen this honour.
- **1901** Newsflash from St. John's, Newfoundland: *Lucitania* wrecked off Cape Ballard; 350 rescued.
- **1906** The first Grand Prix is held at Le Mans.
- **1909** The Victoria and Albert Museum, which now houses art, was opened in London by Edward VII.
- **1963** US President John F. Kennedy arrived for his historic visit to Berlin, where he made his famous "Ich bin ein Berliner" speech to an adoring crowd.

Very Important Birthdates **26** JUNE

Name(print) _____
Comments _____
_____
Autograph _____ Year of Birth _____

Insomnia gets most of the blame that conscience deserves.

Name(print) _____
Comments _____
_____
Autograph _____ Year of Birth _____

On This Date in...

- **1693** The first magazine for women, the *Ladies' Mercury*, was published.
- **1939** Sheer luxury took to the air on the first scheduled transatlantic airline service. Using Boeing 314 luxury class flying boats, Pan Am operated the service from Newfoundland to Southampton.
- **1954** The first nuclear power station was opened in Obninsk, 55 miles from Moscow in the USSR.
- **1989** Boatloads of Vietnamese refugees arrived in droves to Hong Kong. Refugee camps were filled to overflowing as people tried to arrange immigration.

Very Important Birthdates **27** JUNE

Name(print) _____
Comments _____
_____
Autograph _____ Year of Birth _____

An illiterate man is not half as dangerous as an educated fool.

Name(print) _____
Comments _____
_____
Autograph _____ Year of Birth _____

On This Date in...

- **1902** The United States committed itself to building a shipping canal through Panama.
- **1904** Directors of the Knickerbocker Steamboat Co. where found guilty of extreme negligence in the June 15 fire and sinking of the steamboat *General Slocum*, and the resulting deaths of 693 people.
- **1914** Serbian Archduke Ferdinand was assasinated in Sarajevo. It was the event that sparked WWI.
- **1926** Mackenzie King resigned his seat after a liquor-related scandal.
- **1970** The first gay pride march was held in New York.

Very Important Birthdates **28** JUNE

Name(print) _____
Comments _____
_____
Autograph _____ Year of Birth _____

Actions speak louder than words, but not nearly so often.

Name(print) _____
Comments _____
_____
Autograph _____ Year of Birth _____

VIP Birthdates – 1 Year Calendar

VIP Birthdates – 1 Year Calendar

29 JUNE — Very Important Birthdates

Name(print) _____

Comments _____

_____

Autograph _____ Year of Birth _____

Success that goes to your head usually pays a short visit.

Name(print) _____

Comments _____

_____

Autograph _____ Year of Birth _____

On This Date in...

• **48BC** Julius Caesar defeated his brother-in-law Pompey, to become the absolute ruler of Rome.
• **1900** French aviator and writer Antoine de Saint-Exupery was born.
• **1901** Singer and actor Nelson Eddy was born.
• **1905** The AA (Automobile Association) was formed in Britain to counter police harassment.
• **1917** The Ukraine proclaimed its independence from Russia. Others were destined to follow.
• **1974** As a result of her husband's illness, Isabel Peron was sworn in as president of Argentina.

30 JUNE — Very Important Birthdates

Name(print) _____

Comments _____

_____

Autograph _____ Year of Birth _____

Humanity is what you are apt to recognize in some people if you have some yourself.

Name(print) _____

Comments _____

_____

Autograph _____ Year of Birth _____

On This Date in...

• **1894** London's Tower Bridge was officially opened.
• **1906** US President Roosevelt passed the Pure Food and Drug Act, cracking down on adulterated foods.
• **1936** Margaret Mitchell's bestselling book *Gone With The Wind* was first published.
• **1960** The blood ran in the shower for the first time to a paying audience with the premiere of Hitchcock's thriller film *Psycho* in New York.
• **1966** US boxing champion Mike Tyson was born.
• **1974** Soviet born ballet dancer, Mikhail Baryshnikov, defected while on tour in Canada.

1 JULY — CANADA DAY

Name(print) _____

Comments _____

_____

Autograph _____ Year of Birth _____

Counting time is not so important as making time count.

Name(print) _____

Comments _____

_____

Autograph _____ Year of Birth _____

On This Date in...

• **1837** Britain began its first Register of Births, Deaths and Marriages.
• **1847** The first adhesive stamps in the US (five cents and ten cents) went on sale.
• **1916** The distinctive Coca-Cola contoured-shaped bottle was adopted to fend off competitors.
• **1929** The cartoon character Popeye the sailor was created by Elzie Segar in the US.
• **1949** Linus Pauling described sickle-cell anemia.
• **1974** Laura Ashley opened her first American womens clothing shop in San Francisco, California.

2 JULY — Very Important Birthdates

Name(print) _____

Comments _____

_____

Autograph _____ Year of Birth _____

Time is so powerful it is given to us only in small doses.

Name(print) _____

Comments _____

_____

Autograph _____ Year of Birth _____

On This Date in...

• **1865** William Booth formed the Salvation Army during a revival meeting in London, England.
• **1937** US pilots Amelia Earhart and Fred Noonan took off from New Guinea, attempting to fly around the world; they where never seen again.
• **1941** Baseball player Joe DiMaggio set a record, hitting safely for 45 straight games.
• **1951** Kansas and Missouri had the worst floods in US history; 41 died and 200,000 were left homeless.
• **1961** US novelist Ernest Hemingway, fearing ill health, committed suicide.

On This Date in...

- **1608** French explorer Samuel de Champlain founded what is now the Canadian city of Quebec.
- **1905** To restore order during a general strike in Odessa, Russian troops killed over 6000 people.
- **1920** William Tilden became the first US tennis player to win the men's singles title at Wimbledon.
- **1962** French President de Gaulle signed the declaration granting independence to Algeria.
- **1986** US singer and actor Rudy Valley died.
- **1987** Former SS officer Klaus Barbie, age 73, got a life sentence for war crimes committed in France.

Very Important Birthdates **3** JULY

Name(print) _____
Comments _____
_____
Autograph _____ Year of Birth _____

To know what is right and not do it is almost as bad as doing wrong.

Name(print) _____
Comments _____
_____
Autograph _____ Year of Birth _____

On This Date in...

- **1817** Work began on the Erie Canal.
- **1840** The Cunard Line began its first Atlantic crossing when the paddle steamer *Britannia* sailed from Liverpool.
- **1848** *The Communist Manifesto*, written by Karl Marx and Frederik Engels, was published.
- **1881** Infamous wild west outlaw Billy the Kid, was shot while trying to escape from police custody.
- **1934** Marie Curie, discoverer of radium, died.
- **1946** The Philippines declared their independence from the US, raising thier own flag for the first time.

Very Important Birthdates **4** JULY

Name(print) _____
Comments _____
_____
Autograph _____ Year of Birth _____

These are the good old days we will be longing for a few years from now.

Name(print) _____
Comments _____
_____
Autograph _____ Year of Birth _____

On This Date in...

- **1945** Winston Churchill, having led Britain throughout the Second World War, was defeated in the general election; the Labour Party swept the polls.
- **1969** A free concert by the Rolling Stones was given in Hyde Park, London, to an audience of 250,000, three days after guitarist Brian Jones' death.
- **1979** The Isle of Man celebrated 1000 years of its 'Tynewald' or Parliament.
- **1989** A $150,000 fine and a suspended prison sentence was given to Colonel Oliver North, a former marine, for his involvement in the Iran-Contra affair.

Very Important Birthdates **5** JULY

Name(print) _____
Comments _____
_____
Autograph _____ Year of Birth _____

Too many of us worry about what people think of us when they don't.

Name(print) _____
Comments _____
_____
Autograph _____ Year of Birth _____

On This Date in...

- **1535** English politician and author (of *Utopia*) Sir Thomas More was executed for treason. Being a devout Catholic, he refused to recognize Henry VIII as the head of the church over the Pope.
- **1946** American actor Sylvester Stallone, best known for the *Rocky* movies, was born.
- **1971** US jazz trumpeter, singer, bandleader and film star Louis 'Satchmo' Armstrong died. He was 71.
- **1988** An explosion aboard the *Piper Alpha* was the worst off-shore oil rig disaster in history, it took place in the North Sea killing 166 men.

Vory Important Birthdatos **6** JULY

Name(print) _____
Comments _____
_____
Autograph _____ Year of Birth _____

The only thing worse than a quitter is the man who is afraid to begin.

Name(print) _____
Comments _____
_____
Autograph _____ Year of Birth _____

VIP Birthdates - 1 Year Calendar

VIP Birthdates – 1 Year Calendar

7 JULY — Very Important Birthdates

Name(print) _____

Comments _____

_____

Autograph _____ Year of Birth _____

Look backward with gratitude and forward with confidence.

Name(print) _____

Comments _____

_____

Autograph _____ Year of Birth _____

On This Date in...

• **1814** Sir Walter Scott's historical novel *Waverley* was published.
• **1922** Fashion designer Pierre Cardin was born in Venice, Italy. His work in France pioneered high fashion for men and ready-to-wear fashion,
• **1982** The Queen awoke to find Michael Fagin, an intruder, sitting on the end of her bed. The incident revealed serious flaws in Buckingham Palace security.
• **1988** The youngest pilot to ever fly the Atlantic was an 11-year-old Californian boy who took off from San Diego. He landed at Le Bourget, Paris.

8 JULY — Very Important Birthdates

Name(print) _____

Comments _____

_____

Autograph _____ Year of Birth _____

Today's mighty oak is just yesterday's nut that held its ground.

Name(print) _____

Comments _____

_____

Autograph _____ Year of Birth _____

On This Date in...

• **1497** Portuguese navigator Vasco da Gama set sail from Lisbon in search of a sea route to India.
• **1892** A huge fire destroyed three-quarters of the city of St. John's, Newfoundland, levelling 2000 buildings and leaving more than 11,000 people homeless.
• **1907** Florenz Ziegfeld's first Follies show opened in New York. His theme: 'Glorifying the American Girl'.
• **1943** French Resistance leader Jean Molin, known as 'Max', was tortured and executed by the Gestapo.
• **1967** English actress Vivien Leigh, star of *Gone With the Wind*, died of tuberculosis at the age of 53.

9 JULY — Very Important Birthdates

Name(print) _____

Comments _____

_____

Autograph _____ Year of Birth _____

He who stands for nothing is apt to fall for anything.

Name(print) _____

Comments _____

_____

Autograph _____ Year of Birth _____

On This Date in...

• **1819** Elias Howe, sewing machine inventor, was born.
• **1892** Pioneering missionary doctor Sir Wilfred Grenfell first arrived in Newfoundland.
• **1925** The first female member was admitted to the floor of the Dublin Stock Exchange, 40 years before a woman was allowed to join in Britain.
• **1938** Britain issued gas masks to the civilian population in anticipation of the Second World War. 35 million masks went into the shops that day.
• **1969** The US Dept. of Agriculture suspended the use of the pesticide DDT pending further investigation.

10 JULY — Very Important Birthdates

Name(print) _____

Comments _____

_____

Autograph _____ Year of Birth _____

You are not tempted because you are evil; you are tempted because you are human.

Name(print) _____

Comments _____

_____

Autograph _____ Year of Birth _____

On This Date in...

• **138** Death of Hadrian, the Roman emperor who built a wall across Britain to keep out the Scots.
• **1932** King Camp Gillette, inventor of the safety razor, died.
• **1985** The Greenpeace ship *Rainbow Warrior* sank in Auckland harbour after two explosions. The French secret service was suspected. The ship would have led a protest into French nuclear testing sites in the Pacific.
• **1989** US actor Mel Blanc died. He was the voice of Bugs Bunny, Woody Woodpecker and Daffy Duck.

On This Date in...

- **1767** The 6th US President John Quincy Adams, who campaigned against slavery, was born.
- **1937** American composer, George Gershwin, dies.
- **1975** Chinese archeologists found more than 8000 statues of warriors, horses and chariots, located just one mile from the tomb of the leader who built the Great Wall.
- **1977** Britain's *Gay News* was fined £1000 in a rare blasphemy trial for a poem about a homosexual Jesus.
- **1989** Laurence Olivier, the great Shakespearian actor, died. His roles included Hamlet and Henry V.

Very Important Birthdates **11** JULY

Name(print) _____

Comments _____

_____

Autograph _____ Year of Birth _____

A woman's tears is the greatest power known to man.

Name(print) _____

Comments _____

_____

Autograph _____ Year of Birth _____

On This Date in...

- **100BC** Gaius Julius Caesar, the most famous general and dictator in Roman history, was born.
- **1536** Renaissance classicist Erasmus died.
- **1817** Naturalist and writer Henry Thoreau was born.
- **1920** President Wilson opened the Panama Canal.
- **1927** An earthquake in Palestine kills 1000 people.
- **1937** American comedian Bill Cosby was born.
- **1966** The Trans Canada Highway was officially opened in Newfoundland by Premier Smallwood.
- **1969** Tony Jacklin became the first British golfer to win the British Open since 1951.

Very Important Birthdates **12** JULY

Name(print) _____

Comments _____

_____

Autograph _____ Year of Birth _____

Crime's story would be shorter if the sentences were longer.

Name(print) _____

Comments _____

_____

Autograph _____ Year of Birth _____

On This Date in...

- **1883** Famous midget General Tom Thumb of P.T. Barnum Circus, died at 45 (and 40 inches).
- **1923** British Parliament passed a bill banning the sale of alcohol to people under 18.
- **1939** Frank Sinatra made his first record, *From the Bottom of My Heart* with the Harry James Band.
- **1942** US actor Harrison Ford, who starred in *Star Wars* and *Raiders of the Lost Ark*, was born.
- **1973** While performing on stage in California, the Everly Brothers broke up. Phil smashed his guitar and stormed off, leaving Don to finish the show alone.

Very Important Birthdates **13** JULY

Name(print) _____

Comments _____

_____

Autograph _____ Year of Birth _____

Laughter is the sweetest music that ever greeted the human ear.

Name(print) _____

Comments _____

_____

Autograph _____ Year of Birth _____

On This Date in...

- **1789** Bastille Day, a French national holiday, commemorates the storming and razing of the hated Parisian state-prison, the Bastille, at the outset of the French Revolution.
- **1902** During a safety inspection of the famous bell tower of Venice in the Campanile of St. Mark's Cathedral, the tower collapsed.
- **1912** American folksinger Woody Guthrie was born.
- **1959** The 14,000-ton cruiser *US Long Beach* was launched. It was the first nuclear-powered warship.
- **1967** The British parliament legalized abortion.

Very Important Birthdates **14** JULY

Name(print) _____

Comments _____

_____

Autograph _____ Year of Birth _____

Be not simply good - be good for something.

Name(print) _____

Comments _____

_____

Autograph _____ Year of Birth _____

VIP Birthdates - 1 Year Calendar

15 JULY — Very Important Birthdates

Name(print) _____
Comments _____
_____
Autograph _____ Year of Birth _____

Success is getting what you want; happiness is wanting what you get.

Name(print) _____
Comments _____
_____
Autograph _____ Year of Birth _____

On This Date in...

- **1099** Jerusalem was captured by the Crusaders led by Godfrey and Robert of Flanders and Tancred of Normandy.
- **1606** Rembrandt, Dutch painter, one of the great masters who was influenced by Italian art, was born.
- **1881** The notorious US outlaw, Billy the Kid was murdered by Sheriff Pat Garrett.
- **1954** The first Boeing 707 jetliner, made its maiden flight from Seattle.
- **1948** The British branch of Alcoholics Anonymous began.

16 JULY — Very Important Birthdates

Name(print) _____
Comments _____
_____
Autograph _____ Year of Birth _____

No one can be caught in places he does not visit.

Name(print) _____
Comments _____
_____
Autograph _____ Year of Birth _____

On This Date in...

- **1918** Nicholas II, the last Russian Tsar, along with his entire family, were shot by the Bolsheviks.
- **1935** The first parking meters appeared in Oklahoma City.
- **1945** The first atomic bomb developed by Robert Oppenheimer and his team at Los Alamos was detonated in New Mexico, thus officially beginning the atomic age.
- **1969** US astronauts Neil Armstrong, Edwin Aldrin and Michael Collins launched *Apollo 11*.

17 JULY — Very Important Birthdates

Name(print) _____
Comments _____
_____
Autograph _____ Year of Birth _____

Opportunity knocks only once; temptation leans on the doorbell.

Name(print) _____
Comments _____
_____
Autograph _____ Year of Birth _____

On This Date in...

- **1790** Thomas Saint of London, England, patented the first sewing machine.
- **1935** Canadian actor, Donald Sutherland, whose films included *Mash,* was born.
- **1945** Planning for the future peace at the conclusion of the Second World War, the Potsdam Conference began with world leaders Truman, Stalin and Churchill.
- **1959** Billie Holiday, US jazz singer died.
- **1968** The animated film with the Beatles sound track, *Yellow Submarine*, was premiered.

18 JULY — Very Important Birthdates

Name(print) _____
Comments _____
_____
Autograph _____ Year of Birth _____

He who wants to finish the race must stay on the track.

Name(print) _____
Comments _____
_____
Autograph _____ Year of Birth _____

On This Date in...

- **1870** The Vatican Council proclaimed the dogma of Papal infallibility as it regards to faith and morals.
- **1877** The first successful experiment in recording and storing the human voice was carried out by Edison.
- **1925** *Mein Kampf* (My Struggle), which Adolf Hitler wrote while in jail, was published.
- **1955** Walt Disney's 160 acres of fantasy and fun, Disneyland, opened in Anaheim, California.

On This Date in...

• **1545** Henry VIII's battle fleet, the *Mary Rose,* keeled over in the Solent and sank, with the loss of 700 lives. The ship was raised 437 years later.
• **1848** Female rights campaigner Amelia Bloomer, introduced Bloomers to the world, which she described as 'the lower part of a rational dress'.
• **1860** Lizzie Borden, alleged US axe murderess of her father and stepmother, was born.
• **1865** Charles Horace Mayo, US surgeon and one of the three brothers who co-founded the Mayo Clinic, was born.

Very Important Birthdates **19** JULY

Name(print) _____
Comments _____
_____
Autograph _____ Year of Birth _____
Men who know the least always argue the most.

Name(print) _____
Comments _____
_____
Autograph _____ Year of Birth _____

On This Date in...

• **1588** After its initial setback on June 19 when the fleet was dispersed by a severe storm, the Spanish Armada set sail from Corunna.
• **1973** Bruce Lee, US martial arts actor whose films created the Kung-fu craze, died at the age of 32.
• **1976** The US *Viking* spacecraft made a soft landing on Mars and sent back television pictures of the rock-strewn Gold Plain.
• **1982** Two guardsmen and seven army horses were killed when an IRA bomb exploded en route to Horse Guards Parade for the changing of the guard.

Very Important Birthdates **20** JULY

Name(print) _____
Comments _____
_____
Autograph _____ Year of Birth _____
A lady is a woman who makes it easy for a man to be a gentleman.

Name(print) _____
Comments _____
_____
Autograph _____ Year of Birth _____

On This Date in...

• **1798** Napoleon defeated the Mamelukes at the Battle of the Pyramids, after invading Egypt.
• **1897** The Tate Gallery opened on the site of the Millbank Prison, London, England.
• **1899** Ernest Hemingway, US novelist was born.
• **1960** Ceylon became the first modern parliamentary government to have a woman leader, Mrs. Sirimavo Bandaranaike of the Sri Lanka Freedom Party.
• **1969** Neil Armstrong, with other US astronauts stepped out of *Apollo II* onto the Moon, and began their first exploratory walk.

Very Important Birthdates **21** JULY

Name(print) _____
Comments _____
_____
Autograph _____ Year of Birth _____
A person usually criticizes the individual whom he secretly envies.

Name(print) _____
Comments _____
_____
Autograph _____ Year of Birth _____

On This Date in...

• **1284** The Pied Piper appeared in Hamlin, Brunswick, struck his bargain to rid the town of rats, and took his revenge when the burghers refused to pay.
• **1890** Rose Kennedy, wife of Senator Joseph Kennedy, mother of US president John F., was born.
• **1917** Alexander Kerensky became prime minister of the Russian provisional government following the overthrow of the Tsar.
• **1950** Mackenzie King, three-time Canadian prime minister, died.

Very Important Birthdates **22** JULY

Name(print) _____
Comments _____
_____
Autograph _____ Year of Birth _____
If a man defrauds you one time, he's a rascal; if he does it twice, you're a fool.

Name(print) _____
Comments _____
_____
Autograph _____ Year of Birth _____

VIP Birthdates – 1 Year Calendar

23 JULY — Very Important Birthdates

Name(print) _____
Comments _____
_____
Autograph _____ Year of Birth _____

Money can't buy friends, but it can get you a better class of enemy.
- Spike Milligan

Name(print) _____
Comments _____
_____
Autograph _____ Year of Birth _____

On This Date in...

• **1885** Ulysses Simpson Grant, American general and 18th president died.
• **1916** Sir William Ramsy, Scottish chemist and Nobel prize winner who discovered helium, died.
• **1940** Winston Churchill renamed The Local Defense Volunteers as the Home Guard.
• **1967** British cyclist Tony Simpson, 29, collapsed and died, in the heat of the mountain stage in the Tours de France.
• **1986** The wedding of Prince Andrew to Lady Sarah Ferguson took place at Westminster Abbey.

24 JULY — Very Important Birthdates

Name(print) _____
Comments _____
_____
Autograph _____ Year of Birth _____

Success is the ability to hitch your wagon to a star while keeping your feet on the ground.

Name(print) _____
Comments _____
_____
Autograph _____ Year of Birth _____

On This Date in...

• **1704** Admiral Sir George Rooke, with Sir Cloudesley Shovel, captured Gibraltar from the Spaniards.
• **1824** The first public opinion poll was conducted in Wilmington, Delaware, on voting intentions in the forthcoming US presidential election.
• **1898** US aviator Amelia Earhart, who was the first woman to fly solo over the Atlantic, was born.
• **1925** Six-year-old Patricia Cheeseman was successfully treated with insulin at Guy's Hospital, London, England. A first.

25 JULY — Very Important Birthdates

Name(print) _____
Comments _____
_____
Autograph _____ Year of Birth _____

Success can be measured in dollars and sense.

Name(print) _____
Comments _____
_____
Autograph _____ Year of Birth _____

On This Date in...

• **1843** Scottish chemist, Charles Macintosh, who invented waterproof clothing, died.
• **1917** The Dutch spy Margaretha Geertruida Zelle, known as 'Mata Hari', was sentenced to death.
• **1943** Fascism was outlawed in Italy after Mussolini was deposed.
• **1957** Tunisia became a republic with Habib Bourguiba as first president.
• **1978** The world's first test-tube baby, Louise Brown, was born.

26 JULY — Very Important Birthdates

Name(print) _____
Comments _____
_____
Autograph _____ Year of Birth _____

Success is a journey, not a destination. -Ben Sweetland.

Name(print) _____
Comments _____
_____
Autograph _____ Year of Birth _____

On This Date in...

• **1788** New York became the 11th state of the Union.
• **1908** The FBI (Federal Bureau of Investigation) was formed in Washington, DC.
• **1952** King Farouk of Egypt was forced to abdicate by General Neguib.
• **1956** The nationalization of the Suez Canal by President Nasser of Egypt, triggered off confrontations with Britain, France and Israel.
• **1987** Steve Roche won the Tour de France, the first Irishman and only the second cyclist not from continental Europe to win.

On This Date in...

• **1921** Canadians Sir Frederick Banting and Charles Best isolated insulin, the first effective treatment for diabetes.
• **1949** The *de Havilland Comet*, the world's first jet airliner, made its maiden flight.
• **1953** The Korean armistice was signed in Panmunjom, ending three years of war, which killed 116,000 UN troops including 54,000 US troops.
• **1988** Jeff Gutteridge, national pole vault record holder became the first British athlete to be banned for life for taking anabolic steroids.

Very Important Birthdates **27** JULY

Name(print) _____
Comments _____
_____
Autograph _____ Year of Birth _____

If a man defrauds you one time, he's a rascal; if he does it twice, you're a fool.

Name(print) _____
Comments _____
_____
Autograph _____ Year of Birth _____

On This Date in...

• **1586** The first potatoes arrived in Britain from Columbia. The ship docked at Plymouth.
• **1750** Johann Sebastian Bach, German composer died.
• **1929** Jacqueline (Kennedy) Onassis (nee Bouvier), widow of the assassinated US President, John F. Kennedy, was born.
• **1988** A father and son saved each other from leukemia. In 1980, Alan Lack donated bone marrow to his son; eight years later his son donated marrow to his father to save him from the disease.

Very Important Birthdates **28** JULY

Name(print) _____
Comments _____
_____
Autograph _____ Year of Birth _____

Some learn from experience - others never recover from it.

Name(print) _____
Comments _____
_____
Autograph _____ Year of Birth _____

On This Date in...

• **1565** Mary Queen of Scots married her cousin, Lord Arnley.
• **1948** The 14th Olympic Games, the first for 12 years and the first after the War, opened at Wembley Stadium.
• **1966** Bob Dylan did not perform for a year after crashing his motor cycle and suffering serious injuries.
• **1981** Prince Charles married Lady Diana Spencer at St. Paul's, watched by over 700 million on television.

Very Important Birthdates **29** JULY

Name(print) _____
Comments _____
_____
Autograph _____ Year of Birth _____

The wheels of progress are not turned by cranks.

Name(print) _____
Comments _____
_____
Autograph _____ Year of Birth _____

On This Date in...

• **1863** US motor car engineer Henry Ford was born.
• **1941** Paul Anka, Canadian singer and songwriter was born.
• **1963** 'Third Man' Kim Philby turned up in Moscow after escaping arrest in Britain for spying.
• **1973** After 11 years with compensation of £20M, the Thalidomide Case, taken up by the *Sunday Times* on behalf of the victims, ended.
• **1990** Close friend of Margaret Thatcher, Ian Gow, MP, was killed by the IRA when his car blew up in the driveway of his home.

Very Important Birthdates **30** JULY

Name(print) _____
Comments _____
_____
Autograph _____ Year of Birth _____

Advice is least heeded when most needed.

Name(print) _____
Comments _____
_____
Autograph _____ Year of Birth _____

VIP Birthdates - 1 Year Calendar

31 JULY　Very Important Birthdates

Name(print) _____

Comments _____

_____

Autograph _____ Year of Birth _____

When success turns your head, you're facing failure.

Name(print) _____

Comments _____

_____

Autograph _____ Year of Birth _____

On This Date in...

- **1556** St. Ignatius Loyola, founder of the Jesuit Order, died.
- **1917** The third Battle of Ypres (Passchendale) began.
- **1919** The Weimar Republic was established in post-war Germany.
- **1950** Britain's first self-service store, Sainsburys, opened in Croydon.
- **1964** Jim Reeves, US country singer, died.
- **1965** Cigarette commercials were banned on British television.

1 AUGUST　Very Important Birthdates

Name(print) _____

Comments _____

_____

Autograph _____ Year of Birth _____

This year's success was last year's impossibility.

Name(print) _____

Comments _____

_____

Autograph _____ Year of Birth _____

On This Date in...

- **1714** With the death of Queen Anne, George Louis, Elector of Hanover, was proclaimed King George I of Great Britain.
- **1831** King William IV and Queen Adelaide opened New London Bridge.
- **1873** San Francisco's cable car system began running (the Clay Street Hill Railroad).
- **1876** Colorado became the 38th state of the Union.
- **1939** Glen Miller and his band recorded *In the Mood*, which became his theme tune.
- **1975** The Helsinki Agreement was signed.

2 AUGUST　Very Important Birthdates

Name(print) _____

Comments _____

_____

Autograph _____ Year of Birth _____

A successful man keeps on looking for work after he has found a job.

Name(print) _____

Comments _____

_____

Autograph _____ Year of Birth _____

On This Date in...

- **1865** One of the rarest 19th century books, *Alice's Adventures in Wonderland* by Lewis Carroll was published, but it was soon withdrawn because of bad printing. Only 21 copies of the first edition survived.
- **1876** 'Wild Bill' Hickok (James Butler), US frontier scout and law enforcer known as the fastest gun in the West, died.
- **1894** Death duties were introduced into Britain.
- **1932** Peter O'Toole, Irish actor, was born.
- **1990** Iraq invaded Kuwait causing an international crisis.

3 AUGUST　Very Important Birthdates

Name(print) _____

Comments _____

_____

Autograph _____ Year of Birth _____

Your reputation is made by searching for things that can't be done - and doing them.

Name(print) _____

Comments _____

_____

Autograph _____ Year of Birth _____

On This Date in...

- **1492** Christopher Columbus set sail from Andalusia, Spain, on the first Voyage of discovery in the *Santa Maria*, accompanied by the *Pinta* and the *Nina*.
- **1914** The first ships passed through the Panama Canal.
- **1926** Britain's first traffic lights were installed at Piccadilly Circus.
- **1963** The Beatles played The Cavern in Liverpool for the last time. *Please, Please Me* had just been released.

On This Date in...

• **1870** The Red Cross Society was founded in Britain.
• **1914** The First World War began with Britain declaring war on Germany.
• **1966** On a US radio station, John Lennon of the Beatles claimed that they were probably more popular than Jesus Christ. Beatles records were banned in many US states and in South Africa.
• **1984** Mary Decker, US champion, was accidentally tripped by Zola Budd, during the 3000m in the Los Angeles Olympics to cause one of the most dramatic upsets ever.

Very Important Birthdates **4** AUGUST

Name(print) _____
Comments _____
_____
Autograph _____ Year of Birth _____

Money isn't everything ... but it's a sure cure for poverty.

Name(print) _____
Comments _____
_____
Autograph _____ Year of Birth _____

On This Date in...

• **1891** The first traveller's cheque, devised by American Express, was cashed.
• **1914** The first electric traffic lights were installed in Cleveland, Ohio.
• **1962** Marilyn Monroe, US actress and legendary sex symbol, was found dead.
• **1962** African Nationalist leader Nelson Mandela was given a life sentence for attempting to overthrow the South African government.
• **1984** Richard Burton, who became a Hollywood legend, died in Geneva of a stroke, aged 58.

Very Important Birthdates AUGUST

Name(print) _____
Comments _____
_____
Autograph _____ Year of Birth _____

Life is a constant struggle to keep up appearances and keep down expenses.

Name(print) _____
Comments _____
_____
Autograph _____ Year of Birth _____

On This Date in...

• **1890** Murderer William Kemmler became the first person to die in the electric chair, in Auburn Prison, New York.
• **1911** Lucille Ball, US comedienne in films and television was born.
• **1917** Robert Mitchum, US actor, was born.
• **1926** Gertrude Ederle of the US became the first woman to swim the English Channel.
• **1945** The US Boeing B-29 bomber *Enola Gay* dropped the first atomic bomb. Seconds later the Japanese city of Hiroshima was devastated.

Very Important Birthdates **6** AUGUST

Name(print) _____
Comments _____
_____
Autograph _____ Year of Birth _____

The actions of men are the best interpreters of their thoughts.

Name(print) _____
Comments _____
_____
Autograph _____ Year of Birth _____

On This Date in...

• **1556** A Flying Saucer, or UFO, appeared over the city of Basle in Switzerland and was captured as an illustration on a woodcut.
• **1711** With the attendance of Queen Anne at the horse races, Ascot became 'Royal'.
• **1840** The British parliament passed an act prohibiting the employment of climbing boys as chimney sweeps.
• **1913** Samuel Cody, US aviator was killed when his aircraft crashed at Farnborough. It was Britain's first air tragedy.

Very Important Birthdates AUGUST

Name(print) _____
Comments _____
_____
Autograph _____ Year of Birth _____

Small talk wouldn't be so irritating if it weren't handed out in such large quantities.

Name(print) _____
Comments _____
_____
Autograph _____ Year of Birth _____

VIP Birthdates – 1 Year Calendar

VIP Birthdates – 1 Year Calendar

8 AUGUST — Very Important Birthdates

Name(print) _____
Comments _____
_____
Autograph _____ Year of Birth _____

In an argument, the best weapon to hold is your tongue.

Name(print) _____
Comments _____
_____
Autograph _____ Year of Birth _____

On This Date in...

- **1923** Esther Williams, US actress, was born.
- **1937** Dustin Hoffman, US actor whose first success was in *The Graduate*, was born.
- **1963** The US, Britain and the USSR signed the Test Ban Treaty in the Kremlin.
- **1963** The Great Train Robbery took place at Cheddington, Buckinghamshire; over £2.6M was stolen.
- **1974** Richard Nixon resigned from office in the face of threats to impeach him for his part in the Watergate affair.

9 AUGUST — Very Important Birthdates

Name(print) _____
Comments _____
_____
Autograph _____ Year of Birth _____

The man who loses his head is usually the last one to miss it.

Name(print) _____
Comments _____
_____
Autograph _____ Year of Birth _____

On This Date in...

- **1945** Nagasaki's devastation finally forced the Emperor to surrender to the Allies, after the second atomic bomb was dropped on a Japanese city.
- **1969** The bodies of Sharon Tate, and four others were found butchered at a Beverly Hills Mansion.
- **1974** The first non-elected president of the US was Gerald Ford following Nixon's resignation the day before.
- **1979** Brighton established the first nudist beach in Britain, despite protests from those who feared great depravity.

10 AUGUST — Very Important Birthdates

Name(print) _____
Comments _____
_____
Autograph _____ Year of Birth _____

Take care of your character, and your reputation will take care of itself.

Name(print) _____
Comments _____
_____
Autograph _____ Year of Birth _____

On This Date in...

- **1787** Mozart completed his popular *Eine Kleine Nachtmusik* (A Little Night Music).
- **1821** Missouri became the 24th state of the Union.
- **1846** To foster scientific research, English scientist James Smithson established the Smithsonian Institution at Washington.
- **1889** Dan Rylands of Hope Glass Works, Barnsley, Yorkshire, patented the screw bottle top.
- **1928** Eddie Fisher, US crooner and actor, was born.
- **1966** The first US moon satellite, *Orbiter I,* was launched.

11 AUGUST — Very Important Birthdates

Name(print) _____
Comments _____
_____
Autograph _____ Year of Birth _____

Some people won't suffer in silence because that would take the pleasure out of it.

Name(print) _____
Comments _____
_____
Autograph _____ Year of Birth _____

On This Date in...

- **1921** Alex Haley, author of *Roots,* was born.
- **1942** The *Leningrad*, Dimitri Shostakovich's Seventh Symphony, was first performed in that city with many members of the orchestra in their military uniforms, some on leave from the Front, many half-starving.
- **1952** Crown Prince Hussein was named to succeed his father, King Talal of Jordan, who suffered from schizophrenia.
- **1960** The French colony of Chad became independent.

On This Date in...

- **1774** Robert Southey, English poet and Poet Laureate, was born.
- **1887** Thomas Edison made the first sound recording when he recited *Mary Had a Little Lamb*.
- **1908** Affectionately known as the 'Tin Lizzie', the first Ford Model T, was produced, replacing the Model A.
- **1960** The first US communications satellite, *Echo I*, was launched.
- **1980** The first giant panda born in captivity was delivered naturally in a zoo in Mexico.

Very Important Birthdates **12** **AUGUST**

Name(print) _____
Comments _____
_____
Autograph _____ Year of Birth _____

Things that never happen worry us most.

Name(print) _____
Comments _____
_____
Autograph _____ Year of Birth _____

On This Date in...

- **1814** The Cape of Good Hope was made a British colony when it was ceded by the Dutch.
- **1910** English founder of modern nursing and the first woman to win the Order of Merit, Florence Nightingale, died.
- **1964** The last executions took place in Britain when Peter Allen at Walton Prison, Liverpool and John Walby at Manchester's Strangeways, were hanged.
- **1989** A hot air balloon disaster, the worst in history, took place in central Australia when two hot-air balloons collided killing the pilot and 12 passengers.

Very Important Birthdates **13** **AUGUST**

Name(print) _____
Comments _____
_____
Autograph _____ Year of Birth _____

The one thing that children can wear out faster than shoes is parents.

Name(print) _____
Comments _____
_____
Autograph _____ Year of Birth _____

On This Date in...

- **1908** The first International Beauty Contest took place in Folkestone, Kentucky. Young women paraded at the Pier Hippodrome.
- **1945** The Second World War was finally over. Japan surrendered unconditionally to the Allies. V-J (Victory over Japan) Day would be celebrated on the 15th.
- **1951** William Randolph Hearst, US newspaper proprietor whose life was as colourful as his journalists' prose, died.
- **1969** The first British troops were deployed in Northern Ireland to restore order.

Very Important Birthdates **14** **AUGUST**

Name(print) _____
Comments _____
_____
Autograph _____ Year of Birth _____

There are too many different ways to spend money and not enough new ways to get it.

Name(print) _____
Comments _____
_____
Autograph _____ Year of Birth _____

On This Date in...

- **1947** The Union Jack was run down for the last time in New Delhi as India gained independence from Britain.
- **1965** There were 20,000 National Guardsmen required to control race riots in Watts, Los Angeles, which left 28 dead, including children, and 676 injured.
- **1969** The legendary rock festival, the Woodstock Music and Arts Fair began on a dairy farm in upstate New York. It included Janis Joplin, The Who, Jimi Hendrix, Joan Baez and Jefferson Airplane.

Very Important Birthdates **15** **AUGUST**

Name(print) _____
Comments _____
_____
Autograph _____ Year of Birth _____

Some people dream of worthy achievement, while others stay awake and experience it.

Name(print) _____
Comments _____
_____
Autograph _____ Year of Birth _____

VIP Birthdates – 1 Year Calendar

VIP Birthdates – 1 Year Calendar

16 AUGUST — Very Important Birthdates

Name(print) _____

Comments _____

_____

Autograph _____ Year of Birth _____

Reputation is made in a moment; character is built in a lifetime.

Name(print) _____

Comments _____

_____

Autograph _____ Year of Birth _____

On This Date in...

- **1819** Troops including Waterloo veterans broke up a crowd meeting to demand Parliamentary reforms on St. Peter's Field, Manchester. Eleven died in what became known as the Peterloo Massacre.
- **1960** Cyprus became a republic at midnight, with Archbishop Makarios as president.
- **1962** The original drummer with the Beatles, Pete Best, was fired by Brian Epstein and replaced by Ringo Starr.
- **1975** When Peter Gabriel departed, Phil Collins, drummer with Genesis, took over as lead singer.

17 AUGUST — Very Important Birthdates

Name(print) _____

Comments _____

_____

Autograph _____ Year of Birth _____

If silence is golden, not many people could be accused of hoarding.

Name(print) _____

Comments _____

_____

Autograph _____ Year of Birth _____

On This Date in...

- **1896** Bonanza Creek, a small tributary of the Klondike River in Canada's Yukon Territory where the big gold rush was discovered. This led to the great gold rush of 1898, and the settlement of Dawson would grow into a city.
- **1920** Maureen O'Hara, Irish born actress, who starred in *How Green Was My Valley,* was born.
- **1977** *Artika*, the Soviet nuclear-powered ice-breaker, became the first to reach the North Pole.
- **1989** An Australian commercial airliner became the first to fly non-stop from London to Sydney.

18 AUGUST — Very Important Birthdates

Name(print) _____

Comments _____

_____

Autograph _____ Year of Birth _____

When arguing with a stupid person, be sure he isn't doing the same thing.

Name(print) _____

Comments _____

_____

Autograph _____ Year of Birth _____

On This Date in...

- **1922** Shelley Winters, US actress who won Oscars for her supporting roles in *The Diary of Anne Frank* and *The Poseidon Adventure* was born.
- **1930** The two halves of Sydney Bridge met in the centre and were formally joined.
- **1939** The film *The Wizard of Oz*, starring Judy Garland, opened in New York.
- **1960** The Searle Drug Company in the US, marketed the first oral contraceptive.
- **1964** South Africa was banned from participating in the Olympics because of its racial policies.

19 AUGUST — Very Important Birthdates

Name(print) _____

Comments _____

_____

Autograph _____ Year of Birth _____

He who is the slowest in making a promise is the most faithful in keeping it.

Name(print) _____

Comments _____

_____

Autograph _____ Year of Birth _____

On This Date in...

- **1940** Johnny Nash, US singer and songwriter who had a big hit with his song *I Can See Clearly Now*, was born.
- **1960** The Soviet court sentenced Gary Powers, US U-2 spy plane pilot who was brought down by the Russians, to ten years detention.
- **1977** Groucho Marx, US comedian, the fast-talking member of the famous Marx Brothers, died.
- **1989** Solidarity's Tadeuz Mazowiecki became prime minister of Poland; Poland then became the first country in east Europe to end one-party rule.

On This Date in...

• **1912** English founder of the Salvation Army, William Booth, died.
• **1913** Stainless steel was first cast in Sheffield by Harry Brearley.
• **1924** US country and western singer Jim Reeves was born.
• **1940** While the Battle of Britain raged in the skies above him, Winston Churchill spoke in reference to the War, "Never in the field of human conflict was so much owed by so many to so few."
• **1968** Russian troops invaded Czechoslovakia.

Very Important Birthdates **20** **AUGUST**

Name(print) _____
Comments _____
_____
Autograph _____ Year of Birth _____
We cannot help being old, but we can resist being aged.

Name(print) _____
Comments _____
_____
Autograph _____ Year of Birth _____

On This Date in...

• **1901** The Cadillac Motor Company was formed in Detroit, named after the French explorer.
• **1911** Leonardo da Vinci's masterpiece, the Mona Lisa - probably the world's best known painting, was stolen from the Louvre in Paris.
• **1959** Hawaii became the 50th state of the Union.
• **1983** Benigno Aquino, exiled Philippine opposition leader, was shot and killed in full view of the television cameras as he stepped out of the plane at Manila airport. He had been assured a safe return by President Marcos.

Very Important Birthdates **21** **AUGUST**

Name(print) _____
Comments _____
_____
Autograph _____ Year of Birth _____
Quite a few people owe their success to advice they didn't take.

Name(print) _____
Comments _____
_____
Autograph _____ Year of Birth _____

On This Date in...

• **1485** Henry VII led his troops to victory over Richard III, who was killed, in the last of the War of the Roses on Bosworth in Leicestershire.
• **1642** The Civil War began in England when Charles I erected his standard in front of a few hundred of his Royalists in Nottingham.
• **1920** Ray Bradbury, US poetic science-fiction writer of the classic *Martian Chronicles,* was born.
• **1950** Lt. Abdel Rehim of Egypt won the first swimming race across the English Channel in 10 hours, 50 minutes.

Very Important Birthdates **22** **AUGUST**

Name(print) _____
Comments _____
_____
Autograph _____ Year of Birth _____
Tend to your goals. He who aims at nothing is sure to hit it.

Name(print) _____
Comments _____
_____
Autograph _____ Year of Birth _____

On This Date in...

• **410** An end to an era of Roman civilization and influence occured when the Visigoths sacked Rome.
• **1914** The VC (Victoria Cross) was awarded for gallantry to the British Expeditionary Forces in the Battle of Mons during the First World War.
• **1939** Germany and Russia signed a short-lived non-aggression pact which left Hitler free to attack Poland.
• **1940** The Blitz began as German bombers began an all night raid on London, England.
• **1988** The first husband and wife pilot recruits for British Airways were Morten and Anna Riis.

Very Important Birthdates **23** **AUGUST**

Name(print) _____
Comments _____
_____
Autograph _____ Year of Birth _____
It's more important to know where you're going than to see how fast you can get there.

Name(print) _____
Comments _____
_____
Autograph _____ Year of Birth _____

VIP Birthdates - 1 Year Calendar

24 AUGUST — Very Important Birthdates

Name(print) _____

Comments _____

_____

Autograph _____ Year of Birth _____

You can fix anything but a broken promise.

Name(print) _____

Comments _____

_____

Autograph _____ Year of Birth _____

On This Date in...

• **AD79** The cities of Pompeii and Herculaneum were buried in hot volcanic ash when Mount Vesuvius erupted.
• **1690** What is considered to be the official founding of India's largest city, Calcutta, started when Job Charnock established a trading post on behalf of the English East India Company in the small village of Kalikata in West Bengal.
• **1847** Charlotte Brontë sent her manuscript of *Jane Eyre*, written under the name Currer Bell, to her London publishers, Smith, Elder & Company.

25 AUGUST — Very Important Birthdates

Name(print) _____

Comments _____

_____

Autograph _____ Year of Birth _____

Money can't buy happiness ... but it makes searching for happiness a lot easier.

Name(print) _____

Comments _____

_____

Autograph _____ Year of Birth _____

On This Date in...

• **1530** Ivan the Terrible, first Tsar of Russia, was born.
• **1841** Three women graduated with Bachelors of Arts at the Oberlin Collegiate Institute, Ohio. They were the first women to be granted degrees.
• **1919** Daily flights between Paris and London began, starting the first scheduled international air service.
• **1930** Sean Connery, Scottish actor who starred as James Bond, Agent 007, was born.
• **1978** The Shroud of Turin, later proved to be a fake, went on display for the first time at the high altar at St. John's Cathedral, Turin.

26 AUGUST — Very Important Birthdates

Name(print) _____

Comments _____

_____

Autograph _____ Year of Birth _____

If only men took the nation's problems as seriously as they do its sports, our problems would be lessened!

Name(print) _____

Comments _____

_____

Autograph _____ Year of Birth _____

On This Date in...

• **1789** The Declaration of the Rights of Man was adopted by the French Assembly.
• **1920** American women were first given the right to vote by the 19th Amendment.
• **1940** The RAF bombed Berlin for the first time.
• **1952** The Soviets announced the first Intercontinental Ballistic Missile tests.
• **1987** Two people were killed and a radio centre was flattened by a sex-crazed elephant in Bangkok.
• **1989** Lucille Ball died at the age of 78, following open heart surgery.

27 AUGUST — Very Important Birthdates

Name(print) _____

Comments _____

_____

Autograph _____ Year of Birth _____

The problem is that the key to success doesn't always fit your ignition.

Name(print) _____

Comments _____

_____

Autograph _____ Year of Birth _____

On This Date in...

• **1783** The world's first hydrogen-filled balloon was launched.
• **1859** The world's first oil well was drilled at Titusville, Pennsylvania.
• **1882** Movie mogul Sam Goldwyn was born.
• **1910** Mother Teresa (Agnes Gonxha Bojaxhui) was born in Yugoslavia.
• **1910** Thomas Edison demonstrated the world's first sound film projection.
• **1979** Lord Louis Mountbatten, cousin to Queen Elizabeth, was killed by the IRA.

On This Date in...

- **1828** Leo Tolstoy (Lev Nikolayevich), author of *War and Peace*, was born.
- **1850** A telegraph cable was laid across the English Channel from Dover to Cap Gris Nez.
- **1953** Martin Luther King made his famous 'I have a dream' speech after over 300,000 made the civil rights march from the South to the Lincoln Memorial.
- **1967** Charles Darrow, inventor of Monopoly, died.
- **1988** Over 30 people were killed and over 500 injured when three Italian Airforce jets collided during an aerobatic show in West Germany.

Very Important Birthdates **28** AUGUST

Name(print) _____
Comments _____
_____
Autograph _____ Year of Birth _____

All men are created equal, but ambition, or lack of it, soon separates them.

Name(print) _____
Comments _____
_____
Autograph _____ Year of Birth _____

On This Date in...

- **1831** The world's first electrical transformer was demonstrated at the Royal Institute, London, England.
- **1842** The Opium War between Britain and China ended with the signing of the Treaty of Nanking.
- **1885** The world's first motorcycle was patented.
- **1918** British policemen went on strike for the first time, demanding better pay.
- **1958** US pop megastar Michael Jackson was born.
- **1966** The Beatles played their last live concert at Candlestick Park in San Francisco.
- **1987** US Actor Lee Marvin died.

Very Important Birthdates **29** AUGUST

Name(print) _____
Comments _____
_____
Autograph _____ Year of Birth _____

He who is carried away by his own importance seldom has far to walk back.

Name(print) _____
Comments _____
_____
Autograph _____ Year of Birth _____

On This Date in...

- **30BC** Cleopatra of Egypt was killed by a snake.
- **1797** Mary Shelley, author of *Frankenstein*, was born.
- **1881** The world's first stereo system was patented.
- **1862** General Stonewall Jackson and the Confederates achieved victory over the Union Army at the second Battle of Bull Run during the Civil War.
- **1896** Canadian actor Raymond Massey was born.
- **1901** The world's first vacuum cleaner was patented by Cecil Booth, who simply reversed the actions of a dust-blowing machine he had seen in operation.
- **1933** Air France was formed.

Very Important Birthdates **30** AUGUST

Name(print) _____
Comments _____
_____
Autograph _____ Year of Birth _____

He who has an inflated opinion of himself is likely a poor judge of human nature.

Name(print) _____
Comments _____
_____
Autograph _____ Year of Birth _____

On This Date in...

- **AD12** Roman Emperor Caligula was born.
- **1888** Jack the Ripper's first victim Polly Nicholls, a 42-year-old prostitute, was found disembowelled.
- **1900** Coca Cola went on sale in Britain for the first time.
- **1957** Malaya (later called Malasia) became independent.
- **1969** Undefeated world heavyweight champion boxer Rocky Marciano died in an air crash.
- **1972** US swimmer Mark Spitz won 5 of the 7 gold medals he was to win at the Munich Olympics.

Very Important Birthdates **31** AUGUST

Name(print) _____
Comments _____
_____
Autograph _____ Year of Birth _____

Authority is a poor substitute for leadership.

Name(print) _____
Comments _____
_____
Autograph _____ Year of Birth _____

VIP Birthdates - 1 Year Calendar

VIP Birthdates – 1 Year Calendar

1 SEPTEMBER Very Important Birthdates

Name(print) _____

Comments _____

_____

Autograph _____ Year of Birth _____

Our problems should make us better, not bitter.

Name(print) _____

Comments _____

_____

Autograph _____ Year of Birth _____

On This Date in...

- **1715** King Louis XIV (The Sun King) of France died.
- **1830** The poem *Mary Had a Little Lamb* was published by Sarah J. Hales in Boston.
- **1875** US novelist Edgar Rice Burroughs, creator of Tarzan (even though he never visited Africa) was born.
- **1904** Although blind and deaf from infancy, Helen Keller graduated with honours from Radcliffe College.
- **1923** A huge earthquake devastated Tokyo and Yokohama killing over 300,000 people.
- **1939** The Second World War started when Germany invaded Poland.

2 SEPTEMBER Very Important Birthdates

Name(print) _____

Comments _____

_____

Autograph _____ Year of Birth _____

Problems shouldn't be faced; they should be attacked.

Name(print) _____

Comments _____

_____

Autograph _____ Year of Birth _____

On This Date in...

- **1666** The Great Fire of London started at a bakery and went on to destroy 13,000 buildings.
- **1726** John Howard, for whom the John Howard Society is named, was born.
- **1945** The Japanese surrendered to General Douglas MacArthur aboard the aircraft carrier *Missouri*.
- **1973** J. R. R. Tolkien, author of *Lord Of The Rings,* died.
- **1987** The first CD-video, combining digital sound and high definition video, was launched by Philips Electronics.

3 SEPTEMBER Very Important Birthdates

Name(print) _____

Comments _____

_____

Autograph _____ Year of Birth _____

He who has not prepared for the trip should not begin his journey.

Name(print) _____

Comments _____

_____

Autograph _____ Year of Birth _____

On This Date in...

- **1658** Oliver Cromwell, Lord Protector of England, died.
- **1752** The date changed to September 14 when the Gregorian Calendar replaced the Julian Calendar in Britain.
- **1783** US independence was officially recognized by Britain when a treaty was signed in Paris.
- **1913** US Actor Alan Ladd was born.
- **1939** Britain and France officially declared war on Germany.
- **1967** Sweden changed from driving on the left to driving on the right.
- **1976** US spacecraft *Viking 2* landed on Mars.

4 SEPTEMBER Very Important Birthdates

Name(print) _____

Comments _____

_____

Autograph _____ Year of Birth _____

What is planned ahead of time can be done quickly.

Name(print) _____

Comments _____

_____

Autograph _____ Year of Birth _____

On This Date in...

- **1893** Peter Rabbit was introduced in an illustrated note to 5-year-old Noel Moore by Beatrix Potter.
- **1909** The first Boy Scout rally was held in London.
- **1957** The Arkansas National Guard was called out to turn nine black students away from the formerly whites-only Central High School.
- **1962** The Beatles began recording at EMI's famous Abbey Road studios, with producer George Martin.
- **1965** Nobel Prize winner Albert Schweitzer died.
- **1970** Ballerina Natalia Makarova of the Kirov Ballet defected to the West.

On This Date in...

- **1800** The French surrendered to the British at Malta.
- **1847** Outlaw Jesse (Woodson) James was born.
- **1922** The first coast-to-coast US flight was made.
- **1940** US actress Raquel Welch (Racquel Tejada) was born.
- **1969** Britain's commercial television network began broadcasting in colour.
- **1980** The St. Gotthard, the world's longest road tunnel was opened in Switzerland.
- **1987** The world's longest-running comedy show, *No Sex Please - We're British*, closed after over 16 years.

On This Date in...

- **1666** The Great Fire of London was finally extinguished.
- **1852** The first free-lending library opened in Britain.
- **1907** The *Lusitania* left on her five day maiden voyage to New York.
- **1941** Nazi Germany made the wearing of the hated yellow Star of David badges compulsory for all Jews.
- **1989** Citizens of Paris received 41,000 letters charging them with everything from murder and extortion to organized prostitution instead of a traffic violation, because of a computer error.

On This Date in...

- **1533** Queen Elizabeth I, daughter of Henry VIII, was born.
- **1812** Napoleon's army defeated the Russians at the Battle of Borodino, 40 miles west of Moscow.
- **1892** Boxing Champ John L. Sullivan was defeated by Gentleman Jim Corbett in the first fight where boxers wore gloves and rounds were only 3 minutes long.
- **1901** The Boxer Rising ended in China.
- **1936** Superstar Buddy Holly was born.
- **1943** Italy surrendered to the Allies.
- **1973** Jackie Stewart, a Scotsman, became world champion racing driver for a third year.

On This Date in...

- **1157** Richard I (The Lion Hearted) was born.
- **1886** Public diggings for gold were permitted in present day Johannesburg, now South Africa's largest city.
- **1944** The first V2 'flying bombs' killed 3 people in Chiswick, west London, England.
- **1945** General Toyo, who was prime minister of Japan during Pearl Harbor, tried to commit suicide to avoid being tried as a war criminal.
- **1974** President Ford pardoned Nixon for his part in Watergate.

Very Important Birthdates **5** SEPTEMBER

Name(print) _____
Comments _____
_____
Autograph _____ Year of Birth _____

It's easy to keep from becoming a bore. Just praise the person to whom you're talking.

Name(print) _____
Comments _____
_____
Autograph _____ Year of Birth _____

Very Important Birthdates **6** SEPTEMBER

Name(print) _____
Comments _____
_____
Autograph _____ Year of Birth _____

A wise man changes his mind; a fool never does.

Name(print) _____
Comments _____
_____
Autograph _____ Year of Birth _____

Very Important Birthdates **7** SEPTEMBER

Name(print) _____
Comments _____
_____
Autograph _____ Year of Birth _____

The world changes so fast that you couldn't stay wrong all the time if you tried.

Name(print) _____
Comments _____
_____
Autograph _____ Year of Birth _____

Very Important Birthdates **8** SEPTEMBER

Name(print) _____
Comments _____
_____
Autograph _____ Year of Birth _____

It's what you do when you have nothing to do that reveals what you are.

Name(print) _____
Comments _____
_____
Autograph _____ Year of Birth _____

VIP Birthdates - 1 Year Calendar

9 SEPTEMBER — Very Important Birthdates

Name(print) _____

Comments _____

_____

Autograph _____ Year of Birth _____

Perseverance has been defined as sticking to something you're not stuck on.

Name(print) _____

Comments _____

_____

Autograph _____ Year of Birth _____

On This Date in...

• **1583** Sir Humphrey Gilbert and his ship the *Squirrel* were lost after establishing a colony in Newfoundland.
• **1754** William Bligh, captain of the *Bounty,* was born.
• **1835** The British Municipal Corporations Act paved the way for local governments to come into being.
• **1850** California became the 31st state of the Union.
• **1948** North Korea proclaimed independence.
• **1971** Thirty-two guards were taken hostage by inmates at Attica Prison in New York.
• **1975** Eighteen-year-old Czech tennis player, Martina Navratilova defected to the US.

10 SEPTEMBER — Very Important Birthdates

Name(print) _____

Comments _____

_____

Autograph _____ Year of Birth _____

Failure is the path of least persistence.

Name(print) _____

Comments _____

_____

Autograph _____ Year of Birth _____

On This Date in...

• **1894** The first conviction for impaired driving was assessed on an electric cab driver in London.
• **1942** In a single raid, the RAF dropped 100,000 bombs on Dusseldorf, Germany.
• **1945** Vidkun Quisling of Norway was sentenced to death for collaborating with the conquering Germans while he was premier of that country during the war.
• **1987** Despite protests from doctors, a 35-year ban on stage hypnotists was lifted in London, England.
• **1989** Hungary allowed thousands of East German refugees to leave, there by angering East Germany.

11 SEPTEMBER — Very Important Birthdates

Name(print) _____

Comments _____

_____

Autograph _____ Year of Birth _____

The accent may be on youth, but the stress is still on the parents.

Name(print) _____

Comments _____

_____

Autograph _____ Year of Birth _____

On This Date in...

• **1777** British troops defeated George Washington's troops in the Battle of Brandywine Creek.
• **1841** The world's first commuter train between London and Brighton began regular service.
• **1971** Former Soviet premier Nikita Kruschev died in obscurity.
• **1973** A US supported military junta overthrew the elected government of Chile.
• **1978** Georgi Markov, a Bulgarian defector, died when he was stabbed by the poisoned umbrella tip of an unknown secret agent in London, England.

12 SEPTEMBER — Very Important Birthdates

Name(print) _____

Comments _____

_____

Autograph _____ Year of Birth _____

Parents can tell but never teach, until they practice what they preach.

Name(print) _____

Comments _____

_____

Autograph _____ Year of Birth _____

On This Date in...

• **1908** Winston Churchill married Clementine Hozier.
• **1910** Mrs. Alice Stebbins Wells, the world's first police woman, was appointed in Los Angeles.
• **1935** US multimillionaire Howard Hughes set his first of several flying records by flying a plane of his own design at 352.46 MPH.
• **1953** Nikita Kruschev was elected First Secretary of the Communist Party in the USSR.
• **1953** John F. Kennedy married Jacqueline Bouvier.
• **1972** Two British trawlers were sunk by Iceland during the Cod War.

On This Date in...

- **490BC** The Greeks defeated the Persians at the Battle of Marathon, after Philippides had made a marathon run of 150 miles, seeking the help of the Spartans (which later proved to be unneeded).
- **1759** Both French General Montcalm and British General Wolfe died after the French were defeated on the Plains of Abraham above Quebec City.
- **1788** New York City became the capital of the US.
- **1925** US jazz singer Mel Torme was born.
- **1955** Little Richard recorded *Tutti Fruitti*.

Very Important Birthdates 13 SEPTEMBER

Name(print) _____

Comments _____

_____

Autograph _____ Year of Birth _____

You are what you are when no one is around.

Name(print) _____

Comments _____

_____

Autograph _____ Year of Birth _____

On This Date in...

- **1752** Eleven days were lost with the introduction of the Gregorian calendar, making Sept. 3 this date.
- **1812** Napoleon entered Moscow, which had been abandoned by the Russians.
- **1868** The world's first hole-in-one was recorded by Tom Morris on the 8th hole (166 yards) at Preswick.
- **1901** Theodore Roosevelt became the 26th president of the US after President McKinley died, also on this date.
- **1959** The Soviet's *Lunik II*, became the first spaceship to land on the moon.
- **1982** Princess Grace (Kelly) died in a car crash.

Very Important Birthdates   14 SEPTEMBER

Name(print) _____

Comments _____

_____

Autograph _____ Year of Birth _____

Ability will enable a man to get to the top, but it takes character to keep him there.

Name(print) _____

Comments _____

_____

Autograph _____ Year of Birth _____

On This Date in...

- **1789** US author James Fenimore Cooper was born.
- **1916** British Army tanks went into battle for the first time at Fleurs in the Somme.
- **1917** Russia was declared a republic by Kerenski.
- **1928** Britain's first robot was demonstrated.
- **1966** Britain's first nuclear submarine, *HMS Resolution*, was launched by the Queen Mother.
- **1973** Carl Gustav became King of Sweden upon the death of his father, King Gustavus VI.
- **1975** Civil war between Christians and Muslims began in Beirut, Lebanon.

Very Important Birthdates 15 SEPTEMBER

Name(print) _____

Comments _____

_____

Autograph _____ Year of Birth _____

Believers eventually become achievers.

Name(print) _____

Comments _____

_____

Autograph _____ Year of Birth _____

On This Date in...

- **1620** The *Mayflower* set sail with the Pilgrims.
- **1736** Gabriel Daniel Fahrenheit, who devised the Fahrenheit thermometer scale, died.
- **1847** The house in Stratford-On-Avon where Shakespeare was born became the first building in Britain to be bought for preservation.
- **1857** The song *Jingle Bells* was copyrighted.
- **1908** The Buick and Oldsmobile automobile manufacturers merged to become General Motors.
- **1963** The British Embassy in Malaysia was burned by a mob of 100,000 when that country became independent.

Very Important Birthdates   16 SEPTEMBER

Name(print) _____

Comments _____

_____

Autograph _____ Year of Birth _____

Mutual confidence is the pillar of friendship.

Name(print) _____

Comments _____

_____

Autograph _____ Year of Birth _____

VIP Birthdates – 1 Year Calendar

VIP Birthdates – 1 Year Calendar

17 SEPTEMBER — Very Important Birthdates

Name(print) _____

Comments _____

_____

Autograph _____ Year of Birth _____

Many children would take after their parents if they knew where they went.

Name(print) _____

Comments _____

_____

Autograph _____ Year of Birth _____

On This Date in...

- **1701** King James II of England died.
- **1908** The world's first airplane passenger victim, Lt. Selfridge, died during a military assessment flight with Orville Wright, when the plane suddenly nosedived.
- **1931** The world's first long-playing (33 1/3 rpm) records were demonstrated by RCA-Victor.
- **1961** Former Turkish prime minister, Adnan Menderes was hanged by the new military rulers.
- **1987** A hunter shot at a duck that was just taking flight, but instead shot the big fish (a pike) that was attempting to make a meal of the duck.

18 SEPTEMBER — Very Important Birthdates

Name(print) _____

Comments _____

_____

Autograph _____ Year of Birth _____

Talking is sharing, but listening is caring.

Name(print) _____

Comments _____

_____

Autograph _____ Year of Birth _____

On This Date in...

- **1851** The *New York Times* was first published.
- **1895** Canadian Prime Minister John George Diefenbaker was born.
- **1905** Swedish actress, Greta Garbo, one of the most legendary film stars of all time, was born.
- **1914** The Irish Home Rule Bill received Royal Assent.
- **1933** US singer, songwriter, poet and cult figure, Bob Dylan (Robert Allen Zimmerman) was born.
- **1939** The first Nazi propaganda broadcasts to Britain were made by Irishman William Joyce.

19 SEPTEMBER — Very Important Birthdates

Name(print) _____

Comments _____

_____

Autograph _____ Year of Birth _____

One reason so many children are seen on the streets at night is that they're afraid to stay home alone.

Name(print) _____

Comments _____

_____

Autograph _____ Year of Birth _____

On This Date in...

- **1783** The world's first hot air balloon flight, which had a rooster, a duck and a sheep as passengers, was witnessed by King Louis XVI and Marie Antoinette.
- **1876** The world's first carpet sweeper was patented by US inventor, Melville Bissell.
- **1893** New Zealand became the world's first country to give women the right to vote.
- **1945** Irishman William Joyce was sentenced to hang for treason for being a Nazi propagandist during WWII.
- **1955** Juan Peron was overthrown and later exiled to Paraguay by a military junta in Argentina.

20 SEPTEMBER — Very Important Birthdates

Name(print) _____

Comments _____

_____

Autograph _____ Year of Birth _____

An optimist is one who makes the best of it when he gets the worst of it.

Name(print) _____

Comments _____

_____

Autograph _____ Year of Birth _____

On This Date in...

- **1519** Ferdinand Magellan set off from Seville, Spain, to circumnavigate the world in a fleet of five small ships.
- **1854** The Crimean War's Battle of Alma, between Britain and Russia, produced 6 Victoria Cross winners.
- **1863** Fairy tale collector Jakob (Karl) Grimm died.
- **1928** The Fascists took over the supreme legislative body in Rome, and replaced the Chamber of Deputies.
- **1934** Italian movie star Sophia Loren was born.
- **1984** Forty people were killed by a suicide bomber who drove his explosive-laden vehicle into the US Embassy in Beirut, Lebanon.

On This Date in...

- **1327** The deposed and imprisoned King Edward II of England was murdered with a red hot poker to insure that his son, Edward III, succeeded to the throne.
- **1866** English author, H. G. Wells, was born.
- **1745** The English were defeated by Bonnie Prince Charlie and his Jacobite army during the Battle of Prestonpans in Scotland.
- **1903** The 21-minute-long *Kit Carson*, probably the world's first western movie, opened in the US.
- **1934** Canadian poet, Leonard Cohen, was born.

Very Important Birthdates **21** SEPTEMBER

Name(print) _____
Comments _____
_____
Autograph _____ Year of Birth _____
A conscience is something that hurts us when everything else feels terrific.
Name(print) _____
Comments _____
_____
Autograph _____ Year of Birth _____

On This Date in...

- **1776** American Revolutionary, Nathan Hale, was hanged.
- **1927** World heavyweight boxing champion Gene Tunney was given the extra 5 seconds needed to come back and win after being knocked down by Jack Dempsy when Dempsy failed to return to his corner.
- **1972** Eight thousand Asians were given 48 hours to leave Uganda by Idi Amin.
- **1985** A devastating earthquake killed 2000 people in Mexico.
- **1989** Ten people were killed when an IRA bomb was set off at the Royal Marines School of Music.

Very Important Birthdates **22** SEPTEMBER

Name(print) _____
Comments _____
_____
Autograph _____ Year of Birth _____
What the world needs is an amplifier for the still, small voice.
Name(print) _____
Comments _____
_____
Autograph _____ Year of Birth _____

On This Date in...

- **1779** John Paul Jones, aboard the *Bonhomme Richard* defeated the British ships *Serapis* and *Countess of Scarborough* in a naval battle.
- **1780** British agent John André was captured and later hanged by the Americans for spying.
- **1846** The planet Neptune was discovered by astronomer Johann Galle.
- **1920** Actor Mickey Rooney (Joe Yule Jr.) was born.
- **1939** Psychoanalyst Sigmund Freud died.
- **1973** After being ousted almost 18 years previously, Juan Peron was re-elected President of Argentina.

Very Important Birthdates **23** SEPTEMBER

Name(print) _____
Comments _____
_____
Autograph _____ Year of Birth _____
A man will fight harder for his interests than for his rights. - Napoleon Bonaparte
Name(print) _____
Comments _____
_____
Autograph _____ Year of Birth _____

On This Date in...

- **1846** Bramwell Brontë, brother of the famous Brontë sisters, and drunken model of Emily Brontë's Hindley Earnshaw in *Wuthering Heights,* died of drugs and drink.
- **1852** The world's first hydrogen-filled, steam-powered airship made its maiden flight at Versailles.
- **1896** US novelist F. Scott Fitzgerald was born.
- **1936** Muppets' creator Jim Henson was born.
- **1960** The US *Enterprise*, the world's first nuclear-powered aircraft carrier, was launched in Virginia.
- **1980** The conflict between Iran and Iraq became a full-scale war when Iraq blew up the Abadan refinery.

Very Important Birthdates **24** SEPTEMBER

Name(print) _____
Comments _____
_____
Autograph _____ Year of Birth _____
Conscience is something inside that bothers you when nothing outside does.
Name(print) _____
Comments _____
_____
Autograph _____ Year of Birth _____

VIP Birthdates - 1 Year Calendar

25 SEPTEMBER — Very Important Birthdates

Name(print) _____

Comments _____

_____

Autograph _____ Year of Birth _____

The optimist has no brakes; the pessimist has no motor.

Name(print) _____

Comments _____

_____

Autograph _____ Year of Birth _____

On This Date in...

• **1818** The world's first human blood transfusion took place in Guy's Hospital, London, England.
• **1944** Film star Michael Douglas was born.
• **1952** Actor Christopher Reeve, who played Superman, and actor Mark Hamill, who played Luke Skywalker in *Star Wars,* were both born on this day.
• **1954** Haiti's elections were won by 'Papa' Doc (Dr. Francois Duvalier).
• **1957** Nine black children were escorted into Central High by over 1000 National Guardsmen during forced de-segregation in Little Rock, Arkansas.

26 SEPTEMBER — Very Important Birthdates

Name(print) _____

Comments _____

_____

Autograph _____ Year of Birth _____

He who says the days of opportunity are over is copping out.

Name(print) _____

Comments _____

_____

Autograph _____ Year of Birth _____

On This Date in...

• **1580** After circumnavigating the world in 33 months, Sir Frances Drake, sailed into Plymouth, England, in his ship *The Golden Hind.*
• **1687** A mortar bomb fired by the Venetian Army at the Turks, who were holding the Acropolis, severely damaged the Parthenon.
• **1887** A patent was granted to Emile Berliner for his gramophone invention.
• **1961** Bob Dylan made his debut at Greenwich Village.
• **1984** Britain and China agreed that Hong Kong would revert to control by China in 1997.

27 SEPTEMBER — Very Important Birthdates

Name(print) _____

Comments _____

_____

Autograph _____ Year of Birth _____

There's something in life that never returns - a lost opportunity!

Name(print) _____

Comments _____

_____

Autograph _____ Year of Birth _____

On This Date in...

• **1825** The world's first public railway service came into being when a 10 MPH locomotive pulled 32 passenger wagons along a 27-mile track in England.
• **1888** A letter signed 'Jack The Ripper' was received by the Central News Agency in London, the first time the name was ever used.
• **1922** King Constantine I of Greece abdicated following the defeat of Greece in Turkey.
• **1930** The US National Amateur Championships was won by US golfer Bobby Jones to complete the first ever golfing grand slam.

28 SEPTEMBER — Very Important Birthdates

Name(print) _____

Comments _____

_____

Autograph _____ Year of Birth _____

Today's opportunity is yesterday's dream and tomorrow's memory.

Name(print) _____

Comments _____

_____

Autograph _____ Year of Birth _____

On This Date in...

• **1745** At London's Drury Lane Theatre, *God Save The King* was sung for the first time in response to a threat from the Young Pretender, Bonnie Prince Charlie.
• **1894** Retail giant, Marks and Spencer, got its start when Polish immigrant Simon Marks partnered with Tom Spencer to open a penny bazaar in Manchester.
• **1909** Al Capp of *L'il Abner* comic strip fame, was born.
• **1934** French actress Brigitte Bardot was born.
• **1978** Pope John Paul I was found dead after only 33 days as pope.

On This Date in...

- **1399** Richard II became the first British monarch to abdicate.
- **1907** Cowboy star/singer Gene Autry was born.
- **1916** John D. Rockefeller became the world's first billionaire.
- **1930** George Bernard Shaw turned down a peerage.
- **1935** US Rock star Jerry Lee Lewis was born.
- **1950** The world's first automatic telephone answering machine was tested by Bell in the US.
- **1952** World water speed holder, John Cobb, was killed on Loch Ness when *Crusader* disintegrated.

Very Important Birthdates **29** SEPTEMBER

Name(print) _____

Comments _____

_____

Autograph _____ Year of Birth _____

If you correct yourself, others won't have to.

Name(print) _____

Comments _____

_____

Autograph _____ Year of Birth _____

On This Date in...

- **1888** Jack The Ripper killed two women in London's East End.
- **1929** The world's first rocket-powered aircraft made its maiden flight.
- **1938** Prime Minister Neville Chamberlain returned from Germany with his 'peace in our time' agreement, which he had signed with Hitler.
- **1939** The German 'blitzkrieg' cracked Poland.
- **1988** Five astronauts returned to earth completing the first successful space flight since the disastrous 1986 *Challenger* flight.

Very Important Birthdates **30** SEPTEMBER

Name(print) _____

Comments _____

_____

Autograph _____ Year of Birth _____

Remember, you are your own doctor when it comes to curing cold feet.

Name(print) _____

Comments _____

_____

Autograph _____ Year of Birth _____

On This Date in...

- **1792** The first money orders were issued in Britain.
- **1880** The world's first practical electric light bulbs were manufactured by Edison Lamp Works.
- **1908** The first Model T, the world's most popular 'affordable' car was introduced by Henry Ford. It was also the first left-hand-steering-wheel vehicle.
- **1969** The sound barrier was broken for the first time by Concorde 001 during testing in France.
- **1971** Disney World opened in Florida.
- **1974** The Watergate trial began.
- **1974** The first McDonald's opened in London.

Very Important Birthdates OCTOBER

Name(print) _____

Comments _____

_____

Autograph _____ Year of Birth _____

One of the hardest decisions to make in life is when to start middle age.

Name(print) _____

Comments _____

_____

Autograph _____ Year of Birth _____

On This Date in...

- **1187** Jerusalem was captured by Saladin, the Muslim sultan, after an 88-year occupation by the Franks.
- **1608** The world's first telescope was demonstrated.
- **1870** Rome was named the capital of Italy.
- **1871** Mormon leader Brigham Young was arrested for bigamy.
- **1925** London's first red double-decker buses went into service.
- **1935** Mussolini's Italian forces invaded Abyssinia.
- **1950** The first *Peanuts* comic strip by Charles M. Schultz appeared.

Very Important Birthdates OCTOBER

Name(print) _____

Comments _____

_____

Autograph _____ Year of Birth _____

Tact is the ability to shut your mouth before someone else wants to.

Name(print) _____

Comments _____

_____

Autograph _____ Year of Birth _____

VIP Birthdates – 1 Year Calendar

3 OCTOBER — Very Important Birthdates

Name(print) _____
Comments _____
_____
Autograph _____ Year of Birth _____

The cost of obedience is nothing compared with the cost of disobedience.

Name(print) _____
Comments _____
_____
Autograph _____ Year of Birth _____

On This Date in...

- **1899** J.S. Thurman patented a motor-driven vacuum cleaner in the United States.
- **1906** The international distress signal SOS replaced the earlier used CDQ (often called Come Damn Quick).
- **1922** The first facsimile picture was transmitted between buildings in Washington, DC.
- **1941** Aerosol was patented.
- **1941** Chubby Checker, creator of the Twist, was born.
- **1961** Tony Armstrong Jones, husband of Princess Margaret, was made Lord Snowdon by Queen Elizabeth.

4 OCTOBER — Very Important Birthdates

Name(print) _____
Comments _____
_____
Autograph _____ Year of Birth _____

He who thinks by the inch and talks by the yard deserves to be kicked by the foot.

Name(print) _____
Comments _____
_____
Autograph _____ Year of Birth _____

On This Date in...

- **1878** The first Chinese embassy opened in Washington.
- **1905** Orville Wright became the first to fly an aircraft for over 33 minutes.
- **1910** Portugal was proclaimed a republic after King Manuel II fled to Britain.
- **1952** The world's first external pacemaker was fitted to David Schwartz at the Harvard Medical School.
- **1957** Russia beat the US into space by launching *Sputnik I*, the world's first orbiting satellite.
- **1965** Pope Paul VI addressed the UN, thereby becoming the first pope to visit the US.

5 OCTOBER — Very Important Birthdates

Name(print) _____
Comments _____
_____
Autograph _____ Year of Birth _____

All mothers are physically handicapped. They have only two hands.

Name(print) _____
Comments _____
_____
Autograph _____ Year of Birth _____

On This Date in...

- **1880** The world's first ball point pen which carried its own ink supply was patented by Alonzo T. Cross.
- **1908** Bulgaria declared independence from Turkey.
- **1930** *R101*, a British air ship, crashed in France killing 48 of the 54 passengers and crew.
- **1969** *Monty Python's Flying Circus* was screened for the first time by the BBC.
- **1970** Anwar Sadat became Premier of Egypt, replacing Nasser.
- **1982** Two-inch flat pocket television sets were introduced to the market by Sony.

6 OCTOBER — Very Important Birthdates

Name(print) _____
Comments _____
_____
Autograph _____ Year of Birth _____

A family budget is a device to make you worry about money before you spend it.

Name(print) _____
Comments _____
_____
Autograph _____ Year of Birth _____

On This Date in...

- **1890** Bigamy was renounced by the Mormons in Utah.
- **1892** English Poet Laureate Alfred Lord Tennyson died.
- **1902** A 2000-mile-long railway line between Cape Town and Bera, Mozambique, was completed.
- **1921** *April Showers*, when sung by Al Jolson on Broadway, brought no fewer that 36 curtain calls.
- **1928** Chang Kai-shek became President of China.
- **1941** Two men named Willburn and Frizzel were fried in the electric chair in Florida.
- **1951** US breakfast food pioneer Will Keith Kellogg died.

On This Date in...

- **1571** The Ottoman Turks lost 117 galleys and thousands of men in a 4-hour battle with Christian allies during the Battle of Lepanto.
- **1806** Ralph Wedgewood patented carbon paper.
- **1849** US writer Edgar Allan Poe died.
- **1908** Crete united with Greece and revolted against Turkish domination.
- **1913** Henry Ford's new 'moving assembly line' to speed up production was unveiled in Michigan.
- **1959** Russia's *Lunik III* photographed the far side of the moon for the first time.

Very Important Birthdates **7** OCTOBER

Name(print) _____

Comments _____

_____

Autograph _____ Year of Birth _____

This fast age seems more concerned about speed than direction.

Name(print) _____

Comments _____

_____

Autograph _____ Year of Birth _____

On This Date in...

- **1085** St. Mark's Cathedral was consecrated in Venice.
- **1806** Rocket-propelled missiles were used by the British for the first time in an attack on Boulogne.
- **1869** Former US President Franklin Pierce died.
- **1871** The Great Fire of Chicago, which left 95,000 homeless, was started by Mrs O'Leary's cow.
- **1941** Reverend Jesse Jackson, US Senator and black civil rights campaigner, was born.
- **1952** Britain's second worst rail crash, involving 3 trains, killed 112 people and injured 200 in Harrow.

Very Important Birthdates **8** OCTOBER

Name(print) _____

Comments _____

_____

Autograph _____ Year of Birth _____

When people start off on the right foot, there's a better chance that they'll get in step sooner.

Name(print) _____

Comments _____

_____

Autograph _____ Year of Birth _____

On This Date in...

- **28BC** The Temple of Apollo in Rome was dedicated.
- **1940** John Lennon of the Beatles was born.
- **1947** The world's first telephone call was made between a car and an airplane.
- **1967** Guerrilla leader and Marxist revolutionary, Che Guevara, who supported Fidel Castro was captured and shot in the village of Higuera, Bolivia.
- **1973** Elvis Presley divorced Priscilla who received a settlement of $1.5 million, as well as 5% interest in two publishing companies and $4200 a month.

Very Important Birthdates **9** OCTOBER

Name(print) _____

Comments _____

_____

Autograph _____ Year of Birth _____

It would be better to be a little late down here than too early up there.

Name(print) _____

Comments _____

_____

Autograph _____ Year of Birth _____

On This Date in...

- **1913** Forty tons of explosives were detonated by remote control from the White House by President Wilson to clear the last obstacles and open the Panama Canal.
- **1930** TWA (Transcontinental and Western Airways) was formed when three US airlines merged.
- **1940** The high altar of St. Paul's was destroyed in London by a German bomb.
- **1973** US Vice-President Spiro Agnew resigned because of tax evasion charges.
- **1985** High profile film stars, Orson Wells and Yul Brynner, both died at the age of 70.

Very Important Birthdates **10** OCTOBER

Name(print) _____

Comments _____

_____

Autograph _____ Year of Birth _____

Always try to drive so that your licence will expire before you do.

Name(print) _____

Comments _____

_____

Autograph _____ Year of Birth _____

VIP Birthdates – 1 Year Calendar

11 OCTOBER — Very Important Birthdates

Name(print) _____

Comments _____

_____

Autograph _____ Year of Birth _____

The father is the head of the house; the mother is the heart of the house.

Name(print) _____

Comments _____

_____

Autograph _____ Year of Birth _____

On This Date in...

• **1521** The title 'Defender of the Faith' was conferred on Henry VIII by Pope Leo X because of Henry's book supporting Catholic principals. Henry broke with Rome 12 year later so he could marry Ann Boleyn.
• **1689** Peter the Great became Tsar of Russia.
• **1899** The Anglo-Boer War began.
• **1871** The Great Fire of Chicago was finally put out.
• **1884** Eleanor Roosevelt, wife and cousin of President Franklin D Roosevelt, was born.
• **1968** *Apollo 7* was launched.
• **1978** Singer Sid Vicious's girlfriend was found murdered.

12 OCTOBER — Very Important Birthdates

Name(print) _____

Comments _____

_____

Autograph _____ Year of Birth _____

Money talks, but it doesn't say when it's coming back.

Name(print) _____

Comments _____

_____

Autograph _____ Year of Birth _____

On This Date in...

• **1537** King Edward VI of England was born.
• **1609** *Three Blind Mice* was published in England.
• **1845** English prison reformer Elizabeth Fry died.
• **1870** Confederate General Robert E. Lee died.
• **1901** The Executive Mansion was renamed The White House by Franklin D. Roosevelt.
• **1928** The world's first iron lung was used.
• **1971** *Jesus Christ Superstar* opened on Broadway.
• **1984** Prime Minister Margaret Thatcher escaped injury when an IRA bomb killed four and injured 30 at the Conservative Party Conference in Brighton.

13 OCTOBER — Very Important Birthdates

Name(print) _____

Comments _____

_____

Autograph _____ Year of Birth _____

He who makes a mistake and doesn't correct it is making another mistake.

Name(print) _____

Comments _____

_____

Autograph _____ Year of Birth _____

On This Date in...

• **AD54** Roman Emperor Claudius I ate poisoned mushrooms and died as a result of a plot inspired by his wife, the Empress Agrippina.
• **1792** The foundation stone of the White House was laid by President George Washington.
• **1884** Greenwich, England, was adopted as the Prime Meridian.
• **1904** Sigmund Freud had his *Interpretation Of Dreams* published.
• **1925** British Prime Minister Thatcher was born Margaret Hilda Roberts.

14 OCTOBER — Very Important Birthdates

Name(print) _____

Comments _____

_____

Autograph _____ Year of Birth _____

A mistake proves that someone at least tried.

Name(print) _____

Comments _____

_____

Autograph _____ Year of Birth _____

On This Date in...

• **1066** The Battle of Hastings saw King Harold slain by William of Normandy's (the Conqueror) troops.
• **1830** Belgium became an independent kingdom.
• **1884** George Eastman patented photographic film.
• **1912** President Theodore Roosevelt was shot in an assassination attempt by a mentally unstable man.
• **1947** The sound barrier was broken for the first time by Chuck Yeager in his *Bell XI* rocket plane.
• **1964** Martin Luther King received the Nobel Peace Prize.
• **1973** Egyptian and Syrian forces invaded Israel.

VIP Birthdates – 1 Year Calendar

On This Date in...

• **1815** Napoleon and a party of followers were exiled to the island of St. Helena.
• **1917** Dutch spy Mata Hari was executed for collaborating with the Germans during WWI.
• **1945** Pierre Laval, French leader of the Vichy government, was executed for collaboration with the Germans during WWII.
• **1946** Nazi war criminal and founder of the Luftwaffe, Herman Goering, took poison and beat the hangman.
• **1964** Nikita Kruschev was deposed and replaced by Leonid Brezhnev while he was away on vacation.

Very Important Birthdates **15** OCTOBER

Name(print) _____
Comments _____
_____
Autograph _____ Year of Birth _____
Blowing one's horn only succeeds in deafening the listener.
Name(print) _____
Comments _____
_____
Autograph _____ Year of Birth _____

On This Date in...

• **1846** An anaesthetic (diethyl ether) was successfully used for the first time at Massachusetts General Hospital.
• **1847** *Jane Eyre* by Currer Bell (Charlotte Brontë) was published.
• **1859** Anti-slavery activist, John Brown, a white man, seized the US armoury at Harper's Ferry.
• **1916** The world's first birth control clinic was opened in Brooklyn, New York.
• **1978** Cardinal Karol Wojtyla of Poland became the youngest pope in the 20th century, and the first non-Italian pope since 1542.

Very Important Birthdates **16** OCTOBER

Name(print) _____
Comments _____
_____
Autograph _____ Year of Birth _____
People who are all wrapped up in themselves usually make pretty small packages.
Name(print) _____
Comments _____
_____
Autograph _____ Year of Birth _____

On This Date in...

• **1651** Charles II fled to France, destitute and friendless, after being defeated by Cromwell's troops.
• **1777** The American colonists, under general Horatio Gates, won a victory over the British at Saratoga.
• **1855** Sir Harry Bessemer patented a new steel-making process.
• **1860** The world's first golf championship was held.
• **1902** The first Cadillac was built in Detroit.
• **1945** Juan Peron was asked to take over the government of Argentina, eight days after being ousted by the army.

Very Important Birthdates **17** OCTOBER

Name(print) _____
Comments _____
_____
Autograph _____ Year of Birth _____
Experience is yesterday's answer to today's problems.
Name(print) _____
Comments _____
_____
Autograph _____ Year of Birth _____

On This Date in...

• **1887** The US bought Alaska from Russia for $7,200,000.
• **1898** The US took possession of Puerto Rico from Spain.
• **1966** Queen Elizabeth pardoned Timothy Evans for the murder of his wife and child. Unfortunately, Timothy had been hanged in 1953, three years before the real killer was hanged for mass murder.
• **1970** The body of Quebec's Minister of Labour, Pierre Laporte, who had been kidnapped by the FLQ, was found.

Very Important Birthdates **18** OCTOBER

Name(print) _____
Comments _____
_____
Autograph _____ Year of Birth _____
Experience is compulsory education.
Name(print) _____
Comments _____
_____
Autograph _____ Year of Birth _____

VIP Birthdates – 1 Year Calendar

19 OCTOBER — Very Important Birthdates

Name(print) _____

Comments _____

_____

Autograph _____ Year of Birth _____

The man who never makes a mistake must get tired of doing nothing.

Name(print) _____

Comments _____

_____

Autograph _____ Year of Birth _____

On This Date in...

• **1745** Jonathan Swift, author of the politically satirical, *Gulliver's Travels*, died insane.
• **1781** Lord Cornwallis surrendered to George Washington, thus ending the American War of Independence.
• **1970** An oil find in the North Sea was announced by British Petroleum.
• **1987** Wall Street ended the day down 22% lower than the 1929 crash, and wiped out millions on the stock markets around the world on a day that became known as 'Black Monday'.

20 OCTOBER — Very Important Birthdates

Name(print) _____

Comments _____

_____

Autograph _____ Year of Birth _____

Don't worry about your mistakes. Some of the dullest people don't make any.

Name(print) _____

Comments _____

_____

Autograph _____ Year of Birth _____

On This Date in...

• **1714** King George I of England was crowned.
• **1818** The 49th parallel became the official border between the US and Canada.
• **1944** General Douglas MacArthur kept his word and returned to the Philippines as a liberator from the Japanese forces.
• **1960** Author D.H. Lawrence and Penguin Books were taken to court under the Obscene Publications Act for publishing *Lady Chatterly's Lover*.
• **1964** Herbert Hoover, 31st US President, died.
• **1968** Jackie Kennedy married Aristotle Onassis.

21 OCTOBER — Very Important Birthdates

Name(print) _____

Comments _____

_____

Autograph _____ Year of Birth _____

He who takes the wrong road makes the journey twice.

Name(print) _____

Comments _____

_____

Autograph _____ Year of Birth _____

On This Date in...

• **1805** Admiral Horatio Nelson's fleet defeated Napoleon's combined French and Spanish fleet at Trafalgar, but Nelson himself was killed.
• **1833** Alfred Bernhard Nobel, creator of the Nobel Peace Prize, was born.
• **1923** The world's first planetarium was opened in Munich, Germany.
• **1967** An Israeli destroyer was sunk by Egyptian missiles off the coast of Sinai, killing over 40.
• **1969** Willy Brandt became Chancellor of West Germany.

22 OCTOBER — Very Important Birthdates

Name(print) _____

Comments _____

_____

Autograph _____ Year of Birth _____

Many a domestic explosion has been touched off by an old flame.

Name(print) _____

Comments _____

_____

Autograph _____ Year of Birth _____

On This Date in...

• **1797** The world's first parachute jump was made from a balloon 6000 feet above Paris, France.
• **1811** Composer Franz Liszt was born.
• **1844** French actress Sarah Bernhardt was born.
• **1962** President Kennedy announced a naval blockade against Cuba which became known as the 'Cuban Missile Crisis'.
• **1962** Nelson Mandela went on trial for treason in South Africa.
• **1966** Russian spy, George Blake, escaped from jail in London, where he was serving a 40-year sentence.

On This Date in...

- **42BC** Marcus Junius Brutus committed suicide after his army was crushed by Anthony and Octavian.
- **1642** Cromwell's Parliamentary Roundheads clashed with the Cavaliers of Charles I in the Battle of Edgehill.
- **1844** Louis Riel, leader of Metis, was born.
- **1925** US entertainer Johnny Carson was born.
- **1954** The US, Britain and France agreed to end occupation of Germany.
- **1956** Hungarians began a revolt against Soviet leadership.

Very Important Birthdates **23** **OCTOBER**

Name(print) _____
Comments _____
_____
Autograph _____ Year of Birth _____

If you could sell your experience for what it cost, you would never need a pension.

Name(print) _____
Comments _____
_____
Autograph _____ Year of Birth _____

On This Date in...

- **1861** The famous Pony Express mail service stopped running after only 18 months in operation.
- **1901** Mrs. Ann Edison-Taylor went over Niagara Falls in a padded barrel to help pay her mortgage.
- **1930** US singer/songwriter 'The Big Bopper' was born.
- **1931** Gangster Al Capone was given an 11-year jail sentence and fined $80,000 for tax evasion.
- **1957** French fashion designer Christian Dior died.
- **1989** Television preacher Jimmy Bakker was given a 45-year jail sentence for swindling his followers of millions of dollars.

Very Important Birthdates **24** **OCTOBER**

Name(print) _____
Comments _____
_____
Autograph _____ Year of Birth _____

Some people profit by their experiences; others never recover from them.

Name(print) _____
Comments _____
_____
Autograph _____ Year of Birth _____

On This Date in...

- **1415** The Battle of Agincourt took place in France.
- **1854** An ambiguous order from a commander saw the British suffer many casualties from a 3-way crossfire during the Charge of the Lights Brigade.
- **1881** The airbrush was patented in the US.
- **1906** A glass radio tube capable of amplification was patented, thereby making broadcasting possible.
- **1936** The world's first radio request program was broadcast in Berlin, Germany.
- **1971** Taiwan was expelled from the UN so that the People's Republic of China could become a member.

Very Important Birthdates **25** **OCTOBER**

Name(print) _____
Comments _____
_____
Autograph _____ Year of Birth _____

One reason experience is such a good teacher is that she doesn't allow any dropouts.

Name(print) _____
Comments _____
_____
Autograph _____ Year of Birth _____

On This Date in...

- **1881** The Gunfight at the OK Corral in Tombstone, Arizona, saw Wyatt Earp and his two brothers, Virgil and Morgan, along with Doc Holliday, kill Billy Clanton and two others of Ike Clanton's gang members.
- **1825** The Erie Canal, which linked the Niagara River and the Hudson River, was opened.
- **1905** Norway and Sweden ended their union.
- **1956** The International Atomic Energy Agency was formed.
- **1965** The Beatles received their MBEs at Buckingham Palace.

Very Important Birthdates **26** **OCTOBER**

Name(print) _____
Comments _____
_____
Autograph _____ Year of Birth _____

There's no free tuition in the school of experience.

Name(print) _____
Comments _____
_____
Autograph _____ Year of Birth _____

VIP Birthdates – 1 Year Calendar

27 OCTOBER — Very Important Birthdates

Name(print) _____

Comments _____

_____

Autograph _____ Year of Birth _____

Starting from scratch is easy; starting without it is tough. - *Peter's Almanac*

Name(print) _____

Comments _____

_____

Autograph _____ Year of Birth _____

On This Date in...

• **1662** Dunkirk was sold to Louis XIV of France by Charles II for 2,500,000 livres.
• **1936** Mrs. Simpson, who caused a king to abdicate for love, was divorced from her second husband.
• **1951** Winston Churchill became Prime Minister of Britain again when the Labour Government fell.
• **1971** The Republic of the Congo became the Republic of Zaire.
• **1978** The Nobel Peace Prize was won by President Sadat of Egypt and Prime Minister Begin of Israel for trying to establish peace between their two countries.

28 OCTOBER — Very Important Birthdates

Name(print) _____

Comments _____

_____

Autograph _____ Year of Birth _____

Success in marriage is not so much a matter of finding the right person as it is being the right person.

Name(print) _____

Comments _____

_____

Autograph _____ Year of Birth _____

On This Date in...

• **1636** Harvard University was founded.
• **1746** The Peruvian cities of Lima and Callao were demolished by earthquakes.
• **1886** The Statue of Liberty was presented to the US by France.
• **1914** The invention of a colour photographic process was announced by George Eastman of Eastman Kodak.
• **1929** Mrs. T. W. Evans gave birth over Florida to the first baby ever born in a plane. It was a girl.
• **1962** The Cuban Missile Crisis ended with Kruschev agreeing to withdraw missiles from Cuba.

29 OCTOBER — Very Important Birthdates

Name(print) _____

Comments _____

_____

Autograph _____ Year of Birth _____

A man who gives in when he is wrong is wise. A man who gives in when he is right is married.

Name(print) _____

Comments _____

_____

Autograph _____ Year of Birth _____

On This Date in...

• **1618** Sir Walter Raleigh was beheaded by Queen Elizabeth I, after being falsely accused of treason.
• **1927** The tomb of Genghis Khan was discovered by Peter Kozlov, a Russian archaeologist.
• **1929** 'Black Tuesday' hit Wall Street when the stock market crashed, leading to the Great Depression.
• **1948** US actor Richard Dreyfuss was born.
• **1956** Israel invaded the Sinai Peninsula.
• **1964** Tanganyika and Zanzibar united to become Tanzania.
• **1967** Expo 67 opened in Montreal.

30 OCTOBER — Very Important Birthdates

Name(print) _____

Comments _____

_____

Autograph _____ Year of Birth _____

Marry in haste, and repent in leisure.

Name(print) _____

Comments _____

_____

Autograph _____ Year of Birth _____

On This Date in...

• **1918** Czechoslovakia was proclaimed a republic.
• **1922** Benito Mussolini, Italy's youngest prime minister at 39, formed a Fascist party in Rome.
• **1925** The first live person appeared on a television set in John Baird's workshop in London.
• **1938** Panic, and one death through heart failure, was caused by Orson Welles' radio adaptation of H.G. Wells' *War of the Worlds*, when people really thought the US was being invaded by Martians.
• **1974** Muhammed Ali knocked out George Foreman to regain his world heavyweight boxing title.

On This Date in...

- **1915** The first steel helmets were issued to British troops.
- **1940** The Battle of Britain ended with the Royal Air Force losing 915 aircraft to the Luftwaffe's 1733.
- **1952** The first hydrogen bomb was exploded by the US at the Marshall Islands in the South Pacific.
- **1958** The first internal heart pacemaker was implanted in Stockholm by Dr. Ake Senning.
- **1971** An IRA bomb closed the revolving restaurant at the top of the London Post Office Tower for good.
- **1984** Indira Ghandi, Prime Minister of India, was shot dead by Sikh members of her own bodyguard.

Very Important Birthdates **31** **OCTOBER**

Name(print) _____

Comments _____

_____

Autograph _____ Year of Birth _____

Unused experience is a dead loss.

Name(print) _____

Comments _____

_____

Autograph _____ Year of Birth _____

On This Date in...

- **1695** The Bank of Scotland was founded.
- **1755** Lisbon, Spain, was two-thirds reduced to rubble by an earthquake which took 60,000 lives.
- **1895** The American Motor League, the world's first motoring organization, was founded.
- **1927** Betting taxes were first levied in Britain.
- **1950** An attempt was made on President Truman's life by two Puerto Ricans who killed Truman's guard and wounded two others.
- **1961** Stalin's body was removed from Lenin's Mausoleum in Red Square.

Very Important Birthdates **1** **NOVEMBER**

Name(print) _____

Comments _____

_____

Autograph _____ Year of Birth _____

Failure is a better teacher than success, but she seldom finds an apple on her desk.

Name(print) _____

Comments _____

_____

Autograph _____ Year of Birth _____

On This Date in...

- **1734** US Frontiersman Daniel Boone was born.
- **1871** The world's first 'Rogues Gallery' began when photographs of prisoners were taken for the first time in Britain.
- **1930** Ras (Prince) Tafari, whose Jamaican followers call themselves *Rastafarians*, was crowned Haile Selassie, Emperor of Ethiopia.
- **1950** British playwright George Bernard Shaw died.
- **1963** Ngo Dinh Diem, first president of the Republic of South Vietnam, died.
- **1976** Jimmy Carter was elected 38th President of the US.

Very Important Birthdates **2** **NOVEMBER**

Name(print) _____

Comments _____

_____

Autograph _____ Year of Birth _____

There are a great many more trapdoors to failure than there are to success.

Name(print) _____

Comments _____

_____

Autograph _____ Year of Birth _____

On This Date in...

- **1706** An earthquake destroyed the town of Abruzzi in Italy, killing 15,000 people.
- **1843** Admiral Horatio Nelson's statue was placed on top of the column in Trafalgar Square.
- **1942** Nine thousand prisoners were taken when Montgomery's Eighth Army broke through Rommel's front line in Africa.
- **1957** Laika, the Russian dog became the first dog in space, aboard *Sputnik II*.
- **1975** The North Sea pipeline, which carries 400,000 barrels of oil a day, was opened by Queen Elizabeth II.

Very Important Birthdates **NOVEMBER**

Name(print) _____

Comments _____

_____

Autograph _____ Year of Birth _____

Failure isn't bitter if you don't swallow it.

Name(print) _____

Comments _____

_____

Autograph _____ Year of Birth _____

VIP Birthdates - 1 Year Calendar

VIP Birthdates – 1 Year Calendar

4 NOVEMBER — Very Important Birthdates

Name(print) _____
Comments _____
_____
Autograph _____ Year of Birth _____

Many a man wishes he were as smart as his wife thinks he is.

Name(print) _____
Comments _____
_____
Autograph _____ Year of Birth _____

On This Date in...

- **1879** The world's first cash register was patented.
- **1914** The first fashion show was held at the Ritz-Carlton Hotel in New York by Vogue magazine.
- **1916** US news journalist Walter Cronkite was born.
- **1918** US actor Art Carney was born.
- **1952** Queen Elizabeth II opened her first Parliament.
- **1952** Dwight D. Eisenhower was elected 34th President of the United States.
- **1979** Over 60 staff and US Marines were taken hostage when Iranian students stormed the US Embassy in Tehran.

5 NOVEMBER — Very Important Birthdates

Name(print) _____
Comments _____
_____
Autograph _____ Year of Birth _____

Love is like a vaccination - when it takes hold, you don't have to be told.

Name(print) _____
Comments _____
_____
Autograph _____ Year of Birth _____

On This Date in...

- **1605** Guy Fawkes was arrested for his 'gunpowder plot' to blow up the Houses of Parliament in England.
- **1854** Russian forces were defeated at the Battle of Inkerman by French and British forces during the Crimean War.
- **1912** Singing cowboy star Roy Rogers (Leonard Sly) was born.
- **1919** Rudolph Valentino, the world's greatest screen lover, was locked out by his bride, actress Jean Acker, on the night of their wedding, a wedding which lasted only 6 hours.

6 NOVEMBER — Very Important Birthdates

Name(print) _____
Comments _____
_____
Autograph _____ Year of Birth _____

The most important thing a father can do for his children is love their mother.

Name(print) _____
Comments _____
_____
Autograph _____ Year of Birth _____

On This Date in...

- **1429** Henry VI was crowned King of England.
- **1813** Mexico gained its independence from Spain.
- **1860** Abraham Lincoln became the 16th US president.
- **1923** The German mark sank to an incredible 4.2 trillion to the US dollar, as opposed to only 4.2 marks to the dollar ten years earlier.
- **1935** The RAF's *Hawker Hurricane* flew for the first time.
- **1988** Six thousand US Defense Department computers were crippled by a virus spread by the 23-year-old son of the head of the country's computer security agency.

7 NOVEMBER — Very Important Birthdates

Name(print) _____
Comments _____
_____
Autograph _____ Year of Birth _____

A practical nurse is one who falls in love with a wealthy patient.

Name(print) _____
Comments _____
_____
Autograph _____ Year of Birth _____

On This Date in...

- **1867** Physicist Madam Marie Curie was born.
- **1872** The brigantine *Marie Celeste* sailed from New York and was found sailing, with all sails set and without crew or passengers, some days later. The mystery of what happened was never known.
- **1885** The last spike was driven to complete the Canadian Pacific Railway.
- **1918** William Franklin (Billy) Graham was born.
- **1962** Eleanor Roosevelt, lecturer and wife of President Franklin D. Roosevelt, died.
- **1972** Richard Nixon was re-elected President.

On This Date in...

• **1674** Blind English author of *Paradise Lost*, John Milton, died.
• **1793** The Louvre was opened in Paris.
• **1895** X-rays were discovered by accident when William Rontgen was experimenting with the flow of electricity through a partially evacuated glass tube.
• **1939** A bomb exploded in the Buergerbraukeller in Munich, after Hitler left after giving a speech.
• **1989** The US elected its first black governor, Douglas Wilder of Virginia, and its first black mayor, David Dinkins of New York.

Very Important Birthdates **8** NOVEMBER

Name(print) _____

Comments _____
_____

Autograph _____ Year of Birth _____

Falling down doesn't make you a failure, but staying down does.

Name(print) _____

Comments _____
_____

Autograph _____ Year of Birth _____

On This Date in...

• **1799** Napoleon became leader of France at age 30.
• **1847** Wilhemina Carstairs became the first baby born using anesthetic.
• **1859** Flogging was banned in the British Army.
• **1960** John F. Kennedy became the youngest president of the US at age 43.
• **1965** A power outage caused a black-out in 10 US States and many parts of Canada, which saw a large increase in birth rates nine months later.
• **1989** East Germany lifted the 'iron curtain', allowing free access between East and West Berlin.

Very Important Birthdates **9** NOVEMBER

Name(print) _____

Comments _____
_____

Autograph _____ Year of Birth _____

Feed your faith, and your doubts will starve to death.

Name(print) _____

Comments _____
_____

Autograph _____ Year of Birth _____

On This Date in...

• **1483** Martin Luther, German religious leader and father of 'Protestantism', was born.
• **1913** The world's first black mayor, John Archer, was elected in Battersea, England.
• **1938** Nazis burned 267 synagogues and thousands of Jewish homes and businesses.
• **1982** Leonid Ilyich Brezhnev, who led Soviet Russia for 18 years, died at age 75.
• **1987** The US brig, *Somers*, on which Herman Melville based his novel, *Billy Budd*, was found wrecked after being lost for over 50 years.

Very Important Birthdates NOVEMBER

Name(print) _____

Comments _____
_____

Autograph _____ Year of Birth _____

If a man carries his own lantern, he need not fear darkness.

Name(print) _____

Comments _____
_____

Autograph _____ Year of Birth _____

On This Date in...

• **1889** Washington became the 42nd US state.
• **1918** The armistice between the Allies and Germany was signed in a guarded railway carriage.
• **1918** Kate Smith sang Irving Berlin's patriotic song, *God Bless America*, for the first time.
• **1952** Bing Crosby Enterprises in Beverly Hills witnessed the first demonstration of a video recording.
• **1965** The all-white government of Rhodesia, under Ian Smith, declared independence from Britain.
• **1940** The Jeep, which got its name from the initials GP, or General Purpose (vehicle), was launched by Willys.

Very Important Birthdates NOVEMBER

Name(print) _____

Comments _____
_____

Autograph _____ Year of Birth _____

Wise men think without talking; fools talk without thinking.

Name(print) _____

Comments _____
_____

Autograph _____ Year of Birth _____

VIP Birthdates – 1 Year Calendar

VIP Birthdates – 1 Year Calendar

12 NOVEMBER — Very Important Birthdates

Name(print) _____

Comments _____

_____

Autograph _____ Year of Birth _____

Money can build a house, but it takes love to make it a home.

Name(print) _____

Comments _____

_____

Autograph _____ Year of Birth _____

On This Date in...

• **1035** Canute II, The Viking king who was king of England as well as Denmark, died.
• **1859** Leotard, 'the daring young man on the flying trapeze', made his sensational debut in Paris.
• **1923** Hitler was arrested after his failed 'Beer Hall putsch'.
• **1942** Polyurethane was patented by Bayer, makers of pharmaceutical products, including Aspirin.
• **1945** Canadian rock singer Neil Young was born.
• **1987** A painting by Van Gogh, entitled *Irises*, sold for a record $75 million.

13 NOVEMBER — Very Important Birthdates

Name(print) _____

Comments _____

_____

Autograph _____ Year of Birth _____

Love - what you keep to yourself you lose; what you give away you keep forever.

Name(print) _____

Comments _____

_____

Autograph _____ Year of Birth _____

On This Date in...

• **1850** Robert Louis Stevenson, author of *Treasure Island* and *Dr. Jekyll and Mr. Hyde*, was born.
• **1907** The world's first helicopter took flight, rising 6 1/2 feet above the ground and hovered there for 60 seconds in Normandy.
• **1936** King Edward VIII told the Prime Minister that he intended to marry Wallis Simpson, a divorcee.
• **1945** Charles de Gaulle was elected President of France.
• **1950** The first World Bridge Championship was held in Bermuda.

14 NOVEMBER — Very Important Birthdates

Name(print) _____

Comments _____

_____

Autograph _____ Year of Birth _____

Life is just one fool thing after another; love is just two fool things after each other.

Name(print) _____

Comments _____

_____

Autograph _____ Year of Birth _____

On This Date in...

• **1770** The source of the Blue Nile was discovered in northeast Ethiopia by Scottish explorer, James Bruce.
• **1889** Nellie Bly, star reporter with the *New York World*, set out to beat Phileas Fogg's record 'around the world in 80 days', and did beat it by nearly 8 days.
• **1896** The speed limit for horseless carriages (motor vehicles) was raised from 4 mph to 14 mph in Britain.
• **1940** The Luftwaffe bombed Coventry, England, killing 554 people and seriously injuring 865.
• **1963** A new island was created when a volcano erupted off Iceland.

15 NOVEMBER — Very Important Birthdates

Name(print) _____

Comments _____

_____

Autograph _____ Year of Birth _____

Love is a feeling that makes a woman make a man make a fool of himself.

Name(print) _____

Comments _____

_____

Autograph _____ Year of Birth _____

On This Date in...

• **1864** Atlanta was burned by General Sherman and the Union soldiers during the American Civil War.
• **1899** Winston Churchill, then a war reporter for the *Morning Post*, was captured by the Boers in South Africa, but he managed to escape a few weeks later.
• **1901** A hearing aid, powered by electricity, was patented in New York by Miller Reese.
• **1956** *Love Me Tender*, the first film staring Elvis Presley, was premiered in New York.
• **1968** The *Queen Elizabeth*, the world's largest passenger liner, docked for the last time in Southampton.

On This Date in...

- **1824** The Murray River, Australia's longest at 1609 miles, was discovered by Hume and Howell.
- **1869** The 100-mile-long Suez Canal was officially opened.
- **1937** The British House of Commons, with opposition from the Labour Party, voted to build air raid shelters.
- **1959** Broadway saw *The Sound of Music* performed for the first time.
- **1960** US film star Clark Gable died.
- **1965** *Venus III*, an unmanned spacecraft that successfully landed on Venus, was launched by the USSR.

Very Important Birthdates **16** NOVEMBER

Name(print) _____

Comments _____

_____

Autograph _____ Year of Birth _____

Only fools test the depth of the water with both feet.

Name(print) _____

Comments _____

_____

Autograph _____ Year of Birth _____

On This Date in...

- **1558** Mary Tudor, the Catholic queen in Protestant Britain, also known as 'Bloody Mary', died.
- **1603** Sir Walter Raleigh went on trial for treason.
- **1800** The US Congress met for the first time, and John Adams became the first president to move into what is now known as the White House.
- **1925** US film star Rock Hudson (Roy Sherer) was born.
- **1938** Canadian folk singer and song writer Gordon Lightfoot was born.
- **1954** King Farouk of Egypt was exiled and replaced by General Nasser.

Very Important Birthdates **17** NOVEMBER

Name(print) _____

Comments _____

_____

Autograph _____ Year of Birth _____

The reason a dog is a man's best friend is because he does not pretend; he proves it.

Name(print) _____

Comments _____

_____

Autograph _____ Year of Birth _____

On This Date in...

- **1626** St. Peter's church in Rome was consecrated.
- **1905** Norway became independent of Denmark and Prince Carl of Denmark became King Haakon VII of Norway.
- **1963** Push-button telephones were introduced by Bell.
- **1977** President Anwar Sadat became the first Egyptian leader to visit Israel.
- **1978** A US congressman and 3 newsmen were murdered by cultist, Jim Jones in Guyana, which led to the suicide of Jones and 900 of his followers in the biggest mass suicide in modern times.

Very Important Birthdates **18** NOVEMBER

Name(print) _____

Comments _____

_____

Autograph _____ Year of Birth _____

Those who seek faultless friends remain friendless.

Name(print) _____

Comments _____

_____

Autograph _____ Year of Birth _____

On This Date in...

- **1850** Alfred Lord Tennyson became Britain's Poet Laureate.
- **1863** Abraham Lincoln uttered the immortal words, "that government by the people, for the people, shall not perish from the earth," during his famous Gettysburg Address after the American Civil War.
- **1960** The world's first VTOL (vertical take-off and landing) airplane was flown for the first time.
- **1963** US actress Jodie Foster was born.
- **1988** The US-born daughter of Aristotle Onassis, Christina, died from a heart attack at age 37.

Very Important Birthdates **19** NOVEMBER

Name(print) _____

Comments _____

_____

Autograph _____ Year of Birth _____

Almost anything can be bought at a reduced price except lasting satisfaction.

Name(print) _____

Comments _____

_____

Autograph _____ Year of Birth _____

VIP Birthdates – 1 Year Calendar

20 NOVEMBER — Very Important Birthdates

Name(print) _____

Comments _____

_____

Autograph _____ Year of Birth _____

A college education never hurt anybody who was calling to learn other things after he got it.

Name(print) _____

Comments _____

Autograph _____ Year of Birth _____

On This Date in...

• **1818** Venezuela was declared independent from Spain by Simon Bolivar.
• **1906** The Rolls-Royce company was formed by Charles Stewart Rolls and Frederick Henry Royce.
• **1925** Robert Kennedy, who became US Attorney General, and who was assassinated in 1968, was born.
• **1929** Salvador Dali's first one-man show was held in Paris.
• **1945** The Nazi war crime trials began at Nuremberg.
• **1947** Princess Elizabeth married Lt. Philip Mountbatten in Westminster Abbey.
• **1975** Spanish dictator General Franco died.

21 NOVEMBER — Very Important Birthdates

Name(print) _____

Comments _____

Autograph _____ Year of Birth _____

Anyone can steer the ship when the sea is calm.

Name(print) _____

Comments _____

_____

Autograph _____ Year of Birth _____

On This Date in...

• **1783** A hot air balloon took man on his first free-flight when Jean de Rosier and the Marquis d'Arlandes rose 500 feet above Paris and landed a few miles south 25 minutes later.
• **1789** North Carolina became the 12th US state.
• **1843** Vulcanized rubber was patented by Thomas Hancock in Britain.
• **1888** US comedian Harpo Marx was born.
• **1922** US actor Telly (Aristotle) Savalas, who became famous for his TV role as *Kojak* was born.
• **1945** US film star Goldie Hawn was born.

22 NOVEMBER — Very Important Birthdates

Name(print) _____

Comments _____

Autograph _____ Year of Birth _____

He who rolls up his sleeves seldom loses his shirt.

Name(print) _____

Comments _____

_____

Autograph _____ Year of Birth _____

On This Date in...

• **1497** Vasco da Gama rounded the Cape of Good Hope on his way to find a short route to India.
• **1718** Edward Teach, also known as Blackbeard the Pirate, was killed by Lieutenant Robert Maynard of *HMS Pearl* in hand-to-hand combat.
• **1955** Elvis Presley signed with RCA Victor Records.
• **1963** President John F. Kennedy was assassinated by Lee Harvey Oswald in Dallas, Texas.
• **1980** US show business legend Mae West died.
• **1986** Mike Tyson became the youngest-ever world heavyweight boxing champion at age 20.

23 NOVEMBER — Very Important Birthdates

Name(print) _____

Comments _____

_____

Autograph _____ Year of Birth _____

The road to knowledge begins with the turn of a page.

Name(print) _____

Comments _____

_____

Autograph _____ Year of Birth _____

On This Date in...

• **1859** William H. Bonney, who became known as the notorious *Billy the Kid*, was born.
• **1887** Actor and star of many horror shows, Boris Karloff (William Henry Pratt), was born.
• **1889** The world's first jukebox was installed in San Francisco at the Palais Royal Saloon.
• **1910** Dr. Hawley Harvey Crippen was hanged in Britain for murdering and dissecting his wife, then fleeing with his new love, who was disguised as a boy.
• **1915** The famous WWI song, *Pack Up Your Troubles In Your Old Kit Bag,* was published.

On This Date in...

• **1859** *The Origin Of Species*, the controversial work of Charles Darwin, which described evolution as opposed to the 'Adam and Eve' theory, was published.
• **1864** French painter and lithographer Henri (Marie Raymond) de Toulouse-Lautrec was born.
• **1939** British Overseas Airways Corporation (BOAC) came into being when Imperial Airways and British Airways merged.
• **1963** Lee Harvey Oswald, the man accused of shooting President John F Kennedy was shot and killed by Jack Rubinstein.

Very Important Birthdates **24** NOVEMBER

Name(print) _____
Comments _____
_____
Autograph _____ Year of Birth _____

One thing the future can guarantee - anything can happen.

Name(print) _____
Comments _____
_____
Autograph _____ Year of Birth _____

On This Date in...

• **1884** Evaporated milk was patented in St. Louis.
• **1896** The first parking ticket in Britain was given to William Marshall, but the case was later dismissed.
• **1914** US baseball star Joe Di Maggio, who was at one time married to Marilyn Monroe, was born.
• **1935** The monarchy was restored in Greece.
• **1969** In a protest against Britain's support of the US in the Vietnam War, John Lennon returned his MBE.
• **1989** Vietnamese boat people rioted in Hong Kong's detention camps when they were told they would be repatriated back to Vietnam.

Very Important Birthdates **25** NOVEMBER

Name(print) _____
Comments _____
_____
Autograph _____ Year of Birth _____

A man who isn't his own worst critic, is his own worst enemy. *- Frank Tyger*

Name(print) _____
Comments _____
_____
Autograph _____ Year of Birth _____

On This Date in...

• **1688** King Louis XIV of France declared war on the Netherlands.
• **1832** New York City got its first street cars.
• **1939** US singer Tina Turner was born.
• **1942** Soviet forces counterattacked the German Sixth Army at Stalingrad, completely surrounding and routing a quarter million of General Von Paulus's troops.
• **1956** US bandleader Tommy Dorsey choked to death in his sleep at the age of 51.
• **1966** Charles de Gaulle opened the world's first tidal power station near St. Malo.

Very Important Birthdates **26** NOVEMBER

Name(print) _____
Comments _____
_____
Autograph _____ Year of Birth _____

It's better to look where you're going than to see where you've been.

Name(print) _____
Comments _____
_____
Autograph _____ Year of Birth _____

On This Date in...

• **1582** William Shakespeare married Anne Hathaway.
• **1868** Lieutenant George Armstrong Custer killed 103 Indians when he attacked and burned a Cheyenne village.
• **1942** A French fleet was scuttled in Toulon to prevent it from falling into the hands of the approaching Germans.
• **1967** President de Gaulle vetoed British attempts to enter into the European Common Market.
• **1970** A knife-wielding man was arrested in Manila when he attempted to attack Pope John Paul.

Very Important Birthdates **27** NOVEMBER

Name(print) _____
Comments _____
_____
Autograph _____ Year of Birth _____

Those who fear the future are likely to fumble the present.

Name(print) _____
Comments _____
_____
Autograph _____ Year of Birth _____

VIP Birthdates – 1 Year Calendar

VIP Birthdates - 1 Year Calendar

28 NOVEMBER — Very Important Birthdates

Name(print) _____

Comments _____

_____

Autograph _____ Year of Birth _____

Knowing without doing is like plowing without sowing.

Name(print) _____

Comments _____

_____

Autograph _____ Year of Birth _____

On This Date in...

- **1660** The Royal Society was founded in England.
- **1905** Sinn Fein, the Irish political party, was founded by Arthur Griffith.
- **1924** Australian anthropologist Raymond Dart proclaimed that evolution's missing link was found when he noted that the skull of a fossil child, found in Taung, was a southern ape with a brain size capable of human intelligence.
- **1931** US actress Hope Lange was born.
- **1948** The world's first Polaroid camera, invented by Dr. Edwin Land, went on sale in Boston.

29 NOVEMBER — Very Important Birthdates

Name(print) _____

Comments _____

_____

Autograph _____ Year of Birth _____

Kind words do not wear out the tongue - so speak them.

Name(print) _____

Comments _____

_____

Autograph _____ Year of Birth _____

On This Date in...

- **1780** Maria Theresa, Empress of Austria and Queen of Hungary, died.
- **1832** Louisa May Alcott, author of *Little Women,* was born.
- **1864** Twelve hundred US troops attacked a Cheyenne and Arapaho Indian camp at Sand Creek, Colorado, and shot dead over 400 men, women and children, despite the fact that the chief had raised a US flag and a white flag of truce.
- **1929** US Admiral Richard Byrd and his pilot Bernt Balchen became the first men to fly over the South Pole.

30 NOVEMBER — Very Important Birthdates

Name(print) _____

Comments _____

_____

Autograph _____ Year of Birth _____

A kind word picks up a man when trouble weighs him down.

Name(print) _____

Comments _____

_____

Autograph _____ Year of Birth _____

On This Date in...

- **1835** Author Samuel Clemens (Mark Twain) was born.
- **1840** The body of Napoleon was removed from St. Helena and taken to Paris.
- **1874** Sir Winston Leonard Churchill, British statesman, journalist and Nobel Prize winner, was born.
- **1900** Irish-born playwright Oscar Wilde died, poverty-stricken, in self-imposed exile in France.
- **1919** French women were given the right to vote for the first time.
- **1956** Floyd Patterson knocked out Archie Moore to become world heavyweight boxing champion at 21.

1 DECEMBER — Very Important Birthdates

Name(print) _____

Comments _____

_____

Autograph _____ Year of Birth _____

The person who sows seeds of kindness will have a perpetual harvest.

Name(print) _____

Comments _____

_____

Autograph _____ Year of Birth _____

On This Date in...

- **1640** Portugal drove out the Spanish and became independent.
- **1939** The movie, *Gone With The Wind*, staring Clark Gable and Vivian Leigh, premiered in New York.
- **1945** Singer and comedienne Bette Midler was born.
- **1953** Hugh Heffner's first *Playboy* magazine, which he started with only $10,000, featuring a nude photograph of Marilyn Monroe, went on the stands.
- **1990** A construction team from Britain and one from France met under the English Channel to complete the Chunnel, an automobile link between the two countries.

On This Date in...

- **1697** St. Paul's Cathedral in London, which had been rebuilt by Sir Christopher Wren, reopened.
- **1804** Napoleon had himself crowned Emperor by Pope Pius VII in Paris.
- **1823** The Monroe Doctrine, which warned European countries about interfering with North and South American politics, was proclaimed by President Monroe.
- **1859** Abolitionist John Brown was hanged for his attack on the Federal arsenal at Harper's Ferry.
- **1901** The safety razor with the double-edged disposable blade, patented by Gillette, went on sale.

Very Important Birthdates **2 DECEMBER**

Name(print) _____

Comments _____

_____

Autograph _____ Year of Birth _____

Fear of the future is a waste of the present.

Name(print) _____

Comments _____

_____

Autograph _____ Year of Birth _____

On This Date in...

- **1818** Illinois became the 21st US state.
- **1894** Writer Robert Louis Stevenson died.
- **1910** Neon lighting was displayed for the first time at the Paris Motor Show, by its inventor, George Claude.
- **1926** Mystery writer Agatha Christie disappeared, and was presumed kidnapped from her Surrey home.
- **1930** US singer Andy Williams was born.
- **1967** The world's first human heart transplant was performed on a 53-year-old grocer by Dr. Christian Barnard in Cape Town, South Africa.

Very Important Birthdates **3 DECEMBER**

Name(print) _____

Comments _____

_____

Autograph _____ Year of Birth _____

No matter how much a person dreads the future, he usually wants to be around to see it.

Name(print) _____

Comments _____

_____

Autograph _____ Year of Birth _____

On This Date in...

- **1154** Nicholas Breakspear became Adrian IV, the only Englishman to ever become pope.
- **1642** Cardinal Richelieu (Armand du Plessis), who practically ran France for young King Louis XIII, died at the age of 57.
- **1915** The State of Georgia officially recognized the Ku Klux Klan.
- **1949** US film actor Jeff Bridges was born.
- **1948** Orwell's *Nineteen Eighty-Four* was completed.
- **1961** The birth control pill became available on the National Health Service in Britain for the first time.

Very Important Birthdates **4 DECEMBER**

Name(print) _____

Comments _____

_____

Autograph _____ Year of Birth _____

Some carve out the future while others just whittle away the time.

Name(print) _____

Comments _____

_____

Autograph _____ Year of Birth _____

On This Date in...

- **1872** The *Marie Celeste* was found sailing on the Atlantic, but without her captain, his crew and family.
- **1901** Cartoon film producer Walt Disney was born.
- **1904** The Japanese destroyed the Russian fleet.
- **1906** Film director Otto Preminger was born.
- **1933** Alcohol again became legally available in the US when the 14-year prohibition ended.
- **1935** Rock and roll innovator, Little Richard (Richard Penniman), was born.
- **1945** Five US Navy bombers vanished over what is known as the Bermuda Triangle.

Very Important Birthdates **5 DECEMBER**

Name(print) _____

Comments _____

_____

Autograph _____ Year of Birth _____

A pessimist burns his bridges before he gets to them.

Name(print) _____

Comments _____

_____

Autograph _____ Year of Birth _____

VIP Birthdates – 1 Year Calendar

6 DECEMBER   Very Important Birthdates

Name(print) _____

Comments _____

_____

Autograph _____ Year of Birth _____

The man who raises roses in his garden also does a kindness to his neighbours.

Name(print) _____

Comments _____

Autograph _____ Year of Birth _____

On This Date in...

• **1492** Christopher Columbus discovered what is now known as Haiti and the Dominican Republic.
• **1774** The world's first state-run education system began in Austria.
• **1877** The first recording of a human voice was made when Thomas Edison recited *Mary Had a Little Lamb* into his new phonograph.
• **1921** The 26 southern states of Ireland became independent and were called the Irish Free State.
• **1989** A gunman shot 14 female students dead at the University of Montreal in Canada's worst mass murder.

7 DECEMBER   Very Important Birthdates

Name(print) _____

Comments _____

_____

Autograph _____ Year of Birth _____

You can judge a man not only by the company he keeps, but by the jokes he tells.

Name(print) _____

Comments _____

_____

Autograph _____ Year of Birth _____

On This Date in...

• **1783** William Pitt, the Younger, became Britain's youngest Prime Minister at age 24.
• **1941** Japan made a sneak attacked on the US Fleet at Pearl Harbour, killing 2400 people.
• **1972** *Apollo 17* was launched to make the sixth landing on the moon by the US.
• **1982** Charles Brooks Jr. became the world's first person to be executed by lethal injection at Fort Worth Prison.
• **1988** An earthquake killed thousands and caused wide-spread destruction in Soviet Armenia.

8 DECEMBER   Very Important Birthdates

Name(print) _____

Comments _____

_____

Autograph _____ Year of Birth _____

Friendship doubles our joy and divides our grief.

Name(print) _____

Comments _____

_____

Autograph _____ Year of Birth _____

On This Date in...

• **1542** Mary Queen of Scots was born.
• **1925** US entertainer Sammy Davis Jr was born.
• **1941** The US and Britain declared war on Japan following the Japanese attack on Pearl Harbor.
• **1980** The Beatles' John Lennon was shot dead outside his New York apartment by a mentally deranged 'fan' while returning from a recording session with his wife, Yoko Ono.
• **1987** The first-ever treaty to reduce USSR and US ground-based, intermediate-range missiles was signed by President Gorbachev of Russia and US President Reagan.

9 FEBRUARY   Very Important Birthdates

Name(print) _____

Comments _____

_____

Autograph _____ Year of Birth _____

The only reason some people are lost in thought is that they're total strangers there.

Name(print) _____

Comments _____

_____

Autograph _____ Year of Birth _____

On This Date in...

• **1902** The Venezuelan navy was seized by British and German warships in an effort to regain losses incurred by the coup of 1899.
• **1909** Actor Douglas Fairbanks Jr. was born.
• **1918** Kirk Douglas (Issur Danielovitch) was born.
• **1955** Sugar Ray Robinson regained his middleweight title by knocking out Carl Olson.
• **1960** ITV screened the first episode of *Coronation Street*.
• **1990** Lech Walesa was elected president of Poland in the country's first-ever direct presidential elections.

On This Date in...

- **1830** US poet Emily Dickinson was born.
- **1898** Cuba became independent of Spain.
- **1901** The first Nobel prizes, valued at $30,000 each, were awarded in Oslo and Stockholm, for chemistry, literature, medicine, physics and peace.
- **1921** Albert Einstein was awarded the Nobel prize for physics.
- **1979** Mother Teresa of Calcutta was awarded the Nobel Peace prize for her work in helping the destitute.
- **1990** The Communist Party won in a free election in Yugoslavia.

Very Important Birthdates **10** DECEMBER

Name(print) _____
Comments _____
_____
Autograph _____ Year of Birth _____

Gossip is something that goes in one ear and in another.

Name(print) _____
Comments _____
Autograph _____ Year of Birth _____

On This Date in...

- **1688** King James II fled from England.
- **1769** Venetian blinds were patented in London.
- **1894** The first motor show opened in Paris with nine exhibitors.
- **1920** Martial Law was declared in parts of Ireland.
- **1936** Edward VIII abdicated the Throne of England to marry twice-divorced American, Wallis Simpson.
- **1944** Singer Brenda Lee (Brenda Mae Tarply) was born.
- **1987** The famous cane, boots and bowler hat worn by Charlie Chaplin were sold for a total of £121,000.

Very Important Birthdates **11** DECEMBER

Name(print) _____
Comments _____
_____
Autograph _____ Year of Birth _____

A gossiper is a newscaster without a sponsor.

Name(print) _____
Comments _____
Autograph _____ Year of Birth _____

On This Date in...

- **1889** English poet Robert Browning died.
- **1901** Marconi received the first transatlantic wireless radio message, sent from Poldhu, Cornwall, England to St. John's, Newfoundland.
- **1913** The *Mona Lisa* was recovered after it was stolen from the Louvre in Paris.
- **1915** The first all-metal plane was flown in Germany.
- **1938** US singer Connie Francis was born.
- **1939** US actor Douglas Fairbanks Sr. died.
- **1941** US singer Dionne Warwick was born.

Very Important Birthdates **12** DECEMBER

Name(print) _____
Comments _____
_____
Autograph _____ Year of Birth _____

Happiness is a rebound from hard work.

Name(print) _____
Comments _____
Autograph _____ Year of Birth _____

On This Date in...

- **1577** Francis set out from Plymouth, England, on the *Golden Hind*, to circumnavigate the world.
- **1642** Dutch navigator Abel Tasman became the first European to sight New Zealand.
- **1847** *Wuthering Heights* by Emily Brontë and *Agnes Grey* by Anne Brontë were both published, with the sisters using the pseudonyms of Ellis and Acton Bell.
- **1884** The coin-operated weighing machine was patented.
- **1903** The ice cream cone was patented in New York.
- **1925** US actor Dick Van Dyke was born.

Very Important Birthdates **13** DECEMBER

Name(print) _____
Comments _____
_____
Autograph _____ Year of Birth _____

Happiness walks on busy feet.

Name(print) _____
Comments _____
Autograph _____ Year of Birth _____

VIP Birthdates – 1 Year Calendar

14 DECEMBER — Very Important Birthdates

Name(print) _____

Comments _____

_____

Autograph _____ Year of Birth _____

Many people have minds like concrete: mixed up and permanently set.

Name(print) _____

Comments _____

_____

Autograph _____ Year of Birth _____

On This Date in...

- **1799** George Washington, first US President, died.
- **1900** The *Quantum Theory* was revealed in Berlin.
- **1906** The first German U-boat entered service.
- **1911** Roald Amundsen and his party reached the South Pole over a month ahead of the British team under Captain Robert Scott.
- **1935** US actress Lee Remick was born.
- **1973** The teenage grandson of John Paul Getty, John Paul Getty II, was released when his grandfather paid $750,000 in ransom after receiving a part of the teenager's ear in the mail from the kidnappers.

15 DECEMBER — Very Important Birthdates

Name(print) _____

Comments _____

_____

Autograph _____ Year of Birth _____

It is not the IQ but the I WILL that is important in education.

Name(print) _____

Comments _____

_____

Autograph _____ Year of Birth _____

On This Date in...

- **AD37** Nero, the Roman Emperor who had both his mother and his wife put to death, was born.
- **1654** A weather office in Tuscany began recording daily temperatures.
- **1890** Sioux Indian Chief Sitting Bull died.
- **1939** Nylon yarn was first produced commercially.
- **1964** The maple leaf flag was adopted as the official Canadian flag by Parliament.
- **1966** Walt Disney, creator of Disneyland, died.
- **1979** The game of Trivial Pursuit was conceived by two 30-year-old Canadians.

16 DECEMBER — Very Important Birthdates

Name(print) _____

Comments _____

_____

Autograph _____ Year of Birth _____

An inventor is a crackpot who becomes a genius when his idea catches on.

Name(print) _____

Comments _____

_____

Autograph _____ Year of Birth _____

On This Date in...

- **1653** Oliver Cromwell became Lord Protector of England.
- **1773** A group of citizens disguised as Indians dumped 342 chests of tea into Boston Harbor to protest the British tea tax, in what became known as the Boston Tea Party.
- **1914** German warships attacked the English resort town of Scarborough, thinking it was a major port.
- **1944** US band leader Glen Miller, and all on board his plane, perished when the plane was lost over the English Channel, never to be seen again.

17 DECEMBER — Very Important Birthdates

Name(print) _____

Comments _____

_____

Autograph _____ Year of Birth _____

Do not follow where the path may lead. Go instead where there is no path, and leave a trail.

Name(print) _____

Comments _____

_____

Autograph _____ Year of Birth _____

On This Date in...

- **1830** Simon Bolivar, 'the Liberator', who drove the Spanish out of Columbia, died.
- **1843** Charles Dickens' *A Christmas Carol* was published.
- **1903** Wilbur and Orville Wright made history when their heavier-than-air machine flew at Kitty Hawk, NC.
- **1939** The German battleship *Graf Spee* was scuttled.
- **1989** Brazil elected Fernando Collor de Mello as presidnt in the first free elections in 20 years.
- **1991** Joseph Roberts Smallwood, who brought Newfoundland into Canada, died at the age of 90.

On This Date in...

- **1825** Tsar Nicholas I succeeded to the throne in Russia.
- **1865** With the ratification of the 13th Amendment, the US officially abolished slavery.
- **1916** US singer, actress and dancer, Betty Grable, who had her legs insured for $1 million, was born.
- **1919** Six months after he made his famous first transatlantic flight from Newfoundland to Ireland with Sir Arthur Brown, Sir John Alcock was killed when his amphibian plane crashed off Normandy.
- **1947** US film director Steven Spielberg was born.

Very Important Birthdates **18** DECEMBER

Name(print) _____

Comments _____

_____

Autograph _____ Year of Birth _____

Happiness is a way station between too much and too little.

Name(print) _____

Comments _____

_____

Autograph _____ Year of Birth _____

On This Date in...

- **1154** Henry II, the English monarch who started the conquest of Ireland, became king of England.
- **1848** English poet and author of *Wuthering Heights*, Emily Brontë, died of tuberculosis at age 30.
- **1863** Linoleum was patented in London.
- **1984** Britain and China agreed that Hong Kong would retain its capitalistic lifestyle for at least 50 years after Britain's 99-year lease ran out, and possession of the Crown colony would be reverted to China in 1997.
- **1985** Senator Edward Kennedy announced that he would not run in the 1988 presidential election.

Very Important Birthdates DECEMBER

Name(print) _____

Comments _____

_____

Autograph _____ Year of Birth _____

The heart is happiest when it beats for others.

Name(print) _____

Comments _____

_____

Autograph _____ Year of Birth _____

On This Date in...

- **1957** Elvis Presley was drafted into the US Army at the height of his career.
- **1973** Luis Carrero Blanco, prime minister of Spain, was killed in his car by a bomb hidden in a tunnel.
- **1973** US singer Bobby Darrin (Robert Waldon Casotto) died during open heart surgery.
- **1987** A Philippine ferry went down in shark-infested waters, after colliding with an oil tanker near Manila, causing more deaths than the sinking of the *Titanic*.
- **1989** US invasion forces overthrew General Manuel Noriega, Panama's dictator and alleged drug baron.

Very Important Birthdates **20** DECEMBER

Name(print) _____

Comments _____

_____

Autograph _____ Year of Birth _____

Happiness is like a potato salad - when shared with others, it's a picnic.

Name(print) _____

Comments _____

_____

Autograph _____ Year of Birth _____

On This Date in...

- **1620** The *Mayflower*, carrying the Pilgrim Fathers, landed at Plymouth Rock in Massachusetts.
- **1846** Anesthetic was used for the first time when a leg was amputated by Dr. Robert Liston in London.
- **1937** US actress Jane Fonda was born.
- **1945** General George Patton, whose 3rd Army swept across France in 1943, died in a car crash.
- **1958** Charles de Gaulle became president of France.
- **1988** A bomb hidden in a transistor radio exploded, causing a US jumbo jet, carrying 270 passengers, to crash at Lockerbie, Scotland.

Very Important Birthdates DECEMBER

Name(print) _____

Comments _____

_____

Autograph _____ Year of Birth _____

Happiness is not perfected until it is shared.

Name(print) _____

Comments _____

_____

Autograph _____ Year of Birth _____

VIP Birthdates - 1 Year Calendar

22 DECEMBER — Very Important Birthdates

Name(print) _____
Comments _____
_____
Autograph _____Year of Birth _____

Horse sense is stable thinking coupled with the ability to say nay.

Name(print) _____
Comments _____
_____
Autograph _____Year of Birth _____

On This Date in...

- **1715** The failed Jacobite rebellion in Scotland, led by James Stuart, the 'Old Pretender', began.
- **1864** General Sherman's Union troops captured Savannah, Georgia.
- **1877** Liquid oxygen was first formulated.
- **1895** The X-ray was used for the first time.
- **1943** Beatrix Potter, creator of Peter Rabbit, died.
- **1949** The Brothers Gibb, Maurice and Robin (The Bee Gees), were born on the Isle of Man.
- **1975** Carlos the Jackal and pro-Palestinian terrorists seized 70 hostages at OPEC's Vienna headquarters.

23 DECEMBER — Very Important Birthdates

Name(print) _____
Comments _____
_____
Autograph _____Year of Birth _____

Hope is putting faith to work when doubting would be easier.

Name(print) _____
Comments _____
_____
Autograph _____Year of Birth _____

On This Date in...

- **1810** German Egyptologist and founder of modern archaeology, Karl Richard Lepsius, was born.
- **1888** Artist Vincent Van Gogh cut his own ear off.
- **1922** The BBC began daily news casts.
- **1948** General Tojo, Prime Minister of Japan from 1941 to 1944, and chief instigator of the attack on Pearl Harbor, unsuccessfully attempted suicide to avoid execution for his 'crimes against humanity'.
- **1973** The Shah of Iran increased oil prices 100%.
- **1973** Strongman Charles Atlas died at age 79.

24 DECEMBER — Very Important Birthdates

Name(print) _____
Comments _____
_____
Autograph _____Year of Birth _____

Hope is grief's best music.

Name(print) _____
Comments _____
_____
Autograph _____Year of Birth _____

On This Date in...

- **1818** *Silent Night* was sung publicly for the first time.
- **1900** Joseph Roberts Smallwood, author, editor, union leader and Newfoundland's first premier, was born.
- **1914** The first-ever bomb was dropped on British soil at Dover by a German monoplane.
- **1942** The world's first surface-to-surface missile, the *V1*, was launched against Britain by Germany.
- **1943** General Dwight D. Eisenhower was made commander-in-chief of the European invasion.
- **1944** The first jet airplane for wartime use was flown by Germany.

25 DECEMBER — Very Important Birthdates

Name(print) _____
Comments _____
_____
Autograph _____Year of Birth _____

He who loses honesty has nothing else to lose.

Name(print) _____
Comments _____
_____
Autograph _____Year of Birth _____

On This Date in...

- **1642** English mathematician Isaac Newton was born.
- **1899** US film star Humphrey Bogart was born.
- **1914** The war in the trenches of France was halted for a while as German and British troops celebrated Christmas together by singing carols and swapping gifts in no-mans land, before the shooting resumed at midnight.
- **1949** US actress Sissy Spacek was born.
- **1957** Queen Elizabeth gave her first televised Christmas message.
- **1972** An earthquake killed over 10,000 in the Managua, the capital city of Nicaragua.

On This Date in...

- **1898** Radium was discovered by Marie and Pierre Curie while experimenting with pitchblende.
- **1906** *The Story of the Kelly Gang*, the world's first feature film, was shown in Melbourne, Australia.
- **1908** Jack Johnson of Texas beat Canadian world heavyweight champion Tommy Burns in Sydney, Australia, to become the first black world champion.
- **1943** The *Scharnhorst*, Germany's last big battleship, was sunk by the Royal Navy.
- **1972** Harry Truman, the 33rd US President, died.
- **1974** Comedian Jack Benny (Benjamin Kubelsky) died.

Very Important Birthdates **26** **DECEMBER**

Name(print) _____
Comments _____
_____
Autograph _____ Year of Birth _____

It's easy to entertain some people. All you have to do is sit and listen.

Name(print) _____
Comments _____
_____
Autograph _____ Year of Birth _____

On This Date in...

- **1822** French scientist Louis Pasteur was born.
- **1831** The recent BA graduate, 22-year-old Charles Darwin, set out on the Royal Navy's *HMS Beagle* on his famous voyage of scientific discovery, which eventually led to Darwin's disproving the 'Adam and Eve' understanding of the 'origin of the species'.
- **1927** Florenz Ziegfield presented Jerome Kern's musical, *Show Boat,* on Broadway.
- **1945** The International Monetary Fund was set up.
- **1972** Nobel prize winner, Chairman of Nato and Prime Minister of Canada, Lester B. Pearson, died.

Very Important Birthdates **27** **DECEMBER**

Name(print) _____
Comments _____
_____
Autograph _____ Year of Birth _____

The one who listens is the one who understands.

Name(print) _____
Comments _____
_____
Autograph _____ Year of Birth _____

On This Date in...

- **1694** Queen Mary II of England died of smallpox.
- **1734** Scottish outlaw Rob Roy (Robert Macgregor) died.
- **1846** Iowa became the 29th US state.
- **1856** Woodrow Wilson, 28th US president, was born.
- **1879** Ninety people died when the Edinburgh to Dundee train plummeted into the icy river after the Tay railway bridge collapsed.
- **1904** The first wireless weather reports were published in London, England.
- **1908** Over 75,000 died in an earthquake in Sicily.
- **1984** US film director Sam Peckinpah died.

Very Important Birthdates **28** **DECEMBER**

Name(print) _____
Comments _____
_____
Autograph _____ Year of Birth _____

A winner listens; a loser can't wait until it's his turn to talk.

Name(print) _____
Comments _____
_____
Autograph _____ Year of Birth _____

On This Date in...

- **1890** US forces massacred 200 Sioux under Chief Big Foot, at Wounded Knee, South Dakota.
- **1937** US actress Mary Tyler Moore was born.
- **1937** The Irish Republic changed its name to Eire.
- **1951** The world's first transistor hearing aid went on sale.
- **1952** A prehistoric fish, the Coelacanth, previously believed to be extinct, was caught off Africa.
- **1972** The 16 survivors of the airliner that crashed in the Andes mountains on October 13, 1972, who had resorted to cannibalism to survive, were rescued.

Very Important Birthdates **29** **DECEMBER**

Name(print) _____
Comments _____
_____
Autograph _____ Year of Birth _____

You can win more friends with your ears than with your mouth.

Name(print) _____
Comments _____
_____
Autograph _____ Year of Birth _____

VIP Birthdates - 1 Year Calendar

30 DECEMBER — Very Important Birthdates

Name(print) _____

Comments _____

_____

Autograph _____ Year of Birth _____

A good way to forget your troubles is to help others out of theirs.

Name(print) _____

Comments _____

_____

Autograph _____ Year of Birth _____

On This Date in...

- **1865** Author (Joseph) Rudyard Kipling was born.
- **1880** Transvaal became a republic.
- **1916** Grigory Yefimovich Rasputin, Russia's 'Mad Monk' and favourite of Tsar Nicholas II's wife, was given cyanide by a group of extreme conservatives, but it seemed to have no affect on him, so he was shot, and when he still didn't die, he was beaten unconscious and his body dumped in an icy river.
- **1922** Russia officially became the Union of Soviet Socialist Republics (USSR).
- **1979** *Sound of Music* composer Richard Rodgers died.

31 DECEMBER — Very Important Birthdates

Name(print) _____

Comments _____

_____

Autograph _____ Year of Birth _____

It's better to keep a friend from falling than to help him up after he falls.

Name(print) _____

Comments _____

_____

Autograph _____ Year of Birth _____

On This Date in...

- **1491** French navigator Jacques Cartier was born.
- **1687** The first 'Protestant' Huguenots left France for the Cape of Good Hope to escape religious prosecution, taking vines with them to start a new wine industry there.
- **1911** Marie Curie became the first person to receive two Nobel prizes, this time for chemistry.
- **1935** The game of *Monopoly* was patented.
- **1943** John Denver (Henry John Deutsohendorf) was born.
- **1977** Cambodia broke off relations with Vietnam.
- **1985** US singer Ricky Nelson and his fiancee died in a plane crash in Texas.

NOTE: For the benefit of those who own both Volumes 1 and 2 of Downhomer Household Almanac & Cook Book, this index covers recipes for both volumes.

NOTE: For the benefit of those who own both Volumes 1 and 2 of Downhomer Household Almanac & Cook Book, this index covers recipes for both volumes.

NOTE: For the benefit of those who own both Volumes 1 and 2 of Downhomer Household Almanac & Cook Book, this index covers recipes for both volumes.

NOTE: For the benefit of those who own both Volumes 1 and 2 of Downhomer Household Almanac & Cook Book, this index covers recipes for both volumes.

NOTE: For the benefit of those who own both Volumes 1 and 2 of Downhomer Household Almanac & Cook Book, this index covers recipes for both volumes.

NOTE: For the benefit of those who own both Volumes 1 and 2 of Downhomer Household Almanac & Cook Book, this index covers recipes for both volumes.

NOTE: For the benefit of those who own both Volumes 1 and 2 of Downhomer Household Almanac & Cook Book, this index covers recipes for both volumes.

NOTE: For the benefit of those who own both Volumes 1 and 2 of Downhomer Household Almanac & Cook Book, this index covers recipes for both volumes.

NOTE: For the benefit of those who own both Volumes 1 and 2 of Downhomer Household Almanac & Cook Book, this index covers recipes for both volumes.

NOTE: For the benefit of those who own both Volumes 1 and 2 of Downhomer Household Almanac & Cook Book, this index covers recipes for both volumes.

NOTE: For the benefit of those who own both Volumes 1 and 2 of Downhomer Household Almanac & Cook Book, this index covers recipes for both volumes.

NOTE: For the benefit of those who own both Volumes 1 and 2 of Downhomer Household Almanac & Cook Book, this index covers recipes for both volumes.

NOTE: For the benefit of those who own both Volumes 1 and 2 of Downhomer Household Almanac & Cook Book, this index covers recipes for both volumes.

NOTE: For the benefit of those who own both Volumes 1 and 2 of Downhomer Household Almanac & Cook Book, this index covers recipes for both volumes.

NOTE: For the benefit of those who own both Volumes 1 and 2 of Downhomer Household Almanac & Cook Book, this index covers recipes for both volumes.

NOTE: For the benefit of those who own both Volumes 1 and 2 of Downhomer Household Almanac & Cook Book, this index covers recipes for both volumes.

NOTES

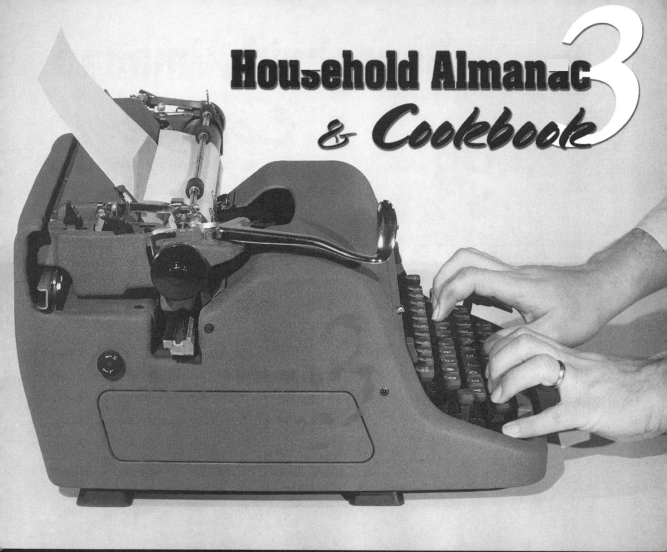

Household Almanac & Cookbook 3

We're in the Process of Putting Together Downhomer Household Almanac & Cookbook 3

Send us your recipes - especially Diabetic - Lo-Cal and Vegetarian recipes - as well as stories, poems, jokes and Life's Funniest Experiences to:
Downhomer Magazine
303 Water Street, St. John's, NF, Canada, A1C 1B9
Be sure to include your name, address, place of origin and phone number in case we need to clarify anything.

You can also contact us by fax (709) 726-2135
or E-mail: ron@downhomer.com